AMERICAN
Car Spotter's
BIBLE
1940-1980

Tad Burness

©2005 Tad Burness
Published by

kp books
An Imprint of F+W Publications

700 East State Street • Iola, WI 54990-0001
715-445-2214 • 888-457-2873

Our toll-free number to place an order or obtain
a free catalog is (800) 258-0929.

Library of Congress Catalog Number: 2005924821

ISBN: 0-89689-179-8

Designed by Donna Mummery
Edited by Tom Collins

Printed in China

Acknowledgments

The majority of pictures and details in this book are drawn from the author's long-time collection of reference materials, though I'm deeply grateful to individuals and organizations graciously providing additional details.

(The car makes in which certain individuals specialize are in parenthesis after their names.)

Bill Adams (Mopar)
Ronald Adams
Jeff Allen
Jeff Anderson
Warren J. Baier
Scott Boettcher
Larry Blodget (Ford)
Jim Bollman
Paul Bridges
Edwill H. Brown (Hudson)
Emmett P. Burke
Ken Buttolph
John A. Conde (AMC)
Virginia Daugert (Kaiser-Frazer)
Howard De Sart (Mopar)
Wallea Draper
Jim Edwards
Gerry Emich (Studebaker)
Jim Evans (Ford)
Fred K. Fox (Studebaker)
Norm Frey (Mopar)
Jeff Gibson (Edsel)

Bruce Gilbert
Dick Grove (Studebaker)
Allan Gutcher (Canadian)
Albert R. Hedges
Larry C. Holian
O. H. Hood
David Huff (Kaiser-Frazer)
Alden Jewell
Elliott Kahn
Bruce Kennedy
Wayne Kielisch
Jean-Paul Labrecque (Canadian)
Mike Lamm
Dale Long
Daisy Lowenstein
Rick Markell
Bob Martin
Keith Marvin
Bill Mason
Larry Mauck
Carl Mendoza (Hudson)

Dave Newell (Corvair)
Paul M. Newitt (Mustang)
Walter O' Kelley (De Soto)
G. Reichow
Walter F. Robinson
Charles Rowe
Jay Sherwin (Jeepster)
Mark Simon
Phil Skinner
Robert Smith (Mopar)
Bob Snyder
Bryon Stappler (Canadian)
John Stempel
Nina Taylor
Ty Thompson
Jim Van Northwick
R. A. Wawryzyniak
Ken Wilson (Mopar)
Paul Woudenberg
Bob Young Jr.
Robert Zimmerman

Thanks, also, to the following corporations and organizations for their kind help:

AACA (Antique Automobile Association of America)
American Motors Corporation
Autophyle Magazine
Buick Club of America
Cadillac-La Salle Club
Cars & Parts Magazine
Contemporary Historical Vehicle Association (CHVA)
Corvair Society of America (CORSA)

Crosley Automobile Club
Daimler-Chrysler (Mopar)
De Soto Club of America
Edsel Owner's Club
Fabulous 50s Ford Club of America
Ford Motor Company (FoMoCo)
General Motors Corporations and Divisions (GM)
Hudson-Essex-Terraplane Club
International Edsel Club

Kaiser-Frazer Owner's Club
Milestone Car Society
Oldsmobile Club of America
Pontiac-Oakland Club
Society of Automotive Historians (SAH)
Special Interest Autos Magazine
Studebaker Driver's Club
Vintage Corvette Club of America
WPC / Chrysler Product Restorers Club

1940s

Convertible Cabriolet.
(11,820 BLT.)
$898.

Cabriolet
ic Top

40 CHEVROLET

Hudson

new PACEMAKER 6 19
LOWER-PRICED SERIES
(119" WB)

$1933.

50

• NOW—3 GREAT SERIES • LOWER-PRICED PACEMAKER • FAMOUS SUPER • CUSTOM COMMODORE

1950s

MERCURY

$2631.

2-DR. H/T (MONTEREY)

MONTCLAIR

2 DR.
MONTEREY

(21,557 BLT.)

CVT.

(6062 BLT.)

4-DR H/T

(RESTYLED) **60**

1960s

302 CID 2V V-8—220 hp; 4.00" bore x 3.00"
stroke; 9.5 to 1 comp. ratio; regular fuel.
302 CID 4V "Boss" V-8—290 hp; 4.00" bore x
3.00" stroke; 10.6 to 1 comp. ratio; premium fuel.
351 CID 2V V-8—250 hp; 4.00" bore x 3.50"
stroke; 9.5 to 1 comp. ratio; regular fuel.
351 CID 4V V-8—300 hp; 4.00" bore x 3.50"
stroke; 11.0 to 1 comp. ratio; premium fuel.
428 CID 4V Cobra V-8—335 hp; 4.13" bore x
3.98" stroke; 10.6 to 1 comp. ratio; premium fuel.
428 CID Cobra Jet Ram-Air 4V V-8—335 hp;
4.13" bore x 3.98" stroke; 10.6 to 1 compression
ratio; premium fuel.
429 CID 4V "Boss" V-8—375 hp; 4.36" bore x 3.60"
stroke; 10.5 to 1 comp. ratio; premium fuel.

70
new GRILLE

$3720.
Boss 302

(63/9 BLT.)

FRONT
SPOILER

(39316 BLT.)

1970s

BOSS 302 WHEEL COVER

BOSS 302 CID,
290-H.P. V-8,
F60 × 15 TIRES.
(new E78 × 14, MOST OTHER
MODELS)

SPORTSROOF H/T

$2771. MUSTANG-70

CUTLASS SUPREME

20 EPA EST. MPG	360 EST. DRIVING RANGE
27 HWY EST. MPG	486 EST. HIGHWAY RANGE

80B (CONT'D.)

1980s

AVAILABLE
5.7~litre
(350 CID)
DIESEL V8
ENGINE

AVAILABLE
INTERIOR

For special distinction, a new "Renaissance" interior trim, available exclusively
on Cutlass Supreme Brougham models.
Features complementary shades of blue
and camel in a bold, contemporary
pattern of rich velour.

(BELOW)

SUPREME BROUGHAM

COUPE (77875

Contents

V8 ENGINE *ONLY*, 1956 ON (265 CID, 1956; 283 CID, 1957 THROUGH '61)

H.P. IN 1957 =
220 (STD.)
245-270 (OPT.) 250-283 w. FUEL INJECTION

new TOP

56-57

$2900.
('56)

SINCE '56, new SIDE TRIM

$3437.
('57)

(3467 BLT., 1956)

new REAR FENDERS

(6339 BLT, 1957)

new 4 HEADLIGHTS

102" WB 230 HP

DASH

58
(9168 BLT.)

RESTYLED

new VENT LOUVRE GROUP ON TOP OF HOOD (1958 ONLY)

$3631.

new BUMPERS

MODEL 867 (THROUGH 1964)

230 HP (STD.) 245-270 (OPT.)
250-290 (1959 W. FUEL INJ.)
275-315 (1960 W. FUEL INJ.)

59-60

(10,261 BLT., 1960)

$3872.
(IN '60; $3 LESS THAN '59)

(9670 BLT., 1959)

XX-8956

6

Introduction

Welcome to this big new color edition, much of which has never been seen in any previous book!

For some time, I've been assembling various car, truck, van and bus spotter's guides—books showing the different makes year by year to help you positively identify older vehicles by their appearances or special features. All the previous books in this series were in black and white because, until recently, the cost of doing a book of this size in color would be four or five times what it now costs! Thanks to improved technology, a book like this is now more affordable.

The use of color here is dramatic and exciting—and more artistic and much more interesting! It's the same improvement as when young Dorothy left Kansas in a black-and-white cyclone and landed in Oz in full color!

The cars here are shown mostly in their original factory colors, along with official color charts, in some cases. However, I must add that even the original sales catalogs contained disclaimers stating that, due to the reprinting process, some colors might not be 100 percent accurate in their hue. I've encountered two copies of some old sales catalogs where the colors varied slightly from one copy to another. On the whole, these color charts are quite helpful.

We don't mean to be presumptuous by using the word "bible" in the title of this new book. However, the dictionary explains that "bible" can refer to any authorative book on a particular subject.

At any rate, I'm convinced that God definitely had a hand in helping me complete this large project, as so many pieces fit together perfectly, like parts of a pre-planned picture puzzle!

This was no coincidence, as it happened over and over as I was assembling the pages. You'll find much new material here that never appeared in any other book! Nearly all illustrations are from original sales catalogs and ads—except in a handful of cases where artists' conceptions from the catalogs were so exaggerated in length and width that I had to supply a photo that was more accurate.

You'll find all kinds of cars from 1940 through 1980 here, along with original prices, specifications, and other tidbits of helpful information. You'll also find powerful muscle cars, family cars, luxury cars, economy cars, rare ones seldom ever seen, as well as many that nearly everyone will recognize!

Studebaker—Nash—Edsel—De Soto—Hudson—Packard—Kaiser and Frazer. They're just some of the long-discontinued makes you'll become familiar with, along with your more recent favorites!

As space permits, often several body styles and variations are shown of a given year and make. I had to be careful to avoid making some pictures too small by reducing them to fit. A magnifying glass might help, in the case of some color names that were reduced—along with their accompanying color charts—to fit in.

Since some prices and specifications could change from month to month, I couldn't include all those changes but did include both east/ Midwest and West Coast prices, in many instances.

You'll find many an old four-wheeled friend among these many colorful pages and we hope you'll want to keep and enjoy this book for a long time—for sheer enjoyment!

With best wishes,
Tad

Tad Burness
PO Box 247
Pacific Grove, CA 93950

P.S. By the way, one of my favorite projects, a labor of love, is my comic strip series "Michael, Mark and Stevie" about a family of hobbyists, their dog and their neighbors. It appears in a local newspaper and I hope to get it published nationally as a book, as a syndicated newspaper feature, or best, in both forms! Two episodes of "Michael, Mark and Stevie" appeared in my recent Vintage House Book, 1880 to 1980, also from KP Books. More are included on the last pages of this book.

I very much enjoy writing and drawing these and hope you will find them entertaining as a tailpiece to this collection.

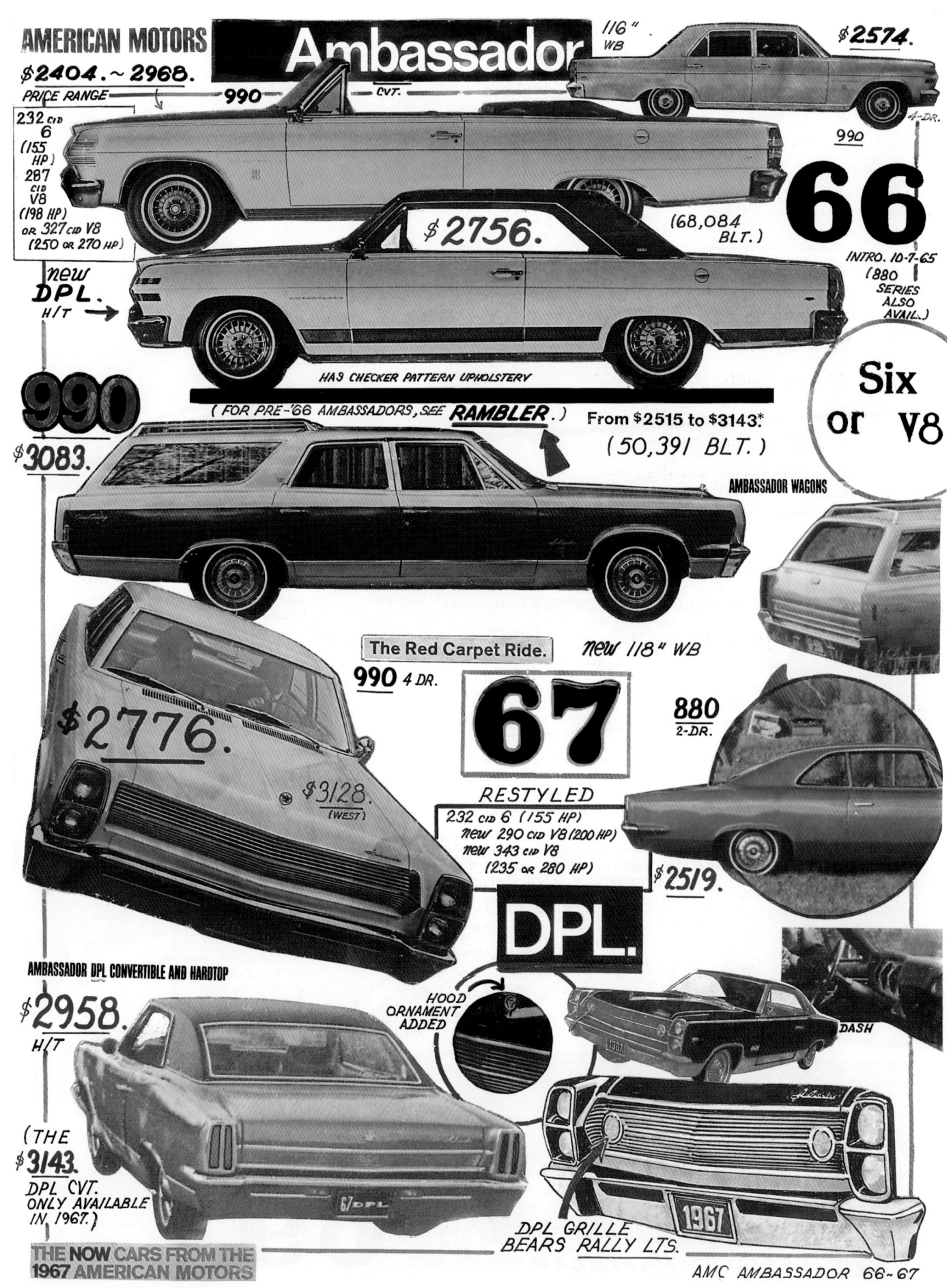

AMERICAN MOTORS Ambassador

$2404. ~ 2968.
PRICE RANGE

990 CVT.

116" WB $2574.

232 CID 6 (155 HP) 287 CID V8 (198 HP) or 327 CID V8 (250 or 270 HP)

new DPL. H/T →

$2756.

990

4-DR.

990

66

(68,084 BLT.)

INTRO. 10-7-65 (880 SERIES ALSO AVAIL.)

HAS CHECKER PATTERN UPHOLSTERY

990
$3083.

(FOR PRE-'66 AMBASSADORS, SEE **RAMBLER**.) From $2515 to $3143*
(50,391 BLT.)

Six or V8

AMBASSADOR WAGONS

The Red Carpet Ride.

new 118" WB

990 4 DR.

67

880 2-DR.

$2776.

$3128. (WEST)

RESTYLED
232 CID 6 (155 HP)
new 290 CID V8 (200 HP)
new 343 CID V8 (235 or 280 HP)

$2519.

DPL.

AMBASSADOR DPL CONVERTIBLE AND HARDTOP

$2958. H/T

HOOD ORNAMENT ADDED

DASH

(THE $3143. DPL CVT. ONLY AVAILABLE IN 1967.)

1967

1967

DPL GRILLE BEARS RALLY LTS.

THE NOW CARS FROM THE 1967 AMERICAN MOTORS

AMC AMBASSADOR 66~67

9

AMERICAN MOTORS AMBASSADOR, DPL, OR SST

MODELS; NO MORE 880 OR 990 SERIES)

SEDAN *$3065.

* WEST COAST PRICE

DASH

new DOOR HANDLES

$2820.

new SIDE SAFETY LIGHTS

new GRILLE

$2947.

DPL

(INTRO. 9-26-67) **68**

AIR COND. NOW STD. EQUIP.

NO MORE HOOD ORNAMENT UNTIL 1974

$2820.~3207. 1968 PRICE RANGE

SST (ABOVE) has RALLY LIGHTS ON GRILLE.

(1969 MODELS INTRO. 10-1-68)

AMBASSADOR SEDAN, DPL and SST SEDANS, WAGONS and H/Ts AVAILABLE
$2914.~3998. PRICE RANGE

(NO MORE AMBASSADOR MODELS AFTER 1974.)

REAR FENDER DETAIL

"Ambassador" NAME ON new GRILLE; HORIZONTAL ROW OF HDLTS.

new HORIZONTAL SHAPE FOR FRONT SIDE SAFETY LIGHTS.

$3,165 (SALE)

69

SEE ALSO **RAMBLER**

AMBER LTS. NOW IN NARROWER SLOTS

REAR

AMC AMBASSADOR

68 ~ 69

10

AMERICAN MOTORS AMBASSADOR, DPL, OR SST

232 CID 6 (155 HP) IN STD. SEDAN $3020.

$3739 SST H/T

DPL

70

$3588.

The instrument panel of the Ambassador SST

SST SEDAN $3722.

1970

SST WAGON $4122.

V8s
304 CID (210 HP)
360 CID (245 or 290 HP)
or
390 CID V8 (325 HP)

(FINAL DPL MODELS)

new "BAVARIAN OAK" WOODGRAIN PATTERN ON DASHBOARD

A/C STD. EQUIP.

1971 EXT. COLORS

	Hornet and Gremlin	Javelin	Matador and Ambassador
P1	●	●	●
A1	●	●	●
A2	●	●	●
A4	●	●	●
A5	●		●
A6			●
A7	●		●
A8		●	
A9			●
B2	●	●	●
B3	●	●	●
B4			●
B5			●
B6	●	●	●
B7	●	●	●
B8	●	●	
B9	●	●	
C1	●	●	●

P1 Classic Black   A1 Snow White   A2 Canary Yellow
A4 Skyline Blue
A5 Midway Blue, Metallic   A6 Midnight Blue, Metallic   A7 Limelight Green, Metallic   A8 Meadow Green, Metallic
A9 Raven Green, Metallic

B2 Burnished Brown, Metallic

B3 Quick Silver, Metallic

B4 Charcoal Gray, Metallic

B6 Electric Blue, Metallic

B7 Brilliant Green, Metallic

Eighteen exterior colors, all in "Lustre-Gard" ACRYLIC ENAMEL. For durable, long-lasting beauty (triple-coated baked finish).

★ = NOT AVAIL. ON MATADOR AMBASSADOR

SST

$3852.

$4253.

AMBASSADOR 1971 PROD. = 41674

DASH

71

All colors shown are available as two-tone with White or Black (except no Black for Midnight Blue, Raven Green and Deep Maroon), for the following models:

Hornet SST Sedans (roof)
Matador Sedans and Hardtops (roof)
Matador Wagons (side panel)
Ambassador Sedans and Hardtops (roof)
Ambassador SST Wagon

B5 Deep Maroon, Metallic

new GRILLE

B8 Mustard Yellow   B9 Matador Red   C1 Golden Lime, Metallic

BROUGHAM H/T

$3999.

AMC AMBASSADOR 70~71

11

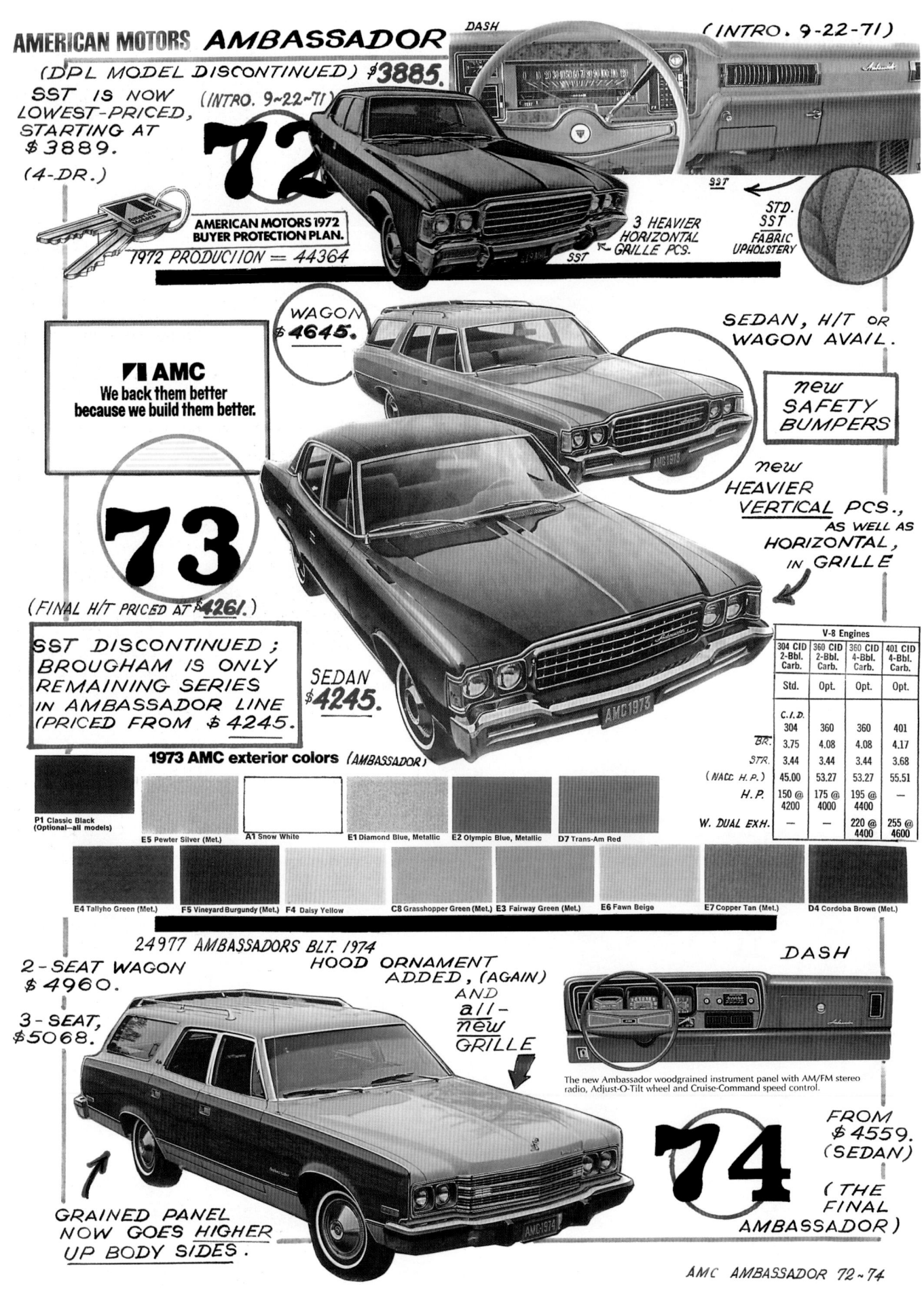

AMERICAN MOTORS **AMBASSADOR** DASH (INTRO. 9-22-71)

(DPL MODEL DISCONTINUED) $3885.

SST IS NOW LOWEST-PRICED, STARTING AT $3889. (4-DR.)

(INTRO. 9~22~71)

72

AMERICAN MOTORS 1972 BUYER PROTECTION PLAN.

1972 PRODUCTION = 44364

3 HEAVIER HORIZONTAL GRILLE PCS. SST

SST

STD. SST FABRIC UPHOLSTERY

WAGON $4645.

SEDAN, H/T OR WAGON AVAIL.

◢ AMC
We back them better because we build them better.

new SAFETY BUMPERS

new HEAVIER VERTICAL PCS., AS WELL AS HORIZONTAL, IN GRILLE

73

(FINAL H/T PRICED AT $4261.)

SST DISCONTINUED; BROUGHAM IS ONLY REMAINING SERIES IN AMBASSADOR LINE (PRICED FROM $4245.

SEDAN $4245.

	V-8 Engines			
	304 CID 2-Bbl. Carb.	360 CID 2-Bbl. Carb.	360 CID 4-Bbl. Carb.	401 CID 4-Bbl. Carb.
	Std.	Opt.	Opt.	Opt.
C.I.D.	304	360	360	401
BR.	3.75	4.08	4.08	4.17
STR.	3.44	3.44	3.44	3.68
(NACC H.P.)	45.00	53.27	53.27	55.51
H.P.	150 @ 4200	175 @ 4000	195 @ 4400	—
W. DUAL EXH.	—	—	220 @ 4400	255 @ 4600

1973 AMC exterior colors (AMBASSADOR)

P1 Classic Black (Optional—all models)
E5 Pewter Silver (Met.)
A1 Snow White
E1 Diamond Blue, Metallic
E2 Olympic Blue, Metallic
D7 Trans-Am Red

E4 Tallyho Green (Met.)
F5 Vineyard Burgundy (Met.)
F4 Daisy Yellow
C8 Grasshopper Green (Met.)
E3 Fairway Green (Met.)
E6 Fawn Beige
E7 Copper Tan (Met.)
D4 Cordoba Brown (Met.)

24977 AMBASSADORS BLT. 1974

HOOD ORNAMENT ADDED, (AGAIN) AND all-new GRILLE

DASH

2-SEAT WAGON $4960.

3-SEAT, $5068.

The new Ambassador woodgrained instrument panel with AM/FM stereo radio, Adjust-O-Tilt wheel and Cruise-Command speed control.

74

FROM $4559. (SEDAN)

(THE FINAL AMBASSADOR)

GRAINED PANEL NOW GOES HIGHER UP BODY SIDES.

AMC AMBASSADOR 72~74

AMERICAN MOTORS AMX

(new) (INTRO. 2-24-68)

(ASSOCIATED WITH JAVELIN SERIES THROUGH '74)

EA. AMX CAR'S PRODUCTION NUMBER IS SET IN DASH.

97" WB

$3485. ('68)
$3571. ('69)

V8 ENGINES
290 CID (225 HP)
343 CID OR
390 CID (315 HP)

E70 x 14 TIRES

READILY IDENTIFIED BY UNIQUE DUAL WEDGES ON HOOD, EACH BEARING 5 PARALLEL LOUVRES.

1969 MODEL INTRO. 10-1-68.

$3245. ('68) (6725 BLT.)

$3297. ('69) (8293 BLT.)

68-69

A-8 SERIAL # PREFIX

A-9 PREFIX FOR 1969, MORE STRIPE COMBINATIONS.

new STD. 360 CID V8 (290 HP) (INTRO. 9-25-69)

new ROCKER PANEL DECORATION

70 $3679.

new E78 x 14 TIRES
new BODY STRIPE

new GRILLE and HOOD SCOOP

1971~1974 AMX IN AMC-JAVELIN SECTION →

(NO 1975 OR 1976 AMX)

HORNET-AMX

108" WB

77

(AMX BECOMES OWN SERIES IN 1978.)

"AMX" LETTERING AT CENTER OF GRILLE IN 1980, AS ON WHITE AMX, LOWER LEFT.'

258 CID 6 (95 HP) OR 304 CID V8 (120 HP)

(V8 AVAIL. THROUGH '79)

6-CYL. PRICES = $5624. ('78)
7019. ('79)
6766. ('80)

'78 V8 = $5391.
'79 V8 = 6769.

78-80

WITH SUNROOF and HOOD DECAL

AMX-citement.

AT RIGHT, 1979 MODELS ILLUSTRATED →

('80)

AMX

AMC

96" WB

A higher level of excitement.

American Motors AMX 68~80

American Motors ———— **Classic** —— *(1961 to 1966)*

("RAMBLER CLASSIC")

(CONT'D. FROM "RAMBLER" SECTION)

intermediate size car   *112" WB*

WAGONS FROM $2888.

AVAILABLE IN "550," "770" OR "REBEL" SUB-MODELS.

2 SIXES and 3 V8s AVAILABLE. STANDARD ENGS.: 287 CID V8 (198 HP) OR 232 CID 6 (145 HP) 6.95/7.35 × 14 TIRES

770 CVT. $3065.

66

(THE FINAL "CLASSIC" LINE)

new GRILLE

(WHITE VINYL TOP ALSO AVAIL., 3-66)

new "CRISP-LINE" ROOF (Rebel/ H/T)

$2972.

(MARLIN ALSO IN CLASSIC LINE, '65 - '66.)

(SEE AMC MARLIN)

Rebel

(INTRO. 10-7-65)

(AVAIL. ONLY AS 2-DR. H/T)

(CLASSIC REPLACED BY THE **AMERICAN MOTORS** **1967 Rebel** *)*

FOR 1965 and EARLIER "CLASSIC" SERIES, PLEASE SEE "RAMBLER" SECTION.

AMC CLASSIC   66

AMC Concord

(REPLACES HORNET)

(SINCE 1978)

78 NEW

232 CID 6, (90 HP) OR 304 CID V8 (120 HP)

D/L 2-DR. $3999.

SALE = $3949.

(REG. $4700 WESTERN PRICES)

DASH

PRICE RANGE === $3749. - 4299.

108" WB

(HATCHBACK, 4 DR. and WAGON AVAIL.)

121 CID 4-CYL. ENGINE and 258 CID 6-CYL. ENGINE ADDED; OTHER 6-CYL. and V8 STILL AVAIL. (FINAL CONCORD V8)

$4788.

D/L 4-DR. $5701. (WEST)

$4988.

D/L WAGON $5901. (WEST)

4 new RECTANGULAR HEADLIGHTS

79

$4623.

$5701. (WEST)

$4324. - 6688. PRICE RANGE

new GRILLE

$6188. LIMITED 4-DR. $6459. (WEST)

(FINAL) D/L **HATCHBACK**

1980 PRICES = $5868. TO $7323.

(NO 1980 HATCHBACK COUPE)

new WRAP-AROUND TAIL LIGHTS

FROM $5219.

151 CID 4 OR 258 CID 6

80

$5419. UP

new GRILLE

14" WHEELS

SEDAN

$5094. UP

COUPE

DASH

AMC CONCORD 78~80

15

American Motors EAGLE 4-WD (INTRO. 1980)

GRILLE CLOSE-UP (STD.)

REAR

COUPE $7168. WT. 3382

80 LIMITED MODELS (LTD) COST $397. MORE.

ALL NEW

WT. 3450

SEDAN $7418.

DASH

109.3" WHEELBASE
258 CID 6 (110 HP) 22-GAL. GAS TANK
3.08 OR 3.31 GEAR RATIO

BUT BEARS A CLOSE RESEMBLANCE TO THE 1980 AMC CONCORD. (EAGLE'S BODY RIDE HIGHER ABOVE THE WHEELS.) CHASSIS FEATURES

INDEPEND. FRONT SUSPENSION

4-W-D TRANS.

POWER FRONT DISC BRAKES

P195/75R x 15 TIRES

WAGON WT. 3470

$7718.

1980 AMC COLOR SELECTOR

Cardinal Red	Russet, Met. 1)	Bordeaux, Met. 1)
Cameo Blue 1)	Med. Blue, Met. 1)	Navy Blue 1)
Dk. Green, Met. 2)	Saxon Yellow 1)	Cameo Tan 1)
Caramel 3)	Med. Brown, Met. 1)	Dk. Brown, Met. 1)
Quick Silver, Met. 1)	Smoke Gray, Met. 1)	Classic Black 1)
Olympic White 1)		

AVAILABILITY
1) all lines
2) Concord/Eagle only
3) Spirit only

The American Eagle. Totally new. Totally exciting. And totally right for the 1980s!

Eagle Interior — Durham Plaid (optional)

AMC EAGLE 80

16

American Motors Gremlin *new*

standard 6-cyl. engine.

(1970 TO 1978)

Gremlin	
$1,879[1]	$1,959[1]
2-Passenger	4-Passenger

ORIG. 1970 PRICES

6.00 x 13 TIRES (THROUGH '72)

('70)

W/O BUMPER GUARDS

WITH BUMPER GUARDS

DASHBOARD VISIBLE

199 or 232 CID 6 (128 or 145 HP)	96" WB

If you had to compete with GM, Ford and Chrysler, what would you do?

American Motors

1971 MODELS ILLUSTR., UNLESS OTHERWISE INDICATED

Gremlin X

Gremlin X
X

GRILLE

70½-71

(INTRO. WED., 4-1-70)

(INTRO. TUES., 9-15-70)

HATCH WINDOW OPENS

REAR SEAT UP

('70)

"GREMLIN" FIGURE ON FENDER

REAR SEAT DOWN

THIS HUB CAP STILL AVAIL. 1971.

AMC GREMLIN 70½-71

('70)

AMC Gremlin
AMERICAN MOTORS BUYER PROTECTION PLAN

72 (617,17 BLT.)

"THE BEST PUT-TOGETHER CARS OUT OF DETROIT THIS YEAR MAY COME OUT OF WISCONSIN. THAT'S WHERE AMERICAN MOTORS MAKES THEM." —Popular Mechanics

GREMLIN $1999. (6-CYL.)

(8500 + V8s, FROM $2153.)

"5-LITRE V8" DESIGNATION INDICATES new 304 CID 304 CID V8.

(INTRO. WED., 9-22-71) new V8 OPTIONAL

Gremlin X

new CURVE IN BODY STRIPE.

Gremlin STD.

STD. FROM $2098.

'73 Gremlin can wear LEVI'S®. All you have to do is ask for our special LEVI'S® custom trim option. One of the many interiors and options

LEVI'S

73

new SAFETY BUMPERS new 6.45 × 14 TIRES

AMC Gremlin
We back them better because we build them better

1973 AMC exterior colors

A1 Snow White	E1 Diamond Blue, Metallic	E2 Olympic Blue, Metallic
F2 Maxi Blue	C8 Grasshopper Green (Met.)	E3 Fairway Green (Met.)
E4 Tallyho Green (Met.)	F1 Blarney Green	E5 Pewter Silver (Met.)
E6 Fawn Beige	E7 Copper Tan (Met.)	D4 Cordoba Brown (Met.)
F4 Daisy Yellow	E9 Mellow Yellow	D7 Trans-Am Red
F5 Vineyard Burgundy (Met.)	F3 Fresh Plum (Met.)	P1 Classic Black (Optional—all models)

	A1	E1	E2	F2	C8	E3	E4	F1	E5	E6	E7	D4	F4	E9	D7	F5	F3
Gremlin	•	•	•	•		•		•	•				•		•	•	•
Gremlin LEVI'S®	•	•	•		•		•		•				•		•		
Gremlin "X"	•	•	•		•		•		•				•		•	•	•
Hornet	•	•	•		•		•		•		•		•		•	•	•
Sportabout Gucci	•	•	•		•		•		•		•		•		•	•	•
Javelin & AMX	•	•	•		•		•		•		•		•		•	•	•
Cardin Javelin	•	•					•		•		•				•	•	•
Matador	•	•	•			•	•		•		•	•			•	•	•
Ambassador	•	•	•			•	•		•		•	•			•	•	•

74 (119,642 = 6 CYL. 12263 = V8s)

new GRILLE, MINOR RESTYLING

6 $2481. V8 $2635.

1974 AMC

CHANGE INSIDE '74 DOOR

AMC Gremlin 72-74

18

AMC Gremlin

$2798. UP
(6~CYL.)
(42630 BLT.)
2694 lbs.

FROM $3127.
(WEST)
(ADD $169. FOR BUCKET SEATS)

STD.
232 CID
6 (100 HP)

258 CID 6
OR 304 CID V8 OPTIONAL

VINYL INTERIOR

DASH

6-CYL. ENGINE

Levi's® Gremlin in H1 Deep Blue Metallic.

LEVI'S GREMLIN (ABOVE) and LEVI'S INTERIOR

75

See all the '75 economy cars from AMC and you'll see why people call AMC dealers **THE ECONOMY EXPERTS**

LEVI'S®

$2952. (V8)
(3218 BLT.)
2952 lbs.

X

P1 Classic Black	G7 Alpine White	G8 Pastel Blue	H1 Deep Blue Met.	G3 Dark Green Met.	E6 Fawn Beige		H9 Silver Dawn Met.	E9 Mellow Yellow
J7 Ivory Green		G9 Medium Blue Met.	H5 Green Apple	J8 Caramel Tan	H8 Autumn Red Met.	H4 Dark Cocoa Met.	G6 Sienna Orange	F9 Copper Met.
						D7 Red		

AMC GREMLIN 75

AMC /II Gremlin

note "X" ON CENTER BAR OF GRILLE

Gremlin X

Gremlin X instrument panel. Options shown include: AM/FM stereo radio, air conditioning, leather-wrapped sports steering wheel, rear window defogger.

96" WB (1970 to 1978)

FINAL YEAR THAT GREMLIN NAME APPEARS HERE

STD. MODEL

new GRILLE

$2889. UP

COLORFUL AMC FLOOR MATS

76

232 CID 6 (100 HP)
304 CID V8 (150 HP)

6.45 x 14 TIRES

21-GALLON GAS TANK

the only full 2 year, 24,000 mile warranty on engine and drive train.

INTRODUCING
BUYER PROTECTION PLAN II ('77)

There's more to an AMC /II

note STRIPE PATTERN

FROM $2995. ('77)
$3539. ('78)

new 4-CYL. ENGINE ALSO AVAILABLE (COSTS $253 MORE THAN 6!) (121 CID, 57 HP) (22 CITY, 35 HWY., EPA)

6 CUT TO 90 HP

LEVI'S DENIM UPHOLSTERY STILL AVAIL. IN '78

GREMLIN "X"

ROOF RACK OPTIONAL

new GRILLE

77-78

THE FINAL GREMLIN

CB RADIO AVAIL.

JOHNSON Messenger 4175
CHANNEL SELECTOR OFF VOLUME SQUELCH

R 1 3
2 4

American Motors Sales Corporation

AMC /II Gremlin 76~78

20

AMC ◢◣ Hornet (REPLACES RAMBLER American) (1970~1977)

S/D.

232 OR 258 CID 6 (135 OR 150 HP)

← SST →

1970

1970

STD. □ 2-DR.

304 CID V8 AVAIL. (210 HP)

Hornet. The little rich car.

'70

1970

WITH 360 CID V8 (245 HP @ 4400 OR 285 HP @ 4800)

new 1 SC 360

(INTRO. 10-6-70)

71

DASH

STD. SEDAN

UN-GRAINED

new

THE SPORTABOUT. STATION WAGON

WOOD-GRAINED

Spring Special

Hornet 1971½

"SPECIALLY EQUIPPED" MODELS IN SPRING, 1971 INCLUDE

Free sunroofs

new AMERICAN MOTORS BUYER PROTECTION PLAN ◢◣

new IMPROVED "TORQUE-COMMAND" AUTO. TRANS. AVAIL.

new 3-SPOKE STEERING WHEEL AVAIL.

GUCCI UPH.

DASH

72

SPORTABOUT

(INTRO. 9-22-71)

HORNET AMC HORNET 70~72

AMC Hornet

SPORTABOUT wagon

$2675. UP

ALSO USED IN GREMLIN, LEVI'S JEANS MATERIAL AVAIL. FOR INTERIOR (SPRING, 1973)

WEST: $2903. UNGRAINED SPORTABOUT ALSO AVAIL.

new GRILLE

GUCCI INTERIOR

Introducing the Hornet Hatchback.

73 108" WB

HORNET SPORTABOUT

We back them better because we build them better.

2-DR. $2298. UP

$2449. UP

$2715. UP (WEST) new!

Hornet

$2824. UP

HORNET 2 AND 4-DOOR SEDAN

H/B

$3049.

232 CID 6 (100 HP)
258 CID 6 (110 HP)
304 CID V8 (150 HP)
360 CID V8 (175 HP)

74

HORNET SPORTABOUT
(67709 BLT.)

Blue "Venetian" custom fabric trim. Available on Sportabout reclining seats. Includes custom upholstery door panels and moldings.

WITH WOODGRAIN

new 1974 ENERGY ABSORBING SAFETY BUMPERS AMC Hornet 73~74

UNGRAINED

AMC ⧄ Hornet

For 1975 . . .
17 "Luster-Guard" Acrylic Enamel Color Choices

1975 HORNETS PRICED FROM $3902.
1977 HORNETS FROM $4343. (WEST)

FINAL 3 YEARS
FOR HORNET.
FEW VISIBLE
CHANGES FROM
1975 – 1977 EXCEPT
FOR BUMPER IMPROVEMENT
NOTED (1976.)

HORNET
Sportabout
wagon

Hometown AMC

Service

AMC BUYER PROTECTION PLAN.™

$3374. UP ('75)

new
GRILLE

D/L 2~DR.

$3074. UP

75-77

(1975 EASTERN PRICES
IN **RED**.)

('76)

('75)   HATCHBACK "X" $3312.

1976 *has* THIN RUBBER STRIPS AT BUMPER EDGES

STD. AM RADIO

American Motors
5·7·9·12·14·16

(AM/FM
ALSO AVAIL.)

(REPLACED BY
CONCORD,
1978)

('75) 4-DR.

$3124. UP

AMC ⧄ Hornet 75-77

23

AMERICAN MOTORS

(1968~1974)

109" WB*
232 CID 6 (145 HP)
290 " V8 (225 ")
343 " V8 (280 ")
390 " V8 (315 ")

6.95/
7.35
×
14
TIRES
(THROUGH
'69)

Javelin.

VINYL TOP →
OPTIONAL

SST H/T
$2587.

(INTRO. 9-26-67)

(56,462 BLT.)

68 New

$2848.
WESTERN PRICE

(STANDARD H/T
PRICED AT
$2482.)
$2743.
WESTERN PRICE

"JAVELIN"
NAME ON GRILLE OF
1968 MODEL.

*=(THROUGH
'70)

DASH HAS DEEPLY-RECESSED
ROUND GAUGES and
CONTROLS

68 JAVELIN

REAR VIEW (W/O VINYL TOP)

AMC JAVELIN 68

AMERICAN MOTORS *JAVELIN* $2512. $2633. (SST)

(INTRO. 10-1-68)

69

SCRIPT "JAVELIN" NAME NOW ABOVE GRILLE.

SPECIAL

Big Bad Javelin

IN "BIG BAD ORANGE," "BIG BAD BLUE" OR "BIG BAD GREEN," WITH PAINTED FRONT and REAR BUMPERS, OTHER OPTIONS.

new "BULL'S EYE"

(40,675 BLT.)

(ASSOCIATED WITH JAVELIN SERIES THROUGH '74)

AMX A-8 SERIAL # PREFIX

(INTRO. 2-24-68)

A-9 PREFIX FOR 1969, MORE STRIPE COMBINATIONS.

$3485. ('68)
$3571. ('69)
(WEST COAST)

ENGINES :
290 CID V8 (225 HP)
OR OPTIONAL
343 CID V8 (280 HP)
390 CID V8 (315 HP)

EA. AMX CAR'S PRODUCTION NUMBER IS SET IN DASH.

E70 x 14" TIRES

97" WB

1969 MODEL INTRO. 10-1-68.

DETAILS OF HOOD

68-69

(new)

BASE PRICES =
$3245. ('68)
3297. ('69)

6725 BLT. 1968
8293 " 1969

AMC JAVELIN/AMX 68~69

READILY IDENTIFIED BY UNIQUE DUAL WEDGES ON HOOD, EACH BEARING 5 PARALLEL LOUVRES.

AMERICAN MOTORS *JAVELIN* $2848.
360 OR 390 V8

AMX DASH

JAVELIN SST

(28210 BLT.) (ALL MODELS)

AMX
(4116 BLT.)
$3395. (V8)

STD. JAVELIN $2720.
WITH 6 CYL. 232 CID (145 HP)

70

(29/30 BLT.)
$2874.

71
UP TO 401 CID V8

← JAVELIN →
SST $2999.

AMX
(2054 BLT.)
$3432.

IF YOU'RE GOING TO BUY A SPORTY CAR, BUY ONE THAT'S BEEN PLACES.

JAVELIN SST

INTRO. 9-22-71
(23455 BLT.)

BUMPER GUARDS

new GRILLE $2807. UP

72

AMX $3109.
(2729 BLT.)

• A. Javelin instrument panel. Notice how it wraps right around

new JAVELIN MESH GRILLE WITH RALLY LTS.

(AMX PROD.=4980 IN '73 and also '74)
$3191. ('73)
$3299. ('74)

AMX

AMX RADIO/TAPE

TACH./ CLOCK

CARDIN UPH.

REAR

JAVELIN and AMX

73-74

$3347. ('73)
(WEST)
$3867. ('74)

FROM $2889. ('73)
$2999. ('74)
(1974 IS FINAL JAVELIN.)

JAVELIN

AMC JAVELIN 70-74

American Motors MARLIN

Marlin BY RAMBLER — Newest of the Sensible Spectaculars
(ANNOUNCED 2-65)

(1965 - 1967)

116" WB
232 CID 6 (155 HP)
OR
287 CID V8 (198 HP)
OR
327 CID V8
270 HP @ 4700 RPM

65

POWER DISC BRAKES STANDARD

10,327 '65 MARLINS BLT.

WIRE WHEEL DETAIL

EASILY IDENTIFIED BY UNIQUE FASTBACK "KNIFE-EDGE" REAR STYLING

7.35 OR 7.75 × 14 TIRES

$**3143.** f.o.b. and up

Marlin GRILLE and SEATS (RECLINING)

Introducing excitement!
The swinging new man-size sports-fastback – MARLIN!

6557
2~DR. FASTBACK H/T IS ONLY MODEL AVAIL.

SEE ALSO:
RAMBLER

INTERIOR, THROUGH LONG SIDE WINDOW AREA

AMC MARLIN 65

AMERICAN MOTORS MARLIN

(1965 - 1967)

6 CYL. OR V8

IN 1965, 1966, A PART OF THE CLASSIC LINE

112" WB (THROUGH '66)

66 (INTRO. 10-7-65)

(ONLY 4547 BLT.)

SALE $2601.

REG. $3051.

SOME WITH CORRUGATED ROCKER PANEL TRIM

232 CID 6 (145 HP @ 4300 RPM) OR 287 CID V8 (198 HP @ 4700 RPM) 2 OTHER V8s AVAIL., TO 327 CID)

NOW A PART OF AMBASSADOR LINE FOR '67.

new 118" WB

ROUND MEDALLION REMOVED FROM REAR DECK ↓

6 CYL. has new 155 HP @ 4400 RPM; STD. V8 with new 290 CID (200 HP @ 4600 RPM) OR 2 new 343 CID V8s (TO 280 HP @ 4800 RPM)

67 (ONLY 2545 BLT.)

$3315. (WEST COAST)

new SMOOTHER BODY SIDES, RECTANGULAR GAS FILLER DOOR

RALLY LTS. IN GRILLE

THE FINAL MARLIN

BASE PRICE RAISED TO $2963.

REPLACED 1968 BY *REBEL* and *JAVELIN*

AMC MARLIN 66~67

28

AMERICAN MOTORS Matador

(1971 TO 1978)

232 CID 6 (135 HP) OR STANDARD 304 CID V8 (210 HP)

(INTRO. 10-6-70)

(REPLACES Rebel)

If you were to compete against G.M., Ford and Chrysler, what would you do?

71

118" WB
E78/G78 × 14 TIRES

TAIL LIGHTS

H/T (ABOVE) $3306.

4 - DR. SEDAN $3277.

ROOF RACK and WITH WOODGRAIN

THE MATADOR STATION WAGON

2- SEATS = $3680.
3 " 3798.

← UNGRAINED WAGON AT LEFT

Engines	Carb. Type	H.P. @ R.P.M.	Torque @ R.P.M.	Comp. Ratio & Fuel	Bore & Stroke
232 CID Six (Standard)	1-Barrel	135 @ 4000	210 @ 1600	8.0:1 Reg.	3.75" x 3.50"
258 CID Six	1-Barrel	150 @ 3800	240 @ 1800	8.0:1 Reg.	3.75" x 3.90"
304 CID V-8	2-Barrel	210 @ 4400	300 @ 2600	8.4:1 Reg.	3.75" x 3.44"
360 CID V-8	2-Barrel	245 @ 4400	365 @ 2600	8.5:1 Reg.	4.08" x 3.44"
360 CID V-8	4-Barrel	285 @ 4800	390 @ 3200	8.5:1 Reg.	4.08" x 3.44"
401 CID V-8	4-Barrel	330 @ 5000	430 @ 3400	9.5:1 Pre.	4.17" x 3.68"

CUSTOM SERAPE FABRIC (H/T)

FRONT CLOSE-UP

AMC MATADOR 71

AMERICAN MOTORS MATADOR.

A CAR YOU PROBABLY NEVER HEARD OF.
(INTRO. 9-22-71)

72

WAGONS FROM $3140.

The L.A. Police Department discovers the Matador.
1972 PROD.= 54813

H/T $2818. UP
$3330. (WEST)

MATADOR IS BACKED BY THE AMERICAN MOTORS BUYER PROTECTION PLAN.

$2784. UP
STD. 304 CID V8 HP CUT TO 150
SEDAN
$3227. (WEST)
new GRILLE

SEDAN
$2853. (6)
$2952. (V8)

Matador 4-dr. Sedan shown in Copper Tan Metallic.

FINAL 2-DR. H/T IN MATADOR SERIES
$2887. UP
$3261. (WEST)

73

The roomy intermediate.
2-WAY TAILGATE

"TROPICANA" UPHOLSTERY

WAGON

new GRILLE
$3179.

Matador Wagon shown in Grasshopper Green Metallic.
2-SEAT-$3652.   3-SEAT-$3760. (WEST)

FROM $3652 (WEST)

wagon
(6734 V8 WAGONS BLT.)
$3477.

SEDAN and WAGON = 118" WB
new COUPE (NEXT PG.) has 114" WB

6-CYL. WAGONS (2975 BLT.)
$3378.

74
A

(CONT'D. NEXT PAGE)

new LARGER WOODGRAINED AREA

AMC MATADOR 72~74(A)

PRESENTING THE ONLY ALL-NEW MID-SIZE CAR FOR 1974
FROM **AMERICAN MOTORS**
118" WB
$3096. UP

ONLY COUPES
ARE TOTALLY
RESTYLED.

OLEG CASSINI MODEL
BEARS A SIDE
MEDALLION.

$4428.
('74)

BLACK
TUFTED
NYLON-
KNIT FABRIC
WITH COPPER
BUTTONS IN ILLUSTRATED
"OLEG CASSINI" INTER. OPT.

'74 OLEG C. DASH
SHOWN AT LEFT CENTER

('75)

HVY. STRIPE, BLACK
GRILLE
ON
"X"

$3699.

Matador X ('1500 BLT.)

1974
COUPES
PRICED
FROM
$4029.
($5660 IN
1978.)

('74)

('76)

74-78
B

$4373.

Matador Barcelona instrument panel.

FROM $3844.

UNGRAINED

('76)

('75)

$3985. (WEST) ('74)

"BARCELONA" UPH.

('76)

1975 AMC
COLORS

1974 SIMILAR,
DARKER GRAIN

$4549. UP

$5302. WEST ('77)

MATADOR SERIES
ENDS 1978.
(6 OR V8)

COUPE (ONLY)
GETS NEW
GRILLE ('76)

('76)

$3452. UP

American Motors

AMC Pacer (1975-1980)
new! 75-76

6 CYL. 232 CID

22-GAL. FUEL TANK
100" WB

BERRY "BASKETRY PRINT"

('76)

(72/58 BLT.)
('75)
$3299.

AMERICAN MOTORS
$3,499
WITH A/C
('76)

The first wide small car.

MODEL 66-7
2-DR. HATCHBACK CONTINUES

57.1"   60.7"

('77)

MODEL 68-7
$4153. Wagon 77
(WEST)   (new)

htchb. sdn 3d	$3649.	3,156 lbs.
wgn 3d	3799.	3,202

INTERIOR

There's more to an AMC

('76)   AMC PACER 75-77

32

AMC ⫽ Pacer

WAGON REAR W. HATCH OPEN

'78

304 CID V8
ALSO AVAIL.
('78-'79)

100" WB

new GRILLE

4193. (6)
4443. (V8)

(HATCHBACK $4048. UP)

WAGON $4519. (WEST)

232 CID
6 CYL.
(90 HP)

new V8
120 HP

COLOR SELECTOR

Olympic White *	Quick Silver, met. **	Classic Black *	Cumberland Green, met. **	Wedgewood Blue	Starboard Blue, met. **	Khaki **
Saxon Yellow *	Morocco Buff *	Alpaca Brown, met. **	Sable Brown, met. **	Firecracker Red *	Russet, met. **	Bordeaux, met. **

1979 COLORS

Misty Beige Clearcoat ***

British Bronze, met. **

Availability (on most models): * all carlines ** all carlines except AMX *** Pacer only

LIMITED HATCHBACK $6222. ('79) (WEST)

NEW DL *and* LIMITED SERIES

(1979 EXAMPLES ILLUSTR.) (UNLESS OTHERWISE NOTED)

$6039. *new* WHEELS

new 258 CID 6 — —(100 H..

$6189. UP

NEW UPRIGHT HOOD ORNAM'T.

←LIMITED WAGON   INTERIORS

79-80

('80) WAGON

DL WAGON → $5189.

(DL HATCHBACK ALSO)

$5407. UP HATCHBK.

('80) (4 OR 6-CYL. ONLY)

(THE FINAL PACER)

BLACK GRILLE

('80)

NO V8s IN 1980

$5456. ('79) (WEST)
5980. ('80)   AMC PACER 78~80

33

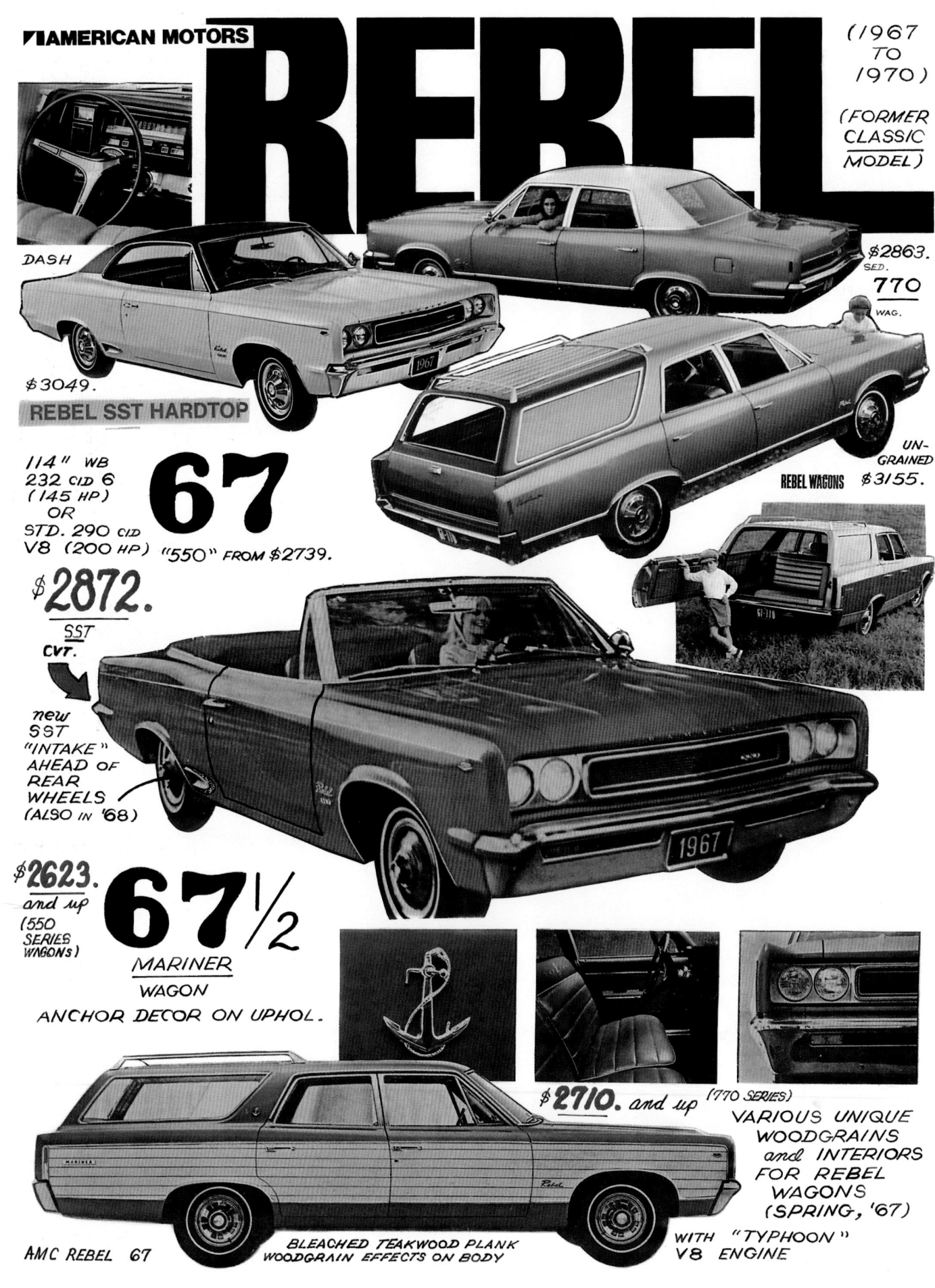

AMERICAN MOTORS

REBEL

(1967 TO 1970)

(FORMER CLASSIC MODEL)

DASH

$2863. SED.

770 WAG.

$3049.

REBEL SST HARDTOP

114" WB
232 CID 6
(145 HP)
OR
STD. 290 CID
V8 (200 HP)

67

"550" FROM $2739.

UN- GRAINED

REBEL WAGONS $3155.

$2872.
SST
CVT.

new SST "INTAKE" AHEAD OF REAR WHEELS (ALSO IN '68)

$2623.
and up
(550 SERIES WAGONS)

67½

MARINER
WAGON

ANCHOR DECOR ON UPHOL.

$2710. and up (770 SERIES)

VARIOUS UNIQUE WOODGRAINS and INTERIORS FOR REBEL WAGONS (SPRING, '67)

AMC REBEL 67

BLEACHED TEAKWOOD PLANK WOODGRAIN EFFECTS ON BODY

WITH "TYPHOON" V8 ENGINE

AMERICAN MOTORS *REBEL*

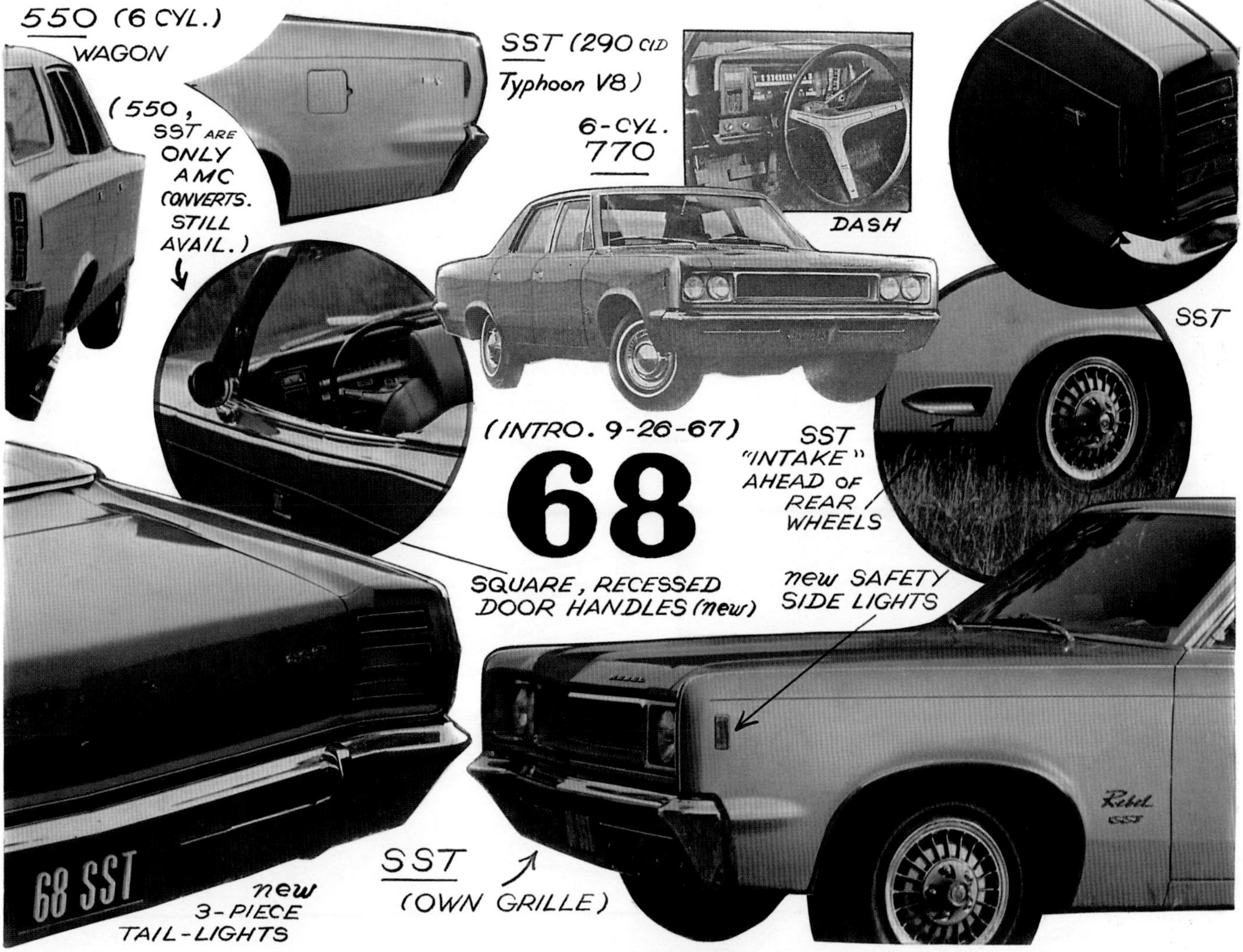

550 (6 CYL.) WAGON

SST (290 CID Typhoon V8)

6-CYL. 770

DASH

(550, SST ARE ONLY AMC CONVERTS. STILL AVAIL.)

SST

(INTRO. 9-26-67)

68

SST "INTAKE" AHEAD of REAR WHEELS

SQUARE, RECESSED DOOR HANDLES (new)

new SAFETY SIDE LIGHTS

68 SST

new 3-PIECE TAIL-LIGHTS

SST (OWN GRILLE)

ENGINES = 232 CID 6 (145 OR 155 HP); 290 CID V8 (200 HP); 343 CID V8 (235 OR 280 HP)

An intermediate-sized car for the price of a compact.

114" WB

Rebel $2,484[1]
(SALE)

69

new GRILLE
new TAIL-LTS.,
WIDER TRACK

(INTRO. 10-1-68)

(REG. $2944.)

AMC REBEL 68~69

AMERICAN MOTORS *REBEL*

Both the front and rear of the '70 Rebels are new:

In back, the massive full-width bumper—with new horizontal taillights, each with a back-up light in the middle. (Wagons, however have taillights vertically stacked, to stay out of the way during loading and unloading)

REBEL "MACHINE" H/T (340 HP V8) (2326 BUILT) **$3475.**

RED, WHITE and BLUE BODY STRIPES GLOW IN THE DARK!

(STD. and "SST" H/Ts ALSO AVAIL.)

1970 REBEL WAGON **$2766.**

($3072. FOR "SST" WAGON)

SEDAN **$2636.**

FINAL YEAR FOR REBEL

70 114" WB (SINCE '67)

● = ENGINES AVAIL. IN REBEL

"SST" SEDAN **$2684.**

AMC REBEL '70

AMC ENGINES

	CARB. TYPE	H.P. @ R.P.M.	TORQUE @ R.P.M.	COMP. RATIO & FUEL	BORE & STROKE
199 Cu. In. Six	1-Barrel	128 @ 4400	182 @ 1600	8.5:1/Reg.	3.75" X 3.00"
232 Cu. In. Six ●	1-Barrel	145 @ 4300	215 @ 1600	8.5:1/Reg.	3.75" X 3.50"
232 Cu. In. Six ●	2-Barrel	155 @ 4400	222 @ 1600	8.5:1/Reg.	3.75" X 3.50"
304 Cu. In. V-8	2-Barrel	210 @ 4400	305 @ 2800	9.0:1/Reg.	3.75" X 3.44"
360 Cu. In. V-8 ●	2-Barrel	245 @ 4400	365 @ 2400	9.0:1/Reg.	4.08" X 3.44"
360 Cu. In. V-8 ●	4-Barrel	290 @ 4800	395 @ 3200	10.0:1/Pre.	4.08" X 3.44"
390 Cu. In. V-8 ●	4-Barrel	325 @ 5000	420 @ 3200	10.0:1/Pre.	4.17" X 3.57"
390 Cu. In. V-8 ●	4-Barrel	340 @ 5100	430 @ 3600	10.0:1/Pre.	4.17" X 3.57"

AMC SPIRIT

(REPLACES AMC Gremlin)

New

STARTS 1979

INTERIOR

4 CYL. (121 CID)
6 CYL. (232 OR 258 CID)
OR V-8 OPTIONAL
(304 CID)

LIFTBACK
FROM **$3953.**

$5090.
and up

$5420.

G.T.

96" WB

79

LIMITED

RELATIONSHIP TO FORMER GREMLIN CAN BE SEEN.

SEDAN
(2~DR.)

FROM
$4090. **DL**
(WEST COAST = $4504.)

DASH

121 CID 4 (90 HP) OR 258 CID 6 (110 HP)
V8 NOT AVAIL. FOR SPIRIT

80

IN 1980, AMERICAN MOTORS WILL BE THE ONLY CAR MAKER IN AMERICA WITH...

LIFTBACK COUPES and 2 DR. SEDANS IN STD., DL or LIMITED MODELS

ZIEBART FACTORY RUST PROTECTION

AMERICAN MOTORS BUYER PROTECTION PLAN

AMERICAN MOTORS 5-YEAR NO RUST-THRU-WARRANTY

ALL THIS AT NO EXTRA COST.

BUILT FOR TODAY. BUILT TO LAST FOR TOMORROW.

LIFTBACK
$4605. and up

AMC SPIRIT

(SINCE 1903)

Buick

(A DIVISION OF GENERAL MOTORS)

TOTAL 1940 PRODUCTION = 278,784

$1359.

ROADMASTER SEDAN (13733 BLT.)

Model 71

~ MODEL SERIES ~
40 SPECIAL (121" WB)
50 SUPER (121" WB)
60 CENTURY (126" WB)
70 ROADMASTER "
80 LIMITED (133" WB)
90 LIMITED (140" WB)

40 A RESTYLED

81 SEDAN (3898 BLT.)

$1553.

LIMITED

SUPER SPT. CPE.
56~S   (26462 BLT.)

$1058.

STREAMLINED FORMAL SEDAN (ONLY 7 BLT.!) 87~F

$1727.

$1211.

56~C (4804 BLT.)

The Buick **SUPER** Convertible Coupe with Press-A-Button Top of full-weight top material in choice of three colors. Full-width rear seat. Wheel shields extra, white sidewall tires standard.

$1620.

61-C

CONVERT. SEDAN ("SPT. PHAETON") (203 BLT.)

(CONT'D. NEXT PAGE)

TRUNK

248 C.I.D. TYPE

Side sectional view of the Buick series 40 and 50 engine

(A) BUICK **1940**

Buick

AN EYE FOR A BUY HAS RUBY KEELER JOLSON *

For instance, here she is with her Buick Estate Wagon, smart, comfortable, useful in no end of ways, and a bargain at $1242, delivered at Flint, Mich., white sidewall tires extra. If you haven't looked into its smoother-than-a-watch engine, close-to-five-foot front seats, Foamtex-cushioned comfort, and endless possibilities for fun, better ask your dealer when you can see one.*

* MOVIE STAR and WIFE OF AL JOLSON

BUICK IN 4TH PLACE IN U.S. SALES, 1938 TO 1942.

NEW!

"Best buy's Buick!"
EXEMPLAR OF GENERAL MOTORS VALUE

50 SERIES SUPER

MODEL 59

40 B **(CONT'D.)**

(501 BLT.)
$1242.

SUPER (50) SERIES IS <u>new</u> FOR '40, CONTINUES THROUGH 1958.

(THERE WAS A 50 SERIES IN 1935 and EARLIER, BUT WAS NOT NAMED "SUPER.")

Aft Flash-Way direction signal.
↳

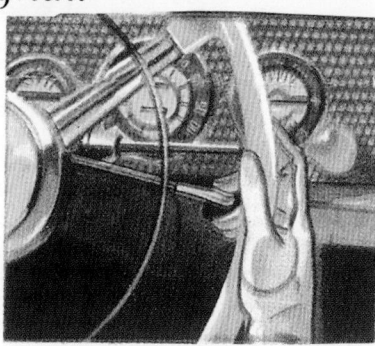

new~STYLE DASH WITH MACHINE~TURNED METAL and COPPER DECOR, WITH "WOODGRAIN"

STRAIGHT~8 O.H.V. ENGINES

248 c.i.d., 107 HP (IN SPECIAL, SUPER)
320.2 c.i.d., 141 HP (IN ALL OTHERS)

(B) BUICK **1940**

SPORT COUPE INTERIOR ←

COMPARE ITS SIZE AND PRICE!

This big new Buick SPECIAL straight-eight for '41 costs even less than some sixes ...and has more room inside!

"Best Buick Yet"

1941

SERIES 40-A SPECIAL (118" WB)

BUICK PRICES BEGIN AT
$915
for the Business Coupe

★delivered at Flint, Mich. State tax, optional equipment and accessories — extra. Prices subject to change without notice.

MODEL 44 (3251 BLT.)

BUICK FIREBALL VALVE-IN-HEAD ENGINES—115, 125 and 165 horsepower. Higher compression, better combustion, greater economy from design that makes the most of modern fuels.

41 A

new 40~A LOWER~ PRICED SERIES JOINS 40 SERIES SPECIAL

new "FASTBACK" SEDANS and 2-DOOR SEDANETS

A four-door sedan with a long, sweeping rear is a new body type on the 40 and 60

NEW

(19876 BLT.)

56-S CLUB COUPE **$1113.**

SEDANET (A.K.A. "SEDANETTE")

(CONT'D. NEXT PAGE)

The sedanet is a new body style on the 40 and 60, a two-door six-passenger car with a highly streamlined back panel

41 BUICK (A)

DASH

Buick

41 B
(CONT'D.)

56-C
Super Convertible
(12391 BLT.)
$1267.

CVT.
SEDAN
IN
50
OR
70
SERILS

MODEL
49

ESTATE WAGON (850 BLT.)
(NOW IN 40 SPEC. SERILS)

$1463.

1941-B

COMPARE LENGTHS OF SPECIAL
and LIMITED

Buick SPECIAL 4-door
Sedan, model 47, $1021.

SERIES 40-A
(14139 BLT.)

LANDAU BODY
BY BRUNN

LIMITED

COIL SPRINGS ALL AROUND
—no lubrication, no spring covers,
no breakage, softer ride.

**"MASS-STREAM"
BODIES,** BIGGER, ROOMIER —
Unisteel Bodies by Fisher

REAR DETAILS

ENGINES =
248 C.I.D. (115 OR
125 HP)
320.2 C.I.D. (165 HP)

40-A SPECIAL (118" WB
40 SPECIAL (121" WB)
50 SUPER   "   "
60 CENTURY (126" WB)
70 ROADMASTER (128" WB)
90 LIMITED (139" WB)
   (80 LIMITED
   DISCONTINUED)

(white sidewall tires and two-tone colors extra)

41 BUICK (B)

$1230.

SUPER (14629 BLT.)

HUB CAP

1942 ENGINE

Buick

SEDANET

ROADMASTER (2475 BLT.)
$1395.

STRAIGHT~ EIGHT O.V. ENGINES IN ALL 1931 TO 1952 BUICKS.

The 50 and 70 two-door sedanet and convertible have front fenders which reach the rear fenders.

FRONT BUMPER DETAIL

248 CID ENG. CUT IN HP (110 OR 118)
320.2 CID ENG. RETAINS 165 HP.

42 RESTYLED

ROADMASTER

TOTAL 1942 PROD. = 92,573

'42 BUICK COUPES ARE RARE!

CVT. (511 BUILT)
$1675.

$990.   118" WB

SPECIAL 40A "UTILITY COUPE" (461 BUILT)

1942 AND LATER BUICK CVTS. HAVE REAR QUARTER WINDOWS

NEW 129" WB ON ROADMASTER (THROUGH 1948)

40 (B) SPECIAL CONTINUES 121" WB (THROUGH 1949)

INTERIOR

$1280.   SUPER   SEDAN (16265 BUILT)

LIMITED

BUICK 1942

$2545.   Series 90 with limousine body   (250 BUILT)

42

GM | BY GENERAL MOTORS

BUICK

(full-sized)

(SINCE 1903)

(STARTS OCT., 1945)

46

PRICE RANGE $1391. - $2594.

SERIES		
40	SPECIAL	121" WB
50	SUPER	124"
70	ROADMASTER	129"

SPECIAL (RARE) HAS MORE HORIZ. CHROME FENDER STRIPS. (SEE 1948 ALSO.)

CLOCK

DASH (WOODGRAIN EFFECTS ON ROADMASTER)

CLOSE-UP OF SPEEDOMETER

RE-SETTABLE TRIP ODOMETER (TO 999.9 MILES)

STRAIGHT-8 O.H.V. ENGINES (SINCE 1931)
SPECIAL, SUPER = 248 CID (110 HP)
ROADMASTER = 320.2 CID (144 HP)

ESTATE WGN. (SUPER)

748 BLT.

$2594.

$1741.

34,425 BLT.

SUPER

$2046.

5987 BLT.

new GRILLE (FEWER VERTICAL PCS. THAN '42)

SUPER

77,724 BLT.

5TH PLACE IN U.S. SALES

$1822.

6.50 x 16" TIRES (7.00 x 15" ON ROADMASTER)

$2110.

20,864 BLT.

TOTAL 1946 BUICK PROD.: 153,627

ROADMASTER

REAR VIEW

BUICK 46

43

MODEL 51

SUPER SEDAN 19 BEST-SELLING MODEL (83,576 BLT.)

MODEL 56-C

$2333.

When better automobiles are built
BUICK
will build them

TRADITIONAL SLOGAN

$1929.

Super

$2940.   MODEL 59

(28,297 BLT.)   CONVERT. has POWER-OPERATED TOP, FRONT SEAT and SIDE WINDOWS!

47

(272,827 BLT.)

new GRILLE has EMBLEM AT TOP, PLUS "BUICK EIGHT" LETTERING

WAGON (2036 BLT.)

POSTWAR "BOMBSIGHT" (ROCKET-THRU-RING) HOOD ORNAMENT (SINCE '46)

1947 PRICE RANGE:
$1497.
TO
$3030.

($1611. TO 3249. PRICE RANGE LATER IN '47 SEASON)

ROADMASTER SEDAN (47,152 BLT.)
$2232.
MODEL 71

USA 1947

note 1947 MODEL NAME AT UPPER CENTER OF BUMPER GUARD

(213,599 BLT., 1948)

SPEC.-SU.-RDMSTR. PRICES: (1948) $1735. TO $3433.

SUPER   MODEL 56-S
SEDANET (46,917 BLT.)

'48 SUPER and ROADMASTER NAMES ALSO APPEAR ON FRONT FENDERS.

MODEL 41 SEDAN $1809.
(14,051 BLT.)

SPECIAL
(CONTINUES WITH 46-48 STYLING INTO 1949)

MODEL 76-C
CVT.

$1987.

48

(11,503 BLT.)
ROADMASTER
$2837.

SEDAN $2418.

OPTIONAL:
new
Dynaflow AUTO. TRANS.

(47,569 BLT.)

MODEL NAME

BUICK 47~48

44

BUICK

Super MODEL 51 SEDAN (136,423 BLT.)
has 3 "PORTHOLES" **$2157.**
(SPECIAL RETAINS 1948 STYLING)

1949 HORSEPOWER RATINGS

SPECIAL	110
SUPER	115 or 120
ROADMASTER	150

248 or 320 CID STRAIGHT-8

CVT. TOP REAR DETAIL

1949 PRICE RANGE :
$1787. TO $3734.

49
TOTALLY RESTYLED (EXCEPT SPECIAL)

ROADMASTER
has 4 "PORTHOLES"
MODEL 71 SEDAN
(55,242 BLT.)
$2735.

BACK SEAT (W. FOLD-DOWN ARM REST)

ROADMASTER
with Dynaflow Drive

SEDANET

MODEL 79
STEEL-BODIED WAGON
$3734. → (653 BLT.)

$3203.

(4343 BLT.)

new DASH

"RIVIERA" (new H/T) 4343 BLT.
(EARLY MODEL with ALL-HORIZONTAL SIDE TRIM)

LATER 1949 CVTS. and RIVIERAS have new "SWEEP-SPEAR" SIDE TRIM (AS ILLUSTRATED)

$3150. CVT. (8244 BLT.)

1949 **TOTAL PRODUCTION** : 324,276

45

BUICK

$1856.

115 HP SPECIAL

SPECIAL INTRODUCED EARLY (IN AUG., '49)

121½" WB EXCEPT ON "52" SUPER SEDAN (125½") and ON 126½" and 130¼" RDMSTRS.

$1941. UP

ONLY THE SPECIAL RETAINS 2-PC. WINDSHIELD

STARTLING *new* "BUMPER-GRILLE"

new EASY-EYE TINTED GLASS IS OPTIONAL

50

TOTALLY RESTYLED

MODEL YEAR PRODUCTION :
(552, 827 CAL. YR.) 588,439
256, 514 SPECIALS ; 253,352 SUPERS ;
78, 573 ROADMASTERS

ESTATE WAGON

THE ESTATE WAGON is yours on either SUPER or ROADMASTER chassis. Three power ranges to choose from.

SUPER (2480 BLT.)
ROADMASTER (420 BLT.)

128 HP *Super*

DASH (SPC.)

BACK SEAT (SEDAN)   MODEL 75-R

(55672 BLT.) 121½" WB **$2139.**

(114,745 BLT.) 4-DR. SEDAN 125½" WB

$2738. MODEL 72

152 HP **ROADMASTER** (66,762 BLT.) RIVIERA H/T

(54,512 BLT.) 130¼"WB ON "RIVIERA SEDAN"

ELONGATED "PORTHOLES"

(4 ON RDMSTR.)

BUICK 50

46

BIIICK

SPECIAL   SPECIAL DE LUXE

('51)

ESTATE WAGON

120 TO 128 HP

('51)

SUPER

128 HP

(999 LOW-PRICED '51~'52 SPECIALS had 2-PC. WINDSHIELDS. = _RARE!_)

152 HP

170 HP

DASH ('52) →
(NEW SINGLE SPEEDO. DIAL IN FRONT OF STEER. WHEEL)

ROADMASTER

('51) ROADMASTER ('52)

PRODUCTION		1951	592,511
(MODEL			404,695
YEAR		1952	367,760
and CALENDAR YEAR)			321,048

('51)

('51)

← 1951 DASH (ABOVE) had **2** DIALS OF GAUGES IN FRONT OF STEERING WHEEL.

51-52

SUPER ↓

Buick Eight

'52 has BROADER HUBCAP MARGINS, FULL-HEIGHT VERTICAL BUMPER GUARDS, NO REAR FENDER CHROME STRIPS.

SPECIAL BUSINESS/CLUB COUPE (RARE!) ↓

('51)

'51 BUMPER GUARDS DO NOT RUN DOWN FRONT OF BUMPER, BUT REST ON TOP.

Equipment, accessories, trim and models are subject to change without notice.

BUICK $2255.

100,312 BLT.

FINAL BUICK STRAIGHT-8 IN SPECIAL

SPECIAL RIVIERA 2-DR H/T

SPECIAL (125 HP @ 3800 RPM)
CVT.
$2553.

$2295.

58,780 BLT.

121½ W.B. ON ALL EXCEPT 125" RIVIERA SEDAN WB
(4282 BLT.)

SPORT WIRE WH. AVAIL.

LOWER PORTION OF DASH FINISHED IN BRIGHT MACHINE-TURNED METAL

1903-1953

53

BUICK'S GOLDEN ANNIVERSARY

1953 PRODUCTION:
485,353

new V8

322 CID ENGINE IN ALL BUT "SPECIAL"

SUPER $2696.
"RIVIERA" SED

164-170 HP (SUPER)

LIMITED-PRODUCTION "SKYLARK" CVT.
$5000.

1690 BLT.

ROADMASTER RIVIERA
$3358.

$4031.

ONLY 670 BLT.

ROADMASTER
(188 HP @ 4000)

$3506.

BUICK 53

48

BUICK

46-R $2305.

$3163.   ALL V8s

143 OR 150 HP
SPECIAL
(40 SERIES)
122" WB

71,186 BLT.

1650 BLT.

1563 → BLT.

49

66-R

195 OR 200 HP
CENTURY
122" WB

45,710 BLT. $2534.

69   $3470.

CENTURY (60 SERIES)
RETURNS (1ST SINCE 1942)

DASH

54
RESTYLED

100-M

(100 SERIES)
SKYLARK *
$4483.

ONLY 836 BLT. '54

* AFTER 1954, NO MORE
SKYLARKS UNTIL NAME
RETURNS IN 1961 AS PART OF
new COMPACT "SPECIAL" SERIES.)

264 OR 322 CID V8s
(THROUGH '55)
(264 CID IN SPECIAL ONLY) $3269.

72-R
26,862 BLT.

new "PANORAMIC"
WRAP-AROUND
WINDSHIELDS (ALL MODELS)

1954 PRODUCTION:
442,903

$2626.   73,531 BLT.
56-R

127" WB   SUPER
(50 SERIES)

(70 SERIES) ROADMASTER

$2964. →

3343 BLT. 56-C

177 OR 182 HP
SUPER

3305 BLT.

ROADMASTER   127" WB
200 HP @ 4100 RPM
76-R $3373.

BUICK SPECIAL

CENTURY

SUPER

$2876.

150 to 236 HP
$3453.

NOW 4 PORTHOLES ON ALL EXCEPT SPECIAL.

ROADMASTER

new GRILLE and TAILLIGHTS (4-DR. HARDTOPS NOW AVAIL.)

55

DASH (SUPER)

BUICK

new MESH GRILLE

1955 PRODUCTION : 737,035

MODEL 49 "SPECIAL" WAGON 13,770 BLT.

$2775.

new TEARDROP-SHAPED PORTS

SPECIAL (220 HP @ 4400 RPM)

ALL MODELS NOW HAVE 322 CID V8s; SUPER, CENTURY and ROADMASTER HAVE 255 HP @ 4400 RPM

56

CENTURY "RIVIERA" 4-DR H/T 20,891 BLT. 63

$3025.

new GRILLE *new* TAILLIGHTS

76-R 12,490 BLT.

$3591.

ROADMASTER

122 OR 127" WB (SINCE '54)

1956 PROD. : 635,158

new V-GRILLE with FINE HORIZONTAL PCS.

MODEL 56-R DASH

$3204.

SUPER 29,540 BLT.

"RIVIERA" 2-DR. HARDTOPS

BUICK

BUICK 55-56

BUICK

SPECIAL

122" WB
SPECIAL

CVT.
48-C
8505 BLT.

$2987.

57
new GRILLE

$3047.
49
7013 BLT.

66-C

REAR
QUARTER WINDOW
DETAILS ON
CONVERTIBLE (WITH
TOP UP) (CENTURY)

$3270.

1957 PRODUCTION:
404,049
26,589 BLT.

63
"RIVIERA"
4-DR. H/T

$3354.

66-R
17,029
BLT.

ALL
WITH
new
364 CID
ENGINE (CONT'D.
IN
SPECIAL
and
LE SABRE
MODELS
THROUGH
1961)

MODEL NAME
ABOVE DIP IN
SIDE CHROME
TRIM (EXCEPT
ON SPECIAL,
WHICH HAS NO
NAME HERE, OR ON
SUPER (with 3
CURVED CHROME
PCS. HERE.)

CENTURY
122" WB

$3706.

69

new
CENTURY CABALLERO
WAGON
(H/T
STYLE)

10,186 BLT.

PILLARED
2-DOOR
SEDAN ONLY
AVAIL. IN
SPECIAL and
CENTURY (ONLY 2 BLT.)
SERIES (MODELS
48 OR 68)
(23,180 SPECIAL 2-DRS.)

new
127½" WB
SUPER

CVT.
56-C

56-R
$3536.

DASH

4 DR. H/T

ROADMASTER
new 127½" WB
SERIES
70 OR 75

note
UNUSUAL
REAR
DOOR
TREATMENT
ON THIS MODEL

2-DR. H/T

300 HP @ 4600 RPM
(EXCEPT SPECIAL,
WHICH HAS 250 HP @
4400 RPM
(THROUGH '58)

BUICK 57

51

BUICK

new BLOCK-STYLE GRILLE

HEAVY USE *of* CHROME TRIM

58
RESTYLED

SIDE "PORTHOLES" DISCONTINUED (UNTIL '60)

250-HP SPECIAL

$2820.

FOR MODEL 43 "RIVIERA" 4-DR. H/T 31921 BLT.

1958 PRODUCTION: 240,659

$3041.
46-C CVT. (5502 BLT.)

(ONLY 2-DR., 4-DR. H/TS *in* SUPER SERIES)

THE AIR BORN B-58 BUICK

SPECIAL

$3154.
49 WAGON 3663 BLT.

DASH (RDMSTR.)

$3436.
CENTURY

63

15,171 BLT.

300 HP IN CENTURY, SUPER, RDMSTR., LIMITED

$2636. 48 2-DR. SEDAN (PILLARED) 11,566 BLT.

$4557.
75-R "RIVIERA" 2-DR. H/T 2368 BLT.

75

10,505 BLT.

ROADMASTER

$4667.

DIAGONAL CHROME STRIPS ON LIMITED RR. FENDERS

$5112.
750   5571 BLT.

new LIMITED (NAME REVIVED)

ONLY 839 BLT.

$5125.
CVT. 756

BUICK

ALL-NEW MODEL NAMES FOR 1959 :
LE SABRE, INVICTA, ELECTRA, ELECTRA 225

LE SABRE

4411 2-DR.   13,492 BLT.

123" WB

$2740.

$3129.

LE SABRE has 364 CID V8, 250 HP @ 4400 RPM

PACE CAR AT INDIANAPOLIS 500 RACE

DASH

MODEL 4419 4 DR. SED.
51,379 BLT.

$2804.

new CANTED HEADLIGHTS

INVICTA

The most spirited Buick

123" WB

4639 4-DR. HARDTOP 20,156 BLT.

$3515.

59 TOTALLY RESTYLED

new SQUARED-OFF ROOFLINE ON 4-DR. H/T

(10,491 BLT.)

INVICTAS and ELECTRAS have 401 CID V8, 325 HP @ 4400 RPM

MODEL 4619 INVICTA SEDAN

1959 PRODUCTION :
284,248
$2740. ~ 4300.
PRICE RANGE

(10,566 BLT.)

$3357.

$4300.

ELECTRA , ELECTRA 225

The most luxurious Buick

TOP-OF-LINE ELECTRA 225 IS ILLUSTRATED.

$4300.

10.5 COMPRESSION IN 1959

BUICK 59

BUICK

$3145. $2915.

LE SABRE
has 210, 235, 250 or 300 HP

364 CID = LE S.
401 CID = OTHERS
(SAME CHOICES IN '61)

60

A RETURN
TO VARIOUS "PORTHOLE" TYPE SIDE
DECORATIONS AS USED ON
1949-1956 BUICKS

new "Mirromagic"
INSTRUMENT
CLUSTER
LETS DRIVER SEE
GAUGES IN A
MIRROR THAT
CAN BE TILTED
TO SUIT DRIVER'S
OWN
EYE LEVEL.

INVICTA WAGON
$3841. UP

INVICTA

1960 PRODUCTION: 253,807

123" WB = LE S., INVICTA
126.3" WB = EL., EL. 225

$3357.

HEADLTS. PLACED HORIZONTALLY,
new GRILLE
WITH CONCAVE
VERTICAL
PIECES
and new
3-SHIELD
BADGE

INVICTA $3515.

1960 BUICK INVICTA 4-DOOR HARDTOP IN MAGIC-MIRROR TAHITI BEIGE AND CORDOVAN

INVICTA and
ELECTRAS have
325 HP @ 4400 RPM

$2756.~4300. PRICE RANGE

4 PORTHOLES ON ELECTRAS, 3 ON OTHERS

H/T $3818.   ELECTRA

ELECTRA 225

TOP OF
III L
LINE!

$4300.

BUICK (INTRO. WED., OCT. 5, 1960, AS _SEPARATE COMPACT SERIES_ of BUICK)

SPECIAL-SIZE
BUICKSPECIAL
THE BEST OF BOTH WORLDS ⊕→

(and **SKYLARK**)

NEW!

BUICK'S REVOLUTIONARY ALUMINUM V-8. This hot 155 HP Fireball V-8 weighs just 318 pounds for a .487 horsepower to weight ratio — highest in the industry!

3 VIEWS OF SPECIAL (SEDAN)

61 A

WAGON _has_ 1-PIECE SWING-UP REAR DOOR

$2384.

PRICES START AT $2659. (WEST) (STD. CPE

SPECIAL WAGON

$2681. UP   112" WHEELBASE

$3091. UP (WEST)

THE CLEAN LOOK of action

$2330. ~ 2816.
PRICE RANGE (BASE)

PRODUCTION: 99,893

(CONT'D. NEXT PAGE)

BUICK **skylark** _new!_

SKYLARK IS _new_ LUXURY 185-HP MODEL of SPECIAL SPT. CPE.

SKYLARK IS AVAILABLE IN TWO-TONE OR SOLID COLORS (AS ILLUSTRATED)

$2949. (WEST)

112" WB _and_ 6.50 x 13 TIRES (THROUGH '63)

note THAT SKYLARK _has_ OWN REAR STYLING

BUICK 61 (A)

BUICK

$2993. ~ 4350.
PRICE RANGE

(new ROOFLINE)
$3228.

Lͤ SABRE

123" WB
250 HP
LE SABRE

4439 4-DR. H/T
37,790 BLT.
(MOST POPULAR
1961 BUICK)

"SPECIAL" RETURNS

SPECIAL-SIZE
BUICK SPECIAL
new COMPACT SERIES,
STARTING 1961
SEE SPECIAL
(PRECEDING PAGE)

SCARCEST
1961 BUICK
IS MODEL
4445
3-SEAT
WAGON
(2423 BLT.)
(ITS COMPACT
"SPECIAL" 3-SEAT
COUNTERPART SAW
ONLY 798 BLT.)

4639 4-DR. H/T
18,398 BLT.

INVICTA

$3515.

123" WB   325 HP

MODEL 4829 4-DR.
"RIVIERA" H/T $4350.

(TOTALLY
RESTYLED)
61
B
1961 PRODUCTION:
(FULL-SIZED MODELS) 191,392

126" WB   ELECTRA 225   13,719
BLT.

STD. ELECTRA
SERIES INCLUDES
4719 SEDAN
(13,818 BLT.) $3825.
4737 2-DR. H/T
(4250 BLT.) $3818.
4739 4-DR. H/T
(8978 BLT.) $3932.

THORNWOOD

ELECTRA 225
CONVT.
MODEL 4867
7158 BLT.
$4192.

BUICK 61 (B)

56

BUICK

2-DR.

4-DR. H/T

4439

4-DR. H/T

4447

LE SABRE

GL·1378

$3567.

DASH

GAUGES HOODED, TO PREVENT WINDSHIELD GLARE

401 CID V8s IN LE SABRE and LARGER MODELS

62 A

(CONT'D.)

FULL-SIZED BUICK PRODUCTION: 256,766

4-DR. H/T

INVICTA

H/T

ADVANCED THRUST

LE S. 265 HP @ 4400
INV. 280 HP @ 4400
ELEC. 325 HP @ 4400

CVT.

$3815.

INVICTA ESTATE WAGON →

EL. 225 CVT.

$4034. (6-PASS.)

4-DR. H/T

ELECTRA 225

H/T

ELECTRA has 126" WB (OTHERS 123")

SEDAN

Close-up of Wildcat! shows you new medalion and unique fabric overlay (available in black or white)

BR-3950

new **WILDCAT!** 325 HP

H/T

62 W 4647

$4125.

BUICK 62 (A)

57

BUICKSPECIAL

$2304.

SPECIAL
2-DR. CPE.
(19,135 BLT.)

$2358. 4-DR. SEDAN
(23,249 BLT.)

CONVERTIBLE
$2587.

(7918 BLT.)

SPECIAL

(2814 BLT.)

SPECIAL
DLX.

1962

3-SEAT
WAGON
2736.

$2890.

WAGON
(10,380 BLT.)

155 OR
185-HP V8 (215 CID)
OR new V6 (198 CID, 135 HP)
ENGINE

**$2304. ~
3012.**

PRICE
RANGE

62 B
(CONT'D.)

$3012.

$2879.

CVT.
(8332
BLT.)

SPECIAL DE LUXE

CVT.
(8913
BLT.)

SKYLARK

(34,060 BLT.)

H/T
$2787.

SPECIAL
2-DR. SPORT COUPE

6.50 × 13 TIRES
(SINCE '61)

$2818.
WAGON (8771
BLT.)

SPECIAL
DE LUXE

SEDAN

$2682.
(WEST COAST)

135, 155 OR
200 HP

PRODUCTION :
159,126 ('62); 152,226 ('63)

(37,695
BLT.) **$2521.**

$2309. ~ 3011. PRICE RANGE

63
A

$2857.

(10,212
BLT.) **$3011.**

SKYLARK

(32,109 BLT.)   H/T

CVT.   BUICK 62 (B) and 63 (A)

BUICK

401 c/d V8s IN ALL MODELS
265 or 280 HP

LE SABRE

SEDAN

$3004.
(64,995 BLT.)

1963 PRODUCTION:
327,123 (FULL-SIZED)

DASH

ROOF RACK

57-847

INVICTA
(FINAL YR.)
STATION WAGON is THE ONLY '63 INVICTA

INVICTA WAGON
$3969.

(3495 BLT.)

$4167. (WEST)

new V-SHAPED FRONT

63
B

325 HP
(EXCEPT LE SABRE)

$3961.

WILDCAT CVT. (6021 BLT.)

4-DR. H/T
(17,519 BLT.)
$3871.

new!

WILDCAT has ITS OWN UNIQUE GRILLE, BUT TAILLIGHTS LIKE OTHER FULL-SIZED 1963 BUICKS.

WILDCAT

BUICK

2-DR. H/T
(12,185 BLT.)
$4047.
(WEST COAST)

$4365.

$3849.
BASE PRICE

(6347 BLT.)

(14,268 BLT.)

$4051.

Electra 225

$4141.
(WEST COAST)

$2869.~4365.
PRICE RANGE

BUICK 63 (B)

ELECTRA TAIL-LIGHT DETAIL

(19,714 BLT.) $4186.

59

$2689.

4035
Special 2-seat Station Wagon
6270 BLT.

BUICKSPECIAL DELUXE 4-DOOR SEDAN

SPEC.
$2397.

4069

$2490.
SPEC. DLX.

31,742 BLT.

4169

17,983 BLT.

4337

$2669.

MODEL 4369 SEDAN
19,635 BLT.

SKYLARK

has HEAVIER SIDE TRIM WHICH ENCOMPASSES THE 3 RECTANGULAR "PORTHOLE" PCS. IN COWL SECTION.

SKYLARK →

SPORT COUPE
42,356 BLT.

$2680.

64A

new 115" WB
new 6.50 x 14 TIRES

4367 CONVERT.
10,225 BLT.

SKYLARK

$2834.

new SPORTS WAGON

new RAISED PANORAMIC ROOF WINDOWS, AS ALSO FOUND IN new OLDS "VISTA-CRUISER" WAGON.

MODEL 4265
(9-PASS.)
$3124.*
(CUST.)

*$3562.
(WEST COAST)

REAR FENDER TRIM (WAGON)

Skylark

225 CID V6 (155 HP) OR 300 CID V8 (210 OR 250 HP)

PRODUCTION: 188,980

INTERIOR VIEWS

MODELS 4255, 4265, 4355, 4365

This is the new Buick Skylark Sports Wagon. It has a raised roof so you can sit tall, and a new kind of shaded glass so you can look up and out, and a forward-facing third seat.

(CONT'D. NEXT PAGE)

BUICK 64 (A)

120" WB (WAGON)

300 CID "WILDCAT" V8 IN WAGON

BUICK

4467 CVT.

$3314. $3635.

6685 BLT.

4447 H/T

$306l.   24,177 BLT.

LE SABRE

ESTATE WAGON
4645 3-SEAT

4003 BLT.

64 B
(257,438 BLT.)
(CONT'D.)

$3164.

4669
THE WILDCAT 4-DOOR SEDAN

WILDCAT
325 HP

THE WILDCAT CONVERTIBLE
4667

7850 BLT.

WILDCAT (CLOSE-UP) →

DASH

ELECTRA 225

THE ELECTRA 225 4-DOOR HARDTOP
(9045 BLT.)

$3267.

(ABOVE) WILDCAT
MODEL 4647 H/T
22,893 BLT.

$4357.

(7181 BLT.)   THE ELECTRA 225 CONVERTIBLE

$4070.

new 425 CID V8
(340 OR 360 HP) IS
OPTIONAL (LE SABRE
WAGONS, WILDCAT,
ELECTRA 225)
BUICK 64 (B)

LE SABRE 4400 HAS
new 300 CID V8 (210
OR 250 HP.) LARGER
MODELS USE 401 CID V8
(325 HP) AS STD. EQUIPMENT.

BUICK SPECIAL

PRODUCTION: 243,441

new 5-DIGIT MODEL NUMBERS

44337 H/T

4549 BLT.   SKYLARK

43369 SPECIAL SED.

$2605. UP

$2397.

SPECIAL CVT.
43367 OR 43467
(3357 BLT.) (3365 BLT.)

INDICATOR LIGHTS   HIGH BEAM

LEFT TURN   RIGHT TURN

65 A

new V-SHAPED FRONT ENDS, new GRILLE.

SKYLARK GRAN SPORT
H/T 44437
47034 BLT. **$2751.**

SKYLARK GRAN SPORT CPE.

11,877 BLT.
$2608.   44427

INDICATOR LIGHTS   FUEL GAUGE   HEATER-AIR CONDITIONING CONTROLS   AIR CONDITIONER OUTLETS

CLOCK

GLASS WIPER   ACCESSORY   IGNITION   LIGHTER   RADIO   **DASH**   SPEAKER GRILLE

5309 BLT.   43427 (V8)
12 945 "   43327 (V6)

REAR

SPECIAL
2-DR. COUPE $2343.
2414. (V8)

SKYLARK WITH *new* FULL-WIDTH TAIL-LIGHTS

SKYROOF→ SPORTS WAG.

(CONT'D. NEXT PAGE)

H/T

1965 BUICK
Skylark
HARDTOP COUPE

BUICK 65 (A)

BUICK

LE SABRE CUSTOM CVT. (6543 BLT.)

LE SABRE

$3030. UP

$3325.
123" WB
300 CID
210 HP
8.15×15 TIRES

45467

H/T (VINYL TOP)
(21,049 BLT.)
(CUSTOM)

$3100.

$2948. TO 4440.
PRICE RANGE

LE SABRE 400

123 OR 126" WB
(SINCE '59)

65B
new GRILLES

$3345. TO $4530.
PRICE RANGE
(WEST COAST)

ELECTRA 225 4 DR. H/T
(12,842 BLT.)
$4206.

(MORE ELECTRA 225s AT BOTTOM OF PAGE)

TOTAL 1965 PRODUCTION : 653,838
FULL-SIZED (EXC. RIVIERA): 368,973

4-DR. H/T

H/T

8.45×15 TIRES
126" WB
401 CID
(325 HP)
425 CID V8 AVAIL.
(340 OR 360 HP)

46639

WILDCAT
(STD., DLX. and CUSTOM MODELS)

$3286. UP

(8505 BLT.) CVT.

SEE ALSO :
RIVIERA
(FOLLOWING 1940~1980 BUICK)

$4440.
ELECTRA 225

$4206. H/T UP

8.85×15 TIRES

BUICK

120" WB
Buick Sportwagon
FROM $3390. (WEST)

DASH (GS)

GS
2~DR. H/T
WITH
WILDCAT V8
ENGINE 401 CID
(325 HP)

66

note COWL DECORAT'N.

SKYLARK GS (GRAN SPORT) (1835 BLT.)
$2956. H/T $3384. (WEST)

216,709 COMPACTS
315,639 FULL~SIZE,
EXCEPT RIVIERA.
TOTAL 1966
PRODUCTION =
553,870
(7TH PLACE IN
U.S. SALES)

(SPECIAL IS LOWEST-PRICED
MODEL, FROM $2783.)
$2348. (WEST)

1966 Buick.
The tuned car.

LE SABRE (BELOW) 123"WB

WILDCAT (325 HP)
(GS - 340 HP)
126" WB
$3547.

WILD.
CUSTOM H/T
$4037. (WEST)
(10800 BLT.)

CUSTOM MODELS IN
EACH SERIES ARE
HIGHER~PRICED.

4 DR. H/T
(17740 BLT.)
$3081.

WILDCAT has
UNIQUE GRILLE

ENGINES
155 TO
225 CID V6 (160 HP) } SPECIAL
300 CID V8 (210 HP) } and SKYLK.
340 CID V8 (220 HP) WAGON, LESAB.
401 CID V8 (325 HP)
SKYLARK GS, WILDCAT, ELECTRA 225
401 CID V8 (340 HP) RIVIERA,
AVAIL. FOR WILDCAT, ELECTRA 225

ON
COWL
SIDES,
Electra 225 has
4 CHROME SEGMENTS,
LE SABRE has 3, and
WILDCAT has NONE,
EXCEPT LOWER
PARALLEL BANDS.

Electra
225
$4153.

4 DR. H/T
(10792 BLT.)

BUICK 66

126"WB

64

225 CID 6 (160 HP) OR 300 CID V8 (210 HP)

BUICK

120" WB

GS-400.

CVT.
(2140 BLT.)

SPORTWAGON

WAGONS FROM
$2742.

$3167.

GS 400

Skylark

CONVERTIBLE (6319 BLT.)
$2945.
115" WB

H/T
(10659 BLT.)

$3019.

$2845.

67 new GRILLES

4~DR. H/T (13721 BLT.)
$2950.

GS 400
401 CID V8
(340 HP)

(41084 BLT.)
$2798.

115" WB

new GS-340.

SPECIALS FROM
$2411. (6 CYL.)
($2844., WEST)

(3692 BLT.)

SCARCEST MODEL (ONLY 894 BLT.) 19 STANDARD SKYLARK V6 CPE.

$2665.

(36220 BLT.)

SEDAN
$3002.

340 CID V8 IN LE SABRE OR SKY. WAGON
(220 OR 260 HP)

LE SABRE
123" WB

note NEW SWEEP BODY SIDE MOLDINGS
$3388.
CONVERTIBLE
(4624 BLT.)

DASH

4~DR. H/T
(17464 BLT.)
$3142.

$3084.

H/T
(13760 BLT.)

WILDCAT
126" WB

SEDAN
(14579 BLT.)

$3277.

EXTRA COST CUSTOM VINYL BUCKETS (SPORT COUPE ONLY).

$3084. UP

CVT.
(2276 STD.,
2913 CUSTOMS
BLT.)

$3536.
STD.

$3757.
CUSTOM

1967s INTRO. 9-29-66

new 430
CID V8 IN WILDCAT OR ELECTRA (360 HP)

ELECTRA 225
LIMITED (RARE)

ELECTRA 225
(126" WB)

$4363. UP

2~DR. H/T
(6845 BLT.) $4075.

TOTAL 1967 PRODUCTION =
562,507 (5TH PLACE IN U.S.
SALES, THRU 1970)
BUICK 67

4~DR. H/T

(12491 BLT.)

$4184.

65

BUICK

SPORT WAGON FR. $3711. (WEST)

Skylark (SKYLARK CUSTOM)

$2956.

9.25/8.55 x 14" TIRES ON SPORTWAGON

WAGON and SEDAN have 115" WB; CPE. and CVT. have 112" WB.

$3127.

P-17

VINYL COVERED TOP

$3326. (WEST)

(44,143 BLT.) 2-DR. W.B. SHORTENED TO 112"

PLAIN TOP

GS-400

$3528. (WEST)

GS-400

(10,743 BLT.)

"400" CID V8 (401) (340 HP @ 5000 RPM) 3 SP. STICK SHIFT OR 3-4 SP. " " WITH HURST SHIFTER OR SUPER TURBINE AUTOMATIC

GS 400 CVT. ALSO AVAIL.

KL 0256

68 A

RESTYLED

GS 400

1968

7.75 x 14" TIRES

GS 400 DASH

(GS = GRAN SPORT)

(CONT'D. NEXT PG.)

GS-350 (H/T)

(GS-400 LOOKS SIMILAR) 350 CID V8 (280 HP @ 4600 RPM)

NEW 350 CID (230 HP) V8 (STD. IN SKYLARK CUSTOM) RUNS ON REGULAR GAS.

(8317 BLT.)

$2926.

$3295. (WEST)

GS

1968

BUICK 68 (A)

BUICK

Wouldn't you really rather have a Buick?

(ABOVE)
LE SABRE 123" WB
(SHOWN with and without VINYL TOP)

4 DR. H/T
(18,058 BLT.)
$3281.

8.45 x 15" TIRES

WILDCAT 126" WB
CUSTOM H/T
(11,276 BLT.)

ENGINES:
350 CID V8
(230 or 280 HP)
430 CID V8
(360 HP)

new GRILLE

68B
(INTRO.
9-21-67)

$3742.

ELECTRA 225
LIMITED 126" WB

$4597.
(WEST COAST)
8.85 x 15"
TIRES

PRODUCTION (FULL SIZED) = 384,575
ALL 1968 BUICKS = 651,823

INTERIOR
(ELEC. 225 LTD.)

BUICK
68 (B)

126" WB
*ELECTRA
225*
CUSTOM SEDAN
(10,910 BLT.)
$4415.

(FULL-SIZED)
$3141.~4541. PRICE RANGE

BUICK

SPECIAL DELUXE
SKYLARK
SPORTWAGON
GRAN SPORT

112" WB (2-DR.)
116" WB (4-DR.)
121" WB (WAGON)

WITH *new* "DUAL ACTION" TAILGATE →

"350"

Sportwagon

8.55 x 14" TIRES

$4195. (WEST)

350 CID V8
3 SIDE PORTS LIKE SPECIAL (DLX.)

GS-350
350 CID V8 (280 HP)

(4933 BLT.)
7.75 x 14" TIRES
$2980. $3810. (WEST)

(155 HP)
250 CID 6
OR
350 CID V8 (230 OR 280 HP)
401 CID V8 (340 HP, IN GS-400 OR SPORTWAGON 400)

GS-400 (BELOW)
400 CID V8 (340 HP)
$3181.
(6356 BLT.)
7.75 x 14" W.S.W. TIRES
$3954. (WEST)

69A
new GRILLES

SKYLARK
CUSTOM H/T
(35,639 BLT.)

$3739. (WEST)

"400 LETTERING

MODIFIED STAGE I GS-400 has "STAGE I" LETTERING INSTEAD, ALSO HI-LIFT CAM, 3.64 GEAR RATIO, ETC.

7.75/ 8.25 x 14" TIRES

$3009.

350 CID V8 STD. ON SKYLARK CUSTOM; AVAIL. ON OTHER SKYLARKS.

No wonder Buick owners keep selling Buicks for us.

Wouldn't you really rather have a Buick?
BUICK 69 (A)

68

BUICK

No wonder Buick owners keep selling Buicks for us.
Wouldn't you really rather have a Buick?

4-DR. H/T (17235 BLT.)

350 CID V8
230 or 280 HP

LE SABRE
4-DR. H/T FROM $3740.
$3356. (WEST COAST)

69 B

(INTRO. 9-26-68)

LE SABRE GRILLE has 5 HORIZONTAL PCS.; (ILLUSTR. WILDCAT GRILLE has JUST ONE.)

WILDCAT

$3596.

430 CID V8 (360 HP)

2-DR. H/T (12416 BLT.)

123.2" WB
(12/36 WILDCAT CUSTOM 2-DR. H/Ts BLT.)

WILDCAT COWL DETAILS

FORMAL ROOFLINE

ELECTRA 225

(ELECTRA GRILLE AT LOWER LEFT)

GRILLE

2-DR. H/T (13128 BLT.)
CUSTOM 2-DR. H/T (27018 BLT.)

430 CID V8 (360 HP)

ELECTRA 225 2-DR. H/Ts FROM
$4323.

TOTAL 1969 PROD.: (ALL MODELS) 665,422
$3216. ~ 4643. PRICE RANGE (FULL-SIZED)

2 DR. H/T, 4-DR. H/T, 4 DR. SEDAN and CONVERTIBLE IN EACH MODEL SERIES.

BUICK 69 (B)

$2859.
(WEST=$3737.)
SKYLARK 350

$2838.
Skylark 350 4-door Sedan
(3028/ BLT.)
Skylark

"SPECIAL"
MODEL NAME DISCONTINUED

WITH 350 CID V8 (260 HP)
(70918 BLT.)

(12241 BLT.)

70 A

FROM $3210. **SPORTWAGON.**
FROM $3977.
(WEST)

$2736.
$3614.
(WEST)

(13420 BLT.)

SKYLARK

4-door Sedan.
(SKYLARK CUSTOM 4-DR. SED. IS SIMILAR)

(VINYL TOP EXTRA)

2-door Sedan.
(COUPE)

1970

(CONT'D. NEXT PAGE)

(18620 BLT.) $2685.
($3563.. WEST)

1970 Buick Exterior Colors

REGAL BLACK 1
GLACIER WHITE 2
GULFSTREAM BLUE 3
DIPLOMAT BLUE 4
CORNET GOLD 5

SEA~ MIST GREEN
BURNISHED SADDLE
AQUA MIST
SHERWOOD GREEN
BURGUNDY MIST
SILVER MIST 11
FIRE RED 12
DESERT GOLD 13
BAMBOO CREAM 14
HARVEST GOLD 15

6 7 8 9 10 11 12 13 14 15

BUICK 70 (A)

BUICK

$3220.
(12411 BLT.)

Skylark Custom 4-door Hardtop

$3283.

$3098. **($3865., WEST)**

(8732 BLT.)
GS 455 Sport Coupe (H/T)

(OTHER GS-455s AT BOTTOM OF PAGE)

GS 455 Stage I Convertible

$3132. ↓ **$3868.** (WEST)

2-DR. H/T
(36367 BLT.)

4-DR. H/T
(12411 BLT.)

STEREO TAPE OPTIONAL

$3220. ($3899., WEST)

SKYLARK CUSTOM

$3275. CVT. **$3987.** (WEST)

70B (CONT'D.)

(4954 BLT.)

GS-455 STAGE I H/T

(360 HP)

Introducing automobiles to light your fire.

(GS H/T $3098. OR $3865.) WEST

GS-455

(1416 BLT.)

GS 455 Convertible.

$4257. (WEST)

$3469. (EASTERN PRICE)

new 455 C/D V8 (350 HP)

BUICK 70 (B)

1970 BUICK
SOMETHING TO BELIEVE IN.

LE SABRE 2-DR. H/T (SPT. CPE.)
(14163 BLT.)

$3419.

$3477.

(14817 BLT.)
LeSabre 4-door Hardtop

LeSabre Custom
455 Sport Coupe
(5469 BLT.)

SPECIAL SIDE
MIRRORS PART OF
OPTIONAL TRAILER-TOW
PACKAGE

LE SABRE STEER.
WHEEL HUB UNIQUE.

$3675. ($4570. WEST)

LeSabre 4-door Sedan.
(35404 BLT.)

LeSABRE

new 124" WB
(THROUGH
1976)

$3337.
($4169., WEST)

LeSabre Custom Convertible.
(2487 BLT.)

$3700.

($4532. WEST)

(INTRO.
9~18~69)

70 C

LeSabre Custom
4-door Hardtop.
(43863 BLT.)

$3571. ($4403., WEST)

LE SABRE
CUSTOM 455
IS ADDED,
TOPPING 3
LE SABRE
LINES.

$3739. (6541 BLT.)
LeSabre Custom 455 4-door Hardtop

$4079. (1244 BLT.)
Wildcat Custom Convertible

$3949. Wildcat Custom Sport Coupe
(9447 BLT.)

Wildcat Custom

Wildcat Custom 4-door Hardtop.
(12924 BLT.)

WILDCAT CUSTOM
IS NOW ONLY
WILDCAT LINE.

$3997.
($4892.,
WEST)

NAME ON
GRILLE

(CONT'D. ON
NEXT PAGE)

BUICK 70 (C)

BUICK

Wildcat Custom Convertible (ABOVE)

CHILD SAFETY SEATS AVAILABLE

CVT. (1244 BLT.)
$4079. ($4974..WEST)

LE SABRE, ESTATE WAG., WILDCAT CUSTOM and ELECTRA 225 HAVE THIS STYLE OF DASH. (ABOVE)

$5272. TO (WEST)

124" WB

ESTATE WAGON

(new) (1st LARGE-SERIES BUICK WAGON SINCE 1964.)

ESTATE WAG. 6~PASS. (11427 BLT.) 9~PASS. (16879 BLT.)

ELECTRA 225 CUSTOM SPT. CPE. (H/T) (26002 BLT.)

$4661.

new 127" WB on ALL ELECTRA MODELS (THROUGH '76)

Electra 225 Custom Limited 4-door Hardtop

70 (CONT'D.)
D

TOTAL 1970 BUICK PRODUCTION = 666,501

CONTROL SWITCH

No more opening your window to adjust your outside mirror. Buick's remote control outside mirror adjusts easily from the interior of the car, enabling the driver to get a clear view to the rear with a simple flick of the finger. It's available on all 1970 Buick models.

Electra 225 Custom Convertible

(6045 BLT.)

$4802.

($5312., WEST)

new 455 CID V8 (350~360 HP IN GS 455 ; 370 HP IN WILDCAT, ESTATE WAGON, LE S. 455, ELECTRA 225)

BUICK 70 (D)

BUICK

SKYLARK

$2897.

4-DR. SEDAN (34037 BLT.)

2-DR. H/T (61201 BLT.)

WILL RUN ON LOW~LEAD OR UNLEADED FUELS.

$2918.

Buick Motor Division, General Motors Corporation, reserves the right to make changes at any time, without notice, in prices, colors, materials, equipment, specifications, and models and also to discontinue models.

$3397.

SKYLARK CUSTOM

4-DR. H/T (10814 BLT.)
116" WB

CVT. (3993 BLT.)

$3462.

SportWagon! $3515.

V8 ENGINES
350 CID
(230 OR
260 HP)
455 CID
(315,
330 OR
345 HP)

6 CYL.
(145 HP)
AVAIL. IN
SKYLARK

DASH

1971   3.08 GEAR RATIO

(12525 BLT.)

SPORTWAGON FRONT DETAILS

GS~455

2-DR. H/T

CONSOLE AVAIL. FOR SKYLK. 2-DR. H/T and GS

GS 112" WB

71 A
(INTRO. 10~3~70)

WITH OPTIONAL "GSX" PACKAGE

CVT. (902 BLT.)

$3476

(CONT'D. NEXT PAGE)
BUICK 71 (A)

74

$3992.

BUICK

new WRAP-AROUND INSTRUMENT PANEL

4-DR. SEDAN (26348 BLT.)

$4213.

LE SABRE CUSTOM 4-DR. H/T (41098 BLT.)

LE SABRE
new LOW OBLONG REAR SIDE LTS. (THRU '73)

$4061.

2-DR. H/T (13385 BLT.)

TOTAL 1971 PRODUCTION 551,188 (CONT'D.)

71 B

MODEL NAME ON COWL — Centurion

CENTURION

CVT. (2161 BLT.)

$4678.

124" WB

CENTURION (*new*) (REPLACES WILDCAT CUSTOM)

455 CID V8 (315 HP)

$4678. ($5170. WEST)

2-DR H/T

(11892 BLT.)

L78 x 15" TIRES

The Buick Estate Wagon.

$4640. OR $4786.

127" WB (8699 2-SEATERS ; 15335 3-SEATERS)

ON EST. WAGON and ELECTRA 225

2-DR. H/T $4801. up

CUSTOM 4-DR. H/T $5093.

ELECTRA 225 CUSTOM LIMITED

ELECTRA 225

1971 Buick exterior colors.
1. Regal Black, Code A*
2. Arctic White, Code C
3. Cascade Blue, Code D
4. Nocturne Blue, Code E**
5. Cornet Gold, Code G**
6. Willowmist Green, Code K
7. Verdemist Green, Code M
8. Rosewood, Code N*
9. Platinum Mist, Code P
10. Fire Red, Code R*
11. Burnished Cinnamon, Code U*
12. Sandpiper Beige, Code W
13. Silver Fern, Code Z

*Not available on Riviera.
**Not available on Skylark, SportWagon and GS.

Exclusive GS, Sportwagon and Skylark colors.
14. Stratomist Blue, Code B
15. Lime Mist, Code H
16. Cortez Gold, Code Q
17. Bittersweet Mist, Code T

Exclusive Electra 225, Estate Wagon, Centurion and LeSabre colors.
18. Twilight Turquoise, Code I
19. Tealmist Gray, Code L

STOP

POWER DISC BRAKES on ALL EXCEPT SKYLARKS

FRONT OF ELECTRA 225 and ESTATE WAGON

BUICK 71 (B)

BUICK Something to believe in.

1972 Buick Skylark.

350 CID V8 WITH 150 OR 190 HP
Skylark 2-Door Coupe
shown in Flame Orange
with a White vinyl top.

Skylark Custom 4-Door Hardtop.

ALL WITH V8 ENGINES IN 1972.

3331.

(12925 BLT.)

SKYLARK CUSTOM

(14552 BLT.)
$2925.
(FINAL SKYLARKS UNTIL 1975)

SKYLARK 350

(INTRO. 9~23~71)

IN "STRATOMIST BLUE"

IN "HERITAGE GREEN"

SKYLARK 350

72

$3124.

Buick Bargain Days.

LeSabre Custom 4-Door Sedan shown in Hunter Green.

LeSabre.

$4047.
(35295 BLT.)

IN "ROYAL BLUE"

1972 Buick LeSabre.

LE SABRE (REAR)

FROM $3958.

Custom Convertible.

$4291.
(2037 BLT.)

455 CID V8 (225 HP) STANDARD IN LE SABRE ESTATE WAGON and ELECTRA 225

$4508. UP

DASH (CENTURION, ETC.)

CENTURION (VERTICAL GRILLE PCS.)

H78 X 15" TIRES

1972 Estate Wagon.
(28968 BLT.)

REAR

4-DR. H/T FROM $4890.

Electra 225.

TOTAL 1972 PROD. = 679,921

1972 Buick   3 SEATS = $4728.   2 SEATS = $4589.

76

BUICK

Century 350 Colonnade Hardtop Coupe

PRICE OF $3811. WEST
FOR
EITHER BODY TYPE
$3057. UP (EAST)

Century 350 Colonnade Hardtop Sedan.

Gran Sport Colonnade Hardtop Coupe.

Century MODEL SERIES RETURNS FOR FIRST TIME SINCE 1942.

"BUICK" NAME ABOVE GRILLE ON **CENTURY 350**

(CENTURY WAGONS ON NEXT PAGE)

CENTURY is new, REPLACES SKYLARK. SERIES.

73 A

REGAL IS new TOP MODEL IN new CENTURY LINE.

Regal instrument panel.

(91557 BLT.)

CENTURY REGAL

VERTICAL PCS. IN REGAL GRILLE

$3470.

$4210. (WEST)

Regal Colonnade Hardtop Coupe.

TOTAL 1973 BUICK PROD. = 821,165

(CONT'D. NEXT PAGE)

BUICK 73 (A)

77

BUICK

WAGONS

Century Station Wagon. **$3486.** UP

$4222. UP (WEST)

(7760 BLT.)

73 B
(CONT'D.)

WOODGRAIN OPTIONAL AT EXTRA COST

(10645 BLT.)

$3652. UP

Century *LUXUS*

$4385. UP (WEST)

Introducing Apollo. By Buick.

4-DR. **$2883.** (WEST)

2-DR. HATCHBACK **$3009.** (WEST) (A.K.A. 3~DR. HATCHBK.)

E78 × 14 TIRES

111" WB
250 CID 6 (100 HP) OR
350 CID V8 (150 HP)
(THIS OPTIONAL V8
IS ALSO AVAIL. WITH
175 HP)(ALSO USED IN
CENTURY and LE SABRE.)

EARLY BUICK APOLLOS COULD BE CONSIDERED AS "1973½" MODELS

2-DR. CPE. **$2860.** (WEST)

(INTRO. APRIL, 1973)

(CONT'D. NEXT PAGE)

instrument panel with wood-grain vinyl accents.

Custom interior available.

APOLLO BODY TYPES and PRODUCTION (EASTERN PRICES)	
2~DR. SEDAN (14475 BLT.)	$2605.
2/3~DR. HATCHBACK (9868 BLT.)	2754.
4~DR. SEDAN (8450 BLT.)	2628.

BUICK 73 (B)

DASH

REAR END
DETAIL

1973 Centurion.

BUICK.
The solid feeling.

CVT.
$4993.
(WEST)

(5739
BLT.)

Centurion

H/T $4803.
(WEST)

(FINAL YEAR FOR
CENTURION)
(NO DECORATIVE UPPER COWL STRIPS AS SEEN
ON LE S., ELECTRA)

Electra 225

FROM
$4815.

73
C

(CONT'D.)

$4645. UP

Electra 225
FROM $5428.
(WEST)

Estate Wagon
$5551.
(WEST)

BUICK

ESTATE WAGON

DASH
CLOSE-UP

CUSTOM SEDAN →
(42854 BLT.)

LE SABRE

$4091.

LE S.
GRILLE
SIMILAR
TO
CENTURION'S

BUICK 73 (C)

BUICK

1974 Apollo

GRILLE MODIFIED →

2-DR. (28286 BLT.)

$3037. →
($3877. WEST)

SEDAN →

$3060. (16779 BLT.)
$3900. (WEST)

(11644 H/Bs BLT.)

$3160.

Space-saver spare tire.
Standard with the Apollo Hatchback Coupe is a space-saver spare tire. If it's needed, the included inflation cylinder pops the folded spare into a full-size, functioning emergency tire.

DASH **Apollo**

6 OR V8

Apollo

74 A

495,063
TOTAL 1974 BUICK PRODUCTION

175, 210 OR 245 HP

455-cubic-inch 4-barrel V-8.
The biggest engine available for the '74 Century. Complete with dual exhaust.

DASH

Century Regal

new SEDAN JOINS REGAL CPE. →

(9333 BLT.) $4221. ($4734. WEST)

116" WB

UN-RESTORED CARS STILL HAVE COLLECTOR VALUE

112" WB

(33/66 GS and 350 COUPES BLT.)

Gran Sport $3904.

SEDAN (11159 BLT.) 4109.

Century Luxus ($4622. WEST)

Century 350 ←

$3790.

new TAIL LTS. →

116" WB

1974 Buick CENTURY Station Wagons
CENT. LUXUS $4371. UP
(6791 BLT.)

$4303. (WEST)

LUXUS COLONNADE COUPE (44930 BLT.)

$4089.

$4602. (WEST)

BUICK 74 (A)

80

BUICK

LeSabre Luxus Convertible (3627 BLT.)

$5256. WEST

$4696.

LUXUS COUPE (27243 BLT.) $4575.

LeSabre
FROM $4915.

(11879 BLT.)

SEDAN

$4482.

LUXUS SED. (23910 BLT.)

$4629.

GRAINED 3-SEAT WAG. $6043. (WEST)

Estate Wagon

(4581 2-SEAT LRS BLT.)
(9831 3-SEAT LRS)

ESTATE WAGON GRILLE

127" WB

REAR

VARIOUS new UPHOLSTERIES

74ᴮ

new~ STYLE QUARTER WINDOWS ON COUPES

White/Blue Oxen–

Electra 225
FROM $5428. (WEST)

$6425. (WEST)

(16086 BLT.)

1974 Electra Limited
$5886.

COUPE

Low-fuel indicator. Available on all Electras. The red light warns you when the fuel level drops to approximately 4½ gallons.

HIGHER BUMPER GUARDS ON SOME CARS

ELECTRA PANEL

new INSTR. PANELS

(COMPARE SMALL DETAILS)

LE SABRE (FULL VIEW)
BUICK 74 (B)

Skyhawk Instrument Panel

BUICK

97" WB

$4173.

Skyhawk.
HATCHBACK

(29448 BLT.) **new**

BR 78 x 13" TIRES

(BUDGET "S" MODEL $3860.)

DASH
USED IN
SKY. and AP.

Skylark/Apollo.

SKYLARK
RETURNS TO
JOIN (AND
THEN REPLACE)
APOLLO

(3746 BLT.)

APOLLO
SEDAN
(21138 BLT.)
6 CYL. (106 HP)
250 CID

$4136.

260 CID V8 AVAIL.
IN BOTH SERIES
(110 HP)

SKYLARK S/R
COUPE
new V6 ENGINE
231 CID (110 HP)

111"
WB

SKYLARK GRILLE (APOLLO IS SIMILAR)

←— Inside —→

V-6 Buick Century
SPECIAL $3815. ($4665. WEST)
COUPE

75
A

BUICK "Dedicated to the Free Spirit in just about everyone."

COLORS
(R=AVAIL.
ON
RIVIERA
ONLY)
R-

REGAL
LANDAU
COUPE

SOME COLORS
AVAIL. ON
CERTAIN MODELS
ONLY.

SEDAN 116" WB
(9995 BLT.) $4211.

CENTURY CUSTOM (REPLACES LUXUS)

According to E.P.A. figures,

In dynamometer tests recently conducted by the Environmental Protection Agency, a Buick Century equipped with a 3.8-litre V-6 got 24 miles per gallon in the highway tests. (And 16 mpg in the city test.)

(10726 REGAL SEDANS
ALSO BUILT)

$4257. UP

(56646 BLT.)
$5098. (WEST)

REGAL
BUICK 75 (A)

Buick
Station Wagons
THE EXTERIORS

BUICK

$5133.

LE SABRE

CUSTOM CVT.   (5300 BLT.)

FINAL BUICK CVT. LE SABRE

LeSabre.

127" WB

CUSTOM COUPE (25016 BLT.) $5007.

ESTATE WAGON (13740 BLT.)

$5447. UP

Century Wagon

(11494 BLT.)

$4636. UP

350 CID V8 (165 HP)

$4771.
(14088 BLT.)

LE SABRE SEDAN

75 B

LeSabre Custom Vinyl Notchback Seat

LeSabre Custom
CUSTOM H/T
SEDAN

Electra Limited Leather 60/40 Notchback Seat

LE SABRE

ELECTRA 225 $6041. UP

it delivers what a luxury car should deliver—superb luxury, superb comfort, superb convenience—but without, well, *flaunting* the fact. Like an iceberg, most of Electra's substance is beneath the surface. Inside. Underneath. Contained within. Where it really matters.

The 1975 Electra Park Avenue you see on the right is the most elegant Electra of all. The headlamps are rectangular. The roof is covered with special vinyl in a halo motif. Inside, shag carpeting and soft velour reside. The seats are upholstered with velour; likewise, the mammoth executive center console. Even the ceiling is lined with velour.

$5061. (30005 BLT.)

Electra Park Avenue Cloth 40/40 Seats

LE SABRE DASH (ELECTRA SIMILAR)

75-502

455 CID V8 (205 HP) *

BUICK ELECTRA PARK AVENUE.

TOTAL 1975 BUICK PRODUCTION =
481,768

*=SAME V8 IN ESTATE WAGON

New

REAR

127" WB   BUICK 75 (B)

Be Happy at BUICK

GM MARK OF EXCELLENCE

BUICK

97" WB

SKYHAWK   DASH

SKYHAWK

231 CID V6 (110 HP)

SKYHAWK
(15768 BLT.)
$4216.   ("S" $3903.)

231 CID V6 or V8s: (3243 BLT.)
(260 or 350 CID) $4324.

SEDAN   SKYLARK S/R

coupes $4281
(3880 BLT.)

SKYLARK

SKYLARK S/R.

76
A

CENTURY
SPECIAL
$3935.
$4836.
WEST

59448 BLT.
(INCL. REGULAR CENT.
COUPE)

CENTURY

CPE.
(124,498
SOLD)
$4465. BEST SELLER!

note VERTICALLY-STACKED HEADLTS.

CENTURY CUSTOM WAGON.

(16625 BLT.)
$4987.
UP

CENTURY and REGAL
have SAME V6 and V8
CHOICES AS SKYLARK.

CENTURY
REGAL

REGAL DASH

UNUSUAL
ROOF OF
REGAL TYPE
(SINCE '73)

BUICK Dedicated to
the Free Spirit in just about everyone.
BUICK 76 (A)

350 CID
V8 (165 HP)   116" WB

84

BUICK

76 B

(CONT'D.)

EXTERIOR COLORS

Special Colors

TOTAL 1976 PRODUCTION:
737,466

GM

PACE CAR REPLICA

A LIMITED NUMBER of "INDIANAPOLIS 500" CENTURY V-6 PACE CAR REPLICAS (IN SPECIAL SILVER, RED and BLACK PAINT COMBINATION) AVAIL. AT BUICK DEALERS. (RARE)

CENTURY

OFFICIAL PACE CAR
BUICK Free Spirit

(20374 BLT.) **Estate Wagon.** $5591. UP

EST. WAG. and LE SABRE DASH

350 CID V8 (165 HP) IN **LeSabre** CUSTOM.

LE SABRE Custom 4-door Sedan (34841 BLT.) $5046.

new 124" WB 231 CID V6 (110 HP) IN STD. LE SABRE.

LIMITED H/T SEDAN (51067 BLT.) $6852.

(46109 BLT.) $5166.

4-DR. HARDTOP SED.

Electra 225 INTERIOR

PARK AVE. **Electra 225** 455 CID V8 (205 HP) (SAME ENGINE IN ESTATE WAGON)

ELECTRA

BUICK 76 (B)

BUICK

SKYHAWK $3981. UP
FROM $4299. (WEST)

Nighthawk.

(12345 BLT.)

SKYHAWK 231 CID V6 (105 HP)

(NIGHTHAWK → has SPECIAL PAINT)

SKYHAWK DASH

REAR

SKYLARK $3825.

SEDAN

V6 OR V8

SKYLARK CPE. (49858 BLT.)

3 COWL "PORTS"

$3642. UP ("S")

77 A

(48121 BLT.)

$4713.

REGAL COUPE

TOTAL 1977 BUICK PROD. = 845,234

Century V6 OR V8

SEDAN (29065 BLT.) (52864 COUPES)

$4364.

OPT. SUNROOF

REGAL CPE. (174 560 SOLD! BUICK'S TOP SELLER IN '77.)

T-BAR ROOF OPT.

AVAIL. FINNED WHEELS

W. BUMPER GUARDS

Regal

CENTURY SPECIAL $4170.

FROM $5219. →

CENTURY CUSTOM WAGON

(19282 BLT.)

(CONT'D. NEXT PAGE)
BUICK 77 (A)

BUICK

(25075 BLT.)

$5903. UP

ESTATE WAGON
(DOWNSIZED) new 116"
(115.9") WB

SEDAN (LE SABRE)
(119827 BLT.)

$5093.

$5322. UP   (58589 BLT.)   CUSTOM COUPE

LeSabres.
(DOWNSIZED)
new 116" WB

I'M OPEN TO OFFERS

BUICK SALESMEN'S 1977
SALES CAMPAIGN
BADGE

REAR
(WRAP-
AROUND
TAIL-
LTS.)

$5382.

'77 LeSABRE CUSTOM.

SEDAN
(103,855
BLT.)

AVAILABLE
SPORT STEERING WHEEL

LE SABRE DASH
(ELECTRA's
SIMILAR)

BRUSHED
ALUMINUM
DIALS
(new)

3 COWL "PORTS"
ON LE SABRES, EST. WAG.,
4 ON ELECTRAS.

new
SMALLER 350 CID V8
in ELECTRA

$7033.
LTD.
CPE

(37871 BLT.)

Electra 225 (DOWNSIZED)

LIMITED COUPE

new SHORTER
119" WB

INTERIORS

77 B

VARIOUS
ENGINES :

231 CID BUICK V6
(105 HP @ 3400 RPM)
350 CID V8s (2)
CHEVROLET = 160 HP @ 3800
OLDS = 170 HP @ 3800
403 CID V8 (OLDS)
185 HP @ 3600

ELECTRA 225 SEDAN

BUICK 77 (B) $6866.   (25633 BLT.)

ELECTRA PARK AVENUE
LIMITED (8236/ BLT.) $7226.

87

BUICK Skyhawk

A little science.. A little magic.
(20014 BLT.)

231 CID V-6 $5233.

$4414. (24589 BLT.)

Skylark Custom Sedan

$4367. (14523 BLT.)

$4520.

$4413. (10818 BLT.)

new 2-door or 4-door

MPG.= 27 HWY. 19 CITY

CUSTOM **Wagon**

CENT

SQUARE DASH GAUGES

(12533 BLT.)

$6098. (WEST) (4-DR.)

note DIFF. BETWEEN ROCKER PANEL / LOWER DOOR TRIM ON CENTURY AND CENT. CUSTOM

$4768.

"3.2 Litre" ON COWL

new FASTBACK REAR

Century Custom

196 OR 231 CID V6 (86/102 HP)

305 CID V8 (145 HP)

"CENTURY CUSTOM" ON REAR FENDERS

78 A

(TOTALLY RESTYLED) all-new BODY SHAPES 108" WB

231 CID V6 TURBO (151/175 HP)

TURBO REGAL

STD. WH. CVR.

$5958. $6480. (WEST)

REGAL

(236,652 REGAL COUPES BLT., MOST W/O TURBO OPT.)

HOOD ORNAMENT (TURBO) Turbo 3.8 Litre

CLOSE VIEW OF REGAL FRONT END

BUICK

Regal 1976

REGAL DASH has GRAINED STRIP

REGAL FROM $6197. (WEST)

GM MARK OF EXCELLENCE

TURBOCHARGING

MORE DETAILS ON NEXT PAGE

THE TURBOCHARGED V-6 **new** BUICK 78 (A)

An idea whose time has come.

...within the confines of a V-6. The turbocharger is powered by exhaust gases that normally go out the tailpipe. In effect, it recycles energy that would otherwise be wasted.

Since turbocharging permits the efficient burning of fuel, the LeSabre Sport Coupe and Regal Sport Coupe, equipped with an available 3.8 litre (231 CID) turbocharged V-6 with 4-barrel carburetor and automatic transmission, is not too much lower in fuel economy figures than the LeSabre and Regal equipped with a 3.8 litre (231 CID) non-turbocharged V-6 and automatic trans- The standard 2-barrel version of this engine is not offered in California. An available 4-barrel version is required and will be available in California after January 1, 1978.

BUICK

America's only turbocharged production automobile engine.

A little science. A little magic.

231 CID TURBO V6 (151/175 HP) AVAIL. in LeSabre Sport Coupe

OTHER ENGS.
231 CID STD. V6
301 CID V8
305 CID V8
350 CID V8
403 CID V8

2 OF THE WORLD'S TURBO CARS ARE BUICKS.

The other two cars are the Porsche Turbo Carrera and the Turbo Saab.

$ 6346. (WITH TURBO)

LE SABRE SEDAN (23354 BLT.) CUSTOM SED. (86638 BLT.)

$5536. UP

Buick LeSabre. Under $5800.

LeSabre Custom Coupe (53675 BLT.) $5727.

DASH

ESTATE WAG. $7399. w. GRAIN (WEST)

$6394. (25964 BLT.)

REAR

78 B

new GRILLES

THE NEW ELECTRA:

22 HIGHWAY **15** CITY **18** COMBINED*

EPA mileage estimates

ELECTRA 225; ELECTRA LTD. OR ELECTRA PARK AVE. MODELS WITH 350 CID V8 (153 HP) (405 CID V8 ALSO AVAIL.)

ELECTRA

$7431. UP

ELECTRA SEDANS $7996. UP (WEST)

ELECT. CPES. PRICED FROM $7821. (WEST)

LTD. CPE. (33365 BLT.) $7638.

INTERIOR

FRONT CLOSE-UP

DASH

ELECTRA

PARK AVE. SEDAN $8208.

BUICK 1978 (B)

BUICK

(23139 BLT.)

DASH

Skyhawk.

Skyhawk and Skylark Colors

Bright Blue*
• Code 24

Bright Red
• Code 75

Bright Yellow
• Code 51

$4778.
("S" MODEL = $4560.)

79A

HATCHBACK
$5543.
(ONLY 608 BLT.)
$4357.

Skylark.

$4308.

SEDAN
$5493.
(WEST)
(10849 BLT.)

196 c/b V6 (105 HP)

turbocharged
Regal.
$7144.
WEST
$6497.
(236652 REGAL COUPES BLT.)
BEST-SELLER

Century Special.

$5021.
(7363 BLT.)

WEST:
$6497.
$5473.

Century Limited and Century Custom.

DASH

TURBO
Century Sport Coupe
$6928.
(WEST)

BUICK
After all, life is to enjoy.
Buick 1979 exterior colors.

$5806.

Century Wagon

(21100 BLT.)
$7154.
(WEST)

Century Wagons.

(UNGRAINED ALSO AVAIL.)

Available on all models

Silver*
• Code 15

Medium Blue*
• Code 22

Black
• Code 19

Dark Blue*
• Code 29

Light Green
• Code 40

White
• Code 11

Dark Gold*
• Code 63

Red*
• Code 77

Medium Green
• Code 44

Tan
• Code 61

Dark Brown*
• Code 69

Available on all models except Skyhawk, Skylark, Century Sport Coupe, Sport Wagon Option & LeSabre Sport Coupe

Light Blue
• Code 21

Dark Red*
• Code 79

Light Yellow
• Code 54

Available on all models except LeSabre Sport Coupe, Century Sport Coupe & Sport Wagon Option

BUICK
79 (A)

SPT. CPE
(TURBO V6)
$6497.

LE SABRE CPE.
(7542 BLT.)
$6010.

BUICK

$6620.

(ABOVE)
Buick LeSabre 4-door $6110, 18 EPA-esti mpg.

79
B

TOTAL 1979 PROD.= 727,275

DASH

BUICK
After all, life is to enjoy.

LTD. SEDAN
(75939 BLT.)

(EST. WAG. (NOW has ONLY 3 HOOD PORTS, LIKE LE SABRE) ('79 ONLY)

SEDANS $8878. UP

(21312 BLT.)
$7169. ESTATE WAGON
REAR

Electra

Special Electra and Riviera Colors (extra cost)

Gold Firemist*
• Code 33

Saffron Firemist*
• Code 99

Gray Firemist*
• Code 98

Additional Designers' Accent Colors

Gray Accent

Blue Accent

COUPES $8703. UP

Ask your Buick salesperson about selected standard car colors that are also used as Accent Colors.

*Metallic Paint

1979 BUICK
ENGINES AVAIL.
196 CID V6 (105 HP) 231 CID V6 (115 HP, 175 TURBO)
301 CID V8 (140 or 150 HP) 305 CID V8 (130 or 155 HP)
350 CID V8 (170 HP) 403 CID V8 (185 HP)
ENG. MFD. BY CHEVROLET • PONTIAC • OLDSMOBILE
(350 CID V8s BY BUICK (CHEVROLET or OLDS.)

Silver • Code 15

Green • Code 40

White • Code 11

Blue • Code 22

Buick 1979 vinyl top colors.

Available at extra cost on all models except Skyhawk, Station Wagons and Century Sport Coupe. Top Codes 11, 15, and 22 available at extra cost on Century Sport Coupe to match car color. Riviera S TYPE vinyl tops available only when matching lower car color is ordered.

Red • Code 79

Black • Code 19

Tan • Code 61

BUICK 79 (B)

BUICK
FINAL SKYHAWK
(DISCONT'D. 1-80)

WITH "ROAD HAWK" OPTION PACKAGE

ROAD HAWK REAR DESIGN DIFFERS

EPA EST MPG	EST. HWY	EST. DRIVING RANGE	EST. HWY RANGE
15	24	277	444

231 CID V6 (110 HP)

Skyhawk

SKYHAWK DASH

(8322 BLT.)

$5211. ($4993. "S" MODEL)

80 A

Available on Skyhawk and Skylark only

Bright Red • Code 72

BUICK 1980 EXTERIOR COLORS.

Available on all models

White • Code 11
Silver* • Code 15
Medium Yellow • Code 50
Tan* • Code 63
Cinnabar • Code 77

new SHORTER 104.9" WB new 151 CID 4 (90 HP) OR 173 CID V6 (115 HP)

LTD. CPE. (42652 BLT.)

$5765.

LTD. SEDAN (86948 BLT.)

Skylark

WITH FRONT-WHEEL DRIVE

$5912.

Available on all models except Century Sport Coupe & Sport Wagon Option

Black • Code 19
Medium Blue* • Code 21
Dark Blue* • Code 29
Dark Green* • Code 44
Beige • Code 59
Medium Brown* • Code 69

*-METALLIC

REAR DETAILS

Skylark is equipped with GM-built engines produced by various divisions. See your dealer for details.

525 UMG

SKYLARK DASH

Dark Red* • Code 76
Light Gray • Code 85

SPORT COUPE (new)

$5955.

($6102. SPORT SEDAN AVAIL.)

Skylark has OWN 6-SLOT GRILLE

BUICK 80 (A)

BUICK

LeSabre

STD. COUPE
$6845.

(LTD. COUPE
(20561 BLT.) $7100.

Buick Diesels

AVAILABLE
(SEE LOWER LEFT
OF PAGE)

LeSabre

LTD. SEDAN
(37676 BLT.)

$7242.

SPORT CPE.
231 CID V6
TURBO
$8003.

LE SABRE MODELS NO LONGER
BEAR IDENTIFYING
HOOD PORTS.

AS BEFORE,
LE SABRE SPORT COUPE
has DIFFERENT (BLACKED) GRILLE.

AVAILABLE
LE SABRE
INTERIOR

LE SABRE   DASH

LeSabre and Electra Estate Wagons

(9318
BLT.)

$7844.
UP

80
C

$10806. UP

New
105 HP
350 CID DIESEL V8
OPTIONAL IN ESTATE
WAGONS AND ELECTRA

OPTIONAL COVER

The new 4.1 Liter
Electra. America's
first and only
traditional luxury
car powered by a
V-6 engine.

ELECTRA
PARK AVE. has
WIRE WHEELS,
FULL-LENGTH
CHROME BELT

ELECTRA DASH

Electra   (14058 BLT.)

LTD.
CPE. $9425.

LTD.
SED. $9580.

(54422
BLT.)

EPA EST. 17 MPG
23 HWY.

PARK AVE. SEDAN
$10,676.

ANOTHER AVAIL. WHEEL COVER
(PARK AVE.)

BUICK 80 (C)

94

BUICK *RIVIERA*

luxury cars.
(STARTS 1963)

(by Buick)

(DASH)

401 CID
V8
325 HP @
4400 RPM

(40,000 BLT.)

117" WB

7.10 x 15
TIRES

63 MODEL 4747

America's bid for a great new — international classic car

new 425 CID V8
(340 OR 360
HP)

(37,658 BLT.)

64 $4385.

MODEL 4747

'64 DASH

ADVENTURE IS A CAR CALLED RIVIERA — AND IT'S A BUICK

(VINYL TOP ALSO AVAIL.)

new
TAIL-LIGHTS
IN BUMPER

65

MODEL 49447

new
CONCEALED
HEADLIGHTS

WIRE
WHEEL
OPTION

Wouldn't you really rather have a Buick?

$4408.

(34,586 BLT.)

2 ENGINES NOW AVAIL.: 401 CID V8 (325 HP)
OR 425 CID V8 (340 OR 360 HP)

BUICK RIVIERA 63~65

BUICK
RIVIERA
new GRILLE

new 119" WB

$4424.

1966 Buick. The tuned car.
425 CID V8 (360 HP)
8.45 × 15 TIRES
(45,348 BLT.)

CONCEALED HEADLIGHTS

66

GS WHEEL COVER

"Riviera GS" ON COWL, JUST AHEAD OF DOOR

(INTRO. 9-29-66)
HAZARD FLASHERS AT ALL CORNERS

67

$4469.

TAIL LIGHTS

(42,799 BLT.)

$4557. (WEST COAST)

new ENERGY-ABSORBING STEERING COLUMN

CENTER CONSOLE AVAIL.

new 430 CID V8 (360 HP)
(THROUGH '70)

MODEL 49487
$4703.
$5245. (WEST COAST)

VINYL TOP COVERING

PLAIN TOP

(INTRO. 9-21-67)

"RIVIERA" NAME ON COWL IS NOW IN BLOCK LETTERS.

68

(49,284 BLT.)

new SPLIT GRILLE

new SIDE SAFETY LTS.

MODEL 49487

8.45 × 15" TIRES

| 1968 PRODUCTION | = 49,284 |
| 1969 PRODUCTION | = 52,872 |

430 CID V8

$4701.

69

new 8.55 × 15" TIRES

$5321. (WEST COAST)

new GRILLE SPLIT, AS IN 1968.

(INTRO. 9-26-68)

new GRILLE has FINE VERTICAL PCS. and JUST 2 HEAVIER HORIZONTAL PCS.

1969

Wouldn't you really rather have a Buick?

BUICK RIVIERA   66~69

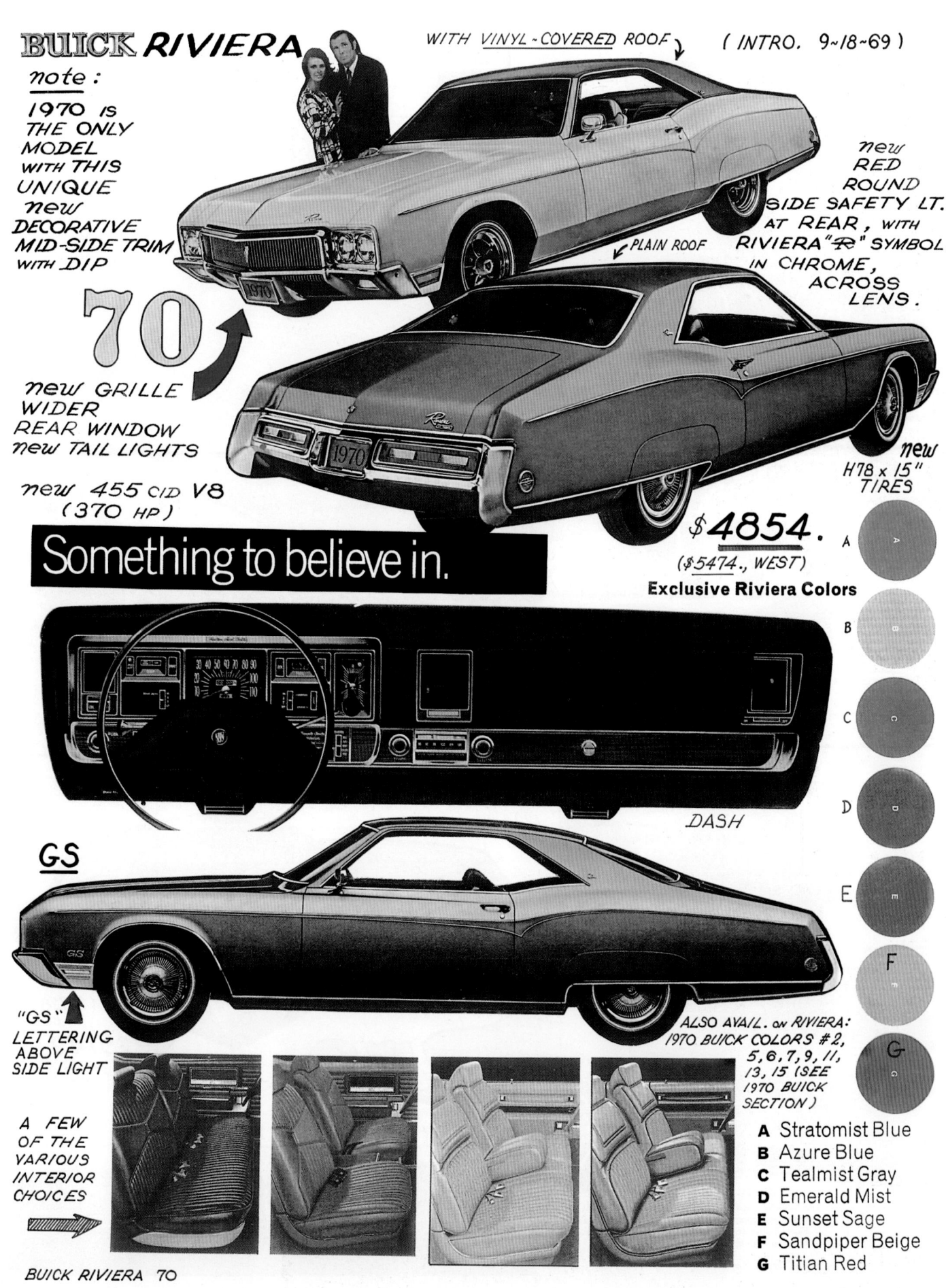

BUICK RIVIERA WITH VINYL-COVERED ROOF (INTRO. 9-18-69)

note:
1970 IS THE ONLY MODEL WITH THIS UNIQUE new DECORATIVE MID-SIDE TRIM WITH DIP

new RED ROUND SIDE SAFETY LT. AT REAR, WITH RIVIERA "R" SYMBOL IN CHROME, ACROSS LENS.

← PLAIN ROOF

70

new GRILLE WIDER REAR WINDOW new TAIL LIGHTS

new 455 CID V8 (370 HP)

new H78 x 15" TIRES

Something to believe in.

$4854.
($5474., WEST)
Exclusive Riviera Colors

DASH

GS

"GS" LETTERING ABOVE SIDE LIGHT

A FEW OF THE VARIOUS INTERIOR CHOICES

ALSO AVAIL. on RIVIERA: 1970 BUICK COLORS #2, 5,6,7,9,11, 13,15 (SEE 1970 BUICK SECTION)

A Stratomist Blue
B Azure Blue
C Tealmist Gray
D Emerald Mist
E Sunset Sage
F Sandpiper Beige
G Titian Red

BUICK RIVIERA 70

97

BUICK *RIVIERA* EMPHASIS ON *all-new* POINTED BOAT-TAIL REAR END STYLING.

$5253.

(INTRO. 10~ 3~ 70)

71 TOTALLY RESTYLED

445 CID V8 CUT TO 315 HP (330 OPT.)

(338/0 BLT.)

3.42 GEAR RATIO

DASH

GS

new GRILLE

122" WB

new TAIL~LTS.

(33728 BLT.)

$5149.

$5790., WEST

72

(INTRO. 9~23~71)

HP CUT AGAIN, TO 250 IN 455 CID V8

DASH

new SIDE TRIM

SOME SPECIAL RIVIERA FEATURES.
AccuDrive, variable ratio power steering, power front disc brakes with composite cast iron rear drum brakes, Full-Flow oil filter, semi-closed cooling system, Delcotron generator with integral voltage regulator,

BUICK RIVIERA 71~72

BUICK

RIVIERA

AccuDrive, variable ratio power steering, power front disc brakes, new durable stamped steel rocker arms, new computer-selected chassis springs for superb ride and handling, new windshield washer and radiator overflow coolant reservoirs integrated with the fan shroud, solenoid actuated throttle stop, new Exhaust Gas Recirculation (EGR) and Air Injection Reactor (AIR) emission control systems, evaporative emission control system, integral voltage regulator and Delcotron, brake proportioning valve

DASH

$5795.
(WESTERN PRICE)

new GRILLE
73

(34080 BUILT)

$5221.

new THICKER ROCKER PANEL TRIM COVERS PART OF DOOR

Engine, standard:
455 C.I.D. V-8.
Carburetion: 4-barrel.

Engine, available: Stage 1 modified 4-barrel 455 C.I.D. V-8 engine with performance ratio, positive traction axle and special ornamentation.

Transmission, standard:
Turbo Hydra-matic 400 automatic.

Axle Ratios: with standard engine: 2.93:1; with Stage 1 engine: 3.23:1 with positive traction.

STD. HP 250
REAR LIC. PLATE NOW IN CENTER

FINAL YR. FOR POINTED REAR

Bravo Cloth and Madrid-grain Vinyl 60/40 Notchback seat available in Riviera in Blue, Sandalwood or Saddle.

Newport Knit Vinyl and Madrid-grain Vinyl 40/40 seats standard in Riviera in Sandalwood or Black.
ALSO:
Oxen-grain Expanded Vinyl and Madrid-grain Vinyl 60/40 Notchback seat available in Riviera in Green, Sandalwood, Saddle, Black or Burgundy.

Oxen-grain Expanded Vinyl and Madrid-grain Vinyl 40/40 seats available in Riviera in White, Saddle or Black.

INTERIORS

BUICK RIVIERA 73

OPT. DIGITAL CLOCK

METAL TOP

6:45

BUICK

BUICK *RIVIERA*

MODEL Y~87
(20/29 BLT.)

455 C/D V8
(HP CUT TO 245 OR 210)

Outside thermometer. Available on the new outside thermometer is built into the left remote-control outside mirror for easy driver visibility. '74 Riviera, the

PARTIAL VINYL~COVERED TOP

$5678.
$6308., WEST

new J78 x 15" TIRES

new DASH

74 RESTYLED

HOOD ORNAMENT ADDED

NEW

Three-speed, variable delay windshield wiper. Available on the '74 Riviera, the new three-speed windshield wiper features a low-speed delay position. In addition to high, medium and slow, there's a variable-delay setting less than slow that lets you match wiper speed to misty or occasional rain conditions.

HI
MED
DELAY
OFF
WIPE   WASH

CONTROL9

BLACK LEATHER OPT.

new GRILLE, WITH "RIVIERA" NAME ABOVE

CLOTH

VINYL

Riviera Cloth Notchback Seat

Riviera Vinyl 60/40 Notchback Seat

new RECTANGULAR HEADLTS.

MODEL Z~87
(HP CUT AGAIN, TO 205)

(17306 BLT.)

$6420.
$6993., WEST)

VINYL

Riviera Vinyl 40/40 Seats

new GRILLE

75

new CORNER LTS. "BUICK" NAME ABOVE GRILLE
"*Riviera*" NAME IN SCRIPT, ON GRILLE

JR/ 78 x 15" TIRES (THROUGH '76)

LEATHER OPTION

new DASH

BUICK RIVIERA 74~75

100

BUICK *RIVIERA*

BUICK *Dedicated to the Free Spirit in just about everyone.*

MODEL Z~87
(20082 BLT.)
$6798.
$7401.
(WEST)

122" WB (SINCE '71)

"X-RAY" VIEW ➔

FINAL 455 CID V8 (205 HP)

DASH SIMILAR TO 1975 MODEL.

Riviera vinyl 40/40 seats

Riviera leather and vinyl 60/40 notchback seat

Riviera cloth and vinyl notchback seat

Riviera cloth and vinyl 60/40 notchback seat

'76

new DASH WITH ROUND GAUGES ➔

MODEL Z~37
DOWNSIZED and RESTYLED

SMALLER 350 CID V8 (155 OR 170 HP) OR 403 CID V8 (185 HP)

new UPSWEPT REAR QUARTER MOLDING

(26138 BLT.)
$7385.
($7988., WEST)

new 116" WB (THROUGH '78)

GR 78 x 15" TIRES (THROUGH '78)

"RIVIERA LXXV"

A little science. A little magic.

'78

(SAME ENGINES and HP as '77)

(20535 BLT.)

(OPT. SILVER-AND-BLACK BUICK 75TH ANNIVERSARY COLOR SCHEME)

$9224.

BUICK RIVIERA 76~78

BUICK RIVIERA
After all, life is to enjoy.
('79)

$10,960.¹⁰ (S) ('79)
11,822.¹¹ (S) ('80)

DASH

"S" (TOP, LEFT) ('79)
(has BLACK GRILLE and SIDE MIRRORS, OWN WHEEL CVRS.)

RESTYLED and DOWN SIZED

new FRONT-WHEEL-DRIVE

V6 OR V8

new 114" WB

(52181 BLT.)
79-
(48621 BLT.)
80

AVAIL. "LANDAU TOP" ('80)

Z-57
$10,683.¹⁰ ('79)
11,491.¹⁰ ('80)

1980 has new INTERIORS and REAR VIEW MIRRORS PLACED FURTHER FORWARD ON DOORS (arrow)

Y-57
S

('80)

WHEEL COVERS (OPT.)

OPT. CHROME ROAD WHEELS

231 c.i.d. V6 TURBO (185 HP) or 350 c.i.d. V8 (160 HP)

1980 DASH

BUICK RIVIERA 79~80

102

Cadillac
(SINCE 1902)

A DIV. OF GENERAL MOTORS

COUPE (1322 BUILT) $**1685.**

(white sidewall tires extra)

62

V-8 ENGINE (SINCE '15) 346 CID (SINCE '36) 135 or 140 HP @ 3400 RPM (SINCE '38)

62
129" WB
$**1745.**
(SEDAN)
(4302 BLT.)

Cadillac PRESENTS

THE NEW SIXTY-TWO

62

40 A

CVT. COUPES and CVT. SEDANS AVAILABLE IN 62, FLEETWD. 75 and V-16 90 SER.

DASH DETAILS

WITH RADIO (ABOVE, RT.)

W/O RADIO (LEFT)

(CONT'D. NEXT PAGE)

40 CADILLAC (A)

62 and FLEETWOOD 72 are new FOR 1940.

MOST EXPENSIVE IS V~16 "9053" 7-PASS. TOWN CAR (2 BUILT) $7175. EACH

Cadillac

HOOD ORNAMENT

2 VERTICAL CHROME POS. DIVIDE 60~S BACKLIGHT ↓

CADILLAC-FLEETWOOD SIXTY SPECIAL
A brilliantly restyled exterior, a greatly enriched interior, and a wealth of engineering advancements again place "the most imitated car in America" far beyond competition.

127" WB

SEDAN (4472 BLT.) DIVISION SEDAN, TOWN CARS AVAIL.

60~S

$2090.

(60~S FIRST INTRO. 1938 with OWN "CONTINENTAL" STYLING)

* Three New Series . . . Four Others Continue

FOR 1940, Cadillac will have seven series of chassis, namely the LaSalle 50, 52 and Cadillac 62, 60S, 72, 75 and 90. The LaSalles are equipped with the 322 cubic inch V-8 engine

(*~INCLUDING LA SALLE 52, also new)

THE NEW **CADILLAC-FLEETWOOD SEVENTY-TWO**
This smart, lower-priced addition to the Fleetwood line is *completely* new.

72

72 (new) 138" W.B.

$2670. (455 BLT.)

FLEETWOOD 75 $2995. and up, FOR 4-DR. SEDAN (155 BLT.)

FLEETWOOD (VARIOUS *FORMAL BODY TYPES* ALSO AVAIL. IN 72, 75 and 90 SERIES.)

40 B (CONT'D.)

2~PASS. COUPE IS RARE, (ONLY 12 BLT.)

FLEETWOOD 75 SIMILAR STYLE TO 72, BUT 75 has LONGER (141.3") WHEELBASE and A WIDE SELECTION OF *FORMAL* and LUXURY BODY TYPES.

IN 11 BODY TYPES, A TOTAL OF ONLY 60 V~16s BLT. IN 1940, PLUS 1 BARE CHASSIS. (V~16 AVAILABLE 1930 TO 1940) FLEETWOOD 90 V~16 431 C.I.D. (SINCE '38) 185 HP @ 3600 RPM 141.3" WB

CADILLAC'S FINAL **V-16** 16~CYL. MODEL has OWN GRILLE and TEARDROP HOOD LOUVRES. →

ALSO SEE: # LaSalle

CVT. SEDAN (2 BLT.) $6000.

40 CADILLAC (B)

CADILLAC NOW ONLY $1345

For the Cadillac Sixty-One 5-Pass. Coupe delivered at Detroit. State tax, optional equipment and accessories — extra. Prices subject to change without notice.

NEW 150 HP (THRU 1948)

(SERIES 61 REPLACES LA SALLE.)

61
$1345. UP

Concealed runningboard steps on some models

A four-door sedan is the only body type in the 63 line

$1695.

STYLIZED EMBLEM ON FRONT OF HOOD (ITS ACTUAL COLOR SEEN IN "61" VIEW, TOP CENTER OF PAGE)

62 CONVERTIBLE (3100 BLT.) $1645.

63 (5050 BLT.)

MODEL SERIES		
61	126" WB	$1345. UP
62	"	1420. "
63	"	1695. "
60~S	"	2195. UP
67	138"	2595. "
75	"	2995. "
ALL WITH 346 CID V8		

41 A RESTYLED

FINAL YEAR FOR "62" 4-DR. CONV'T. (400 BLT.) $1965.

Hinged lamp uncovers fuel tank filler

CREST

(CONT'D. NEXT PAGE)

41 CADILLAC (A)

CADILLAC-FLEETWOOD *Sixty Special*

SEDAN
(3878 BUILT)
$2195.   (220 DIVISION SEDANS ALSO, $2345.)

NEW
"FADE~
AWAY"
FENDERS
ON
60
SPECIAL

new

AUTOMATIC TRANSMISSION

41B

(CONT'D.)

Fleetwood
75
GENERAL MOTORS' FINEST CAR

Announcing the New Cadillac-Engineered

HYDRA·MATIC DRIVE

(Optional on All Cadillacs at Extra Cost)

SELECTOR →

**ELIMINATES
CLUTCH PEDAL AND
GEARSHIFTING
•
INCREASES
ECONOMY,
SAFETY, AND
PERFORMANCE**

"75" MODELS AVAILABLE	
SEDAN	422 BLT.
DIVISION SEDAN	132
7~PASS. SEDAN	405
9~PASS. BUSINESS SED.	54
7~PASS. IMPERIAL SED.	757
7~PASS. FORMAL SED.	98
BUSINESS IMPERIAL	
7~PASS. SEDAN	6
FORMAL SEDAN	75
CHASSIS	5
LONG CHASSIS (163"W.B.)	150

... AND OWNERS SAY "14 TO 17 MILES PER GALLON!"   41 CADILLAC (B)

Cadillac

2-DR. FASTBACK "CLUB COUPE"
(2482 BLT.)
$1450.

Cadillac Sixty-One—again available at a surprisingly low price

4-DR. SEDAN
(3218 BLT.)
$1530.

61

OF DEFENSE PRODUCTION

LARGER
PCS. IN
GRILLE and
RESTYLED
IN

SIX GREAT NEW SERIES

FOR 1942

new "FADEAWAY"
FENDERS ON
ALL BUT "75"
SERIES.

42 A

DELUXE SEDAN
(1827 BLT.)
$1705.

62

6~PASS. CONVERT.
(ONLY 308 BLT.) **$1880.**

On four-door, four-window sedans, fenders are carried into both front and rear doors. The portion of the fender on the door is known as a fender cap which is readily detached in case of accident. The 62 is illustrated

MODEL 63
SEDAN IN FINAL YR.
(1750 SOLD)
$1745.

DASH WITH
LEFT HAND
INSTRUMENT CLUSTERS and
"WOODGRAIN" PANELS
EXTENDING ON DOORS.

**FORTIETH YEAR
OF FINE-CAR BUILDING**

CONT'D.
NEXT PAGE

42 CADILLAC (A)

A MUCH DIFFERENT 1942 DASH DESIGN SHOWN WITH MODEL 67.

Cadillac

42

B

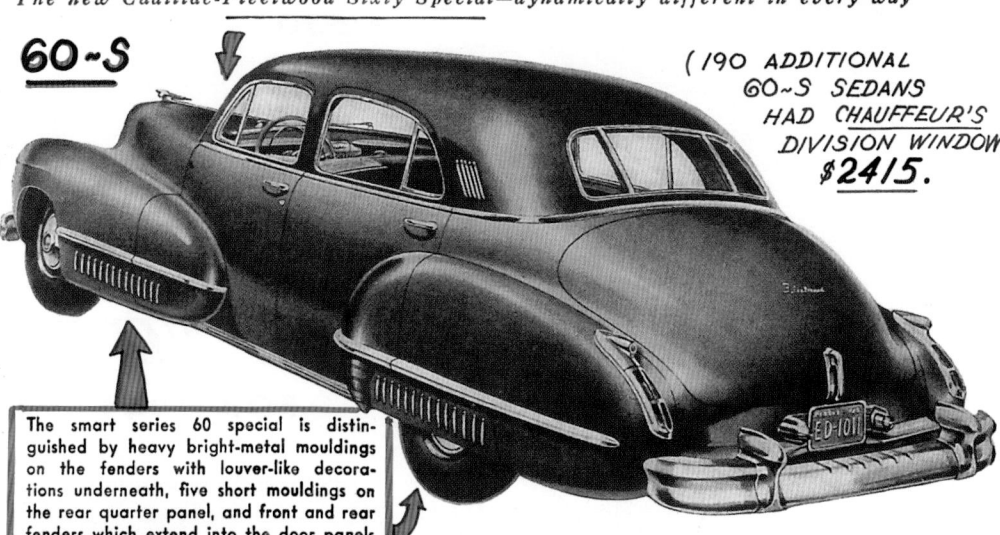

1684 60~SPECIAL SEDANS BUILT, AT $2265.

The new Cadillac-Fleetwood Sixty Special—dynamically different in every way

60~S

(190 ADDITIONAL 60~S SEDANS HAD CHAUFFEUR'S DIVISION WINDOW) $2415.

The gasoline filler is reached by lifting the **signal lamp**. The other **two** lamps in the unit are **tail** and **stop**

The smart series 60 special is distinguished by heavy bright-metal mouldings on the fenders with louver-like decorations underneath, five short mouldings on the rear quarter panel, and front and rear fenders which extend into the door panels

"67" DASH

STYLED TO THE MINUTE
AND BUILT FOR THE YEARS

SERIES 67 BLT. 1941 and 1942 ONLY, WITH 138" WB $2845. 4 VARIETIES OF SEDANS

67

7~PASS. SEDAN (260 BUILT)

FLEETWOOD 75

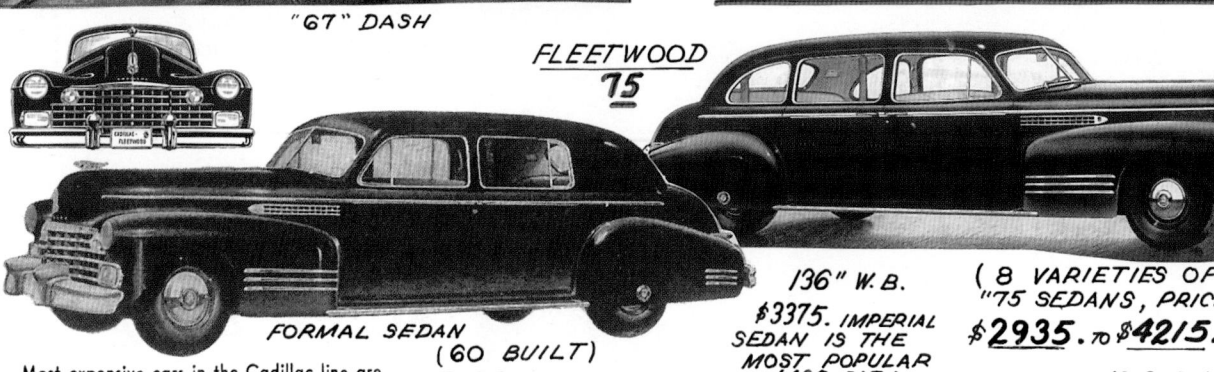

FORMAL SEDAN (60 BUILT) $4060.

Most expensive cars in the Cadillac line are found in series 75. The formal sedan is shown

136" W.B. $3375. IMPERIAL SEDAN IS THE MOST POPULAR (430 BLT.)

(8 VARIETIES OF "75 SEDANS, PRICED $2935. to $4215.)

42 CADILLAC (B)

Cadillac
Standard of the World

126" WB 61 (2200 BLT.) 6267 CVT. D $2556.

$2176.

$2359.

62 129" WB (1342 BLT.)

TOTAL 1946 PRODUCTION: 29,214

(14,900 BLT.)

FLEETWOOD 60-S

(60-S has 5 SLOPING CHROME STRIPS ON REAR QUARTER PANEL.)

$3095.

46

(5700 BLT.)

AS IN 1942, A TOTAL OF 6 HORIZONTAL GRILLE MEMBERS, BUT WITH new RECTANGULAR GRILLE LTS.

75 (136" WB THROUGH '49) $4153. TO 4669.

FRONT VIEW

(5160 BLT.)

Cadillac
Standard of the World

$2523. 61 126" WB

$2324.

6289 SEDAN (25,834 BLT.) 62 129" WB

TOTAL 1947 PROD.: 61,926

$2060. TO $4590. PRICE RANGE

62 6267 CVT. (6755 BLT.)

$2902.

TOTAL OF 5 HORIZONTAL MEMBERS IN 1947 GRILLE.

new SMALL ROUND PARKING LIGHTS

47

Cadillac NAME ON FENDERS IS NOW IN SCRIPT STYLE.

AS BEFORE, CHROME STRIPS IDENTIFY 60-S

133" WB

MODEL 6069 SEDAN

8500 BLT. $3195.

new HEAVY FLANGES ON 1947 HUBCAPS.

ALL MODELS HAVE L-HEAD 346 CID V8 (150 HP @ 3600 RPM) (SINCE 1941)

Cadillac
STANDARD OF THE WORLD

61 6169 SEDAN (5081 BLT.) **$2833.**

new "FISHTAIL" REAR FENDER FINS

126" WB ON BOTH "61" AND "62" SERIES

PLAIN ROCKER PANEL ON "61."

48 TOTALLY RESTYLED! (EXCEPT FOR SERIES "75")

Cadillac

REAR DETAILS

CLOSE VIEW OF ENAMELED CREST and CHROMED "V" ON FRONT OF HOOD

PRESENTS THE *New* STANDARD OF THE WORLD!

$2728. ~ 5199. PRICE RANGE

62 → $2912.

6207 (4764 BLT.)

has CHROME ROCKER PANEL STRIP

75

"75" RETAINS OLD STYLING (THROUGH 1949) $4679. TO $5199.

FLEETWOOD 60-S (6561 BLT.)

(60 SPECIAL SEDAN) 6069

$3820.

133" WB

60-S REAR FENDER HAS UNIQUE CHROME TRIM.

TOTAL 1948 PRODUCTION: 52,706

Cadillac
Standard of the World

61 2-DR.
$2840. (6409 BLT.)

49

IMPROVED V-8 ENGINE NOW HAS OVERHEAD VALVES.

160 HP (THROUGH '51)
126" WB (61, 62)
GRILLE MODIFIED *

...The world's newest engine—for the world's finest car!

62
6269 SED.
(37,977 BLT.)

* EXCEPT ON 75, 1949 GRILLE has ONE LESS HORIZONTAL PIECE THAN 1948. new CHROME WRAP-AROUNDS EXTEND GRILLE at EITHER END.

$3050.
($3103., WEST COAST)

6237 HARDTOP (2150 BLT.)
$3497.

new "COUPE DE VILLE" (CADILLAC'S FIRST H/T (HARDTOP CVT.) (PILLARLESS)

62

TOTAL 1949 PRODUCTION: 92,554

6267 CONVERTIBLE (8000 BLT.)

$3442. ($3549., WESTERN PRICE)

WESTERN PRICE
$5253.

75

133" WB FLEETWOOD 60 SPECIAL

$3891. (11,399 BLT.)

"75" RETAINS OLDER STYLING. 136¼" WB

CADILLAC 49

111

Cadillac
Standard of the World
6169 SEDAN
14,931 BLT.

61

AS
ILLUSTRATED,
NO REAR
QUARTER
WINDOWS ON
61 SEDAN

$2866. 122" WB

$3234.

6237 D
H/T

4507
BLT.

$3523.

62

$3654.

6219 SEDAN
62
126" WB

41,890 BLT.

$2761.
TO
$4959.
PRICE RANGE

new
GRILLE

TOTAL 1950
PRODUCTION:
103,857

6267 CONVERTIBLE   6986 BLT.

new 1-PIECE
WINDSHIELD

ALL MODELS
RESTYLED
(INCLUDING "75")

6019 SEDAN (BELOW)
13,755 BLT.

50

60-S   130" WB
NOW HAS
SMALL
LOUVRES
HERE

$3797.

$4770. UP   75
(new 146 3/4" WB)

CADILLAC 50

CONVERTIBLE WITH
CUSTOM INTERIOR
(USUALLY LEATHER)

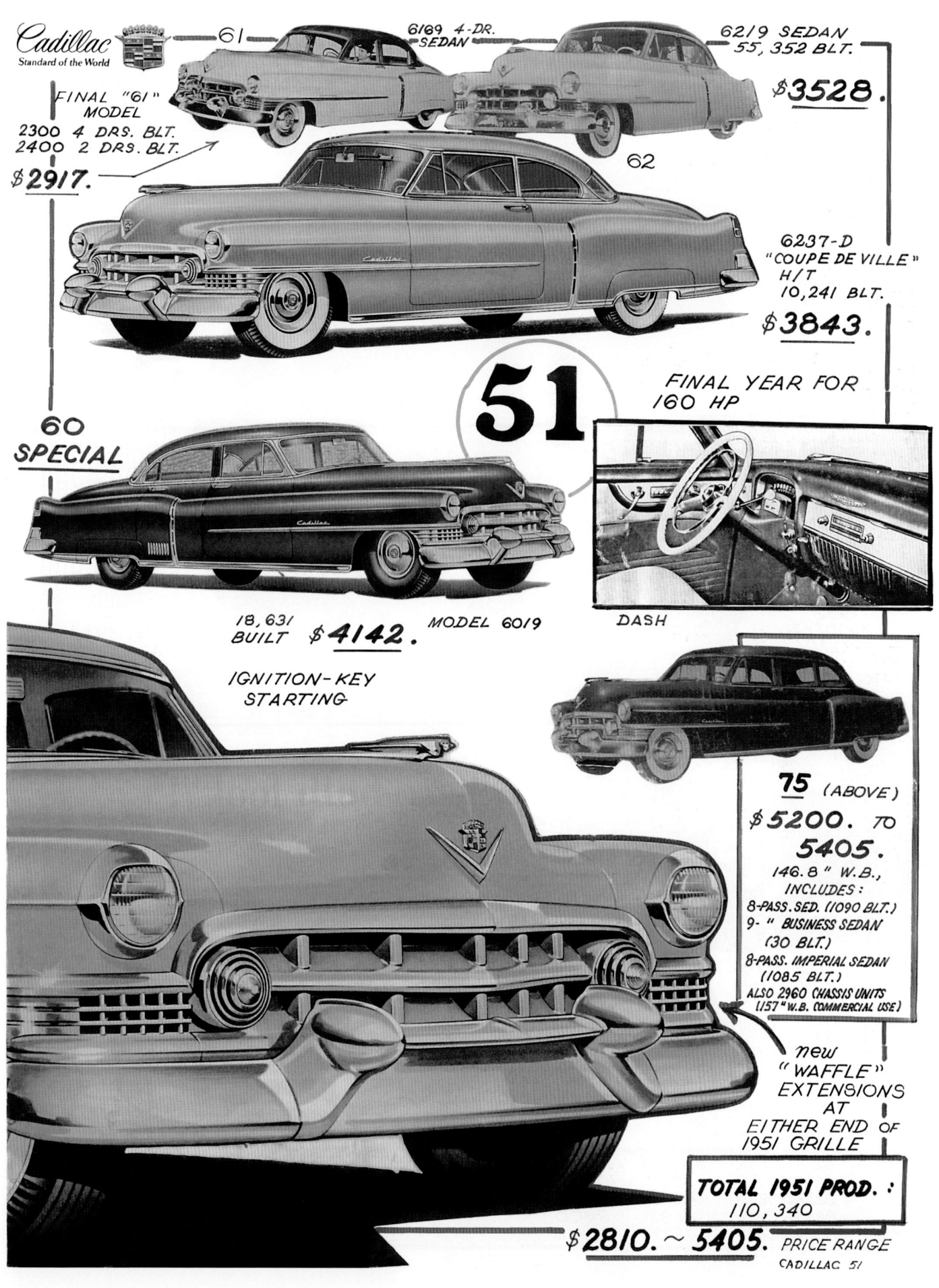

Cadillac
Standard of the World

61   6169 4-DR. SEDAN

6219 SEDAN 55, 352 BLT.

$3528.

FINAL "61" MODEL
2300 4 DRS. BLT.
2400 2 DRS. BLT.

$2917.

62

6237-D "COUPE DE VILLE" H/T 10,241 BLT.

$3843.

51

FINAL YEAR FOR 160 HP

60 SPECIAL

DASH

18,631 BUILT   **$4142.**   MODEL 6019

IGNITION-KEY STARTING

75 (ABOVE)
$5200. TO **5405.**
146.8" W.B.,
INCLUDES:
8-PASS. SED. (1090 BLT.)
9- " BUSINESS SEDAN (30 BLT.)
8-PASS. IMPERIAL SEDAN (1085 BLT.)
ALSO 2960 CHASSIS UNITS (157" W.B. COMMERCIAL USE)

new "WAFFLE" EXTENSIONS AT EITHER END OF 1951 GRILLE

TOTAL 1951 PROD.:
110,340

$2810. ~ 5405.   PRICE RANGE
CADILLAC 51

GOLDEN ANNIVERSARY

Cadillac
Standard of the World

BEAUTIFUL NEW INTERIORS IN ALL MODELS

"COUPE DE VILLE" H/T

CVT. (6400 BLT.)

$4163.

62 (NOW THE LOWEST-PRICED SERIES)

1902 52

52

"GOLDEN ANNIVERSARY" MODELS INCREASED BY 30 H.P.

"V" INSIGNIA NOW COLORED GOLD, TO COMMEMORATE CADILLAC'S 50TH ANNIVERSARY.

STANDARD OF THE WORLD

THESE new DECORATIONS FOUND ON 1952 MODELS ONLY

8-PASS. "75" SEDAN

147" WB

(16,110 BLT.)

60-S

$4323.

NEW 190-HORSEPOWER ENGINE

★ NEW HYDRA-MATIC DRIVE

★ NEW FRONT AND REAR END APPEARANCE

★ NEW CADILLAC POWER STEERING

★ NEW DUAL EXHAUST SYSTEM

MODELS:	6219 SEDAN = $3684. (42,625 BLT.)	75 SERIES:	7523 8-PASS. SEDAN $5428.
	6237 COUPE 3587. 10,065		(1400 BLT.)
	6237D H/T 4013. 11,165		7533 IMPERIAL SEDAN $5643.
	6267 CVT. 4163. 6400		(800 BLT.)
60 SPL.	6019 SEDAN 4323. 16,110		

1952 PRODUCTION : 90,259 CADILLAC 52

114

Cadillac
Standard of the World

62

126" WB   6237D 14,550 BLT.

6267-S
EL DORADO
CVT. (*new*)
(*has* WRAP-AROUND
WINDSHIELD)
$7750.
(ONLY 532
BUILT)

60-S has
MORE CHROME
ALONG LOWER
EDGE, PLUS THE
CHARACTERISTIC
VERTICAL STRIPS.

60-S $4341.
130" WB
6019   20,000
BLT.

$4144.
62
CVT.

53

6267
CVT.
8367 BLT.

new
PARKING/
DIRECTIONAL
LIGHTS

DASH

TOTAL 1953 PRODUCTION:
109,651

PRICE RANGE
(ALL MODELS)
$3571.
TO
$7750.

75 SERIES (146.75" WB)
BELOW: 7523 8-PASS.
SEDAN-LIMO. (1435 BLT.)

$5408.

(THROUGH 1955)
331 CID
ENGINE
210 HP @
4150 RPM

Cadillac
Standard of the World

62

new 129" WB ON "62"

$**4261.**

CPE. DE VILLE
MODEL 6237D
(17,170 BLT.)

(also, 17,460 new
STD. H/Ts AT $3838.)

DASH
(CONVERTIBLE)
6267 (6310 BLT.)

$**4404.**

SPEEDOMETER
CLOSE-UP

$**4863.** 60-S

MODEL
6019
(16,200
BLT.)

new 133" WB ON 60-S

new PANORAMIC
WINDSHIELD

54

75
LIMOUSINE
new 149.75" WB

RESTYLED
new 230 HP
@ 4400 RPM

SPECIAL
ELDORADO REAR
FENDER BRIGHTWORK

6267S ELDORADO
CVT. (2,150 BLT.)
$**4738.**

FRONT
VIEW

CADILLAC 54

TOTAL 1954
PRODUCTION:
96,680

"75" COMMERCIAL CHASSIS (#8680S)
INCREASED FROM 157" TO 158" WB)
(1635 BLT.)
"75" 8-PASS. SEDAN $5875. (889 BLT.)*
" " " IMPERIAL SEDAN $6090.
(611 BLT.)*   * 149.75" WB

Cadillac
Standard of the World

129" WB
62

$3882.
TO
6402.
PRICE
RANGE

HIGHLIGHT FEATURE
of CADILLAC and OLDSMOBILE for '55!

AUTRONIC -EYE

AUTOMATIC
LIGHT CONTROL

REAR VIEW

PADDED DASH DETAIL

1955

(18,300 BLT.)
$4728.

←60-S (133" WB)
MODEL 6019 SEDAN

new 250 HP @ 4600 RPM

BRIGHT
DIM
BRIGHT
Automatically AT NIGHT!

new GRILLE with HEAVIER PIECES

55

('55 has VERTICAL CHROME STRIP RUNNING TO BOTTOM OF REAR FENDER.)

TOTAL 1955 PRODUCTION:
140,777

ELDORADO MODEL 6267S

CONVERTIBLE
(3950 BLT.)
$6286.

270 HP @ 4800 RPM
(ELDORADO ONLY)

129" WB

ELDORADO has OWN STYLE OF new POINTED FIN REAR FENDERS

2 VIEWS OF ELDORADO

IMPORTED, HANDCRAFTED LEATHER UPHOLSTERY in ELDORADO

CADILLAC 55

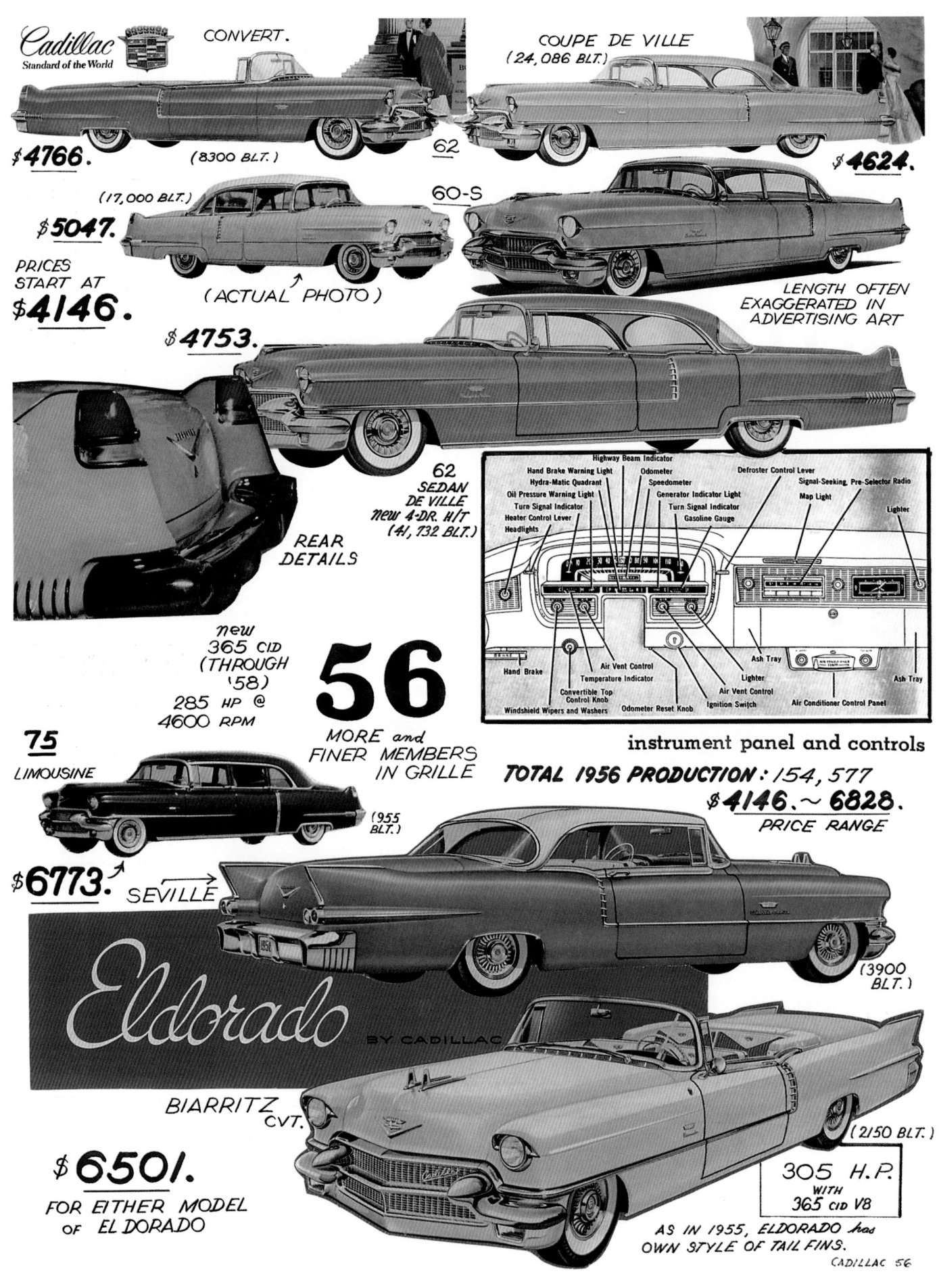

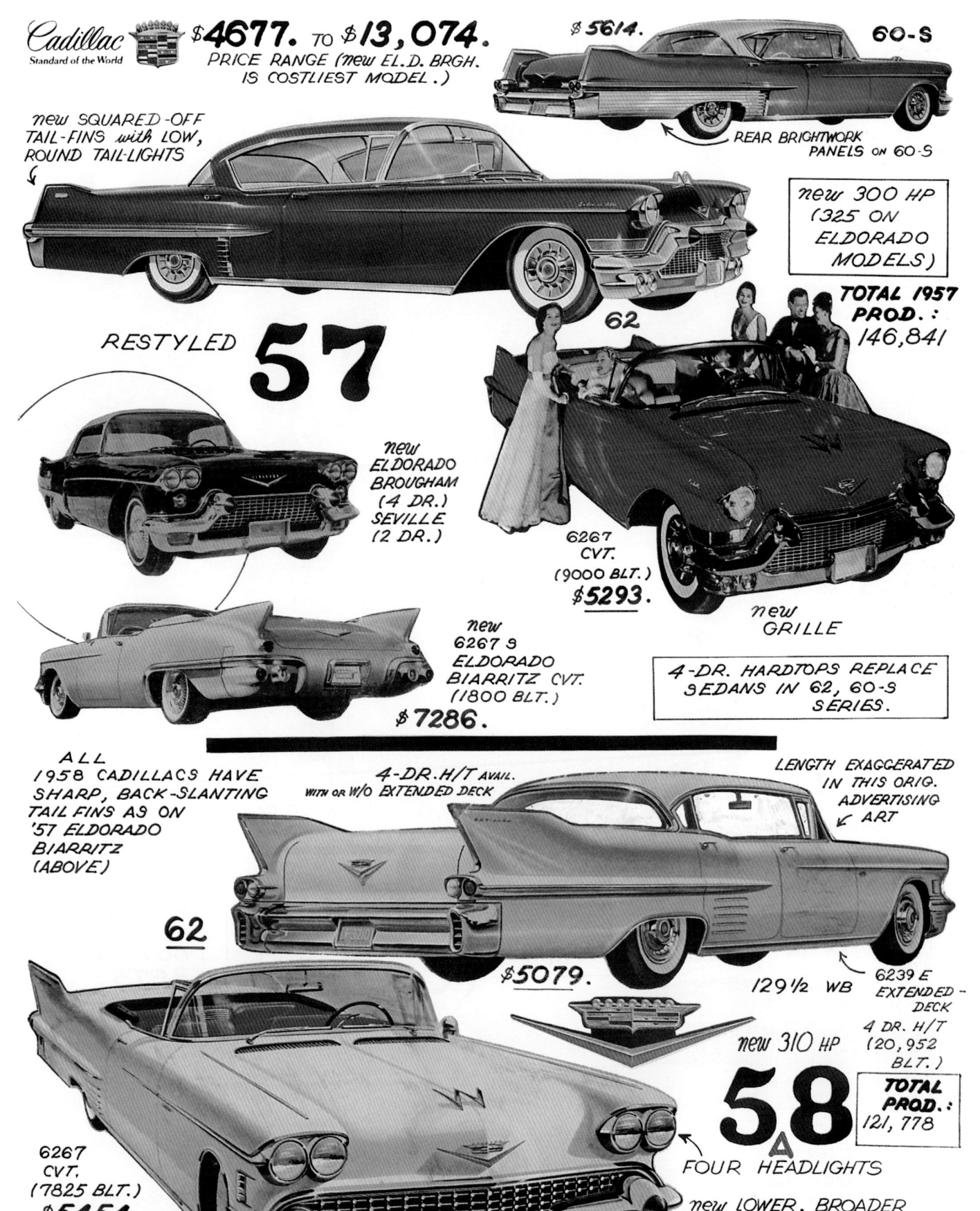

Cadillac
Standard of the World

$4677. TO **$13,074.**
PRICE RANGE (new EL.D. BRGH. IS COSTLIEST MODEL.)

$5614.

60-S

new SQUARED-OFF TAIL-FINS with LOW, ROUND TAIL-LIGHTS

REAR BRIGHTWORK PANELS on 60-S

new 300 HP (325 ON ELDORADO MODELS)

TOTAL 1957 PROD.: 146,841

RESTYLED **57**

62

new ELDORADO BROUGHAM (4 DR.) SEVILLE (2 DR.)

6267 CVT. (9000 BLT.) **$5293.**

new GRILLE

new 6267 S ELDORADO BIARRITZ CVT. (1800 BLT.) **$7286.**

4-DR. HARDTOPS REPLACE SEDANS IN 62, 60-S SERIES.

ALL 1958 CADILLACS HAVE SHARP, BACK-SLANTING TAIL FINS AS ON '57 ELDORADO BIARRITZ (ABOVE)

4-DR. H/T AVAIL. WITH OR W/O EXTENDED DECK

LENGTH EXAGGERATED IN THIS ORIG. ADVERTISING ART

62

$5079.

129½ WB

6239 E EXTENDED-DECK 4 DR. H/T (20,952 BLT.)

new 310 HP

58

TOTAL PROD.: 121,778

6267 CVT. (7825 BLT.) **$5454.**

WIDTH EXAGGERATED IN THIS ORIGINAL ADVERTISING ART

FOUR HEADLIGHTS

new LOWER, BROADER GRILLE

1958

MORE 1958 MODELS ON NEXT PAGE

$6232. *Cadillac* STANDARD OF THE WORLD

60-S CONTINUES LOWER BRIGHTWORK PANELS ON REAR FENDERS. 133" WB

MODEL 6039
(12,900 BLT.)

AS IN 1957, EL DORADO BROUGHAM HAS ITS OWN UNIQUE FRONT END STYLING.
$13,074.
SERIES 70 MODEL 7059 (304 BLT.)

AIR SUSPENSION ON ELD. BROUGHAM, OPTIONAL ON *OTHER* 1958 CADILLACS.

A PRICE OF
$7500.
FOR SEVILLE OR BIARR.

(855 BLT.)

62
6239 4 DR. H/T (STANDARD-LENGTH DECK)
(13,335 BLT.)
$4891.

20-GAL GAS TANK

TIRES:
8.00 × 15 OR
8.20 × 15

58 B (CONT'D.)

75 STYLED LIKE 62 SERIES, BUT W. 149 3/4" W.B.
AVAIL. MODELS:
7523 9-PASS. SEDAN (802 BLT.)
$8460.
7533 9-PASS. LIMO. (730 BLT.)
$8675.
ALSO 156" WB CHASSIS- UNITS (1915 BLT.)

Cadillac Eldorado

EL DORADO SEVILLE 6237S
(335 HP, 129 1/2" WB ON EL DORADOS)

EL DORADO BIARRITZ 6267S

note ROUNDED-DOWN REAR FENDER/DECK PANELS ONLY ON THESE 2 EL DORADO TYPES.

(815 BLT.)

Cadillac
STANDARD OF THE WORLD

62

6237 H/T
(21,947 BLT.)

ENORMOUS
TAIL-
FINS!

new
"DOUBLE-
DECK" GRILLE

DETAILS
OF
THE
UNIQUE
REAR
END
DESIGN
IN
1959

CLOSER
VIEW OF
TRADITIONAL "V"
ON REAR DECK

GRILLE MOTIF
IS ALSO
CARRIED ON
AT REAR

new 390 CID V8s
ON ALL EXCEPT ELDORADO
new 325 HP
(THROUGH '63)

new 130" WB
(ON ALL EXCEPT
75 SERIES)

TOTALLY
RESTYLED

59A

DE VILLE NOW
A SEPARATE SERIES
FROM 62.

6267 "62"
CONVT.
(11,130 BLT.)
$5455.
(NO DEVILLE
CVT.)

6339 "SWEEP-ROOF"
SEDAN DE VILLE
(12,308 BLT.)

2 DR. H/T
$4892. (62)

NOTE THE
ROOFLINE
DIFFERENCES
BETWEEN THESE
4-DOOR
HARDTOPS

$5498.

DE VILLE

$5252.
(DE V.)

1959 PRICES START AT
$4892.

6329 "FLAT TOP" SEDAN DE VILLE
(19,158 BLT.)

'59 HP FIGS. @ 4800 RPM

FLEETWD.
75

6733
LIMOUSINE
$9748.
(CONT'D.)

(149.87" WB)

(690 BLT.)

Cadillac
STANDARD OF THE WORLD

MODEL 6039 4-DR. H/T
(12,250 BLT.)

59_B_
(CONT'D.)

FLEETWOOD
60 SPECIAL

(note ITS
OWN UNIQUE
SIDE and FENDER
TRIM)

$6233.

note "FLEETWOOD" NAME
ON FRONT FENDER PANEL. (60-S)

DASH

345-HP
EL DORADO MODELS BELOW:

("ELDORADO" NAME
on FRONT FENDER
PANELS of
BIARRITZ and
SEVILLE ONLY.)

$7401. (EITHER
MODEL)

6929
BROUGHAM
(ONLY 99 BLT.)

6467
BIARRITZ
(1320 BLT.)

EL DORADO
BROUGHAM STYLING
DIFFERS FROM
OTHER 1959
CADILLACS.

$13,075.

6437
SEVILLE
(975 BUILT)

2102 MODEL 6890 COMM. CHASSIS UNITS ALSO PRODUCED IN
"75" SERIES, ON A 156" WHEELBASE

TOTAL 1959 PRODUCTION: 142,272

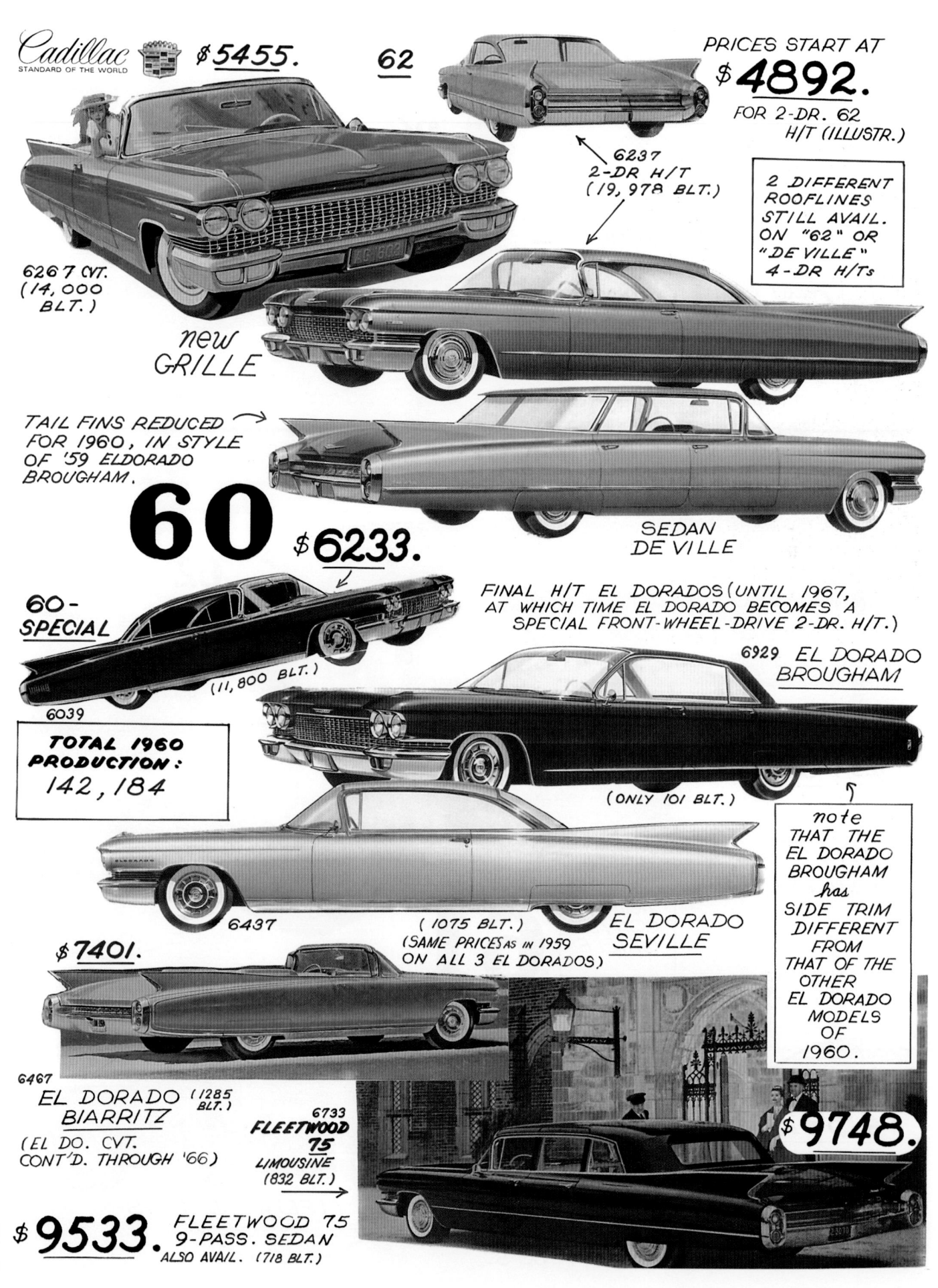

Cadillac STANDARD OF THE WORLD

$5455.

62

PRICES START AT $4892. FOR 2-DR. 62 H/T (ILLUSTR.)

6237 2-DR H/T (19,978 BLT.)

2 DIFFERENT ROOFLINES STILL AVAIL. ON "62" OR "DE VILLE" 4-DR H/Ts

6267 CVT. (14,000 BLT.)

new GRILLE

TAIL FINS REDUCED FOR 1960, IN STYLE OF '59 ELDORADO BROUGHAM.

60

SEDAN DE VILLE

$6233.

60-SPECIAL

(11,800 BLT.)

6039

FINAL H/T EL DORADOS (UNTIL 1967, AT WHICH TIME EL DORADO BECOMES A SPECIAL FRONT-WHEEL-DRIVE 2-DR. H/T.)

6929 EL DORADO BROUGHAM

TOTAL 1960 PRODUCTION: 142,184

(ONLY 101 BLT.)

note THAT THE EL DORADO BROUGHAM *has* SIDE TRIM DIFFERENT FROM THAT OF THE OTHER EL DORADO MODELS OF 1960.

6437

(1075 BLT.) (SAME PRICES AS IN 1959 ON ALL 3 EL DORADOS)

EL DORADO SEVILLE

$7401.

6467 EL DORADO BIARRITZ (1285 BLT.)

(EL DO. CVT. CONT'D. THROUGH '66)

6733 *FLEETWOOD 75* LIMOUSINE (832 BLT.)

$9748.

$9533. FLEETWOOD 75 9-PASS. SEDAN ALSO AVAIL. (718 BLT.)

Cadillac

$5080.

62

6229 4-DR. H/T
(26,216 SOLD)

new 6399 "TOWN
SEDAN" 6 WINDOW
H/T IN DE VILLE
SERIES (3756 BLT.)

6237 2-DR H/T
(16,005 BLT.)

6267 CVT.
(15,500 BLT.)

$4892.

$5455.

62

DE VILLE
PRICE RANGE =
$5252-5498.

new
LOWER SIDE FIN,
TO BALANCE
EFFECT OF
UPPER TAIL FIN

new
CONVEX
GRILLE
61

new 129½" WB
RESTYLED, SLIGHTLY DOWNSIZED and
LIGHTENED

TOTAL 1961 PRODUCTION:
138,379

$6233.

$4892.
TO
$9748.
PRICE
RANGE
(62 TO 75)

CHROME BANDS NEAR
END OF REAR FENDER
IDENTIFY 60-S.

FLEETWOOD 60-S

124

Cadillac
STANDARD OF THE WORLD

DASH

RADIO, CLOCK DETAIL

62 new GRILLE and TAIL LTS.

"CONVERTIBLE-STYLE CREASE IN REAR ROOF LINE

COUPE DE VILLE

COUPE (2-DR. H/T)

SEDAN DE VILLE 6339 (27,378 BLT.)

DE VILLE

DE VILLE 6347 (25,675 BLT.) **$5385.**

$5189. (OR $5025.) "62" 6247 2DR. H/T (16,833 BLT.)

Fog Lamps (OPT.)

* ALSO PRICED AT $5631.

new "TOWN SED." MOVED TO 62 SERIES IN 1962, THEN DISCONT'D.

new 6389 "PARK AVE." 4 DR. H/T in DE VILLE SERIES (THROUGH 1963)

62

6267 CONVERTIBLE (16,800 BLT.) **$5588.**

$9937. OR **$10,100.**

TOTAL 1962 PRODUCTION: 160,840

FLEETWD. 60-S

BACK SEAT

6733 FLEETWOOD 75 LIMO. (904 BLT.)

REAR COMPARTMENT (75)

$6366. OR $ **6529.**

125

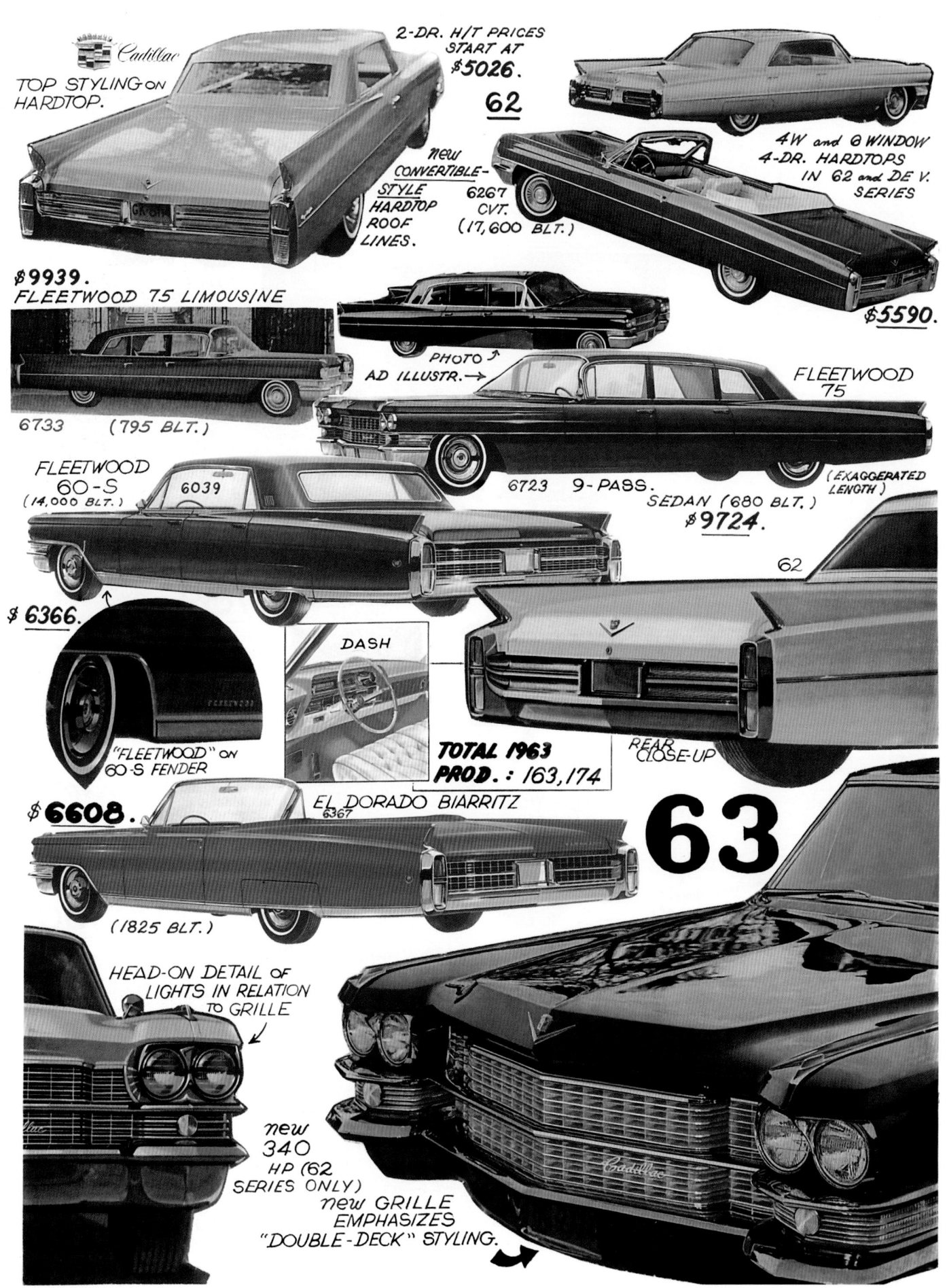

Cadillac

TOP STYLING ON HARDTOP.

2-DR. H/T PRICES START AT $5026.

62

4W and 6 WINDOW 4-DR. HARDTOPS IN 62 and DE V. SERIES

new CONVERTIBLE-STYLE HARDTOP ROOF LINES.

6267 CVT. (17,600 BLT.)

$5590.

$9939.
FLEETWOOD 75 LIMOUSINE

6733   (795 BLT.)

PHOTO ↑
AD ILLUSTR. →

FLEETWOOD 75

FLEETWOOD 60-S
(14,000 BLT.)

6039

6723   9-PASS. SEDAN (680 BLT.)
$9724.

(EXAGGERATED LENGTH)

62

$6366.

"FLEETWOOD" ON 60-S FENDER

DASH

TOTAL 1963 PROD.: 163,174

REAR CLOSE-UP

$6608.

EL DORADO BIARRITZ
6367

63

(1825 BLT.)

HEAD-ON DETAIL OF LIGHTS IN RELATION TO GRILLE

new 340 HP (62 SERIES ONLY)

new GRILLE EMPHASIZES "DOUBLE-DECK" STYLING.

Cadillac STANDARD OF THE WORLD **62**

60-S

DASH AND INTERIOR VIEWS

new "COMFORT CONTROL"

new CONVEX GRILLE

64

ALL MODELS NOW HAVE 340 HP @ 4600 RPM *and new* 429 CID

PRICED FROM $5048. (62 H/T)

6267 CVT. (17,900 BLT.) $5612.

62

60-S

FLEETWOOD 75
6723 9-PASS. SED. (617 BLT.) $9746.
6733 LIMO. (808 BLT.) $9960.

75

"62" PRICES FROM $5191.

Comfort Control combines heating and air conditioning in a single unit, the interior weather never changes. Even humidity is under perfect control. This system now available as an extra-cost option.

DE VILLE $5247.

68357 H/T
(43,345 BLT.)

new CALAIS (REPLACES 62 SERIES) $5247.

CALAIS

68239 4-DR. H/T
(13975 BLT.)

129½" WB

$5419.

DE VILLE

TOTAL 1965 PRODUCTION:
182,435

Cadillac

new TAIL-LIGHTS

65

new 4-DR. SEDANS AVAIL., IN ADDITION TO ONGOING 4-DR. H/Ts.

PRICE RANGE:
$5224. TO $10,125.

new LARGE 1-PC. GRILLE

FLEETWOOD BROUGHAM

60 S (new 133" WB)
68069 SED. (18,100 BLT.)
$6479.

new VERTICALLY-PLACED HEADLIGHTS

1965

DASH

Cadillac
STANDARD OF THE WORLD

RADIO DETAIL

Cadillac

DE VILLE $5339.

COUPE DE VILLE H/T

(50,580 BLT.)

RJF 217

FLEETWOOD 75
LIMO. OR 9-PASS. SEDAN
$10,312. UP

DE VILLE CVT.

$5555.

66

new GRILLE

$6695.

Interior (FLEETWOOD)

(13,630 BLT.)

FLEETWOOD BROUGHAM
JOINS 60-S SEDAN

TOTAL 1966 PRODUCTION: 196,685

(INTRO. 10-6-66)

TOTAL 1967 PRODUCTION: 200,000

new GRILLE

67

FLEETWOOD BROUGHAM

CALAIS 5215.

(2865 BLT.)

FRONT DETAIL

$6277.

New

ELDORADO H/T

$6739.

(17,930 BLT.)

ELDORADO'S GRILLE
DIFF. FROM OTHER
MODELS

FLEETWOOD 75
(BELOW)

(has 8.20 × 15 TIRES)

SEDAN = $10,522.
LIMOUSINE = 10,733.
149.8" WB

75 INTERIOR
(7-PASS.)
IN
LIGHT GRAY
DEVONSHIRE
CLOTH

front to rear: DeVille Convertible; Fleetwood Eldorado; Coupe deVille; Fleetwood Brougham; Fleetwood Seventy-Five Sedan; Hardtop Sedan deVille; Sedan deVille; Fleetwood Sixty Special; Calais Coupe; Calais Hardtop Sedan; Fleetwood Seventy-Five Limousine.

FULL LINE OF 11 MODELS ILLUSTR.

new CONCEALED WINDSHIELD WIPERS

new 472 CID V8 375 HP (AVAIL. THROUGH '74. HP CUT TO 345 IN '71, TO 220 IN '72, TO 205 IN '74.)

Cadillac

SEDAN DE VILLE 4 DR. H/T (72,662 BLT.)

68

new GRILLES

H/T (AVAIL. IN CALAIS OR DEVILLE SERIES.

CVT. (18,025 BLT.) $5736.

TOTAL 1968 PROD.: 230,003

DETAILS OF ELDORADO'S RETRACTABLE HEADLIGHTS

ELDORADO H/T $6605. (24,528 BLT.)

COUPE DE VILLE H/T $5721. (65,755 BLT.)

$7110.

DE VILLE $5905.

FLEETWOOD BROUGHAM (17,300 BLT.)

DeVille Convertible (16,445 BLT.)

69 new GRILLES

9.00 x 15" TIRES

$6711.

Eldorado H/T ⟶ PLAIN TOP

(23,333 BLT.)

VINYL TOP

(A TOTAL OF 23,333 1968 ELDORADO COUPES BLT.)

TOTAL 1969 PRODUCTION: 223,237

new ELD. GRILLE w. FINER PCS. new UNCONCEALED HEADLIGHTS

Cadillac

IN BACKGROUND 1935 CADILLAC SEDAN

SHOWN IN PATINA SILVER WITH BLACK VINYL~PADDED ROOF

OPT. Automatic Climate Control

IN A 1970 SALES BROCHURE, OLDER CADILLACS WERE SHOWN WITH 1970 CADILLACS, FOR COMPARISON.

129½" WB

(76043 BLT.) $5884.

COUPE DEVILLE H/T

IN BACKGROUND = CLASSIC 1931 CADILLAC V~12 PHAETON

new GRILLES.

FINAL DEVILLE CONVERTIBLE.

70

TOTAL 1970 PROD.: 238,744

REAR DETAILS

1970 Brougham's luggage area.

new CORNERING LTS.

133" WB (16913 BLT.)

$7284.

60 SPECIAL
FLEETWOOD BROUGHAM
IN
REGENCY BRONZE WITH BLACK VINYL~ PADDED ROOF

472 CID V8 (375 HP) IN ALL BUT ELDORADO

REMOTE~CONTROL TRUNK OPENER

$6903.

FLEETWOOD ELDORADO

has new 500 CID V8 (400 HP)

120" WB

IN COTILLION WHITE WITH BLACK VINYL~ PADDED ROOF

(28842 BLT.)

Eldorado is the one luxury car

to provide

front-wheel drive,
power front disc brakes,
and Automatic Level Control.

70 CADILLAC

Cadillac

FROM
$5899.
(CALAIS H/T)

DASH

HORSEPOWER CUT TO
345 @ 4400
RPM (GROSS)
OR
220 @ 4000 RPM (NET)
2.93 GEAR RATIO
(3.15 ON 75)

$6983.
(WEST)

CPE. DE VILLE H/T
(66081 BLT.)
$6264.
new
1-PC. TAIL-LIGHTS

DE VILLE
new 130" WB

$6498.

4-DR. H/T
$7177.
(WEST)

new
RUBBER-TIPPED
BUMPER GUARDS
(ON ALL MODELS)

(69345 BLT.)

TOTAL 1971 PROD. =
188,537

AM/FM STEREO RADIO
AND 8-TRACK TAPE
PLAYER AVAIL.

71
(INTRO. 9-29-70)

new GRILLE
new WIDELY-
SPACED
HEADLTS.

(CONVERTIBLE
MOVED TO
EL DORADO
LINE, 1971-
76)

note ARCHED
WINDOWS

SIDE VIEW
(60-S)

$7763. ($8502., WEST)

One of the most appreciated new Cadillac luxuries
available is the lamp monitoring system that tells you
whether your headlights, rear lights and turn signals are
functioning properly. Coupled with the lamp monitoring
system is a warning light that tells you when your windshield washer fluid is low.

FLEETWOOD
SIXTY SPECIAL
BROUGHAM

133" WB
FLEETWOOD
60 SPECIAL
BROUGHAM

INTERIOR

(15200 BLT.)

ATOP FRONT FENDERS
27-GAL. GAS TANK
(CAN RUN ON
LEADED OR UNLEADED
FUEL)

ELD. WHEEL COVER

EL DORADO
CUT TO
365 HP

new
CVT.
(6800 BLT.)

FLEETWOOD
SEVENTY-FIVE
INTERIOR

FLEETWD.
75 GETS
new
151½" WB
$11,869. UP

75

new
QUARTER
WINDOWS
ON
EL DORADO
H/T

(20568 BLT.)
$7383.

$7751.

CADILLAC 71

132

Cadillac

(1972 CADILLACS INTRO. 9~23~71)

CALAIS

H/T (3900 BLT.) $5771.

4~DR. H/T (3875 BLT.) $5938.

CALAIS was LOWEST~ PRICED CADILLAC SERIES FROM 1965 THRU 1976.

HP CUT AGAIN, TO 220 (THROUGH '73)

AUX. LTS. MOVED UP FROM BUMPER and PLACED BETWEEN HEADLTS.

ELECTRIC SUNROOF OPTION

POWER DOOR LOCKS

DEVILLE

$7637. (20750 BLT.) **FLEETWOOD** BROUGHAM (60~S)

AUTO. CLIMATE CONTROL (CAPACITY INCREASED FOR 1972)

80 75 70   CLIMATE CONTROL
OFF VENT LO AUTO HI BI-LEVEL DEF

H/T (95280 BLT.) $6168.

new GRILLES TOTAL 1972 PROD. = 267,787

72

1972 DASH LIKE 1971 TYPE (SEE 1971 PAGE)

The Seventy- Five INTERIOR

AUTO DIMMING OFF OFF LIGHTS SENTINEL

"TWILIGHT SENTINEL"

151½" WB **FLEETWOOD 75**

9~PASS. LIMOUSINE (960 BLT.) $11880 SEDAN (955 BLT.) $11748.

CONVERT. (7975 BLT.) $7546.

Eldorado 126.3" WB

ELDORADO HP CUT TO 235 (THROUGH '73)

H/T (32099 BLT.) $7230.

CADILLAC 72

133

CALAIS

H/T (4275 BLT.)
$5866.

Cadillac

DASH

DEVILLE
4-DR. H/T
(103,394 BLT.)
(112,849 2-DR. DEVILLE H/Ts)

new GRILLES **73**

TOTAL 1973 PROD.=304,839

1973

$7765

FLEETWOOD 60-S BROUGHAM (24800 BLT.)

AS BEFORE, A WREATH AROUND EMBLEM IDENTIFIES THE FLEETWOOD.

Fleetwood
Seventy-Five

$11748. UP

75 PROD.
(955 SEDANS)
(960 LIMOS.)

Eldorado

$7360.

ELDORADO   H/T (42136 BLT.)
CVT. (9315 BLT.)
$7681.

1973

CADILLAC 73

134

Cadillac

CALAIS 4-DR. H/T (2324 BLT.) $7545.

DEVILLE $7867. UP

The Coupe de Ville

11/1 COUPE (4559 BLT.) $7371.

472 CID V8 HP CUT TO 205

EARLY '74 HAS EMBLEM ABOVE GRILLE

new WITH WARNING LIGHTS and GAS GAUGE ABOVE INST. PANEL

new FRONT STYLING

74

(112,201 DEVILLE CPES.)

new DASH

NEW

$9537. (18250 BLT.)

FLEETWOOD BROUGHAM 60-S

Stereo with Tape Deck.

AM/FM RADIO WITH 8-TRACK TAPE

HOOD ORNAMT. "FLIP-UP" ADDED DURING 1974 BUT AVAILABLE ON EARLY "SPECIAL MODELS."

new BUMPERS ABSORB MINOR IMPACTS (ELDORADO TYPE SHOWN)

12:45

new DIGITAL CLOCK →

FLEETWOOD 75

$13120. UP

(895 SEDANS BLT.)

(1005 LIMOS. BLT.)

75 GRILLE

$9437.

ELDORADO

$9110.

H/T (32812 BLT.)

(VT. (7600 BLT.)

500 CID V8 HP CUT TO 210

CADILLAC 74

135

Cadillac

CALAIS

$8377. 4-DRS.

AVAIL. CALAIS INTERIOR

available
New

Air Cushion Restraint System. Alternative to seat belt/ignition interlock system. "Air bags" are designed to provide restraint to front seat occupants in front accident situations. (Not available on Convertible and Limousine.)

DEVILLE
$8801.

FLEETWOOD
BROUGHAM

(18755 BLT.)

WITH POP-UP ORNAMENT ATOP HOOD   TALISMAN

(Talisman.) Also available without wreath on DeVilles and Calais.

COUPE

$10414.

new RECTANGULAR HEADLIGHTS and new GRILLES

75

WITH V AND CREST BUT NO HOOD ORNAMENT ABOVE

FLEETWD. 75 LIMO.
$14557.

TOTAL 1975 PROD. = 264,732

(795 BLT.)

ALL MODELS HAVE 500 cid EL.D. V8   HP CUT TO 190 (THRU '76)

Eldorado

INTERIOR (CVT.)

ELDORADO CVT.

CPE. (35802 BLT.)
$9935.

(8950 BLT.)
$10354.

NAME NO LONGER APPEARS ON SIDE OF COWL

SIDE SAFETY LT. NOW MOVED

BACK FROM FRONT CORNER

"... a Standard for the World in American-Built Cars"

CADILLAC 75

136

Cadillac **Seville** (43772 BLT. 1976) $12,479. (INTRO. SPRING, 1975) (16355 BLT. DURING 1975)

114.3" WB
350 CID V8 (180 HP)
(IN SEVILLE ONLY)

Cornering Lights.

Tilt and Telescope Steering Wheel.

NEW

International size luxury car,

FINAL YEAR FOR
CALAIS
(ONLY 1700 SEDANS BLT.)

CPE. (4500 BLT.)
$8629.

FLTWD. BROUG. TALISMAN SEDAN (24500 BLT.)

TOTAL 1976 PROD. =
309,139

$10935.
($12748. WEST)

76

DEVILLE SEDAN (67677 BLT.)
$9265.

DEVILLE

new FINER "CROSSHATCH" GRILLE PIECES

COUPE DEVILLE (114,482 BLT.) = **$9067.**
(BEST SELLER)

(834 BLT.)
FLEETWOOD 75 LIMO. **$15239.**

(CPE. 35184 BLT.) *Eldorado*

THE FINAL CONVERTIBLE
MFD. BY A MAJOR AMERICAN FACTORY UNTIL 1982.

Eldorado Convertible
Last of a magnificent breed.
(CPE. PRICE = $10,586.)
"Cadillac" NAME NOW ABOVE GRILLE.

(14000 BLT.)

$11049.

CADILLAC 76

It is the only convertible now built in America. And it will be our last. The very last. Because the Eldorado Convertible will not be offered in 1977.

Cadillac

SEVILLE $13359.
(45060 BLT.)

350 CID V8 (180 HP)

V8 CUT TO 425 CID (180 HP) IN ALL BUT SEVILLE (195 HP OPT.)

CB RADIO!

with Citizens Band.

DASH

(95421 BLT.)

SEDAN DE VILLE $10,020.

COUPE DE VILLE (2 VIEWS) $9810.

new 77
"DOWNSIZED" MODELS (TOTALLY RESTYLED)

WB CUT TO 121½"

FLEETWD. BRGHM.

$11546.
(28000 BLT.)

(138,750 BLT.)

TAIL~ LTS. (FLEET~ WOOD)

Dual rub strip for bumper protection.

(1032 BLT.)

FLEETWOOD LIMO. $19014. (FORMAL)

new SHORTER 144½" WB

new SMALLER 425 CID V8 (180 HP)

new GRILLE WITH MORE, FINER VERTICAL PCS. and "ELDORADO" NAME ABOVE.

Automatic Level Control Adjusts for changing loads automatically.

PHANTOM VIEW

ELDORADO
(47344 BLT.)

Four Wheel Disc Brakes Ventilated discs have cooling fins for rapid heat dissipation

Automatic Climate Control Redesigned for 1977 Compressor works only when necessary

COUPE = $11,187.

126.3" WB (THRU '78)

$12947.
(BIARRITZ CPE.)

TOTAL 1977 PROD. = 358,488

CADILLAC 77

$14710. AND UP

"ELEGANTE" $16867.

Seville

(56985 BLT.)

REAR DETAILS (SEVILLE)

SEDAN DEVILLE(88951 BLT.)

CLOSER VIEW OF REAR~ QUARTER PANEL

Elegante

COUPE DE VILLE (117,750 BLT.)

$10924.

DEVILLE

IN DRIVER'S DOOR
New driver's power-seat control location

$10584.

new TAIL~ LTS.

1978

78

New GRILLE with "Cadillac" NAME ABOVE IN SCRIPT

DASH

FLEETWOOD BROUGHAM (36800 BLT.)

$12842.

TOTAL 1978 PROD.= 349,684

LIMOUSINE LANDAU "CABRIOLET ROOF" (FORMAL)

Limousine with Landau Cabriolet Roof.

FLEETWOOD LIMO.
8~PASS.-848 BLT.
FORMAL-682 "

$20742.
(FORMAL, WITH PARTITION and LEATHER FRNT. SEAT)

(CPE. PRICED FROM $11,921.)

Eldorado Custom Biarritz

QUARTER~ PANEL LIGHT

new GRILLE WITH HEAVIER HORIZONTAL PCS.

ELDORADO

"ELDORADO" NAME ABOVE GRILLE

(46816 BLT.)

CADILLAC 78

$13786.

139

Cadillac

$14710.

(53487 BLT.)

Seville

INTERIOR

OLDSMOBILE DIESEL POWER FOR CADILLAC
Available now for Seville and Eldorado... Later in the model year for Fleetwood Brougham and DeVilles.

350 CID V8 DILSLL

125 HP

"ELEGANTE" OPTION

DASH

SED. DEVILLE
(93211 BLT.)
$12093.

DEVILLE

CUSTOM PHAETON SEDAN
Similar to the Phaeton Coupe

DEVILLES WITH SPECIAL ROOFS

DISTINGUISHED ROOFS

$14102.
FLTWD. BROUGHAM

(42200 BLT.)

425 CID V8
(180 OR 195 HP)

79

"Cadillac" NAME RETURNS TO UPPER BORDER OF new GRILLE
TOTAL '79 PRODUCTION = 383,138

GLENRIDGE LODGE

COUPE DVL.
(121,890 BLT.)

$11728. UP

FLEETWOOD FORMAL LIMOUSINE
$22640. (2025 BLT.)

new "TRIP COMPUTER"
(AVAILABLE ON ELDORADO AND SEVILLE)

1 MPG	2 SPEED	3 TIME	RESET
4 RANGE	5 DEST	6 ARRIVE	CLOCK
Cadillac Trip Computer			
7 RPM	8 °F	9 VOLTS	ENT 0 MILES

ELDORADO
TOTALLY RESTYLED

$14668. UP

BIARRITZ

ELDORADO DASH
350 CID V8
(160 HP)
ALSO IN SEVILLE
WB CUT TO 113.9"

CADILLAC 79

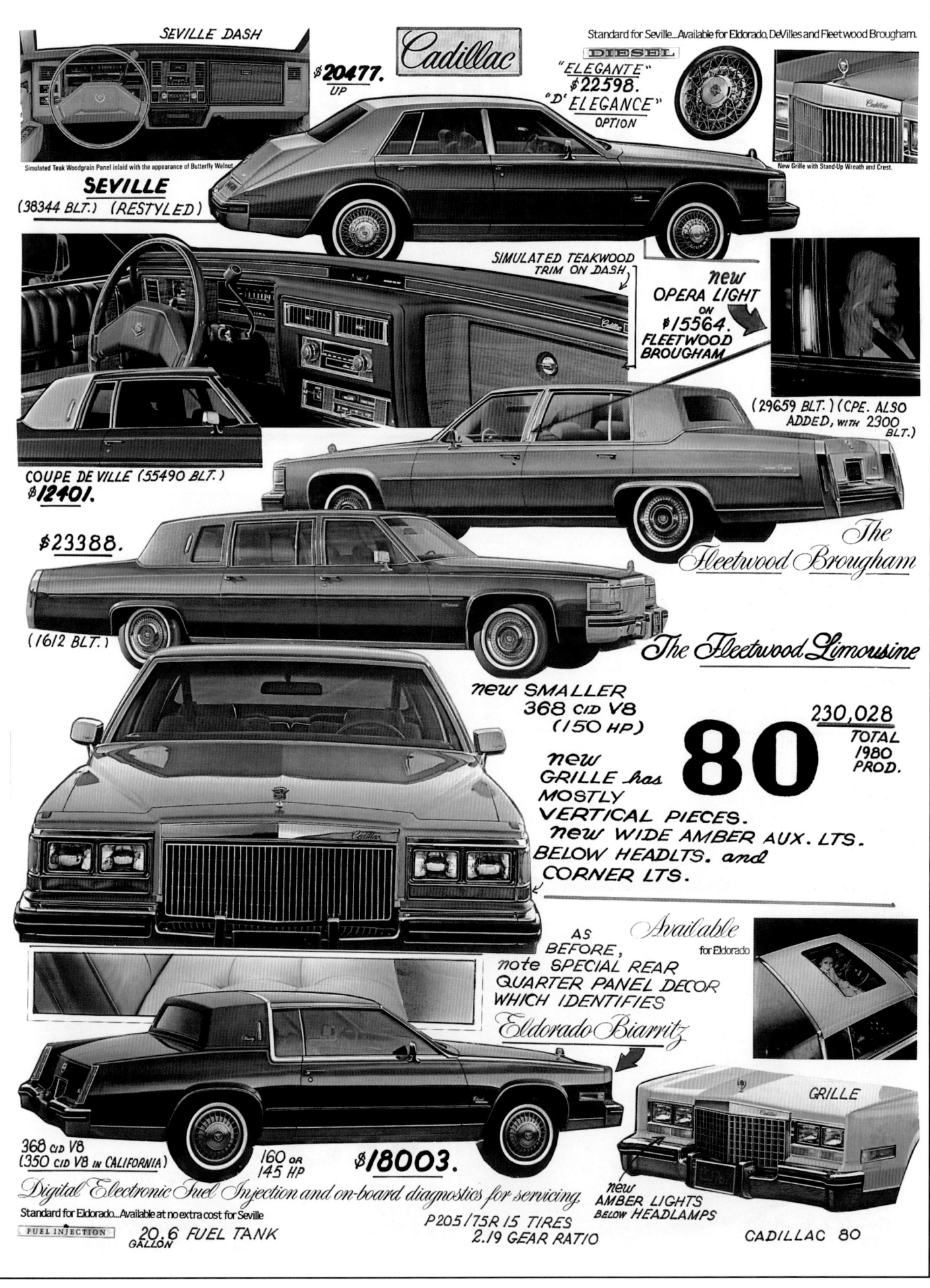

SEVILLE DASH

Cadillac

$20477. UP

Standard for Seville...Available for Eldorado, DeVilles and Fleetwood Brougham.

DIESEL

"ELEGANTE" $22598. "D' ELEGANCE" OPTION

Simulated Teak Woodgrain Panel inlaid with the appearance of Butterfly Walnut.

New Grille with Stand-Up Wreath and Crest.

SEVILLE
(38344 BLT.) (RESTYLED)

SIMULATED TEAKWOOD TRIM ON DASH

new OPERA LIGHT ON $15564. FLEETWOOD BROUGHAM

(29659 BLT.) (CPE. ALSO ADDED, with 2300 BLT.)

COUPE DE VILLE (55490 BLT.) $12401.

The Fleetwood Brougham

$23388.

(1612 BLT.)

The Fleetwood Limousine

new SMALLER 368 CID V8 (150 HP)

230,028 TOTAL 1980 PROD.

80

new GRILLE has MOSTLY VERTICAL PIECES. new WIDE AMBER AUX. LTS. BELOW HEADLTS. and CORNER LTS.

AS BEFORE, note SPECIAL REAR QUARTER PANEL DECOR WHICH IDENTIFIES *Eldorado Biarritz*

Available for Eldorado

GRILLE

368 CID V8 (350 CID V8 IN CALIFORNIA)

160 OR 145 HP

$18003.

new AMBER LIGHTS BELOW HEADLAMPS

Digital Electronic Fuel Injection and on-board diagnostics for servicing.

Standard for Eldorado...Available at no extra cost for Seville

FUEL INJECTION

20.6 FUEL TANK GALLON

P205/75R 15 TIRES
2.19 GEAR RATIO

CADILLAC 80

"The Hugger" Camaro

(SINCE 1967)

BY CHEVROLET

(INTRO. 9-29-66)

230 CID 6 CYL. OR V8 {327 OR 350 CID}
(140 TO 325 HP)
108" WB

$2466. UP

NEW 67

STOCK CAMARO 6 COUPE

SS CONVERTIBLE

SS 350

CAMARO

SS-350 CPE. w. CONCEALED LTS.

1967 PRODUCTION:
6 = 58,808
V8 = 182,109

SS HAS DUAL ROWS OF SQUARE PORTS ATOP HOOD

1968 PRODUCTION:
6 = 50,937
V8 = 184,178

68

$2588. UP

new DASH

ENGINES
230 CID 6 (140 HP)
250 CID 6 (155 HP)
327 CID V8 (210 HP) (275 HP AVAIL.)
350 CID V8 (295 HP)
396 CID V8 (325 HP)

NOTE new FRONT and REAR SIDE (RECTANGULAR) SAFETY LIGHTS, AS REQUIRED BY LAW

REAR FENDER

Chevrolet Camaro

(FINAL CONVERTIBLE AVAILABLE)

SS SPT. CPE. WITH RALLY SPORT EQUIP.

V-SHAPE and CRISS-CROSS PCS. IN new GRILLE (BLK.)

69

(CONTINUES TO FEB., 1970)

140 HP 6 TO 396 CID 325 HP V8
(EARLY 327 CID, 210 HP V8 REPL. BY new STD. 307 CID, 200 HP)

1969 PRODUCTION:
6 = 65,008   V8 = 178,087

Camaro

Chevrolet

New Camaro. Feb. 26th.

We've never announced a car at this time before. But then nobody's ever announced a car like this before.

$2749. UP
(1970)

REAR QUARTER SECTION

SPORT CPE. WITH DELUXE BUMPER

'70 FROM $3089.
(WEST)

(1970 (SOMETIMES REFERRED TO AS THE 1970½ CAMARO, BY REASON OF ITS LATE DEBUT.)

Spoilers OPT.

Z-28 PKG.: $573. EXTRA

70 -71

(RESTYLED)

$2921. UP
(1971)

Z-28
1970 (8733 BLT.)
1971 (4862 ")

Z-28 has BROAD DUAL STRIPES on HOOD and DECK

TW·572

FRONT DISC BRAKES NOW STD.

(BLUE OR BROWN VINYL TOPS NOT AVAIL. UNTIL '71)

RS (RALLY SPORT) CPE.) (note ROUND INBOARD PARK./DIR. LTS., PROTRUDING GRILLE)

STD. 250 C.I.D 6 (155 HP) OR 307 C.I.D V8 (200 HP)

360 HP V8 AVAIL.

Super Hugger.

TOTAL PRODUCTION =
124,889 (1970)
114,630 (1971)

See it. At your Chevrolet Sports Dept.

Center Console

The instrument panel wraps around you. A new invisible resilient bumper surrounds the grille of RS models.

There are four transmissions available. And six power plants up to the 360-hp 396.

FLAT BLACK DASH

Camaro Option

AIR CONDITIONING — HEATING

Forget the tack-on tach. Ours is on the instrument panel, along with a temperature gauge and an ammeter. There's even a clock

RS GRAINED DASH

GM
MARK OF EXCELLENCE

Special Instrumentation

CAMARO 70~71

143

Camaro Sport Coupe

Chevrolet
Building a better way
to see the U.S.A.

$2730. UP (6-CYL.)

$2820. UP (V8)

DASH

Sport Coupe / Rally Sport / SS / Z28

STD. 307 CID V8 (130 HP) (6 -250 CID— ALSO AVAIL.) (110 HP)

72

FEWER PCS. IN new STD. GRILLE

FROM $3580. (V8) (WEST)

Rally Sport

Super Sport

Remote-Control Sport Mirror.

"SS 350"

TOTAL 1972 PROD. = 68656

4-SPOKE STEER. WHEEL

new STD. EQUIP.

"Z28"

Z28 (2575 BLT.)

(REAR)

CUSTOM INTERIOR

note "Z-28" ON GRILLE

Front and Rear Spoilers. Include lower front spoiler and a special full-width rear spoiler that extends down sides of rear fenders.

Wheel Covers. Two styles

New "Wet Look" Vinyl Roof. Comes in black, white, green, covert and tan. Black and white available with all exterior colors. Others available depending on exterior color.

CAMARO 72

307 CID V8 CUT TO 115 HP
(6 CYL. AVAIL.
$2781.)

$2872.
V8
SPORT
COUPE
$3608.
(WEST)

(NOT
AVAIL.
ON
Z-28)
TURBINE
I WHEEL

UNIROYAL
TIGER PAW F70-14

73

new
FRONT BUMPER

AVAIL.
ONLY
FOR
SPT.
CPE.
OR
RS

LT DASH
(LT = "LUXURY
TOURING")

$3884.
(V8)
(WEST)

$3268.
(EAST)

LT (new)

TOTAL
1973
PROD. =
96751

(32327 BLT.)

(SS
NOT
AVAIL.)

RALLY
SPORT

($90. LESS
FOR 6-CYL.)

Available Engines*			
145-hp Turbo-Fire 350-2 V8**	Std.	Avail.	Avail.
175-hp Turbo-Fire 350-4 V8♦	Std.	Avail.	Avail.
245-hp Turbo-Fire Special 350-4 V8†	—	Avail.‡	Avail.

*Horsepowers shown are SAE net (as installed) ratings. **Standard engine with Type LT. ♦Power brakes required. †Z28 only. ‡Close ratio also available (except with air conditioning).

Transmissions			
	3-Speed	Wide range 4-Speed	Turbo Hydra-matic
	Std.	—	Avail.
	Std.	—	Avail.

Standard Engines*
100-hp Turbo-Thrift 250 Six
115-hp Turbo-Fire 307 V8

V8 Building a better way to see the U.S.A.

CAMARO 73

Camaro

STD. $4091.

(LT = $4438.)
(48963 LT's BLT.)

SPORT COUPE INTERIOR

CHEVROLET MAKES SENSE FOR AMERICA.

DASH

WIDE 60 OVAL FIRESTONE

Z-28

Z-28
(13082 BLT.)

Chevrolet

TOTALLY RESTYLED

74

TOTAL 1974 PROD. = 151,008

Z28's 350 4-barrel V8.

REAR Z-28 COWL

250 CID (100 HP) 6-CYL. STILL AVAIL.; STANDARD V8 IS 350 CID, (WITH *new* 145 HP) (6 CYL. $212. LESS)

TAIL-LT. DETAIL

$4424. Sport Coupe or Type LT. ($4796.)
(105 HP 6 CYL. $145 LESS)
SPORT COUPE

2-TONE

WITH RALLY SPORT TRIM

('75)

new RECTANGULAR EMBLEM, NOW ON HOOD and REAR DECK

camaro

75 -76

('75) **TYPE LT** LT WOODGRAINED

CAMARO 74-76

Chevrolet
Camaro

Z-28
Z-28 SPOILER

STD. 305 CID V8 (145 HP) OR 250 CID 6 (100 HP)
SPT. CPE.
$5082.

$5767.
(WEST)

STD.
E/FR78 × 14/B
TIRES

(Z-28 = GR70 × 15)

SPECIAL PAINT JOB ON Z-28

Z28 **77**

RETURNS!
Z-28 350 CID V8
has 170 HP
(ENG. AVAIL. FOR "LT" also)

(14349 BLT.)

SEE WHAT'S NEW TODAY IN A CHEVROLET.

OVERHEAD VIEW of
new T-BAR ROOF
AVAIL.

$5604. (Z-28)

new ALL-MOLDED FRONT APPEARS "BUMPERLESS"

(6-CYL. has new 110 HP)

78

Camaro Z28

has new SLANTING LOUVRES ON SIDE OF COWL.

$6236.
(WEST)

new T-BAR AVAIL.

(STD. $5562. UP)
(WEST)

DASH

LT
FR. $5962.

ANNUAL PRODUCTION TOTALS =
1977 — 218,853   1978 — 272,631

EASTERN PRICES BEGIN AT =
$4113. ('77) $4414. ('78)

CAMARO 77~78

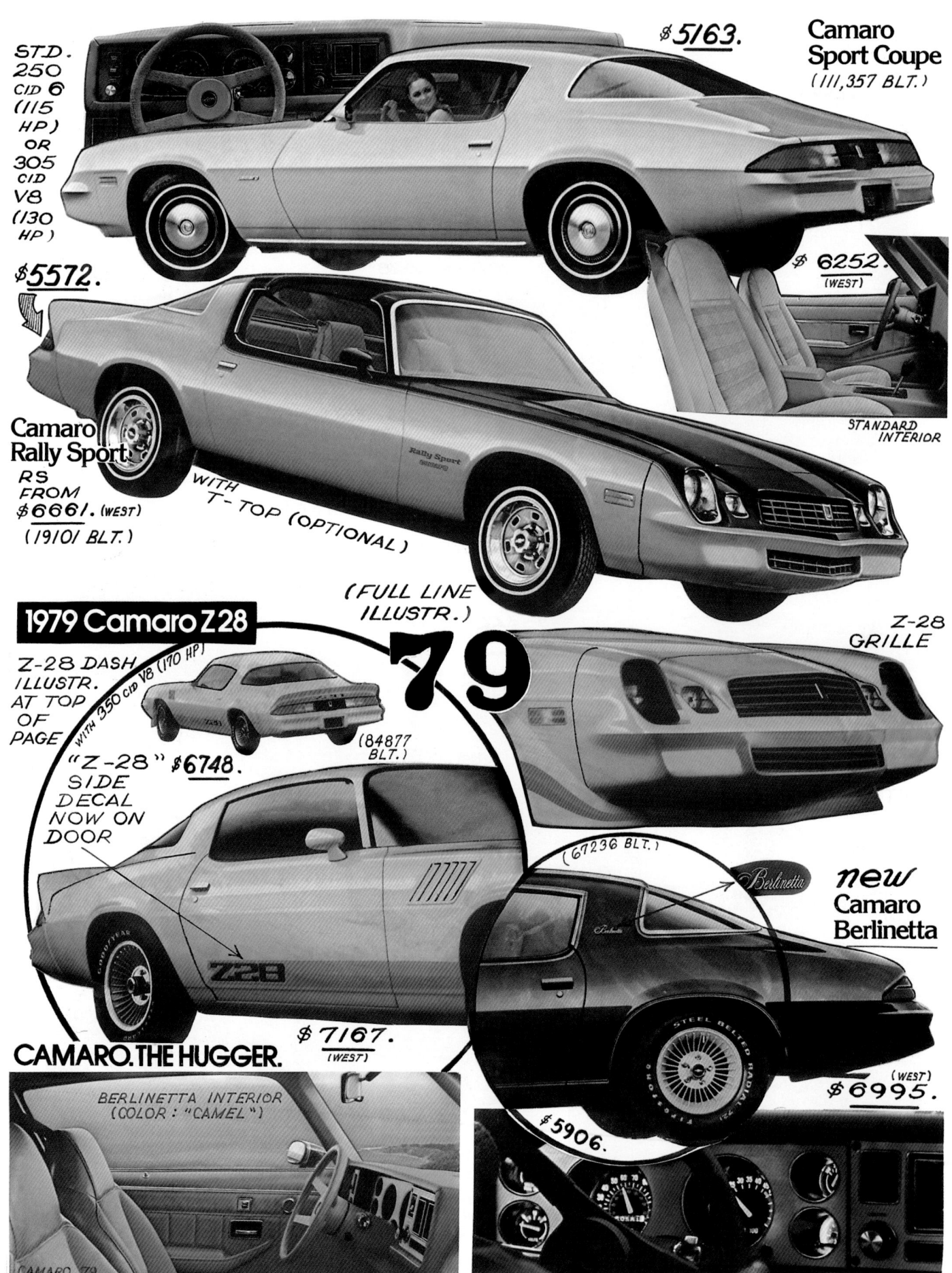

STD. 250 CID 6 (115 HP) OR 305 CID V8 (130 HP)

$5163.

Camaro Sport Coupe
(111,357 BLT.)

$6252. (WEST)

STANDARD INTERIOR

$5572.

Camaro Rally Sport
RS FROM $6661. (WEST)
(19101 BLT.)

WITH T-TOP (OPTIONAL)

(FULL LINE ILLUSTR.)

79

Z-28 GRILLE

1979 Camaro Z28

Z-28 DASH ILLUSTR. AT TOP OF PAGE

WITH 350 CID V8 (170 HP)

(84877 BLT.)

"Z-28" $6748.

"Z-28" SIDE DECAL NOW ON DOOR

(67236 BLT.)

new Camaro Berlinetta

CAMARO. THE HUGGER.

$7167. (WEST)

BERLINETTA INTERIOR (COLOR: "CAMEL")

CAMARO '79

$5906.

(WEST) $6995.

Camaro

Chevrolet

$5843.

$6699. WEST (68174 BLT.)

EPA MPG:
20 CITY
26 HWY. (6)

80

TAIL-LT.
DETAILS

(26679 BLT.)

BERLINETTA

$6606.

$7462 (WEST)

$6086.

RALLY
SPORT

$7116.
(WEST)

AVAIL. FOR
RALLY SPT.
OR SPT. CPE.

NOT TO
BE CONFUSED
WITH WIRE WHEELS
SHOWN ON BERLINETTA

(12015
BLT.)

new STD.
ENGINES
229 CID V6 (115 HP)
267 CID V8 (120 HP)
305 CID V8 AVAIL. (155 HP)
350 CID V8 (IN Z-28)

231 CID V6 (110 HP) IN CALIFORNIA

Z 28 FOR 1980.
THE MAXIMUM
CAMARO.

Z28 DASH

$7363.

WITH
350 CID
V8
(new
190 HP)
IN Z-28

(45/37
BLT.)

Black	Blue, Bright (Metallic)	Blue, Dark (Metallic)	Brown, Dark (Metallic)	Charcoal (Metallic)	Claret, Dark (Metallic)	Gold (Metallic)	Green, Lime (Metallic)	Red	Red Orange	Bronze (Metallic)	Silver	White	Yellow, Bright

CAMARO 80   **EXTERIOR COLORS** (Except Rally Sport)

TOTAL 1980
PRODUCTION
152,005

EXTERIOR COLORS
(Rally Sport Only)

Bronze with Dark Brown (Metallics)	Bright Blue with Dark Blue (Metallics)	Red with Black	Silver with Black	Lime Green (Metallic) with Black	Silver with Charcoal (Metallic)

CHECKER

(1922 TO 1982)

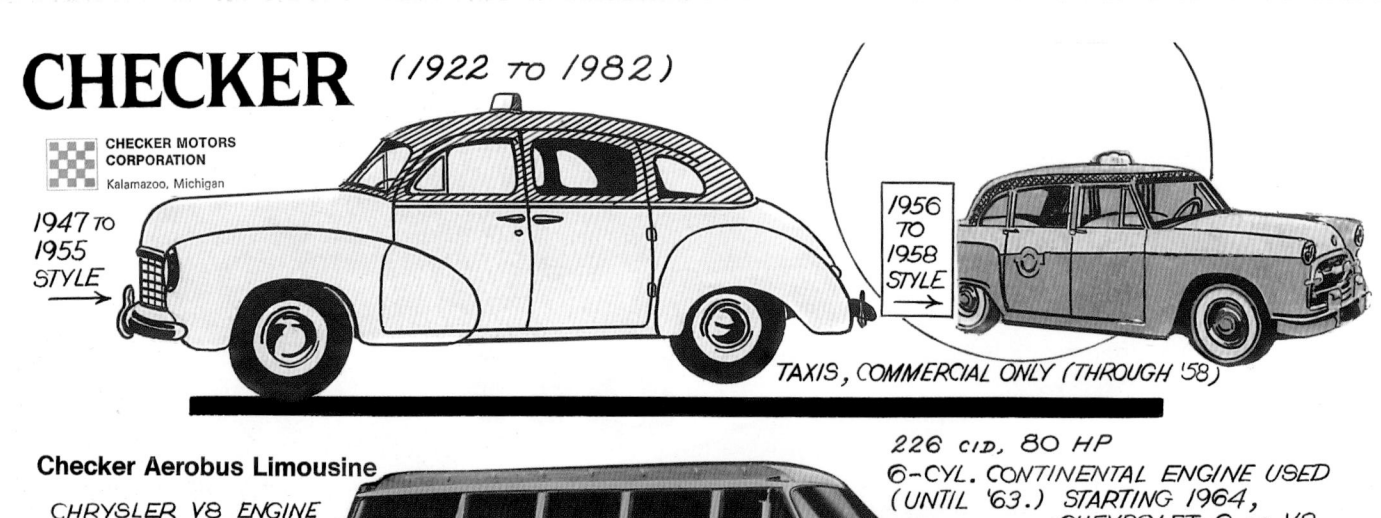

CHECKER MOTORS CORPORATION
Kalamazoo, Michigan

1947 TO 1955 STYLE →

1956 TO 1958 STYLE →

TAXIS, COMMERCIAL ONLY (THROUGH '58)

Checker Aerobus Limousine

CHRYSLER V8 ENGINE IN PRE-'64 AEROBUS

226 CID, 80 HP 6-CYL. CONTINENTAL ENGINE USED (UNTIL '63.) STARTING 1964, CHEVROLET 6 OR V8.

DASH ('68)

Checker Marathon Deluxe Limousine

NON-COMMERCIAL SEDANS and WAGONS NOW AVAIL. TO PUBLIC.

59
ON
NO YEARLY STYLE CHANGES.

120" WB

Checker Marathon 4-door sedan

Checker Marathon 4-door station wagon

SAFETY-BUMPERS (ENERGY-ABSORBING) ADDED IN MID-1970s.

1.
2.
3. INTERIOR ('69)

1965 ENGINES = 230 CID 6 (140 HP) 283 " V8 (195") 327 " " (250") (SMALLER V8 DROPPED IN 1966, REPL. BY 307 CID (200 HP) IN 1968)

SEDAN PRICE $2542 ('60-61) $2642 ('62-63) $2814 ('64) $2793 ('65) $2874 ('66-67) $3221 ('68) $3290 ('69)

6-CYL. LOW-PRICED "SUPERBA" SERIES AVAIL. 1959 TO 1963.

PRODUCTION PEAK OF 8173 IN 1962 (DOWN TO 5417 IN 1969) CHECKER

CHEVELLE
(NEW)
by Chevrolet

(2-DR. WAGON ALSO AVAIL.)

INTERIOR (MALIBU)

64

194 OR 230 CID 6 (120 OR 155 HP @ 4400 RPM)

ALSO 283 CID V8 (195 OR 220 HP @ 4800 RPM)

300

$2231. UP

PRODUCTION : MALIBU : 149,000
300 : 68,300 ; MALIBU SS : 78,800

115" W.B.

MALIBU (ABOVE) $2376. (6)
($2484. (V8))

1965 PRODUCTION :
300 : 31,600 ; MALIBU : 152,200 ; MALIBU SS : 101,577
MALIBU SS-396 : 201

$2156. ~ 2858. PRICE RANGE

$2269.

300 DELUXE 13369 (6)

$2156.
300 2-DR. 13111 (6)

300 2-DR. 6-PASS. WAGON (MALIBU 4-DR. WAGON has CHROME STRIP ALONG SIDE.)

MALIBU SS

new HORIZONTALLY-SPLIT GRILLE

65

MALIBU SS
13767 (6) $2750. CVT.
13867 (V8)   2858. "

194 OR 230 CID 6 (120 OR 140 HP @ 4400 RPM)
ALSO :
(283 CID V8 AVAIL. ONLY WITH 195 HP @ 4800 RPM)
3 new 327 CID V8s (250, 300, OR 350 HP)

CHEVELLE 64~65

FULL COIL SUSPENSION

CHEVELLE

MALIBU CVT. = $3030.
(241,600 MALIBU MODELS BLT.)

MALIBU

H/T SPT. CPE.
$2821.

194 cid 6 (120 HP)
230 cid 6 (140 HP)
283 cid TURBO FIRE V8
(195 or 220 HP)
327 cid V8
(275 HP)
396 cid V8
(325 or 360 HP)

300 SERIES has
PLAINER REAR DECK w/o CHROME ORNAMENTATION.
6.95 / 7.35 x 14 TIRES

66 new GRILLE

(72,300 SS MODELS BLT.)
(SS CVT. ALSO
AVAIL.)

H/T $2434. UP

UPHOLSTERY
CHOICES

MALIBU CVT.
2637. UP

MALIBU

(227,000 MALIBU MODELS
BLT.)

67 new GRILLES and TAIL-LIGHTS

COLORS

7.35 x 14 TIRES

TOTAL '67 PROD.:
375,831

$2825. SS 396

note
"SS 396" IN
GRILLE
CENTER

Turbo-Jet V8
H/T

(63,000
SS MODELS BLT.)

SS 396

152

LARGER STD. 307 CID V8
(200 HP) USES REG. GAS
230 CID STD. 6
(140 HP)

CHEVELLE
MALIBU

1968 PRODUCTION:
432,302

68 (RESTYLED)

AT CENTER:
Chevelle Nomad Custom
WAGON (new)
$3303.
(3-ST.)

new WB
112" 2 DR.
116" 4 DR.
(THROUGH '77)

WITH OPT. VINYL TOP

SS-396
H/T = $3249.

BE SMART. BE SURE. BUY NOW AT YOUR CHEVROLET DEALER'S.

$2458. ~ 3266. PRICE RANGE

$2601. UP

FRONT VENT WINDOWS ELIMINATED

STD.
230 CID 6
(140 HP)
307 CID V8
(200 HP)

69 new GRILLES

new LOCKING STEERING COLUMN and TRANS. LEVER

MALIBU H/T
$3025.
$3372 WITH OPTIONAL ILLUS.
SS-396 PACKAGE
(also NOMAD, GREENBRIER, CONCOURS, CONCOURS EST. WAGONS AVAIL.)
116" WB

153

CVT. $**2919**. UP

CHEVELLE BY CHEVROLET

SS PKG.

$**3342**. UP   CONCOURS EST.

(4-DR. SEDANS and 4-DR. H/Ts ALSO)

CHEVROLET On The Move.

70

(354,855 BLT.)

TOP TO BOTTOM: NOMAD, GREENBRIER, CONCOURS, CONCOURS ESTATE WAGONS

REAR

new 2-TIER GRILLE

$**2719**. UP

MALIBU H/T

SS PKG.

1971. You've changed. We've changed. new GRILLE and BUMPERS

(186,337 BLT.) $**2885**. UP

new TAIL-LTS. (ROUND, RECESSED IN REAR BUMPER

new CORNER LTS.

new SINGLE HEADLTS.

Putting you first, keeps us first.

71

CHEVROLET

DASH

ENGINES	Gross hp	SAE net hp	3-Speed	4-Speed	Power-glide	Turbo Hydra-matic
250-cu.-in. Six*	145	110	*		■	
307-cu.-in. V8*	200	140	*		■	■
350-cu.-in. V8	245	165		■	■	■
350-cu.-in. V8	270	175	†	■		■
400-cu.-in. V8	300	260	‡	■		■
454-cu.-in. V8 (SS only)	365	285		●●		■

*Standard. **Special 4-Speed. †Floor shift. ‡Special 3-Speed with floor shift.

350 CID V8

SCARCEST 1971 CHEVELLE WAS GREENBRIER 3-SEAT WAGON (2129 BLT.)

CHEVELLE 70~71

CHEVELLE
Building a better way to see the U.S.A.

SCENE:
6 FLAGS AMUSEMT. PK., ATLANTA, GA.

250 CID 6
(110 HP)
307 CID
V8
(130 HP)
350 CID
V8 (165
OR 175 HP)
400 CID V8 (240 HP)
454 CID
V8 (SS)
(270 HP)

WAGON

← W. VINYL TOP

CONVERTIBLE
SS

MALIBU
$3187.
(4853 BLT.)

'72

new GRILLE

$2636.
UP

PLAIN
TOP

$2833.
4790-6 CYL.
207,598-V8s

MALIBU
H/T

SEDAN
6764-6-CYL.
12881-V8s

INTERIOR

"HEAVY CHEVY" SPT. CPE.
has BLACK GRILLE, SPECIAL
STRIPING (INTRO. MID-'71)

3562-6-CYL.
450/3-V8s →

SS

MALIBU
SEDAN

$2801.

BLACK GRILLES ON
SS and
"HEAVY CHEVY"

STD.
DASH

OPT.
SPORT
DASH
WITH
ROUND
GAUGES

ARROW INDICATES
A CHANGE FROM '71

CHEVELLE '72

155

OTHER *new* TYPE BUMPER AT TOP (GUARDS OPT.)

CHEVELLE

new ENERGY-ABSORBING SAFETY BUMPERS

(MALIBU SS *has* "SS" IN CENTER OF BLACK GRILLE *and* ON COWL.)

LAGUNA FRONT END IS ENTIRE BUMPER.

LAGUNA ESTATE

MALIBU FR. $3997.

wagon (22,533 BLT.)

DLX. WAGON $3909. UP

(10940 BLT.)

MALIBU

5261·CE

SEDAN (60679 BLT.) 100 TO 245 HP (400 CID V8 DISCONTINUED '73 ONLY)

TOTALLY RESTYLED

73

CPE. (168,784 BLT.) $3743.

(20755 BLT.) DLX. 4-DR. = $3566.

DASH (LAGUNA)

DELUXE

(21377 BLT.)

Malibu

DLX. CPE. $3599.

(60679 BLT.)

OPTION. SWING-OUT (90°) BUCKET SEATS

COLONNADE 4-DR. $3711.

COLONNADE CPE. (BELOW)

(WEST COAST HIGHER PRICES SHOWN)

Laguna

(New)

Laguna Estate

IIM·984

(7370 BLT.) $4373.

(42941 BLT.) $3932.

CHEVELLE 73

CHEVELLE

(CHEVELLE DELUXE DISCONTINUED)

MALIBU 6 COUPE $2878*
(15790 BLT.)

74 new GRILLES

$2873* MALIBU 6 SEDAN
(11399 BLT., PLUS 26841 V8s)

(DURING 1974, MALIBU 6 CPE. PRICE INCREASED TO $3954.!)
(WEST)

(PLUS 37583 V8s)

GM Love Seats.
One size for infants up to 20 lbs.; a second size for youngsters 20-40 lbs. and up to 40" in height. Infant seat faces backward, older child's forward.

(MALIBU, CLASSIC and CLASSIC EST. WAGONS AVAIL.)

$4590.
(WEST)

(351~6 CYL., 27490~V8s)
● Color-keyed steering column and wheel ● Luxury seat and upper door panel trim ● E78-14 (Six) or G78-14 (V8) bias belted tires

Malibu Classic

new HOOD ORNAMENT (MAL.CLASSIC ONLY)

NEW

SEDAN

Malibu Classic

LANDAU CPE.

Malibu Classic

FROM $3304.
$4376.
(WEST)
(4457~6 CYL., 51468~V8s)

Building a better way to see the U.S.A.
Chevelle Laguna Type S-3.

LAGUNA S-3
S-3 GRILLE

NEW

LAGUNA TYPE S-3

S~3

(note 2 AVAILABLE TOP STYLES)

(ALL LAGUNA S~3s ARE V8s)

(15792 BLT.)

$3723.
$4504.
(WEST)
REQUIRES 91 or HIGHER OCTANE UNLEADED OR LOW~LEAD GAS.
(ALL MODELS)

CHEVELLE 74

Chevrolet makes sense for America.

Engines	Power Rating*	Carb./ Exh.**	Engine Usage	3-Speed Manual	4-Speed Manual	Turbo Hydra-matic
Turbo-Thrift 250 Six	100-hp	1/SE	Std.(1,4)	Std.	NA	A
Turbo-Fire 350 V8	145-hp	2/SE	Std.(2)	Std.	NA	A
Turbo-Fire 350 V8	160-hp	4/SE	(3)	Std.	NA	A
Turbo-Fire 400 V8	150-hp	2/SE	(2)	NA	NA	A
Turbo-Fire 400 V8	180-hp	4/SE	(3)	NA	NA	A
Turbo-Jet 454 V8	235-hp	4/DE	(4,5)	NA	(6)	A

*The horsepowers shown here are SAE net (as installed) ratings **First number indicates number of carburetor barrels, followed by letters for Single Exhaust or Dual Exhaust. (1) Available for Malibu Classic and Malibu models only. (2) Not available in State of California. (3) Available only when California Emission Equipment is ordered. (4) California Emission Equipment required in State of California. (5) Available only with power brakes, heavy-duty battery and power steering. (6) Available only with Special Front and Rear Suspension—RPO F40 (except on Laguna Type S-3, or on Malibu Classic and Malibu models equipped with radial ply tires). A—Available. NA—Not available.

Integral litter container.
Attached to right cowl side panel.
(GR70 × 15 TIRES ON Laguna)

Simulated wire wheel covers.
So carefully detailed they could be mistaken for wire wheels. Brushed metal gives a casting look. 48 bright metal spokes.

CHEVELLE

MALIBU
coupe.
$3407.*

The lowest-priced sedan.
$3402.*

Malibu Wagon

$4989.
(WEST)

MALIBU CLASSIC

Malibu Classic instrument panel, with new speedometer calibrated in both miles per hour (mph) and kilometers per hour (kph).

22% higher gas mileage with standard V8

WAGON (MAL. CLASSIC ESTATE) → (3-ST.) $5412.

(ALSO AVAIL. W/O GRAIN.)

$4744.
(WEST)

SEDAN

REAR WINDOW DE-FOGGER (OPT.)

catalytic converter.

75
(RESTYLED FRONT and REAR ENDS)

Special instrumentation. Includes tachometer, voltmeter, temperature gauge, clock.

NEW

$4867.
(WEST)

8-TRACK STEREO TAPE OPT.

new SLOPING FRONT ON

LAGUNA TYPE S-3

DASH

LAGUNA TYPE S-3

POWER TEAMS				
Engine	Horse-power	Engine Usage	3-Speed	Turbo Hydra-matic
250-1 barrel Six	105	Std. (1)	Std.	A
350-2 barrel V8	145	Std. (2)	Std.	A
350-4 barrel V8	155	A (3)	Std.	A
400-4 barrel V8	175	A (1)	NA	A
454-4 barrel V8	215	A (2)	NA	A

(1) California Emission Equipment required in State of California
(2) Not available in California
(3) Available only for sale and/or registration in California
A—Available   NA—Not Available   CHEVELLE 75

MALIBU

REG. $4711. **Two roomy Chevelles priced under $3671.** (SALE)
26 MPG Highway, 18 MPG City, EPA.*

'76 Chevelle. A size whose time has come.

* = WITH 250 CID 6 (105 HP)
20 HWY., 14 CITY
WITH 305 CID V8 (new, 140 HP)

(454 CID V8 DISCONT'D.)

MALIBU CLASSIC

$5185. (LANDAU)

MALIBU REG. $4746.

new GRILLES

76

(MAL. CLASSIC has OWN 4 HEADLIGHTS, MESH-TYPE GRILLE)

FINAL S-3

(NO MORE TYPE 9-3)
new GRILLES, FEWER ENG. CHOICES

77

250 CID 6 (110 HP)
305 CID V8 (145 HP)
350 CID V8 (170 HP)

Smart, complete, mid-size Chevelle.

COUPE (28793 BLT.)

$5466. (WEST)

MALIBU WAGON (ABOVE) $4734. UP

MALIBU CLASSIC

(50592 BLT.)

$5065. UP
$5651. (WEST)

DASH ('76 SIMILAR)

MALIBU

$3885.

(MALIBU CLASSIC)

SEDAN (76776 BLT.)

(illustr. LARGE SIDE MIRROR IS OPTIONAL.)

TAIL-LT. DETAILS

$4475. UP
WEST, $5327.

CHEVELLE 76~77

CHEVELLE

TOTAL 1978 PRODUCTION = 358,366

(NOW KNOWN AS **CHEVY MALIBU**)

MALIBU WAGON CLASSIC

EST. $6221.

MPG 29 HWY. 21 EPA WITH 200 CID V6

23 HWY., 16 EPA 231 CID V6

$6025.

$5543.

95 TO 170 HP

MALIBU COUPE

NEW-SIZE 78 (RESTYLED)

new SHORTER 108" WB

DASH (MALIBU CLASSIC)

MALIBU, MALIBU CLASSIC

'SPEC. INSTRUMENTATION PKG. has SMALL ROUND GAUGES.)

NOW SHARE GRILLE, BUT MAL. CLASSIC has CHROME → TRIM AROUND WINDOWS, ETC.

new 200, 231 CID V6s (305, 350 CID V8s ALSO)

" SEE WHAT'S NEW TODAY IN A CHEVROLET. "

1978

5902.

(22) EPA estimated MPG / (28) Highway estimate

"A FRESH NEW SLICE OF APPLE PIE"

$5215. up $6512. (WEST)

(104,222 CLAS. SEDANS)

MALIBU CLASSIC

(WAGONS, COUPES ALSO AVAIL.)
(DASH LIKE '78, BUT WITH "Malibu Classic" LETTERING AT RT.)
(new 267 CID V8 ADDED)

79 new GRILLE (59674 MALIBU SEDANS)

MALIBU 4-D SEDAN $4915.

VALUE IS WHAT MAKES A MALIBU A CHEVROLET.

MAL. PRICED FROM $6543.

MPG: 20 EPA 26 HWY.

80 Malibu CLASSIC

new GRILLE TOTAL 1980 PRODUCTION = 278,348

$7063.

EXTERIOR COLORS

Beige | Black | Blue, Dark (Metallic) | Blue, Light (Metallic) | Camel, Light (Metallic) | Camel, Medium (Metallic) | Cinnabar | Claret (Metallic) | Claret, Dark (Metallic) | Gray | Green, Dark (Metallic) | Silver | White | Yellow

Vinyl roof colors available: White, gray, black, light blue, dark green, light camel and dark claret. Check your dealer for complete information on vinyl roof color availability. *Metallic

CUSTOM TWO-TONE COLORS AVAILABLE:

Black/ Lt. Camel*	Black/ Silver*	Lt. Blue*/ Med. Blue*	Lt. Camel*/ Beige	Lt. Camel*/ Med. Camel*	Dark Claret*/ Claret	Gray*/ Med. Gray*
Int. Colors: Black or Camel	Int. Colors: Black or Claret	Int. Color: Blue	Int. Color: Camel	Int. Color: Camel	Int. Colors: Camel or Claret	Int. Colors: Black or Claret

REAR

CHEVELLE 78~80

160

HIGH ENERGY IGNITION.
Standard on every Chevette,
Engine
4 CYL.

STD. 85 CID (52 HP)
OR

OPT. 97.6 CID (60 HP)
(OPT.)
97.6 CID (60 HP)

(1976 TO 1987)
Chevette
Chevrolet's new kind of American car.
(SOLD BY 6,030 CHEVROLET DEALERS)
New

CHEVETTE SCOOTER NAME ON COWL

SCOOTER INTERIOR

LOW~PRICED "SCOOTER" HAS NO BACK SEAT OR GLOVE BOX DOOR.

ALL HATCHBACKS

EPA rating
40 MPG highway
28 MPG city

$**2899**. UP

(9810 BLT.)

76 **Chevette Scooter.**

SCOOTER COLORS. Select from light blue, antique white, cream and light red.

INTERNATIONAL TAILLIGHTS.
It's the red, white, and amber combination found in most world-type cars. Outside—stop. Middle—signal. Inside—backup.

Chevette Woody Coupe.

155 x 80 - 13" TIRES
13~GAL. GAS TANK

94.3" WB

DELUXE DASH

TOTAL 1976 PROD. 187,817

77

new 57 HP (85 CID ENG.) (OPT. 63 HP 97.6 CID)

('76)

RALLY SPORT PKG.

('77)

Bright and happy. That's Sandpiper with the special Custom Interior that features richly patterned "Reef" cloth-and-vinyl upholstery in tones of Yellow, Cream and Gold. Carpeting, instrument panel and seat belts are Yellow Gold. Also included: deluxe door trim, wood-grain vinyl accents, sport steering wheel, day-night rearview mirror, carpeted cargo area and added acoustical insulation.

sandpiper

Shown below is Sandpiper's special interior trim.

new SANDPIPER PKG. OPT.

ZJX 362

$**2999**. UP

TOTAL 1977 PROD.: 133,469

BUMPER RUB STRIPS AND GUARDS. Front and rear. Protect from minor dings. Add styling appeal.

JZX 187

(OPT.)

SPECIAL INSTRUMENTA-TION. For the well-informed driver. Has tachometer and voltmeter. Included with available Rally Sport equipment.

(OPT.)
SWING-OUT WINDOWS.
CHEVETTE 76~77

Chevette

STANDARD: Deluxe grille.

STANDARD: AM radio.

STANDARD: Console.

STANDARD: Swing-out rear windows.

STANDARD: Wheel trim rings.

STANDARD: Cigarette lighter.

STANDARD: Color-keyed instrument panel.

STANDARD: Glove compartment lock.

78 all new $3764.
4-DR.
(WEST, $3805.)
("97.3" WB)

(167,769 BLT.)

MANY *new* STANDARD FEATURES (ILLUSTR.)

(118,375 BLT.)

$3644.

2-Door

(WEST, $3695.)

STANDARD: Carpeting.

97.6 CID 4 (63 HP) NOW STANDARD

94.3" WB CONTINUES ON 2-DR.

STANDARD: Bumper rub strips.

STANDARD: Sport steering wheel.

STANDARD: Body side moldings.

STANDARD: Fully synchronized 4-Speed transmission.

'78 Chevette. A lot more car for a lot less money.*

$3149. SCOOTER ($3340. WEST) WITH FEWER FEATURES
(12829 BLT.)

(208,865 BLT.)

$4072.

('79)

BEST-SELLING SMALL CAR IN AMERICA.

79 *new* GRILLE

70 HP

$3437. SCOOTER (NO SIDE TRIM) $3724. WEST
(24099 BLT.)

($4220., WEST)

$3948.

$4100. WEST

1979 and 1980 DASH SIMILAR EXCEPT FOR MINOR CHANGES IN SPEC. INSTRUMENTATION PKG. (illustrated)

JEH-916

(136,145 BLT.)

70 HP (74 HP AVAIL.)

TOTAL 1980 PROD.= 451,161

2-TONE PAINT AVAIL.

$4057. and up

('80)

70 HP OR 74

80 *new* 4-PIECE WRAP-AROUND TAIL-LIGHTS

100377

CHEVROLET

A lot of car for the money.

$4756. (2-DR. and SCOOTER AVAIL.)

TACHOMETER. Constantly monitors engine speed.

*Except Scooter

CUSTOM TWO-TONE COLORS AVAILABLE:*

Black/ Lt. Camel	Black/ Silver	Lt. Blue/ Dk. Blue	Gray/ White	Red/ Silver

Recommended interior colors: (Other choices also available.)

Black/ Camel	Black/ Oyster	Blue/ Oyster	Oyster/ Black	Carmine/ Oyster

EXTERIOR COLORS

SS Beige	All Black	All Blue, Bright (Metallic)	SS Blue, Dark (Metallic)	SS Blue, Light (Metallic)	SS Camel, Light (Metallic)	SS Claret, Dark (Metallic)	All Gray	SS Green, Dark (Metallic)	All Red	All Red Orange	All Silver (Metallic)	All White	All Yellow, Bright

CHEVETTE 78~80

SS—Scooter and Standard

Chevrolet 6

CHEVROLET HAS MORE THAN 175 IMPORTANT MODERN FEATURES!

CHEVROLET
Special De Luxe Sport Sedan
Also available in Master De Luxe and Master 85 Series

$802.

DASH →

FIRST AGAIN!

SPECIAL DELUXE TOWN SEDAN (2-DR. COACH) (205,910 BLT.)

216½ CID 6 (85 HP) (SINCE '37)

$761.

Eye it—and you'll recognize the "Beauty Leader" for '40. *Try it*—and you'll agree we've put the wind on wheels. *Buy it*—and you'll thank your own good judgment for the choice!

MASTER 85 BUSINESS COUPE

(CLUB COUPES ALSO AVAIL.)   (25,734 BLT.) $659.

40 RESTYLED new 113" WB

NEW "ROYAL CLIPPER" STYLING • BIGGER INSIDE AND OUTSIDE • LONGEST OF ALL LOWEST-PRICED CARS—Measuring 181 inches from front of grille to rear of body • NEW FULL-VISION, BODIES BY FISHER • NEW EXCLUSIVE VACUUM-POWER SHIFT • "THE RIDE ROYAL"—Chevrolet's Perfected Knee-Action Riding System* • SUPER-SILENT VALVE-IN-HEAD ENGINE • PERFECTED HYDRAULIC BRAKES • ALL-SILENT SYNCRO-MESH TRANSMISSION • LARGER TIPTOE-MATIC CLUTCH • NEW SEALED BEAM HEADLIGHTS WITH SEPARATE PARKING LIGHTS • IMPROVED SHOCK-PROOF STEERING* • NEW CRYSTAL-CLEAR SAFETY PLATE GLASS • STABILIZED FRONT-END CONSTRUCTION • FOUR-WAY LUBRICA-TION • HIGH-OUTPUT GENERATOR WITH VOLTAGE AND CURRENT CONTROL • BODIES AND SHEET METAL COMPLETELY RUST-PROOFED • ILLUMINATED LUGGAGE COM-PARTMENT • BOX-GIRDER CHASSIS FRAME • NO DRAFT VENTILATION

*On Special De Luxe and Master De Luxe Series

HUB CAP

$903. UP

(2804 BLT.)
This handsome new Chevrolet Station Wagon . . . seating eight passengers com-fortably, and available on either the Special De Luxe or Master 85 Chevrolet chassis . . . is the ideal carrier for general suburban use and for resort hotels, clubs and estates.

NEW A TOUCH OF THE BUTTON PUTS THE TOP UP OR DOWN

Convertible Cabriolet.
(11,820 BLT.)
$898.

Special De Luxe Cabriolet
Equipped with Automatic Top

40 CHEVROLET

CHEVROLET

$800.
(155,889 BLT.)

$769.
(17,602 BLT.)

Special De Luxe Business Coupe
Also available in the Master De Luxe Series

Special De Luxe Five-Passenger Coupe
Also available in the Master De Luxe Series

Special De Luxe Town Sedan
Also available in the Master De Luxe Series

(11,820 BLT.)   **$949.**

Special De Luxe Cabriolet
Equipped with Automatic Top

EYE IT ·· TRY IT ·· BUY IT!

new 116" WB (THROUGH '48)

41
RESTYLED

$810.
228,458 BLT.
MOST POPULAR
MODEL OF 1941
CHEVROLET.

new 90 HP (THROUGH '49)

FOG LIGHTS
OPTIONAL

AG MASTER DLX. **$795.**

AH SPECIAL
DELUXE
$851.

4-DR. SPORT SEDAN
(208,199 TOTAL AG, AH BLT.)

HEADLTS. SUNKEN FURTHER INTO FENDERS

DASH
(SPEC. DLX.)

HEAVIER
PCS. IN
GRILLE

41 CHEVROLET

The Finest CHEVROLET

Of All Time

3 new MODEL SERIES:
BG STYLEMASTER
BH FLEETMASTER
BH FLEETLINE (w. 3 HORIZ. CHROME STRIPS ON FENDERS)

The instrument panel has new color treatment

CARS BLT. SEPT. TO DEC., 1941 have CHROME GRILLES and TRIM.

PRICE RANGE:
$760. ~ 1095.

The Fleetline Sportsmaster, introduced last March, is a companion model to the Aerosedan

(14,530 BLT.)
$920.

new "FADEAWAY FRONT FENDERS BLEND INTO DOOR.

new GRILLES 42

NEW CHEVROLET Fleetline SPORTSMASTER

JANUARY, 1942: "BLACKOUT" MODELS have PAINTED GRILLES and TRIM, TO CONSERVE CHROME.

IT PAYS TO BUY THE LEADER AND GET THE LEADING BUY

FLEETMASTER SPORT SEDAN (31,441 BLT.)
$895.

FASTBACK "AERO~SEDAN"

$880.

THIS "BLACK~OUT" MODEL ONE OF THOSE HELD IN STORAGE IN '42 AND SOLD AS A "1943."

(61,885 BLT.)

FOR THE SERVICE OF AMERICA

CHEVROLET AIDS NATIONAL DEFENSE

MAKING MILITARY TRUCKS

MAKING AIRPLANE ENGINES

MAKING 75-MM. SHELLS

TRAINING MAINTENANCE OFFICERS

42 CHEVROLET

WHY PAY MORE? WHY ACCEPT LESS?

CHEVROLET

(SINCE 1912)

A DIVISION OF GENERAL MOTORS CORP.

90 H.P.

6-CYL. (216½ CID) ON ALL 1937 TO 1949 CHEVROLETS and ON 1950 TO 1952 W/O POWERGLIDE AUTO. TRANS.) (CARS)

DK "FLEETMASTER" has CHROME TRIM AROUND WINDOW MOULDINGS

SPORT SEDAN (73,746 BLT.) $1280.

46

(CHEVROLET TRUCKS ALSO AVAILABLE)

TOTAL '46 PROD. = 398,028

FASTBACK ONLY ON THIS "AERO" MODEL.

DK "FLEETLINE" AEROSEDAN (2-DR.) (57,932 BLT.) $1249.

'46 MEDALLION

HORIZONTAL CHROME STRIPS ON FLEETLINE FENDERS

NEW POSTWAR GRILLE

DJ "STYLEMASTER" NO CHROME TRIM AROUND WINDOW MOULDINGS.

SPORT SEDAN (75,349 BLT.) $1205.

PRICE RANGE: $1098. (BUSINESS COUPE, DJ) TO $1712. (STATION WAGON, DK, w. WOODEN BODY)

166

CHEVROLET

FLEETMASTER SPORT SEDAN $1345.

FLEETLINE AERO $1313.

FLEETLINE SPORTMASTER SED. $1371.

FLEETMASTER STATION WAGON (4-DOOR, 8-PASS.) $1893.

EJ, EK
47
new GRILLE has PROTRUDING CENTER SECTION

new MEDALLION

THIS DELCO STEERING-COLUMN RADIO CONTROL BOX IS **RARE!** MOST HAVE RADIO CONTROLS ON LOWER SECTION OF **DASH**.

FLEETMASTER CONVT. $1628.

	PRODUCTION
EJ STYLEMASTER	
4 DR. SPORT SEDAN	42,571
2 DR. TOWN SEDAN	88,534
SPORT (CLUB) COUPE	34,513
BUSINESS COUPE	27,403
EK FLEETMASTER	
4 DR. SPORT SEDAN	91,440
2 DR. TOWN SEDAN	80,128
SPORT (CLUB) COUPE	59,661
CONVERTIBLE	28,443
STATION WAGON (8-PASS.)	4912
EK FLEETLINE	
4 DR. SPORTMASTER SEDAN	54,531
2 DR. AERO SEDAN (FASTBACK)	159,407

$1439.

DASH →

1948 CHEVROLET "FLEETMASTER" Four Door Sedan
(93,142 BLT.)

48
FJ, FK

← USUAL LOCATION OF RADIO

FJ STYLEMASTER 2-DR. TOWN SEDAN $1313.

(70,228 BLT.)

new "T"-SHAPED PIECE ADDED AT CENTER OF GRILLE

2144 FK FLEETLINE AERO (211,861 BLT.) $1434.

PRICE RANGE : $1244. TO $2013.
90 HP (1941 THROUGH 1949) @3300 RPM

OFFICIAL PACE CAR AT 1948 INDIANAPOLIS 500 RACE

167

CHEVROLET

STYLELINE

2134 CVT. $1857. (32,392 BLT.)

2152 2-DR.

FLEETLINE

new FASTBACK 4-DR. (2153)

METAL-BODIED WAGON

PRICES START AT $1339.

(STYLELINE SPEC. BUS. CPE.)

GJ, GK

49

TOTALLY RESTYLED

GJ = SPECIAL (1500 SERIES)
GK = DE LUXE (2100 SER.)

1949 TRUNK LID _has_ SMALL "T" HANDLE _which_ TURNS.

2103 4-DR. SPORT SEDAN

2102 2-DR. TOWN SEDAN

STYLELINE

2124 SPORT CPE.

VERTICAL PIECES IN LOWER HALF OF GRILLE

new SHORTER 115" WB (THROUGH '57)

1949 HUBCAP _has_ RED CENTER.

6.70 x 15

new DASH

all-new INTERIOR (LEFT AND RIGHT VIEWS)

new PONTOON-STYLE REAR FENDERS

DLX. MODELS _have_ CHROME AROUND WINDOWS _and_ ON FRONT FENDERS

CHROME (DLX.) BLACK RUBBER (SPEC.)

2 VARIETIES OF STATION WAGON MODELS AVAILABLE (4 DR.)
#2109 (WOOD BODY) (3342 BLT.) ('49 ONLY)
OR 2119 (STEEL ") (6006 BLT.) ('49 ON)
($2267. FOR EITHER ONE)

DASH

CHEVROLET

$1741. (76,662 BLT.)

2154
new "Bel-Air" 2-DR. HARDTOP
has WIDE BACKLIGHT →

DASH

1950 TRUNK LID has new
RE-DESIGNED HANDLE.

$1529. ↘

HJ, HK
50

TOTAL
1950 PRODUCTION:
1,498,590
new AUTOMATIC
TRANSMISSION
AVAILABLE

First low-priced car
with POWER*Glide* No-Shift driving *

FEWER VERTICAL PCS.
IN 1950 GRILLE.

HJ = SPECIAL
HK = DE LUXE
2103 STYLELINE DLX.
SPT. SEDAN (316,412 BLT.)
(BEST-SELLING MODEL)

PRICE RANGE:
$1329. TO $1994.

* = POWERGLIDE
SOMEWHAT LIKE BUICK'S
"DYNAFLOW." (NOT
INCLUDED IN
ABOVE PRICES)

FLEETLINE DELUXE
#2152 2-DR. SEDAN
(189,509 BLT.)

STYLELINE DLX.
BACK SEAT (4-DR.)

$1482.
FOR EITHER →

The Styleline De Luxe 2-Door Sedan
(248,567 BLT.)

1950 HUBCAP has
YELLOW CENTER.

CHEVROLET

MODEL 2154

BEL AIR
H/T (103, 356 BLT.)
$1914.

"See the U.S.A. in your Chevrolet..."

$1629.

1500 SERIES SPEC. STYLELINE
PRICES START AT
$1460.

STYLELN. DLX.
2102 2-DR.
(262,933 BLT.)

new GRILLE JJ, JK
and SIDE TRIM
51

FLEETLINE DLX.
2152 2-DR.
(131,910 BLT.)
$1629.

DE LUXE

Chevrolet

MODEL 2103 4-DR.
STYLELINE DLX.
(380,270 BLT.)
$1680.

TOTAL 1951 PROD.: 1,229,986

NEW Safety-Sight Instrument Panel

INTERIOR

NEW Modern-Mode Interiors

170

CHEVROLET

$1620.

$1707.

#1524 STYLELINE SPECIAL SPORT CPE. IS SCARCE, WITH ONLY 8906 BLT. →

(37,164 BLT.)

2-DR. ONLY

STYLELINE SPECIAL (HAS MINIMUM OF CHROME TRIM)

FLEETLINE DLX. (NO MORE FLEETLN. SPECIAL OR 4-DRS.)

NEW

26 Exterior Colors and two-tone color combinations to choose from.

New Softer, Smoother Ride with new and improved shock absorber action.

Improved Carburetion with Automatic Choke in Powerglide models.

New Centerpoise Power is smoother — "screens out" engine vibration.

Color-Matched Two-Tone Interiors bring new beauty to De Luxe models.

52

KJ, SPECIAL. KK DELUXE

STYLELINE DE LUXE 2-DR.

$1707.

(215,417 BLT.)

new 5 RIDGES RUN DOWN CENTER HORIZ. MEMBER OF GRILLE.

new MEDALLION

$1519. TO $2281.
PRICE RANGE

(2 VIEWS)

$1726.

STYLELINE DE LUXE SPORT COUPE (ABOVE)
(36,954 BLT.)

$1992.

BEL AIR (IN STYLELINE DLX. SERIES) H/T (74,634 BLT.)

TOTAL 1952 PRODUCTION: 818,142

1952 IS FINAL YEAR FOR STYLELINE and FLEETLINE MODEL NAMES.

CHEVROLET

CLUB CPE. **$1620.** BUS. CPE. **$1524.**

150

150 HAS NO SIDE CHROME

210 HAS SINGLE SIDE CHROME STRIP

210 2-DR.

$1707.

ABOVE: 210 SEDAN (IN SAN FRANCISCO, CALIF.)

(53) (TOTALLY RESTYLED)

FIRST 1-PC. WINDSHIELD ON A CHEVROLET SINCE 1935! BEL AIR IS NEW TOP-OF-LINE SERIES.

$2010.

"Handyman" (two of them) 6-PASS. 150 station wagons 210

$1874.

BEL AIR SEDAN (INTERIOR)

H/T

$2051.

$2123.

235 CID ENGINE (THROUGH '62, ON 6-CYL.) 108 OR 115 HP @ 3600 RPM)

BEL AIR (note EXTRA TRIM and CONTRASTING COLOR STRIP on REAR FENDER.)

$2175.

$2273.

WITH IMITATION WOODGRAIN TRIM

"Townsman" 8-PASS.

DASH

150 SPECIAL
1502 2 DR. SED. (79,416)
1503 4 DR. " (54,207)
1504 BUSINESS CPE. (13,555)
1509 WAGON (22,408)
1524 CLUB COUPE (6993)

PRODUCTION

210 DELUXE
2102 2 DR. SED. (247,455)
2103 4 DR. " (332,497)
2109 HANDYMAN WAGON (18,258)
2119 TOWNSMAN 8-PASS. " (7988)
2124 CLUB CPE. (23,961)

2134 CONVERTIBLE (5617)
2154 H/T CPE. (14,045)
240 BEL AIR = 2402 2 DR. SED. (144,401)
2403 4 DR. " (247,284)
2434 CONVERTIBLE (24,047)
2454 H/T CPE. (99,028)

CHEVROLET 53

CHEVROLET

new MEDALLION
new TAIL-LIGHTS

54

5 VERTICAL GRILLE
PCS. INSTEAD OF 3

Push Button Window Controls*
Toe-Touch Power Brake Pedal*
Extra-Easy Power Steering*
Powerglide Automatic Transmission*
Push Button Door Latches
Push Button Door Locks (Keyless Locking)
Automatic Dome Light Switches†
Push Lever Heater Controls*
Push Button Radio Controls*
Pull Knob Light Switch
Push Button Glove Compartment Lock (Automatic Light†)
Finger-Touch Horn Blowing Ring†
Pull Knob Ventilation Controls
Key-Turn Starter (Automatic Choke)
Turn Knob Windshield Wiper Control (Push Button Washer*)
Toe-Touch Accelerator Treadle
Push Button Headlight Dimmer
Lever Action Direction Signal Control (Automatic Return)*
Push Button Automatic Seat Adjustment Control*

Advanced Chevrolet Engineering brings
CYBERNETIC CHEVROLET
(Cybernetic = Automatic Control)

$1782.

210 DELRAY COUPE 2124
(66,403 BLT.)

$1884.

BEL
AIR

2403
BEL AIR SEDAN
(248,750 BLT.)

115 HP @ 3700 RPM
OR 125 HP @ 4000 RPM

new
OBLONG
PARKING LIGHTS

PRICE RANGE = $1539. TO $2283.
"150" 2-DR., 3-PASS.   "240" BEL AIR
UTILITY SEDAN   TOWNSMAN 8-PASS.
(10,770 BLT.)   (8156 BLT.)

DASH

CHEVROLET 54

CHEVROLET

185,562
BEL AIR H/Ts
BLT.

150 UTILITY SED.
(3-PASS.)
(11,196 BLT.)
$1593.
#1512

"ONE-FIFTY" HANDYMAN
$2030.
(17,936
BLT.)
#1529

BEL
AIR

$2206.

#2103
$1819.
(317,724 BLT.)
THE "TWO-TEN" 4-DOOR SEDAN in Skyline Blue.

(ABOVE)
210
HANDYMAN
(28,918
BLT.)
$2079.

(TOTALLY
RESTYLED)

55

new V-8

(1ST CHEVROLET V8
SINCE 1918!)

(ABOVE) BEL AIR CVT.
(41,292 BLT.)

(82,303
BLT.) #2109

210
"TOWNSMAN" WAGON
$2127.

A = GAS GAUGE   C = WATER TEMP.

WITH CONVENTIONAL TRANSMISSION

265 CID V8   162 HP @
4400 RPM, 170 HP,
OR 180 HP @ 4600 RPM

235½ CID 6
123 HP @ 3800 RPM OR
136 HP @ 4200 RPM

DASH

REVERSE SECOND
NEUTRAL
FIRST
(LOW)   THIRD
(HIGH)
CLUTCH
PEDAL

2409
$2262.

THE BEL AIR BEAUVILLE
(24,313 BLT.)

new "NOMAD"
2-DR. WAGON

(CHROME STRIPS
RUNNING DOWN
TAILGATE.)

(8386
BLT.)

CVT. IS
PACE CAR AT
1955 INDY 500 RACE

$2472. (6)

174

CHEVROLET

1529
THE "ONE-FIFTY" HANDYMAN
2 doors, 6 passengers, versatile and thrifty..
(13,487 BLT.)
$2171.

56

2129
THE "TWO-TEN" HANDYMAN
2 doors, 6 passengers, all-vinyl interior.

2119
THE "TWO-TEN" BEAUVILLE
4 doors, 9 passengers.

2109
THE "TWO-TEN" TOWNSMAN
4 doors, 6 passengers, loads of cargo space.

BEL AIR 4-DOOR HARDTOP and interior

AIR COND. DETAIL

(103,602 BLT.)
MODEL 2413
$2329.

Now in the low price field...

All components are located "up front" ... out of sight and out of the way! Harrison air conditioning is available on four great GM cars—Chevrolet, Pontiac, Oldsmobile and Buick.

AIR CONDITIONING!

2419
BEL AIR BEAUVILLE 9-PASS. WAGON (13,279 BLT.)
$2482.

new SMALL ROUND LENSES IN TAIL-LIGHTS →

$1912.
210

AA·1956

2403
$2068.
BEL AIR SEDAN
(269,798 BLT.)

2102 2-DR. SID.
(205,545 BLT.)

CORVETTE

2429
NOMAD

new FULL-WIDTH GRILLE

BEL AIR 2-DR. **2402**
(104,849 BLT.)
$2025.

235½ CID 6 has new 140 HP

265 CID V8 AVAIL. WITH 162, 170, 205 OR 225 HP

6.70 x 15 TIRES

CHEVROLET

PRICES
START AT
$1885.
(150 2-DR. UTIL. SED.)

150

210

#1503 SEDAN   (52,266 BLT.)

$2048.

1957 IS 3RD AND FINAL YEAR
THAT THE NOMAD IS A
SUPER-DELUXE
2-DOOR
SPORT
WAGON.

$2757. (6)

#2429   (6103 BLT.)

NOMAD
and BEL AIR
have new
ANODIZED REAR
FENDER PANEL.

NEW TRIPLE-TURBINE TURBOGLIDE*

It's the last word in automatic drives. Super-smooth—
and there's even a HILL RETARDER position on the
selector, for safer control on the steepest down grades!

57

#2403
4-DR. SED.
(254,331
BLT.)

$2290.

BEL AIR   (27,375 BLT.)

$2580.

4-DOOR
WAGON
(#2409 "TOWNSMAN")

new
GRILLE
COMBINED
with
BUMPER

2454

$2299.   2-DR. H/T   (166,426 BLT.)

DASH

HEADLIGHT-HOOD AIR VENTS

COMMAND POST CONTROL PANEL

new
7.50 x 14
TIRES

ENGINES = 235½ CID 6 has 140 HP.
265 CID V8 has 162 HP.
new 283 CID V8 ALSO,
AVAILABLE WITH 185,
245, 250, 270 OR 283 HP.

new
TAILFINS
and ARCHED
TAIL LIGHTS

4-DR.
H/T
SPORT
SEDAN

$2464.   2413   (137,672 BLT.)

CHEVROLET

NOMAD 6-PASS. 4-DR.

DASH

BEL AIR

$2571. and up

new 117½" WB (1958 ONLY)

TOTALLY RESTYLED

58

BISCAYNE

235 CID 6 has 145 HP @ 4200 RPM

4-DR., 6 OR 9-PASS. BROOKWOOD

2-DR. 6-PASS. YEOMAN

#1191 (6 CYL.) YEOMAN IS LOWEST-PRICED CHEV. WAGON, AT $2413.

CROSS-SECTION OF "TURBO THRUST" V8 ENGINE

283 OR 348 CID V8s (TO '62) (185 TO 280 HP)

new MODEL SERIES IN 1958
DELRAY = $2013. UP
BISCAYNE = 2236. UP
BEL AIR and
IMPALA =
$2386. TO
2841.

IMPALA (new)

#1867 CVT. $2841.

IMPALA DASH

#1847 H/T $2693.

new WAGON TAILGATE

IMPALAS have 6 REAR LIGHTS, AND EXTRA "AIR SCOOP" DECORATIONS.

CHEVROLET

1—*Biscayne Utility Sedan.* Chevy's prices start right here—a handy, handsome 2-door with 31 cu. ft. of cargo space behind front seat.

2—*Brookwood 2-Door,* Chevy's lowest priced wagon, is as dutiful as it is beautiful. Seats 6, holds up to 92 cu. ft. of cargo.

3—*Impala 4-Door,* most elegant family sedan in the line, makes you wonder why anyone would want a car that costs more.

4—*El Camino* combines stunning passenger car styling with the load space of a pickup. Good looks never carried so much weight!

5—*Impala Convertible.* Chevy's got a special formula for carefree top-down fun.

6—*Biscayne 2-Door.* This beauty's the lowest priced 6-passenger Chevy you can buy!

7—*Nomad 4-Door,* 6-passenger station wagon—finest of Chevrolet's 5 wonderful wagons.

8—*Bel Air 4-Door.* As luxurious as it looks, yet priced just above Chevy's thriftiest sedans.

9—*Brookwood 4-Door,* Chevy's lowest priced 4-door wagon seats 6, holds 92 cu. ft. of cargo with rear seat down.

2-DR. BROOKWOOD
(18800 BLT.~V8)
(6 CYL. AVAIL.)

135 TO 315 HP

10—*Bel Air 2-Door,* distinctively styled inside and out, carries a price tag just a notch above Chevy's thriftiest 2-door sedan.

11—*Impala Sport Sedan.* Here's a 4-door hardtop with the kind of looks and luxury you'd expect only on the most expensive makes.

12—*Kingswood 4-Door,* 9-passenger station wagon, offers rear-facing third seat and power-operated rear window at no extra cost.

13—*Impala Sport Coupe.* It's one of Chevy's full series of elegant Impalas for '59. And you won't find a handsomer hardtop anywhere!

14—*Parkwood 4-Door,* 6-passenger station wagon, distinctively trimmed inside and out, priced a shade above the thrifty Brookwoods.

15—*Bel Air Sport Sedan.* It's Chevy's lowest priced hardtop—and it makes beautiful sense!

16—*Corvette.* Take the wheel of America's only authentic sports car and treat yourself to the snappiest, happiest driving you've known.

17—*Biscayne 4-Door,* thriftiest 4-door sedan in the line, is another big reason

PRICE RANGE $2160. TO $3009.

BEL AIR
$2440. and up

$2891. and up

NOMAD 4-DR., 6-PASS. WAGON

HUGE new TAIL-LIGHTS

59 (TOTALLY RESTYLED)

BIG "GULL WING" REAR DECK IS UNIQUE!

1959

GENERATOR AND OIL PRESSURE INDICATOR LIGHTS
TEMPERATURE GAUGE
SPEEDOMETER
BRIGHT BEAM INDICATOR
FUEL GAUGE
CLOCK
ODOMETER
BRAKE SIGNAL LIGHT
LIGHT SWITCH
WINDSHIELD WIPER SWITCH
RIGHT AND LEFT TURN SIGNALS
HEATER CONTROL
IGNITION SWITCH

NEW INSTRUMENT PANEL

#1737 (6)
1837 (V8)

IMPALA SPORT COUPE (H/T)
$2599. (6) $2717. (V8)

(TOTAL 1959 PROD. 1,462,140)

new 119" WHEELBASE (THROUGH 1970)

CHEVROLET 59

178

CHEVROLET

BISCAYNE
(NO SIDE CHROME)

NOMAD

KINGSWOOD

60

PRICE RANGE: $2230. TO $2996.

BEL AIR

BEL AIR

#1511
2 DR.
SEDAN
$2384.

new GRILLE

#1737
IMPALA
SPORT CPE.

$2597.

Impala 4-Door Sport Sedan

"GULL-WING"
REAR STYLING
MODIFIED.
new ROUND
TAIL LIGHTS and
BACKUP LIGHTS.

DASH

#1739 SPORT SEDAN
4 DR. H/T $2662. UP

ENGINES = 235½ CID 6 (135 HP)
283 CID V8 (170 HP)
348 CID V8 (250 OR 335 HP)

CHEVROLET
$2316. (6)

BROOKWOOD
$2653. UP

$2230. UP

BISCAYNE

NOMAD

PRODUCTION:
1,201,811

135 TO 360 HP
new 409 CID V8
JOINS OTHER
ENGINES

$3099. 9-PASS. V8.

new ROOFLINE
(SPT. CPE.)

1961

(HT)
SPT.
CPE.

BISCAYNE
(PHOTO) $2423. (V8)

(ARTIST'S
CONCEPTION, TOP LEFT)

(RESTYLED)

61

$2230.
TO $3099.
PRICE RANGE

$2954. (V8)

(64,600
BLT.)
CVT.

BEL AIR

$2489. UP

IMPALA
$2590. (6)

new
ROOFLINE →

BEL AIR
SPT. SED.

$2554. UP

1961

IMPALA
H/T

$2597.
(6)

INSTRUMENT PANEL

LIGHT CONTROL
SWITCH

CIGARETTE LIGHTER
AND ASH TRAY

RADIO CONTROLS

LEFT VENT
CONTROL

WIPER AND WASHER
CONTROL

HEATER
CONTROLS

RIGHT VENT
CONTROL

IGNITION
SWITCH

GLOVE BOX
AND LOCK

CHEVROLET

$2725./UP

BISCAYNE $2378.→

FINAL 235 CID 6 has 135 HP @ 4000 RPM

$2819./UP

BEL AIR SPT. CPE. ROOFLINE

DASH

$2510./UP

BEL AIR

$3026.

new GRILLE

M-1042

IMPALA

AG-1400

IMPALA has ALUMINIZED PANELING AROUND TAIL-LIGHTS.

OUTER-EDGE TAIL-LTS. DO NOT OPEN WITH TRUNK.

IMPALA

RESTYLED 62

CY 7144

(IMPALA I.D.)

JET-SMOOTH RIDE

IMPALA 4 DR. H/T

ENGINES (V8s)

283 CID V8 (170 HP)
new 327 CID V8 (250 OR 300 HP)
409 CID V8 (380 OR 409 HP)

1962 PROD.= 1,495,476

$2734. (6)
2841. (V8)

LIGHT CONTROL SWITCH   CIGARETTE LIGHTER AND ASH TRAY   RADIO CONTROLS

LEFT VENT CONTROL   WIPER AND WASHER CONTROL   HEATER CONTROLS   RIGHT VENT CONTROL   IGNITION SWITCH   GLOVE BOX AND LOCK

CONTROLS

62 CHEVROLET

181

CONTROLS

WIPER WASHER · IGNITION · VENT · HEATER · LIGHTER · RADIO · ASH TRAY · GLOVE BOX

1963 PROD. : 1,625,931

DASH

$2976. (6) — BISCAYNE

$2519. — BEL AIR

63

PRICE RANGE : $2558. TO $3417.

IMPALA SPORT SEDAN

$2732. (6) — $2839. (WITH V8)

note CONVERTIBLE-STYLE "CREASES" STAMPED INTO STEEL ROOF OF THIS IMPALA SPORT COUPE

new DIP IN MIDDLE OF DECK LID ON 1963 MODELS $2786.

new
230 CID 6 (140 HP @ 4400 RPM)
283 CID V8 (170 HP)
327 CID V8 (250 OR 300 HP)
409 CID V8 (340 OR 425 HP) @ 6000

#1847 H/T SPT. CPE. (V8) $2774.

BISCAYNE

$2417. UP

BISCAYNE

BISCAYNE

BISCAYNE 2-DR.

$2363.

$2590. (WEST)

new STRAIGHT-ACROSS DECK LID with CENTER RIDGE

BEL AIR

$2519. UP

BEL AIR 4-DR. SED.
#1569 (6)
1669 (V8)

64

RESTYLED

REAR DECK DETAILS (IMPALA)

1964 PRODUCTION: 1,420,304

PRICE RANGE = $2363. TO $3196.

283, 327, 409 CID V8
ENGINES, SAME
SIZES AS IN
'63   6 = 140 HP
V8s = 195, 250, 300,
340, 400 OR
425 HP

3.08 TO 4.56 GEAR RATIOS

THERE'S 5 IN **64** CHEVROLET

CHEVROLET • CHEVELLE • CHEVY II • CORVAIR • CORVETTE

C-1964

SPT. SEDAN 4-DR. H/T

$2742. UP

IMPALA

IMPALA SS

H/T

9-PASS. WAGON #1745 6 CYL.

$3073.

#1447 new IMPALA SS

$3185., (WEST COAST)

$2947. ELSEWHERE

new GRILLE

C-1964

IMPALA V8 CONVERT.

$3035. (SS, $3196.)

DASH

CHEVROLET

$2669.. 4 DOOR BISCAYNE

7.35 × 14 TIRES

$2519. UP

BEL AIR

(107, 700 BISCAYNE 6s; 37,600 BISCAYNE V8s)

(163,000 BEL AIR V8s; 107,800 6s)

$2742. (6)

IMPALA 4 DR. H/T

$2850. (V8)

IMPALA 3-SEAT WAGON

FY-1588

$3181.

8.25 × 14 TIRES ON WAGONS

803, 400 IMPALAS BLT. (6 or V8)

POPULARLY REFERRED TO AS THE "COKE BOTTLE" PROFILE

$2947.

#16637 IMPALA SS H/T

(243,100 IMPALA SS H/Ts and CVTS., 6 or V8)

PRICE RANGE = $2363. TO $3212.

65

(TOTALLY RESTYLED)

1965 PRODUCTION: 1, 821, 266

CONTROLS

VENT

LIGHTS

WIPER WASHER

IGNITION SWITCH

LIGHTER

ASH TRAY

RADIO

HEATER

GLOVE BOX

VENT

IMPALA SUPER SPORT

(WITH OPTIONAL EQUIPMENT)

243,100 IMPALA SS BLT. (H/T or CVT., 6 or V8)

AVAIL. with VINYL TOP COVERING

with SPORT WHEEL COVERS →

WEST COAST: $3210.,

184

Chevrolet

CHEVROLET

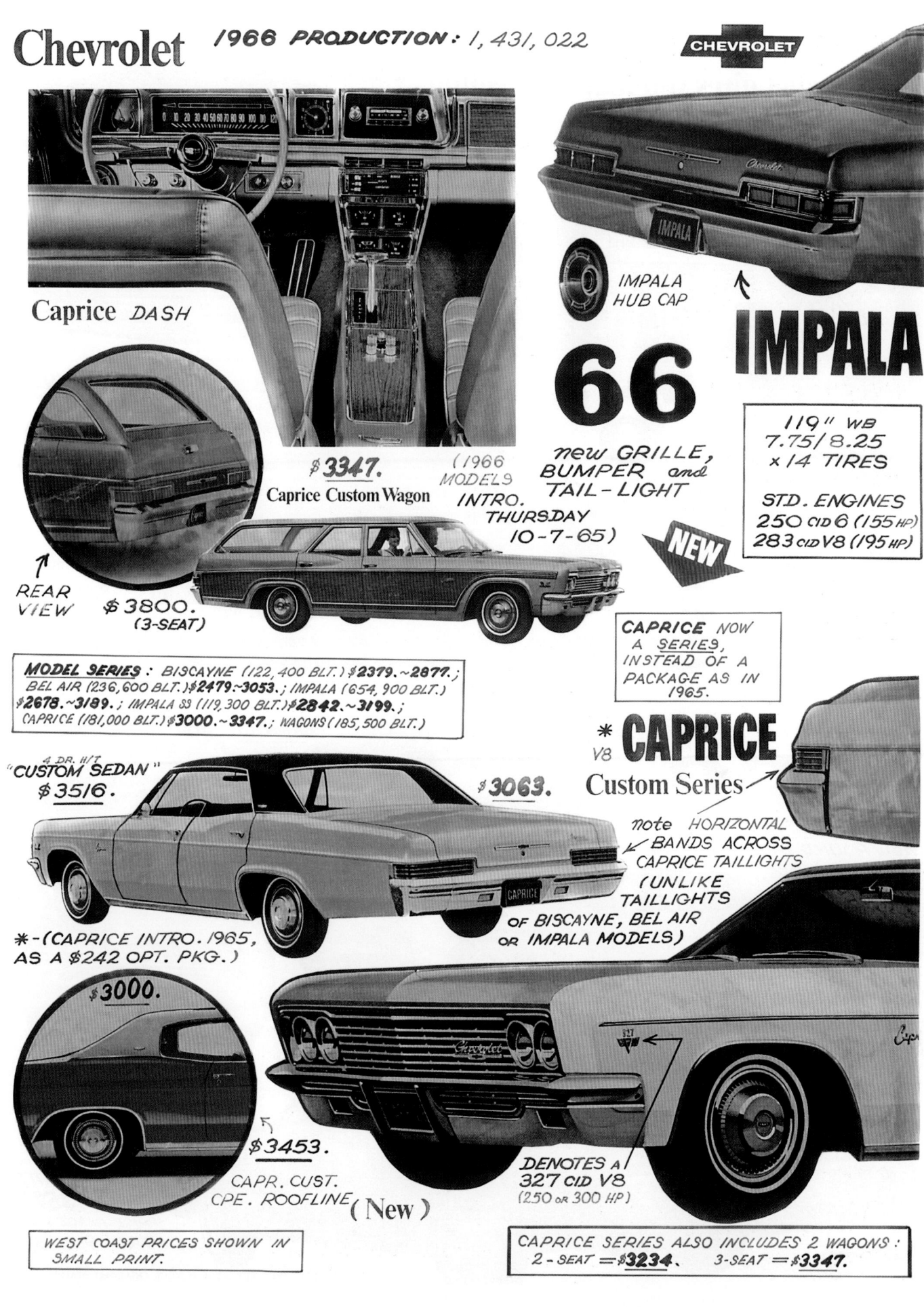

Caprice DASH

IMPALA HUB CAP

REAR VIEW

$3347.
Caprice Custom Wagon

$3800.
(3-SEAT)

66

(1966 MODELS INTRO. THURSDAY 10-7-65)

new GRILLE, BUMPER and TAIL-LIGHT

NEW

IMPALA

119" WB
7.75/8.25
x 14 TIRES

STD. ENGINES
250 CID 6 (155 HP)
283 CID V8 (195 HP)

MODEL SERIES : BISCAYNE (122,400 BLT.) **$2379.~2877.**;
BEL AIR (236,600 BLT.) **$2479.~3053.**; IMPALA (654,900 BLT.)
$2678.~3189.; IMPALA SS (119,300 BLT.) **$2842.~3199.**;
CAPRICE (181,000 BLT.) **$3000.~3347.**; WAGONS (185,500 BLT.)

CAPRICE NOW A SERIES, INSTEAD OF A PACKAGE AS IN 1965.

V8 **CAPRICE**
Custom Series

"CUSTOM SEDAN"
4 DR. H/T
$3516.

$3063.

note HORIZONTAL BANDS ACROSS CAPRICE TAILLIGHTS (UNLIKE TAILLIGHTS OF BISCAYNE, BEL AIR OR IMPALA MODELS)

*-(CAPRICE INTRO. 1965, AS A $242 OPT. PKG.)

$3000.

$3453.
CAPR. CUST.
CPE. ROOFLINE (New)

327
V8

DENOTES A 327 CID V8 (250 OR 300 HP)

WEST COAST PRICES SHOWN IN SMALL PRINT.

CAPRICE SERIES ALSO INCLUDES 2 WAGONS:
2-SEAT = **$3234.**   3-SEAT = **$3347.**

185

1967 CHEVROLET PRICE RANGE : $2442. ~ 3413.

'67 Chevrolet gives you that sure feeling

Biscayne **2484.**
$ 3036.
(WEST)

NO SIDE CHROME ON BISCAYNE

$2971. UP

WEST COAST, $3469. UP

(INTRO. 9-29 66)

Impala

STANDARD ENGINES
155-hp Turbo-Thrift 250 Six
195-hp Turbo-Fire 283 V8
EXTRA-COST OPTIONAL ENGINES
275-hp Turbo-Fire 427 V8
325-hp Turbo-Jet 396 V8
385-hp Turbo-Jet 427 V8

'67 IMPALA

67

new GRILLE

$3192. (WEST)

Impala SS $ 3350. (WEST COAST)

Impala Sport Coupe

Caprice Custom Sedan $3477. (WEST COAST)

$ 3130.

$ 2845. (V8)

TOTAL 1967 PRODUCTION : 1,201,700 (CALENDAR YEAR : 1,150,264)

LARGEST ENGINE (1967 and 1968) is 427 cid V8 (385 HP) (OPT.)

TOTAL 1968 PRODUCTION : 1,235,800 (CALENDAR YEAR : 1,217,255)

new GRILLE IS HORIZONTALLY BISECTED BY BUMPER CROSS BAR

68

new ROUND TAIL LTS. IN BUMPER

(WEST COAST) $3809. UP

CAPRICE

CUSTOM SEDAN $3621.

STD. 250 CID 6 (155 HP)
307 CID V8 (200 HP)
(327, 396, 427 CID V8s AVAIL.)

CUSTOM CPE.
formal $3021.

$3371. (WEST)

Impala coupes

$ 2968.

1968

note SMALL new SIDE LIGHTS

$2581. ~ 3570.
PRICE RANGE
(INTRO. 9-21-67)

Fastback SPORT CPE.

BE SMART! BE SURE! BUY NOW AT YOUR CHEVROLET DEALER'S.

CHEVROLET

ALL ENGINES
EXCEPT 427 CID V8s
USE REGULAR GAS.

GM
MARK OF EXCELLENCE

$2981. UP
$3427.
(WEST)

new
PLASTIC
GRILLE

119" WB

Impala

H/T $2927.

69
(INTRO. 9-26-68)
(RESTYLED)

new
KINGSWOOD
ESTATE
(3-SEAT)
$4019.

Caprice.

ENGINES:
250 CID 6 (155 HP); 327 CID V8 (235 HP);
350 CID V8 (255 OR 300 HP);
396 CID V8 (265 HP);
427 CID V8 (335 OR 390 HP)

$2645.~3678.
PRICE RANGE

"walk-in wagon"
has
2-WAY TAILGATE

wagon

327 CID
V8
AVAIL.

new CONCEALED
HEADLIGHTS

OPTIONAL
"LIQUID TIRE CHAIN"
TRACTION IMPROVER
SQUIRTS ONTO REAR
WHEELS AT THE
PUSH OF A BUTTON.

TOTAL 1969
PRODUCTION:
1,227,600

new
BROOKWOOD,
TOWNSMAN, KINGSWOOD
and KINGSWOOD ESTATE
WAGONS

note THE
FLARED
FENDERS

Caprice
$3294.
2. DR. H/T

(4-DR. H/T, WAGON
ALSO IN CAPRICE
SERIES)

Putting you first, keeps us first.

CHEVROLET 69

187

BROOKWOOD, TOWNSMAN, KINGSWOOD $3294.UP
KINGSWOOD ESTATE WAGONS
(FROM TOP, DOWN)
(119" WB)

2-ST. $4088.

On the move: The Chevrolet '70s.

Right Car. Right Price. Right Now.

KINGS. EST.

Impala

(7 Wagons MODELS)
3-ST. $4201.
(WEST)

(new MONTE CARLO IN SEPARATE SECTION.)

'70
(INTRO. 9-18-69)

$3886.

250 CID 6 (155 HP); 350 CID V8 (250 OR 300 HP); 400 CID V8 (265 HP); 454 CID V8 (345 OR 390 HP)

TOTAL 1970 PRODUCTION = 1,456,574

IMPALA CONV'T.

new V-GRILLE 119" WB

(9652 BLT.)
$3377.

Our big one: '70 Caprice

2-DR. CUST. H/T $3474. ($3815., WEST)

(LOWER-PRICED BISCAYNE and BEL-AIR 4 DR. SEDANS ALSO = $2787. UP)

IMPALA

REAR DETAILS

IMPALA CUSTOM H/T $3607. (WEST)

$3266.

CHEVROLET 70

BROOKWD.

Impala

(BISCAYNE 4-DR. SED. FR. $3885.)

(INTRO. 9-29-70)
STD. HP CUT (6-145) (V8-245)

$4239.

new GRILLES

Caprice.

CAPR. CUSTOM SED. 4-DR. H/T $4545.

TOTAL 1971 PROD. = 1,830,319

71 new 121½" WB

Caprice TYPE WITH MID-SIDE TRIM SPEAR (TYPE W/O, ABOVE RT.)

1971. You've changed. We've changed.

CAPRICE GRILLE DETAIL

Impala Custom Coupe (183,493 BLT.)

Impala Sport Coupe

(52692 BLT.)

FINE HORIZ PCS. IN IMPALA GRILLE

(FINAL BISCAYNE 4-DR. PRICED AT $3878.)

H/T Caprice Sedan

350 CID V8 HP CUT AGAIN, (TO 165)

(65513 BLT.) WITH 400 CID V8 (170 HP) CAPRICE

$3882.

Bel Air 4-Door Sedan (41888 BLT.)

72

125" WB ON WAGONS (SINCE '71)

$3969. UP

Brookwood Station Wagon (8150 BLT.)

(INTRO. 9-23-71)

(83400 BLT.)

Townsman Station Wagon (25149 BLT.)

FROM $4056. (WITH DISAPPEARING TAILGATE)

$4314. UP (55004 BLT.)

Kingswood Station Wagon

Kingswood Estate Wagon

TOTAL 1972 PROD. 2,420,564

CHEV. IN 1ST PLACE IN SALES (1ST TIME SINCE '69)

IMPALA DASH

CHEVROLET 71~72

189

CHEVROLET

LOWEST-PRICED IS NOW THE **BELAIR** 👉

$3247. UP

4-DR. SEDAN AT $4018 (WEST)

100 HP 250 CID 6 OR 350 CID V8

(41832 BLT.)

1973 Chevrolet. Building a better way to see the U.S.A.

IMPALA

73 NEW GRILLES

BELAIR

(20870 BLT.)

New
improved front bumper system that retracts on minor impact and hydraulically cushions the shock.

$4022. UP

The Bel Air Station Wagon has Chevrolet's practical Glide-Away tail-gate (with power-operated rear window) that disappears out of your way when you're loading or unloading. Or if you're trailering you needn't unhitch. Bel Air Station Wagons are available in either 2- or 3-seat models. (See our 1973 Wagon Catalog for details.)

($4196., WEST)

SPORT COUPE

Impala SEDAN (190.536 BLT.) $3752.

CAPRICE

$4345.

The Caprice Estate Wagon, with translucent woodgrain vinyl panels that let the body colors show through and a Glide-Away tailgate (with power rear window) that disappears. (See Wagon Catalog for complete details.)

CVT. NOW IN CAPRICE SERIES.

(7339 BLT.)

FROM $4382. ($4784. WEST)

(62504 BLT.)

IMPALA CUSTOM CPE. HAS INDENTED REAR WINDOW 👉

DASH

CAPRICE

OPT. WIRE WHEEL COVERS

IMPALA FRONT END

350 CID V8 CUT TO 145 HP. CAPRICE 400 CID V8 CUT TO 150 HP; 454 CID CUT TO 215 OR 245 HP G78 x 15 TIRES (L78 x 15, WAGONS)

$4082.

CAPRICE H/T

(77134 BLT.)

CHEVROLET 73

190

CHEVROLET

$4162. (50036 BLT.)

(BEL-AIR 4-DR. SED. PRICED AT $4473.)

CHEVROLET MAKES SENSE FOR AMERICA
Chevrolet

IMPALA SPT. CPE. $4675.
CUSTOM CPE. $4742. (WEST)

IMPALA

(76492 BLT.) IMPALA SPT. SED. $4728. (WEST)

$4215.

new GRILLE TOTALLY ABOVE BUMPER. new FRONT CORNER LIGHTS ADDED.

EXTERIOR COLORS

11 Antique White
13 Cosworth Silver
19 Tuxedo Black
24 Light Blue*
25 Medium Blue
29 Bright Blue*
29 Midnight Blue*
36 Aqua Blue*
40 Lime Yellow
44 Medium Green
46 Bright Green*
47 Medium Green*
49 Medium Dark Green
50 Cream Beige
51 Bright Yellow
53 Light Gold*
55 Sandstone
59 Golden Brown*
64 Silver*
66 Bronze*
67 Bright Orange
69 Dark Taupe*
74 Medium Red*
75 Medium Red *Metallic

CARPET COLORS

B–Black
D–Midnight Blue
E–Accent Blue
E–Accent Blue
G–Green
H–Dark Red
K–Gold
N–Neutral
R–Red
S–Saddle
T–Taupe
U–Russet *Accent carpet @ Vega only

IMPALA COUPES & SEDANS
UPHOLSTERY
BEL AIR SEDAN
IMPALA COUPES & SEDANS...CAPRICE ESTATE & IMPALA WAGONS
UPHOLSTERY

VINYL ROOF COVER COLORS
AA–White
BB–Black
DD–Blue
EE–Beige
FF–Brown
GG–Green
HH–Red
LL–Russet
WW–Taupe

Caprice Estate wagon

FROM $5313.

New Flip-Down seats (WAGON)

REAR
74

$4464. UP (9350 BLT.)

BEL AIR WAGON

BEL AIR SEDAN & WAGON
UPHOLSTERY
CAPRICE CLASSIC COUPE & SEDANS

(59484 BLT.) $4483.

Caprice

(4670 BLT.) $4745.

TOTAL 1974 PROD.= 2,333,839

$5258. (WEST)

Caprice Classic

CUST. CPE. $4996. (WEST)

note GIANT new RR. QUARTER WINDOW ON **Caprice Classic**

CHEVROLET 74

CHEVROLET

IMPALA

(FINAL CAPRICE CLASSIC CVT.)

FINAL
BEL-AIR
(15871 BLT.)
$4345.

BEL AIR 4-DOOR SEDAN

$5113.
(8349 BLT.)

IMPALA 4-DOOR
(9/330 BLT.) $4548.

LANDAU CPE. WITH
LARGE
QUARTER WINDOWS
STILL AVAILABLE

NEW CATALYTIC CONVERTER
(Standard, all '75 Chevrolet cars, and trucks
6.000 GVW and below.)

CAPRICE CLASSIC
SPORT SEDAN

NEW

Caprice Classic
$4819.

CHEVROLET
MAKES SENSE
FOR AMERICA
**Now that
makes sense**

(33715
BLT.)

75

Chevy Suburban

$4707.
UP
129"
WB

SHOWN
ONLY AS
EXAMPLE.
USUALLY
LISTED
WITH
TRUCKS.

**CAPRICE
ESTATE**

FROM
$5758.

CAPRICE/IMPALA/BEL AIR   **Chevrolet**

IMPALA TAIL LIGHTS

4190 ED

$4507.
(18265 BLT.)

EPA M.P.G.
13 CITY, 18 HWY.
(w. STD.
350-2 V8)

76 IMPALA
A

NO MID-
SIDE CHROME
STRIP.

(new) Impala **S**

SEDAN
$5068.
(WEST)

$5323.

INTERIOR

(CONT'D.
NEXT
PAGE)

CHEVROLET 75-B and 76

1976 DASH

CHEVROLET

↗ SIMILAR TO 1975 DASH BUT GRAIN CHANGED TO "ROSE~WOOD."

Caprice Classic instrument panel has conveniently located controls and easy-to-see instruments surrounded by tasteful accents.

76 B (CONT'D.)
Caprice Classic

(FINAL 4-DR. H/T) (55308 BLT.) $5078.

1976.Chevrolet makes room for America.

new SHORTER 116" WB

TOTAL 1977 PROD.= 2,543,153

REAR →

Impala

The 1977 Caprice Classic Sedan

$6427. (WEST)

CAPR. ESTATE **WAGON**

(56569 BLT.)

$5617. UP

ENGINES: 250 CID 6 (110 HP)
305 CID V8 (145 HP)
350 CID V8 (170 HP)

$5187. UP

New

SIZE

CAPRICE CLASSIC CPE. $5917. (WEST)
(62366 BLT.)

77

Caprice Classic.   22 mpg. hwy.   17 mpg. city

TOTALLY RESTYLED and DOWNSIZED

DELUXE DASH (CAPRICE)

STANDARD PANEL

20.2-cubic-foot trunk

REAR ←

CHEVROLET 76-B and 77

Now that's more like it.

193

CHEVROLET

305 CID V8 (145 HP)

SEE WHAT'S NEW TODAY IN A CHEVROLET.

IMPALA

DASH

$5208. UP (33990 BLT.)

$6012. UP

$6042. (WEST)

WAGON (CAPR. CLASSIC) (57742 BLT.)

78 (INTRO. THURS., 10-8-77)

new GRILLES

POWER SKY ROOF AVAIL. (above)

IMPALA

TOTAL 1978 PROD.= 2,375,436

EPA M.P.G. 17 CITY, 24 HWY. WITH 250 CID 6 (110 HP)

(203,837 BLT.)

$6460. (WEST)

CAPRICE CLASSIC

Impala

CAPR. CLSSC. (REAR) ('79)

new HORIZ. STRIPS ACROSS CORNER LTS.

Impala

new GRILLES **79**

2,284,749 = TOTAL 1979 PROD.

Caprice Classic

$6323. UP

SEDAN (203,017 BLT.)

$7324. (WEST)

America has driven it to the top.

CPE. FROM $5828.

$6829. UP

(26589 BLT.) (CPE.)

250 CID 6 (110 HP)

305 CID V8 CUT TO 130 HP

350 CID V8 (170 HP)

CAPRICE CLASSIC ESTATE WAGON (6894 IMPALA WAGONS ALSO BLT.)

(56261 BLT.)

$7754. UP (WEST)

$6800. UP CHEVROLET 78~79

116" WB (SINCE '77)

CHEVROLET

EST. RANGE*
450 CITY 650 HWY

WITH 25-GAL. FUEL TANK

FROM $7041.

IMPALA WAGON FR. $7526. (WEST)

(17990 BLT.)

18 26

EPA EST. MPG* HWY. ESTIMATE

WITH STD. 229 V6 ENG. (115 HP)

New engines.

IMPALA SPT. CPE. (10756 BLT.)

$6535. UP $7105. (WEST)

IMPALA $6650. UP

IMPALA SEDAN $7214. (WEST) (70801 BLT.)

new P205/75R×15 TIRES (P225 ON WAGONS)

TOTAL 1980 PROD. = 2,288,745

80 new GRILLES   new V6

CAPRICE CLASSIC LANDAU CPE. has BRIGHTWORK BAR EXTENDING UP OVER ROOF $7400. UP $7954. (WEST)

STD. 267 CID V8 (120 HP) 305 OR 350 CID AVAIL.

DASH (CAPRICE CLASSIC)

RICH WOODGRAIN EFFECTS

CAPRICE CLASSIC

SEDAN $7635. (WEST)

FROM $7369.   CAPR.   WEST, $8125. UP

ESTATE WAGON (23304 BLT.)

BOTH IMPALA AND CAPRICE CLASSIC GRILLES ARE **NEW**

BODY COLORS   (91208 BLT.)

We made it right for the '80s

85 GRAY · 84 CHARCOAL METALLIC · 80 BROWN METALLIC · 79 RED ORANGE · 77 CINNABAR · 76 DARK CLARET METALLIC · 75 CLARET METALLIC · 72 RED · 69 MEDIUM CAMEL METALLIC · 67 DARK BROWN METALLIC · 63 LIGHT CAMEL METALLIC · 59 BEIGE · 57 GOLD METALLIC · 51 BRIGHT YELLOW · 50 YELLOW · 44 DARK GREEN METALLIC · 40 LIME GREEN METALLIC · 29 DARK BLUE METALLIC · 24 BRIGHT BLUE METALLIC · 21 LIGHT BLUE METALLIC · 19 BLACK · 15 SILVER · 11 WHITE

SOME COLORS AVAILABLE ON CHEVROLET'S SUBSIDIARY BRANDS (EXCEPT CORVETTE)

CHEVROLET 80

195

(STARTS WITH 1980 MODEL)

CHEVROLET Citation
A whole new kind of compact car.
(REPLACES NOVA)

(FRONT WHEEL DRIVE)
TRANSVERSE ENGINE
104.9" WB
P185/80R x 13 TIRES

$5422. UP
(210,258 BLT.)

2-DR. HATCHBACK
$6427.
(STD. CPE = $5965.)
(WEST)
(42909 BLT.)

EPA MPG 24 CITY, 38 HWY. WITH

151 CID 4 (90 HP)   173 CID V6 (110 OR 115 HP) ALSO AVAIL.

$5552. UP   4-DR. HATCHBACK
$6293.
(WEST)
(ALSO KNOWN AS "CHEVY" CITATION.)

(458,033 BLT.)

STD. DASH

80
NEW
(INTRO. 4-19-79)

$5214. UP WEST, $6300.
Club Coupe.

(100,340 BLT.)

Custom Interior (ROUND GAUGES)

"THE FIRST CHEVY OF THE '80s"

SLIP STREAM STYLING

Full Wheel Covers.

X-11 SPORT PACKAGE - $500.

WITH SPECIAL PAINT JOB, P205/70R-13 TIRES

CHEVROLET CITATION

X-11 STEERING WHEEL

(X-11 CL. CPE. ALSO AVAIL.)

196

CHEVROLET Monte Carlo

(2-DR. H/Ts ONLY)

$3123.

(INTRO. 9~18~69)

$3464. (WEST)

70

116" WB **NEW**

V-8 ENGINES:
350 CID (250 HP)
350 CID (300
400   265
400   330 (130,657 BLT.)
454 CID (360 HP) (IN SS MODEL)

G78 × 15/B TIRES

IMITATION (VINYL)
CARPATHIAN BURLED ELM GRAIN
ON INSTRUMENT PANEL

DASH

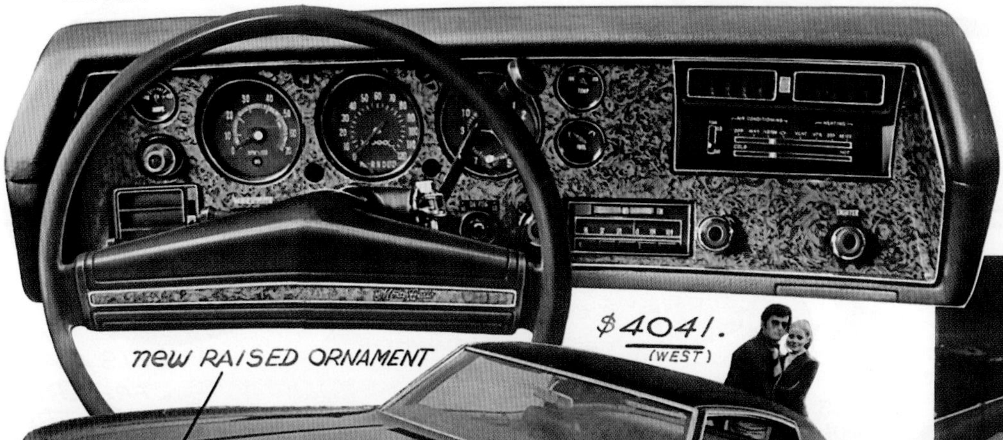

71

new GRILLE

new RAISED ORNAMENT

$4041. (WEST)

$3416.

(128,600 BLT.)

SAME 3 V8 SIZES
245, 270, 300 OR 365 HP

1971. You've changed.
We've changed.

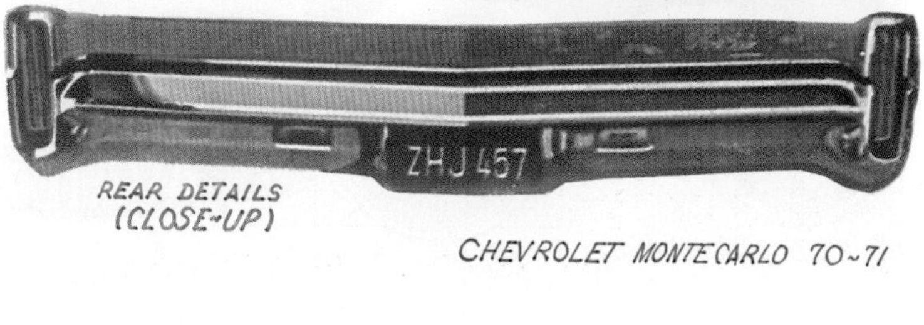

REAR DETAILS
(CLOSE-UP)

ZHJ 457

ZHJ 457

CHEVROLET MONTE CARLO 70~71

197

DASH

CHEVROLET MONTE CARLO

new GRILLE

72

$4009. (WEST)

STD. 350 CID V8 CUT TO 165 HP

$3362.

180,819 BLT.

STD. 350 CID V8 CUT TO 145 HP * *175 AVAIL.

new S and LANDAU COUPES JOIN STD. SPT. COUPE

new OPERA WINDOWS

$3415. UP

new DASH (RESTYLED)

290,693 BLT.

73

454 CID V8 OPTIONAL (245 HP)

3 CPE. MODELS AVAIL., FR. $3827. (WEST)

117 984

AVAILABLE ONLY ON S, LANDAU MODELS

"WIRE WHEEL" COVERS

TURBINE II

REAR WINDOW DE-FOGGER DUCTS

POWER DOOR LOCKS

AVAILABLE

SUN ROOF

CHEVROLET MONTE CARLO 72~73

CHEVROLET Monte Carlo

TURBINE II WHEEL

$4129. *Landau* (127,344 BLT.)

DASH

S OR LANDAU TYPES (BOTH ILLUSTR.)

$4858. (WEST)

new TAIL-LTS. **74** new GRILLE

$3885.

$4614. (WEST)

Monte Carlo S (184,873 BLT.) SIMULATED WIRE WHEEL COVER →

new GR70 x 15/B TIRES

CHEVROLET MAKES SENSE FOR AMERICA

LANDAU CPE. $5273. (WEST)

new TAIL-LTS.

75 new GRILLE

S COUPE $5003. (WEST) (148,529 BLT.)

$4519.

(110,380 BLT.)

RALLY WHEEL   DASH

new DLX. WHEEL COVER

22-gallon fuel tank. $4249.
unleaded fuel •

***California Emission Equipment required in California.*

Engine	Horse-power (NET)	Engine Usage	3-Speed Manual	Turbo Hydra-matic
350 2-barrel V8	145	Std.*	Std.	Avail.
350 4-barrel V8	155	Avail.** (IN CALIF. ONLY)	Std.	Avail.
400 4-barrel V8	175	Avail.***	Not Avail.	Req.
454 4-barrel V8	215	Avail.*	Not Avail.	Req.

CHEVROLET MONTE CARLO 74~75

*Not available in California.

199

Monte Carlo

When a car makes you feel good about its looks, that's style. When it makes you feel good about yourself, that's character.

'76

DASH
191,370 S COUPES

new GRILLE

w/o $4673. VINYL TOP $5218. (WEST)

DELUXE WH. COVER

Wire wheel covers.

Rally wheels.   Turbine II wheels. (Std. on Landau.)

WITH VINYL TOP → $5511. (WEST)

new TAIL-LIGHTS
new 305 CID V8 (140 HP) (161,902 BLT.) $4966.

LANDAU CPE.

224,327 S COUPES BLT. $4968.
Like you, it's an original.
w/o OPTIONAL VINYL TOP   S (STANDARD) $5539. (WEST)
(186,711 BLT.)
LANDAU CPE. W/VINYL TOP

305 CID (145 HP) V8, OR 350 CID (170 HP) V8

new TAIL-LIGHTS

$5869. (WEST) $5298.

RALLY WHEELS

1977 DASH IS SIMILAR IN MOST RESPECTS TO 1976 TYPE ILLUSTR.

'77

DELUXE WHEEL CVR.

GR 70 × 15 TIRES

new

SPORT WIRE WHEEL COVER   new GRILLE →

OPT. AIR COND.

INTERIORS →

CHEVROLET MONTE CARLO 76~77

200

CHEVROLET

Monte Carlo
$4785. UP

new 108" WB
78
RESTYLED

$5678. UP
LANDAU
CPE.
$6451.
(WEST)
(141,461 BLT.)

SPORT CPE. (216,730 BLT.)
$6086.
(WEST)

new 205/70R×14 TIRES

DASH

105 HP, 231 CID V-6 IS new STANDARD ENGINE. 305 CID V8 ALSO AVAIL. (145 HP)

**The Third Generation Monte Carlo.
A new dimension in affordable luxury.**

TOTAL 1978 PROD. = 358,191

WESTERN PRICES LISTED

DASH SIMILAR TO 1978
200/231 CID V6s (94/115 HP)
267/305 CID V8s STD. (125/160 HP) (350 CID V8 AVAIL.)

79
new FRONT and REAR CORNER LIGHT LENSES
(w. HORIZONTAL STRIPS)

T-TOP (OPT.)

RALLY WHEEL

(LANDAU CPE. $7561.)

SPORT CPE. $6711.

TOTAL '79 PROD. = 316,923

"OYSTER" UPHOLSTERY

with 55/45 split seat and center armrest shown in oyster

EXTERIOR COLORS: YELLOW, LIGHT / WHITE / SILVER / GREEN, MEDIUM (METALLIC) / GREEN, LIGHT / CARMINE, DARK (METALLIC) / CARMINE (METALLIC) / CAMEL (METALLIC) / BROWN, DARK (METALLIC) / BLUE, PASTEL / BLUE, LIGHT (METALLIC) / BLUE, DARK (METALLIC) / BLACK / BEIGE

Custom Two-Tone colors available:

Lt. Blue/ Med. Blue (Metallic)*	Camel (Metallic)/ Beige	Carmine/ Dk. Carmine (Metallic)	Med. Green (Metallic)/ Lt. Green	Silver/ Gray (Metallic)*	Silver/ Black
Int. Colors: Black, Blue or Oyster	**Int. Colors:** Black or Camel	**Int. Colors:** Black, Camel, Carmine or Oyster	**Int. Colors:** Black or Green	**Int. Colors:** Black, Carmine or Oyster	**Int. Colors:** Black, Carmine or Oyster

*Not available on Landau.

Vinyl roof colors available:
Black, light blue, light green, white, beige, dark carmine, silver. Check your dealer for complete information on vinyl roofs available.

CHEVROLET MONTE CARLO 78~79

201

CHEVROLET MONTE CARLO

80

WITH T-TOP AND 2-TONE PAINT OPTION (NOT AVAIL. ON LANDAU COUPE)

(116,580 SPORT COUPES)

new GRILLE has FEWER PIECES. 4 new RECTANGULAR HEADLIGHTS

LOW SIDE LIGHT REPLACES CORNER TYPE.

SPORT CPE. $7040. (WEST)

$6524. UP

AVAILABLE SPECIAL CUSTOM INTERIOR WITH 55/45 SPLIT BENCH SEAT

new STYLE OF RALLY WHEEL

new DASH

(32262 LANDAU CPES.)

LANDAU CPE. $6772. UP $7288. (WEST)

P-205/70R-14 TIRES STANDARD

115 HP, 229 CID V-6 IS new STD. ENG. (231 CID IN CALIFORNIA)

AVAIL. TURBO V6

267/305 CID V8s AVAIL. (120/155 HP)

CUSTOM TWO-TONE COLORS AVAILABLE

Light Camel Metallic	Light Blue Metallic	Black	Dark Claret Metallic	Dark Claret Metallic	Black	Gray
Beige	Dark Blue Metallic	Light Camel Metallic	Claret Metallic	Gray	Silver	White

Vinyl roof colors available for full roof and Landau roof covers
Black, Dark Claret,* Dark Green,* Gray, Light Blue,* Light Camel,* White.
Check your dealer for complete information on vinyl roof and Custom Two-Tone availability.   *Metallic

EXTERIOR COLORS

Beige · Black · Blue, Dark (Metallic) · Blue, Light (Metallic) · Camel, Light (Metallic) · Camel, Medium (Metallic) · Cinnabar · Claret (Metallic) · Claret, Dark (Metallic) · Gray · Green, Dark (Metallic) · Silver · White · Yellow

CHEVROLET MONTE CARLO 80

(1975~1980)

$3570. ('75)

Chevrolet
Chevrolet makes sense for America

Monza

('75)

NEW 75-76

97" WB 87 HP
4-CYL.(140 CID)
OR
2 V-8s)

POWER VENT SLOTS

(69238 BLT. '75)
(46735 " '76)

New Towne Coupe.

(TOWNE CPE.
INTRO. As '75½
SPRING, 1975.)

$3648.

(1975 ONLY)

THE NEW MONZA "S" HATCHBACK COUPE.
$3946 (9795 BLT.)

TROMPE L'OEIL WHEEL COVERS. That's French for "fool the eye." Which is what these standard wheel covers do beautifully. They look like expensive metal wheels but they're tough molded polycast.

$3953. ('75)

$4250.

18½-GAL. FUEL TANK

(57170 BLT. '75)
(34170 " '76)

2+2

Monza 2+2
COWL LETTERING

BR 78 × 13 TIRES

"V8 4.3 LITRE" PLAQUE DESIGNATES A 262½ CID V8 (110 HP) (125 HP, 305 CID V8 AVAIL. ALSO)

INTERIOR ('75)

CHEVROLET MONZA '75~'76

Chevrolet MONZA
DASH
TOWNE COUPE

76

Special gauge instrumentation, including tachometer, voltmeter, temperature, "Add Coolant" light and electric clock.

Chevrolet makes sense for America.

"PRADO VELOUR" CLOTH

Deluxe instrument panel. (Standard on 2+2 Hatchback; also, included with Cabriolet or Sport Equipment when ordered with Special Custom Interior.)

Special two-spoke steering wheel with wood-grain vinyl insert. Wheel, shroud and column color-keyed to interior.

New "stitched" instrument panel pad with added wood-grain vinyl ornamentation color-keyed to interior.

1976

EPA **35** HIGHWAY **24** MPG CITY

Towne Coupe
$3359 A small car and then some.

$3359.

"CABRIOLET STYLE" STILL AVAIL.

new PROFILE WITH LARGE REAR QUARTER WINDOWS (70 OR 84-HP VERSIONS OF 140 4 CYL. ENG.)

5 YEAR 60,000 MILES
This 5-year/60,000-mile guarantee is an added value feature included in your 1976 Monza.

DASH

BHB 093

Monza Coupe.

$3560.

(34/33 BLT.)

Get a little road magic.

77

2+2 for the road.

new OPT. GRILLE ON MONZA (TOWNE) COUPE, BUT EARLIER STYLES ALSO AVAIL.

$3840.

"SPYDER" HOOD DECAL

SPYDER *SPORT STEERING WHEEL*

Monza 2+2
(392/5 BLT.)

"SPYDER" DOOR DECAL and STRIPLS

"SPYDER" SPORT PACKAGE IS AN OPTION FOR

Monza 2+2
CHEVROLET MONTE CARLO 76-77

4 CYL. OR 305 CID V8 AVAIL. (145 HP)

REAR SPOILER

204

Chevrolet **MONZA 4 CYL. OR V6**

(V8 AVAIL. ALSO)

NEW (24555 BLT.)

('78)

$3698

EPA ESTIMATES

34/24
HWY / CITY

(ESTATE WAG. ALSO, '78 ONLY) (2478 BLT.)

WAGON ('78 and '79 ONLY)

WAGON (1979 FINAL YR., AT $4646.) (WEST)

('79)

(15190 BLT.)

BODY SIDE MOULDINGS BECOME STD. EQUIPMENT IN 1979.

$3850. ('79)

78-80
new GRILLES

(1979 MODELS ILLUSTRATED, UNLESS OTHERWISE INDICATED.)

COUPE

(WEST)
$4080. ('78)
4517. ('79)
5041. ('80)
(4497. SALE)

Monza 2+2

$4161. ('79)

WITH OPT. "SPYDER" PACKAGE

DASH

SAME SINGLE-TONE BODY COLOR CHOICES AS SHOWN with 1980 MONTE CARLO, PLUS RED.
(NO 2-TONES)

TOTAL MONZA PRODUCTION =
{ 1978 = 138,632
  1979 = 163,833
  1980 = 169,418

2+2 *Sport*

$4624. ('79)

('80)

COUPE

REMOVABLE SUNROOF (OPT.)

1980 INSTR. PANEL (SPORT, WITH TACH.)

WITH OPT. EXT. DECOR PKG. ('80)

$4433. ('80)

CHEVROLET MONZA 78~80

CHEVY Nova

CPE. FR. $2589. (WEST)
4-DR. FR. $2617. (WEST)

FROM $2528. COUPE (135,819 BLT.)

BACKGROUND SCENE: HISTORIC PLYMOUTH, MASS.

SEDAN (60283 BLT.) $2407. UP

New

Hatch back

SS

new LOOK, FRONT and REAR

73

$2528. UP

new 2-TONE ROOF ACCENT TRIM AVAILABLE (ON CAR ILLUSTR. ABOVE, CENTER)

4 TAIL-LIGHTS (new)

187 GII

FROM $2738 (WEST)

TOTAL 1973 PRODUCTION = 369,509

UPHOLSTERY

NOVA/NOVA CUSTOM

new GRILLE with PARK./DIR. LTS. BUILT IN

250 CID 6 (100 HP)
307 CID V8 (115 HP)

350 CID V8 AVAILABLE (145 or 175 HP)

SKY ROOF (OPT.)

New Nova Custom. A lot more Nova for you to enjoy. We added the Nova Custom series for one reason: to give you Nova's famed practicality, dependability and economy in a luxury package.

Outside, bright parking light and taillight accents; bright roof drip and body sill moldings; deluxe bumpers with black full-width impact strips; special Custom nameplates.

Inside, color-keyed deep-twist carpeting; bright instrument cluster accents; glove compartment light; wide 10" non-glare rearview mirror; right front door light switch; cigarette lighter.

Chevrolet. Building a better way to see the U.S.A.

1973 DASH (1974 SIMILAR)

$2580.

NOVA CUSTOM SEDAN **New**

CHEVY NOVA 73

CHEVY Nova 74

250 CID 6 (100 HP)

new 350 CID V8 (145 HP)

DASH

CPE. FROM $3/01.

CHEVROLET EMBLEM ADDED TO 1974 GRILLE

□ **Nova Hatchback Hutch.** This handy camping tent attaches quickly and easily to Nova Hatchback models, transforming them into economy two-sleeper campers.

SEDAN FROM $3131.

new BRIGHT ANODIZED ALUMINUM HUBCAPS

□ **Full wheel covers.** Shown left. □ Rally wheels with bright trim rings (included with SS). Shown right.

CUSTOM SS

SS has OWN GRILLE.

new "NOVA BY CHEVROLET" ON DECK (ALSO ON HOOD ON DRIVER'S SIDE)

Nova Custom cloth-and-vinyl interior.

EMBLEM ON GRILLE (CLOSE-UP)

TOTAL 1974 PRODUCTION = 390,477

CHEVY NOVA 74

AJN·256

NOVA SIX.

$3218.*

* REG. $3966. (WEST)

TOTAL 1975 PROD. = 334,728

(RESTYLED) '75

EPA mileage: 16 city, 21 highway.

HATCHBACK CPE. $4214. (WEST)

NOVA

FR78 × 14 TIRES (EXCEPT ON $3966. "S" CPE. AT TOP, LEFT)

NOVA CUSTOM $4270. (WEST)

So we've distinguished the exterior of our '75 Nova LN— front, rear and sides— with this classic LN emblem.

NOVA LN

It appears inside, too (on the steering wheel), along with some of the nicest things that ever happened to a compact.

250 CID 6 (105 HP) new 262 CID V8 (110 HP)

4.3 LITRE

$4650. (WEST)

$3782. UP

LN (new)

DASH (LN) $3795. UP

NOVA

CHEVROLET MAKES SENSE FOR AMERICA

Improved ventilation is a new air exhaust lower.

A swing-out quarter window is available for all coupes, including the Custom and LN.

CHEVY NOVA 75

208

$3417.
HATCHBACK
$4366. (WEST)

Nova

$3283* *6
Nova 4-Door Sedan
$4232. (WEST)

E78 × 14/B TIRES ON STD. NOVA

Nova SS Coupe.

250 CID 6 (105 HP)
305 CID V8 (140 HP)

76

(Introducing **Concours**.)
(1976 and 1977 ONLY)

$3830. UP

note THAT GRILLE OF NEW CONCOURS has HEAVY PANEL OF BRIGHTWORK ABOVE

Concours

NEW

4-Door Sedan
$4780. (WEST)

$3795. UP

$4745. (WEST)

• Instrument cluster with rosewood vinyl accents, smoked lenses, bright framing.

• Available electric clock.

Concours Coupe (52298 BLT.)

• Built-in heater and defroster system.

(ALSO, 7574 CONCOURS HATCHBACKS)

CONCOURS has HOOD ORNAMENT and FULL-LENGTH SIDE TRIM. (CONCOURS TIRE SIZE = FR 78 × 14/B)

CONCOURS HATCHBACK AVAIL., AT $4922. (WEST)

NOVA DASH RESEMBLES ILLUSTRATED CONCOURS DASH, BUT DOES NOT have WOOD GRAIN.

Concours

• Concours identification on steering wheel.

• Cigarette lighter.

• Glove compartment light and lock.

• Soft-rim steering wheel with cushioned center.

TOTAL 1976 PRODUCTION = 334,728*

*(INCL. 60383 CONCOURS) **NOVA**

• Nova nameplate on steering wheel center.

• Speedometer reads to 100 mph with metric equivalents.

CHEVY NOVA 76

CHEVY NOVA 77

new GRILLES

TOTAL 1977
PRODUCTION =
365,264

SEDAN
$4539.
(WEST)

$3482.UP

CPE.
FR.
$4489.
(WEST)

THE
LOS ANGELES
SHERIFF'S DEPT.
ORDERED A
RECORD
NUMBER
OF
NOVA
POLICE
CARS.

NOVA RALLY

UNIQUE
MESH
GRILLE

NOVA
CUSTOM RALLY
(IN '78, WITH SIMILAR
STYLING)

DASH

- Soft-rim
  steering wheel
  with cushioned center.
- Speedometer indicates both
  miles per hour and
  kilometers per hour.
- Available Four-Season air
  conditioning and Delco-
  GM AM/FM stereo radio.
- Glove compartment lock.

new 110 HP (6) 145 HP (V8)
(250 CID)   (305 CID)
350 CID V8 (170 HP)

TRIPLE
TAIL
LTS.
(*new*)

THE FINAL
CONCOURS

CONCOURS GRILLE →

$4066.UP

$5073.
(WEST)

CHEVY NOVA 77

Concours:
A world class luxury compact from Chevrolet.

GM
MARK OF EXCELLENCE

26 MPG. HWY., 19 CITY

CHEVY NOVA 4-DR. $4852.)

$3823.*

SEE WHAT'S NEW TODAY IN A CHEVROLET.

2-DR.
$3702.*

*(REG. $4777.)

EMBLEM ADDED ABOVE GRILLE, new BUMPERS (STD. NOVA)

78

HOOD ORNAMENT NOT INCL. on new CUSTOM

RETURN OF NOVA CUSTOM
(FORMERLY THE CONCOURS)

RALLY WHEELS

NOVA

Nova Models.

$5260.

RALLY

$5306.

Nova Custom Models.

79

BUMPER RUB STRIP and GUARDS OPTION.

$5406.

WIRE WHEEL COVER

new GRILLE WITH ALL-HORIZONTAL PCS.

250 CID 6 (115 HP)
305 CID V8 (130 HP)
or 350 CID V8 (170 HP)

CABRIO-LET ROOF COVER (OPT.)

REPLACED BY 1980 CITATION.

"Chevrolet" NAME

CHEVY NOVA 78~79

CHRYSLER FOR 1940

L~HEAD 6 OR STRAIGHT~8 (THROUGH '50)

"HIGHLANDER" PLAID INTERIOR ➡

$1185. and up

New

A CVT. WITH SCOTCH PLAID UPHOLSTERY!

CHRYSLER "HIGHLANDER"

.. the talk of the smart set everywhere!

6~CYL. 241½ CID
  (108 OR 112 HP)
  (122½" OR 139½" WB)
8~CYL. 323½ CID
  (132, 135 OR 143 HP)
  (128½" OR 145½" WB)

40

RESTYLED; LONGER WBs

ROYAL COUPE $895.

MODELS
ROYAL 6
WINDSOR 6
TRAVELER 8
SARATOGA 8
NEW YORKER 8
CROWN IMPERIAL 8

ROYAL CLUB COUPE INTERIOR

BIGGEST SELLER : WINDSOR SEDAN = 28,477 BLT.

NEW PLASTIC INSTRUMENT PANEL

$895. ~ $2445. PRICE RANGE

SEDAN INTERIOR (8~PASS. ALSO AVAIL.)

SEMI~AUTOMATIC "FLUID DRIVE" AVAIL. FOR ONLY

CLOSE~UP OF DASH GAUGES

$38 EXTRA.

SEDAN REAR

40 CHRYSLER

CHRYSLER

NEW

The dashing Coupe for three also has four-foot doors and a perfectly enormous luggage locker.

$1385.
NEW YORKER 8
3~WINDOW COUPE
(158 BLT.)

3 WINDOW BUSINESS COUPE has UNUSUALLY LONG TRUNK COMPARTMENT, AVAIL. in ROYAL WINDSOR SARATOGA or NEW YORKER SERIES.

41 A RESTYLED

$1075. INTERIOR

(479 BLT.) Chrysler Royal Coupe

CLUB COUPE REAR

CLUB COUPE

...the way You want it

HAVE IT YOUR OWN WAY!
upholstery

Tailored to Your Taste!

CLUB COUPE INTERIOR

(CONT'D. NEXT PAGE)

Instrument panel plastic made for a rich-looking assembly and complemented the various interior colors.

the Beautiful 1941 Chrysler!

213

Chrysler for 1941!

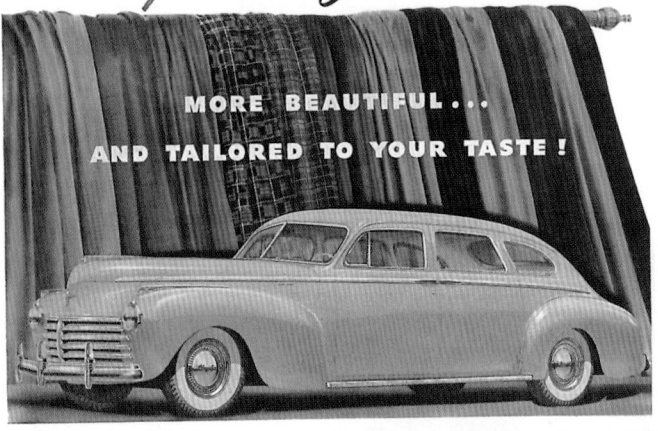

MORE BEAUTIFUL...
AND TAILORED TO YOUR TASTE!

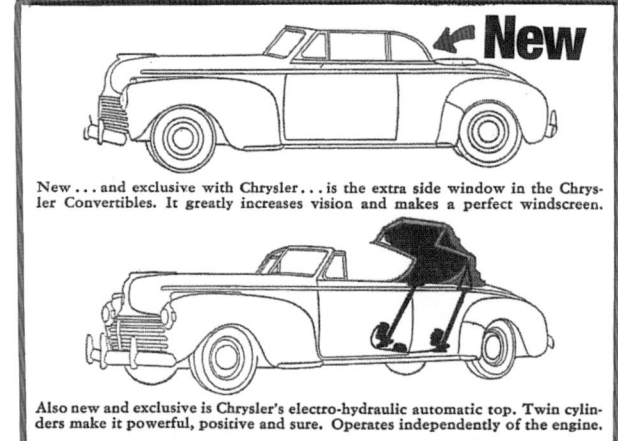

New

New... and exclusive with Chrysler... is the extra side window in the Chrysler Convertibles. It greatly increases vision and makes a perfect windscreen.

Also new and exclusive is Chrysler's electro-hydraulic automatic top. Twin cylinders make it powerful, positive and sure. Operates independently of the engine.

six-passenger Convertible

NOW—*Fluid Drive* with Automatic Safety Control !

Fluid Coupling For All Models ... New Four-Speed Transmission ... Bodies Are Lower and Roomier

THE ROOMINESS OF A SEDAN !

NEW

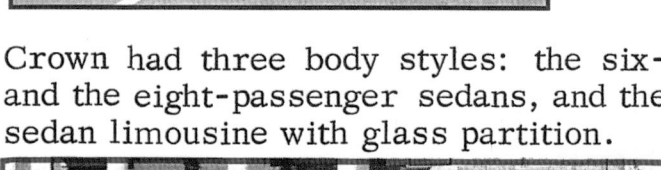

TOWN and COUNTRY 6 **$1412.** UP

41 B
(CONT'D.)

Crown had three body styles: the six- and the eight-passenger sedans, and the sedan limousine with glass partition.

CROWN IMPERIAL 8

C-33 **$2595.** and up

SIX =
108,
112 OR
115 HP

EIGHT =
137,
140 OR
143 HP

SPITFIRE ENGINES !

Smooth, Jerkless Ride for Everybody! Smooth as oil ... that's Chrysler's Fluid Drive! Because it *is* a drive through oil ... without any metal to metal connection between the engine and rear axle. Eliminates noise, jars, jolts and shocks. Try it!

41 CHRYSLER (B)

The Beautiful Chrysler

CVTS. IN WINDSOR 6 OR NY 8 SERIES.

(ROYAL 6 COUPES PRICED FROM $1075.)

"BLACKOUT" MODEL OF JAN., 1942 (PAINTED TRIM)

TOTAL CVTS. BLT. = 3100

NO REAR FENDER TRIM

new 250.6 cm 6 (120 HP)

ALL 8s WITH 140 HP

Windsor two-door luxury brougham (317 BLT.) $1220.

NEW YORKER 8 TOWN SEDAN (1648 BLT.)

C-34

NO "PRIORITIES" ON

Color and Charm!

$1520.

NEW YORKER 8 SEDAN C-36
(7045 BLT.) $1475.

new "BEAUTY RINGS" INSTEAD OF WHITE SIDEWALL TIRES

42 new WIDE "WRAPAROUND" GRILLE WITH 5 HARMONIZING CHROME STRIPS ON REAR FENDERS.

TOWN and COUNTRY 6 CYL. (OR STRAIGHT 8) (1000 BLT.) $1595. UP

DASH

The fluid coupling is a simple design without a torus tube running through the vanes

FLUID DRIVE STD.

CROWN IMPERIAL C-33

$2815. UP

42 CHRYSLER

215

CHRYSLER

ROYAL 6 (C-38-S)
WINDSOR 6,
TOWN and COUNTRY 6
SEDAN (C-38-W)
SARATOGA 8 (C-39-K)
NEW YORKER 8,
TOWN and COUNTRY 8
CVT. * (C-39-N)
CROWN IMPERIAL 8
(C-40)

*=100 T+C 8
SEDANS
ALSO

EMBLEM

Chrysler

WINDSOR 6
CVT. $1861.

6 CYL. has 250.6 CID
(1942 THROUGH 1951)
114 HP @ 3600 RPM
(THROUGH '49)

STRAIGHT-8 has
323.5 CID (1935
THROUGH 1950)
135 HP @ 3400 RPM
(THROUGH '49)

WHITE "BEAUTY RING"

(ABOVE = SARATOGA 8
SEDAN
$1863.

WHITE
"BEAUTY RINGS"
USED, BECAUSE OF SCARCITY OF
WHITE SIDEWALL TIRES.

NEW YORKER 8 CLUB COUPE
$1948.

(3-
WINDOW
BUSINESS CPES.
HAVE LONG
REAR DECKS!)

PRICE RANGE :
$1415. TO $4767.

46-48 A

CONTINUES NEARLY UNCHANGED
TO FEB., 1949

121½" WB (6)
127½" " (8)
145½" " (CROWN
IMPERIAL 8, THROUGH
'54)
139½" WB (6-CYL.
LIMOUSINE)

TEMP. BEAM TURN
SIGNAL
LITE
OIL CLOCK

AMPS

C-38
SERIES

FUEL

SPEEDO.

SHIFT
LEVER

DASH

HORN RING

BEAUTIFUL DASH
OF METAL, CHROME
and PLASTIC,
COLOR KEYED TO
BODY COLOR.

AT NIGHT,
SPEEDOMETER
NUMERALS
CHANGE COLOR
FROM GREEN
TO AMBER TO
ORANGE TO
RED AS THE
SPEED
INCREASES !

new
CAST-METAL
"HARMONICA
STYLE"
GRILLE

ROYAL 6 CLUB COUPE
$1551.

1946 CHRYSLER CORP.
CARS HAVE FLAT
DOOR LOCK COVERS;
1947-48 PROTRUDE.

"TOWN and COUNTRY"
MODELS,
NEXT PAGE

TOWN + CNTRY.
H/T (ONLY 7
BUILT)

CONVENTIONAL
CONVERTIBLE
INTERIOR →

46-48
(CONT'D.)

TOWN -
-and-
COUNTRY

REAR DETAILS
(SEDAN)

(FIRST
1941-1942
T + Cs ARE
FASTBACK
HATCHBACKS.)

SEDANS ═══
MOST 1946-48 T+C
6 CYL., BUT SOME 8s ALSO.

Natural wood

'46 - EARLY 1947
"TOWN and
COUNTRY"
MODELS have
GENUINE
WOODEN
PANELS of
ASH and
MAHOGANY.
(DK. PANELS
on LATER
MODELS
ARE
DECALS)

TOWN and COUNTRY

$ 3123.
('48) ↗

CONVT. (8-CYL.)

ONE-OFF
2-DR. BROUGHAM
(EXPERIMENTAL) ←

6.50x15
TIRES

CHRYSLER

WINDSOR 6

(55,879 BLT.)

(4524 BLT.)

CLUB COUPE

NEW YORKER 8

(C-45) 125½" WB (THROUGH '54)

(LENGTH EXAGGERATED)

$3206.

(1137 BLT.)

WINDSOR 6 LIMOUSINE has 139½" WB (73 BLT.) $3144.

NEW YORKER 8

ACTUAL LENGTH

(18,799 BLT.)

NEW YORKER 8 (C-46) 131½" WB (THROUGH '52)

ROYAL 6 and SARATOGA 8 ALSO AVAIL.

49

(TOTALLY RESTYLED FEB., 1949)

CHRYSLER

PRESTOMATIC FLUID DRIVE* TRANSMISSION
*gyrol Fluid Drive

PRICE RANGE:
$2114.
TO
$5334.

$3970.

TOWN and COUNTRY 8 CONVERTIBLE (SAME SPECS. as NEW YORKER) (1000 BLT.)

CROWN IMPERIAL 8 (C-47)

LIMOUSINE

(45 BLT.)

$5334.

145½" W.B.

(FINAL 1948 CHRYSLERS SOLD AS "EARLY 1949" DURING JAN. and FEB., 1949.)

CHRYSLER (FINAL YEAR FOR CHRYSLER STRAIGHT-8.)

ELECTRIC POWER TOP OPERATION DOESN'T DEPEND ON RUNNING ENGINE

WINDSOR CONVERTIBLE COUPE

(2201 BLT.)

$2741.

(179,299 TOTAL 1950 PROD.)

PRICE RANGE = **$2114.~5334.**

(22633 BLT.)

NY 8 $2758.

NEW LOW LOOK! NEW LONG LOOK! NEW LOVELY LOOK!

50

ROYAL 6, WINDSOR 6 (C-48)
SARATOGA 8, NEW YORKER 8, TOWN and COUNTRY 8 (C-49)

REAR WINDOW LOWERS INTO TAILGATE. NO UPPER HINGED SECTION

(599 BLT.) (100 ALL-STEEL WAGONS ALSO)

ROYAL STATION WAGON **$3163.**

WINDSOR NEWPORT

(9925 BLT.)

$2637.

INTERIOR

T + C AVAIL. ONLY AS 2 DR. H/T (700 BLT.)

FINAL TOWN and COUNTRY 8

new GRILLE FOR 1950

$4003.

BEST-SELLER: WINDSOR 4-DR. (78199 BLT.)

$5334. *Crown Imperial*

LIMOUSINE (205 BLT.) (C-50)

8-CYL. MODELS DEVELOP 135 HP @ 3200 RPM.

CRN. IMP. REAR COMP. has QUARTER WINDOWS.

CHRYSLER 50

219

CHRYSLER

C51-1
Windsor
6

NEWPORT H/T
$3798. UP

NY V8
(C-52)
131½" WB

(ABOVE) "TOWN and COUNTRY" WAGON AVAIL.
IN WINDSOR, SARATOGA or NY SER.

new WINDSOR DLX. 6 (C-15-2) $2608.

125½" W.B. (LENGTH EXAGGERATED IN THIS ADVER-TISING ILLUSTR.)

FORMER STR.-8 REPLACED '51 BY new V8 ENGINE (331.1 cID, 180 HP, O.H.V.) @ 4000 RPM

new GRILLES, WIDER REAR WINDOWS in 1951.

6-CYL. ENGINE CHANGES
(1951) 250.6 cID, 116 HP @ 3600 RPM
(1952) 264.5 cID, 119 HP @ 3600 RPM

FRONTAL RESTYLING

51-52 A

ROYAL 6 DISCONT'D.

C-55 SARATOGA V8

(new "HYDRA-GUIDE" POWER STEERING AVAILABLE, 1951 ON)

125½" WB

$3016. UP

New V8 ENGINE!

V8 MODELS HAVE CHROME "V" ABOVE GRILLE

FOG LIGHTS OPTIONAL

C-52 NEW YORKER V8
131½" W.B.

CVT. WAS INDIANAPOLIS 500 PACE CAR '51.

$3916. UP

PREST O MATIC DRIVE (OPT.)

TOTAL PRODUCTION
163,613 (1951)
87,470 (1952)

IMPERIALS, CUSTOM MODELS NEXT PAGE)

CLUB CPE. $3348. UP

Note the taillight design change FOR 1952

1952

CHRYSLER 51-52 (A)

K-310 CUSTOM-BUILT COUPE

125 ½" W.B.
(ITALIAN GHIA BODYWORK)
HAND~CRAFTED, EXPERIMENTAL

CUSTM BLT.

PHAETON   147½" W.B.
(FOR PARADE USE, ETC.)

C-54
Imperial
BY CHRYSLER

$4042. ('51)
4224. ('52)

A VARIETY OF ROSE WAS NAMED "CHRYSLER IMPERIAL."

NEWPORT IMPERIAL H/T
(1180 + BLT., 1951-52)

IMPERIAL V8
(C-54)

51-52 B (CONT'D.)

IMPERIAL SEDAN PROD.
(EST.)
13,600 + ('51)
8000 + ('52)

8-passenger

LIMOUSINE
213 BLT. ('51)
125 " ('52)

(C-53)
V8

131½" W.B.
(IMPERIAL)

145½" W.B.
(CROWN IMPERIAL)

$6690. ('51)
$6994. ('52)

CROWN IMPERIAL LIMOUSINE

CHRYSLER 51~52 (B)

CHRYSLER

WINDSOR 6

(C-60-1)
$2442.

WINDSOR 6

CLUB CPE.
(11,646
BLT.)

("TOWN and
COUNTRY" WAGON IN
WINDSOR
and NY
SERIES)

$3217. ↗
WINDSOR
DELUXE 6
(C-60-2)
CVT. (1250 BLT.)

$3653.

$3487. ↘

NEW YORKER
V8 ↓

NEWPORT
(2525 BLT.) (C-56-1)

NEW YORKER DELUXE
NEWPORT H/T
(3715 BLT.)

SEDAN
(20,585 BLT.)
$3293.

POWER STEER.,
POWER BRAKES
AVAIL.

(W. and NY
8-PASS.
SEDANS have
139½"WB)

(NEW YORKER
DELUXE V8 IS
C-56-2) (new)

OTHERWISE,
ALL EXCEPT IMPERIAL
have 125½" WB (THROUGH '54)

53 New 1-PIECE
WINDSHIELDS)

(RESTYLED)

TOTAL PROD.=
170,006

CUSTOM IMPERIAL V8
(C-58) new 133½"WB

CROWN IMPERIAL V8
(C-59)
145½"WB

Imperial
BY CHRYSLER

IMPERIAL (STYLIZED
EAGLE) HOOD ORNAMENT (new)

$4225. TO 6872.

FOR
1954 TO
1965
IMPERIALS,
SEE:
IMPERIAL

CHRYSLER
WINDSOR DELUXE
(C-62)

CLUB COUPE

NEWPORT

(3655 BLT.) **$2831.**

FINAL CHRYSLER
6 CYL. L-HEAD
"SPITFIRE"
ENGINE

(5659 BLT.) **$2541.**

264½ CID
119 HP @ 3600 RPM

CLUB COUPE INTERIOR

RNDL

54 A *New* GRILLE

SPECIAL 139½" WB
$3492.

(500 BLT.)

EIGHT~PASSENGER SEDAN

INTERIOR

2 FOLDING "JUMP SEATS"

$3321.
(650 BLT.)

TOWN & COUNTRY WAGON

new
REAR
DETAILS

MODEL
NAME
(*Windsor
Deluxe*)

CONVERTIBLE
TAILORED-TO-TASTE

(500 BLT.)

$3046.

GLOVE COMPARTMENT
NEW glove compartment
with plenty of storage space
flips open at a touch . . . locks
securely. Lid bears handsome
Chrysler script in chrome.

DASH

V8
MODELS
ON NEXT PAGE
(SEE ALSO "IMPERIAL" SEC.)

$2562.

SIX~PASSENGER SEDAN
(33563 BLT.)

CHRYSLER 54 (A)

CHRYSLER

SEDAN (15788 BLT.) $3229.

CLUB COUPE (1861 BLT.) $3406.

(C-63-1)
NEW YORKER V8

$3202. (STD. NY) (2079 BLT.)

$3707.

NY DLX. NEWPORT (4814 BLT.)

NY 331.5 CID V8s have 195 OR 235 HP @ 4400 RPM

ON C-63-2 NEW YORKER DELUXE (note SMALL EXTRA HORIZONTAL CHROME PIECE ON REAR FENDER)

7.60 x 15 TIRES

54 B (CONT'D.)

DASH

IMPROVED TAMPER-PROOF VENT-WINDOW LOCKS

TOTAL 1954 PROD.: 105,030

new 126" W.B. on ALL 1955 CHRYSLERS

NASSAU OR NEWPORT H/Ts

WINDSOR DELUXE (C-67)
new 301 CID V8, 188 HP @ 4400 RPM "SPITFIRE" ENG.

$2660.

4-DR. SEDAN (63,896 BLT.)

(WINDSOR DELUXE and N.Y. DELUXE SERIES ONLY)

(7.60 x 15" TIRES)

55 (RESTYLED)

V-8s ONLY

N.Y. DELUXE ST. REGIS H/T (11,076 BLT.)

$3690.

TOWN and COUNTRY WAGON (N.Y. DLX.) (1036 BLT.) $4209.

INTRO. OCT. 11, 1954

NEW YORKER DELUXE (C-68)
331 CID V8, 250 HP @ 4600 RPM "FIREPOWER" ENG.

$4109.

(1725 BLT.)

300 (new!)

300 HP @ 5200 RPM

126" WB

EMBLEM

NEWPORT H/T (5777 BLT.) $3652.

TOTAL '55 PROD.: 142,776

55 ½ NEWPORTS (new TRIM)

300

CHRYSLER 54-55

CHRYSLER

New Pushbutton PowerFlite!
(Illustrated at right)

$3336.

(C-71) WINDSOR

CVT. (1011 BLT.)

SEDAN (53,119 BLT.)

DASH

$3041.

WINDSOR NEWPORT

(10,800 BLT.)

$2870.
new GRILLES

4-DR. H/Ts NOW AVAIL.

56

WINDSOR has 331.1 CID V8 (225 HP @ 4400 RPM or 250 @ 4600)

N.Y. has new 354 CID V8 (280 HP @ 4600 RPM)

N.Y. ST. REGIS H/T (6686 BLT.)
$3995.

(C-72) NEW YORKER

NEW "PowerStyle" CHRYSLER

"DELUXE" DESIGNATIONS DISCONTINUED

126" WB

$4523.
(1070 BLT.)

N.Y. TOWN and COUNTRY

NEWPORT H/T $3951.
(4115 BLT.)

MORE HORIZONTAL PCS. IN NEW YORKER GRILLE
NOW DIFFERENT FROM OTHERS.

BELOW:
300-B (C-72-300)
(1102 BLT.)

354 CID V8 (340 OR 355 HP @ 5200)

NEW YORKER INTRODUCES VERTICAL CHROME STRIPS ON REAR FENDER (THROUGH '62.)

TOTAL 1956 PROD. = 128,322

CHRYSLER

(17,639 BLT.)

SEDAN

$3088.

WINDSOR (C-75-1)

$3575.

WINDSOR TOWN and COUNTRY WAGON

(2035 BLT.)

2-DR. H/T

(14,027 BLT.) $3153.

4 HEADLIGHTS ON MOST MODELS

(11,586 BLT.) 4-DR. H/T

$3832.

(C-75-2) SARATOGA

TORQUEFLITE AUTO. TRANS. AND POWER STEER. ARE STD. EQUIPMNT. ON ALL MODEL SERIES EXC. WINDSOR. (OPTIONAL ON WINDSOR AT EXTRA COST)

WINDSOR and SARATOGA HAVE 354 CID V8 (285 OR 295 HP @ 4600 RPM)

SARATOGA 4-DR. SEDAN (14,977 BLT.) $3718.

SEDAN

note ONLY 2 HEADLTS.

(C-76) NEW YORKER

(8863 BLT.)

2 DR. H/T

$4202.

4-DR. H/T

57 (TOTALLY RESTYLED)

126" W.B. CONT'D. ON ALL

TOTAL 1957 PROD.: 124,675

$4929.

NEW YORKER has new 392 CID V8 (325 HP @ 4600 RPM)

4 DR. H/T $4259.

(10,948 BLT.)

(1918 BLT.)

H/T

300-C

(C-76-300)

300-C has new HIGH and NARROWER GRILLE, ALSO new 392 CID V8 (9.25 OR 10 COMPR.) TWO 4-BBL. CARBS.

CVT. (484 BLT.) $5359.

THE MIGHTY CHRYSLER

300 C

America's Most Powerful Car!

300-C ENGINE 375 HP @ 5200 OR 390 HP @ 5400 RPM

CHRYSLER

$5173. (6/8 BLT.)

300-D (LC3-S) →
380 OR 390 HP
@ 5200 RPM

$3616.

WINDSOR
(LC1-L)

58

126" WB
(new
SHORTER 122" WB
ON WINDSOR)

WINDSOR
T+C WAGON   791 6-PASS.
            862 9-PASS.

PROD.

WINDSOR
has
290 HP
@ 4600 RPM
(354 CID)

WINDSOR *DART*LINE

note DIFFERENT SIDE TRIM on '58½ "DARTLINE" (ABOVE)

(ONLY 2 WINDSOR CONVERTIBLES BLT.)

$4347.

N.Y. 2 DR. H/T
(3205 BLT.)

SARATOGA
(LC2-M) $3955.
4 DR. H/T
(5322 BLT.)

310 HP @
4600 RPM (354 CID)

NEW YORKER
(LC3-H)
345 HP @ 4600 RPM (SAME
SIZE V8 [392 CID] as 300-D)

TOTAL 1958 PRODUCTION:
63681

new FRONTAL STYLING

new ENGINES: 383 OR
413 CID
V8s

59A

MC
SERIES

305, 325, 350 HP @ 4600,
OR 380 HP @ 5000 RPM

MORE 1959 CHRYSLERS
ON NEXT PAGE

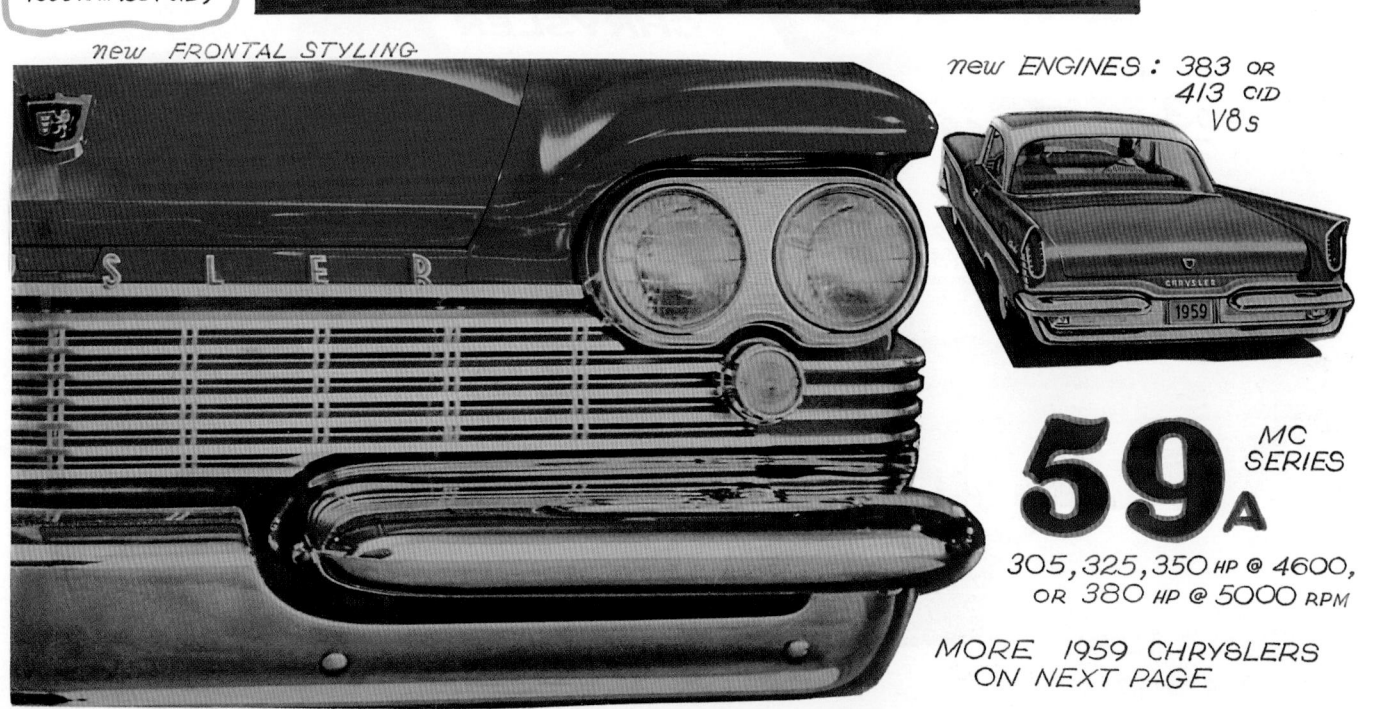

CHRYSLER

#512 2-DR. H/T (6775 BLT.)

(MC2-M)

SARATOGA

#534 4-DR. H/T (4943 BLT.)

$4104.

(MC1-L)
WINDSOR

$3289.

LION-HEARTED
CHRYSLER '59

59 B
(CONT'D.)

(MC3-H)

NEW YORKER

$3353.

#514 4-DR. H/T (6084 BLT.)

#578 - 6 PASS. (444 BLT.)   #579 - 9 PASS. (564 BLT.)

N.Y.
TOWN and COUNTRY
WAGON

#554 N.Y. 4 DR. H/T
(4805 BLT.)

$4633.

#555 N.Y. CVT. (286 BLT.)

$4890.

CHRYSLER   300   (REAR FENDER BAND)

The international classic   ...made in America

300-E

(MC3-H)

TOTAL 1959
PRODUCTION:
69970

#592 2-DR. H/T
(550 BLT.)

#595 CONVERTIBLE
(140 BLT.)

$5749.

300~E
$5319.

413 CID V8
380 HP (IN 300~E)
@ 5000 RPM
CHRYSLER 59 (B)

300-E

228

CHRYSLER

$4067. 4-DR. H/T

WINDSOR CVT.

60

$3623.

SARATOGA (PC2-M) has 383 CID V8 (325 HP @ 4600 RPM)

has 383 CID V8 (305 HP @ 4600 RPM)

SAR. SEDAN $3929.

SARATOGA has GRILLE LIKE WINDSOR (ABOVE)

NEW YORKER (PC-3-H has 413 CID V8 (350 HP @ 4600 RPM

NEW PUSHBUTTON DASH PUTS ALL THE CONTROLS AT YOUR FINGERTIPS

H/T $4461.

NEW YORKER TOWN and COUNTRY WAGON

WINDSOR $3733 T+C UP

WNDSR.

NY CVT. $4875.

300/F BY CHRYSLER

The 300F medallion is molded like a gear wheel to express the rugged spirit of the car.

#23 H/T (964 BLT.)

413 CID V8 (375 HP @ 5000 OR 400 HP @ 5200 RPM)

(300-F)

The open grille gives the 300F a "Pure automobile" look.

$5411. (PC3-H)

#27 300 F CVT. ALSO (248 BLT.) $5841.

WINDSOR PRODUCTION:	#23 H/T	6496 BLT.
	27 CVT.	1467
	41 SEDAN	25,152
	43 4 DR. H/T	5897
	46 6-PASS. WAGON	1120
	9-PASS. "	1026

SARATOGA PRODUCTION:	
H/T	2963 BLT.
SEDAN	8463
4 DR. H/T	4099

N.Y. PROD.:	H/T	2835
	CVT.	556
	SEDAN	9079
	4 DR. H/T	5625
WAGON (6-PASS.)-624		(9 PASS.)-671

229

CHRYSLER

wagon NEWPORT T + C (2403 BLT.)

$3541. UP

(RC2-M) FINAL 1961 WINDSOR MODEL

$3303.

NEW → NEWPORT LOW-PRICED SERIES 122" WB (RC1-L)

$3025. (NPT. H/T)

NEWPORT has new 361 CID V8 (265 HP @ 4400 RPM) (OPTIONAL 413 CID V8 has 350 HP @ 4600 RPM)

4 DR. H/T (7789 BLT.) $3104.

61ᴬ (126" WB ON NEW YORKER and 300-G)

300/G

new GRILLES, CANTED HEADLIGHTS

413 CID V8 with 350 HP @ 4600 RPM IN RC3-H NEW YORKER

MODELS: RC-1-L NEWPORT
RC-2-M WINDSOR (FINAL YR.)
RC-3-H NEW YORKER
RC-4-P 300-G

TOTAL 1961 PRODUCTION: 96454

(FRONT END OF 300-G (CLOSE-UP) ILLUSTR. ON NEXT PAGE)

NY

$4133. CHRYSLER

NY TOWN and COUNTRY

NEW YORKER SEDAN

230

CHRYSLER

300-G
new GRILLE
CLOSE-UP

300-G (RC4-P) has SAME ENGINES AS IN 1960

FINAL YR. OF 126" WB FOR 300 SERIES

61^B →

(CONT'D.)

CHRYSLER NAME ON TOP RIM OF GRILLE IN 1961 BUT NOT IN 1962.

300-G		
# 842	2-DR. H/T (1280 BLT.)	$5411.
# 845	CONVERTIBLE (337 BLT.)	$5841.

TOTAL 1962 PROD.: 128,921
(SC1-2)
NEWPORT

note:
STARTING 1962, THERE ARE 2 300 SERIES. THE 300 CVTS. and 2-DR. H/Ts FOLLOWED BY A LETTER DESIGNATION (300-H) HAVE MORE POWER.

SEDAN (54,813 BLT.) $2964.

NEWPORT

62

(435 BLT.)
$5090.

361, 383, 413 OR new 426 CID V8 ENGINES
(10,030 BLT.) $3400.

300

300 CVT. (123 BLT.) $5461. RARE!

728 6-PASS. N.Y.
793 9-PASS. WAGON

265 HP @ 4400 RPM TO 421 HP @ 5400 RPM

300-H
(SC2-M)

$4263. (6646 BLT.)

N.Y. 4-DR. H/T

$4125.

SEDAN (12,056 BLT.)

126" WB

NEW YORKER
(SC3-H)

ALL 122" WB (EXCEPT NY)

CHRYSLER

$3106.

ALL MODELS NOW *have* 122" WB. (THROUGH '64)

PAINTED in ACRYLIC ENAMELS

NEWPORT (TC1-L)

ROUND TAIL-LIGHTS in 1963.

$2964.

63 TC SERIES

(RESTYLED in *new* "KNIFE-EDGE" [CREASE] BODY DESIGN.)

SAME 4 V8 SIZES AS IN 1962, BUT TOP "300" HP FIGURE NOW IS 425 @ 5600, *with new* TOP 13.5 COMP.

PACE CAR at 1963 INDY 500 RACE IS 300-J.

DASH

TOTAL 1963 PRODUCTION: 128,937

#884 SALON (4 DR. H/T) (593 BLT.) (INTRO. 2-14-63)

(TC3-H) NEW YORKER

$5860.

(TC3-H) 1963 NEW YORKERS *have* VERTICAL LOUVRES ON FRONT FENDERS.

(14,884 BLT.) (BELOW) #833 NEW YORKER SEDAN $4981.

NY #878 TOWN and COUNTRY 6-PASS. WAGON (950 BLT.) $4708.

#879 9-PASS. (1244 BLT.) $4815.

CHROME BANDS JOIN ENDS OF GRILLE WITH EDGES OF HOOD. (NY and 300)

300

NEW YORKER

New Yorker

300

(TC2-M) 300

300-J ALSO

232

CHRYSLER

#814 4 DR. H/T
(9710 BLT.)

$3042.

6 OR 9-PASS.

Chrysler Newport   Hardtop Town & Country Wagon

NEWPORT

Chrysler Newport Convertible
(VC1-L)

NEWPORT
#813 SEDAN
(55,957 BLT.)
$2901.

TOTAL 1964 PROD.:
153,319

VC1
SERIES

NEWPORT'S 361 CID V8 HAS
265 HP.

64

new GRILLES
new HEADLIGHT
TREATMENT ON
NEWPORT, N.Y.

COMPRESSION RATIOS
NOW RUN FROM
9.0 TO 10.1
TO 1.

361, 383 OR 413 CID V8s
(265 HP @ 4400 RPM
TO 290 HP @ 4800)

NEW YORKER
(VC1-H)

NY SALON
$5860.

(1621 BLT.)

VINYL TRIM
ON ROOF

#833 SEDAN
(15,443 BLT.) $3994.

note
GRILLE and
SIDE TRIM
VARIATIONS
BETWEEN
"300" CVT. and H/T
MODELS
ILLUSTRATED

300 (K)

WAGON
6 OR 9
PASS.

$4721.
UP

300
(VC1-M)

300~K
HAS 413 CID
V8 (360 OR
390 HP), AVAIL. ONLY
AS H/T OR CVT.
CHRYSLER 64

INTERIOR
300

Chrysler Newport Convertible

(AC1-L) NEWPORT 7-W. SEDAN →

5-W. SEDAN

NEWPORT CVT. (SHOWING DASH)

CHRYSLER DIVISION

CHRYSLER MOTORS CORPORATION

CVT. (3192 BLT.) $3442.

REAR INTERIOR (7-W. N.P. SEDAN)

N.Y.

AC1 SERIES

65

NEW YORKER (AC1-H)

C-32 H/T (9357 BLT.) $4161.

C-24 4-DR. H/T (12,452 BLT.) $4061.

300 (AC1-M)

300 →

note DIFFERENCES IN SIDE TRIM BETWEEN 300 and 300-L.

C-42 H/T (2405 BLT.) $4153.

'65's ONLY ENG. CHOICES ARE 383 OR 413 CID V8s (270 HP @ 4400 TO 360 @ 4800)

NEWPT. PRICES START AT $3442.

300 has LARGE RED CROSS IN CENTER of GRILLE →

300-L

C-45 CVT. (440 BLT.)

$4618. (AC1-M) 300-L's 413 CID V8 has SPECIAL CAM. $4716. WEST COAST (CVT.)

TOTAL 1965 PRODUCTION: 206,089

234

CHRYSLER $4086 up Town & Country Wagon

NEW YORKER

440 CID V8 (350 OR 375 HP) 300 →

$4157.

383 CID V8 (290 OR 330 HP)

PROD.: 264,848

NEWPORT H/T $3112.

66

WRAP-AROUND TAIL LTS.

67

You can tell a 300 by its dash.

300 GRILLE ↓

300

NEWPORT GRILLE

NEW YORKER GRILLE

WAGONS $4264. UP

$3159.~4369. PRICE RANGE

1967 PROD.: 218,742

SLOT-TYPE TAIL LTS.

$3936.

NEW YORKER $4500.

300 has NEW CONCEALED HEADLIGHTS.

300 $4010.

1968 PROD.: 264,853

NEWPORT GRILLE

1968 MODELS EASILY RECOGNIZED BY new SMALL SIDE SAFETY LIGHTS REQUIRED BY U.S. GOV'T. REGULATIONS IN '68.

68

$3730.

NEWPORT CUSTOM

4-DR. H/T $4568. (WEST)

1969 PROD.: 260,773
ENGINES: 383 CID V8 (290 OR 330 HP)
440 CID V8 (350 OR 375 HP)

300 H/T $4104.

$3414.~4669. PRICE RANGE

69

RESTYLED

NEW YORKER GRILLE

1969

235

CHRYSLER

$3861.

Your next car: 1970 Chrysler.

ALSO:
A 2~DR. H/T
(6639 BLT.)

STANDARD-TYPE NEWPORT
DOES NOT HAVE SIDE TRIM
AS SEEN ON THESE MODELS.

(1124 NEWPORT
CONVERTIBLES
BUILT =
$3925.)

4~DR.
H/T
(10873 BLT.)

WITH
ANTIQUE
GOLD
VINYL TOP
COVERING,
AZTEC EAGLE
HOOD
MEDALLION)

1970 Newport Custom

(PILLARED
4 DR. SEDAN ALSO)   (FC~L)

70

FC SERIES

(1868 BLT.)

(ABOVE)

The new Chrysler Cordoba.

FC~P
TOWN and
COUNTRY
WAGON

6~PASS. (5686 BLT.)
$4738. ($5349. WEST)

TOTAL 1970
PROD.:
180,177

(SPECIAL-
EDITION
H/T)

383 CID V8
(290 OR 330
HP)
440 CID V8
(350 OR
375 HP)

$4824.

9~PASS.
(9583 BLT.)

NEW
YORKER
GRILLE SIMILAR,
BUT has UPRIGHT
RECTANGULAR
MEDALLION
AT CENTER.

RUGGED
OVERHEAD-VALVE V-8's

**CHRYSLER
POWER
TEAM**

**CHRYSLER
CORPORATION**

(BELOW)
4~DR. H/T
(9846 BLT.)
$4313.
$4928. (WEST)

FC~M

300

(3 VIEWS)

VARIOUS 1970 ENGINES BUILT BY

MODEL	H-170	HB-170	H-198	HB-198	H-225	HB-225	LH-318	LT-318	HT-361	H-383	HB-383	HT-413	H-440
DISPLACEMENT	170	170	198	198	225	225	318	318	361	383	383	413	440
GROSS HP.	104	104	115	115	132	132	186	180	200	216	216	215	240
ENGINE TYPE	Slant 6	Slant 6	Slant 6	Slant 6	Slant 6	Slant 6	V-8	V-8	V-8	V-8	V-8	V-8	V-8

(INDUSTRIAL ENGINES INCLUDED)

"300" CONVERT.
ALSO AVAIL.
(1077 BLT.)
$4580.

2~DR.
H/T
$4608.
$4849.
(WEST)

(400
"300-H"
"HURST"
2-DR. H/Ts
ALSO)

REAR DETAILS
(300)

CHRYSLER 70

DDA-70

Chrysler comes through for you

(10800 BLT.)
Newport 4-Dr. Hardtop

4~DR. H/T ROYAL (REAR) (5/88 BLT.)

1971 $4216.

$4672. (WEST)

2-DR. H/T $4153. (8500 BLT.)

NEWPORT CUSTOM

(NEWPORT) ROYAL new

71ᴬ new GRILLES

"ROYAL" NAME BELOW "NEWPORT," ON COWL PANEL

ROYAL

DIFFERING DETAILS

$4471. (10207 BLT.)
Newport Custom 4-Dr. Hardtop

$4391. (5527 BLT.)
Newport Custom 2-Dr. Hardtop

11254 BLT.
Newport Custom 4-Dr. Sedan

(13549 BLT.)
Newport 2-Dr. Hardtop

Newport 4-Dr. Sedan (24834 BLT.)

(CONT'D. NEXT PAGE)
CHRYSLER 71 (A)

Chrysler New Yorker & Town & Country

FROM $5596.

DASH →

$5686.

SUN ROOF OPT.

NEW YORKER

TOTAL 1971 PRODUCTION: 175,118

300 4-DR. H/T $5205.

71ᴮ (CONT'D.)

HEAVY CHROME SIDE STRIP ON NEW YORKER 4-DOOR HARDTOP (20633 BLT.)

(6683 BLT.)

2-DR. H/T $5126.

Chrysler 300

CHRYSLER Plymouth **Coming Through.**

(CHRYSLER CONVERTS. NO LONGER AVAIL. UNTIL 1982.)

New Yorker 4-Dr. Sedan

AVAIL. PAINT COLORS

Winchester Gray Metallic | Charcoal Metallic* | Slate Gray Metallic | Glacial Blue Metallic | Evening Blue Metallic | Autumn Bronze Metallic | Spinnaker White | Midnight Blue Metallic* | Rallye Red† | Burnished Red Metallic | Amber Sherwood Metallic | Avocado Metallic

April Green Metallic | Aztec Gold Metallic | Coral Torquoise Metallic | Sparkling Burgundy Metallic* | Tahitian Walnut Metallic | Sandalwood Beige | Formal Black | Lemon Twist† | Honey Dew* | Crystal Dawn Metallic | Tawny Gold Metallic

✳ = IMPERIAL COLORS

CHRYSLER 71 (B)

238

NY BROUGH. DASH WITH "RIM-BLOW" STEERING WHEEL

(1973 DASH SIMILAR)

CHRYSLER

TOTAL 1972 PRODUCTION: 204,704

$4863.

CM **Newport Custom**
(10326 BLT.) 2-DR. H/T

new OUTBOARD TAIL-LIGHTS

ENGINES:
360 c/d V8 (175 HP)
400 c/d V8 (190 HP)
OR 440 c/d V8 (225 HP)
ALL HP DECREASED

CL **Newport Royal**

$4630.

new GRILLES

72

w. 2~SEATS (6473 BLT.)

Town & Country CP

w. 3 SEATS (14116 BLT.)

NEW YORKER H/T $5552.

FROM $5692. (WEST)
$5241. (EAST)

CS

New Yorker Brougham

2-DR. H/T N.Y. BRGHM. $5777. (WEST)
$5413. (EAST)

4-DR. H/T (26635 BLT.) $5492.

(300 DISCONTINUED UNTIL '79)

TOTAL 1973 PROD.: 234,223

NEW

(H78 x 15" TIRES ON NEWPORT and NEWPT. CUSTOM)

2-DR. H/T (27456 BLT.) $4254.

73A

new GRILLES, new FRONT END STYLING. "CHRYSLER" NAME ABOVE GRILLE

4-DR. H/T (20175 BLT.)

$4316.

CHRYSLER 72~73 (A)

Chrysler Newport
Extra care in engineering...it makes a difference.

NEW ENERGY-ABSORBING SAFETY BUMPERS

(CONT'D. NEXT PAGE)

239

CHRYSLER

COLORS

Regal Blue Metallic

Burnished Red Metallic

Blue Sky

True Blue Metallic

Mist Green

Amber Sherwood Metallic

Forest Green Metallic

Silver Frost Metallic

Golden Haze Metallic

Honey Gold

Formal Black

Spinnaker White

Sahara Beige

Tahitian Gold Metallic

Regal Blue Metallic[6]

Coral Turquoise Metallic[6]

Chestnut Metallic[6]

Sun Fire Yellow[6]

Burnished Red Metallic[7]

NEWPORT ✳
DASH

✳ (CUSTOM)
SERIES

LT. COLOR
VARIATION
IN SOME
ADS →

True Blue Metallic

Town & Country Wagon

NEWPORT, NEWP. CUSTOM
have 400 CID V8 (185 HP)

124" WB ON ALL
EXCEPT WAGON

NEW

ENERGY~ABSORBING
Extra-Protection
Bumper System

L84 x 15" TIRES ON
WAGON

122"
WB

WITH 2 SEATS
(5353 BLT.)

$5241. ($5885., WEST)

w. 3 SEATS
(14687 BLT.)

$5266.

73B
(CONT'D.)

NEW

Electronic
Digital Clock

3:55 10
Chronometer

FIRST DIGITAL CLOCK
IN ANY CAR!

(AVAIL. ON 4~DR. MODELS)
Vent Windows
(OPT.)

Steel-Belted, Radial-Ply Whitewall Tires
J78 x 15"

4~DR. H/T
(76/9 BLT.)

$5125.
($5769. WEST)

440 CID V8 (215 HP)
ON NY, T+C
(OPT. ON NEWPTS.)

Chrysler New Yorker
Extra care in engineering...it makes a difference.

REAR

CHRYSLER 73 (B)

240

VERTICAL OUTBOARD TAIL LTS.

CL CHRYSLER NEWPORT
2-DR. H/T (13784 BLT.)

CM NEWPORT CUSTOM
4-DR. H/T (9892 BLT.)

$5190.

CRISS-CROSS PCS. IN NEWPORTS' GRILLES

Optional Newport Navajo Seat

$4752.
($5300., WEST)

NEWPORT CUSTOM

The 1974 Newport Custom's all-new styling is further enhanced by the rich exterior appointments.

The body side accent stripes not only add to Newport Custom's total beauty, but also give it a lower, leaner look. While body, sill, hood, headlamp, and drip-rail moldings are graceful.

This year, Newport Custom—along with all '74 Chryslers—has a safety package that includes a new design collapsible steering column, rugged side impact beams, a new hydraulic impact-absorption bumper system, and a color-keyed passenger restraint system with starter interlock.

RESTYLED
'74
new NARROW "CLASSIC STYLE" GRILLES.
124" WB ON ALL.

CP TOWN & COUNTRY WAGON

2236 2-SEAT
5958 3-SEAT

400 cid V8 (185 OR 205 HP)
440 " " (230 OR 275 HP)

FROM $5767.

Optional Passenger Assist Handles

AVAIL. FEB., 1974, NEW YRKR. ST. REGIS COUPE has new OPERA WINDOWS.

(3066 BLT.)

CH NEW YORKER
4 DR. H/T
$5686.

UPHOLSTERY

New Modular Instrument Panel

CS NEW YORKER BROUGHAM
4-DR. H/T (26635 BLT.)
$6063.
($6611., WEST)

1974 CHRYSLER— EXTERIOR COLORS

Silver Frost Metallic[1]	Powder Blue	Lucerne Blue Metallic	Starlight Blue Metallic[2]	Golden Haze Metallic	Tahitian Gold Metallic
Burnished Red Metallic[4]	Frosty Green Metallic	Deep Sherwood Metallic	Avocado Gold Metallic	Sahara Beige	Golden Fawn
Dark Moonstone Metallic	Sienna Metallic	Dark Chestnut Metallic[2]	Spinnaker White	Formal Black	Sun Fire Yellow[2]

CERTIFIED CAR CARE

KEEP YOUR CAR "FACTORY-NEW" WITH GENUINE MOPAR PARTS

mopar

CHRYSLER

CHRYSLER 74

CHRYSLER

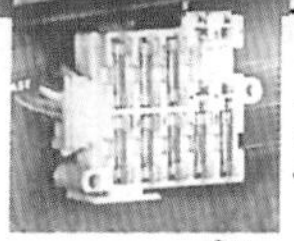

SWING-DOWN FUSE BLOCK

MODULAR INSTRUMENT PANEL

note TUBULAR COURTESY LTS. JUST FORWARD OF OPERA WINDOWS

MEDALLION (BELOW) IS FEATURED IN CENTER OF CORDOBA HOOD ORNAMENT

CORDOBA CPE.

318 CID
V8
150

CORDOBA IS ENTIRELY

NEW!

WITH SMALL (115") WB
WITH VINYL-COVERED TOP

$5581.
(WEST)

75

Cordoba

150,105 BLT.
(CHRYSLER'S BEST-SELLING 1975 MODEL BY FAR!!)

GR 78 x 15" TIRES

The New Small Chrysler $5072.
(EAST)

(TOWN and COUNTRY, NEWPORT, NEWPORT CUSTOM MODELS ALSO AVAIL.)

1975 ENGINES (ALL V8s)

318 CID (150 HP)

360 CID (180 OR 190 HP)

400 CID (165, 175, 190, 195, OR 235 HP)

440 CID (215 OR 260 HP)

FINAL 4-DR. SEDAN N.Y. BROUGH. IN 1975, PRICED AT $6851. (5698 BLT.) ALSO 2-DR. H/T $6908. (7567 BLT.)

ILLUSTR. 4-DR. H/T $6998. (12774 BLT.)
(WESTERN PRICES ABOVE)

$6424.
(EAST)

Chrysler New Yorker Brougham

new DUAL SLOTS IN BUMPER, new BUMPER GUARDS

new CRISS-CROSS PCS. IN GRILLE

CHRYSLER 75

CHRYSLER

CORDOBA

Chrysler Cordoba

NEW CORDOBA GRILLE WITH ALL-VERTICAL PCS.

$5392.

(120,462 BLT.)

NEW ELECTRONIC IGNITION LEAN-BURN ENGINE AVAIL. EXCEPT IN CALIFORNIA.

$5076.

$4993.

•Newport•

4-DR. SEDAN (16370 BLT.)

OPT. "CASTILIAN" UPH.

OPT. PLAID "HIGHLANDER" UPH.

TOTAL 1976 PROD.= 222,153

76

2-Door Hardtop. (6109 BLT.)

OPTIONAL

$5479.
(6448 BLT.)

$5576.
(9893 BLT.)

Town & Country

Newport Custom 2-Door Hardtop

Newport Custom

(FINAL IN THIS SERIES)

$6084. UP

1770 ~ 2 SEAT
3769 ~ 3 "

New Yorker Brougham

$6737.

New Yorker Brougham 4-Door Hardtop.
(28327 BLT.)

DASH

NEW "WATERFALL" GRILLE SIMILAR TO FINAL 1975 IMPERIAL

MANY OPTIONS INCLUDE

Genuine Corinthian leather interior, a superb option available on 50/50 bench seating, with individual front seat adjustment and dual folding armrests. Passenger-side recliner standard in Brougham 4-Door Hardtop.

CHRYSLER 76

an electric rear window defroster, AM/FM Search Tune Radio and stereo 8-track tape system

CHRYSLER

TOTAL 1977 CHRYSLER PROD. = 399,297

Chrysler Cordoba

CORDOBA $5368. UP

115" WB

(new STEEL-TOP CORDOBA "S": $5962.)

($6012. WEST)

(183,146 CORDOBAS BLT.)

FINE CROSS~PIECES ADDED TO CORDOBA GRILLE.

New T~BAR ROOF OPTION

$5,741. AS SHOWN.

VELOUR UPH. STD. (MEDALLION)

INTRODUCING CHRYSLER LEBARON.

WITH 318 CID V8, 112.7" WB (145 HP)

NEW

$5,758.
4~DR.

2~DR.

(STD. "FH" LE BARON) $5066. UP

54851 2~DR. and 4~DR. LE BARONS BLT. (IN "FH" STD., "FP" MEDALLION SER.)

NEW SIZE

77

CHRYSLER LE BARON. THE BEGINNING OF A TOTALLY NEW CLASS OF AUTOMOBILES.

Four-Door LeBaron Medallion
Base Sticker Price	$5,594
318 cu. in. V-8	Std.
Padded Vinyl Roof	Std.
Power Steering	Std.
Power Front Disc Brakes	Std.
Automatic Transmission	Std.
Wire Wheel Covers	$35
Whitewall Tires	$43
Bumper Guards, Front	$21
Light Package	$65
TOTAL	$5,758*

*Sticker price, including options as shown. Taxes and destination charges extra.

Two-Door LeBaron Medallion
Base Sticker Price	$5,436
318 cu. in. V-8	Std.
Power Steering	Std.
Power Front Disc Brakes	Std.
Automatic Transmission	Std.
Landau Vinyl Roof	$132
Wire Wheel Covers	$35
Whitewall Tires	$43
Bumper Guards, Front	$21
TOTAL	$5,667*

*Sticker price, including options as shown. Taxes and destination charges extra.

LEATHER UPH. AVAIL.

AVAIL. IN LE BAR. MEDALLION

V8 ENGINES

318 CID (135 OR 145 HP)
360 CID (155 OR 170 HP)
400 CID (190 HP)
440 CID (195 HP)

FINAL BIG 124" WB T + C WAGONS $6461. UP

$7873. (WEST)

$7215. 4-DR. H/T (56610 BLT.)

2-DR. H/T (16277 BLT.)

1977 Newport. $5374.

CHRYSLER
A PRODUCT OF CHRYSLER CORPORATION

1977 Chrysler New Yorker.
More affordable than you could ever imagine.

(N.Y. 2-DR. ALSO AVAIL.)

CHRYSLER 77

244

1978 Cordoba Colors

1. Dove Gray 2. Pewter Gray Metallic 3. Charcoal Gray Sunfire Metallic 4. Cadet Blue Metallic 5. Starlight Blue Sunfire Metallic 6. Tapestry Red Sunfire Metallic 7. Mint Green Metallic 8. Augusta Green Sunfire Metallic 9. Caramel Tan Metallic 10. Sable Tan Sunfire Metallic 11. Classic Cream 12. Spinnaker White 13. Formal Black

(W. PAINTED STEEL TOP)

CHRYSLER CORDOBA 'S'. $5550.

DASH

TOP VARIATIONS

1978 Chrysler Cordoba
"The picture of style and taste."
(124,825 BLT.)

DON'T SETTLE FOR ANYTHING LESS.

$5811.

114.9" WB

new 2-TIER RECTANGULAR CORDOBA HDLTS.

DETAIL OF TAIL-LIGHT

LeBARON TOWN & COUNTRY.

T + C REAR

LE BARON has new 225 CID 6 (110 OR 90 HP) OR V8s = (318 OR 360 CID)

$5761. (new)
DOWNSIZED (WAGON ADDED)
(25256 WAGONS BLT.)

New

SWING-UP STEERING WHEEL

$5270. (WEST)

LE BARON
$5060. UP

DASH

"S" COUPE
$5114. (WEST)
($4984. EAST)

25 MPG HWY / 17 MPG CITY

FINAL NP 2-DR. $6432. (WEST)

78

TOTAL 1978 PROD.: 354,029

new 6-CYL. JOINS V8s IN LE BARON SERIES

$5526. UP

(37/38 MEDAL. CPES. BLT.)

FINAL 2-DR. NEWPORT and NEW YORKER MODELS; 4-DR. ONLY AFTER 1978.

NEWPORT 2 DR. H/T
$5804.
(8877 BLT.)
123.9" WB
$7831.
(33090 BLT.)

NEWPORT.

NEW YORKER.
(new GRILLE)

NY 4-DR. H/T
$8420. (WEST)

CHRYSLER

New CHRYSLER 300.

$8034.

(FIRST new "300 SINCE 1971)

note UNIQUE GRILLE

79 A

"300" DASH

WITH 360 CID V8 (195 HP)

("300" SHARES CORDOBA CHASSIS)

3/8 CID V8 (135 HP) (360 CID V8 WITH 150 OR 195 HP OPT.)

CORDOBA DASH

$6337. UP

SEAT

CORDOBA

PREMIUM WHEEL COVER

WIRE WHEELS OPT.

REAR DETAIL

new GRILLE

CORDOBA

2-TONE HOOD PAINT VARIATION

WITH OPTION. T-BAR ROOF

(88015 "300s" and CORDOBAs BLT.)

CB RADIO!

CORDOBA

THE CONTEMPORARY CLASSIC. COLORS

Dove Gray/Formal Black
Dove Gray/Nightwatch Blue
With Special Appearance Package:
Linen Cream/Light Cashmere
Pearl Gray/Dove Gray
Two-Tone Colors with Crown Roof:
Linen Cream/Light Cashmere
Light Cashmere/Sable Tan Sunfire Metallic
Dove Gray/Regent Red Sunfire Metallic
Dove Gray/Nightwatch Blue
Pearl Gray/Dove Gray
Two-Tone Colors with Landau Roof:
Formal Black
Spinnaker White
Sable Tan Sunfire Metallic
Light Cashmere
Regent Red Sunfire Metallic
Chianti Red
Teal Green Sunfire Metallic
Teal Frost Metallic
Nightwatch Blue
Frost Blue Metallic
Dove Gray
Colors Single-Tone colors

in-car entertainment communications system . . . Cordoba's optional in-dash-mounted 40-channel CB transceiver with AM or AM/FM stereo.

CHRYSLER 79 (A)

246

CHRYSLER

$6017. UP
(21752 BLT.)

$6835. UP
(WEST)

LeBARON MEDALLION 2-DOOR COUPE

LeBARON. COUPE
$5381. UP

$6124.
(WEST)
(10987 BLT.)

(18843 BLT.)
$5851. (6)
$6162. (V8)
$6361. UP
(WEST)

4~DR. SEDAN

LeBARON SALON.
NEWEST NAME IN THE LeBARON LINEUP.
(MID~RANGE SERIES)

LeBARON TOWN & COUNTRY
(19932)

□ Defroster, rear window,
  (required in New York,
□ Emissions Control Syst
  (required on all vehicle:
  California)
□ Gas cap—locking

225 CID 6 (100 OR 110 HP)
318 CID V8
(135 HP) 360 CID V8
(150 OR 195 HP)

$7055. UP
(WEST)

$6331. UP

79 (CONT'D.)
B

OPT. SUNROOF

REAR DETAILS

DASH

28 MPG HWY. / 18 MPG** CITY
(6~CYL.)

$6556. (V8)

$6425.
(6)

NOTE new GRILLE

CHRYSLER

LeBARON

LeBARON MEDALLION 4-DOOR SEDAN. (25041 BLT.)

$7063.
(WEST)

**GET A LITTLE STYLE IN YOUR LIFE.
ADD A LITTLE LIFE TO YOUR STYLE.**

SUNROOFS
and T~BAR
ROOF 2~DR.
OPTIONAL

1979 LeBaron Colors

Spinnaker White †Not available wagon	Formal Black	Dove Gray†	Cadet Blue Metallic†	Teal Green Sunfire Metallic	Light Cashmere
Chianti Red†	Regent Red Sunfire Metallic	Ensign Blue Metallic†	Teal Frost Metallic†	Med Cashmere Metallic (wagon only)	Sable Tan Sunfire Metallic

CHRYSLER 79 (B)

CHRYSLER

NEWPORT
118½" WB
(78296 BLT.)

NEWPORT

225 CID 6 (110 HP)
OR
318 CID V8
(135 HP)

360 CID
V8s OPT.

new GRILLE

23 MPG HWY 17 MPG CITY*

NEWPORT EMBLEM

**CHRYSLER NEWPORT. $6,089.†
NOW YOU CAN HAVE IT ALL...NOW.**

TOTAL
1979 PROD.:
349,450

79 c **(CONT'D.)**

Designer's Cream & Designer's Beige
(Fifth Avenue Edition Only)

Chrysler New Yorker
Fifth Avenue
EDITION

$10,596.

new GRILLE

SEDANS ONLY,
IN
NEWPORT and
NEW YORKER
SERIES
of 1979 and 1980.

note LOUVRES

DASH (FIFTH AVENUE)

$10,026.

V8s
318 CID (135 HP)
360 CID
(150 or
(195 HP)

COMBINED
REAR PANEL WINDOW/DOOR

Formal Black

NEW YORKER

(54640 BLT.)

118½" WB

NEW YORKER DASH

NEW YORKER. Colors

Dove Gray

Nightwatch Blue

Frost Blue Metallic

Teal Frost Metallic

Teal Green Sunfire Metallic

Sable Tan Sunfire Metallic

Regent Red Sunfire Metallic

Medium Cashmere Metallic

Spinnaker White

CHRYSLER

IMITATION CABRIOLET ROOF AVAIL.

Cordoba.
new 112.7" WB

new GRILLE and SINGLE HEADLIGHTS

80 A

DASH

CORDOBA PRICED FROM $7454. (WEST)
$6745. (EAST)

(31,238 STD. COUPES, 22,233 LS, CROWN, and "300" COUPES BLT.) ("300" WITH 360 CID V8 = 185 HP)

"Cordoba. An American Classic."

225 CID 6 (90 HP) OR 318 CID V8 (120 HP)
(SAME CHOICES IN CORDOBA OR LE BARON)

REAR DETAILS

112.7" WB (SINCE '78)

(CONT'D NEXT PAGE)

GRILLE UNLIKE OTHER 1980 LE BARONS

LeBaron Salon Two-Door LS Limited.
$6643. and up

DASH

80 CHRYSLER (A)

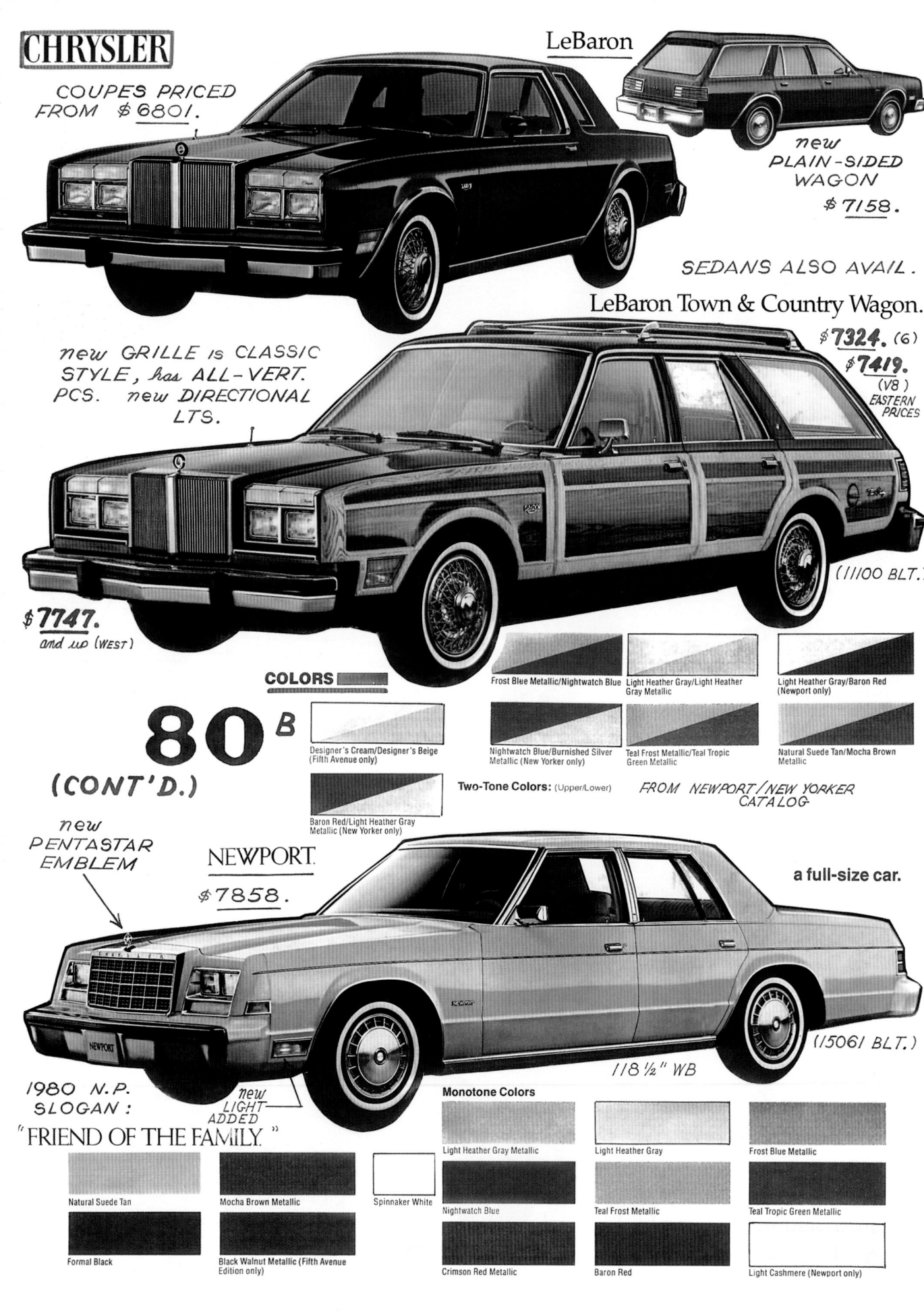

CHRYSLER

LeBaron

COUPES PRICED FROM $6801.

new PLAIN-SIDED WAGON $7158.

SEDANS ALSO AVAIL.

LeBaron Town & Country Wagon.

$7324. (6)
$7419. (V8) EASTERN PRICES

new GRILLE is CLASSIC STYLE, has ALL-VERT. PCS. new DIRECTIONAL LTS.

(11100 BLT.)

$7747. and up (WEST)

COLORS

80 B

(CONT'D.)

Designer's Cream/Designer's Beige (Fifth Avenue only)

Frost Blue Metallic/Nightwatch Blue

Light Heather Gray/Light Heather Gray Metallic

Light Heather Gray/Baron Red (Newport only)

Nightwatch Blue/Burnished Silver Metallic (New Yorker only)

Teal Frost Metallic/Teal Tropic Green Metallic

Natural Suede Tan/Mocha Brown Metallic

Two-Tone Colors: (Upper/Lower)

FROM NEWPORT/NEW YORKER CATALOG

Baron Red/Light Heather Gray Metallic (New Yorker only)

new PENTASTAR EMBLEM

NEWPORT.

$7858.

a full-size car.

(15061 BLT.)

118½" WB

1980 N.P. SLOGAN:

new LIGHT ADDED

"FRIEND OF THE FAMILY."

Monotone Colors

Natural Suede Tan

Mocha Brown Metallic

Spinnaker White

Light Heather Gray Metallic

Light Heather Gray

Frost Blue Metallic

Formal Black

Black Walnut Metallic (Fifth Avenue Edition only)

Nightwatch Blue

Teal Frost Metallic

Teal Tropic Green Metallic

Crimson Red Metallic

Baron Red

Light Cashmere (Newport only)

CHRYSLER

THE INCOMPARABLE NEW YORKER.

ALUMINUM ROAD WHEELS OPT. (NEWPORT OR NEW YORKER)

EARLY PRICE $10,459

BRAKES:	Front—Disc, power
	Rear—Drum, power

$10,872.

new WHEEL COVERS

(13513 BLT.)

80c (CONT'D.)

NEW YORKER.

LITTLE DIFFERENCE BETWEEN '79/'80 N.Y. DASH

FIFTH AVENUE.

$11,759

NOTE 2 new HORIZONTAL STRIPS ON 1980 5TH AVE. FENDER LIGHT

FIFTH AVENUE

" THE ONE AND ONLY. "

CHRYSLER   Mopar

A PRODUCT OF CHRYSLER CORPORATION

80 CHRYSLER (C)

MOPAR parts are engineered by Chrysler Corporation for use in your new Chrysler. When replacement is necessary, be sure to specify MOPAR parts. Used by professional mechanics all over the world.

STANDARD SPECIFICATIONS

ENGINE:	Newport: 3.7-liter (225 CID) 1V, Slant Six (49 states, federal)
	New Yorker: 5.2-liter (318 CID) 2V, V-8 (49 states, federal)
SUSPENSION:	Front—Torsion bar, independent
	Rear—Multi-leaf
AXLE RATIO:	2.9:1 six cylinder, 2.4:1 V-8
TIRES:	Newport: P195/75R15—Glass-belted radial white sidewall
	New Yorker: P205/75R15—Steel-belted radial wide white sidewall

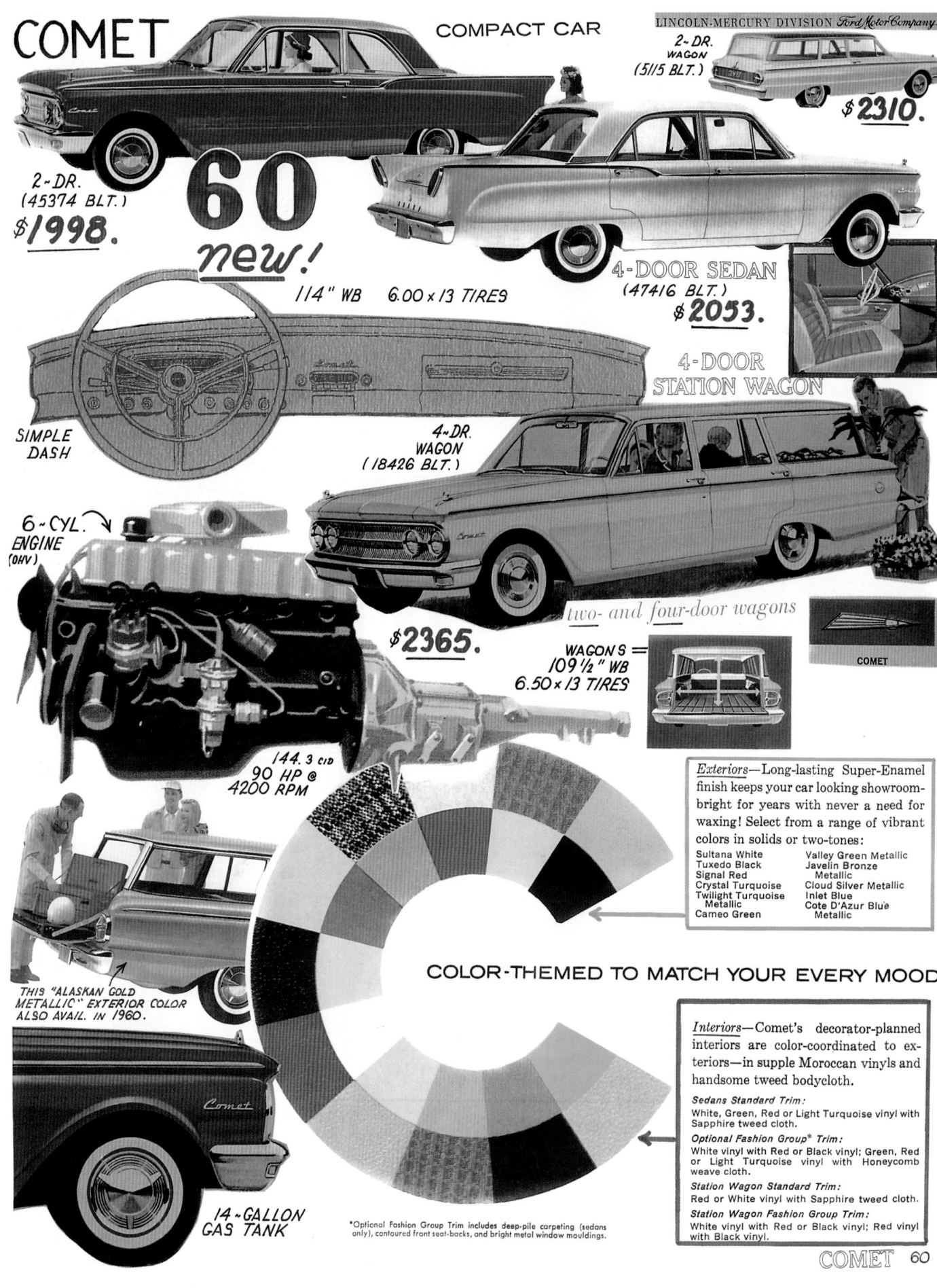

COMET

COMPACT CAR

LINCOLN-MERCURY DIVISION *Ford Motor Company*

2~DR.
WAGON
(5115 BLT.)

$2310.

2~DR.
(45374 BLT.)

$1998.

60
new!

114" WB   6.00 x 13 TIRES

4-DOOR SEDAN
(47416 BLT.)
$2053.

4-DOOR
STATION WAGON

SIMPLE
DASH

4~DR.
WAGON
(18426 BLT.)

6~CYL.
ENGINE
(OHV)

$2365.

two- and four-door wagons

WAGONS =
109½" WB
6.50 x 13 TIRES

COMET

144.3 CID
90 HP @
4200 RPM

Exteriors—Long-lasting Super-Enamel finish keeps your car looking showroom-bright for years with never a need for waxing! Select from a range of vibrant colors in solids or two-tones:

Sultana White
Tuxedo Black
Signal Red
Crystal Turquoise
Twilight Turquoise
  Metallic
Cameo Green

Valley Green Metallic
Javelin Bronze
  Metallic
Cloud Silver Metallic
Inlet Blue
Cote D'Azur Blue
  Metallic

COLOR-THEMED TO MATCH YOUR EVERY MOOD

THIS "ALASKAN GOLD
METALLIC" EXTERIOR COLOR
ALSO AVAIL. IN 1960.

Interiors—Comet's decorator-planned interiors are color-coordinated to exteriors—in supple Moroccan vinyls and handsome tweed bodycloth.

Sedans Standard Trim:
White, Green, Red or Light Turquoise vinyl with Sapphire tweed cloth.

Optional Fashion Group* Trim:
White vinyl with Red or Black vinyl; Green, Red or Light Turquoise vinyl with Honeycomb weave cloth.

Station Wagon Standard Trim:
Red or White vinyl with Sapphire tweed cloth.

Station Wagon Fashion Group Trim:
White vinyl with Red or Black vinyl; Red vinyl with Black vinyl.

14~GALLON
GAS TANK

*Optional Fashion Group Trim includes deep-pile carpeting (sedans only), contoured front seat-backs, and bright metal window mouldings.

COMET 60

252

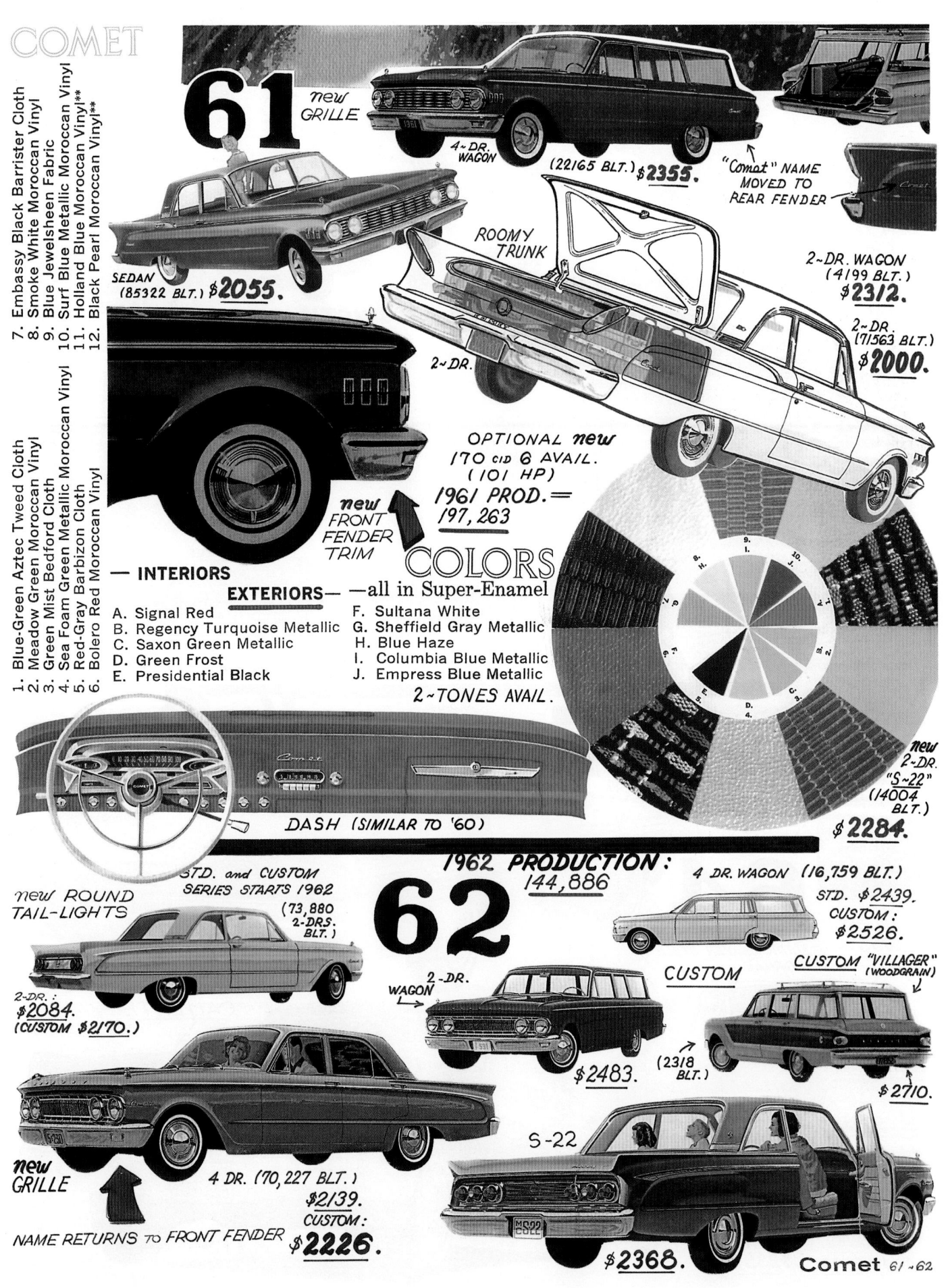

COMET

61 new GRILLE

4~DR. WAGON

(22165 BLT.) **$2355.**

"Comet" NAME MOVED TO REAR FENDER

SEDAN (85322 BLT.) **$2055.**

ROOMY TRUNK

2~DR. WAGON (4199 BLT.) **$2312.**

2~DR. (71,563 BLT.) **$2000.**

2~DR.

new FRONT FENDER TRIM

OPTIONAL new 170 CID 6 AVAIL. (101 HP) 1961 PROD. = 197,263

— INTERIORS —

EXTERIORS—

COLORS —all in Super-Enamel

1. Blue-Green Aztec Tweed Cloth
2. Meadow Green Moroccan Vinyl
3. Green Mist Bedford Cloth
4. Sea Foam Green Metallic Moroccan Vinyl
5. Red-Gray Barbizon Cloth
6. Bolero Red Moroccan Vinyl

7. Embassy Black Barrister Cloth
8. Smoke White Moroccan Vinyl
9. Blue Jewelsheen Fabric
10. Surf Blue Metallic Moroccan Vinyl
11. Holland Blue Moroccan Vinyl**
12. Black Pearl Moroccan Vinyl**

A. Signal Red
B. Regency Turquoise Metallic
C. Saxon Green Metallic
D. Green Frost
E. Presidential Black

F. Sultana White
G. Sheffield Gray Metallic
H. Blue Haze
I. Columbia Blue Metallic
J. Empress Blue Metallic

2~TONES AVAIL.

DASH (SIMILAR TO '60)

new 2~DR. "S~22" (14004 BLT.) **$2284.**

new ROUND TAIL-LIGHTS

STD. and CUSTOM SERIES STARTS 1962 (73,880 2-DRS. BLT.)

62

1962 PRODUCTION: 144,886

4 DR. WAGON (16,759 BLT.) STD. **$2439.** CUSTOM: **$2526.**

2-DR.: **$2084.** (CUSTOM **$2170.**)

2-DR. WAGON

CUSTOM

CUSTOM "VILLAGER" (WOODGRAIN)

$2483.

(2318 BLT.)

$2710.

new GRILLE

NAME RETURNS TO FRONT FENDER

4 DR. (70,227 BLT.) **$2139.** CUSTOM: **$2226.**

S-22

$2368.

Comet 61~62

253

Comet

REAR

fun at its fetching best

#71-B CUSTOM
4-DR. WAGON
$2570.

#71-C VILLAGER
4 DR. WAGON
$2754.

station wagons

63

PRODUCTION
2 DR. (24,351); CUSTOM 2 DR. (11,897);
S-22 2-DR. (6303); CUSTOM H/T (9432);
S-22 H/T (5807); 2 DR. WAGON (623);
CUSTOM 2-DR. WAGON (272); 4 DR. WAGON (4419);
CUSTOM 4-DR. WAGON (5151);
VILLAGER 4-DR. " (1529);

(SEDANS ALSO)

1963 PRODUCTION:
150,694

COMET *SPORTSTER* hardtop

new GRILLE

CUSTOM CVT.
$2557. *fun without a fancy price tag!*

144.3 CID
6 (85 HP);
170 CID 6
(101 HP);
221 CID V8
(145 HP); OR
260 CID V8 (164 HP)

tach, bucket seats,

Vinyl covered roof optional.

114" WB

$2636.

DASH (CYCLONE)

THE COMET CYCLONE
Super 289 cu. in. V-8,
chrome engine parts,
competition-type
wheel covers.
210 H.P.
(7454 BLT.)
$2655.

(MIDSEASON MODEL)

64

new "ELECTRIC SHAVER STYLE" GRILLE

#25 CVT.
(9039 BLT.)

CALIENTE #23 H/T
(31,204 BLT.)

1964 PRODUCTION=
195,227

4-DR. SEDANS
202 $2182.
404 $2269.

CALIENTE
$2350.

$2375.

comet 63-64

254

Comet

(12,347 BLT.)
$2683.

#27 CYCLONE H/T

$2578.

#34 CUSTOM WAGON (5226 BLT.)

#29 CALIENTE H/T

(29,247 BLT.)

$2403.

65

404

$2762. #96 VILLAGER

200 CID 6 (120 HP)
OR
289 CID V8 (200 OR 225 HP)

202
$2154.

(32,425 BLT.)

REAR FENDER DETAIL

40 days
from Cape Horn to Fairbanks

1965 PRODUCTION:
162,335
$2154. ~ 2762.
PRICE RANGE

CYCLONE SEATS

COMET 404 INTERIOR

COMET 404 BUCKET SEATS

Multi-Drive Merc-O-Matic AVAILABLE

Every Comet Cyclone can be rally-ready with this optional "Rally-Pac" gauge cluster of vacuum gauge and elapsed time clock which can be added to the standard tachometer.

COML/ 65

255

COMET

BELOW: CAPRI H/T (CUSTOM SPTS. CPE)
(15,031 BLT.)

COMET *Custom Sports Coupe*

$2400.

There are 13 models
convertibles, wagons, hardtops, sedans.

FORD MERCURY LINCOLN

new 116" WB
(WAGONS 113")
$2475.

(25,862)

Completely equipped with white-
walls, deluxe wheel covers,
vinyl interiors, wall-to-wall
carpeting, heater-defroster,
seat belts (front and rear),
emergency flasher, lots more.

$2908.
(WEST)
Comet Caliente

$2735.

$3168.
(WEST)

(3922 BLT.)

$3152.

"Performance Car
of the Year"
Named Pace Car For
Memorial Day 500

1966 Performance Car of the year SUPER STOCK

Official PACE CAR
Mercury COMET · INDIANAPOLIS 500
CYCLONE GT

(2158 BLT.)

6.95/7.35/7.75 x 14 TIRES

66 new GRILLES

$3510.
(WEST)

200 CID 6 (120 HP)
289 CID V8 (200 HP)
390 CID V8s
(265, 275 or
335 HP) OR
427 CID V8

Cyclone GT

has BODY STRIPES

OPT.
DUAL
HOOD
SCOOPS

$2700.
CYCLONE
H/T
$3028.
(WEST)
(6889 BLT.)

1966

$3250.
(WEST)

A.K.A.
Mercury COMET

"Performance Car of the Year"

1966 PRODUCTION: 170,426
CALENDAR YEAR: 133,165

$2154.~3152. PRICE RANGE

(13,812 BLT.)
$2891.

COMET 66

MODELS:
202, CAPRI, CALIENTE,
CYCLONE, CYCLONE GT

$2535.
$2994.
(WEST)

COMET

HORIZ.-GROOVED DASH →

CALIENTE

Caliente Grandé interior has blue Gossamer nylon or Chambrey nylon in black or parchment. Both framed with crinkle vinyl.

(INTRO. 9-30-66)

67

CYCLONE GT $3034.
(3419 BLT.)

PROD.: 56,451

$3290.

CYCLONE GT (INTRO. 9-22-67)
(RESTYLED)

68

NOTE new SIDE SAFETY LTS.

new MONTEGO

116" WB
200 CID 6
(115 HP) OR
289 CID V8 (195 HP)

MONT./COMET PROD.: 149,391

(16,693 COMETS BLT.)

WHEEL COVER

MONTEGO H/T (17,785 BLT.)
$2605.

(COMET H/T $2532.
14,104 BLT.)

69

(14,104 COMETS BLT.)

STD. ENGINES:

new 250 CID 6 (155 HP)
OR 302 CID V8
(220 HP)

V8s UP TO
428 CID

(INTRO. 9-27-68)

1969 COMET and MONTEGO SHARE THIS GRILLE.

257

(COMET)/ **Montego** /CYCLONE

(3315 BLT.)

$2896.

M X

$2740.

1970

MX BROUGHAM

(1695 BLT.)
CYCLONE H/T

STD.
250 CID 6
(155 HP)
302 CID V8
(200 HP)

351 CID V8
(250 HP)
429 CID V8 (360, 370 OR 375 HP)

("COMET" NAME
SUSPENDED 1970)

1970

$3759.

(10/70 BLT.)
$3226.
F70 x 14 TIRES

70
GT

CYCLONE GT

(1631 BLT.)

(CYCLONE "SPOILER"
(ABOVE)

Comet
RETURNS!

109.9" WB
(4~DR.)

"6" or V-8

(2811/6 BLT.)

4~DR.

SALE
$2276.

2 or 4 doors

Comet GT.

SALE
$2217.
(54884
BLT.)

103" WB
(2~DR.)

71A

(INTRO. 9~11~70)

170 CID 6 OR 250 CID 6 (100, 115 OR 145 HP)
302 CID V8 (210 HP)

SALE
$2395.80

VINYL-COVERED
TOP OPTIONAL.

22 MPG
(6~CYL.,
CITY / HWY
AVG.)

COMET DASH

Better ideas make better cars.
The better small car.

(MONTEGO ON
NEXT PAGE)

COMET / MONTEGO/CYCLONE 70-71(A)

258

$2798

COMET ETC.

(9623 BLT.)

Energy-absorbing steering column with locking features

Printed electrical circuits in instrument cluster

Woodgrain vinyl paneling on the dash

Better ideas make better cars:

MONTEGO

MX WAGON

1971

(3698 BLT.)

$3331.

Exhaust emission control system

Dual brake system, self-adjusting brakes

Front tread 60.5"

Overall length 209.9"

Bias-belted tires

Rear tread 60.0"

Head restraints

Flow-thru ventilation

(STD. CPE. NO SIDE CHROME)

Montego

(REGULAR PRICE, 2-DR. 3694. UP)

117" WB (114" ON WAGONS)

INTERIOR

71B (CONT'D.)

250 CID 6 (145 HP)
302 CID V8 (210 HP)
F78 × 14 TIRES
(G78 × 14, WAGONS)

REAR

MX H/T (13719 BLT.

$3007.

ALL MODEL SERIES AVAIL. IN 1970 ARE CONTINUED. 1971 IS FINAL YR. FOR CYCLONE TYPES.

CENTER OF HOOD PROTRUDES AS BEFORE, BUT MONTEGO *has new* STANDARD GRILLE WITH CRISS-CROSS PIECES *and* EXPOSED HEADLIGHTS.

MONTEGO ← CYCLONE GT

(2287 BLT.)

$3680.

STANDARD CYCLONE ENGINE : 351 CID V8 (285 HP @ 5400 RPM)

GT GRILLE QUITE SIMILAR TO 1970 GT, BUT *has* new "GT" LETTERING IN CENTER CIRCLE.

MONTEGO MX VILLAGER WAGON

$3572. (2121 BLT.)

1971

CYCLONE GT DASH

COMET, ETC. 71 (B)

259

Comet , ETC.

$2398

COMET DASH

Better ideas make better cars.

A BETTER IDEA FOR SAFETY: BUCKLE UP.

(29092 4-DRS.)

4-DR. (STD.) WEST, $2474.
6.45 × 14 TIRES
(53267 2-DRS.)

COMET

1972

Comet GT
$2595.

COMET GT INTERIOR

4-DR. WITH EXTERIOR DECOR GROUP OPTION

72 A

FRONT RESTYLED ON MONTEGOS

(INTRO. 9-17-71)

note GT HOOD SCOOPS (2)

$3346.

$2848.

MONTEGO

Mercury Montego 2-Door Hardtop

MONTEGOS: new 114" WB (118" 4-DR.)

H/T $3639. (WEST)
(9963 BLT.)

302 CID V8 (140 HP) STD. ENG.

MONTEGO GT FASTBACK 2-DR. H/T
(5820 BLT.) $4137. (WEST)

note GT LOUVRES (3)

$3127.
(17540 BLT.)

Mercury Montego MX Brougham

MX DASH

MX 4-DR. PILLARED H/T (SEDAN)

INTERIOR →

$3742. (WEST)

$2951. (EAST)

(WEST)
$3918.

REAR WINDOW WASHERS AVAIL. ON MERCURY WAGONS (VARIOUS)

MX WAGON

MX

(23387 BLT.)

1972

(6268 BLT.)
$3264.

COMET, ETC. 72

COMET ETC. MX VILLAGER
ROOF RACK DPT. (9237 BLT.)
$3438.

Montego MX WAGON (UNGRAINED)
$3264.
302 CID V8 STD. ON WAGONS.
2-SEAT $4229.
3-SEAT 4305.

2-SEAT $4055.
(6268 BLT.)
3-SEAT $4131.

2 VARIETIES OF REAR SEATING AVAIL.

72 B (CONT'D.)

COMETS PRICED FROM $2432.

Built better to ride better.
MERCURY MONTEGO

(24329 BLT.)

MONTEGO MX BROUGHAM $3189.

F78 x 14 TIRES
MONTEGO MX BROUGHAM 4-DR. $3928.

(FINAL YR. FOR MONT. GT FASTBACK)

73

LARGE new ENERGY-ABSORBING SAFETY BUMPERS.

COMET CUSTOM DASH

COMET

MONTEGO MX DASH

2-DR. INT.

2-DR. (55707 BLT.)

COMET 4-DR. (28984 BLT.)

(COMET PRICES FROM $3122.) $3008. (WEST)

MONTEGO TIRE SIZES: G/H/HR 78 x 14

$3646.
GRILLE MOTIF NO LONGER CONT'D. AROUND HEADLIGHTS.

74

new REAR QUARTER OPERA WINDOWS ON MX BROUGHAM 2-DR $4481.

(INTERIOR ALSO ILLUSTRATED)

MONTEGO 2-DRS. PRICED FROM $4162.

Mercury Montego

Montego MX Brougham with optional Custom Trim, radio, remote control mirror, opera windows, white sidewall tires and bumper protection group.

COMET ETC. 72(B)~74

261

COMET, ETC.

$3270.
4-DR. (31080 BLT.)

DASH

Mercury Comet with Custom Option

200 CID 6 (78 HP)
302 CID V8 (122 HP)

Mercury Comet
4-DR.
$3453.

2-DR. (22768 BLT.)
$3236.

COMET 2-DRS. FROM $3419. (GT PKG. $277.)

Mercury Comet standard interior in cloth-and-vinyl

75
new DUAL SLOTS IN FRONT BUMPERS

MX WAGON (4508 BLT.) ($4671.)

MX VILLAGER WAGON (FROM $5450.) (5754 BLT.)

$4909.

1975
(THIS PICTURE ALSO IN 1976 CATALOG WITH 1976 LICENSE PLATE!)

4-DR. (4142 BLT.)

Mercury Montego
$4128.

Mercury Montego MX

351 CID V8 (150 HP) IN MONTEGOS

DASH
Mercury Montego MX instrument panel

$4304.
(13666 BLT.)
$4845.

Mercury Montego MX standard interior in cloth-and-vinyl

2-DR. H/Ts (4-DR. AVAIL.)

(8791 BLT.)

HR 78x14 TIRES

MX BROUGHAM INTERIOR

DASH
Custom Trim Option instrument panel for Montego MX Brougham

Mercury Montego MX Brougham–Custom Trim Option

BROUGHAM H/T
$4453.

$4994.

COMET, ETC. 75

4-DR. $3633.

COMET *ETC.*

2-DR. WITH OPTIONAL SPORTS ACCENT GROUP and SPORTS VINYL-COVERED ROOF

200 CID 6 (78~81 HP)
250 CID 6 (90 HP)
302 CID V8 (138 HP)

C78 x 14 TIRES

Comet Custom interior option

$3398.

BASIC 2-DR. PRICE: $3566. (15068 BLT.)

$3465.

4-DR. (21006 BLT.)

COMET WITH CUSTOM OPTION

76

SLIGHT CHANGE IN COMET GRILLE and AUX. LTS.
MONTEGO ENGS.:
351 CID V8 (152~154 HP)
400 CID V8 (180 HP)
460 CID V8 (202 HP)

FINAL COMETS AVAIL. INTO 1977 SEASON.

(6412 BLT.)

$4343.

MONTEGO

4-DR. $4904. (3403 BLT.)

IMITATION CHERRY WOODGRAIN ON MONTEGO MX VILLAGER
2-SEAT = $5626.
3-SEAT = 5734.
351 CID V8 (152 HP)
new WHEEL COVERS

$5065.

MONTEGO DISCONTINUED AT END of 1976 MODEL RUN.

MX Villager standard interior

2-DR. H/T $5026.

$4465.

MONTEGO MX
H/T (12367 BLT.)

$4670.

$4621.

A distinctive note: Opera window

MONTEGO MX BROUGHAM
2-DR. (3905 BLT.)

4-DR. (5043 BLT.)

COMET, ETC.   76

263

corvair (1960~1969)

compact.

DASH

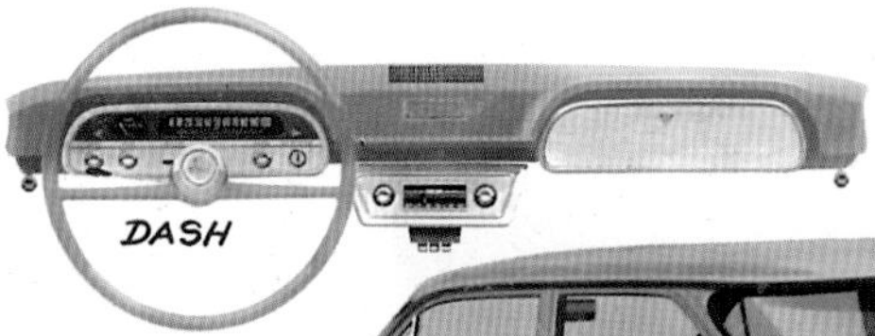

569 SEDAN

500
(NO CHROME BELT TRIM)

60
new!

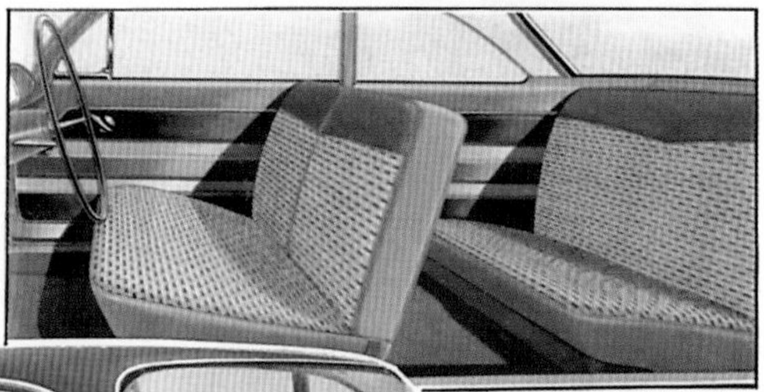

WITH THE ENGINE IN THE REAR

CLUB COUPE and INTERIOR (727)

AIR-COOLED 6-CYL.
REAR ENGINE-TRANSAXLE UNIT
140 CID
80 HP @ 4400 RPM
6.50 x 13
TIRES 108" WB

700

PRODUCTION =				PRICE =
500	527	COUPE	(14,628)	$1984.
	569	4-DR.	(47,683)	2038.
700	727	COUPE	(36,562)	2049.
	769	4-DR.	(139,208)	2103.
900 MONZA	927	COUPE	(11,926)	2238.

900 SERIES
(# 927)
MONZA CPE.
has DELUXE
INTERIOR
and BUCKET
SEATS.

4 DR. SEDAN and INTER.

BACK SEAT FOLDS, FOR CARGO.

$2103.
(769 SEDAN)

CORVAIR 60

264

corvair

500

CLUB
COUPE

$1920.

700

700
INTERIOR

spunkier 145-cu.-in. air-cooled rear engine

$2039.

4-DOOR
SEDANS

$2201.

new OPTION.
ELECTRIC
HOT AIR
HEATER

#969
SEDAN
$2201.

MONZA 900

note UNIQUE WHEEL COVERS
on NEW MONZA

new
CORVAIR MONZA
CLUB COUPE
and INTERIOR

61

CORVAIR
GREENBRIER
SPORTS WAGON

SWINGING
SIDE
DOORS
95"
WB

2 new
WAGON TYPES
and 2 SUB-TYPES

$2651.

GREENBRIER (STD.)

$2331.

700
(735)

LAKEWOOD
500
(535)

$2266.

LAKEWOOD
STATION WAGONS

SMART, DURABLE INTERIORS—Shown here: the 700's
rich fabric-vinyl upholstery, offered in three color-keyed
choices. 500 all-vinyl interior also comes in three color-
keyed blends. Check the push-button locks on rear doors.

735
LAKEWOOD
INTERIOR

700

ENGINE UNDER
REAR FLOOR.

PRODUCTION (CARS)	527 COUPE	(16,857)	769 4-DR. SEDAN	(51,948)
	535 LAKEWOOD WAGON	(5591)	927 MONZA COUPE	(109,945)
	569 4-DR. SEDAN	(18,752)	969 (MONZA) 4 DR.	(33,745)
	727 COUPE	(24,786)		
	735 LAKEWOOD WAGON	(20,451)		

CORVAIR 61

265

corvair

500

527 COUPE (16,245 BLT.)

FLAT 6 (80, 98 OR NEW 150 HP IN SPYDER) (THROUGH 1963)

$1992.

FINAL YEAR FOR LAKEWOOD WAGONS (3716 BLT.)

$2407.

GREENBRIER (AVAILABLE THROUGH '65)

969 MONZA SEDAN (48,059 BLT.)

$2273.

62

MONZA **900**

STD. 927 MONZA CPE. IS BEST SELLING 62 CORVAIR (144,844 BLT.)

700 $2057. UP

727 COUPE (18,474 BLT.)
735 LAKEWOOD (3716 ")
769 SEDAN (35,368 ")

124130

$2636.

MONZA SPYDER COUPE (6894 BLT.)

2056.

700 CLUB CPE. and SEDAN

DASH (ALL BUT SPYDER)

2110.

145 CID FLAT 6 (80 98 OR 150 HP)

500	FROM	1992.
700	FROM	2056
900 MONZA	FROM	2272
900 MONZA SPYDER	FROM	2589.

6.50 × 13 TIRES

BA·3515

note CHANGE IN FRONTAL STYLING

MONZA $2272. MONZA

63

SPORTS WAGON

GREENBRIER

MONZA

$2481.

CORVAIR 62~63

266

corvair

STD. ENGINE RAISED TO 95 HP.

FINAL **700**
#769 SEDAN (16,295 BLT.)
$2119.

64

new FRONT MEDALLION

#927 COUPE (88,440 BLT.)

DASH

$2281.

MONZA

SEDAN (21,926 BLT.)
$2335.

MONZA SPYDER (ABOVE) has 150 HP.

$3008. (4761 BLT.)
(667 CVT.)

ENGINE ENLARGED TO 164 CID (95, 110 OR 150 HP) (LONGER STROKE)

GB 8427

500

←DASH has CIRCULAR GAUGES.
$2066.

H/T (88,954 BLT.)
$2347.

#10137 H/T (36,747 BLT.)

MONZA

$2493.

#10567 CVT. (26,466 BLT.)
new LARGER BODIES

This year, <u>all</u> the coupes and sedans have hardtop styling

FROM **$2281.**
WEST COAST

65

(ONLY MAJOR CORVAIR RESTYLING)
new 5-DIGIT BODY MODEL NOS.

New power choices, too. There's a new 140-hp engine that's standard in Corsa models and can be ordered for all others—and a 180-hp power plant that you can specify for your Corsa.

#10539 (37,157 BLT.)

MONZA SPORT SEDAN

140 HP OR 180 HP
(CORSA IS new TOP OF LINE MODEL.)

$2422.

TOTAL PRODUCTION, 1964 = 195,780
            "   "   1965 = 204,007

CORVAIR 64~65

267

CORVAIR

MONZA

$2350.

A most unusual car for people who enjoy the unusual

(WEST COAST) $2630.

SPT. SEDAN (4-DR. H/T)

H/T $2556. (WEST COAST)

monza

CORSA $2662.

1966 SALES: 88,951

66

108" WB	6 CYL., 164 CID
7.00 × 13 TIRES	95-140 HP

$2424.

CORSA SERIES NO LONGER AVAILABLE 19

95 OR 110 HP ENGINES ONLY, DURING 1967.

'67 Corvair
The rear-engine road car

1967 SALES: 24,736

500 = 2 DR. H/T	$2128.
4 DR. H/T	2194.
MONZA = 2 DR. H/T	2398.
4 DR. H/T	2464.
CONVERT.	2540.

500

('67)

New oval steering wheel—This easy-to-grip wheel sits atop the GM-developed energy-absorbing steering column—one of many new standard safety features. Others include 4-way hazard warning flasher and a lane-change feature incorporated in direction signal control.

THIS BEST IDENTIFIES A 1967 MODEL.

67

('67)

MONZA CVT.

new DASH

OPTIONAL LUGGAGE RACK

(NO 4-DR. HARDTOPS AFTER 1967)

TOTAL PROD. 1968 = 12977
1969 = 3102

new SIDE SAFETY LIGHTS

Corvair 500 H/T $2528.

68-69

1968 Colors and Fabrics

DISCONTINUED MAY 14, 1969

$2641.
MONZA
CONVERTIBLE

1969 PRICES SHOWN

MONZA SPT. CPE. $2522.

CORVAIR 66~69

268

(STARTS 1953)

CORVETTE

(3/5 BLT. 1953, 3640 BLT. 1954)

MODEL 290 (UNTIL '57) (A.K.A. #2934)

102" WB (THROUGH '62)

235½ CID 6 CYL. CHEVROLET ENGINE

53 new! **54**

$3512. ('53)
3523. ('54)

CHEVROLET Corvette

INTERIOR (BROCHURE ILLUSTR.)

FULL-LENGTH SIDE TRIM ON REGULAR-PRODUCTION

Sports Car

6 CYL. OR new V8 (265 CID, 162 HP)

55

ILLUSTRATED with AVAIL. DETACHABLE TOP

(BECAUSE OF COMPETITION with FORD's new THUNDERBIRD,) 1955 CORVETTE PRICE CUT TO

(674 BLT., 1955)

$2799.

FIBERGLASS BODIES ON ALL (TO DATE)

V8 ENGINE ONLY, 1956 ON (265 CID, 1956; 283 CID, 1957 THROUGH '61)

H.P. IN 1957 = 220 (STD.) 245-270 (OPT.) 250-283 w. FUEL INJECTION

new TOP

SINCE '56, new SIDE TRIM

56-57

$2900. ('56)

$3437. ('57)

(3467 BLT., 1956)

new REAR FENDERS

(6339 BLT., 1957)

new 4 HEADLIGHTS

102" WB 230 HP

DASH

58 (9/68 BLT.)

RESTYLED

new VENT LOUVRE GROUP ON TOP OF HOOD (1958 ONLY)

$3631.

new BUMPERS

MODEL 867 (THROUGH 1964)

230 HP (STD.) 245-270 (OPT.) 250-290 (1959 w. FUEL INJ.) 275-315 (1960 w. FUEL INJ.)

59-60

(10,261 BLT., 1960)

$3872. (IN '60; $3 LESS THAN '59)

(9670 BLT., 1959)

XX-8956

269

CORVETTE $4272. **61** $3934.
WEST COAST

SAME HP CHOICES AS IN 1960

(10,939 BLT.) new GRILLE

new 300-340 OR 360 HP (F.I.) OPTIONAL (THROUGH '63)

new 250 HP STD. **62** (14,531 BLT.) $4038.
WEST COAST $4375.
new SIDE-SCOOP DESIGN

new "STINGRAY"

63 new SIDE-SCOOPS AGAIN

new GRILLE, CONCEALED HEADLIGHTS, new 98" WB

WEST $4589.
NEW

new #837 SPORTS COUPE (10,594 BLT.) $4252.

FASTBACK

new SHORTER 98" W.B.

#867 CONVT. RDSTR. (10,919 BLT.) $4037.

H.P. 250 (STD.) 300 (OPT.) 395 (WITH FUEL INJECTION)

(8304 BLT.) (13,925 BLT.) new 1-PC. BACKLIGHT → **64**

Corvette Sting Ray Convertible in Saddle Tan
Corvette Sting Ray Sport Coupe in Riverside Red

$4252. $4037.

WEST COAST $4627.
W. ADD-ON TOP

WEST COAST $4723.

327 CID V-8 HAS 250, 300, 350, 365 OR 375 HP @ 5500 RPM

65 WEST COAST $4508.

#19437 SPT. CPE. (8186 BLT.) $4321.

#19467 CVT. RDS. (15,376 BLT.)

4-WHEEL DISC BRAKES

$4106. new VERTICAL LOUVRE DESIGN

425 HP 396 CID V8 →

1965½ CORVETTE "396"

270

Corvette

327 CID V8 (300 OR 350 HP)
427 CID V8 (390 HP)
(OPT. 425 HP, '66 ; 435 HP, '67)

98" WB
(SINCE '63)

7.75 x 14
TIRES

66-67

CONVERTIBLE AVAIL. ALSO, AT
$4084. ('66) $4141. ('67)
17,762 BLT.   14,436 BLT.

9958 BLT. '66
8504 BLT. '67

COUPE
$4295. ('66)
4353. ('67)

1968 TOTALLY RESTYLED $4320.

COUPE
(9936 BLT.)
$4663.

WEST COAST:
$5157.
CPE.

new F70 x 15 TIRES

OPTIONAL
HARD
TOP →

(18,630 BLT.)

CVT.
$4814.
(WEST COAST)

Corvette simulated wood steering wheel and instrumentation.

new T-TOP (INTERIOR)

68

$4781.
(22,154
BLT.)

COUPE (22,154 BLT.)
$4781.

CONV'T.
$4438.
(16,608
BLT.)

EU·9262

69

"STINGRAY"
NAME ADDED,
ON FRONT FENDERS

327 CID REPL. BY new
350 CID V8
(300 HP)
427 CID V8 CONT'D.
(390, 400, 430
OR 435 HP)

CORVL//L 66~69

CORVETTE 70

98" WB (SINCE 1963)
350 CID V8
(300, 350 OR 370 HP)
427 CID V8
(390 OR 460 HP)

(6648 CVTS. BLT.,
AT $4849.)

$5192.

(10668 COUPES BLT.)

(14680 BLT.)
$5533.

71

350 CID V8
(270 OR 330 HP)
new 454 CID V8
(365 OR 425 HP)

4~SP.
close ratio box is available
with the 425-hp V8.
    With the 270-, 365-, and
425-hp engines, you can
order Turbo Hydra-matic.

CVT.
(7121 BLT.)
$5296.

(BELOW)
Chevrolet Corvette Stingray Convertible with removable hardtop.

DASH

Excitement Center 1971.

The standard all-vinyl
interior comes in black,
dark saddle, dark green,
dark blue and red.

T~BAR ROOF
AVAILABLE

Chevrolet Corvette Custom Interior and Telescopic steering column.

CORVETTE 70~71

272

BLUE-LIGHTED INSTRUMENTS (new)

COUPE (20846 BLT.)

Corvette

F70 x 15 TIRES

$5472.

$5246.

CHEVROLET

72 new SOFT CONTROL KNOBS, MARKED with FUNCTION SYMBOLS.

350 CID V8 (200 OR 255 HP)
454 CID V8 (270 HP @ 4400)

CVT. (6508 BLT.)

WILL RUN ON UNLEAD. FUEL

EU·9262

REMOVAB. T~ ROOF PANELS

new URETHANE RESILIENT FRONT END

($277. EXTRA FOR 2ND TOP FOR CVT.)

DASH SIMILAR TO 1972

73

new DOMED HOOD

350 CID V8
(190 HP @ 4400
OR 250 HP @ 5200)
454 CID V8
(275 HP @ 4400 RPM)

$5399.
CONVERTIBLE
(6093 BLT.)

new GRILLE and PARKING LTS.

COUPE (24372 BLT.)

new GR 70 x 15 TIRES

We gave it radials, a quieter ride, guard beams and a nose job.

350 CID V8 (195 OR 250 HP)
454 CID V8 (270 HP)

DASH

EXTERIOR COLORS
Corvette Dark Green Metallic (New)
Corvette Gray Metallic (New)
Corvette Brown Metallic (New)
Corvette Bright Yellow
Corvette Medium Red Metallic (New)
Corvette Silver Mist
Corvette Medium Blue Metallic
Mille Miglia Red
Corvette Orange Metallic
Classic White

INTERIOR TRIM COLORS
All-Vinyl (Standard)
• Silver (New) • Light Neutral (New)
• Medium Saddle • Dark Blue
• Dark Red • Black
Custom Interior (Available)
• Silver (New) • Medium Saddle (New)
• Black

'74 Corvette Stingray Convertible.

74 REAR RESTYLED (SLOPING)

5474 CVTS. BLT.
$5846.

COUPE (32028 BLT.) $6082.

CORVETTE 72~74

273

Corvette

(350 CID ONLY FROM 165 HP ('75) 180 HP ('76)

new CATALYTIC CONVERTER

(4629 BLT.)

(1975 IS FINAL CONVERT.)

'75

Available Custom interior with leather seat panels.

The roll of radials. Corvette's Efficiency System extends right to the road and those special GR70-15 steel-belted radial ply tires.

IMPROVED BUMPER SYSTEM ('75)

33836 CPES. ('75) $**6797.**

46558 CPES. ('76) $**7605.**

new HIGH ENERGY IGNITION

CORVETTE. AMERICA'S ONLY TRUE PRODUCTION SPORTS CAR.

-76

DASH

The only one.

(49213 BLT.) $**8648.** ($9504., WEST)

new EMBLEM

FRONT SIDE LIGHT LENS

77 new BLACK WINDSHIELD POSTS

INTERIOR

• Soft-Ray tinted glass.
• Black windshield posts give new "thin pillar" look.

CONSOLE

350 CID V8 (180 OR 210 HP)   CORVETTE 75~77

Corvette

the new rear window not only allows for a cleaner styling profile, it also improves driver visibility and adds luggage space. There's a roll shade to screen the luggage space. And there's room inside for storage of removable roof panels.

SEE WHAT'S NEW TODAY IN A CHEVROLET.

Chevrolet

$9645.

$10286. (WEST)

(2500 "SILVER ANNIVERSARY" MODELS, PLUS 6501* "PACE CAR REPLICAS")

*(SOME SOURCES SAY 6200)

(38967 STANDARD MODELS BLT.)

Silver Anniversary Corvette.

PACE CAR REPLICAS PRICED AT $13653.

new FASTBACK REAR WINDOW

78

new

25TH ANNIVERSARY EMBLEM (ALSO ON HOOD)

P225/60R x 15 TIRES (OR 70R)

ENGINE AVAILABILITY				Transmissions/Rear Axle Ratios	
All states except California				Automatic Transmission	
Engines	Power Rating†	4-Speed Manual	4-Speed Close-Ratio Manual	Below 4,000 Ft.	4,000 Ft. and Above
350 Cu. In. V8 (Std.)	185/175▲	3.36	NA	3.08	3.55
350 Cu. In. V8 (Avail. RPO L82)●	220	3.70/3.36*	3.70	3.55	NA
California only					
350 Cu. In. V8	175	NA	NA	3.55	NA

†S.A.E. net horsepower as installed.   *Available highway ratio.
STD.—Standard.   NA—Not available.   ▲Rating with High Altitude Emission Equipment.
●Not available California, Maryland, Florida, Oregon, Washington, also Boston, Chicago, Des Plaines (Ill.), Barrington (Ill.), Grand Rapids (Mi.) and Cook County (Ill.).

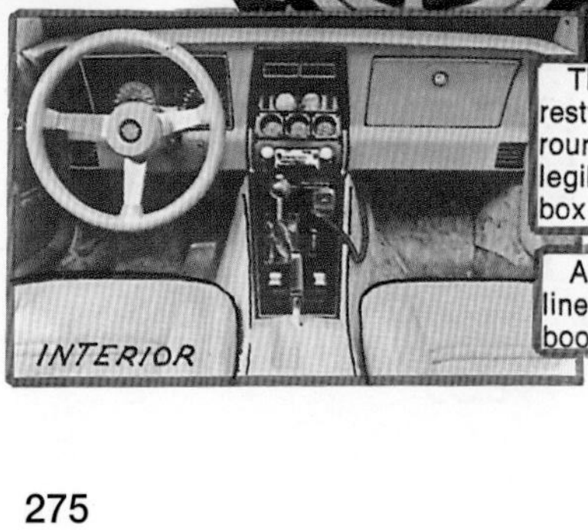

The instrument panel has also been restyled and features face-mounted, round instruments which are extremely legible as well as handsome. A new glove box has been added, too.

Also new for 1978 is a larger, plastic-lined fuel tank. Capacity has been boosted from 17 to 24 gallons.

INTERIOR

CORVETTE 78

CORVETTE

new 3.55 GEAR RATIO

AUTO. TRANS. REQUIRED IN CALIFORNIA

RETURN OF A SIMPLE CROSSED~FLAGS EMBLEM

$12313.

79

DASH AND CONSOLE

(53807 BLT.)

MINOR ENG. IMPROVEMENTS

350 CID V8 STD. (195 - 225 HP)

FIBERGLASS BODIES ON ALL CORVETTES (1953 ON)

P225/70R x15 OR P255/60R x15 TIRES

GOODYEAR POLYSTEEL RADIAL

(RESTYLED)

80

NEW STANDARDS FOR 1980
Air conditioning • Cornering lights • Power windows • Tilt-Telescopic steering wheel • Dual, remote-control Sport mirrors • Convenience group (includes time-delay dome and courtesy lights, headlight warning buzzer, underhood light, low fuel warning light, color-keyed floor mats, intermittent windshield wipers and a passenger-side illuminated visor vanity mirror).

Other exterior highlights include a new hood with a lower profile. New rear bumper cover with integral rear spoiler. New flag emblems. New rear lights. And cornering lights, new to Corvette as well as being standard, are fully automatic.

(40614 BLT.)

305 CID V8 (180, 190 OR 230 HP)

CORVETTE 79~80

(GDYR. GT TIRES, 1980)

new 2-PC. CORNERING LTS.

$13965.

new FRONT END WITH AIR DAM; LOW-PROFILE HOOD

CROSLEY

MFD. IN MARION, IND.

new!
39-42

POWEL CROSLEY, JR.

FOUNDER OF CROSLEY CORP. (KNOWN AFTER WW 2 AS CROSLEY MOTORS)

2-CYL. AIR-COOLED WAUKESHA ENGINE (35.3 CID) (THROUGH '42)

12 HP
MECHANICAL BRAKES

PRICE CUT TO
$299.
IN 1941.

$412.
IN 1942

80" WB
4.25 × 12 TIRES

CVT. (OTHER MODELS ALSO AVAIL.)

PRODUCTION (ALL BODY TYPES): 422 (1940); 2289 (1941); 1029 (1942)

CAR PRODUCTION: CONVERTIBLES:
12 (1946); 4005 (1947); 2845 (1948)

2-DR. SEDANS:
4987 (1946); 14,090 (1947); 2750 (1948, INCLUDING new SPORT UTILITY 2-DR.)

2-DR. WAGON: 1249 (new, 1947); 23,489 (1948)

"CC" SERIES

"a FINE car"

new 4-CYL. WATER-COOLED "COBRA" (COPPER-BRAZED) STAMPED-BLOCK 44 CID ENGINE (26½ HP @ 5400 RPM)

new BODY SIDES COMBINE with FULL-LENGTH FENDERS

WAGON

CVT.
$1035. ('47)
$931. = SEDAN
('47) new GRILLE, BUILT-IN HEADLIGHTS ABOVE

80" W.B.

(TOTALLY RESTYLED)

47-48

(POSTWAR PRODUCTION RESUMES DURING JUNE, 1946)

$799.
('48)

CROSLEY SPORTS-UTILITY

PICKUP

4.50 × 12" TIRES

PANEL DELIVERY   CROSLEY 39-48

CROSLEY

NOW CROSLEY HAS THE NEW LOOK

48½

new GRILLE
ON MID-YEAR
"NEW LOOK" SERIES

FOR 1949, COPPER-BRAZED, 58-lb. STAMPED ENGINE
REPLACED BY IMPROVED CAST-IRON VERSION (CIBA.)

49-50

new GRILLE, "SPEEDLINE"
STYLING

SEDAN

new 85" W.B.
"HOTSHOT"
SPORTS
ROADSTER
← (ALSO "SUPER SPORTS")

$866. ('49)
$882. ('50)

new
HYDRAULIC
DISC
BRAKES (BY
GOODYEAR-
HAWLEY)

CVT.

WAGON

(645 BLT. 1949)
(478 BLT. 1950)

"CD" SERIES
(THROUGH 1952)

(3803 BLT. 1949)
(4205 BLT. 1950,
INCLUDING *new*
$984 "SUPER WAGON")

ROADSTERS : 752 BLT. 1949
742 BLT. 1950

INSTRUMENT
CLUSTER
(HOTSHOT)

new BENDIX
9" HYDRAULIC
BRAKES

new "BUSINESS COUPE" VARIATION
OF 2-DR. SEDAN ($943.)

51-52

Crosley Hotshot

new 2-BLADED GRILLE *with*
CENTER "SPINNER"

"SUPER WAGON"

$952. $1029. (S.S.)
646 RDSTRS. BLT. 1951,
358   "   BLT. 1952

(9500 BLT.,
1951)
(1355 BLT. 1952)
(WAGON, SU. WAGON)

$1450. ('51)
$1077. ('52)

DISCONTINUED DURING 1952

Cougar (STARTS 1967)

BY *MERCURY*

111" WB
289 CID V8
(200 HP)
7.35 × 14 TIRES
390 CID V8
(320 HP) IN "GT PERFORMANCE GRP."

67

Cougar all-vinyl bucket-seat interior (Full-width front seat optional)

H/T (116,260 BLT.)

New
$2851.
$3213.
(WEST)

[LINCOLN/MERCURY'S COUNTERPART TO FORD'S POPULAR MUSTANG]

REAR

COUGAR ADVERTISING MASCOT

(GT H/T 7412 BLT. $3175.)

WITH TRIP ODOMETER

XR-7
$3081.
$3443.
(WEST COAST)

has GRAINED DASH and BEARS THIS SYMBOL

(27,221 BLT.)

XR7

TAILLIGHTS HARMONIZE WITH GRILLE DESIGN

COUGAR

TOTAL 1967 PRODUCTION: 150,893

WESTERN PRICES SHOWN IN BLACK

CALENDAR YEAR PRODUCTION: 131,743

COUGAR 67

STD. H/T
$**2933**.

COUGAR

E 70 × 14 TIRES
289 CID V8 STD.
427 CID V8 (390 HP)
IN GT. E

(GT MODEL ALSO)

electric sunroof

$**3232**.
(32,712 BLT.)

$3296.
(WEST COAST)
(81,014 BLT.)

68

$3594.
(WEST COAST)

XR-7-G has
SPORT-STYLE HOOD
and RALLYE LIGHTS
(GT.E has HORIZ. BAND ACROSS GRILLE)

new SAFETY SIDE LIGHTS

WESTERN PRICES
FROM $3383.
(WEST COAST)

1969½ "ELIMINATOR" (not illustr.) has new FRONT and REAR SPOILERS.

$3016.

VARIOUS V8s AVAIL., INCLUDING
new 351 CID V8 (250 HP @ 4600 RPM)
E 78 × 14 TIRES

69

new DOWNSWEPT SIDE SCULPTURE

new GRILLE

(new STD. or XR-7 CONVERTIBLES ALSO AVAIL.)

H/T (66,331) $3016.
XR7 H/T (23,918) $3315.

CONVERT. (5796) $3382.
XR7 CONVERT. (4024) $3595.

COUGAR 68~69

COUGAR XR-7

CVT. (1977 BLT.) $3692.

ELIMINATOR H/T

70 new GRILLES

"ELIMINATOR" has HOOD SCOOP and STRIPES, BODY STRIPES and BLACK GRILLE)

(18565 BLT.) $3413.

note THAT XR-7 GRILLE DIFFERS FROM STANDARD 1970 COUGAR GRILLE SEEN ON "HOUNDSTOOTH" MODEL

$4170. WESTERN PRICE

CLOSER VIEW OF HOUNDSTOOTH TOP COVERING

AVAIL. TRIP ODOMETER and TACHOMETER

It's wild. It's sophisticated. It's elegant. The sporty look of houndstooth for spring. Cougar sets the trend with houndstooth check vinyl roof and hi-back cloth-and-vinyl buckets. Designer Pauline Trigère comes up with a swaggering houndstooth cape to match. Cougar...far more than just a sporty car. It's styled with European flair. Lean and sculptured, with concealed headlamps and sequential rear turn signals. Powered by a restless 351 cubic-inch V-8. It's the best

INTERIOR

Introducing the Houndstooth Cougar...

"HOUNDSTOOTH" MODEL STARTS SPRING, 1970

with a little something to match by Pauline Trigère.

FROM $3871. WESTERN PRICE

STD. H/Ts (49479 BLT.) $3114.
" CVTS. (2322 BLT.) $3480.

A RETURN OF DOWNWARD EXTENSION OF HOOD AT CENTER, AS IN 1968.

COUGAR 70

COUGAR

STD. CVT. ('71)

BLACK DASH

STD. CVT. — 1971 $3681.
1972 3370.

REAR WINDOW TREATMENT (H/T) →

351 CID V8 CUT FR. 240 TO 164 HP FOR 1972.

new 112"WB (RESTYLED)

71-72

XR-7

H/T

CVT.

('72)

WOOD-GRAINED DASH

PRICE CUTS ON ALL 1972 MODELS

('71)

1971 $3629. '72 3323.

TOTAL PRODUCT. =
1971 – 62864
1972 – 53702

XR-7 ROUND EMBLEM (OTHERWISE, EMBLEM IS UPRIGHT RECTANGULAR.)

COUGAR 71~72

COUGAR

(FINAL COUGAR CONVERTS.)

$3726.
(STD. CONV'T.) (1284 BLT.)

$3903.
(XR-7 CONV'T.)
(3165 BLT.)

73

(PRICED FROM
$3821., AFTER
1972 PRICE CUTS)

INTERIOR

351 CID V8
(168 OR 264 HP)

SUNROOF
DETAILS

STD. H/T
$3372.
(21069 BLT.)

TOTAL 1973 PROD. = 60628
It's not like anybody else's car.

XR-7

DASH

$3679.
(XR-7 H/T)
(35110 BLT.)
$4152.

new
GRILLE
STYLED
LIKE A
"RADIATOR"

PRODUCTION = 91670 ('74); 62987 ('75); 83765 ('76)

74-76

new OPERA WINDOWS

new AND ENLARGED
SERIES (114" WB)
XR-7 H/T

new GRILLE

1974 DASH →
(1975 has
new
2-SPOKE
STEERING
WHEEL.)

1975 and 1976 have
2 OPENINGS IN LOWER
CENTER SECTION OF
FRONT BUMPER

new ORNAMENT

('74)

new UPHOLSTERY PATTERN
XR-7, '74

1974,
(WITHOUT BUMPER OPENINGS)

2-DR. HARDTOP, XR-7,
IS ONLY REMAINING MODEL, (UNTIL '77)

PRICES =
$4706.
('74)
$5218.
('75)
$5125.
('76)

Mercury Cougar XR-7 instrument panel
('76)   COUGAR 73~76

COUGAR

Introducing a new symbol of driving excitement.
The 1977 Cougar XR-7 unleashes 6 new running mates.

WESTERN PRICES SHOWN (IN BLACK)

PRICED FROM $5284. ('77)

$5631. ('78)

$4832. UP ('77)

2 New Hardtops
'77 = $4700. UP
'78 = $5052. UP

FOR 1977 ONLY, 2 New Wagons

(RESTYLED)

77-78

(351 CID V8, 161 HP IN WAGONS)
$5104. UP

2 New Sedans

2-DRS. 114" WB
4-DRS. 118" WB
'77 = 302 CID V8 (130 HP)
OR 351 CID V8 (149 OR 161 HP)

FOR 1978, ONLY STD. and XR-7 HARDTOPS and THE 4-DR. SEDAN ARE CONTINUED.

TOTAL PRODUCTION =
1977 = 184,823
1978 = 213,270

'78 = (400 CID, 166 HP V8 OPT.)

XR-7

('77)

FINAL COUGAR DASH WITH ROUND GAUGES

302 OR 351 CID V8

79

(2831 BLT.)

STD. H/T $5379.

STD. H/T $5379.

BODY-COLOR TAPE STRIPS IN XR-7 GRILLE

STD. H/T $6165.

new TAILLIGHTS WITH HORIZONTAL CHROME STRIPS

1979

$6635. XR-7 $6430.

(163,716 BLT.)

AVAILABLE V8 ENGINES =
302 CID (129 OR 133 HP) (STD.)
351 CID (135 HP) (STD. IN XR-7)
"   " (151 HP) (OPTIONAL)

(4-DR. SEDAN = $5524.)
(5605 BLT.)

TOTAL 1979 PRODUCTION = 172,152

COUGAR 77~79

284

COUGAR
STANDARD DASH

NEW!

new KEYLESS (OPTIONAL) DOOR ENTRY (PUSH-BUTTON) COMBINATION LOCK

new

STD. 255 CID V8 (115 HP) (4.2 L)
OPT. 302 CID V8 (130-131 HP)

XR-7 (ONLY MODEL AVAIL.)

FROM **$7045.**

(58028 BLT.)

RECARO BUCKET SEATS AVAIL.

new REAR STYLING

P185/75R × 14 TIRES

COUGAR XR-7 EXTERIOR COLORS

Standard Colors

1C Black
9D White
1G Silver Metallic
12 Light Grey*
7M Dark Pine Metallic*
8A Dark Chamois Metallic*
6D Pastel Sand*
3L Midnight Blue Metallic*

8N Dark Cordovan Metallic*
2K Candy Apple Red*

Optional Glamour Paints

2H Medium Red Metallic
3H Medium Blue Metallic
8D Medium Bittersweet Metallic*
8W Chamois Metallic*
*New for 1980

Color chips: 1C, 9D, 1G, 12, 7M, 2H, 3H, 8A, 6D, 3L, 8N, 2K, 8D, 8W

ELECTRONIC DASH

80

DOWNSIZED and RESTYLED
new 104.8" WB

XR-7 WITH SPORTS GROUP.* A SPECIAL

FROM **$7271.**
WESTERN PRICE

WHEEL CHOICES (left to right) STANDARD COVER; DECOR GROUP COVER; WIRE WHEEL COVER; CAST ALUMINUM WHEEL.

COUGAR 80

DART

Dodge Division of Chrysler Corporation

FULL-SIZED
LOWER-PRICED
new COMPANION
TO

Dodge

STARTS 1960

(BECOMES A
COMPACT CAR, 1963)

SENECA

$2410. (6)
$2530. (V8)

(STARTS 1960)

M21
2 DR.

PIONEER

L 45 WAGON $2695. (6) $2815. (V8)

H23 2-DR. H/T
$2618. (6) $2737. (V8)

PHOENIX

H43 4 DR. H/T
$2677. (6)   2796. (V8)

118" WB (WAGONS 122")
(THROUGH '61)

60 new!

PD3 (6 CYL.)
PD4 (V8)

225 CID SLANT 6 has
145 HP @ 4000 RPM
318, 361 and 383 CID V8 have
230, 255, 310, 325
or 330 HP.

$2787. UP

PIONEER WAGON
M 45 A (6-PASS.)
M 45 B (9-PASS.)

THE DODGE DART IS PRICED MODEL FOR
MODEL WITH OTHER LOW-PRICE CARS.

DODGE DART	CAR F	CAR P	CAR C
SENECA	Fairlane	Savoy	Biscayne
PIONEER	Fairlane 500	Belvedere	Bel Air
PHOENIX	Galaxie	Fury	Impala

PRODUCTION = SENECA 6   (93,167)
SENECA V8   (45,737)
PIONEER 6   (36,434)
PIONEER V8   (74,665)
PHOENIX 6   (6567)
PHOENIX V8   (66,608)

H27 PHOENIX
CONVERTIBLE AVAIL.,
$2868. UP

(HIGHEST-PRICED MODEL = PIONEER V8 9 PASS. WAGON, $3011.)

WAGON
with
TAILGATE
OPEN

New Economy Slant "6" Uses Exclusive Semi-Ram Intake Manifold!

New design
features
inclined block
with new
Equi-flow fuel
induction, over-
head valves,
for greater
fuel economy.

DART 60

286

DART

$2695. UP

L45G (6)   L55G (V8)

SENECA

145 HP 6-CYL. CONTINUES

SENECA STATION WAGON 6 OR V8, 4 PASSENGER

SENECA 4 DOOR SEDAN 6 OR V8

$2330. UP

M46G, M4G7 (6)
M56G M5G7 (V8)

PIONEER STATION WAGON 6 OR V8, 5 OR 9 PASSENGER

PIONEER 4 DOOR SEDAN 6 OR V8

$2459. UP

$2595. UP

RD3 (6 CYL.)
RD4 (V8)

$2787. UP

PIONEER

PHOENIX 4 DOOR HARDTOP 6 OR V8

61

318, 361, 383 and new 413 CID V8s (230 TO 375 HP)

PHOENIX

H535 CONVT. (V8 ONLY)

convertible

$2988.

PRODUCTION =		
SENECA 6 (60,527)	SENECA V8 (27,174)	FINAL YEAR FOR THESE MODEL NAMES
PIONEER 6 (18,214)	PIONEER V8 (39,054)	
PHOENIX 6 (4273)	PHOENIX V8 (34,319)	

DART 330 2-DOOR HARDTOP 6 OR V8

DART 330 4-DOOR 6-PASSENGER WAGON 6 OR V8

DART 330 2-DOOR SEDAN 6 OR V8

$2463. UP

$2739. UP

$2375. UP

$3092.

DART 440 9-PASSENGER WAGON V8

new 116" WB ('62 ONLY)

62

(TOTALLY RESTYLED)

SAME DISPL. AS '61
145 TO 380 HP

DART 440 CONVERTIBLE V8

$2945.

MODELS

DART 6 =	(SD1-L)
" " 300	(SD1-M)
" " 440	(SD1-H)
DART V8 =	(SD2-L)
" " 330	(SD2-M)
" " 440	(SD2-H)

(BUDGET-PRICED "FLEET SPECIAL", **$2158. UP**)

1962 IS FINAL YEAR THAT DART IS DODGE-SIZED.

DART 61~62

SD SERIES

THE NEW LEAN BREED OF DODGE

DART
713 SEDAN
$2041. 170
(RESTYLED)
63 TL1 SERIES
756 WAGON $2309.
731 2-DR.
8.2 COMPR.
WHEELBASE REDUCED AGAIN, TO 111"
(106" WB ON WAGONS)
compact
$2512.
270
776 WAGON
$2433.
PRODUCTION =
170 (58,536)
270 (61,159)
H/TGT (34,227)
DASH
745 CVT.
GT 742 H/T
$2289.
ALL 1963 DARTS ARE 6-CYL.
170 CID 101 HP @ 4400 RPM
OR 225 CID 145 HP @ 4000 RPM

$2318. #742 H/T
TWO SLANT SIXES AS IN '63
new 273 CID V8
(180 HP @ 4200)
$2315.
170
GT
64
VL1 (6)
VL2 (V8)
"DODGE" NAME ACROSS new GRILLE
(270 STILL AVAIL.)
$2053.
SEDAN

new GRILLE
65
ENGINES AS IN 1964
AL1(6) AL2(V8)
$2407.
$2481.
Dodge Dart 270 convertible. 6 and V8 power.
270
Dodge Dart 4-door station wagon. 2-seat model only. 6 and V8 power.
L-56
DART (EX-170)
GT
Dart GT two-door hardtop.
L-42
Dodge Dart 2-door sedan. 6 and V8 power.
L-11

L-45
(GT CONVERT. ALSO AVAILABLE, $2628.)

1965
PRODUCTION (BY MODEL SERIES) =
DART (AL1-L) (86,013 BLT.) $2074. UP
DART 270 (AL1-H) (78,245 BLT.) $2180. UP
DART GT (AL1-P) (45,118 BLT.) $2404. UP

DART 63~65

Dart

170 CID 6 (101 HP)

225 CID 6 (145 HP) OR

273 CID V8 (235 HP)

2-DR. $2319.

$2661.

Dart 4-door sedan. Six or 273 V8 power.

$2383.

JOIN THE DODGE REBELLION

WAGONS | $2094.~2828. PRICE RANGE
$2319.~2925. WEST COAST PRICES (LISTED HERE)

66 new GRILLE

111" WB (106," WAGONS)

6.50×13 TIRES

DART 270 SERIES

2-DR. $2439.

270 WAGON $2758.

270 CVT. $2795.

270 H/T $2532.

270 4-DR. $2505.

GT

GT HAS CHROME ATOP FR. FENDERS AND ON ROCKER PANELS

GT H/T $2642.

PARTIAL VINYL TOP AVAIL.

GT CVT. $2925.

TOTAL 1966 PRODUCTION = 176,027 (75,990 DARTS; 69,996 DART 270s; 30,041 DART GTs)
(146,361 CALENDAR YEAR)

DART 66

289

$2453. DART

$2416.
(WEST COAST)

DART
WAGONS
DISCONTINUED

(INTRO
9-29-66) **67**

(RESTYLED)

←MODELS (6 OR V8)

CLL DART = (53,043 BLT.) $2187. ~ 2352.
CLH DART 270 = (63,227 ") 2362. ~ 2516.
CLP DART GT = (38,225 ") 2499. ~ 2860.
(WEST COAST PRICES HIGHER)

ENGINES :
170 CID SLANT-6 (115 HP)
225 " " " (145 HP)
273½ " V8 (180 OR 235 HP)

new SUNKEN-IN REAR WINDOW

$2388. (6)
2516. (V8)

$2591.

DART 270

$2617.
(WEST COAST)

The Dodge Rebellion: Operation '67

CONVERTIBLE (GT)
$2732. (6) 2860. (V8)

Go '67 Dart!"

WEST COAST $2961.

GT

$2728.

REDESIGNED RECESSED INSTRUMENT PANEL

note "GT" TAGS

FULL 1967 LINE ILLUSTRATED

DART 67

290

Dart

2-DR.
$2556.

4-DR.
$2593.

270 4-DR.
$2732.

270

(INTRO. 9-14-67) $2323.~3383.
($2556.~3445. WEST COAST)
new GRILLES

68

DODGE fever

TAIL-LT. DETAIL

PLAIN TOP

GT

270 H/T
$2758.

GT H/T
$2860.

GT CVT.
$3064.

GTS CVT.
$3445.

VINYL TOP (OPT.)

GT SPORT (GTS) 340 CID V8

340 CID V8

H/T
$3251.

FULL 1968 LINE ILLUSTRATED

This year, DODGE is turning up the fever

(270 BECOMES CUSTOM)
$2550. UP

69

new GRILLES

(INTRO. 9-19-68)

DASH

Announcing Dart Swinger. (new)

$2400.

$2637.
(WEST COAST)

TOTAL 1968 PRODUCTION = 171,772
TOTAL 1969 " = 221,673
BY MODEL SERIES
DART (106,329, INCL. SWINGER 340); CUSTOM (63,740);
GT (20,914); GTS V8 (6702);

DART 68~69

ENGINES:
170 CID SLANT-6 (115 HP)
225 CID " " (145 HP)
273½ CID V8 (190 HP)
318 CID V8 (230 HP)
340 CID V8 (275 HP); 383 CID V8 (330 HP)

291

Dart

1970 Dart

DART
111" WB

(36499 BLT.)
$2308.
4-DR.

$2807.

DART CUSTOM 4-DR. SEDAN
$2467.
$2972.

(23779 BLT.)

CUSTOM

CUSTOM H/T
$2999.

$2463.

(17208 BLT.)

OPT. WH. CVRS.

* **60 DAY SWINGER AUTOMATIC SALE!**

(NO DART 2-DR. SEDAN AVAIL. 1969 OR 1970)

INCLUDES EXTRAS LISTED AT BOTTOM OF PAGE.

'70

(INTRO. 9-23-69) (BUCKET STS. OPT. IN CUST., SW. 340 H/Ts)

SWINGER 340 H/T
$3171.

$2790.

SWINGER H/T

Dart Swinger 2-door hardtop. Our lowest priced hardtop.

SWINGER

SHOWING ALL-STEEL RALLYE WHEELS

(13785 BLT.) **$2631.**

SWINGER 340
(ABOVE)

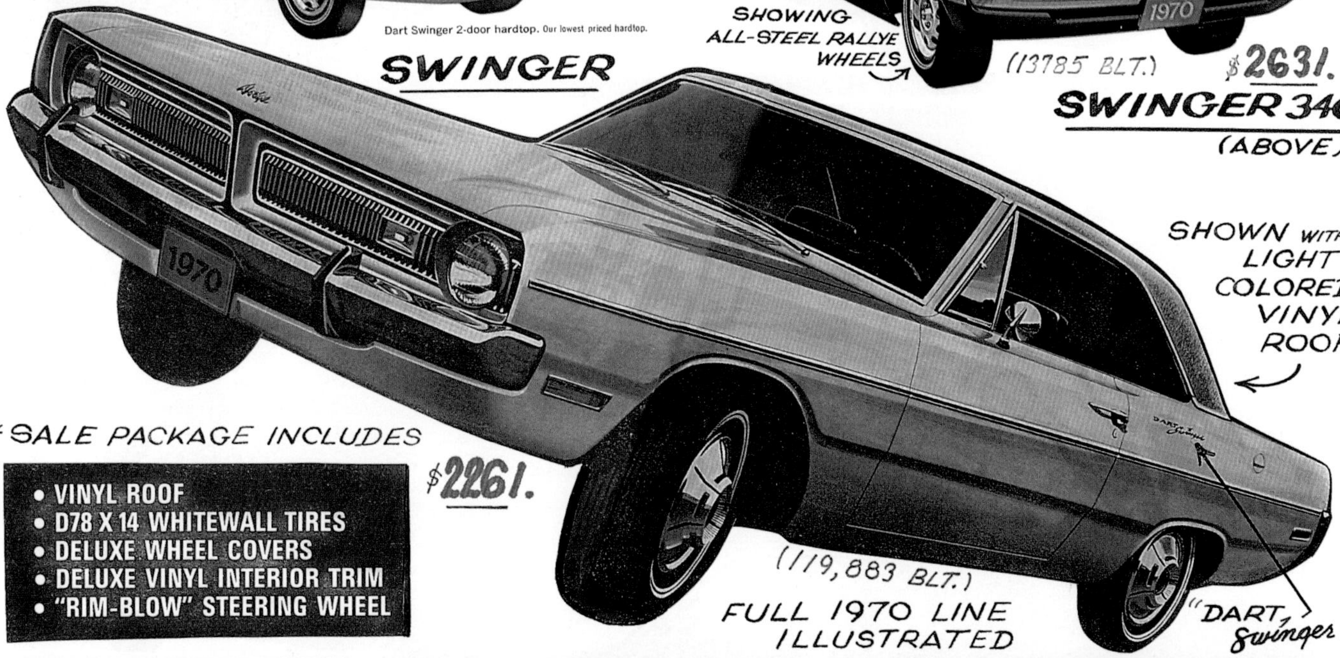

SHOWN WITH LIGHT COLORED VINYL ROOF

$2261.

(119,883 BLT.)

FULL 1970 LINE ILLUSTRATED

"DART, Swinger"

* **SALE PACKAGE INCLUDES**
- VINYL ROOF
- D78 X 14 WHITEWALL TIRES
- DELUXE WHEEL COVERS
- DELUXE VINYL INTERIOR TRIM
- "RIM-BLOW" STEERING WHEEL

DART SWINGER 2-DOOR HARDTOP

America's swingingest compacts: the Dodge Darts! Just what you're looking for. Fun to drive. Economical to run. Easy to own. For '70, there's a brand-new Dart "look." A longer hood, a powerful new rear styling treatment. Five great new Darts for '70: Swinger hardtop, Dart four-door sedan, handsome Dart Custom four-door sedan, and Dart Custom hardtop. And for high performance at a low price, go Swinger 340—

*Optional, at extra cost, on some Dart models.

- LEFT, REMOTE-CONTROL MIRROR
- CARPETS
- VINYL BODY-SIDE MOULDINGS
- BUMPER GUARDS (Frt. & Rr.)
- WHEEL-LIP/BELT MOULDINGS

a hardtop loaded with more goodies (340 V8, disc brakes, three-on-the-floor, etc.) than many cars near its price! Every Dart model has room for six. With a trunk that holds a vacation's worth of luggage. Run-of-the-mill models? On page 14, you'll find over fifty Dart options to add as many personal touches as you want. You can have your '70 Dart any way you want it: as a town car, a suburban shopper, a travel car, or (as a Swinger 340)

one of the greatest "stormers" ever designed. Four engine choices: 198 and 225* Sixes, 318 and 340 V8s. Four boxes: three-on-the-tree, three- or four-on-the-floor,* or the three-speed automatic.* More wheel and wheel cover choices than ever before. Ask your Dealer for all the news. See the '70 Dart. By all means, drive it! *If you won't take small for an answer . . . you could be* **DODGE MATERIAL.**

automatic trans.

1970 Dart

$2561.

Dart
SWINGER
$2808.
(102,480 BLT.)

Dart CUSTOM
$2856. →

(49941 BLT.)
$2609.

(INTRO. 9-15-70)

new GRILLE
$2721.
↙

71
new BODY
(ONLY ON NEW DEMON CPES.)

$3000.
(10098 BLT.)
340 CID V8
(275 HP)
↗

DEMON 340

(new) DEMON
(108"WB) FROM
$2590.
(69861 BLT.)
198 CID 6 (125 HP)
OR 318 CID V8
(230 HP)

DEMON $2343.

DODGE DEMON

ALSO AVAIL. SWINGER SPEC. H/T
($2649.) and
DART SEDAN
($2697.)

WESTERN PRICES SHOWN IN BLACK

DART

SEDAN
$2665.
(20019 BLT.)

$2528.
new GRILLE

72
(INTRO. 9-28-71)

$2420.

DODGE DART

DART SWINGER H/T
$2773.

(119,618 BLT.)

Med. Tan Metallic (B) | Super Blue (B) | Hemi Orange (B)* | Top Banana (B)*

DART

$2561.

Dodge. Depend on it.

DART DEMON H/T

$2316.

1972 DEMON REAR STYLING SIMILAR TO 1971

DASH

COLORS
Lt. Blue (A) | Bright Blue Metallic (A) | Red (A) | Lt. Green Metallic (A) | Dk. Green Metallic (A) | Eggshell White (A) | Black (A) | Lt. Gold (A) | Gold Metallic (A) | Dk. Gold Metallic (A) | Dk. Tan Metallic (A) | Lt. Gunmetal Metallic (B)

DART H/T

DART 71-72

293

Dart

$2898.

NO SIDE CHROME ON *DART SWINGER SPECIAL* H/T

$2702.
$2462.
(17480 BLT.)

$2857.

Dart Custom Sedan & Swinger Hardtop

73
new GRILLE and BUMPERS

(68113 BLT.)

Dart Sport. $2424.
$2664.

DASH

$3124.

SPORT (108" WB) MODELS REPLACE DART DEMONS.

REAR CLOSE-UP (DART)

$2853.

SPORT 340

Dodge invents the Convertriple. Three cars for the price of one.

(11315 BLT.)

Colors

Pale Green (A) · Bronze Metallic (C) · Gold Metallic (A) · Parchment (A) · Dark Green Metallic (A) · Light Blue (A) · Bright Red (A) · Dark Silver Metallic (A) · Bright Blue Metallic (A) · Light Gold (A) · Dark Gold Metallic (A) · Light Green Metallic (A) · Eggshell White (A) · Black (A) · Super Blue (C) · Top Banana* (C)

DART 73

294

DART SWINGER $3873.
3//9.
CUSTOM
$3915.
(16/55 BLT.)
$2918.

TODAY—more than ever—
Dart is right on target.

(SPORT TOPPER, SPORT HANG 10, SPORT RALLYE DELS ALSO)

74

Extra care in engineering makes a difference in Dodge ...depend on it.

$3674.

DART SPORT CONVERTRIPLE '74.

Dart Special Edition. new

74½ MODEL $3837.

1 IT'S A FIVE-PASSENGER COUPE. With the size and features you wouldn't expect from a compact. Features such as torsion-bar suspension, Unibody construction, and the Electronic Ignition System...Dart Sport 1 makes 2 and 3 that much better.

2 IT'S A SUN ROOF CONVERTIBLE. What an option! You get a secure metal sun roof that slides open to give you the sun in the morning and the moon at night. With Dart Sport, the sky's the limit. So sit back, relax, and start to follow the sun.

3 IT'S AN ECONOMY WAGON. With the optional fold-down rear seat, you can flip yourself into a wagon in seconds and have a fully carpeted cargo space that's six-and-a-half feet long. Dart Sport Convertriple '74. Pack it up and get going.

1974

$4349.

The new Dart Special Edition is based on the premise that a small car can be a *very* luxurious car. High-backed seats covered in crushed velour

Dart Special Edition.

WESTERN PRICES SHOWN IN BLACK

$4/59.

$4565. (WEST)

Dart "Hang 10."

DASH

INTERIOR

new GRILLE

(EARLY)

75-76

THE FINAL DART

1975

('75)

REPLACED DURING 1976 BY DODGE ASPEN.

DART 74~76

Dodge is right on target

'48 DAVIS 3-WHEEL CAR

STATION
WAGON
(PROPOSED)

DAVIS MOTOR CAR COMPANY
8055 WOODLEY AVENUE
VAN NUYS, CALIFORNIA

$995.

ONLY 1 7~PASS.
SEDAN BUILT

Presenting the
Davis 7 PASSENGER SEDAN

CONVERTIBLE
WITH REMOVABLE
ALUMINUM TOP
IS ONLY
FULL~PRODCTN.
MODEL,
AVAILABLE
1948 and 1949

108 " W.B.
4 ~ CYL.
HERCULES OR
CONTINENTAL
ENGINE
60 ~ 63 H.P.
WT. = 1385 lbs.

FRONT SEAT
WIDE ENOUGH
TO SEAT 4!
(64 ")

35 TO 50 M.P.G.
TOP SPEED
100 M.P.H. PLUS!

2 DAVIS
3~WHEEL
ARMY JEEPS
ALSO BUILT.

DETAILS

ALUMINUM CONVERTIBLE TOP
64" 4 PASSENGER SEAT
AIR DUCT BETWEEN FAN & RADIATOR
15" FAN
CONCEALED HEADLAMP
SPARE WHEEL
25 CU.FT. OF TRUNK
20 GAL. FUEL TANK
QUICK DISCONNECT CANNON PLUG
4 CYL. 60 H.P. HERCULES ENG.
INDIVIDUAL COIL SPRING & OLEO SHOCK ABSORBER
5.50" X15" TIRES ON ALL WHEELS

DAVIS D-2

PICKUP
(PROPOSED)

DAVIS

296

DE SOTO CUSTOM
COUPE (1929~1961)

DeSoto

TOTAL 1940 PRODUCTION
67,790

AUX. SEATS $60. EXTRA

	Body	Price	Weight	Prod
Deluxe	2dr B cpe	$845	3001	3650
	2dr AS cpe	905	3026	2098
	2dr Tr sdn	905	3066	7072
	4dr Tr sdn	945	3086	18666
Long Wheelbase				
	4dr Tr Sdn/7P	1175	3490	142
	4dr Cal taxi	N/A	N/A	2323

CUSTOM has CHROME TRIM BELOW TAIL~LTS.

MFD. BY CHRYSLER CORPORATION

CUSTOM 7-PASS. SEDAN

DE SOTO
TWO TONE SPORTSMAN

S~7

40 RESTYLED

DE SOTO—America's Family Car

DE LUXE 2~DR.

Custom	2dr Cpe	885	3024	1898
	2dr AS cpe	945	3044	2234
	2dr Conv	1095	3329	1085
	2dr Tr sdn	945	3084	3109
	4dr Tr sdn	985	3104	25221
Long Wheelbase				
	4dr Tr sdn/7P	1215	3490	206
	4dr Limo/7P	1290	3635	34
	Chassis	N/A	N/A	52

Custom

CONVERTIBLE

(1085 BLT.)

IN BRILLIANT TWO-TONE GREEN (AMPHIBIAN GREEN Above GARLAND GREEN)

has POWER~OPERATED TOP

SPLIT GRILLE

DASH

DE LUXE has NO CHROME TRIM BELOW TAIL~LTS.

100 160 212

TEMP

AMPS

35 - 0 + 35

0 40 80

OIL

FUEL

E 1/2 F

000267

HEAD LIGHTS   THROTTLE

GAUGES

"De Soto" ON REAR BUMPER

40 DE SOTO

BROUGH. VENT PANE

1941 DE SOTO

$1085.
(2-TONE PAINT EXTRA)

BACK SEAT

2-DR. SEDAN

2-DR. BROUGHAM SIMILAR, BUT HAS EXTRA "BUTTERFLY" VENT PANES IN BACK-SEAT SIDE WINDOWS.

CLUB COUPE $1025. UP

3-W. CPE

CUSTOM (2033 BLT.)
(VERTICAL CHROME TRIM BELOW TAIL-LTS.)

17 FEET OF *Sheer Beauty!*

SEE THE New 1941 De Soto

(ABOVE)
CUSTOM SEDAN
(30,876 BLT.)

New
SPLIT GRILLE WITH VERTICAL PCS.

SALE $898 *DELUXE* 3-WINDOW COUPE (REG. $945.)

(4449 BLT.)
New 41 BODY TYPE S-8

RESTYLED

CLOCK OPTIONAL

Slip behind De Soto's wheel…relax in an interior "tailored" in every detail! Smart plastic-trimmed fittings, richly-grained mouldings, wide "bolster" seats—all *harmonize* with your choice of body color! Yes, you've 12 to choose from—8 solid colors, 4 superbly blended 2-tones!

65903

FLUID DRIVE
WITH
Simplimatic Transmission
You Don't Have To Shift Or Use The Clutch For Normal Driving
*AVAILABLE ON ALL MODELS AT MODERATE ADDITIONAL COST

REAR (DELUXE)
(NO CHROME TRIM BELOW TAIL-LTS.)

for a new experience! With De Soto Fluid Drive and Simplimatic Transmission, you have the smoothest surging getaway known to driving…without having to shift or use the clutch! Drive De Soto. Discover All that's New in '41!

new DASH DESIGN   1941 *DeSoto*

DeSoto FLUID DRIVE

DELUXE $1147.
TOWN SEDAN
(291 BLT.)

CUSTOM $1046.
3-PASS. COUPE (3-WINDOW)
(120 BLT.)

S~10
42
RESTYLED

Neat switch on instrument panel regulates fan, controls cooling.
TEMPERATURE CONTROL

CUSTOM CONVERTIBLE (489 BLT.) $1317.

CUSTOM
7~PASS. SEDAN
$1504. (139½" WB)
HAS AUXILIARY JUMP SEATS
(79 BLT.)

De Soto's Newest
Engineering Triumph

OPTIONAL
Refrigerated
Cool air outlet is placed inconspicuously in back of the rear seat.

AIR CONDITIONING!

A.C. DETAILS

NEW 236.6 cm SIX (115 HP) 121½ OR 139" WB

The compact cooling unit takes up very little room in rear of the trunk!

TWO—DOOR DELUXE SEDAN
(1781 BLT.)

$1075.

CUSTOM FENDER SKIRTS

BELOW:
"BLACKOUT" MODEL (JAN. 1942) HAS PAINTED GRILLE and TRIM.

DESOTO

HEAD~LIGHTS OPEN CONTROLLED BY LEVER ON DASH (MANUALLY)

US 1942

CONCEALED HEADLIGHTS

DE SOTO 42

DE SOTO

BY CHRYSLER CORP., AVAIL.
1929 TO 1961 MODEL YEARS

SUBURBAN
$2631.
('48)

7 TAXI

ALL '48-STYLE
CHRYSLER CORP. CARS
CONT'D. TO 2-49.

SINCE LATE 1935, LONG-WHEELBASE DE SOTO
7-PASS. OR 8-PASS. SEDANS AND LIMOUSINES
AVAIL., MANY SOLD IN FLEETS TO BIG-CITY
TAXICAB COMPANIES
139½" LONG W.B. AVAIL.
(FROM 1940 THROUGH 1954.)

S-11S =
DELUXE
S-11C =
CUSTOM

S-11
46-48

CUSTOM

6 CYL. (236.6 cid) 109 HP @ 3600 RPM

TIRES : 6.50 × 15 , 6.50 × 16 L.W.B. ('46-47)
7.00 × 15, 7.50 × 15 L.W.B. ('48)

SEMI-AUTOMATIC TRANS.
and "FLUID DRIVE"

CONVENTIONAL
HEADLIGHTS
RESUMED

LARGER DIE-CAST
GRILLE

$1761. ('46) $1965. ('47)

"8 out of 10
say De Soto again*"

$2296.
('48)

*=SLOGAN BASED ON POLL WHICH
INDICATED HOW MANY WOULD BUY ANOTHER DE SOTO.

1946 TO FEB., 1949 { DLX.= CPE. (1950); CLUB CPE. (8580); 2-DR. SEDAN (12,751); 4-DR. SEDAN (32,213)
PRODUCTION { CUSTOM = CLUB CPE. (18,431); CONVT. (3385); 4 DR. SEDAN (48,589); 8-PASS. SEDAN (342)
9-PASS. SUBURBAN SEDAN (129) (ADDITIONAL TAXI SALES, 7500 (?))

"THE CAR DESIGNED WITH YOU IN MIND"

49 A
S-13 { -1=DELUXE
-2=CUSTOM
(STARTS 2-49)

(TOTALLY
RESTYLED)

6000-W

REAR

EMBLEM
DE SOTO 46~49 (A)

new 125½" WB (THROUGH '54)

(1949 CONT'D.
NEXT PAGE)

4 DR. SEDAN
(13,148 BLT.) $1986.

DE SOTO CUSTOM

CONVERTIBLE
(3385 BLT.)
$2578.

DE LUXE
(has NO EXTRA CHROME
FENDER STRIPS.)

CLUB COUPE
(18,431 BLT.)
$2156.

49B
(CONT'D.)

new 112 HP
@ 3600 RPM
(THROUGH
'50)

(139½" W.B.
8 PASS. SEDAN
AVAIL. THROUGH
'54)

"CARRY ALL"
SEDAN
(new)
(IN LOWER-
PRICED
"DELUXE"
SERIES, BUT
HAS ADDITIONAL
CHROME TRIM.
(2690 BLT.)

$2191.

CONVERTIBLE
(2900 BLT.)
$2578.

AS IN 1949,
DE LUXE PRICES
START AT
$1976. (CLUB CPE.)

RE-DESIGNED LIKENESS
OF HERNANDO DE SOTO, HISTORIC
SPANISH EXPLORER FOR WHOM
CAR WAS
NAMED

1950 GRILLE has
PAINTED SECTION
IN CENTER, with
new EMBLEM.

CUSTOM

IN "CUSTOM" SERIES,
2 TYPES OF 4-DR.
STATION WAGON
BODIES IN '50:
WITH WOOD
(600 BLT.)
$3093.
OR
ALL-STEEL
(100 BLT.)
$2717.

50 CUSTOM

new
SPORTSMAN
H/T (4600 BLT.)
$2489.

REAR

SEDAN (72,664 BLT.)
$2174.

new ROUND
PARKING LIGHTS
DE SOTO 49(B)-50

Drive a DeSoto before you decide!

DE SOTO

SPORTSMAN

H/T $2761.

S-15-1 (DE LUXE)

S-15-2 (CUSTOM)

51

6- CYL. DISPLACEMENT RAISED TO 250.6 CID 116 HP @ 3600 RPM (THROUGH '54)

new LOWER, SIMPLER GRILLE

AS ON OTHER '51 CHRYSLER CORP. CARS, new "ORIFLOW" SHOCK ABSORBERS

$2436.

1951 MODELS have SCRIPT LETTERING ABOVE GRILLE

S-15 MODELS CONTINUE CUSTOM 6

SEDAN CUSTOM

new Full Power Steering

52

1952 MODELS have BLOCK LETTERING ABOVE GRILLE

WAGON

new FIRE DOME V8 (BELOW and RIGHT) (S-17)

S-17 CARS with AIR SCOOP HOOD ORNAMENT HAVE new "FireDome" 276.1 CID V8 ENGINE

(850 V8 CVTS. BUILT)

$3183.→

160 h.p. @ 4000 RPM

Power Braking

'51-'52 PRODUCTION : **DE LUXE** = CLUB CPE. (6100); SEDAN (13,506); CARRY-ALL (1700); 8-PASS. SED. (343); **CUSTOM** = CLUB CPE. (19,000); H/T (8750); CVT. (3950); SEDAN (88,491); WAGON (1440); 8-PASS. SED. (769); 9-PASS. SUBURBAN (600); **FIREDOME V8** = CLUB CPE. (5699); H/T (3000); SED. (35,651); WAGON (550); 8-PASS. SED. (50) (FIREDOME V8 NOT AVAIL. 1951)

DASH

L-HEAD 6-CYL. ENG. STILL AVAIL. (THROUGH 1954)

POWERMASTER 6 OR **FIREDOME V8** MODELS

DeSoto

$2893.

new 1-PC. WINDSHIELD

POWERMASTER 6
$2356. (S-18)

6 has a BROAD SHIELD EMBLEM on HOOD; V8 has "V" BELOW A NARROWER SHIELD (THROUGH '54.

V8 SPORTSMAN H/T

RESTYLED **53**

PRODUCTION =
CLB. CPE (6)(8063); (V8)(14,591)
H/T (6)(470); (V8)(4700)
CVT. (V8 ONLY)(1700)
SEDAN (6)(33,644);(V8)(64,211)
WAGON (6)(500); (V8)(1100)
8-PASS. SEDAN (6)(225)
   (V8)(200)

V8 CONVERTIBLE $3114.

REAR DETAILS (V8 SEDAN)

$2643.

new POWER BRAKES *and* OVERDRIVE AVAILABLE

THE FINAL 6-CYL. DE SOTO

7.60 x 15

V8 CLUB CPE.
$2622.

POWERMASTER 6
(S-20)

"POWERFLITE" A.T. AVAIL.

V8 *has* new 170 HP @ 4400 RPM

CORONADO SEDAN

V8 SED. (45,093 BLT.) $2673.

FIREDOME V8 (S-19)

54

GRILLE MODIFIED new SIDE TRIM *and* TAIL-LIGHTS

DASH

DE SOTO

The *Forward* Look

V8s ONLY
(1955 ON)

new 126" WB

FLITE-CONTROL gear selector lever is mounted on De Soto's smart, new instrument panel—out of your way. Yet at your finger tips."

(TOTALLY RESTYLED)

55

new 291 CID
FIREDOME (S-22) 185 HP @ 4400 RPM
FIREFLITE (S-21) 200 HP @ 4400 RPM

7.60 x 15

PRODUCTION : S-22 FIREDOME   SPECIAL H/T ; SPORTSMAN H/T (28,944);
CONV'T. (625); 4-DR. SEDAN (46,388); 4-DR. WAGON (1083)

S-21 FIREFLITE   SPORTSMAN H/T (10,313); CONV'T. (775)
4-DR. SEDAN ; CORONADO (26,637)

PRICE RANGE =
$2498. TO $3170.

DRIVE A DE SOTO
BEFORE YOU DECIDE

(PUSH-BUTTON A.T.)

$3728.
new   341.4 CID
ADVENTURER (S-24)
320 HP @
5200 RPM
(996 BLT.)

DASH

(MINOR CHANGES
FROM 1955)

230 HP @ 4400 RPM
FIREDOME
(S-23)

"HI WAY
HI-FI"
BLT.-IN
RECORD
PLAYER
AVAIL.

7.60 x 15

new MESH
GRILLE

TRIPLE TAIL-LIGHTS
with OVERLAPPING
FIN

(44,909 BLT.)

new
330 CID

$2678.

PACESETTER CVT.
(100 BLT.)
$3615.

56

255 HP @ 4400 RPM
FIREFLITE
(S-24)

SEDAN
$3119.

(18,207 BLT.)

PACE CAR AT 1956
INDY 500 RACE

new
12-VOLT ELEC. SYS.

304

DE SOTO... *the most exciting car in the world today!*

PRICE RANGE = $2777. TO $4272.

SPORTSMAN 2-DR. H/T (13,333 BLT.) $2836.

DE SOTO

$2912. *new* LOWER PRICE

FIRESWEEP (S-27) (*has* OWN FRONT END STYLING)

4-DR. H/T (7168 BLT.)

(S-25) $2958.
FIREDOME

new 325, 341 OR 345 CID

245, 270, 295 OR 345 HP

SEDAN (23,339 BLT.)

(TOTALLY RESTYLED)

57

H/T (1650 BLT.)

(1151 BLT.)
CVT.

2-DR. H/T

$3614.

$3997.

ADVENTURER

(4 HEADLIGHTS, ANODIZED GOLD TRIM) (S-26)

FIREFLITE (S-26)

new 122" WB ON FIRESWEEP, 126" ON OTHERS (THROUGH '59)

$3671.

$3487.

4-DR. H/T (6726 BLT.)

REAR SEAT FACES BACKWARD ON EXPLORER WAGON (3 SEATS) 9-PASS.

BOTH WAGONS ARE AVAIL. IN EITHER FIRE-SWEEP OR FIREFLITE SERIES.

6-PASS.
SHOPPER (2 SEATS)

FIREFLITE SEDAN (11,565 BLT.)

WAGON PRODUCTION = **FIRESWP.** 6-PASS. (2270); 9 PASS. (1198); **FIREFLT.** 6 PASS. (837); 9-PASS. (934)

DE SOTO

18 MODELS, 4 SER.

new "TURBOFLASH"
V8
(350 OR 361 CID)

280 TO 355 HP

(LS2-M)
FIREDOME $3235.

(LS1-L)
FIRESWEEP
$2953.

$3675.

$4172.

FIREFLITE
(LS3-H)

9-PASS.
"EXPLORER" WAGON

LARGE new
"CONTROL TOWER"
WINDSHIELD

CLOSE-UP

58

LS SERIES

DASH

GULFLEX   SERVICE   GULF

$4369.
(LS3-S)
ADVENTURER
has ANODIZED SIDE TRIM

DE SOTO — the exciting look and feel of the future!

PRODUCTION: FIRESWEEP H/T (5635); CVT. (700); SEDAN (7646); 4 DR. H/T (3003);
6-PASS. WAGON (1305); 9-PASS. WAGON (1125) FIREDOME H/T (4325); CVT. (519); SEDAN (9505);
4-DR. H/T (3130) FIREFLITE H/T (3284); CVT. (474); SEDAN (4192); 4-DR. H/T (3243);
6-PASS. WAGON (318); 9-PASS. WAGON (609)
ADVENTURER H/T (350); CVT. (82)

PRICE RANGES:
FIRESWEEP (MS1-L) = $2904. TO $3508.
FIREDOME (MS2-M) = $3234. TO $3653.
FIREFLITE (MS3-H) = $3763. TO $4358.
ADVENTURER (MS3-S) = $4427. (H/T) OR $4749. CVT.

'59 DE SOTO

(MS1-L) FIRESWEEP
#23 H/T
$2967.
(5481 BLT.)
8.00 × 14 TIRES

361 OR NEW 383 CID V8
(THROUGH '60)
295 HP @ 4600 RPM
TO 350 HP @ 5000 RPM

#23 SPORTSMAN H/T (1393 BLT.)
$3831.
(MS3-H)
FIREFLITE
#41 SEDAN (4480 BLT.)

$3763.

FIREFLITE SHOPPER

(ALL BUT FIRESWEEP HAVE
8.50 × 14 TIRES.)
(SINCE '57)

(MS2-M)
FIREDOME
#23 SPORTSMAN H/T
(2862 BLT.)

ADVENTURER
(MS3-H)
#27 CVT.
(97 BLT.)

DASH

307

1960 DE SOTO

#41 SEDAN
(9032 BLT.)

(PS1-L)
FIREFLITE

DASH (*with RAISED INSTRUMENT CLUSTER*)

4-DR. H/T
(2759 BLT.)

(PS3-M)
ADVENTURER   **$3727.**

H.P. CHOICES :

295 @ 4600 ; 305 @ 4600 ;
325 @ 4600 OR
330 @ 4800 RPM

BUILT-IN
45-RPM
RECORD
PLAYER OPTIONAL AGAIN
(AS IN PLYMOUTH)

10.0 TO 1 COMPRESSION

ONLY 2 MODEL SERIES IN 1960:
FIREFLITE OR
ADVENTURER
(NO MORE DE SOTO WAGONS
OR CONVERTIBLES)

#23 H/T
(3092 BLT.)
$3663.

ALL 1960
and 1961
DE SOTOS ON
122" WB and
8.00 × 14 TIRES

$3/67.

1961 DE SOTO

ITS QUALITY SETS IT APART, ITS PRICE KEEPS IT WITHIN YOUR REACH

FROM
$3102.

(THE FINAL
DE SOTO CAR,
AVAILABLE
ONLY IN 2-DR.
OR 4-DR. H/T
BODIES)

(2123 BLT.)

4-DR. H/T
#614

2-DR. H/T
#612

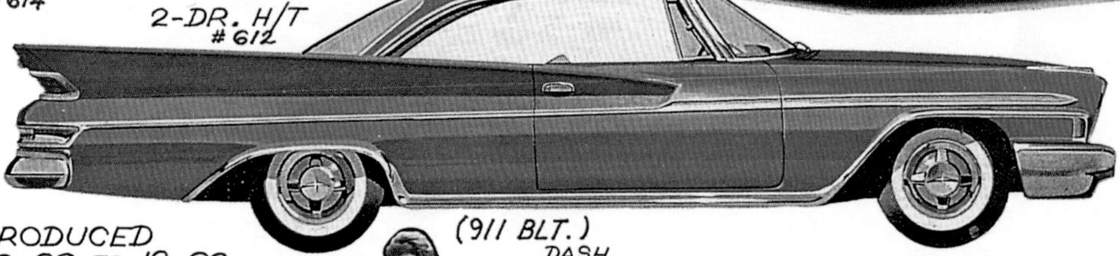

ONLY THE 361 CID V8
IS AVAILABLE, with
COMPRESSION
REDUCED TO 9.0

265 HP @ 4400 RPM

ODD
"SHARK-NOSE"
TAIL-LIGHTS

PRODUCED
8-60 TO 12-60

(911 BLT.)
DASH

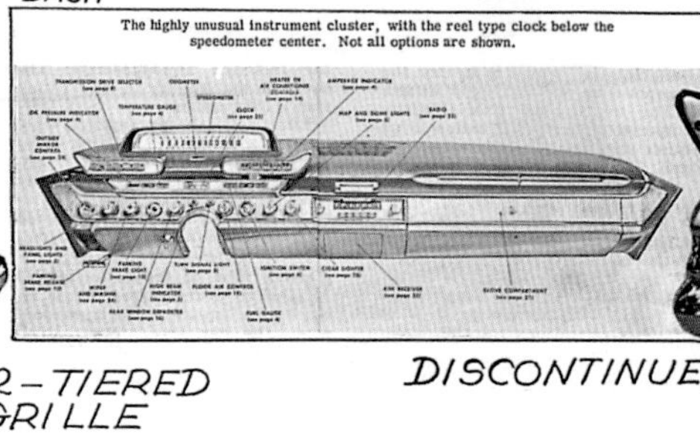

The highly unusual instrument cluster, with the reel type clock below the
speedometer center. Not all options are shown.

2-TIERED
GRILLE

DISCONTINUED

308

DODGE

1940 Dodge Luxury Liner Special, 6-Passenger, 2-door Sedan $815, delivered in Detroit.

DODGE DIVISION OF THE CHRYSLER CORPORATION

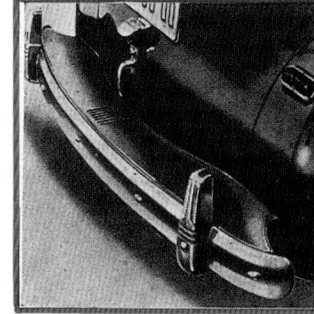

GRAVEL GUARD BETW. REAR BUMPER and BODY

With Longer Wheelbase
(119½")

"SCOTCH DYNA-MITE!" That's what we call this big six-cylinder engine in the new 1940 Dodge Luxury Liner, with its flashing pickup, road-eating performance and its great combination of sensational gasoline and oil-saving features that mean money in your pocket every mile you drive!

217.8 cɪᴅ 6
87 HP
(SINCE '34)
L~HEAD ENGINE

MODEL NUMBER	BODY TYPE	PRICE	WEIGHT	1940 TOTAL PRODUCTION
D17	2-DOOR BUSINESS COUPE	755	2867	12,001
D17	2-DOOR SEDAN	815	2942	27,700
D17	4-DOOR SEDAN	855	2997	26,803
D14	2-DOOR BUSINESS COUPE	803	2905	12,750
D14	2-DOOR A/S COUPE	855	2973	8,028
D14	2-DOOR CONVERTIBLE COUPE	1030	3190	2,100
D14	2-DOOR SEDAN	860	2990	19,838
D14	4-DOOR SEDAN	905	3028	84,976
D14	4-DOOR 7 PASSENGER SEDAN	1095	3460	932*
D14	4-DOOR 7 PASSENGER LIMOUSINE	1170	3550	79*
D14	CHASSIS	NA	NA	298*

* DENOTES ON AN EXTENDED CHASSIS (139" WB)

TOTAL SERIES PRODUCTION FOR THE D17 WAS 66,504.
TOTAL SERIES PRODUCTION FOR THE D14 WAS 129,001.

"LUXURY LINER" SERIES (THROUGH '41)

40

A

D~17 = SPECIAL
D~14 = DELUXE

6.00 x 16" TIRES
(6.50 x 16 ON 7~PASS.)

(CONT'D. NEXT PAGE)

TRUNK

40 DODGE (A)

309

CONVERTIBLE DASH (PAINTED)

DODGE

DE LUXE COUPE WITH AUXILIARY SEATS

CLOSED CAR DASH

WOODGRAIN EFFECTS

BUSINESS COUPE

COMFORT ZONE

PASSENGERS RIDE AHEAD OF REAR AXLE

40 B (CONT'D.)

NEVER BEFORE a ride like this in a car priced so low—the new *Full-Floating Ride* in the New 1940 Dodge! Wheelbase is longer, center of gravity is lower, wheels are moved back, seats forward. All passengers ride in the buoyant "Comfort Zone" *between* axles!

ASH TRAY

2~TONE PAINT OPTIONAL; RUNNING~ BOARDS OPTIONAL ALSO

CLOSE~UP OF DASH GAUGE CLUSTER

Old-Style "Dog-Leg" Door   New Dodge Straight Door

Say good-bye to the narrow old-style rear door, with its "dog-leg" cutaway over the rear wheel. Getting in and out of such doors was always a cramping experience. Now, thanks to the new wide Dodge straight door, you *walk* right in, and you *walk* right out, so easily you'll rub your eyes in astonishment! This new design also permits rear door windows to be rolled all the way down!

Dots on the four instruments show red when their hands read to "off"

40 DODGE (A)

DODGE LUXURY LINER
WITH OR WITHOUT FLUID DRIVE*

41
RESTYLED
D~19

CONVERTIBLE
CUSTOM (3554 BLT.)

$1162.

CUSTOM
4~DR.
TOWN
SEDAN

(16,074
BLT.)

3 HORIZ. CHROME
TRIM STRIPS ON
ALL FENDERS
OPTIONAL
AT
EXTRA
←Cost

$1062.

OPT. GRAVEL
GUARDS
(FRONT
and
REAR)

New

3 WINDOW COUPES

DELUXE 3~WINDOW
COUPE (22,318 BLT.)

$862.

6

FRONT
EMBLEM

ENGINE new 91 HP

LARGE SPLIT GRILLE
EXTENDS TO
HEADLIGHTS ;
BOW~TYPE
BUMPER
GUARDS OPT.

CUSTOM 4~DR. ($999.)
IS BEST SELLER
(72,067 SOLD)

DASH

41 DODGE

DODGE

FACTORY VIEWS →

DELUXE

CUSTOM

DELUXE SERIES			
BODY STYLE	PRICE	WEIGHT	TOTAL
3 passenger coupe	$895	3056	5,257
6 passenger coupe	$995	3131	3,314
6 passenger 2-dr.	$958	3131	9,767
6 passenger 4-dr.	$998	3171	13,343
CUSTOM SERIES			
6 passenger coupe	$1045	3171	4,659
5 passenger conv. cpe.	$1245	3476	1,185
6 passenger Brougham	$1008	3171	4,685
6 passenger 4-dr.	$1048	3206	22,055
6 passenger Town Sdn.	$1105	3256	4,047
CUSTOM SERIES LONG WHEELBASE			
7 passenger sedan	$1395	3693	201
7 passenger limo	$1475	3768	9

TOTAL PRODUCTION
68,522

new 230.2 CID ENGINE
new 105 HP

42 new GRILLE

CUSTOM CVT.

CUSTOM 4~DR. SEDAN

SPEEDOMETER FACE CHANGES COLORS = GREEN TO ORANGE AT 30, TO RED AT 50

BIG~HORN ROCKY MT. RAM HOOD ORNAMENT

NEW →

DASH

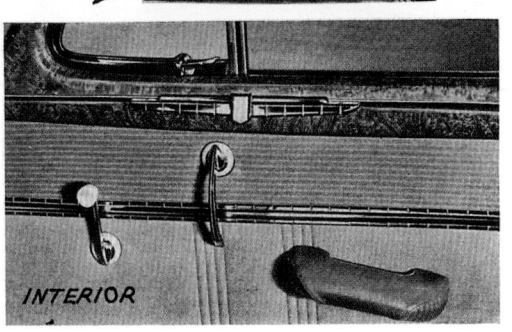

INTERIOR

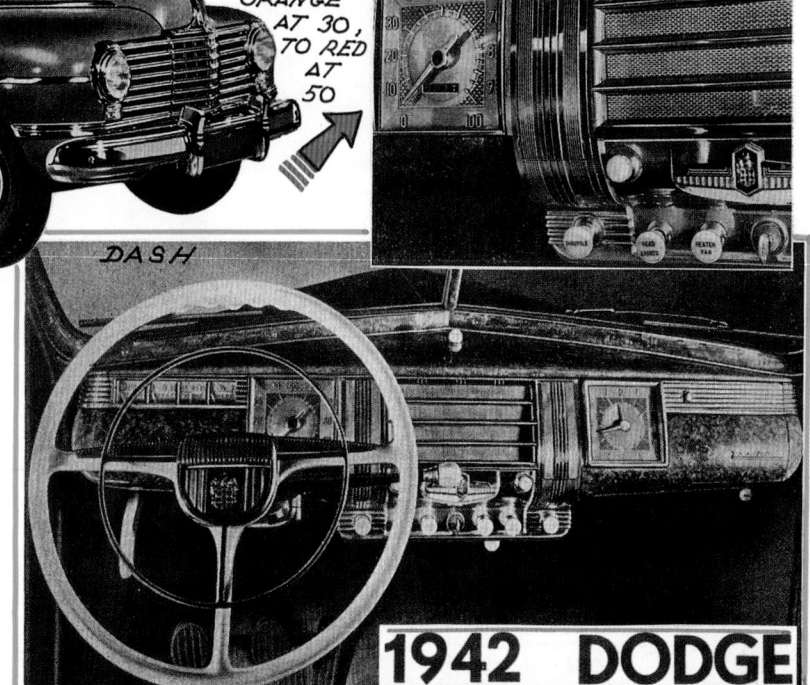

1942 DODGE

DODGE

ESTABLISHED
1914,
MFD. BY CHRYSLER
CORP. SINCE 1928

1946-48 PRODUCTION	
D24S DELUXE =	
BUSINESS CP.	27,600
2.DR.SEDAN	81,399
4 DR. "	61,987
D24C CUSTOM =	
CLUB COUPE	103,800
CONVERTIBLE	9500
4 DR. SEDAN	333,911
TOWN SEDAN	27,800
7-PASS. SEDAN	3698
7-PASS. LIMO.	2
CHASSIS ONLY	302
(SERIES ENDS 2~49	

(ABOVE)
2-DR. SEDAN
$1676.

CLUB COUPE
$1774.

7-WINDOW SEDAN **$1788.**

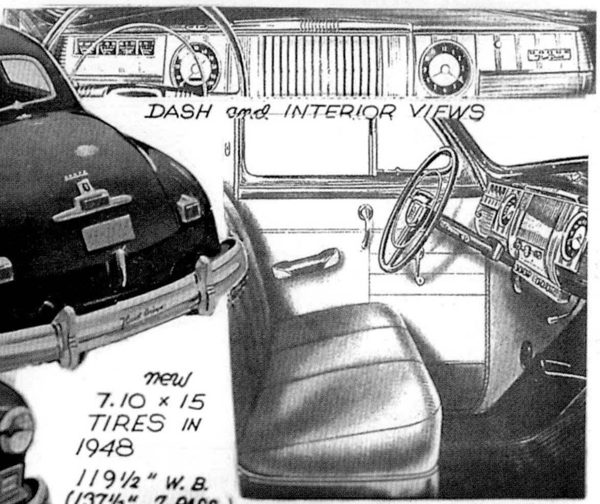

DASH and INTERIOR VIEWS

NEW
7.10 × 15
TIRES IN
1948
119½" W.B.
(137½", 7-PASS.)

CONVERTIBLE
$2189.

D-24S = DE LUXE
D-24C = CUSTOM

46-48

230.2 CID L-HEAD 6
102 HP. @ 3600 RPM

$1872.

TOWN SEDAN
(5-WINDOW SEDAN)
(ALL DOORS FRONT-HINGED)

"FADEAWAY"
FENDERS

Dodge

SMOOTHEST CAR "AFLOAT"

ROADSTER (new)
(TOP UP)

$1611.

((ACTUAL PHOTO)
(TOP DOWN)

3-WINDOW COUPE

2-DOOR $1738.

LOWER PRICED
NEW DODGE *WAYFARER*

The Daring New
DODGE
gyrol Fluid Drive plus GYRO-MATIC
Frees You from Shifting
OPTIONAL ON CORONET MODELS

PRODUCTION =	
WAYFARER	
3-WINDOW CPE.	9342
2-DR. SEDAN	49,058
ROADSTER	5420
MEADOWBROOK	
4-DR. SEDAN	
CORONET	} 144,390
4-DR. SEDAN	
CLUB COUPE	45,345
CONVERTIBLE	1800
4-DR., 9 PASS.	
WAGON	800
CHASSIS ALONE	1

$1727.

(ABOVE) WAYFARER ROADSTER (ARTIST'S CONCEPTION)

49
TOTALLY RESTYLED
(INTRO. 2~49)

D-29 = WAYFARER
(115" WB)

D-30 = MEADOWBROOK
and CORONET
(123½" WB)

(SAME WBs THROUGH '52)

$2865.

MEADOWBRK. 4-DOOR SEDAN, $1848. →

MEADOWBRK. HAS HUB CAPS INSTEAD OF FULL WHEEL COVERS.

New Dodge CORONET

SEDAN $1927.

CORONET WAGON

new 103 HP @ 3600 RPM (TO '53)

new
SWITCH KEY STARTING

LONGER on the inside . . . SHORTER outside!
WIDER on the inside . . . NARROWER outside!
HIGHER on the inside . . . LOWER outside!

DODGE

INTERIOR

BACK SEAT

new DIPLOMAT H/T

WAYFARER ROADSTER $1727.

$2233.

"GYRO-MATIC" AUTO. TRANS. AVAILABLE ON CORONET models (OPTIONAL)

4-DR. SEDAN

REAR WINDOW ENLARGED

MEADOWBROOK $1848.
CORONET $1927.

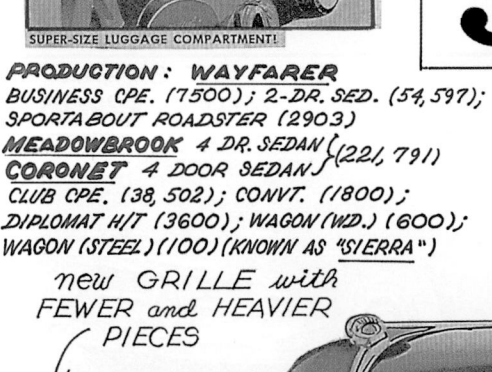

SUPER-SIZE LUGGAGE COMPARTMENT!

50	D-33 = WAYFARER
	D-34 = MEADOWBROOK ; CORONET
	(2 TONE COLORS AVAIL.)

PRODUCTION: **WAYFARER**
BUSINESS CPE. (7500); 2-DR. SED. (54,597);
SPORTABOUT ROADSTER (2903)
MEADOWBROOK 4 DR. SEDAN (221,791)
CORONET 4 DOOR SEDAN }
CLUB CPE. (38,502); CONVT. (1800);
DIPLOMAT H/T (3600); WAGON (W.D.) (600);
WAGON (STEEL) (100) (KNOWN AS "SIERRA")

new GRILLE *with* FEWER *and* HEAVIER PIECES

(8-PASS. SEDAN AVAIL. ON 137½" W.B.)

DODGE

PRODUCTION, 1951-1952 : WAYFARER = SPORTABOUT RDS. ('51 ONLY) (1002);
BUSINESS COUPÉ (6702); 2-DR. (70,700);
MEADOWBROOK, CORONET SEDANS (COMBINED, 329,202);
CORONET = CLUB COUPÉ (56,103); CONVERTIBLE (5550); DIPLOMAT H/T (21,600);
SIERRA WAGON (4000); 8-PASSENGER SEDAN, 137½" W.B. (1150)

51

$1936.

WAYFARER

DASH

ON 1951 MODEL, ENTIRE GRILLE IS CHROMED (INCL. LOWER PIECE)

DEPENDABILITY VALUE

FEATHER-TOUCH BRAKING!
Big Safe-Guard Hydraulic Brakes stop smoothly, surely, safely. Cyclebond linings, with their larger braking surface, last up to twice as long. New feather-touch parking brake holds securely on even steep grades . . . easily released with a twist of the wrist.

D-41 = WAYFARER

D-42   MEADOWBRK.
CORONET

$2059. UP

SHOWN IN SAN FRANCISCO, LOOKING EAST TOWARD OAKLAND.

$2256.

CORONET

D-41 and D-42 SERIES CONTINUE with LITTLE CHANGE

CORONET SIERRA WAGON **$2908.**

new HUBCAPS/WHEEL CVRS.

1952 SERIAL NOs. START AT:

WAYFARER	MEAD./CORONET
3717500I (Detroit)	31867601
48009901 (San Leandro)	45090601
48507601 (Los Angeles)	
45527501 ==	
MD., COR., (L.A.)	

LOWER PART OF GRILLE IS PAINTED.

52

CORONET **$2602.**
"DIPLOMAT" H/T

FINAL YEAR FOR WAYFARER MODEL; REPLACED IN '53 BY MEADOWBROOK SPECIAL

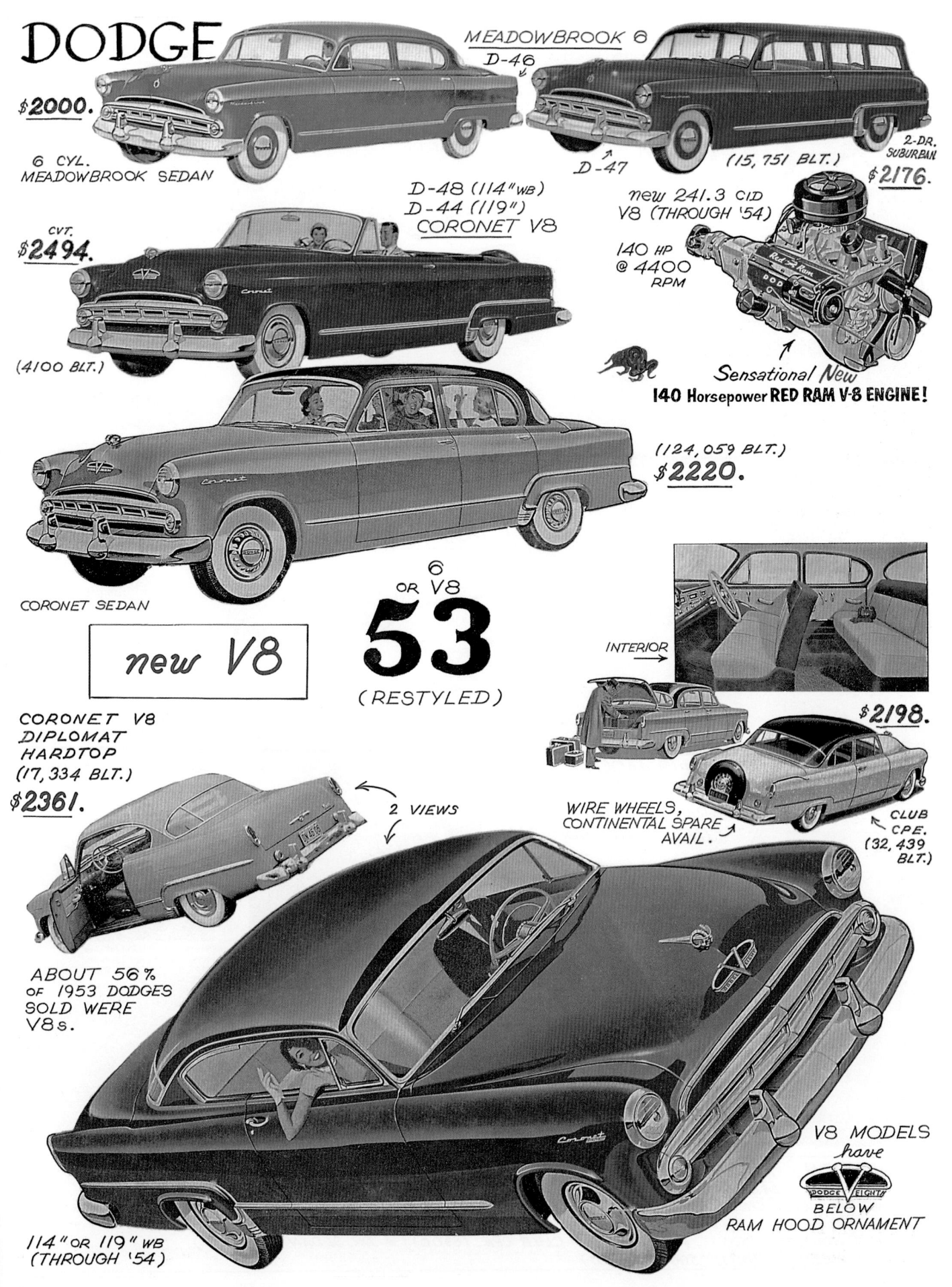

DODGE

$2000.

6 CYL.
MEADOWBROOK SEDAN

MEADOWBROOK 6
D-46

D-47

(15,751 BLT.)

2-DR.
SUBURBAN

$2176.

D-48 (114" WB)
D-44 (119")
CORONET V8

CVT.
$2494.

(4100 BLT.)

new 241.3 CID
V8 (THROUGH '54)

140 HP
@ 4400
RPM

Sensational New
140 Horsepower RED RAM V-8 ENGINE!

(124,059 BLT.)
$2220.

CORONET SEDAN

new V8

OR 6
V8
53
(RESTYLED)

INTERIOR

$2198.

CORONET V8
DIPLOMAT
HARDTOP
(17,334 BLT.)
$2361.

2 VIEWS

WIRE WHEELS,
CONTINENTAL SPARE
AVAIL.

CLUB
CPE.
(32,439
BLT.)

ABOUT 56%
OF 1953 DODGES
SOLD WERE
V8s.

V8 MODELS
have

DODGE V EIGHT
BELOW
RAM HOOD ORNAMENT

114" OR 119" WB
(THROUGH '54)

DODGE

SUBURBAN 2-DOOR WAGON ((ORNT. V8) (3100 BLT.)
$2517.

$2136.

CORONET 6

$2109.

D-51, D-52 (6 CYL.)

54 D-50, D-53 (V8)

6-CYL. NOW HAS 110 HP @ 3600 RPM

$2349. (8900 BLT.)

CLUB CPE.

ROYAL SERIES is new!

new GRILLE

ROYAL V8

ROYAL 500 CVT. IS PACE CAR AT 1954 INDY 500 RACE.

H/T

2373. (50,050 BLT.)

ROYAL V8 SEDAN

V8 has 140 OR 150 HP @ 4400 RPM (7.1 OR 7.5 COMPR.)

VARIOUS INTERIORS (JACQUARD FABRICS)

DEPENDABLE NEW '54 DODGE *Elegance in Action*

Fully-automatic PowerFlite and full-time Power Steering—yours at moderate extra cost.

PRODUCTION: MEADOWBROOK 6 = CLUB CPE. (3501); 4-DR. SEDAN (7894)
        MEADOWBROOK V8 = " " (750); " " (3299)
CORONET 6 = CLUB CPE. (4501); 4-DR. SEDAN (14,900); SUB. WAGON (6389); SIERRA 4-DR. WAGON (312) (6 or 9 PASS.)
CORONET V8 = " " (7998); " " (36,063); " " (3100); " " " (988) " " "
   SPT. H/T (100); CVT. (50)   ROYAL V8 = CLUB CPE. (8900); 4-DR. SEDAN (50,050)
   " (3852); " (1299) "500" CVT. (701)

DODGE FLASHES AHEAD IN '55

SEDAN (6- 15,976 BLT.) (V8 - 30,098 ")

CORONET

REAR

V8 ENGINE NOW 270 CID

$2452. (4867 BLT.)
CORONET V-8 2-DOOR SUBURBAN

$2761. (5506 BLT., 6 or 8 PASS.)
ROYAL V-8 4-DOOR 8-PASSENGER SIERRA

$2473.
CUSTOM ROYAL V-8 4-DOOR SEDAN

new 3-TONE PAINT JOBS AVAIL.

new CUSTOM ROYAL LANCER H/T (30,499 BLT.)

H/T

D56-1= CORONET 6
6 CYL., 230.2 CID
123 HP @ 3600 RPM

$2543.

55

D 55-1= CORONET V8
and
D 55-2= ROYAL V8
270.1 CID V8
(175 HP @ 4400 RPM)

TOTALLY RESTYLED

(MID-1955 "LA FEMME" MODEL FOR WOMEN, "TEXAN" MODEL FOR MEN.)

D 55-3= CUSTOM ROYAL V8
270.1 CID V8 (183 or 193 HP @ 4400 RPM)

2-TONE COLORS on DASH; A/T CONTROL on DASH

$2516.

CUSTOM ROYAL LANCER SEDAN (new)

WITH **THE FORWARD LOOK** ▷

new 120" WB (ON ALL, THROUGH '56)

6 CYL. NOW HAS 131 HP @ 3800 RPM (230 CID)
V8 has 189 TO 340 HP (270, 3/5 OR 354 CID)

$2807.

D-62 (6 CYL.)
D-63 (V8)

56

new FINS and EMBLEM IN GRILLE
new SIDE TRIM
DIPS AT REAR
new BUMPERS
HIGHER REAR FENDERS

CUSTOM ROYAL LANCER 4 DR. H/T

The look, the feel, the power of success: New '56 Dodge Custom Royal Lancer 4-Door

In all the world no car like this

The New Dodge Lancer goes 4 door!

MORE 1956 DODGES
ON NEXT PAGE

319

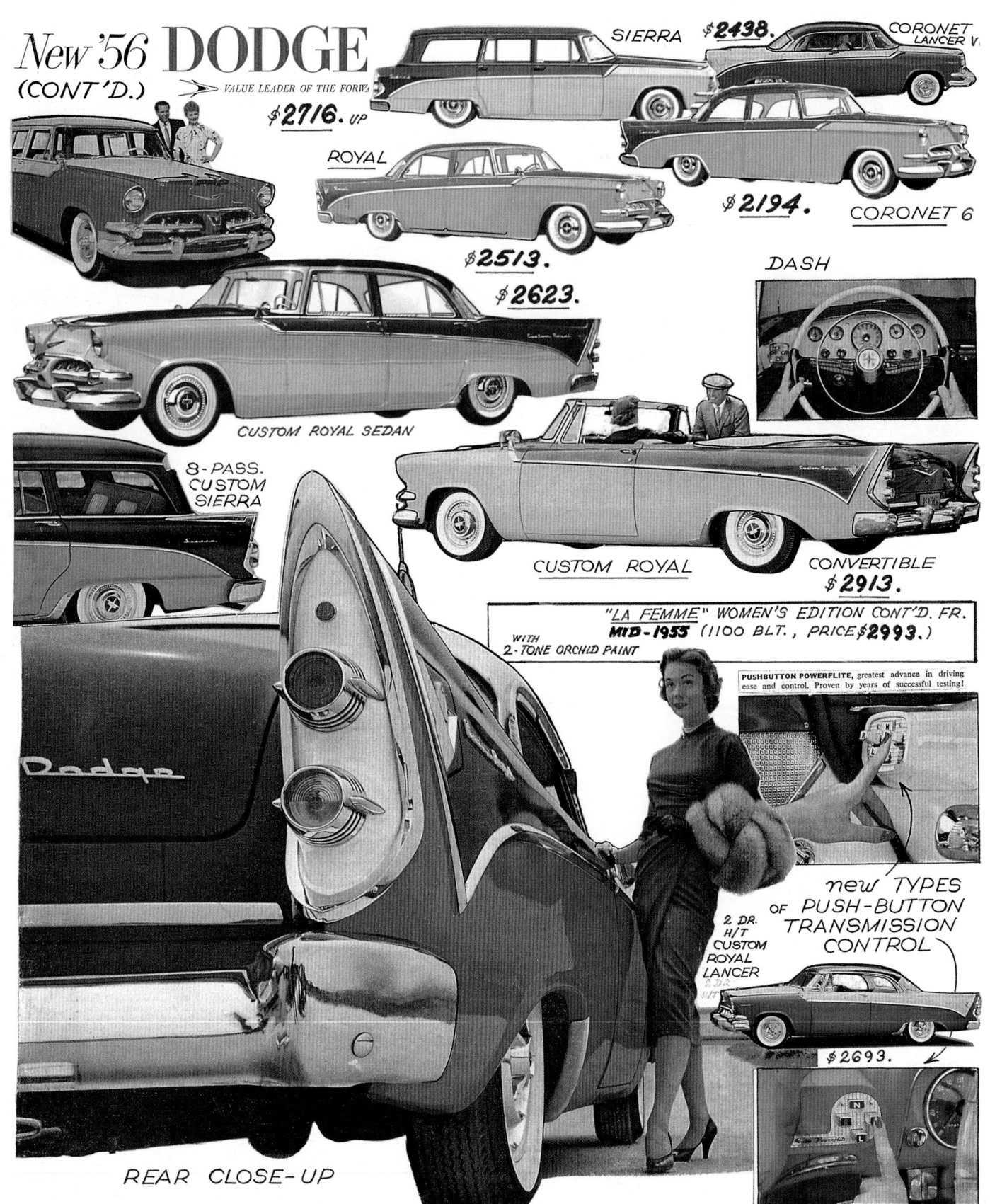

New '56 DODGE
(CONT'D.)

VALUE LEADER OF THE FORWA...

SIERRA $2438.

CORONET LANCER V...

$2716. UP

ROYAL

$2194. CORONET 6

$2513.

$2623.

DASH

CUSTOM ROYAL SEDAN

8-PASS. CUSTOM SIERRA

CUSTOM ROYAL CONVERTIBLE $2913.

"LA FEMME" WOMEN'S EDITION CONT'D. FR.
MID-1955 (1100 BLT., PRICE $2993.)
WITH 2-TONE ORCHID PAINT

PUSHBUTTON POWERFLITE, greatest advance in driving ease and control. Proven by years of successful testing!

new TYPES OF PUSH-BUTTON TRANSMISSION CONTROL

2 DR. H/T CUSTOM ROYAL LANCER

$2693.

REAR CLOSE-UP

MODEL SERIES			
D 62 CORONET 6 (142,613 BLT.)	$2194. to $2491.	230.2 cid 6 (131 HP)	
D 63-1 CORONET V8 (IN ABOVE FIGURE)	$2302. to $2822.	270 cid V8 (189 HP)	
D 63-2 ROYAL V8 (48,780 BLT.)	$2513. to $2974.	new 315 cid V8 (218 HP)	
D 63-3 CUSTOM ROYAL V8 (42,293)	$2623. to $2913.	(SAME)	
(also 260 HP, 315 cid V8 OPTIONAL IN ANY MODEL.)			

'57 Dodge

SWEPT·WING $2861.
(TOTALLY RESTYLED)
D-72 (6) D-66, 67, 70 (V8)

2-DR. SUBURBAN
(D-70)

$2370.

CORONET (6 or V8)
(D-72 or D-66)

$2818.

new 325 or 354 CID V8s

4-DR. SIERRA
(D-70) (D-71 IS
CUSTOM SIERRA)

ROYAL
LANCER (D-67-1)
2-DR.
H/T

$2991. CUSTOM
ROYAL LANCER
(D-67-2)

new
7.50
x 14
TIRES
(8.00 x14
WAGON, CVT.)

138
TO
340 HP

new
122" WB
(ON
ALL MODELS,
THROUGH
'59)

ADDED
LOWER
"TEETH" IN
GRILLE OF ABOVE
LATER MODEL.

REAR FINS "OVERLAP"
FENDER

new COMPOUND-
CURVED WINDSHIELD

138 TO 333 HP
325, 350 or
361 CID V8s

CORONET

CUSTOM
ROYAL
LANCER

ROYAL

$2797.

SIERRA

LD-1 (6)
LD-2, LD-3 (V8)

EARLY MODEL
'58s SHOWN ABOVE

58 new
GRILLE

$3071.

PRODUCTION=
CORONET 6, V8 (77,388) $2449.-$2942.
ROYAL V8 (15,165) $2797.-$2915.
CUSTOM ROYAL V8 (25,000+) $3030.-$3298.
STATION WAGONS, V8 (20,196) $2970.-
$3354.

SPRING SWEPT-WING

by **Dodge**

58½ MODEL with IDENTIFYING
CHARACTERISTICS

1958

PAINTED
HEADLIGHT
AREA, also
new
GRILLE
MEDALLION
ON 58½

new colors

'59 DODGE

CORONET 6, V8
#21 2 DR. $2516. (6); $2636. (V8)

59½ Silver Challenger
two-door sedan

FINAL L-HEAD 230 CID 6 REDUCED TO 135 HP @ 3600 RPM

6 or V8

326,361 OR 383 CID V8s have 255 HP @ 4400 RPM TO 345 HP @ 5000 RPM

#43 LANCER 4-DR H/T

SIERRA

6-PASS. $3103. #45-A
9-PASS. $3224. #45-B

CUSTOM ROYAL $3270.

#27 CONVERTIBLE

$3422.

new TAIL-LIGHTS

SWIVEL-SEATS AVAIL. (new)

INTERIOR (CUSTOM ROYAL CVT.)

59

MD1-L (6)

MD2-L, MD3-M, MD3-L, MD3-H (V8)

PUSH-BUTTON SHIFT PLAN

DASH

new interior

PRODUCTION:
  MD1-L CORONET 6, MD2-L CORONET V8 (96,782) $2516.-$3089.
  MD3-M ROYAL V8 (14,807) $2934.-$3069.
  MD3-H CUSTOM ROYAL V8 (21,206) $3145.-$3422.
  MD3-L SIERRA V8 WAGONS, MD3-H CUSTOM V8 WAGONS (23,590) $3103.-$3439.

'60 DODGE

#23 MATAD. 2-DR H/T
$2996.

#45-A, B MATADOR WAGON
$3239. UP

#43 MATADOR 4-DR. H/T
$3075.

122" WB ON LARGE DODGES (THROUGH '61)

MATADOR·POLARA

$3506. UP

new O.H.V. SLANTED 6-CYL. ENGINE AVAIL. ONLY IN new SUBSIDIARY DART.

361 OR 383 CID V8s (THR.'61) IN ALL DODGES EXCEPT new DART OR '61-2 LANCER

(295 OR 330 HP)

#43 POLARA 4-DR. HARDTOP

#27 CVT.

$3416.

POLARA has BRIGHTWORK ON LOWER REAR FENDER.

$3275.

PD1 and PD2 SERIES

new DART LISTED SEPARATELY.

60 RESTYLED

POLARA has HEAVY BAND ATOP FENDER

UNIBODY CONSTRUCTION

SEE ALSO **DART.**

TOTALLY new FRONTAL APPEARANCE, WITH V-DIP IN LOWER EDGE OF GRILLE.

PRODUCTION:
PD1-L MATADOR (27,908) $2930. — $3354.
PD2-H POLARA (16,278) $3141. — $3621.
(CONVERTIBLE AVAIL. ONLY IN POLARA SERIES) = $3416.

DODGE

POLARA 2 DOOR HARDTOP V8

265 TO 330 HP

122" WB

POLARA CONVERTIBLE V8

DASH

14,032 BLT.

61
RESTYLED

POLARA HARDTOP WAGON V8,
6 OR 9 PASSENGER

MODELS, PRICES #542 H/T $3032.
#543 4 DR. SEDAN $2966.
#544 4 DR. H/T $3110.
#545 CONVERTIBLE $3252.
#578 6-PASS. WAGON $3294.
#579 9-PASS. WAGON $3409.

POLARA V8
IS
ONLY LARGE
SERIES

SEE ALSO DART,
OR
LANCER

$3019. #542 2-DR. H/T

$2960. #544 4-DR. H/T

Dodge Polara 500—2-dr Hardtop

Dodge Polara 500—4-dr. Hardtop

POLARA 500

POLARA 500

361 OR
413 CID
V8
305
OR
380
HP

#545 CVT.

$3268.

(SD2-P)
POLARA MODELS
TOTALLY RESTYLED
116" WB (AS ON
DART)

62

#658 6-PASS. CUSTOM 880 WAGON
#659 9-PASS.

614 CUSTOM 880
4-DR. H/T

$3109.

CUSTOM 880

(CONSERVATIVE
OLDER TYPE
STYLING) 122" WB

(SD3-L)

361 CID V8
265 HP @
4400 RPM

$3292. OR $3407.
6 PASS.   9 PASS.

PRODUCTION:
SD2-P POLARA 500
(12,268) $2960.-$3268.
SD3-L CUSTOM 880
(17,505) $2964.-$3407.

$3030.

#612 CUSTOM 880 2-DR. H/T

1963 DODGE

330 SERIES

330 2-DR. SED.
$2245. UP

$2648. UP

$2470. UP

440 WAGON
$2854. UP

440 SERIES

$2381. UP

116" OR 119" WB

$2438. UP

225 CID 6 (145 HP @ 4000)

318, 383 OR 426 CID V8
(230 TO 425 HP)

POLARA SERIES

DASH

$3196.

(V8) 4-DR. H/T
$2781.

POLARA 500 SERIES
BUCKET SEAT

#642 H/T
$2965.

#L-558, 559
$3292. UP

#L-514 4-DR. H/T

TD SERIES
63

CUSTOM 880
361 OR
383 CID V8
(265 OR 305 HP)

$3109.

122" WB

REAR
VIEW OF CUSTOM 880
WAGON

PRODUCTION :
TD1-L 330 (6)	(51,761)	
TD2-L 330 (V8)	(33,602)	
TD1-M 440 (6)	(13,146)	
TD2-M 440 (V8)	(49,591)	

TD1-H POLARA (6)	(68,262)	
TD2-H POLARA (V8)	(40,323)	
TD2-P POLARA 500 (V8)	(7256)	
TA3 880 (V8)	(9831)	
(CUSTOM 880) (V8)	(18,435)	

'64 Dodge

225 CID 6 OR 318, 383 OR 426 CID V8

440 (VD-2) 7.00 × 14 TIRES

$2264. UP

330

$2637. UP

POLARA

$2994.

SPORTSMAN WAGON

1964

145 TO 425 HP

PRODUCTION:
VDI-L 330 (6)   (57,957)
VD2-L 330 (V8) (46,438)
VDI-M 440 (6)   (15,147)
VD2-M 440 (V8) (68,861)

VDI-H POLARA (6)   (3810)
VD2-H POLARA (V8)   (66,988)
VD2-P POLARA 500 (V8) (17,787)
VA3   880 (V8)   (10,526)
       (CUSTOM 880 (V8) (21,234)

POLARA   A- PARK. LOCK ; B- TRANSMISSION BUTTONS ; C- SPEEDO. ; D- CLOCK ;
E- HEATER CONTROLS ; G- RADIO ; H- GLOVE BOX ; I- ASHTRAY, LIGHTER ;
J- IGNITION ; K- WIPER CONTROL ; L- LIGHTS ; M- PARK. BRAKE RELEASE

DASH

note THAT POLARA DASH (ABOVE) DIFFERS FROM 880 DASH (SEE 880 CVT., BELOW)

$3155. UP

880 WAGON

4-DR. SED.

$2826.

880

64

FINAL YR. OF '61-STYLE ROOFLINE ON 880

CONCAVE GRILLE ON 880

$3264.

WRAPAROUND TAIL LIGHTS ON 880

(VA-3)

8.00 × 14 TIRES

Dodge

AW1 (6)   AW2 (V8)

Dodge Coronet 440 2-door hardtop. 6 and V8 power.

Coronet
7.35 × 14 TIRES

116" and 117" WB

$2622. UP

Coronet

CORONET DASH

Dodge Coronet 440 Station Wagon (3-seat model also offered)
7.75 × 14 TIRES

$2674.

$2403. UP

145, 180, 230, 265, 270, 315, 330 340, 365 OR 425 HP.

$2913. **Polara**   #D-14 4-door hardtop. V8 power.
(AD2-L)

V-8 CHOICES INCLUDE 273, 318, 361, 383, 413 OR 426 CID

new 121" WB

(13,096 BLT.)

Monaco two-door hardtop.

Dodge Monaco. Limited edition. 2-door hardtop. V8 power.

$3355.

MONACO DASH

65 Monaco
(new)(H/T only) (AD2-P)

8.25 × 14 TIRES

$3010.

CUSTOM 880   4 DR. H/T
CUSTOM 880 4-DR. SED.

$3150.

Wagon
has 8.50 × 14 TIRES

CUSTOM 880 (AD2-H)   **$3422.**

44,496 CUSTOM 880s BLT. (6 MODELS)

PRODUCTION (OTHER MODELS):
AW1-L CORONET (6) $2217. UP
AW2-L CORONET (V8) $2313. "
AW2-N CORONET 440 (6) $2377. UP
"   CORONET 440 (V8) $2473. UP

AW2-P
CORONET 500 (V8) (32745) $2674. UP
AW2-L POLARA (V8) (12,705) $2730. UP

327

(WEST COAST) $2736.

$2264. UP

DODGE

STD. CORONET SERIES (lowest priced Coronets
(NO SIDE CHROME)

2-DR. $2303. UP

$2722.

Coronet
DELUXE
(2 DR.
WAGONS ALSO)

CORONET 440
4 DR. WAGON

$2264. ~ 3604.
PRICE RANGE
TOTAL 1966 PROD. :
419, 287
CALENDAR YR. = 435,026 *
* INCL. DART, CHARGER

ALL CORONET
MODELS WITH
225 CID 6,
273½ CID V8
3/8 CID V8
361 CID V8 OR
383 CID V8

JOIN THE DODGE REBELLION

ENGINES:
225 CID 6 (45 HP); 273½ CID V8 (180 HP);
3/8 CID V8 (230 HP);
361 CID V8 (265 HP);
383 CID V8 (270 OR 325 HP);
440 CID V8 (350 HP)

66
(6 CYL. OR V8)
new
GRILLES

Signal when ready. Hidden behind the handsome
grille are Coronet's turn signals and parking lights.

2457. UP

117"
WB

Coronet
440
$2891.

$2611.

1966

CORONET
440

$3045.
(WEST)

Coronet 500.

Coronet
500

440 H/T
INTERIOR
(ABOVE)

$2827. UP
$3261.
(WEST)

CORONET

500 DASH

(CONT'D.
NEXT PAGE)

328

DODGE

$3183. UP

POLARA V8

Polara V8 CVT.
$3161.

FROM $3555. (WEST)

66 (CONT'D.)

$2948.

4-DR. H/T

$3320. (WEST)

$3533. (WEST)

Polara V8

V8
("POLARA 500" MODELS ALSO)

(121" WB and V8 ENGINES=IN EACH POLARA, MONACO)

(WEST) $3405.

$3033.

Monaco V8 4 DR. SEDAN

Slip gracefully and frugally out of the low-price field. It's never been so easy. See what Dodge Monaco and Polara cars offer you as standard equipment. Then slip behind the wheel—and get a kick out of driving!

2 SEAT OR 3 SEAT 4 DR. $3436. OR 3539.

MONACO V8

FROM $3808 (WEST)

wagons

REAR DECK BEARS "MONACO" NAME, INSTEAD OF "DODGE"

A-60

(WEST) $3759.

Monaco 500 2-door hardtop. 383 4-barrel V8 power, standard.

$3604.

MONACO 500—THE VERY FINEST DODGE OF ALL FOR '66.

$2884.

90" WB

CUSTOM SPORTSMAN

($2567. STD. SPORTSMAN ALSO)

MODELS: CORONET BWL (66,161 BLT.) (INCLUDES CORONET DELUXE); CORONET 440 BWH (128,998 BLT.); CORONET 500 BWP (55,683 BLT.); POLARA BD2-L (107,832 BLT.); MONACO BD2-H (49,773 BLT.) MONACO 500 HARDTOP (ONLY BODY TYPE IN MON. 500 BD2-P SERIES)(10,840 BLT.)

SMALL VANS LIKE CUST. SPTSMN. (ILLUSTRATED ABOVE) FOUND FAVOR DUE TO THEIR ROOMY INTERIOR SPACE, SHORT EXTERIORS.

DODGE *Coronet*

$ 3070.

$ 2622. UP

Dodge Coronet 2-seat station wagon.

$ 2693. UP

$ 3141.

Dodge Coronet Deluxe 2-seat station wagon.

440 DLX.

FRONT CLOSE-UP

$ 2397. UP COR. DLX.

440

(INTRO. 9-29-66)

67

new GRILLES

$ 3352.

CORONET R/T

(w. 440 CID V8)

COR. 500 TAIL-LTS. APPEAR INVISIBLE BY DAY.

Dodge Coronet 500 SE (Special Edition)

Coronet 500

The Dodge Rebellion wants you!

FROM $3666. (WEST)

Dodge Polara station wagon, available in 2-seat and 3-seat models.

$3183. UP

POLARA STATION WAGON

(POL. 500 has VERTICAL TRIM STRIPS NEAR FRONT TIP of FRONT FENDER.)

POLARA REAR LIKE MONACO

MONACO

$3170. UP

$3676. (WEST)

Monaco 500

BEARS "DODGE" NAME AT REAR

"MONACO" NAME AT REAR, (EXCEPT ON MONACO 500)

$3896. (WEST)

CORRUGATED STRIP ALONG SIDE

(WEST COAST PRICES IN SMALL PRINT)

$3712.

$ 2359. ~ 3712.
PRICE RANGE

361 CID V8 DISCONTINUED

TOTAL 1967 PRODUCTION: 295,449

DODGE

TOTAL 1968 PRODUCTION: 455,761

$2525.

$2487.

CORONET DELUXE

PLAIN TOP

$2603. CORONET 440

$3379.

CORONET R/T

VINYL TOP

$3613.

$3212. UP

WAGON $2924. UP

a two-way tailgate...

Coronet 500 wagon

FROM $3933. (WEST)

new GRILLES

68

Watch out. You're getting **DODGE fever**

(INTRO. 9-14-67)

CORONET 500

H/T $2879.

POLARA WAGON FROM $4105.

POLARA 122" WB (SINCE '67)

$3483

POLARA 318 CID V8 (230 HP)

MONACO 500 H/T (4568 BLT.)

MONACO WAGONS FROM $4469.

383 CID V8 (290 HP)

new SIDE SAFETY LTS. (CIRCULAR)

$4035.

new FULL-WIDTH TAIL-LT. ASSEMBLY ON POLARA, MONACO.

$3432. 4 DR. H/T $3815. (WEST)

CUSTOM SPORTSMAN

108" WB (AVAIL. SINCE '67)

two sizes— (90" WB $2887. UP)

4 models— to choose from!

MONACO

PRICE RANGE $2487.~3869.

331

DODGE

CORONET

$2692.

440 H/T $3521. (WEST)

White Hat Special Coronet.

The Dodge Coronet White Hat Special comes in a 2-door hardtop or 4-door sedan—with the features listed below—at a special low package price.
■ Vinyl roof in black; white, tan, green—or standard top
■ Whitewall tires ■ Front, rear bumper guards ■ Deep-dish wheel covers ■ Light group ■ Outside, remote-control rearview mirror ■ Bright trim package.

new GRILLES

REAR DETAIL

69
(INTRO. 9-19-68)

new TAIL-LIGHTS

Coronet. 500 V8

$3655. (WEST)

Coronet 500

H/T $2929.

$3138. (SUPER BEE, BELOW)

(32,050 CORONET 500s BLT. '69) (H/T, CVT, SED., WAGON)

FRONT VIEW

TOTAL 1969 PROD.: 611,645

note DUAL HOOD SCOOPS on

'69 CORONET SUPER BEE

STANDARD SUPER BEE EQUIPMENT
• Special 4-bbl. 383-cid Magnum V8 (440 Magnum V8 heads, valve gear, hot cam and manifolds), 335 hp @ 5,200 rpm • Dual exhaust
• Hurst 4-speed with HD clutch • HD suspension • HD shocks • HD brakes • Dodge Charger Rallye instrument panel
OPTIONAL
• 426 Hemi—two 4-bbl. carbs—425 hp @ 5,000 rpm
REAR AXLE RATIOS
• 383 Magnum V8—standard: 3.23:1; optional: 3.55:1, 3.91:1
• Hemi—standard: 3.23:1, optional: 3.54 (with 4-speed manual), 3.55:1 (with automatic), 4.10:1 (with manual or automatic)

H/T $3697. (WEST)

(note BEE FIGURE ON GRILLE)

THIS DECAL and POPULAR ADVERTISING FIGURE IS WELL KNOWN, BUT DIFFERS FROM BEE ON GRILLE.

(27,846 BLT.)

(COUPE or H/T)

EARLY "SUPER BEE"

THIS TYPE AVAIL. in LATE '68 MODEL YEAR.
383 CID V8 (335 HP @ 5200) OR
426 CID HEMI V8 (425 " @ 5000)

(CONT'D. NEXT PAGE)

DODGE

$3188.

4 DR. H/T

a 230-hp V8. Not to mention an all-new instrument panel and concealed windshield wipers.

Polara.

DODGE WHITE HAT SPECIAL POLARA.
The Dodge Polara White Hat Special comes in a 2-door or 4-door hardtop—with the features listed below—at a special low package price.
• Vinyl roof in black, white, tan, green or standard top • Front, rear bumper guards • Fender-mounted turn signals • Outside, remote-control rearview mirror • Whitewall tires • Deep-dish wheel covers • Bright trim package.

WHITE HAT SPECIAL

POLARA **$3117.**

500
$3314.

69
(CONT'D.)

$2554.~ 4046. PRICE RANGE

ENGS.: 225 cid 6 (145 HP)
318 cid V8 (230 HP)
383 cid V8 (290, 330 or 335 HP)
426 cid V8 (425 HP)
440 cid V8 (350 or 375 HP)

TOTAL 1969 PROD.:
324,256

FINAL YEAR FOR POLARA **500**

This year, **DODGE** is turning up the *fever*

Monaco.

$3917. UP

wagon

Dodge CHRYSLER MOTORS CORPORATION

In a test of acceleration, economy, and braking ability, a 1969 Monaco was overall winner, Class II, in the Union/Pure Oil Performance Trials.

MONACO GRILLE (left) DIFFERS ONLY SLIGHTLY FROM POLARA's.

INTERIOR

MONACO 4 DR. H/T

FROM **$4707.** (WEST)
(38,566 MONACOS BLT., INCL. 2-DR. H/T, SED.)

$4381.
(WEST)

all-new aircraft-type instrument panel. And ahead of it all—a big 383-cu.-in. V8. 1969 Monaco.

$3591.

(1966 – 1978)

Dodge CHARGER NEW

66

$3469.

HDLTS. DISAPPEAR INTO GRILLE

BUCKET SEATS, FRONT and BACK

... new leader of the Dodge Rebellion.

117" WB (LIKE Coronet) (THROUGH '70)

V8s : 3I8 CID (230 HP)
361 (265 HP)
383 (325 HP)
426 CID Hemi (425 HP)

7.35 × 14 TIRES

(37,344 BLT.)

FASTBACK STYLING (THROUGH '67)

V8s : 3I8 CID (230 HP); 383 CID (325 HP); 426 CID Hemi (425 HP)
new 440 CID Magnum V8 AVAIL. (375 HP)

($3482., WEST COAST)

VINYL TOP OPT.

67

XP-29 MODEL CONTINUES WITH FEW CHANGES

DODGE CHARGER 66-67   the Dodge Rebellion.

3/28.

15,788 BLT.

Join the fun... catch
DODGE *fever*

DASH

Dodge Charger

$3184. UP

new SIDE SAFETY LTS. (ROUND)

68
(RESTYLED) NO LONGER A FASTBACK

FROM $3371.

$3592.
(20,057 BLT.)

R/T SE

STANDARD CHARGER R/T EQUIPMENT
• 440-cid Magnum (4-bbl.) V8, 375 hp
• Choice of 3-speed automatic or Hurst 4-speed manual • Dual exhausts
• HD suspension • HD shocks • HD brakes
• Dodge Charger Rallye instrument panel • F70x14 wide-treads
OPTIONAL
• 426 Hemi

Success Car of the Year

69
new SPLIT GRILLE

117" WB

$4000.

Charger Daytona:

UNIQUE REAR "TAIL" SPOILER

RARE! (505 BLT.)

Totally new

69½-70A

(1970 PLYMOUTH ROAD-RUNNER "*SUPERBIRD*" SIMILAR)

(TOTAL 1969 PROD. [ALL MODELS] AMOUNTS TO 90,000-PLUS.)

DODGE CHARGER 68~70

335

DODGE

(STD. CHALLENGER IS "DEPUTY" COUPE, AT $3562.)

(WEST)

$2851.

Challenger hardtop, showing deluxe wheel covers
(53337 BLT.)

H/T $3670.

$3083.

SE → WITH FORMAL ROOF, SMALL REAR WINDOW

$3902.

(6584 BLT.)

MORE TOPS...MORE MODELS
Three tops available. Standard (shown), a Special Edition (SE) with vinyl-covered formal roof hardtop, and convertible. All nine models feature concealed wipers, locking steering-wheel column, deep-pile carpeting, dual headlights, and more.

...you could be DODGE MATERIAL.

110" WB
225 CID 6 (145 HP) OR
318 CID V8 (230 HP)
D78/E78 × 14 TIRES

Challenger (NEW)

70 A

(INTRO. 9-23-69)

3535.

18 1970 DODGE COLORS

Plum Crazy (FC7)*
Sublime (FJ5)*
Light Green Metallic (FF4)
Dark Green Metallic (EF8)
Cream (DY3)
Go-Mango (EK2)*
Hemi Orange (EV2)*
Banana (FY1)*
Light Blue Metallic (EB3)
Bright Blue Metallic (EB5)
Bright Red (FE5)
Dark Blue Metallic (EB7)
Dark Burnt Orange Metallic (FK5)
Beige (BL1)
Dark Tan Metallic (FT6)
White (EW1)
Black (TX9)
Light Gold Metallic (FY4)

O = OPTIONAL AT EXTRA COST

$4249.

(1070 BLT.)

DODGE CHALLENGER R/T CONVERTIBLE

$3226.

Challenger R/T, showing bumblebee stripe (12 colors available).

(14889 BLT.)

Challenger R/T

WESTERN PRICES SHOWN *IN BLACK*

18~GAL. GAS TANK

"R/T" EMBLEM ON GRILLE

note HOOD VARIATIONS ON THESE 2 R/T HARDTOPS. CAR ABOVE has 2 LG. VENT SLOTS; CAR AT RIGHT has SHAKER TYPE AIR SCOOP.

F70 × 14 TIRES ON R/T

FROM $4007. (WEST)

(CONT'D. NEXT PAGE) DODGE 70(A)

DODGE

$3048. (3694 BLT.)

(3436 BLT.)

440 $3616.

Coronet Deluxe station wagon, 2-seat model only—Six or V8 power.

Coronet 440 station wagon, 2-seat models—Six or V8 power. 3-seat model 4 V8 power only.

(33258 BLT.)

Coronet 440 4-door sedan.

Coronet Deluxe 2-door coupe

Coronet R/T 2-door hardtop. (Convertible also available.)

CORONET

$3826.

Coronet 500 station wagon, 2-seat and 3-seat models. 318 V8, std.

Coronet 500 2-door hardtop.

(8247 BLT.)

Super Bee

$3188. (924 BLT.)

3919.

70 B (CONT'D.)

Coronet 500

(11154 BLT.)

(11540 BLT.)

H/T

(8247 BLT.)

WESTERN PRICES SHOWN IN BLACK

Polara GRILLE CLOSE UP

Polara

1970

$4022.

Polara station wagon, 2-seat and 3-seat models. 318 V8, std.

Polara convertible.

Polara 2-door hardtop, with optional Gator Grain roof.

$4221.

$3527.

(842 BLT.)

$4305.

Polara Custom 4-door sedan. Polara 4-door sedan also available.

$3743.

FROM $4905.

MONACO

(5475 BLT.)

(10974 BLT.)
4-DR. H/T
$4538.

A-100 SPORTSMAN

FROM $3207.

THOUGH A FEW PASSENGER VANS ARE ILLUSTRATED ON THESE PAGES, BROADER COVERAGE OF ALL BRANDS OF POPULAR PASSENGER (AND CARGO) VANS ARE SEEN IN "ULTIMATE TRUCK AND VAN SPOTTER'S GUIDE, 1925~1990," ALSO FROM KP BOOKS.

INTERIOR (CORONET)

TOTAL 1970 PROD.—543,019   DODGE 70 (B)

Dodge

Challenger convertible

Challenger.
H/T

PRICED FROM $3569.

CHALLENGER T/A
(note STRIPES and SPEC. PAINT)

(INTRO. 10-6-70)

R/T
383 CID V8
(300 HP)
$4009.

CHALLENGER R/T

'71 CORONET

Coronet wagons FROM $3947.

RESTYLED
SPORTSMAN
(ILLUSTRATED with OPTIONAL TRAVCO CAMPER TOP)

new SPORTSMAN
B-100, B-200 OR B-300
new 109" OR 127" WB

Coronet Brougham

SEDANS FROM $3649.

(CONT'D. NEXT PAGE)
DODGE 71 (A)

DODGE

CORONET
CRESTWOOD
$4352.
UP

71ᴮ
(CONT'D.)

WESTERN PRICES
SHOWN

POLARA

$4538
AND UP

POLARA
CUSTOM 4-DR. H/T
$4376.

COLORS

Lt. Gunmetal Metallic (A)	Lt. Blue Metallic (A)	Dk. Blue Metallic (A)	Bright Red (A)	Lt. Green Metallic (A)
Dk. Green Metallic (A)	Dk. Bronze Metallic (A)	Black (A)	Citron Yella (A)*	Gold Metallic (A)
Dk. Gold Metallic (A)	Dk. Gunmetal Metallic (C)	Burgundy (C)	Moss Green Metallic (C)	Turquoise Metallic (C)
Dk. Tan Metallic (C)	White (C)	Gold (C)	Bright Blue Metallic (B)	Plum Crazy (B)*
Green Go (B)*	Butterscotch (B)*	Tan Metallic (B)	Hemi Orange (B)*	Bright White (B)

(A) Available on all cars.
(B) Available on Dart, Challenger, Coronet, Charger.
(C) Available on Polara, Monaco.
* High-impact colors. Optional at extra cost.

**WIRE
WHEEL
COVER**

DASH

MONACO

FROM
$5105.

DELUXE WHEEL COVER

H/T
$4631.

DODGE 71 (B)

339

DODGE

CHALLENGER.
100" WB

150 HP, 318 CID V8 (225 CID 6 AVAIL.)

CHALLENGER

$3634.

7.35 x 14 / F70 x 14 TIRES

DASH

For people who like to know what's going on, a dash you can read. The Rallye Instrument Cluster, standard with Challenger Rallye, optional with Challenger, starts out with a simulated wood-grained instrument panel and continues with a tachometer, trip odometer, and clock, in addition to the gauges you'd expect.

tape cassette
radio/ stereo
● EXTERIOR COLORS

1. Light Blue
2. Bright Blue Metallic
3. Red
4. Light Green Metallic
5. Dark Green Metallic
6. Eggshell White
7. Black
8. Light Gold

*(Hi-impact color, optional at extra cost)

9. Gold Metallic
10. Dark Gold Metallic
11. Dark Tan Metallic
12. Light Gunmetal Metallic
13. Medium Tan Metallic
14. Super Blue
15. Hemi Orange*
16. Top Banana*

CHALLENGER RALLYE

340 CID V8 AVAIL.

72 A (INTRO. 9-28-71)

new GRILLES

CORONET CRESTWOOD

E 78 x 14 TIRES ON all CORONETS (H78 x 14, WAGONS)

9-PASS. $4451.

CORONET CUSTOM

SEDAN

Coronet

118" WB

(CONT'D. NEXT PAGE)

$3766.

DODGE 72 (A)

DODGE

SED. $4096

POL. CST. WAG. $4849.

POLARA

DASH

PROTECTIVE VINYL-FACED RUB MOLDING ALONG BODY SIDES

POLARA CUSTOM H/T $4308.

WESTERN PRICES SHOWN

72 B (CONT'D.)

POLARA CUSTOM 4-DR H/T ROOFLINE

Monaco.

$5105. TO 5566.

note UNUSUALLY HIGH PLACEMENT of GRAINED PANELING on MONACO WAGON.

MONACO UPHOLSTERY

ATTRACTIVE MONACO DOOR PANEL

H/T $4631.

4-DR. H/T $4694.

WITH BUMPER GUARDS (THAT ALSO SERVE AS GRILLE GUARDS)

DODGE 72 (B)

DODGE

$3752.

Challenger Rallye

(FINAL 1974 CHALLENGER has SHORT SIDE PORTS in COWL, BUT NO STRIPS ACROSS DOOR AS SEEN ON 1973 MODEL ILLUSTR. ABOVE.)

Coronet Wagons

$4358. (ABOVE)

Coronet Custom.

CORONET CRESTWOOD WAGON, 6-PASS.: $4449.; 9-PASS.:$4569.

SPORTSMAN. THE LARGEST SELLING COMPACT WAGON BUILT IN AMERICA.

Sportsman.

POLARA 4-DR. SEDAN

CORONET

21

Coronet '73

CORONET SEDAN.

STD. CORONET SEDAN $3757.

SEDAN $3907.

Coronet CUSTOM

73 A
new GRILLES

'73 Dodge Polara.

Polara 2-Dr. Hardtop.

(FINAL POLARA TYPES IN 1973) (CONT'D. NEXT PAGE)

DODGE 73 (A)

342

DODGE

FINAL Polara SERIES

Polara Custom 2-Dr. Hardtop.

Polara Custom Wagon

Polara Custom

DASH

Options & Colors

SHIFT INDICATOR ON SPEEDOMETER

Turquoise Metallic (B)
Parchment (A)
Yellow (B)
Dark Green Metallic (A)
Dark Tan Metallic (B)
Light Blue (A)
Super Blue (C)
Bright Red (A)
Top Banana* (C)
Dark Silver Metallic (A)
Medium Tan Metallic (D)
Bright Blue Metallic (A)
Dark Blue Metallic (B)
Light Gold (A)
Pale Green (A)
Dark Gold Metallic (A)
Bronze Metallic (C)
Light Green Metallic (A)
Gold Metallic (A)
Eggshell White (A)
Black (A)

(A) Available on all cars.
(B) Available on Polara and Monaco only.
(C) Available on Dart/Challenger/Coronet and Charger.
(D) Available on Coronet and Charger only.
*Extra-cost paint.

73 (CONT'D.)
B

Extra care in engineering makes a difference in Dodge...depend on it.

DODGE POLARA

Polara Custom 4-Door Hardtop

Monaco

DAKAR CLOTH ~ AND ~ VINYL UPHOL. (MONACO)

Monaco's luxurious Dakar cloth-and-vinyl interior.

MONACO BROUGHAM 4-DOOR SEDAN

Monaco Brougham 4-Dr. Sedan.

Monaco Wagon

new ELECTRONIC IGNITION STD. EQUIP.

DODGE 73 (B)

DODGE

CHALLENGER

FRONT CLOSE~UP

$3143. (16437 BLT.)

(CHALLENGER DISCONTINUED DURING 1974; NAME RETURNS 1978 on JAPANESE IMPORT VERSION.)

19 TEXAS 74 DGE ★474

WESTERN PRICES SHOWN *IN BLACK*

CORONET CUSTOM
$4333.

new GRILLES WITH "DODGE" NAME ABOVE, CENTER.

74A

(CORONET and CORO. CUST. SEDANS ONLY) $3271. UP

SPORTSMAN

DODGE SPORTSMAN WAGONS (tow up to 6,000 lbs.).

note SIDE DOOR VARIATIONS

new GRILLE, WITH DODGE NAME ABOVE

$5011.- 6155.

B-100, B-200, OR B-300 SERIES

Dodge
Dodge Trucks

CHRYSLER
MOTORS CORPORATION

(NO POLARA SERIES; DISCONTINUED)

(CONT'D. NEXT PAGE)

DODGL 74 (A)

DODGE

WAGONS with 124" WHEELBASE (122" WB on OTHER MONACOS)

WAGON FROM $5860.

MONACO
74 B (CONT'D.)

MONACO, CUSTOM and BROUGHAM DIVISIONS WITHIN MONACO SERIES

$4283. UP

H/Ts FROM $4783.

TOTAL 1974 PROD. = 477,728

Dodge

BACKGROUND SCENERY IN MONACO

1974 is a beautiful time for Monaco

4 DR. H/Ts = CUSTOM (10585 BLT.) $4539.   BROUGHAM (5649 BLT.) $4999.   DODGE 74 (B)

DODGE

Extra care in engineering makes a difference in Dodge. Depend on it.

CORONET SEDAN $3641. UP

CORONET WAGON $4358. UP

Coronet
Two-Door
Hardtop

('75)
FINAL '76
CORONET
has HOOD
ORNAMENT.

$3591.

115" WB ON
2-DRS.,
117½" ON
OTHERS

ALL-NEW CORONET
HARDTOP BROUGHAM '75
a little bit smaller and a little bit sportier.

$4154.

CORONETS AVAIL. IN
STANDARD, CUSTOM
OR BROUGHAM
MODELS.

1975 EXAMPLES and EASTERN
PRICES SHOWN

TOTAL
1975 PROD. = 377,462
1976 PROD. = 430,641

75-76

SINCE 1975,
MOST 6-CYL.
MODELS
COST MORE THAN
COMPARABLE
V8s.

Introducing the Royal Monaco Brougham from Dodge.

Dodge
Dodge Trucks
CHRYSLER MOTORS CORPORATION

For 1975, Dodge introduces the
Royal Monaco Brougham—an
automotive classic that reflects the
beauty and elegance of the proud
principality for which it was named.

H/T $4868. (8117 BLT.)

(SEDANS ALSO AVAIL.)

DODGE 75-76

DODGE MONACO

MONACO NOW *has* FORMER CORONET WHEELBASE: (2-DR., 115"; 4-DR., 117½")

2-DRS. FROM $5061.

BROUGHAM 2-DR. $5297.

77A

MONACO

REAR

PLAID INTERIOR AVAIL.

EXTERIOR COLORS*

Vintage Red Sunfire Metallic	Jade Green Metallic	Burnished Copper Metallic	Bright Red (Monaco only)	Forest Green Sunfire Metallic	Mocha Tan	Moondust Metallic

Russet Sunfire Metallic — Coffee Sunfire Metallic — Eggshell White — Black Sunfire Metallic — Jasmine Yellow — Silver Cloud Metallic — Golden Fawn

Mojave Beige — Cadet Blue Metallic — Inca Gold Metallic (Royal Monaco only) — Spanish Gold Metallic — Starlight Blue Sunfire Metallic — Wedgewood Blue

Monaco Brougham 4-door sedan

Monaco Brougham 2-door hardtop

Monaco 4-door sedan

Monaco 4-door wagon

Monaco 2-door hardtop

Monaco Crestwood 4-door wagon

OXFORD VINYL BUCKET SEATS (MONACO BROUGH. H/T)

STD. SEAT FOR MONACO BRM. 2 or 4-DR. (VERDI VELOUR)

VERDI VELOUR CLOTH and VINYL (AVAIL. MONACO BRM. SEDANS)

MONACO CRESTWOOD WAGON

Dodge   Mopar   CERTIFIED CAR CARE

$5818.

(CONT'D. NEXT PAGE)

DODGL 77(A)

DODGE

77 (CONT'D)

$5619.

BROUGHAM SEDAN

LOW SIDE LIGHTS ON ROYAL MONACO

ROYAL MONACO

MORE MONACO MODELS AND SIZES THAN EVER BEFORE.

Royal Monaco Brougham 2-door hardtop

Royal Monaco 4-door sedan

Royal Monaco 2-door hardtop

Royal Monaco Brougham 4-door wagon

Royal Monaco Brougham 4-door sedan

Royal Monaco 4-door wagon

(W/O GRAIN)

CPE. ROOFLINE VARIETIES

Royal Monaco Brougham Hardtop

WITH DIPLOMAT ROOF PKG. $5634.

$5011.

(8309 BROUGHAM H/Ts BLT.)

$4996.

POMPEII CLOTH ~and~ VINYL INTER. AVAIL. FOR 2 OR 4 ~DR.

WESTERN PRICES SHOWN IN BLACK

OPT. CLOTH ~and~ VINYL INTERIOR (2-DR. or 4-DR.)

TOTAL 1976 PROD. = 526,254

(21440 BLT.)

BROUGHAM SEDAN WITH RED VINYL ROOF

BANCROFT VINYL INTERIOR AVAIL. IN ROYAL MONACO WAGON

BANCROFT VINYL INTERIOR STD. IN ALL ROYAL MONACO MODELS

INTERIOR UPHOLSTERY PATTERNS AVAIL. IN VARIOUS COLOR CHOICES.

wagon

REAR DETAILS

2-SLAI (1418 BLT.)
3-SLAI (4251 BLT.)

$5607.

$6353.

DODGE

standard

Diplomat or

DELUXE MEDALLION MODELS
112.7" WB

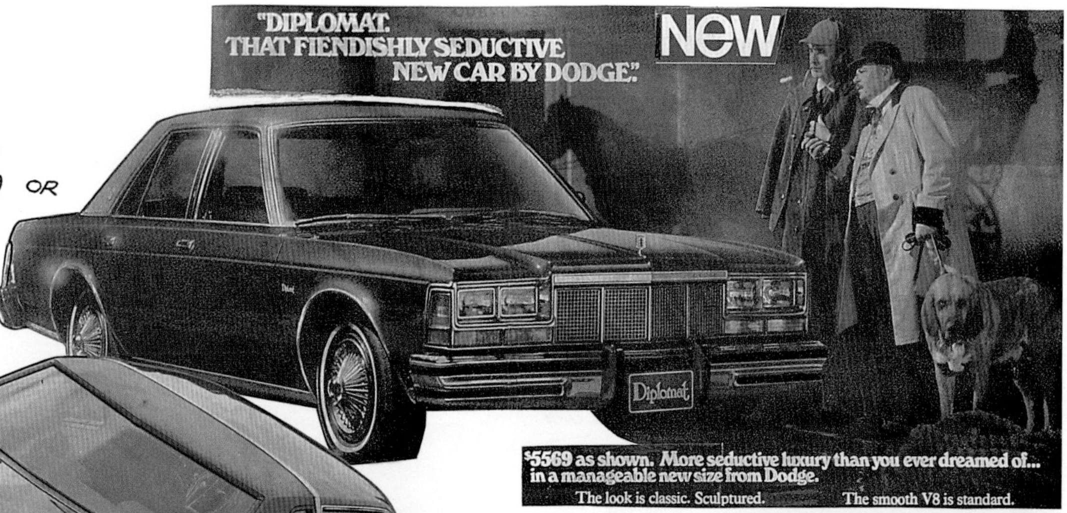

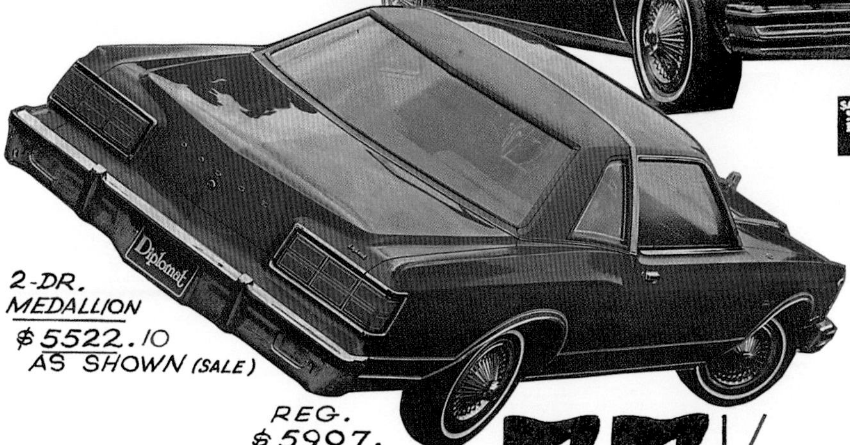

2-DR. MEDALLION
$5522.10
AS SHOWN (SALE)

REG. $5907.

77 1/2

318 CID V8 (145 HP)

FR 78 × 15 TIRES

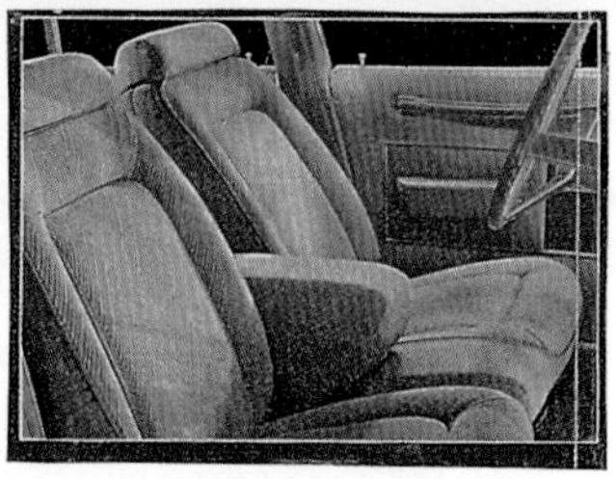

VELOUR STD. IN MEDALLION INTERIOR (4-DR. ILLUSTR.)

DIPLOMAT

(6TH DIGIT IN SERIAL # PREFIX IS NOW 8 ... SIGNIFYING 1978 MODEL.)

25/17
MPG HWY   MPG CITY

WITH T-BAR ROOF

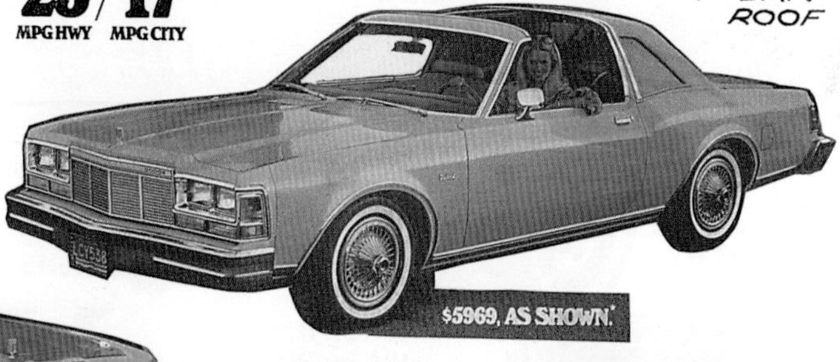

$5969, AS SHOWN.

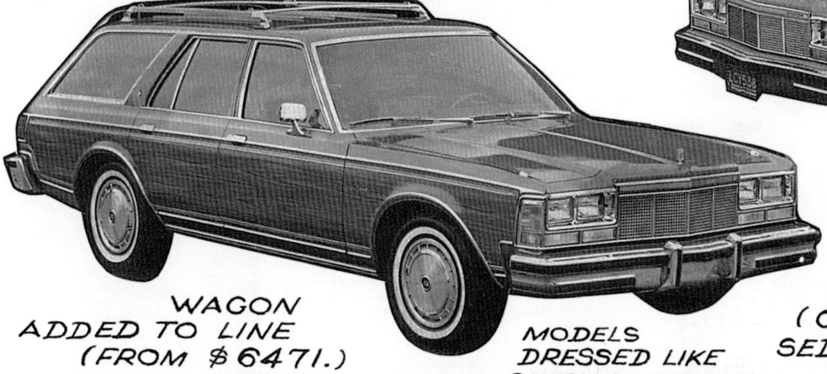

WAGON ADDED TO LINE (FROM $6471.)

LOWER-COST DIPLOMAT "S" ADDED: (CPE., $5726. SED., $5882.)

78 A
(new MODELS ADDED)

MODELS DRESSED LIKE SHERLOCK HOLMES and DR. WATSON CONTINUE APPEARING IN DODGE DIPLOMAT ADVERTISING. (RIGHT, TOP RIGHT)

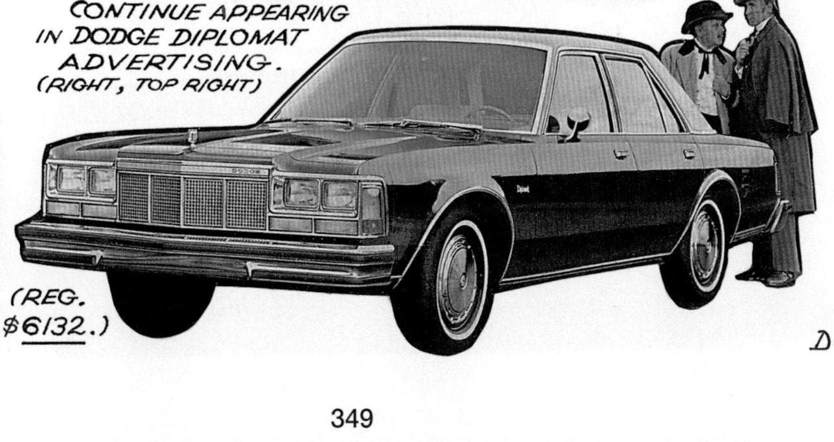

(REG. $6132.)

(CONT'D. NEXT PAGE)

DODGE 77½ ~ 78 (A)

349

DODGE

78 B

Magnum XE.

Magnum GT

1978 Dodge MAGNUM XE

STD. VINYL UPH.

XE WITH VINYL-COVERED TOP and SUN-ROOF

GT

114.9" WB
25½-GAL. GAS TANK
$5509. UP

GT WITH T-BAR ROOF

OPT. CLOTH 60/40 SEATS

WHITE LEATHER UPH. AVAIL.

XE has SLOTTED OPERA WINDOWS

New
(55431 BLT.)

V8
318 CID   360 CID   400 CID
(140-155 HP) (155-170 HP) (190 HP)

TIRE AVAILABILITY
STANDARD — FR78x15 glass-belted, radial-ply black sidewall tires
AVAILABLE — GR78x15 glass-belted, radial-ply black or white sidewall tires
AVAILABLE — GR60x15 Aramid fiber-belted, radial-ply raised white-letter tires (standard with GT Package)
AVAILABLE — GR78x15 steel-belted, radial-ply wider white sidewall tires
AVAILABLE — HR78x15 steel-belted, radial-ply wider white sidewall tires
*Space Saving spare tire or conventional spare tire available at no charge.

CB RADIO OPT.

DASH

Dodge

DODGE 78-B

DODGE

Meet the Diplomats.

28 MPG HWY / 18 MPG CITY

Exterior Colors*
Choice of 11 exterior colors for two- and four-door models. Choice of seven for wagon.†

Dove Gray

Cadet Blue Metallic

Ensign Blue Metallic

Regent Red Sunfire Metallic†

Chianti Red

Teal Green Sunfire Metallic†

Teal Frost Metallic

Sable Tan Sunfire Metallic†

Medium Cashmere Metallic†
(Wagon only)

Light Cashmere†

Eggshell White†

Black†

Buy or lease a Diplomat and say
"Hey that's my Dodge!"

Diplomat Ready-To-Order Form

Medallion 4-door
(5995 BLT.) **$6198.**

Medallion 2-door
(6637 BLT.) **$5966.**

Diplomat wagon
(9511 BLT.) **$6127.**

Models

- [ ] Medallion 4-door
- [ ] Medallion 2-door
- [ ] Diplomat wagon
- [ ] Diplomat Salon 2-door
- [ ] Diplomat Salon 4-door
- [ ] Diplomat 2-door
- [ ] Diplomat 4-door

Power Teams

Engine	Four-Speed Transmission (Overdrive)	TorqueFlite Automatic Transmission
All except California		
☐ 225-1 6-cyl. *(100 HP)* Standard	Standard	NA
☐ 225-2 6-cyl. *110"* NA	NA	Optional
☐ 318-2 8-cyl. *135"* NA	NA	Optional
☐ 360-2 8-cyl. *150"* NA	NA	Optional
☐ 360-4 8-cyl. HD *(195 HP)*		
☐ Dual Exhaust*		
California	†(Optional TorqueFlite required in California)	
☐ 225-1 6-cyl.	NA	Optional
☐ 318-4 8-cyl.	NA	Optional
☐ 360-4 8-cyl.	NA	Optional
☐ 360-4 8-cyl. HD		
☐ Dual Exhaust*		

†Emission Control System and Testing required on California cars and available in other states.
*Requires A 36 Heavy-Duty Trailer-Assist Pkg., at extra cost.

Diplomat

WITH T-BAR ROOF

$5234.

$5234.

(8733 BLT.)

DIPLOMAT

CPE.

5714.

SALON

(5479 BLT.)

79
A

(2159 BLT.)

MEDALLION

SEDAN VINYL ROOF

SEDAN INT.

"HEY, THAT'S MY DODGE!"

TOTAL 1979 PRODUCTION = 404,266

new GRILLE, new FRONT BUMPER, STACKED RECT. HEADLTS. OPT. (SPTSMN.)

SPORTSMAN

DASH

(CONT'D. NEXT PAGE)

DODGL 79 (A)

DODGE

MAGNUM

EXTERIOR COLORS Choice of 14 exterior colors for Magnum XE

Black	Pewter Gray Metallic	Dove Gray	Eggshell White
Frost Blue Metallic	Nightwatch Blue	Teal Frost Metallic	Teal Green Sunfire Metallic
Chianti Red	Regent Red Sunfire Metallic	Light Cashmere	Sable Tan Sunfire Metallic

Optional Two-Tone Paint Colors-

Nightwatch Blue/Pewter Gray Metallic

Black/Pewter Gray Metallic

"HEY, THAT'S MY DODGE."

WESTERN PRICES SHOWN

FINAL **MAGNUM XE**

318 OR 360 CID V8

$6380.

79ᴮ

ST. REGIS COLORS

Two-Tone Package colors:
(includes accent stripe at color break)

Dove Gray (upper)/
Oxford Gray (lower)

Frost Blue Metallic (upper)/
Ensign Blue Metallic (lower)

Teal Frost Metallic (upper)
Teal Green Sunfire Metallic (lower)

Regent Red Sunfire Metallic (upper)
Garnet Red Sunfire Metallic (lower)

Colors
Single Colors: Dove Gray, Frost Blue Metallic, Nightwatch Blue, Teal Frost Metallic, Teal Green Sunfire Metallic, Regent Red Sunfire Metallic, Light Cashmere, Medium Cashmere Metallic, Sable Tan Sunfire Metallic, Eggshell White, Black

ST. REGIS

REAR

Re-introducing the
full-size car. The totally new
St. Regis by Dodge.

NEW

ST. REGIS
DASH

118½" WB

$7429. (6)

St.Regis

A standard two-barrel Super Six provides
exceptional mileage. **(225 CID)**
23 mpg highway/17 mpg city

318 CID
V8 (140 HP)
AVAIL.
$7190. (V8)

ST.REGIS

DODGE 79 (B)

DODGE

$6485.

DIPLOMAT FOUR-DOOR.

(7941 BLT.)

$6202.

$6048.

Dodge Diplomat.

(5884 BLT.)

DIPLOMAT TWO-DOOR.

$5995.

Introducing Diplomat S-Type Coupe. A new level of driving

(S-TYPE DASH ILLUS.)

DIPLOMAT 80 A

CLOTH-and-VINYL SEATS IN SALON INTERIOR

new GRILLE
new 108.7" WB
ON 2-DRS.

COLORS

Burnished Silver Metallic
Crimson Red Metallic
Baron Red

$7311.

$6346.

(2093 BLT.)

$6621. DIPLOMAT WAGON.

(112.7" WB CONT'D. ON 4-DRS.)

Natural Suede Tan
Mocha Brown Metallic
Light Heather Gray*
Light Heather Gray Metallic*
Teal Tropic Green Metallic†
Light Cashmere
Black
Eggshell White
Teal Frost Metallic*†
Frost Blue Metallic*
Nightwatch Blue

*Not available on wagon models.
†Not available with S-Type Package.

$7041.

TOTAL 1980 PROD. = 308,638

WITH WOODGRAIN (SALON WAGON)
(2664 BLT.)

OPT. WIRE WH. COVERS

Buy or lease a Dodge Diplomat.

Tone-Tone Paint Package (4-Door)
Upper/Lower

Two-Tone Paint Package (2-Door)
Body/Lower Body, Rear of Roof, Rear Deck

Light Heather Gray/
Light Heather Gray Metallic
Nightwatch Blue/
Frost Blue Metallic
Natural Suede Tan/
Light Cashmere
Black/
Burnished Silver Metallic

STD. 225 CID 6
(100/110 HP)
STD.
318 CID V8
(140 HP)

$6501.

SALON 4-DR.
(5479 BLT.)

$6772.

WESTERN PRICES SHOWN IN BLACK

Protective rub strips front and rear (std)
Power brakes—front disc, rear drum (std)

(CONT'D. NEXT PAGE)
DODGE 80 (A)

353

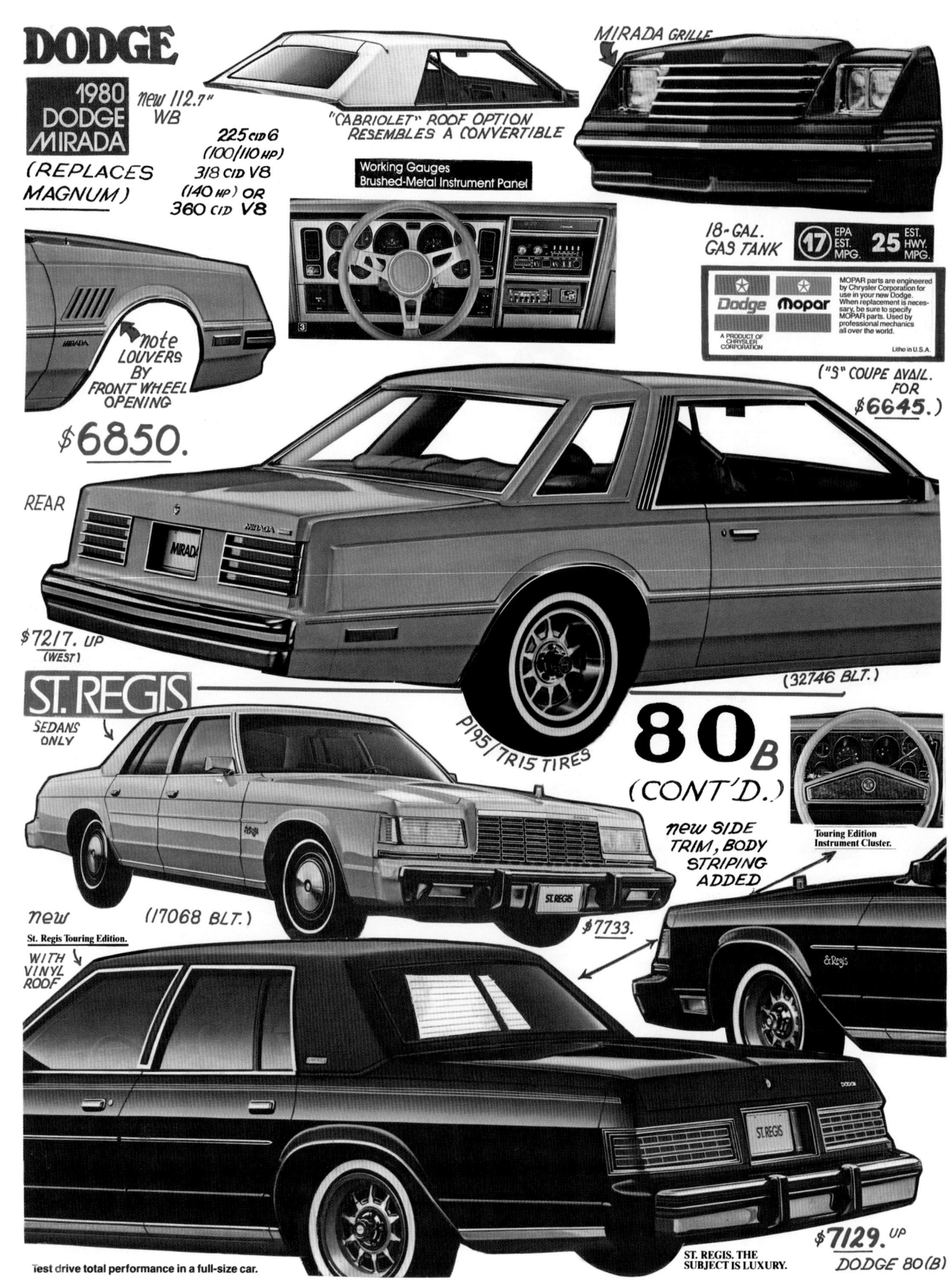

DODGE

1980 DODGE MIRADA

(REPLACES MAGNUM)

new 112.7" WB

225 cid 6 (100/110 HP)
318 cid V8 (140 HP) OR
360 cid V8

MIRADA GRILLE

"CABRIOLET" ROOF OPTION RESEMBLES A CONVERTIBLE

Working Gauges
Brushed-Metal Instrument Panel

18-GAL. GAS TANK

17 EPA EST. MPG.   25 EST. HWY. MPG.

MOPAR parts are engineered by Chrysler Corporation for use in your new Dodge. When replacement is necessary, be sure to specify MOPAR parts. Used by professional mechanics all over the world.

Dodge   Mopar
A PRODUCT OF CHRYSLER CORPORATION
Litho in U.S.A.

note LOUVERS BY FRONT WHEEL OPENING

$6850.

REAR

MIRADA

$7217. UP (WEST)

("S" COUPE AVAIL. FOR $6645.)

(32746 BLT.)

P195/TR15 TIRES

80 B (CONT'D.)

Touring Edition Instrument Cluster.

new SIDE TRIM, BODY STRIPING ADDED

ST. REGIS

SEDANS ONLY

new   (17068 BLT.)

St. Regis Touring Edition.

WITH VINYL ROOF

ST. REGIS

$7733.

St. Regis

Test drive total performance in a full-size car.

ST. REGIS. THE SUBJECT IS LUXURY.

$7129. UP

DODGE 80(B)

1976 WESTERN PRICE RANGE = $4155. TO 4916.

DODGE ASPEN

(REPLACES DART, 1976.)
(REPL. BY ARIES FOR 1981)

"Unbelievable."

Winner of the 1976 Motor Trend Magazine Car of the Year Award.

STD. WAGON ('77)

Aspen R/T has a bold look. With a blacked-out grille, wide rallye wheels, distinctive stripes.

SE

108½" WB (2-DR.)
112½" WB (4-DR.)

EPA MPG: 30 HWY. 18 CITY

Aspen RT

SE

$4872. (WEST)
(34617 BLT.)

6-PASS. WAGONS

225 CID 6 (100 HP)

76-77A

ASPEN, CUSTOM and SPECIAL EDITION MODELS

new T-BAR ROOF AVAIL. '77

('77)

HOOD ORNAMENT ON SPECIAL EDITION MODELS

Winner of the 1976 Motor Trend Magazine Car of the Year Award.

SE CPE. (21564 BLT.)

ASPEN

EXTERIOR COLORS*

Vintage Red Sunfire Metallic	Jade Green Metallic	Forest Green Sunfire Metallic	Spitfire Orange	Mojave Beige	Russet Sunfire Metallic	Eggshell White	Black Sunfire Metallic
Caramel Tan Metallic	Silver Cloud Metallic	Yellow Blaze	French Racing Blue	Regatta Blue Metallic	Spanish Gold Sunfire Metallic	Starlight Blue Sunfire Metallic	Mocha Tan

*=1977

318 CID V8 (140-150 HP)

'76 MODELS SHOWN, EXCEPT WHERE INDICATED OTHERWISE.

(1977 MODELS CONT'D.) DODGE ASPEN 76-77A

355

DODGE ASPEN

3582.

Aspen 2-door coupe (33102 BLT.)

Aspen 4-door sedan
3631. (32662 BLT.)

3953.

Aspen wagon (67294 BLT.)

E70 x 14 TIRES

1977 DODGE ASPEN
The unbelievable small car.

(29946 BLT.)
3764.

Aspen 2-door Custom coupe

Aspen 4-door Custom sedan

77 B

Two-tone paint (all Aspen coupes). Available in Red/Silver. Silver/Black. Black/Silver. Medium Blue/Dark Blue. Dark Blue/Medium Blue. Light Tan/Medium Tan. Medium Tan/Light Tan. Yellow/Gold. Dark Green/Medium Green.

4317.

Aspen Special Edition coupe

Aspen Special Edition sedan

Aspen Special Edition wagon   4283.

"HALO" VINYL TOP

1977 FROM $4515. TO $5216.
(WEST)

$3813.

(45697 BLT.)

OPTIONAL POWER WINDOWS

SE SEDAN
(25949 BLT.)
$4366.

AMERICAN SUNROOF CO. BUILT 25 ASPEN "CALIFORNIA CRUISER" SPECIALS FOR DODGE DEALERS. TOP WAS RIGID, BUT LOOKS LIKE A CONV'T. $7267.05

AVAIL. POWER DOOR LOCKS

R/T

LOUVERED QUARTER WINDOWS new FOR 1977.

SIMILAR VOLARE CONVERSIONS ALSO

OPT. SUN ROOF

The small car at a small price.

DODGE ASPEN 77 (B)

356

Dodge ASPEN

SPECIAL EDITION $5684.

$3783. UP

STD. Aspen two-door sport coupe.

SPECTRUM CLOTH + VINYL UPH.

AVAIL. IN COUPES

SMALLER FEELS BIGGER IN AN ASPEN.

1978

CUSTOM $5513.

SPECIAL EDITION $5410.

CUSTOM $5087.

Aspen Wagon $4294.

(REG. $5203.)

25/18 MPG HWY / MPG CITY

'78 new GRILLE and TAIL-LTS.

DASH

Vinyl roof cover in seven different colors

FULL-LENGTH SIDE STRIPE ON CPE. WITH R/T SPORT PAK

the R/T Sport Pak.

AS BEFORE, NO SIDE CHROME ON STD. ASPEN MODELS; SPEC. ED. MODELS have HOOD ORNAMENTS.

SUPER COUPE (BLACKED-GRILLE, SPOILER, ETC.)

SPECIAL EDITION $5262.
WESTERN PRICES SHOWN IN BLACK

T-BAR ROOF OPTIONAL

NARROWER new GRILLE,

Ten new Aspen colors are featured for 1978.

(1) Not available on wagons.   (2) Coupes only.

• New for 1978.

Spitfire Orange(2)	•Bright Canyon Red	•Tapestry Red Sunfire Metallic
Light Mocha Tan	•Caramel Tan Metallic	•Mint Green Metallic

		Cadet Blue Metallic	Starlight Blue Sunfire Metallic(1)
•Pewter Gray Metallic	•Black		
•Classic Cream	Eggshell White	•Augusta Green Sunfire Metallic	Citron Metallic(1)

DODGE ASPEN 78

DODGE ASPEN

WITH SUNRISE → PACKAGE

WITH 2-TONE PAINT and DECOR PACKAGE

STD. SEDAN
$5201.
(COUPES FROM $5100.)

79

2-TONES →

TWO-TONES

Cadet Blue Metallic/Ensign Blue Metallic

Teal Frost Metallic/Teal Green Sunfire Metallic

Pewter Gray Metallic/Black

Light Cashmere/Medium Cashmere Metallic

Medium Cashmere Metallic/Sabte Tan Sunfire Metallic

WITH **Aspen RT.** PKG.

DASH

ASPEN SED. with 2-TONE PAINT and DECOR PACKAGE

$5675. →
Aspen Special Edition Coupe

WESTERN PRICES SHOWN

$6061. ↓
Aspen Special Edition

SUN-RISE PKG.

SPECIAL EDITION EXT. and INTERIOR PKG.

$5808.

Engines
☐ Standard 225 1-barrel 6-cyl.
☐ Optional 225 2-barrel 6-cyl.
☐ Optional 318 2-barrel V-8
☐ Optional 318 4-barrel V-8
☐ Optional 360 4-barrel V-8

SOLID COLORS

COLORS

Ensign Blue Metallic | Cadet Blue Metallic | Teal Green Sunfire Metallic

Teal Frost Metallic | Regent Red Sunfire Metallic | Oriald Red

Sable Tan Sunfire Metallic | Medium Cashmere Metallic | Light Cashmere

Eggshell White | Light Yellow (coupe only)

Black | Pewter Gray Metallic

SPECIAL EDITION OPT. INTERIORS

DODGE ASPEN 79

358

Dodge **ASPEN**

(FINAL ASPEN)

Special.

SALE $4994.

INTER. and EXT. OF ASPEN CPE. WITH SUNRISE OPTION PACKAGE

Test drive **Total Performance from Dodge.**

SPECIAL *has* MINIMUM OF CHROME TRIM.

80

new GRILLE

6   V8
90 OR 120 HP

Optional T-Bar roof
The next best thing to a convertible. Tinted glass panels lift out and store in the trunk to give that fresh air feeling to any Aspen coupe.

WESTERN PRICES SHOWN

RECTANGULAR HEADLIGHTS

ENGINES & TRANSMISSIONS
Federal
☐ 3.7-liter (225 CID) 1V, Slant Six (std)
☐ 5.2-liter (318 CID) 2V, V-8 (opt)
High Altitude
☐ 5.2-liter (318 CID) 4V, V-8 (opt)
California
☐ 3.7-liter (225 CID) 1V, Slant Six (std)

☐ 5.2-liter (318 CID) 4V, V-8 (opt)
☐ Three-speed manual (std) (N/A Calif. or V-8)
☐ Four-speed manual (opt) (N/A Calif. or V-8)
☐ TorqueFlite automatic (opt)

SEDAN, CPE., WAGON
SHOWN WITH SPECIAL EDITION PACKAGE

REAR

(STD. UNGRAINED WAGONS FROM $6141.)

SEDAN WITH CUSTOM PACKAGE

Spinnaker White

(Upper) Burnished Silver Metallic (Lower) Baron Red

Optional cast aluminum road wheels
Add that sporty road car image to any Aspen with the addition of these great looking optional wheels

(Upper) Frost Blue Metallic (Lower) Nightwatch Blue

Light Cashmere

Natural Suede Tan   Nightwatch Blue

Teal Frost Metallic   Teal Tropic Green Metallic

COLORS

Baron Red   Formal Black

Burnished Silver Metallic   Crimson Red Metallic

Frost Blue Metallic   Graphic Red (coupe only)

Mocha Brown Metallic

WAGON WITH CUSTOM PACKAGE

(Upper) Light Cashmere (Lower) Natural Suede Tan

DASH

3 SP MANUAL TRANS. (3.2 GEAR RATIO) BUT CALIFORNIA-SOLD CARS *have* 2.9 GEAR RATIO WITH TorqueFlite AUTO. TRANS.

⑰ EPA EST. MPG   25 EST. HWY MPG**

(REPLACED BY 1981 ARIES)

DODGE ASPEN 80

359

Dodge Charger

500 WITH FRONT BUCKET SEATS FROM **$3496.**

G78 x 14 TIRES (ON ALL V8s EXC. R/T)

If you don't want another same old brand-new car... you could be **DODGE MATERIAL.**

SE (SPECIAL EDITION) AVAIL. IN 500 oR R/T SERIES

(AVAIL. WITH BUMBLEBEE STRIPE)

(WITH LONGITUDINAL TAPE STRIPE, RALLYE WHEELS)

70 B (117" WB, 1966 THRU 1970)

$3878. F70 x 14 TIRES

R/T w. 440 CID MAGNUM V8 (10,337 BLT., INCL. DAYTONA ON PRECEDING PAGE)

STD. **CHARGER** WITH FULL-WIDTH FRONT SEAT

(39,431 STD. and "500" CHARGERS BLT.)

OPT. SUN-ROOF

AVAIL. CONSOLE SHIFT

18 EXTERIOR COLORS *Optional at extra cost.

Plum Crazy (FC7)*	Light Green Metallic (FF4)
Sublime (FJ5)*	Dark Green Metallic (EF8)
Go-Mango (EK2)*	Dark Burnt Orange Metallic (FK5)
Hemi Orange (EV2)*	Beige (BL1)
Banana (FY1)*	Dark Tan Metallic (FT6)
Light Blue Metallic (EB3)	White (EW1)
Bright Blue Metallic (EB5)	Black (TX9)
Dark Blue Metallic (EB7)	Cream (DY3)
Bright Red (FE5)	Light Gold Metallic (FY4)

318 CID V8 (230 HP)
383 CID V8 (290, 330 oR 335 HP)
426 CID HEMI V8 (425 HP)
440 MAGNUM V8 (375 oR 390 HP)

225 CID 6 (145 HP) NOW AVAIL. IN CHARGER (w. F78 x 14 TIRES)

FOR 1970 DODGE INTRODUCES A NEW MODEL CHARGER AT A NEW LOWER PRICE **$3001.***

* REG. $3358.

RACK OPTIONAL

DASH

CHARGER R/T

LEFT DECK-SIDE SPORT TYPE GAS FILLER CAP

FUEL

DODGE CHARGER 70

Dodge Charger

$4043.

300 HP **Super Bee** with a 383 Magnum... regular gas.

PAINTED GRILLE

VINYL TOP

STEEL TOP

71

(RESTYLED) new SHORTER 115" WB

Charger SE

CHARGER FROM $3579.

OPEN HEADLIGHTS

$4311.

CONCEALED HEADLIGHTS
SPOILER

new FLAT DOOR HANDLES

$4173.

R/T
440 CID (370 HP)

CHARGER 500

$3973.

note DIFFERENCES IN DETAILS BETWEEN THESE VARIOUS MODELS.

WESTERN PRICES SHOWN

DODGE CHARGER 71

Dodge CHARGER

dash

CHARGER

FROM $3527.

ROOF DETAILS

72

new GRILLES

Charger Topper
landau vinyl roof.

CHARGER RALLYE

REAR

BULGE ON RALLYE HOOD IS PAINTED BLACK.

WITH CONCEALED HEADLIGHTS, RALLYE DASH, BUMPER GUARDS and SPECIAL TRIM. (note CONVENTIONAL TYPE STEERING WHEEL USED) (arrow)

DOOR SLOTS

(ON RALLYE ONLY)

RALLYE has OWN GRILLE (HORIZONTAL PCS.) and OPEN HDLTS.

SE GRILLE DETAIL

"Special Edition"

SE

DASH

$4017.

Dodge. Depend on it.

Dodge Charger

COUPE
WESTERN PRICES SHOWN
FROM $3700.

CHARGER COUPE WITH LANDAU TOP

SE.

SE

4153.

new GRILLE

"HALO" TOP

"LANDAU" TOP

73

CHARGER H/T $3949.

new SAFETY BUMPERS; ELECTRONIC IGNITION STD.

E78x14 4 P/R TIRES

225 CID 6
318 CID V8
340, 400 OR 440 CID V8s ALSO
(105 TO 260 HP)

SE with new 3-PC. LOUVRED QUARTER WINDOWS

SE

OPT. SUNROOF AVAIL. with VINYL TOP

SE INT.

Charger Rallye.

CHARGER RALLYE
The Rallye Package is available on V8 Charger hardtops and coupes, and includes the following items: Rallye Instrument Cluster • Power bulge hood • Body side tape stripe • Hood pins • Front and rear sway bars • F70 x 14 tires with raised white letters.

Rallye Hardtop.

Rallye Coupe.

Extra care in engineering makes a difference in Dodge...depend on it.

DODGE CHARGER 73

Dodge Charger

This year, go Charger style.

$4171.

CHARGER COUPE

(FULL 1974 LINE ILLUSTR.)

74

CHARGER H/T $4370.

SE has HOOD ORNAMENT

E78 or F78 × 14 TIRES

CHARGER **SE** $4584.

EXTRA CARE IN ENGINEERING MAKES A DIFFERENCE IN DODGE ...DEPEND ON IT.

Introducing Dodge Charger Special Edition '75

HORIZ.- LOUVRED OPERA WINDOWS ARE *new* AND OPT.

2.45 GEAR RATIO

SE $5412.

318, 360 OR 400 CID V8 s (150 TO 235 HP)

"You'll love the change we made."

DASH

75 (RESTYLED) (RESEMBLES CHRYSLER'S *new* CORDOBA)

GR78 × 15 TIRES, OTHERS

DODGE CHARGER 74~75

CHARGER DAYTONA
(new)

75½

(DAYTONA ADDED IN MID-SEASON)

"CHARGER DAYTONA" NAME on SIDE

4 MODELS, SALE PRICED FROM

Once you've looked, you're hooked.

$3736.

(BASIC CHARGER REG. $4744.)

new SPORT = $5033.

23 MPG. HWY., 16 CITY WITH 6-CYL. 225 CID (100 HP)

76

SE $5334.

'76 DAYTONA

SE $5692.

(MOVES TO MONACO LINE)

FINAL CHARGER SE A PART OF 1978 MONACO LINE AT $5951.

new GRILLE

77

318 CID V8 (145 HP) STD. 6-CYL. STILL AVAIL.

1977½ T-TOP

Dodge **THE NIGHT BELONGS TO CHARGER.**

CHARGER

CHARGER

DODGE CHARGER 75½~77

DODGE OMNI

(81611 BLT. '78)
(141,477 '79)
(138,155 '80)

New *IN 1978*

4-DR. ('78) $3981.

GRAINED SIDE TRIM *OPTIONAL*

SINCE 1978

('78) REAR (OMNI *has* HORIZONTAL STRIPS ACROSS TAIL-LIGHTS; HORIZON DOES NOT.)

O-24 2+2 FASTBACK (HATCHBACK) STARTS 1979. DE TOMASO VERSION ALSO AVAIL. 1980.

IT DOES IT ALL.
4-DR.   2-DR. ('79 ON)
99.2" WB   96.7" WB

78-80

WITH VOLKSWAGEN 4-CYL. ENGINE 104.7 CID

155/80 × 13 TIRES

↑
(LENGTH EXAGGERATED)
2+2
('79)-*new* 2-DR. = $4801.
"   "   5611. ('80)

OPTIONAL SUNROOF WITH GLASS DOOR

('79)

OMNI GRILLE *has* ALL HORIZONTAL PCS.

PLYMOUTH HORIZON SPECS. SIMILAR

DODGE OMNI

EDSEL

$2519. UP

MFD. BY FORD MOTOR CO.
(1958, 1959, 1960 MODELS ONLY)

ROUNDUP #26
2-DR. WAGON
$2876.

note "HORSECOLLAR" CENTER GRILLE

"Teletouch"
AUTO. TRANS.
CONTROL BUTTONS IN
STEERING-WHEEL HUB.
(OPTIONAL) (1958 ONLY)

WAGONS HAVE SPECIAL TAIL-LIGHTS

SLOGAN : "THIS IS THE EDSEL"
(OTHER SLOGANS ALSO)

58

DASH →
(with REVOLVING SPEEDOMETER)

#27, 28
VILLAGER 4-DR. WAGON
$2933. UP

V-8s
361 CID, 303 HP
or 410 CID, 345 HP

#47, 48
BERMUDA 4-DR. (DELUXE WAGON with WOODGRAIN)
$3190. UP
$3801.

RANGER (LOWEST-PRICED)
#21 2-DR.
(has MINIMUM of SIDE CHROME)
$2519.

#84 4 DR. H/T
$3615.

CITATION

PACER
#42 4 DR.
$2735.

CITATION
(TOP of LINE)
has INSET PANEL SET WITHIN REAR FENDER TRIM LOOP.

1958

#85 CONVT.

$3346.
#63 H/T ↓
CORSAIR

W.B.s:
116"
(WAGONS)

118"
(RANGER, PACER)

124"
(CORSAIR, CITATION)

PRODUCTION : RANGER =2 DR. (4615); 4 DR. (6576); H/T (5546); 4-DR. H/T (3077); ROUNDUP WAG. (963); VILLAGER, 6 PASS. (2294); VILLAGER, 9 PASS. (978) **PACER** =4 DR. (6083); H/T (6139); 4 DR. H/T (4959); CONVT. (1876); BERMUDA, 6 PASS. (1456); BERMUDA, 9 PASS. (779)
CORSAIR = H/T (3312); 4 DR. H/T (5880)
CITATION =H/T (2535); 4 DR. H/T (5112); CONVT. (930)

EDSEL 58

EDSEL

RANGER

PACER, CITATION, ROUNDUP and BERMUDA MODELS NO LONGER AVAIL.

223 CID 6-CYL. OHV ENGINE ALSO AVAIL. STARTING 1959. (145 HP @ 4200 RPM)

$2629. UP

3 V8 ENGINES:
Ranger 292 CID (200 HP @ 4500 RPM)
Express 332 CID (225 HP @ 4600)
or Super Express 361 CID (303 HP @ 4600)

CORSAIR

new ROUND TAIL-LIGHTS

1959

VILLAGER

new DASH

CORSAIR has VERTICAL CHROME STRIPS

59 (RESTYLED)

SLOGAN: "MAKES HISTORY BY MAKING SENSE"

INSET ANODIZED TRIM PANEL IDENTIFIES 1959 CORSAIR.

new 120" W.B. (ALL MODELS, THROUGH '60)

new GRILLE INCORPORATES HEADLIGHTS, with HORIZONTAL MEMBERS in CENTER SECTION.

RANGER = #57F 4 DR. H/T (2352); #58D 4 DR. (12,814); #63F H/T (5474); 2-DR.(#64-C)(7778)
CORSAIR = #57B 4 DR. H/T (1694); #58B 4 DR. (3301); #63B H/T (2315); #76E (CONVT.)
VILLAGER WAGONS = #71E 9 PASS. (2133); #71F 6 PASS. (5687)

EDSEL 59

EDSEL

CORSAIR NO LONGER AVAIL.

RANGER and VILLAGER ARE ONLY MODELS OFFERED FOR EDSEL's BRIEF 1960 SEASON.

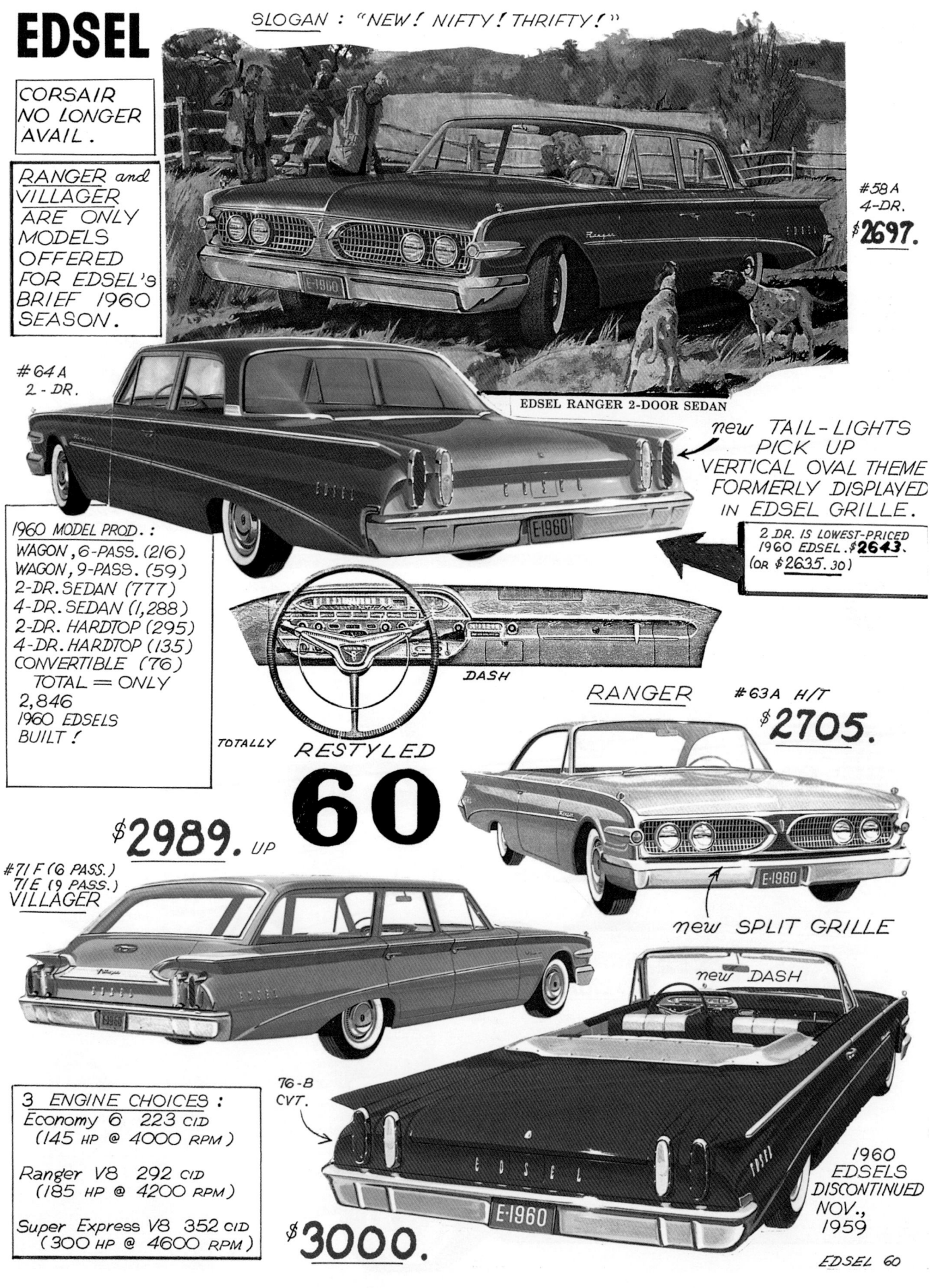

#58A 4-DR. $2697.

EDSEL RANGER 2-DOOR SEDAN

#64A 2-DR.

new TAIL-LIGHTS PICK UP VERTICAL OVAL THEME FORMERLY DISPLAYED IN EDSEL GRILLE.

2-DR. IS LOWEST-PRICED 1960 EDSEL. $2643. (OR $2635.30)

1960 MODEL PROD.:
WAGON, 6-PASS. (216)
WAGON, 9-PASS. (59)
2-DR. SEDAN (777)
4-DR. SEDAN (1,288)
2-DR. HARDTOP (295)
4-DR. HARDTOP (135)
CONVERTIBLE (76)
TOTAL = ONLY 2,846 1960 EDSELS BUILT!

DASH

TOTALLY RESTYLED **60**

RANGER   #63A H/T $2705.

new SPLIT GRILLE

$2989. UP

#71F (6 PASS.) 71E (9 PASS.) VILLAGER

new DASH

3 ENGINE CHOICES:
Economy 6 223 CID
(145 HP @ 4000 RPM)

Ranger V8 292 CID
(185 HP @ 4200 RPM)

Super Express V8 352 CID
(300 HP @ 4600 RPM)

76-B CVT.

$3000.

1960 EDSELS DISCONTINUED NOV., 1959

EDSEL 60

FAIRLANE
BY
(FORD)

new COMPACT / **6** OR **V-8**
INTERMEDIATE
FOR 1962 ; FORMERLY
A FULL-SIZED FORD SERIES

2 -DR.
$2154.

$2242.
"500" 2 -DR.

115 1/2" w.b. (THROUGH '65)

$2304.
"500" 4-DR.

$2392. UP
(WEST COAST)
EASTERN PRICES
FROM $2154.

62
new

223 CID 6
(138 HP)
221 CID V8
(145 HP)
260 CID V8
(164 HP)

PRODUCTION : 54-A 4 DR. (45,342);
62-A 2-DR. (34,264) ; 54-B "500" 4 DR. (129,258); 62-B "500 2-DR. (68,624);
62-C "500" SPT. CPE. (19,628)

SERIES 30 FAIRLANE
(INCLUDES WAGONS)
$2154. - $2781.

SERIES 40 FAIRLANE "500"
$2242. $2504.

$2304.

500

new
CONCAVE
GRILLE

RANCH
WAGON

$2525. UP ↗

SQUIRE →

$2781.

63
new 200 CID 6
(116 HP)
221 CID V8
and 260 CID
V8 CONT'D.

new 289 CID V8
(271 HP)

$2324.

63 1/2 AVAIL. WITH
new VINYL ROOF

H/T
INTERIOR

FAIRLANE 62~63

FAIRLANE

"289" V-8 option

Fairlane wagons:

500 H/T

1964

$2341.
$2502.

64 new GRILLE

CUSTOM
RANCH WAGON
$2612.

FAIRLANE CUSTOM RANCH WAGON
(24,962 BLT.)

SEE
ALSO:

FORD

PRODUCTION:
SERIES 30 = 2 DR. (20,421); 4 DR. (36,693); RANCH WAGON (20,980)
" 40 "500" = 2 DR. (23,447); 4 DR. (86,919); H/T (42,733);
H/T (BUCKET SEATS) (21,431); CUSTOM RANCH WAGON (24,962)

LOWEST-PRICED SERIES 30 2-DR. $2230.

| 1965 FAIRLANE PRODUCTION : 251,647 |

optional features. 4-speed stick. Overdrive. Tachometer.

500 WAGON (20,506 BLT.)
$2648.

500 H/T (41,405 BLT.)
w. BUCKET SEATS (15,141)

FAIRLANE 500

HEADLIGHTS
PAIRED IN
PLATES

271 solid-lifter horsepower
high-shift automatic!

SERIES 30 4-DR.
(25,378 BLT.)
$2271

1965

NO MORE
RAISED "AIR
SCOOP"
EFFECT
ON
HOOD

COBRA
POWERED
FORD

65

new GRILLE

500
2-DR.
(16,092 BLT.)

1965

$2312.

1965

new
OBLONG
TAIL-LIGHTS

FAIRLANE 64~65

Fairlane
$2533.
(23,942 BLT.)

new GRILLE, VERT.-STACKED HDLTS.

H/T 500-XL 116"WB GT

ENGINES:
200 CID 6 (120 HP)
289 CID V8 (200 HP)
OR 390 CID V8 IN
GT (335 HP)

66

$3068.
GT

Fairlane GT –
FRONT END DETAIL

NAME ON REAR FENDER → FAIRLANE

Special GT and GTA identification

new TAIL-LIGHTS

convertible (4327 BLT.)

(GTA has AUTO. TRANS.)

GT DASH

$2718. (INTRO. 9~30~66) FAIRLANE CLUB CPE. $2297.
(10,628 BLT.)

67 116"WB

new TAIL-LIGHTS and GRILLE 500

WAGONS have 113" WB

Fairlane 500 Wagon
(15,902 BLT.)

(WEST)
$3163.

FAIRLANE'S SQUIRE WAGON AVAIL. SINCE '66

$2377. CLUB CPE. (8473 BLT.)

(1943 BLT.) CVT. $3289.
(WEST)

$2950.

$2902.

(8348 BLT.) ↑

SQUIRE → $3347.
(WEST)

500/XL

BADGE INDICATES A 390 CID V8

390

TOTAL
(1967 PROD.: 190,383)

(14,871 BLT.) H/T

$3063. (WEST)

(note SIDE PAINT STRIPES ON GT)
↓ $2839.

GT

INTERIOR (500 / XL)
FAIRLANE C.L.~67

372

Fairlane / TORINO (new!)

FAIRLANE

$2464.

FAIRLANE SEDAN

$2962. (WEST)

1968

TORINO.

$3011. (WEST)

FAIRLANE 500

H/T $2909.
FORMAL H/T $3156

(WESTERN PRICES ABOVE)

68 (INTRO. 9-22-67)

$2710.

$2747.

TORINO
GT
302 CID V8 (210 HP) or
390 CID V8

(74,135 BLT.)
FASTBACK

TORINO INT.

Torino Squire

$2488. ~ 3107. PRICE RANGE

$2488.

$2733.

TORINO

REAR SIDE SAFETY LTS. SMALLER, MOVED FORWARD AND DOWN.

FAIRLANE

(INTRO. 9-27-68)

69 new GRILLES

250 CID 6 (155 HP)
302 CID V8 (220 HP)
351 CID V8 (250 OR 290 HP)
390 OR 428 V8s ALSO (TO 360 HP)

SPORTS-ROOF (FASTBACK) (61,319 BLT.)

$2840.

TORINO

1969

FAIRLANE/TORINO 68-69

TORINO GT

373

FALCON (compact)

BY FORD

$1912. and up

60

(1960 – 1970½ MODELS)

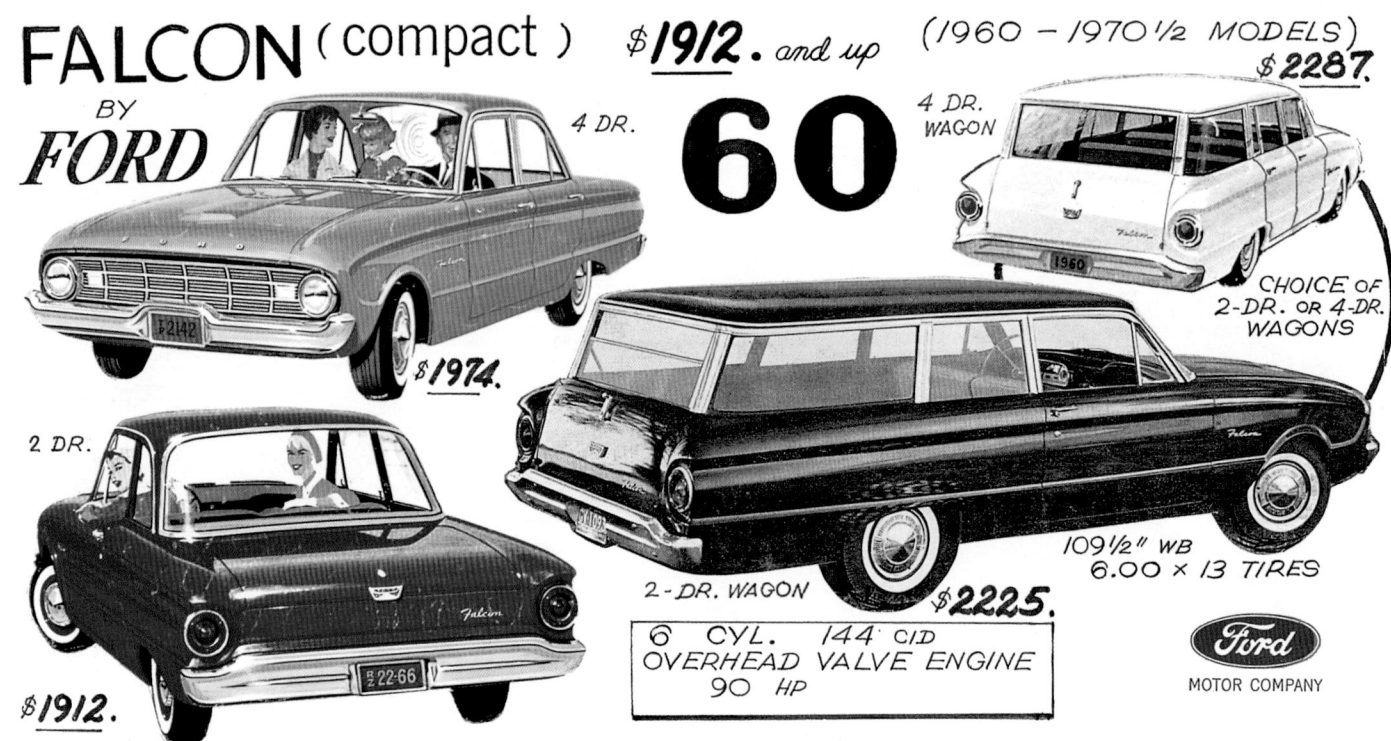

4 DR. — $1974.

4 DR. WAGON — $2287.

2 DR. — $1912.

CHOICE of 2-DR. or 4-DR. WAGONS

2-DR. WAGON — $2225.

109½" WB
6.00 × 13 TIRES

6 CYL. 144 CID
OVERHEAD VALVE ENGINE
90 HP

Ford
MOTOR COMPANY

PRODUCTION:
#64-A 2-DR. (193,470); 58-A 4-DR. (167,896); 59-A 2-DR. WAGON (27,552);
#71-A 4-DR. WAGON (46,758)

PRODUCTION 1961: 4 DR. (159,761); 2-DR. (149,982); 2-DR. ECONOMY SEDAN (150,032);
2 DR. WAGON (32,045); 4 DR. WAGON (87,933) new FUTURA COUPE (44,470)
(FUTURA INTRO. SPRING, 1961)

$1976.

A CHOICE OF TWO SURGING "SIXES"!
STD. 144 CID OR
new 170 CID 6
85 OR 101 HP

2-DR.

4-DR.

85 HP (STD.) $2227.

$1914.

Falcon Tudor Wagon

(4-DR. WAGON ALSO AVAIL., $2270.)

new FUTURA CONSOLE

FORD **Falcon** '61
WORLD'S MOST SUCCESSFUL NEW CAR
new CONVEX GRILLE

Futura
(1961½)
$2162.

FORD

1961

FALCON 60~61

FUTURA has 3 DARTS on REAR FENDERS, and SPECIAL HUBCAPS.

$2273.

Falcon '62
BEST SHAPE ECONOMY'S EVER BEEN IN

$2384.

DELUXE 2-DR.

FUTURA

FALCON SPORTS FUTURA

4-DR.

FUTURAS HAVE SPECIAL
FRONT FENDER TRIM,
AS ILLUSTRATED.

$2133. DELUXE

$2427.

(new)
SQUIRE
$2603.

62

STD. 2-DR.

(STANDARD MODELS HAVE
NO SIDE CHROME TRIM.)

$2243.

new CONVEX GRILLE has ALL-VERTICAL PIECES.

1962 PRODUCTION : 381,558

PRODUCTION :

54A 4-DR. (62,365); 62A 2-DR. (70,630); (THESE 2 STANDARD MODELS KNOWN AS "SERIES O.")
FUTURA SERIES 10 : 62B 2-DR. (27,018); 54B 4-DR. (31,736); 63B H/T (28,496); 63C SPRINT H/T (10,479);
76A CVT. (31,192); 76B SPRINT CVT. (4602) SERIES 20 WAGONS : 59A 2-DR. (7322);
59B DLX. 2-DR. (4269); 71A 4-DR. (18,484); 71B DLX. 4-DR. (23,477); 71C SQUIRE (WOODGRAIN) (8269)

$1985. STD.

new 164 HP V8
ALSO AVAIL.
(260 CID)

$2298.

STD.
2-DR.

STD.
2-DR.

63

new GRILLE

$2384.

DE LUXE

2 DR.

FUTURA

$2603.

4-DR.
SQUIRE

$2116. 2-DR.
$2198. H/T

MID-1963
"SPRINT" V8
H/T and CVT. are new

$2470.

(new)
CONVERTIBLE
FALCON 62~63

375

FALCON

Lively new Sprint $2600. $2320.

THESE MODELS INTRODUCED IN MID-SEASON

63½

new scatback hardtop

Squire (6766 BLT.)

$2622.

new wider tread

$2481. UP
$2325. UP

SPRINT NOW AVAIL. AS 6 OR V8.

64
(RESTYLED)

new '260' cu. in. V-8 power option

new longer springs

$2226. (FUTURA)
$2337. (SPRINT)

$2665.

Squire

H/T

New battery-saving alternator.

65

1965 PRICE RANGE: $2020. TO $2671.

13" OR 14" WHEELS

new GRILLE

DASH

new 170 cu. in. standard Six with optional 3-speed Cruise-O-Matic transmission

PRODUCTION: 2-DR. (35,858); DLX. 2-DR. (13,824); 4-DR. (30,186); DLX. 4-DR. (13,850)
FUTURA = 2-DR. (11,570); H/T (25,754); 4-DR. (33,985); CVT. (6215); DLX. 4-DR. WAGON (12,548)
SPRINT = H/T (2806); CVT. (300)
WAGONS = (DLX. LISTED WITH FUTURA) 2-DR. (4891); 4-DR. (14,911); SQUIRE 4-DR. (6703)

FALCON 63½~65

Falcon

(1960-1970)

FUTURA CLUB CPE. (21,997 BLT.)

$2669. ($2781., FUTURA)

$2183.

FUTURA

new THINNER SIDE TRIM

(20,289 BLT.)

66

new GRILLE

SPT. CPE. WITH VINYL TOP
$2555. (WEST COAST)

$2328.

DASH

111" WB
170 CID 6 (105 HP)
200 CID 6 (120 HP) IN SPT. CPE., WAGON
289 CID V8 (180-200 HP)

6 CYL. OR V8 (SINCE '63)

(FALCON RANCHERO PICKUP ALSO AVAIL.)

CLUB CPE. $2060.

1966

$2284. (WEST COAST)
7.35/7.75 x 15 TIRES

TOTAL 1966 PRODUCTION: 182,669

TOTAL 1967 PRODUCTION: 64,335

new TIRE SIZE = 6.95/7.35 x 14"

289 CID V8 has 225 HP, OTHER ENGINES AS IN 1966.

$2437.

FUTURA SPTS. CPE. (7053 BLT.)

$2663. (WEST COAST)

2 new COWL INDENTATIONS ('67 ONLY)

67

(INTRO. 9-30-66)

new GRILLE

REAR (STD.)

1967

FALCON 66-67

FALCON

('69) WAGON

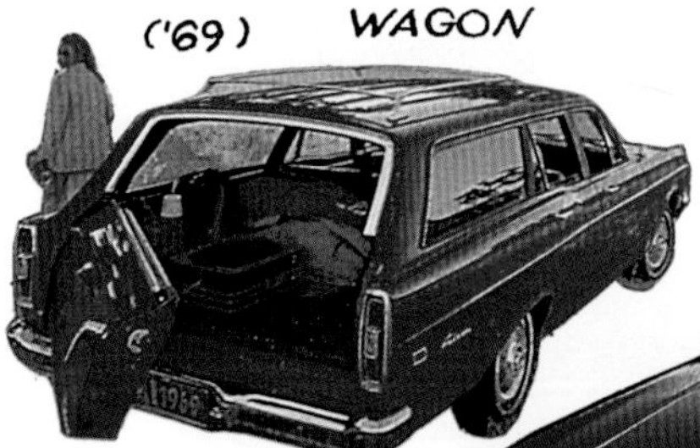

$2301.

('68)

EARLY
68-70

$2579.

170 CID 6 (100 HP)
289 CID V8 (195 HP)
200 CID 6 AVAIL. '69-'70 (115-120 HP)
302 CID V8 (220 HP) '69-70

FALCON. 7 MODELS. MORE THAN ANY OTHER COMPACT.

$2541.

('70)

FUTURA SEDAN

111" WB (WAGONS 113")

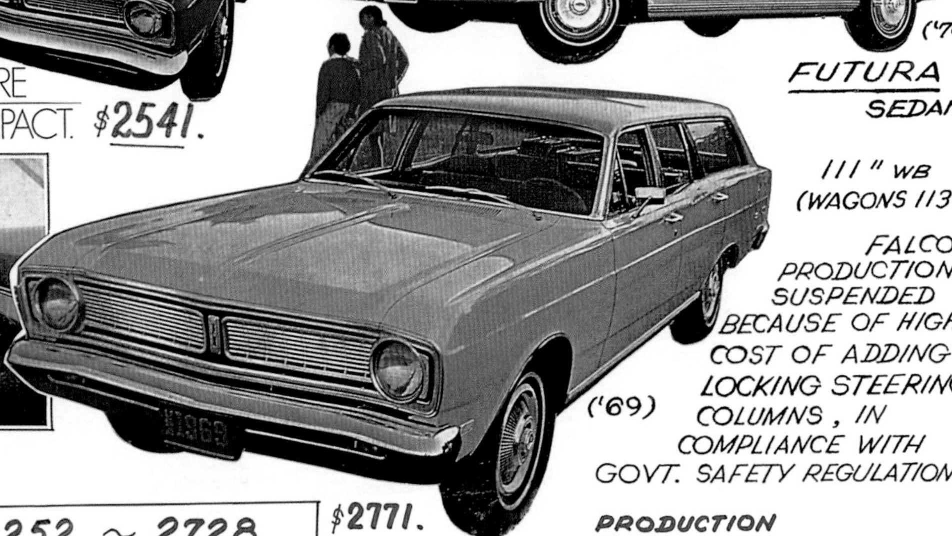

FALCON PRODUCTION SUSPENDED BECAUSE OF HIGH COST OF ADDING LOCKING STEERING COLUMNS, IN COMPLIANCE WITH GOVT. SAFETY REGULATIONS.

B

INTERIOR ('69)

('69)

$2771. ('69)

PRICE RANGE, 1968	$2252. ~ 2728.
" " 1969	2283. ~ 2771.
" " 1970	2390. ~ 2878.

PRODUCTION
1968 = 131,389
1969 = 95,019
1970 = 15,694

new E78/G78 x 14 TIRES

FALCON TEMPORARILY REVIVED, AS A BUDGET-PRICED MODEL OF TORINO.

2-DR. $2460.

70½ NEW

LARGER 117"-WB TORINO SERIES (WAGON - 114")

3 FINAL FALCONS
2-DR. $2827.
4-DR. $2867.
4-DR. WAGON $3163. (WEST COAST PRICES)

(DISCONTINUED SUMMER, 1970)

67,053 BLT.

STD. ENGINES:

new 250 CID 6 (155 HP)
302 CID V8 (220 HP)

AVAILABLE
351 CID V8 (250 OR 300 HP)
429 CID V8 (360 OR 370 HP)

26,071 2-DRS.; 30,443 4-DRS.; 10,539 4-DR. WAGONS
FALCON 68-70½

Firebird BY PONTIAC

(SINCE 1967)
Magnificent Five are here!

(215-HP) SPRINT
230 CID OHC 6

$2667. UP $3127. (WEST)

STD. FIREBIRD
230 CID OHC 6
(165 HP)

108" WB

E70 × 14 W.O. TIRES

67 (new)
(INTRO. 2-23-67)
(67032 COUPES BLT.)

400

Firebird HO.

HO (note STRIPE, "HO" LETTERING on SIDES.
(HO MEANS "HIGH OUTPUT")

V8 326 CID (285 HP)

CVTS. PRICED FROM $2903.

(15526 CVTS. BLT.)

400 CID V8 (325 HP)

TOTAL 1967 PRODUCTION: 82,558

326
326 CID V8 (250 HP)

Firebird 326

TOTAL 1968 PRODUCTION: 107,110

(E70/F70 × 14" TIRES)
"LANDAU TOP" $84. EXTRA

AIR CONDITIONING $370.

CONVERTIBLES, $2996. UP

$3705. (WEST)   (INTRO. 9-21-67)

Firebird 400.

new 250 CID FOR OHC 6 (175 HP)
(SPRINT 6 = 215 HP)
350 CID V8 (265 HP)
400 CID V8 (335 HP)

CVT. (16,960 BLT.)

68
new SIDE SAFETY LIGHTS

H/Ts $2781. UP

400 H/T $3490. (WEST)
400 CID V8 (330 OR 335 HP)

(VARIOUS MODELS CONT'D.)
H/Ts FROM $3238; CVTS. FR. $3453
(WEST COAST PRICES)

FIREBIRD 67~68

H/T (90,152 BLT.)

"400" (V8) OPTION = $252. EXTRA

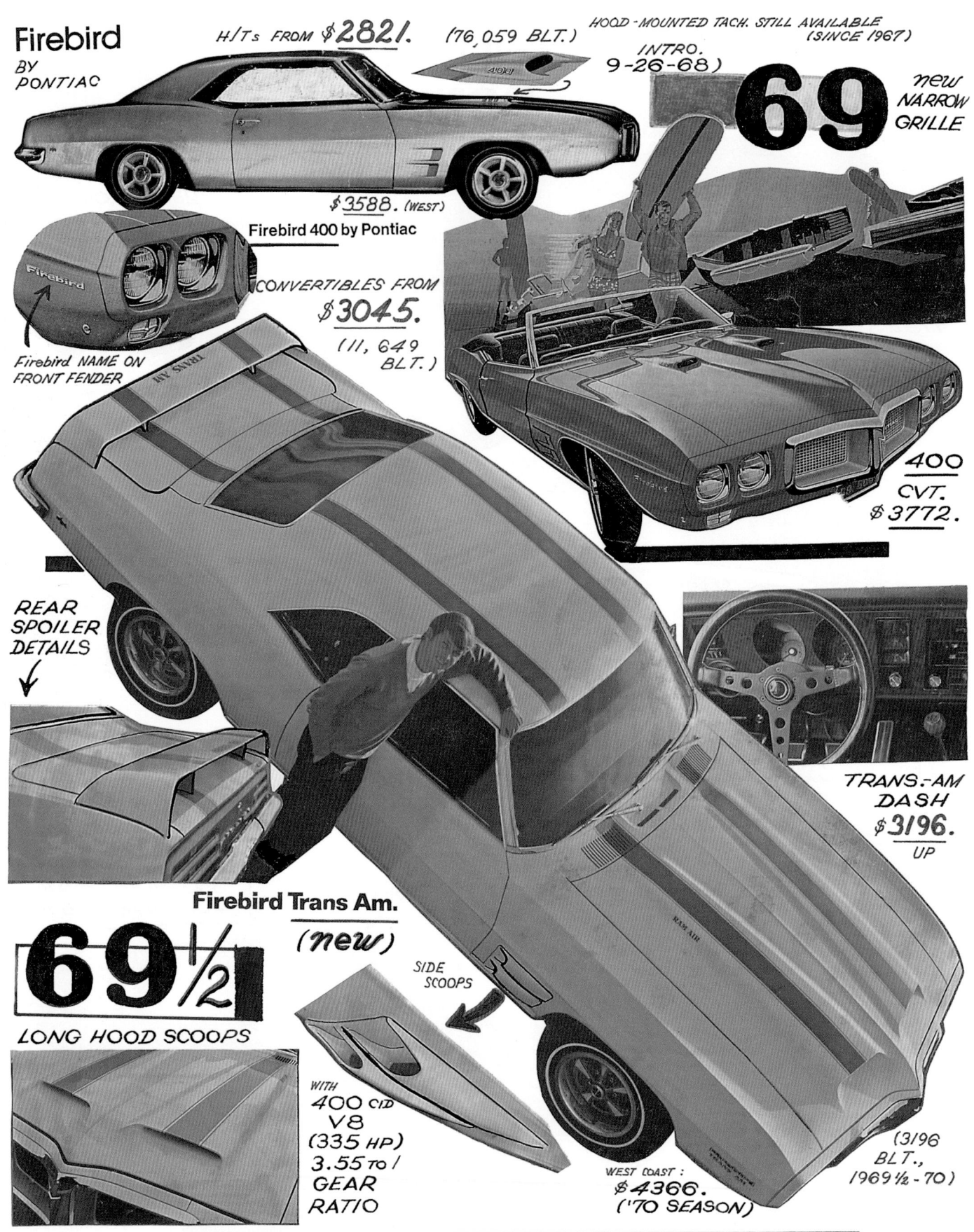

Firebird
BY PONTIAC

H/Ts FROM $2821. (76,059 BLT.)

HOOD-MOUNTED TACH. STILL AVAILABLE (SINCE 1967)

INTRO. 9-26-68)

69 new NARROW GRILLE

$3588. (WEST)

Firebird 400 by Pontiac

Firebird NAME ON FRONT FENDER

CONVERTIBLES FROM $3045. (11,649 BLT.)

400 CVT. $3772.

REAR SPOILER DETAILS

TRANS.-AM DASH $3196. UP

Firebird Trans Am.
(new)

69½

LONG HOOD SCOOPS

SIDE SCOOPS

WITH 400 CID V8 (335 HP) 3.55 TO / GEAR RATIO

WEST COAST: $4366. ('70 SEASON)

(3196 BLT., 1969½-70)

1969 ENGINES: 250 CID 6=(175 OR 230 HP); 350 CID V8=(265, 325 OR 330 HP) 400 CID V8=(330, 335 OR 345 HP)

TOTAL 1969 PROD.=90,904

CALENDAR YR. PROD.=105,526

FIREBIRD BY PONTIAC

Pontiac announces the beginning of tomorrow.
New, even for Pontiac.

TRANS-AM has STRIPE, SPOILER, and AIR DAM BELOW GRILLE

T.A. $4752. (WEST COAST PRICE)

(3196 BLT.)

STD. ENGINE 250 CID 6 (155 HP) (V8 OPT.)

STD. CPE has NO SPECIAL TRIM. $3743.

(18874 BUILT)

DASH

(7708 BLT.)

TRANS-AM (345 HP) 400 CID V8

FORMULA 400

$4149.

FORMULA 400 400 CID V8 (330 HP) (note HOOD SCOOPS

DENT-PROOF PLASTIC "ENDURA" FRONT END

(RESTYLED)

70+

new GRILLE SINGLE HEADLTS. new RECTANGULAR-SPLIT SIDE LIGHTS

(18961 ESPIRITS BUILT) 350 CID V8 (255 HP)

E78×14 TIRES

all two-door hardtops $3999.

ESPRIT (has BIRD EMBLEM ABOVE GRILLE)

FIREBIRD SYMBOL

(KNOWN OFFICIALLY AS "1970½" MODELS. INTRO. 2-26-70)

The all-new Firebirds are here.

FIREBIRD 70+

381

FIREBIRD BY **PONTIAC**

STD. CPE. FROM $3910.

71 (INTRO. 9-29-70)

A bumper you can knock. And a price you can't.

250 CID 6 (145 HP) OR 350 CID V8 (250 HP) STD.

335-HP TRANS-AM has F60×15 TIRES; FORMULA has E70×14 (OTHERS, E78×14)

"Pure Pontiac!"

Esprit $4155. new WHEEL COVERS →

FROM 3716.

STD. WH. CVR.

DASH

STD. H/T

STD. REAR

Formula 400

(STD. 350 CID V8 CUT TO 160 HP)

$3981. (5250 BLT.)

(FORM. 350 and 455 ALSO AVAIL.) (350 CID V8 CUT TO 175 HP.)

ESPRIT $3954. (11415 BLT.)

72 New MESH PATTERN IN GRILLE

(INTRO. 9-23-71)

NOTE: Trans Am model is available only in— C—CAMEO WHITE with Blue striping or F—LUCERNE BLUE with White striping

C—CAMEO WHITE
Recommended Interior Colors: Beige (Covert), Black, Blue, Green, Ivory, Pewter, Saddle, Tan

(12000 STD. CPES.

F—LUCERNE BLUE
Recommended Interior Colors: Black, Blue, Ivory, Pewter

Trans Am (1286 BLT.)

$4256. ($4718., WEST COAST)

TRANS~AM 455 CID H.O. V8 CUT TO 300 HP

FIREBIRD 71~72

382

FIREBIRD BY PONTIAC

($3953. FOR ESPRIT) (17249 BLT.)

note: Trans Am model is available only in—Cameo White with Blue/Black Striping—Brewster Green with White/Black Striping—Buccaneer Red with White/Black Striping.

73 new CRISS~CROSS GRILLE PCS.

$4863.

TRANS~AM 455 cid V8 CUT TO 215 HP

350 cid V8 CUT TO 150 HP

FORMULA (10166 BLT.) $3981.

STD. $3716. (14096 BLT.)

TRANS~AM note "FIREBIRD" HOOD DECAL

(4802 BLT.)

$3865. EASTERN

$4708. TRANS~AM (10255 BLT.)

The Wide-Track people have a way with cars.

(22583 ESPRITS BLT.) $4412.

STD. (26372 BLT.) ($4185. WEST COAST)

FIREBIRD DECAL

note HONEYCOMB~TYPE WHEELS WITH GR70x15 B/WL TIRES

RESTYLED

74

new SLOPING FRONT END WITH VERTICAL PCS. IN GRILLE

ENGINES
250 cid 6 (100 HP)
350 cid V8 (155 HP)
(170 HP IN FORMULA)
new 400 cid
TRANS~AM V8
(225 HP)

DASH FORMULA $4207. (14519 BLT.)

Part engineering. Part soul.

GR70x14 TIRES →

FORMULA (13670 BLT.) $4853. (27274 BLT.) TRANS~AM (HP CUT TO 185) $5244.

STD. $4584. (22293 BLT.)

6~CYL. NOW 105 HP

75 (new AUX. LTS. and HORIZ. PCS. IN GRILLE)

DASH (TRANS~AM)

ESPRIT

(20826 BLT.)

$4829. FIREBIRD 73~75

383

FIREBIRD
PONTIAC

76

new GRILLE "WITH MESH PCS."

PRODUCTION = STD. CPE.—21209
ESPRIT ——22252
FORMULA —20613
TRANS~AM—46701

250 CID 6 (110 HP)	350 CID V8 (160 HP)
STD. = $4834.	
ESPRIT = $5090.	TR. AM.= $5514.

FORMULA
$5092.

PONTIAC *The Mark of Great Cars*

1977 PRODUCTION = STD. COUPE —30642
ESPRIT —34548   FORMULA —21801
TRANS~AM — 68745

STD. = $5174.
ESPRIT = 5455.
FORMULA = 5534.

(SE OR
SKYBIRD
PKG.
AVAIL.)

TRANS-AM
$6013.

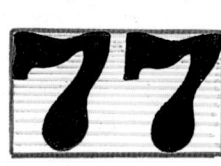

77

new GRILLE
WITH *new*
QUADRUPLE
RECTANGULAR
HEADLIGHTS

231 CID V6 (105 HP)
301 CID V8 (135 HP)

TR. AM 400 CID V8
(180 HP)

GR 70×15 TIRES
(TR. AM)
(OTHERS=FR78×15)

1978 ♦ **Pontiac's best year yet!**

(32672 BLT.) STD. **Firebird** *has* 231 CID V6
$5662.   (105 HP)

OPTIONAL T-BAR ROOF

TRANS-AM
$6390.

180 HP
400 CID V8
(403 CID, CALIF.)
(185 HP)
GR 70×15
TIRES

new
BLACK
GRILLE

(93341 BLT.)

FORMULA
305 CID V8
(145 HP) NOT
AVAIL. IN CALIF.
$6039.
(24346 BLT.)

ESPRIT
$5959.
(36926 BLT.)

78

(SE, SKYBIRD OR
new REDBIRD
PKG. AVAIL.)

FIREBIRD 76~78

384

FIREBIRD BY **PONTIAC**

400 CID V8 (220 HP) ALSO AVAIL.

A NEW BREED OF WOW.

FORMULA

231 CID V6 (115 HP)
301 CID V8 (140 HP)
(305, 350 CID AV.)
403 CID V8 (TR. AM.) (185 HP)

$6633.

X~87
(7500 "LIMITED EDITION" TRANS~AMS. ALSO BLT
$10,620.)

(24850 BLT.)

(Pontiac, Buick, Chev. and Oldsmobile ENGINES USED)

TRANS~AM DASH

2.41 to 3.23 GEAR RATIOS AVAIL.

W87

Trans Am.
(109609 BLT.)
$6914.
($7314., WEST COAST)

TRANS AM 1979

As exciting going as it is coming.

(225/70 R14 TIRES ON TR. AM. OR FORMULA ; FR 78×15 ON OTHERS)

79

(RESTYLED FRONT and REAR)

new SEPARATELY- PORTED HEAD LIGHTS

I~87
ESPRIT
(30853 BLT.)
$6414.

S~87
STD.
(38642 BLT.)

$6046.

UNIROYAL
STEEL BELTED RADIAL

CLOSER DETAILS OF TRANS~AM HOOD and DECAL

FIREBIRD 79

FIREBIRD BY PONTIAC

PONTIAC ANNOUNCES: THE WORLD'S ONLY TURBOCHARGED V-8

$6311.

$5948.

STD. FIREBIRD S~87 $6805.
(WEST COAST)

ESPRIT T~87 $7168.
(17277 BLT.)

108" WB
(SINCE 1967)
(SOMETIMES LISTED AS 108.1 OR 108.2")

80

(29811 BLT.)

enjoy driving again. The manufacturer's suggested retail price for the '80 Firebird including dealer preparation is just... **$5,963** INCLUDES AUTO. TRANS.
Taxes, license, destination charges and additional equipment are extra.
(STD.)

new SMALL V8 265 CID (120 HP) OR
BUICK 231 CID V6 (115 HP) IN STD. OR ESPRIT
CHEVROLET 173 CID V6
(SE OR NEW YELLOWBIRD PACKAGE AVAIL.)

FORMULA V~87
(9356 BLT.) $7256.
$7617.
(SAME ENGINE CHOICES AS TRANS~AM)

205/75 R x 15 OR
225/70 R x 15 TIRES

T~BAR ROOF AVAIL. AS SHOWN, WITH STRIPING

W~87
TRANS~AM
(50896 BLT.)
7841. $7480.
(WEST)

TRANS~AM DASH

V8 TRANS~AM ENGINES =
301 CID (140 HP)
301 CID TURBO (210 HP)
305 CID (150 HP.)
CHEVROLET ENGINE)

20	27	416 MILES	561 MILES
EPA EST. MPG	HWY. EST. MPG	EST. RANGE	HWY. EST. RANGE

WESTERN PRICES SHOWN IN BLACK

MORE PONTIAC EXCITEMENT FOR THE GREAT ONES

FIREBIRD 80

386

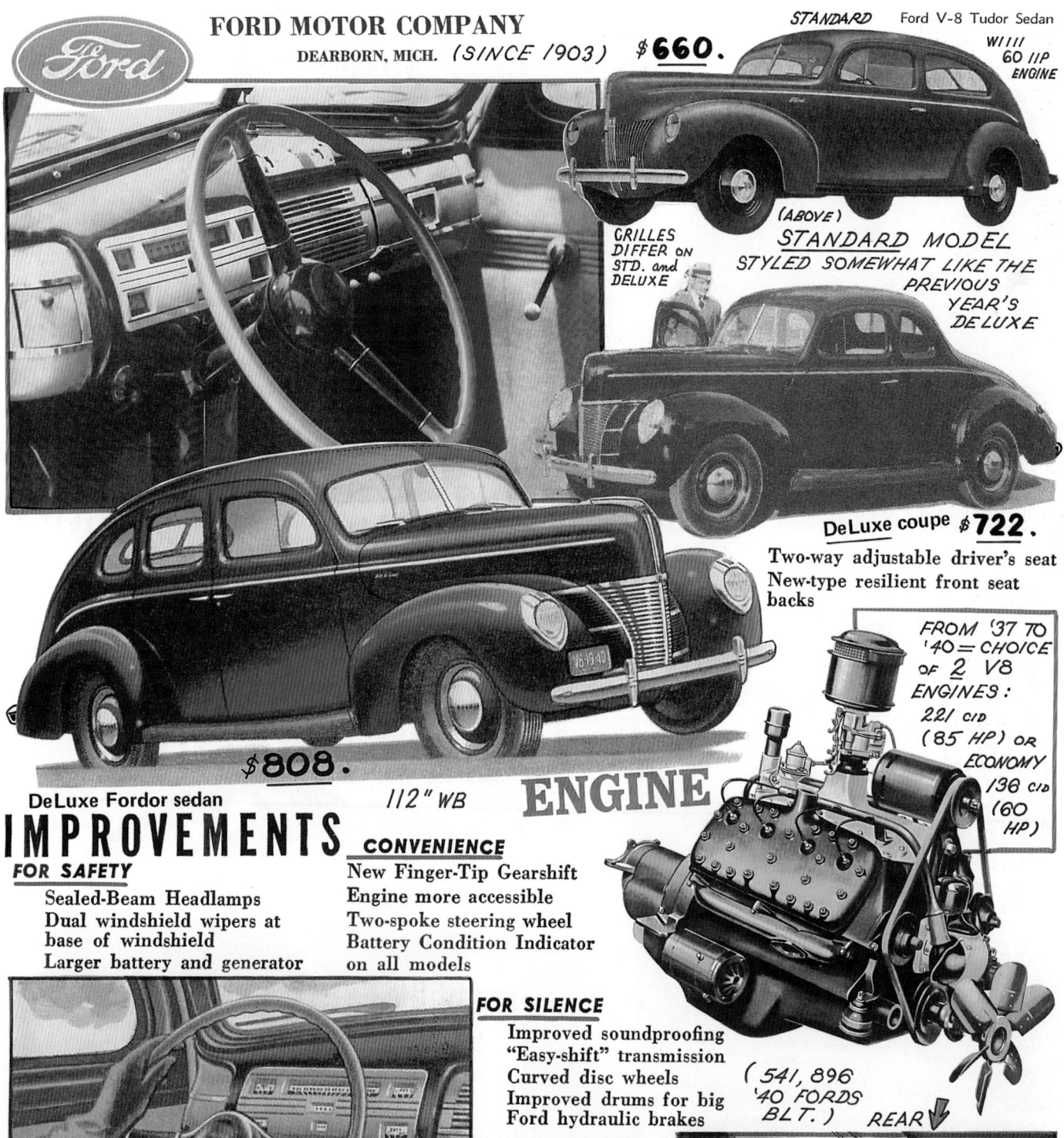

FORD MOTOR COMPANY

DEARBORN, MICH. *(SINCE 1903)*

STANDARD   Ford V-8 Tudor Sedan

$**660**.

W/III 60 IIP ENGINE

GRILLES DIFFER ON STD. and DELUXE

(ABOVE)

STANDARD MODEL STYLED SOMEWHAT LIKE THE PREVIOUS YEAR'S DELUXE

DeLuxe coupe $**722**.

Two-way adjustable driver's seat
New-type resilient front seat backs

FROM '37 TO '40 = CHOICE OF 2 V8 ENGINES: 221 CID (85 HP) OR ECONOMY 136 CID (60 HP)

$**808**.

DeLuxe Fordor sedan   112" WB   ENGINE

IMPROVEMENTS

FOR SAFETY

Sealed-Beam Headlamps
Dual windshield wipers at base of windshield
Larger battery and generator

CONVENIENCE

New Finger-Tip Gearshift
Engine more accessible
Two-spoke steering wheel
Battery Condition Indicator on all models

FOR SILENCE

Improved soundproofing
"Easy-shift" transmission
Curved disc wheels
Improved drums for big Ford hydraulic brakes

(541,896 '40 FORDS BLT.)

REAR

40

A

(CONT'D. NEXT PAGE)

New interior luxury
New instrument panel

"THEN I TOOK THE WHEEL—a clever two-spoke wheel with the Finger-Tip Gearshift right under it. I was amazed at how nicely it shifted. There's nothing tricky about it at all. It's just the regular shift turned on its side.

40 FORD (A)

Ford

New "Floating-Edge" Seat Cushions

849.

(WITH GRILLE GUARD)

DeLuxe Ford V-8 Convertible Coupe

40 B (CONT'D.)

1940

COLORS

FOLKSTONE GRAY	CLOUDMIST GRAY	MANDARIN MAROON	ACADIA GREEN	GARNET MAROON

SAHARA TAN	COMO BLUE	LYON BLUE	YOSEMITE GREEN	COTSWOLD GRAY (POLY)

$947.

DELUXE STATION WAGON

"WATCH THE FORDS GO BY"

(BLACK, WHITE, and SELECTED COLORS ALSO AVAILABLE.)

NINETEEN FORTY

More room inside
New Controlled Ventilation

DASH

NEW 1941 FORD

$833. (6)
$849. (V8)

new FORD 6
INTRO. MAY, 1941
226 c/d 6 (90 HP)

V8 CONTINUES
(221 c/d, SINCE '34)
85 HP
(SINCE '37)

SUPER DELUXE
"SEDAN COUPE"
(RESTORED EXAMPLE WITH AFTER~MARKET 5~GUARD BUMPERS)

new 114" WB
(THROUGH '51)

"Super Deluxe" DESIGNATION NEXT TO LEFT~HAND HEADLT.

LOWER~PRICED SERIES HAVE NO CHROME ON DUAL LOWER GRILLE EXTENTIONS.

(6) $843.
(V8) $859.

Get the facts and you'll get a FORD!

(691,896 BLT.)

40 FORD (B)/NINETEEN FORTY-ONE

$780.~$1125.
PRICE RANGE

8~PASS.　Super DeLuxe four-door station wagon

$1125.

Steel Stampings for Die-Castings

Exterior parts like radiator grilles, and mechanical parts like generators and starter end plates, are now made from steel stampings instead of die-castings, without affecting their usefulness or appearance. This has freed large amounts of zinc, aluminum and other defense-needed materials.

Some Results in Defense Metals Saved

Based on present conditions, here are some examples of how new materials and methods in the 1942 Ford are helping relieve defense "shortages." Figures show the *cut* in use this year of the materials named:

Primary (*new*) Aluminum has been cut out 100% . . . Secondary (*re-melted*) Aluminum has been cut down 70% . . . Nickel has been cut down by 90.7% . . . Magnesium, cut out almost entirely, is down 98.7% . . . Zinc has been reduced by 37.5% . . . Copper, Tin, Lead, and Tungsten cut down in varying amounts from 5.2% to 81%.

MODEL GPW

Contract Number
W-398-qm-11424

FORD TRUCK

¼ TON 4 x 4
BUILT FOR
U. S. GOVERNMENT

Parts are designated in this book under both Ford and Willys part numbers since all parts are interchangeable for vehicles produced by Willys Overland Motors, Inc., under the

FORD
JEEP!
4 CYL.
60 HP @ 3600 RPM

FORD JEEP : U. S. A. Registration Numbers
20100000S to 20163145S

42

DASH IN FORD CIVILIAN 1942 CARS

NEW GRILLE

Plastics Replace Metal for Interior Trim

We have been developing plastics for a long time at Ford. The value of this is now apparent. The wider use of plastics this year in instrument panel, radio grille, door handles and other interior trim has released large quantities of zinc formerly used in metal die-castings, as well as nickel and chromium formerly used in plating bright metal parts. The new plastic parts are lighter in weight, fully as serviceable, and very attractive in appearance.

SPECIAL (6),
DELUXE and SUPER DELUXE MODELS (6 or V8)

SUPER DE LUXE SEDAN **$930.**

JM·547

Molybdenum Replaces Nickel

PAINTED TRIM ON JAN. 1942 "BLACKOUT" MODELS.

IN CIVILIAN CARS:

6 or 8 Cylinders

(160,432 BLT.)
42 FORD

FORD

PRICES START AT **$1003.** (6 CPE.)

V8 Six

NEW OVERSIZED BRAKES (12" DRUMS)

CLUB COUPE

(70,826 BLT.)

TUDOR

FORDOR (101,302 BLT.)

SUPER DELUXE has DESIGNATION RT. of GRILLE.

TUDOR (238,324 BLT.)

There's a *Ford* in your future

1946 MODEL STARTS JULY, 1945

46

new GRILLE

NEW 1946 FORD SPORTSMAN'S CONVERTIBLE (V8) (with GENUINE WOODEN BODY)

(1209 BLT.)

$1865.

Outside and inside, there never was a car like this before! The new Ford Sportsman's Convertible is really *two* cars in one! Ford designers have combined the paneled smartness of the station wagon and the touch-a-button convenience of the convertible!

114" W.B.

ALL—METAL CVT. MORE COMMONLY SEEN (ILLUSTR. ON NEXT PAGE)

PRODUCTION (OF BODY TYPES NOT ILLUSTRATED ABOVE
BUSINESS COUPE (22,919)
STATION WAGON (4 DR. with WOODEN BODY) (16,960)
CUSTOM BLT. VEHICLES ON FORD CHASSIS (123)

FORD 46   LION FIGURE ON HUBCAP

97 HP

118" WB

1946½ **MONARCH** (INTRO. 3-23-46 IN CANADA AS A *MERCURY*-TYPE CAR SOLD BY CANADIAN FORD DEALERS.) SEE *METEOR/MONARCH* PAGES FOR CANADIAN FORD MOTOR CO. VARIATIONS.

FORD

EARLY 47
(SIMILAR TO 1946)

Ford's out Front
(1947 SLOGAN)

$1740. (V8)

CONVERTIBLE (METAL)
(16,359 BLT.)

47½-48

1948 *has* NO STEERING COLUMN LOCK, AS PREVIOUSLY USED.

. . . new stainless steel body molding newly fashioned door handles . . .

. . . new body colors . . .

V8 WAGON

There's a FINER **Ford** in your future

A newly styled instrument panel with big new dials for easy reading

new HOOD MEDALLION IDENTIFIES 6 or V8

MODIFIED GRILLE NO LONGER *has* RED INDENTATIONS.

new ROUND PARKING LIGHTS PLACED BELOW HEADLIGHTS

new wheel rims and hub caps

new heavier bumper guards—And many other new features!

1947 PRODUCTION 2-DR. (180,649); 4-DR. (116,764); COUPE (10,872); CLUB COUPE (80,830); WAGON (16,104) STEEL CONVERTIBLE (22,159); SPORTSMAN CONVERTIBLE (2250); CUSTOM CHASSIS (46)

COMBINATION IGNITION/STEERING LOCK

1948 PRODUCTION 2-DR. (105,517); 4-DR. (71,358); COUPE (5048); CLUB COUPE (44,826) WAGON (8912); STEEL CONVERTIBLE (12,033) SPORTSMAN CONVERTIBLE (ONLY 28) MODEL YEAR ENDS MID-1948, WHEN 1949 FORDS APPEAR. CONVENTIONAL IGNITION LOCK, 1948

FORD 47-48

FORD

COUPE

PRICES START AT
$**1333.**
(DLX. COUPE)
(6 CYL.)

CONVERTIBLE
(AVAIL. ONLY IN CUSTOM)
(51, 133 BLT.)
$**1886.**

CVT.

TUDOR

FORDOR
(292, 739 BLT.)
$**1472.**
UP

(560, 086 BLT.)
$**1425.** UP

CUSTOM
SERIES
REPLACES
"SUPER DELUXE."

226 CID 6 (95 HP)
and
239.4 CID V8 (100 HP)
CONTINUE.

NEW! '49

STARTS
SPRING,
'48

(TOTALLY RESTYLED)

Overdrive

(31, 412 WAGONS BLT.) $**2119.**

Wagon

LIFE
GUARD

Engine speed
42 m.p.h.

Car speed
60 m.p.h.

(OPTIONAL)

57% more luggage space

Ford Custom

FORD

new
"Hydra-
Coil"
FRONT SPRINGS

CHOICE OF COLOR
Hard Tops
1. BLACK
2. COLONY BLUE
3. BAYVIEW BLUE
4. SEA MIST GREEN
5. ARABIAN GREEN
6. MIDLAND MAROON
7. BIRCH GREY
8. GUNMETAL GREY
Convertibles
9. FEZ RED
10. MIAMI CREAM

"6" OR "8"
IN GRILLE
"SPINNER"
INDICATES
NUMBER OF
CYLINDERS.

(new CUSTOM SERIES
DESIGNATED BY NAMEPLATE
JUST AHEAD OF SIDE DOOR.)

New "Flight Panel" dash . . .

(INCLUDING
EARLY '49s
BUILT IN
1948)

FORD 49

TOTAL 1949 PROD.: 1, 118, 308

FORD

"Double Duty"

"Country Squire" STATION WAGON (8-PASS.)

CVT.

(50,299 SOLD)

$1948.

(MOST POPULAR MODEL WAS 2-DR. SEDAN, NEARLY 700,000 SOLD!)

(22,292 WAGONS BLT. 1950)

$2028.

1,000,000 FORDS BUILT 1950; MOST FORD SALES SINCE 1930!

TOTAL SALES (INCLUDING TRUCKS) 1,208,912

CHASSIS (V8)

50

new "KEYSTONE" FORD EMBLEM INTRODUCED

$1511.

CLUB COUPE

(85,111 SOLD) (ALSO 35,120 DLX. BUSINESS COUPES)

new MID-SEASON 2-DR. "CRESTLINER"

$1711.
(17,601 BLT.)

new EMBLEM ON HOOD (ALSO ON DECK LID)

FORD

(325,069 SOLD)

FORDOR

"TEST DRIVE" A '50 FORD

THERE'S A *Ford* IN YOUR FUTURE WITH A FUTURE BUILT IN!

FORD 50

FORD

BIG 1951 NEWS IS FORD'S FIRST H/T ("HARDTOP CONVERTIBLE,") THE *VICTORIA* ! (110,286 BLT.!) **$1925.**

CONVERTIBLE, BUSINESS CPE., CLUB CPE. and TUDOR SEDAN ALSO AVAIL.

TOTAL 1951 PRODUCTION: 1,013,381
FORDOR (232,691 CUSTOM, 54,265 DELUXE) **$1465.**
(CUSTOM HAS MORE CHROME TRIM)

$1553.

$1595.

CRESTLINER

('8703 BLT.)

51
new GRILLE

MORE PRONOUNCED TAIL LIGHT — HOUSING EXTENSION AROUND SIDE OF FENDER w. CHRM. TRIM.

DUAL SPINNERS IN GRILLE

new **VICTORIA**
H/T

VICTORIA INTERIOR

VICT. WRAPAROUND REAR WINDOW

$2029.

COUNTRY SQUIRE
(29,017 BLT.)

new DASH

You can pay more but you can't buy better!

$1925.
VICTORIA H/T with WINDOWS OPEN

REAR (SEDAN) FORD 51

1951

FORD

new MAINLINE (has LEAST AMOUNT OF CHROME TRIM)

(5246 BLT.)

COUNTRY SQUIRE NOW A 4-DOOR METAL WAGON has IMITATION MAHOGANY PANEL DECALS, FRAMED with REAL MAPLE or BIRCH TRIM.

$2186.

$2060.

$1832.

new RANCH WAGON 2 DR.

new COUNTRY SEDAN 4 DR. WAGONS (11,927 BLT.)

FORD'S FIRST WAGONS W/O WOOD PANELING.

Station Wagons

FORD'S FIRST 4-DR. WAGONS SINCE 1948

(32,566 BLT.) **1952 PROD.: 671,733**

52 (TOTALLY RESTYLED)

1952

MAINLINE PRICED FROM
$1389.
$1526., WEST COAST
(BUSINESS CPE.)

New Flight-Style Control Panel

Ford's new Center-Fill Fueling cuts down spillage.

$1570.

DASH

new SUSPENDED PEDALS

CUSTOMLINE 4 DR. (183,303 BLT.) $1615.

HUGE, curved, one-piece windshield and car-wide rear window to match. You can really see what's ahead and what's behind!

(22,534 BLT.) $2027.

"TEST DRIVE" A FORD TODAY
YOU CAN PAY MORE BUT YOU CAN'T BUY BETTER

CRESTLINE SUNLINER V8
CRESTLINE VICTORIA H/T

FORD

new GRILLE has APPEARANCE of 3 "SPINNERS"

$1925., OR $2104. WEST COAST

(77,320 BLT.)

Full-Circle Visibility

CUSTOMLINE 2-DR. SEDAN (175,762 BLT.) SHOWN ABOVE CONVERTIBLE

new OHV 6
215.3 CID
101 h.p. High-Compression
Mileage Maker Six

"Only V-8 in its field"!
110 h.p. High-Compression
L-HEAD 239.4 CID V8 CONT'D. W. MORE H.P
Strato-Star V-8

FORD

CVT. IS PACE CAR AT 1953 INDY 500 RACE

PRICES START AT $1400.

($1537.
MAINLINE 6 CPE.,
WEST COAST)

MAINLINE 2-DR
(152,995 BLT.) $1497.

GENUINE Ford PARTS
SERVICE Ford

GENUINE Ford PARTS
SERVICE Ford

DASH

FORD 50TH ANNIVERSARY
50TH ANNIVERSARY 1903-1953

CUSTOMLINE 4-DR. $1628
(374,487 BLT.)

VICTORIA
(128,302 BLT.)
$1941.

1953

REAR DECK DETAIL

3 SERIES, AS IN '52 { MAINLINE
CUSTOMLINE
CRESTLINE

FRONT CLOSE-UP

new GRILLE

1953 PRODUCTION:
1,247,542

ONLY ONE "SPINNER" IN new GRILLE.

50TH ANNIVERSARY OF FORD MOTOR CO.

Crestline

(11,001 BLT.)

COUNTRY SQUIRE

SUNLINER CVT.
(40,861 BLT.)
$2043.

$2203.

FORD-O-MATIC
(SINCE '51)
P R N Dr Lo

2-DOOR RANCH WAGON $2019. (6)
(66,976 BLT.) $1917. (WEST COAST)

4-DOOR COUNTRY SEDAN $2076.
(37,743)
FORD 53

new! Ford Skyliner (CRESTLINE SERIES)

COUNTRY SQUIRE

$2339.

NO SHIFTING...NO CLUTCHING

$2199.
(V8 $134 EXTRA)
with PLEXIGLASS
ROOF WINDOW

New 130-h.p.
Y-BLOCK V·8

54
new GRILLE

239 CID V8 ENDS '54

MAINLINE
$1701.

New Ball-Joint Front Suspension

New 115-h.p.
I-BLOCK SIX

223 CID (THR. '64)

4. Four-Way Power Seat.

UP FRONT AND BACK DOWN

CUSTOMLINE

4 DR. $1793.

5 optional power assists*

★ Master-Guide power steering does up to 75% of steering work . . . ★ Swift Sure Power Brakes do up to one-third of your stopping work . . . ★ Fordomatic Drive does *all* your shifting

. . .★ Power-Lift Windows open and close at a button's touch. And ★ 4-Way Power Seat adjusts up or down, forward or back, at a touch of the controls.   *At extra cost.

PRODUCTION: **MAINLINE** = RANCH WAGON (44315); 2 DR. (123,329); BUSINESS COUPE (10,665); 4 DR. (55,371) **CUSTOMLINE** = RANCH WAGON (36,086); 2 DR. (293,375); CLUB COUPE (33,951); 4 DR. (262,499); 4 DR. WAGON (COUNTRY SEDAN) (48,384) **CRESTLINE** = VICTORIA H/T (95,464); SKYLINER H/T (13,344); 4 DR. (99,677); SUNLINER CVT. (36,685); COUNTRY SQUIRE 4 DR., 8-PASS. WAGON (12,797)

FORD 54

FORD

PRICES START AT
$1606. (MAINLINE 6 CPE.)

$1753.

SEDAN
MAINLINE

new GRILLE

new FAIRLANE SUNLINER CVT. (ABOVE)

$2224.

$1801. CUSTOMLINE

new "WRAP-AROUND" WINDSHIELD

55

120-H.P. 6 OR V8s with 162 OR 182 H.P.

RANCH WAGON

$2043.

CUSTOM RANCH WAGON

$2156. 6-PASS.

COUNTRY SEDANS

$2109.
$2392.

COUNTRY SQUIRE

8-PASS. (with FAIRLANE SIDE TRIM)

$2287.

"Y" SYMBOLIZES Y-BLOCK V8 *new* 272 CID

FAIRLANE VICTORIA

$2095.

SIDE EMBLEM (ON FAIRLANE TYPES)

$2202.

FAIRLANE CROWN VICTORIA (note BAND WRAPPED OVER ROOF)

new FAIRLANE MODELS IDENTIFIED BY SWEEP SIDE TRIM

FAIRLANE SERIES REPLACES **CRESTLINE**

PRODUCTION: **MAINLINE**=2 DR. (76,698); BUSINESS CPE. (8809); 4 DR. (41,794)
CUSTOMLINE=2 DR. (236,575); 4 DR. (235,417)
FAIRLANE = VICTORIA H/T (113,372); CROWN VICTORIA H/T (33,165); CROWN VICTORIA GLASSTOP ("SKYLINER" STYLE, LG. STATIONARY SUNROOF OVER FRONT SEAT AREA)(1999); 2 DR. CLUB SEDAN (173,311); TOWN SEDAN (254,437); SUNLINER CONVERTIBLE (49,966) **WAGONS**=RANCH WAGON (40,493); CUSTOM RNCH. WGN. (43,671); COUNTRY SEDAN

FORD 55

FORD

V-8 h.p. upped

MAINLINE $1748. UP

CUSTOM RANCH WAG. $2249.

FAIRLANE FORDOR

CTY. SQUIRE

The 272-cubic inch Ford V-8, the standard eight for all Customline and Mainline Fords. Has modern dual carburetor, automatic choke, single exhaust.

223 CID 6 INCREASED TO 137 HP @ 4200 RPM

The 292-cubic inch Thunderbird V-8, the standard eight for all Fairlanes and Station Wagons, is now available in all Customline and Mainline models, too. Has 4-barrel carburetor, dual exhausts.

202 H.P.

CUSTOM COUNTRY SEDAN

new 2-DR. LUXURY PARKLANE WAGON (INTRO. TO COMPETE with CHEVY's NOMAD.) (RARE! 1956 ONLY) (15,186 BLT.) $2428.

56 new GRILLE

MAINLINE	$1748. - 1895.
CUSTOMLINE	$1939. - 1985.
FAIRLANE	$2047. - 2407.
WAGONS	$2185. - 2533.

1956 PRODUCTION: 1,408,478

$1985. (33,130 BLT.)

CUSTOMLINE VICTORIA

$2428. (85,374 BLT.)

SKYLINER   CROWN VICTORIA

The 312-cubic inch Thunderbird Special V-8,

225 h.p.

$2249. new 4-DR. H/T (FAIRLANE FORDOR VICTORIA) (32,111 BLT.)

FORD .56

1956 INTERIOR

FORD

6 CYL. INCREASED TO 144 HP

COUNTRY SEDAN

$2451. UP

SQUIRE

(60,486 BLT.)

RANCH WAGON

LADDER-TYPE CONTOURED FRAME

4-way ball-joint front suspension

CUSTOM
(REPLACES MAINLINE)
(116,963 BLT.)

CUSTOM TUDOR

$1991.

CUSTOM 300 FORDOR
(194,877 BLT.)
$2157.

New deep-offset hypoid axle

FAIRLANE 500 MODELS BELOW

UP TO 245 HP with "SILVER ANNIVERSARY" V8s."

FAIRLANE
(note UNIQUE SIDE TRIM)

TOWN SEDAN (193,162 BLT.)
(52,080 BLT.) (FAIRLANE 500)

RESTYLED

57

(1,522,408 TOTAL PRODUCTION)

AVAIL. ENGINES
223 CID 6 (144 HP)
272 CID V8 (190 HP)
292 CID V8 (212 HP)
312 CID V8 (245 HP)

FAIRLANE 500 4-DR. TOWN VICTORIA H/T

$2404.

(68,550 BLT.)

LOW-SILHOUETTE CARB.

(20766 BLT.)

new V8 SKYLINER has RETRACTABLE HARD TOP (POWER-OPERATED)

SUNLINER CVT.

$2942.↗

$2505.

(77,726 BLT.)

REAR

new FRONT END

(183,202 BLT.)

FORD 57

400

FORD

6 CYL. NOW
145 HP
(THROUGH
'60)

CUSTOM
300

FAIRLANE 500 SKYLINER
(SHOWN *with* TOP IN
MOTION, *and with* TOP
IN PLACE.) $3163.

$2397.

NOTHING NEWER
IN THE WORLD

RANCH WAGON (4-DR.
ALSO
AVAIL.)

DEL RIO RANCH
WAGON
$2503.

DASH

COUNTRY SEDAN
COUNTRY $2557. UP
SQUIRE
(2
VIEWS)

$2794.

58
(TOTALLY
RESTYLED)

NEW INTERCEPTOR V-8
PRECISION FUEL INDUCTION

A TRUE AIR RIDE

FINE-CAR DETAIL

new
ROOF
GROOVES

$2428.

4
HEADLIGHTS

4 TAILLIGHTS

Versatile Cruise-O-Matic Drive! Set selector in D₁ position for brisk, solid-feeling take-off.
Select D₂ for gentle, sure-footed starts. What's
more, when new Cruise-O-Matic Drive is teamed
with a new Interceptor V-8 engine it can give you
up to 15 per cent more gasoline mileage.

*V8s = 292, new 332
and new 352 CID
(THROUGH '59)*

F-1958

FAIRLANE 500

Up to 300 h.p. with new Precision Fuel
Induction.

PRODUCTION: **CUSTOM:** 2 DR. (36,272); BUSINESS SED. (4062); 4 DR. (27,811); **CUSTOM 300:** 2 DR. (137,169);
4 DR. (135,557); **FAIRLANE:** VICT. H/T SEDAN (5868); 4 DR. TOWN SEDAN (57,490); VICT. H/T (16,416); 2 DR. CLUB SED. (38,366)
FAIRLANE 500: SKYLINER RETRACTABLE H/T (14,713); VICT. H/T (36,509); 4 DR. (105,698); VICT. H/T (80,439); " " (34,041);
SUNLINER CVT. (35,029) **WAGONS:** 2 DR. RANCH WAGON (34,578); 2 DR. DEL RIO (12,687); 4 DR. RANCH WAG. (32,854);
COUNTRY SEDAN (68,772); (COUNTRY SEDAN, 9-PASS. (20,702); COUNTRY SQUIRE, 9-PASS. (15,020)
(1,038,560 1958 TOTAL)

FORD 58

FORD

CUSTOM 300

$2132. (6)

WINDSHIELD DOGLEG DETAILS

note "FORD" LETTERING ON HOOD

Fairlane 500

(23,892 BLT.)

$2537.

FAIRLANE 500 VICTORIA ROOFLINE (CLOSE-UP)

note EMBLEM ON HOOD

new GRILLE

FAIRLANE REAR FENDER

(TOTALLY RESTYLED AGAIN)

TOTAL 1959 PRODUCTION: 1,427,835

ENGINES:
223 CID 6 (145 HP)
292 CID V8 (200 HP)
332 CID V8 (225 OR 300 HP)

59A

GALAXIE new MID-SEASON SERIES

NEW FORD GALAXIE CLUB VICTORIA—THUNDERBIRD STYLING IN A 6-PASSENGER, 2-DOOR HARDTOP

(121,869 BLT.)

1959 WAGONS ON NEXT PAGE

$3346.

(12,915 BLT.)

new 1959½ TOP-OF-LINE GALAXIE MODELS ADDED, with T-BIRD ROOFLINE.

THE FINAL SKYLINER (GALAXIE) FORD 59(A)

FORD

$2634.

wagons

(INTERIOR VIEW EXAGGERATED)

4-DOOR *and* 2-DOOR RANCH WAGONS

FENDER CHEVRONS ON THIS '59½ RANCH WAGON

ROOMY NEW FORD RANCH WAGON . . . LOWEST PRICED WAGON OF THE MOST POPULAR THREE

STATION WAGON PRODUCTION

59 (CONT'D.)

B

59-C 2-DR. RANCH WAGON (45,588)
59-D " " DEL RIO (8663)
71-E COUNTRY SEDAN, 9-PASS. (28,811)
71-F " " , 6-PASS. (94,601)
71-C COUNTRY SQUIRE, 9-PASS. (24,336)
71-H 4-DR. RANCH WAGON (67,339)

$2958.   (WEST COAST) **$3076.** *

COUNTRY SQUIRE

1959 DASH
(ILLUSTR. *with* FACTORY-INSTALLED AIR CONDITIONER UNIT)

*WAGON PRICE SHOWN APPLIES TO V-8 9-PASSENGER 6 CYL. OR 6-PASS. MODELS *also avail.*

COUNTRY SEDAN
$2947. *
(WEST COAST)
(ELSEWHERE, **$2745.** OR **$2829.**)
FORD 59 (B)

403

FORD
(91,041 BLT.)

FAIRLANE 500

FAIRLANE PRICES START AT
$**2170.**
(6-CYL. 2-DR.)

(31,866 BLT.)

GALAXIE TUDOR

(TOP UP)

SUNLINER CVT.

(TOP DOWN)

(68,461 BLT.)
new STARLINER
$**2723.** (V8; 6 ALSO AVAIL.)

ARCHED TAIL-LIGHTS ONLY ON 1960 MODELS

292 CID V8 REDUCED TO 185 HP ; OTHER ENGINES AS IN 1959.

$**2860.**

(44,762 BLT.)

GALAXIE FORDOR
$**2603.**

(104,784 BLT.)

(TOTAL 1960 PRODUCTION = 1,004,305)

60 (TOTALLY RESTYLED FOR 3RD SUCCESSIVE YEAR !)

145 TO 300 HP

NEW SLOPING HOOD GIVES INCREASED VISIBILITY

DASH

RANCH WAGON
$**2586.**

(27,136 BLT.)

COUNTRY SEDAN →
(59,302 BLT. 6 PASS.)
(19,277 BLT. 9 PASS.)

$**2967.**

9-passenger Country Squire

(22,237 BLT.)

FORD 60

404

Beautifully built to take care of itself...

FORD WHEEL COVER

(66,875 BLT.)

2 DR. FAIRLANE $2261. (6)

$2432.

4 DR. (98,917 BLT.) FAIRLANE 500

new GRILLE IS CONCAVE, BISECTED HORIZONTALLY

RETURN TO CONSERVATIVE STYLING

61

$2664. (30,342 BLT.)

GALAXIE 4-DR. TOWN VICTORIA H/T

(CLOSER VIEW OF GALAXIE WHEEL COVER AT UPPER RIGHT)

$2588. (12,042 BLT.)

RANCH WAGON

$2754. UP

STATION WAGONS

CNTRY. SEDAN

292, 352 OR new 390 CID V8s (175 TO 401 HP)

SQUIRE

(16,961 BLT.) $2943.

$2599.

GALAXIE VICTORIA H/T (CLOSE-UP and DASH)

(29,669 BLT.)

STARLINER H/T

$2599.

ROUND TAIL LIGHTS RETURN

1961 PRODUCTION = 1,338,790

(75,437 BLT.) FORD 61

405

FORD
(NO MORE 2-DR. WAGONS)

COUNTRY SQUIRE (16,114 BLT.)

RANCH WAGON (33,674 BLT.) $2733.

(47,635 BLT.)

6-PASSENGER COUNTRY SEDAN.
(9-pass. model also)

$2829.

$3018.

"CRUISE-O-MATIC" A/T CONTROL

SLOGAN: live it up with a lively One from FORD

("500")
(27,824 BLT.)

(54,930 BLT.)
$2453.

Galaxie **62**

new BLUNTED REAR END

POWER STEERING

XL H/T
(28,412 BLT.)

Galaxie 500XL

138 TO 405 HP (THR. '63)

GALAXIE 500/XL.

DENOTES 405 HP THUNDERBIRD ENGINE

GALAXIE 500 and XL have ← GRILLE MEDALLION

1962 TAIL LIGHTS

(87,562 BLT.)

Galaxie 500

BUCKET SEATS and FLOOR CONSOLE IN new

Galaxie 500/XL!

new *SIDE TRIM

*=ON 500, XL

$3518.

Galaxie 500XL

(13,183 BLT.)

1962 PRODUCTION: 1,476,031

$2924.
(42,646 BLT.)

Galaxie 500
(SEDAN and CVT. ILLUSTR.)

FORD 62

FORD

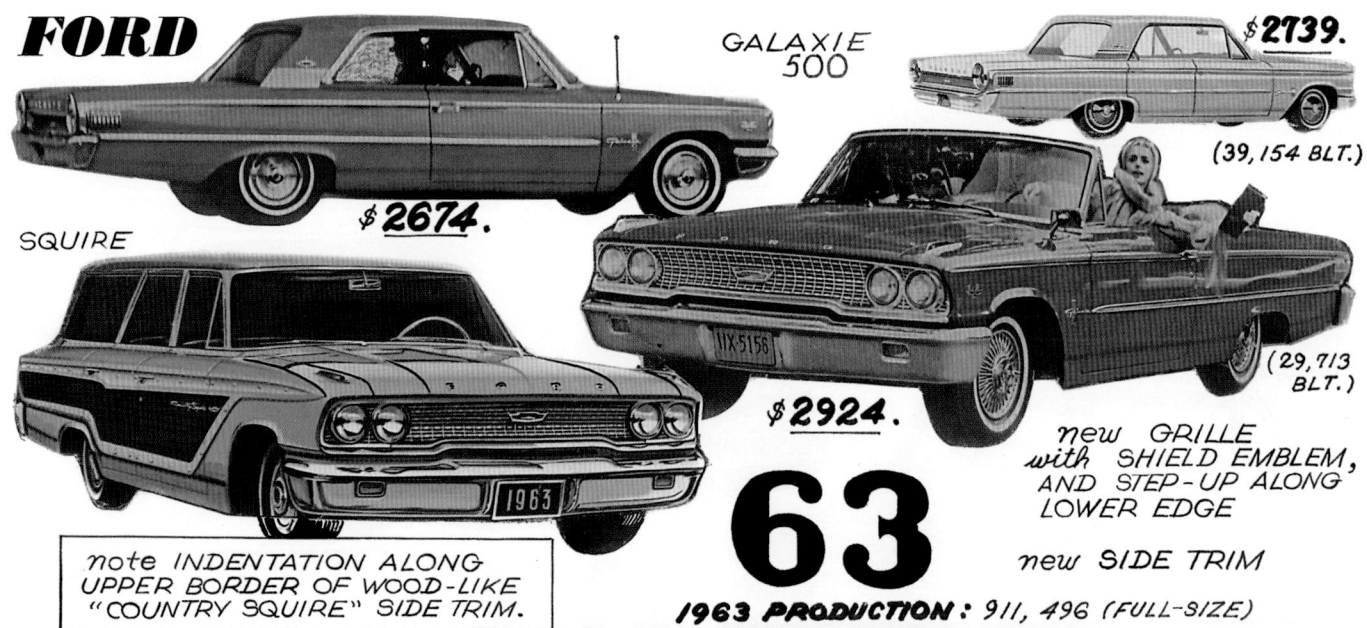

GALAXIE 500

$2739.

(39,154 BLT.)

$2674.

SQUIRE

(29,713 BLT.)

$2924.

63

new GRILLE *with* SHIELD EMBLEM, AND STEP-UP ALONG LOWER EDGE

new SIDE TRIM

note INDENTATION ALONG UPPER BORDER OF WOOD-LIKE "COUNTRY SQUIRE" SIDE TRIM.

1963 PRODUCTION: 911,496 (FULL-SIZE)

SQUIRE (6 PASS.) (20,359 BLT.) $3018.
    (9 PASS.) (19,567 BLT.) $3088.

COUNTRY SEDAN WAGONS ALSO =
  (6 PASS.) (64,954 BLT.) $2829.
  (9 PASS.) (22,250 BLT.) $2933.

ENGINES	223 CID 6 (138 HP)
	289 CID V8 (195 OR 271 HP)
	352 CID V8 (250 HP)
	390 CID V8 (300 OR 330 HP)
new	427 CID V8 (425 HP)

FLOOR CONSOLE *and* DASH

BACKGROUND: MONACO, ON THE RIVIERA

PRICES START AT **$2563.**

6-CYL. "300" 2-DR.

UP TO 425 HP IN *new* '63½

new

Presenting the 63½ Super Torque Ford Sports Hardtop —brand new hardtop that looks like a convertible!

new SWING-AWAY STEERING WHEEL AVAILABLE

FORD 63

407

CLEAR GLASS BACKLIGHT IN CVT.

RANCH WAGON RETURNS

CUSTOM RANCH WAGON

FORD

SQUIRE

138 TO 425 HP

$2750.

$3988. UP

GALAXIE 500 4-DR. H/T (49,242 BLT.)

GALAXIE 500 XL

new GRILLE **64**

PRICES START AT $2586. (CUSTOM 6 2-DR.) ($2600 IN '65)

TOTAL 1964 PRODUCTION = 881,061 (FULL-SIZE)

TOTAL 1965 PRODUCTION = 1,048,388 (FULL-SIZE)

CUSTOM 4 DR. (96,393 BLT.)

$2518.

"CRUISE-O-MATIC" A/T CONTROL

$2361. ~ 3498. PRICE RANGE

(RESTYLED) 150 TO 425 HP (THROUGH '67)

65

CUSTOM 500 (71,727 BLT.) $2415.

new VERTICAL STACKED HEADLIGHTS →

new DIP IN WAGON ROOF →

Convenient face-to-face rear seats add passenger space

SQUIRE

CVT. (9849) BLT.

$3104. UP

GALAXIE 500 XL

$3498.

$3313.

GALAXIE 500 LTD (68,038 BLT.)

TAIL LIGHT SHAPE 19 new FORD 64-65

408

FORD $2533.

CUSTOM 500

RANCH WAGON
(33,306 BLT.)
$2793.

COUNTRY SEDAN ↓

New Magic Doorgate for all our 1966 wagons!

GALAXIE 500

240 CID 6 (150 HP)
289, 352, 390,
427 and
428 CID
V8s AVAIL.
(200 TO
425 HP)

swings down for cargo

$2882. UP

$2685. UP
(7 LITRE ENG.,
$3621.)

GALAXIE 500

new
2-TIERED
GRILLE

66

119" WB (THROUGH '68)

7.35/7.75
× 15
TIRES

COUNTRY SQUIRE

(69,598 BLT.)
FROM
$3182.

Swings open for people

In the Greatest Year Yet
For Total Performance,
There Are . . .
**49 NEW WAYS
TO GO FORD!**

new Stereo-Sonic TAPE

**painting all
our engines blue**

GALAXIE
500
LTD
WITH
SPECIAL HOOD
ORNAMENT (SEE
RED ARROW)

"7 LITRE"
SIGN ON GRILLE

LTD
DASH

STD.
289 CID V8
(200 HP)

TOTAL 1966 PROD. —
2,212,415

FORD 66

409

YOU'RE AHEAD IN A FORD

2-DR. (18,107 BLT.) $2441.

Custom and Custom 500

$3234.

GALAXIE 500 H/T (197,388 BLT.) $2755.

COUNTRY SQUIRE $3816. (WEST)

RANCH WAGON and COUNTRY SEDAN ARE UN-GRAINED FORD WAGONS. (SINCE 1952.)

LTD H/T (46036 BLT.) $3362.

New GRILLE and TAIL-LIGHTS (INTRO. 9-30-66)

67

240 CID 6 (150 HP)
289 CID V8 (200 HP)
390 CID V8 (315 HP)
ALSO 427 and 428 CID V8s
   (TO 345 HP) (427 CID TO 425 HP)

$2441.~3493.
PRICE RANGE

TOTAL 1967 PRODUCTION = 1,730,224

XL

SelectShift transmission you can use automatically or manually.

1967

CUSTOM 500 SEDAN (83260 BLT.)
FORD 67

$2595.

410

FORD
...has a better idea.

Custom Sedans →

GRILLE

CUSTOM 2~DR.

RANCH WAGON $3000. UP

(49839 BLT.)

CUSTOM INTERIOR →

1968 Custom 500 4-Door Sedan

Custom 500   (49398 BLT.)

GALAXIE 500 REAR TRIM

Contoured Headrests. Adjust for any type front seating.

SELECTSHIFT CRUISE-O-MATIC

OPTIONAL ON SOME

Convenience Group has warning lights for door ajar, low fuel, parking brake and to fasten seat belts.

PARK BRAKE | LOW FUEL | DOOR AJAR | SEAT BELTS

1968 Ford Galaxie 500 Convertible
(11832 BLT.)
$3108.

(154,092 BLT.)
$2881. and up

GALAXIE 500 H/T (2 TYPES) UP

$3539. UP

(6066 BLT.)
XL CVT.

68
(INTRO. 9~22~67)
new GRILLES
new 302 CID V8
(210 HP)

TOTAL 1968 PROD.:
1,753,334

$3214. XL H/T

(50048 BLT.)
$2985.

COUNTRY SQUIRE (GRILLE LIKE LTD)
(9/770 BLT.)

CONCEALED HEADLIGHTS (IN "OPEN" POSITION) →

LTD

XL INTERIOR

428 CID V8 (345 HP) OPT.
ON ALL MODELS

FORD 68

LTD H/T
(54163 BLT.) $3153.

new

Lifeguard-designed Front Side Marker Lights

FORD

CUSTOM 2-DR.

(SIDE CHROME STRIP NOT SEEN ON CUSTOM.)

CUSTOM 500 SEDAN

Galaxie 500 SEDAN

TOTAL 1969 PROD.= 1,826,777

69

(INTRO. 9-27-68) new GRILLES new 121" WB (THRU '78)

GALAXIE 500 UPHOLST.

GALAXIE 500

COUNTRY SQUIRE

FORD It's the going thing!

DASH

1969 Ford XL GT SportsRoof

Ford XL GT Specifications—Required engine: 390 CID 2V V-8, bore and stroke 4.05 x 3.78 in., compression ratio 9.5:1, regular fuel, 265 horsepower at 4400 rpm, 390 lbs-ft torque at 2600 rpm. Single exhaust. Optional engines: 429 CID 2V Thunder-Jet V-8. Bore and stroke 4.36 x 3.59 in.

XL CONVERTIBLE ALSO AVAIL.

Ford XL GT—

LTD

LTD INSIGNIA ABOVE GRILLE

XL SPRTSRF. H/T $3536

FORD 69

412

FORD $3026.

F78 x 15 TIRES
(57059 BLT.)
$3094.

H/T

1970

(101,784 BLT.) GALAXIE 500 4-DOOR SEDAN

GALAXIE 500

STEERING
COLUMN
LOCK
(IGN.)

(50825 BLT.)
$3043.

FASTBACK
H/T

GALAXIE 500

CUSTOM SEDAN IS
LOWEST-PRICED MODEL, AT
$2850.
(42849 BLT.)

RIM~BLOW HORN (OPT.)

Under the hood, the quiet, thrifty 240-cu. in. Big Six is smoothly harnessed to a fully synchronized 3-speed manual transmission. More V-8 brawn up to a 429 powerhouse is optional. SelectShift Cruise-O-Matic, which you can shift manually or auto-

121" WB
(SINCE '69)
(INTRO.
9-19-69)

70
new GRILLES

GALAXIE 500
COUNTRY SEDAN WAGON

(27251 BLT.)
$3293.

FASTBACK
H/T

FORD XL CONVERTIBLE
(6348 BLT.)
$3501.

$3488. up

WITH DOOR OPEN

SEDAN (78806 BLT.)
LTD

1970

CONCEALED
HEADLIGHTS
**TOTAL '70 PROD.:
2,096,184**

H/T
(96324 BLT.)
$3356. up

CLOSE-UP! LTD GRILLE

FORD 70

413

FORD Take a Quiet Break... '71 Ford.

FROM $3288. (CUSTOM 4-DR.)

BELOW = CUSTOM 500 4-DR. (33765 BLT.)

CUSTOM 500

CUSTOM 500 RANCH WAGON

Custom 500 Ranch Wagon with Dual-Facing Rear Seats.

(42653 BLT.) $3890. UP

Custom 500 4-Door Sedan.

$3426.

4-DR. H/T

$3665. (46595 BLT.)

TOTAL 1971 PROD. = 2,054,351

GALAXIE 500

2-DR. H/T

(117,139 BLT.) $3628.

$3594.

Ford Galaxie 500 4-Door Sedan.

(98/30 BLT.)

121" WB

71 (INTRO. 9-18-70)

new GRILLE

LTD

$4097.

2-DR. LTD BROUGHAM (43303 BLT.)

DASH

COUNTRY SQUIRE (130,644 BLT.)

ENGINES: 240 CID 6 (140 HP)
302 CID V8 (210 HP)
351 CID V8 (240")
400 CID V8 (260")
(260 HP) PLUS
BIG 429 CID V8
(320 OR
360 HP)

new BUMPER DIPS, TO FOLLOW CONTOUR OF POINTED GRILLE.

INTERIOR

FORD 71

414

FORD

GLAMOUR PAINT OPTION GROUP
Exclusive Thunderbird
Optional at Extra Cost

Ford Custom 4-Door Sedan

Ford Torino Mustang Thunderbird
Maverick Pinto Ranchero

2G — Burgundy Fire (Opt)
3C — Blue Fire (Opt)
4D — Green Fire (Opt)
4G — Lime Fire (Opt)
1C — Black

5C — Walnut Fire (Opt)
5D — Cinnamon Fire (Opt)
5G — Copper Fire (Opt)
6G — Gold Fire (Opt)
2B — Brt Red
2E — Red
2J — Maroon

COLOR GLOW PAINT OPTION
Ford Torino Mustang Maverick Pinto Ranchero
Optional at Extra Cost

3D — Med Blue Met
3F — Grabber Blue
3H — Dk Blue Met

DASH

4C — Ivy Glow (Opt)
5J — Ginger Glow (Opt)
6F — Gold Glow (Opt)

4A — Pastel Lime
4B — Brt Green Gold Met
4E — Brt Lime

4P — Med Green Met
4Q — Dk Green Met
5A — Lt Pewter Met

5H — Med Brown Met
6B — Lt Yellow Gold
6C — Med Yellow Gold

Galaxie 500 Instrument panel puts everything fingertip-handy

6E — Med Brt Yellow
6J — Gray Gold Met
9A — White

CUSTOM SEDAN (33014 BLT.) **$3246.**
240 C/D 6 (103 HP)
302 C/D V8 (140 HP)
351 C/D V8 (153 C/D)
400 C/D V8 (172 HP)
429 C/D V8 (208 HP) H/T

GALAXIE 500

1A — Lt Gray Met

2A — Med Coral

$3572. (80855 BLT.)

3B — Lt Blue

SEDAN (104,167 BLT.) **$3537.**

3J — Brt Blue Met

35I C/D V8 IN **Wagons**

WITH AVAILABLE SIDEWAYS REAR SUNKEN SEATS (ARROW)

4F — Med Lime Met

$4028. COUNTRY SQUIRE FROM **$4792.** (WEST)

DASH

LTD FINAL CVT. (4234 BLT.) **$4057.**

5F — Dk Brown Met

6D — Yellow

(INTRO. 9-24-71)

72
TOTAL 1972 PRODUCTION = 2,246,563

Quiet Plus.

2 SLIGHTLY DIFFERING *new* GRILLES

new STRAIGHT-ACROSS POINTED BUMPER

LTD

GALAXIE 500

FORD 72

$4146. UP

(51290 BLT.)

MAKING AMERICA'S BEST-SELLING WAGONS IS A WAGONMASTER TRADITION.

$3833.

FORD

G78 x15 TIRES
4 DR. H/T
(25802 BLT.)

GALAXIE 500

(CUSTOM 500
4-DR. SEDAN HAS
NO CHROME SIDE
STRIP.)
($4014.)

(6 and 302 CID V8
NOT AVAIL. IN FULL-SIZED LINE)

COUNTRY
SEDAN

(RANCH WAGON
LOOKS
SIMILAR)

351, 400, 429
OR 460 CID V8s,
J78 x15 TIRES
ON WAGONS

The closer you look, the better we look.

RECREATION TABLE OPTION. (with magnetized checkers). Available on Dual Facing Rear Seat models. Use as game board or snack table. Stows under seat.

SQUIRE BROUGHAM OPTION. Includes High Back split bench seats with manual passenger recliner, special vinyl trim (Color KR), cut-pile carpeting, Steel-Belted Radial Ply Tires, front door courtesy lamps and rear door courtesy light switches.

(RESTYLED)

73

TOTAL
1973
PROD. =
2,349,815

COUNTRY SQUIRE
(142,933 BLT.)
$4401. UP

DASH

AVAIL. POWER-OPERATED
SUN ROOF

H/T (120,864 BLT.)
$3950.

LTD

new
INSIDE
HOOD LOCK,
and FRONT
DISC BRAKES
STANDARD
LTD BROUGHAM
PILLARLESS
4-DOOR H/T
also available, AND
2-DR. H/T, 4-DR. PILLARED
H/T

PILLARED
4-DR. H/T
FR. $4364.
(WEST)

CLOSER
REAR
DETAILS
(LTD)

$4001.
(28606 BLT.) FORD 73

FORD $4898. UP.

(64047 BLT.)

LTD Country Squire

3 V8s AVAIL.
351 CID (162 HP)
400 " (170 ")
460 " (220 ")

74

LTD BROUGHAM

LTD BROUGHAM

Ford Custom 500 Ranch Wagon, Green Glow (Code 4Z).

$4488. UP

CUSTOM 500 RANCH WAGON (12104 BLT.)

CUSTOM 500 / GALAXIE 500 GRILLE

new GRILLE; LTD has HOOD ORNAMENT

($4483 CUSTOM 500 4-DR. IS LOWEST-PRICED LARGE FORD.)

(FINAL YR. FOR GALAXIE 500)

400 CID V8 (144 HP)
460 " (216 HP)

new

LTD H/T (47,432 BLT.)
(24005 BROUGHAM 2-DR.)
$5133. (2-DR. BR.)

LTD AND LTD BROUGHAM

REAR

75

FRONT RESTYLED

DASH

$5440. UP
(41550 BLT.)

COUNTRY SQUIRE (3-SEATER)

SQUIRE BROUGHAM INT.

CONCEALED HDLTS. RETURN

$5158.

HOOD ORNAMENT STD. LTD WAGON

LTD. LANDAU (new)

(FINAL YEAR FOR CUSTOM 500)

(32506 BLT., PLUS 26919 2-DRS.)

TOTAL 1975 PROD. = 1,569,608

4-DR. $5453.

FORD 74~75

FORD

4-SEAT COUNTRY SQUIRE WAGON $6213. (WEST)

(4-DR. STD. LTD IS LOWEST-PRICED, AT $5316.) (WEST)

wagon $5649. $5207.

NO MORE CHROME STRIP ALONG GRAINED PANEL.

(47379 BLT.)

(29673 BLT.)

LTD

$5613.

(32917 BLT.)

TOTAL 1976 PROD. 1,861,537

BAND OVER ROOF

76

FEW CHANGES

new WHEEL COVERS

LTD LANDAU NO LONGER HAS BODY-PAINTED SECTIONS BETWEEN THE 3 AMBER LENSES.

MINI-VENT WINDOWS

(OPTIONAL)

LTD. The full-size car WITH STD. 351 CID V8 (161 HP)

77

LTD (UNGRAINED) $5415. UP

LTD Wagon SQUIRE

LTD Wagon

$5866. UP

(LTD GENERALLY SIMILAR TO 1976 MODEL)

(C) Power mini-vent windows. Provide draft-free ventilation. Great for smokers. Available on 4-door and wagon models.

LTD PILLARED H/T (73637 BLT.)

FR. $6012. (WEST)

4-DOOR LTD LANDAU

$5128.

$4870.

TOTAL 1977 PROD. = 1,840,427

(56704 BLT.)

the **new** trimmer, sportier LTD II

(REPLACES TORINO)

FROM $5156. (S)

(65030 BLT.)

$5742.

new LTD II has 302 CID V8 (130 HP) and HR78 x 14 TIRES

BROUGH. 5698.

Now, in addition to the full-size Ford LTD, Ford also offers LTD's kind of quality and luxury in a sportier, trimmer car that's priced and handles like a mid-size.

114"/118" WB 2-DR. 4-DR.

(20979 BLT.) $5121.

WEST $5362. UP (STD. 2-DR.)

(RANCHERO NOW IN LTD II SERIES) FORD 76-77

FORD
$5885. UP

UNGRAINED LTD WAGON

TOTAL 1978 PRODUCTION = 1,923,655

DASH

FINAL BIG 121" WHEELBASE MODELS

78

FORD LTD LANDAU (REAR)

COURTESY LIGHT ACTUATED BY BOTH FRONT AND REAR DOORS

CENTER PILLAR WINDOWS ON LTD and LANDAU 2 DR. H/Ts

V8 ENGINES
302 CID (134 HP)
351 CID (144/145 OR 152 HP)
400 CID (166 HP)
460 CID (202 HP)

$5398. (57466 BLT.) LTD H/T

FORD LTD
FORD DIVISION
75" ANNIVERSARY

LTD, LTD II NOW SHARE STD. 302 CID V8 (134 HP)

$6304.
2-SEAT: $6848. (WEST)

LTD

Ford LTD Country Squire

(TOTAL OF 71285 WAGONS BLT.)

LTD LANDAU (39836 BLT.) $6055. $6614. (WEST)

LTD REAR

$5222. UP

LTD II

"S" COUPE

(9004 BLT.)

LTD II DASH

SEDAN (64133 BLT., INCL. BROUGHAM)

(BROUG.= $5483. UP)

$5112.

LTD II BROUGHAM
(note HEAVY MID-SIDE HORIZONTAL TRIM)
(76285 BLT., INCL. STD. H/T)

H/T CPE.

H/T $5448.

NOW 2 LTD II COUPE STYLES

LTD II

FORD 78

FORD DETAILS OF STD. LTD
2-DR.
(54005 BLT.)
$6184.

1979 NEW AMERICAN ROAD CAR

STD. LTD

LTD II (FINAL YEAR)

"It's like they made it for me... sporty and practical."

LTD II 2-door Brougham in Pastel Chamois

$6135.

LTD DASH

COUNTRY SQUIRE
(29932 BLT.)
$7006.

FROM
$7291.
(WEST)

$6550. UP

LTD WAGON
(37955 BLT.)

LTD SEDAN
(117,730 BLT.)
$6284.

79

TOTALLY
RESTYLED
AND
DOWN-
SIZED
new
114.4" WB

(42314 BLT.)

CARS IN DIRTY
BUT ORIGINAL
CONDITION ARE
WORTH
RESTORING.

1979

$6686.

302 CID V8 (134 HP)
351 CID V8 (144 HP)
(OR 142, 151 HP)

FORD LTD LANDAU

1979 has TALL, NARROW
HOOD ORNAMENT →

CLOSER DETAILS OF LTD LANDAU CPE.
TOTAL 1979 PROD. =
1,835,937

4-DR.
(74599 BLT.)
$6811.

FORD

FORD 79

420

FORD

$6875.

DIFF. GRILLE ON LOW-PRICED LTD "S"

(19283 BLT.)
(ONLY 553 "S" 2-DR. CPES. BLT.)

LTD S Wagon, Light Grey (12)
$7198.
(3490 BLT.)

$7628.
(7725 BLT.)

new P205, P215 75R x 14 TIRES

(new)
FORD LTD
CROWN VICTORIA

SEDAN DETAILS IN CIRCLE AT LOWER LEFT)

LTD WAGON $7463.
(11718 BLT.)

MPH 5 15 25
km/h 10 20
P RN031

80

Ford EXTENDED SERVICE PLAN

NEW LIMITED CORROSION PERFORATION WARRANTY.

new WIDER HOOD ORN. (CNTRY. SQ. and CRN. VICT.)

$7891.

LTD.

(9868 BLT.)

LTD COUNTRY SQUIRE CROWN VICT.

new HIGHER BELT STRIPING FOR 1980

(15333 BLT.)

$7003.

NO HOOD ORNAMENT ON STD. LTDs

$7763.
$7900. (WEST)

CROWN VICTORIA SEDAN

TOTAL 1980 PROD. 1,162,275
new

FORD 80

Ford **Fairmont**

105½" WB
$4754. ('78)
5773. ('80)

Ford Motor Co. = (1978 ~ 1983)

(new) $5474. ('78)
6577. ('80)

Squire Wagon

REAR

2-DR.

78-80

140 CID 4 (88 HP); 200 CID 6 (85 HP)
302 CID V8 (139 HP)(THROUGH '79)
255 CID V8 (1980)

CR78×14 TIRES
(PLAIN-SIDED
WAGONS ALSO,
FROM $5109. ('78) TO
$6059. ('80)

← FUTURA
SPECIAL
COUPE has
OWN GRILLE

$5209. ('78)   6/78.
('80)
BR78×14 TIRES

1978 CARS
ILLUSTRATED,
UNLESS NOTED
OTHERWISE

('80) ←

4-DR.

$4754.
('78)
5157.
('79)
5890. ('80)

DLX. WOOD-TONED
DASH   ('80)

2-TONE COLOR BANDS
AVAILABLE ON
1980 MODELS →

REPL. BY 1984 *TEMPO*

EASTERN
PRICE RANGE AND YEARLY PRODUCTION =
1978 = $3624. TO 4428. 2-DR. (78776); 4-DR. (138,649); *FUTURA* CPE. (116,966); WAGONS (128,390)
1979 = 4102. — 4856. 2-DR. (54798); 4-DR. (133,813); *FUTURA* CPE. (106,065); WAGONS (100,691)
1980 = 4894. — 5390. 2-DR. (45074); 4-DR. and *FUTURA* 4-DR. (143,118); *FUTURA* CPE. (51878);
WAGON (77035: *UNGRAINED* ONLY IN 1980)

FORD FAIRMONT 78-80

FORD Granada

(INTRO. 1975)

GRILLE

...elegance in a new efficient size

109.9" W.B.

DR 78 x 14" TIRES

253-NA1 NEW YORK

STANDARD GRANADA
$3698*...2-Door

14-18⁺ mpg: city/
18-26⁺ mpg: highway

(100,610 BLT.)

$3756*...4-Door

(118,168 BLT.)

On the Inside, Ghia Offers More Luxury

$4225. (40028 BLT.)

Ghia control panel is elegant, easy to read.

1975 MODELS, UNLESS OTHERWISE INDICATED.

GHIA

GHIA HAS HVY. LOW SIDE TRIM.

(43652 BLT.)

Granada Ghia. Rich look, spacious feel, full-scale comfort.

REAR (GHIA)

Granada 2-Door Sedan, Green Glow (4T).

$3707. (161,618 BLT.)

$3798. ('76)

(187,923 BLT.)
4-Door Sedan, Medium Chestnut Metallic (5M).

■ Odense Vinyl Trim High-lights — appear in the roof center pillars — the bodyside moldings which are both protective and decora-tive — and on the distinctive lower back panel applique.

$4283.

$4265.

(46786 BLT.)
Ghia 2-Door Sedan, Medium Slate Blue Metallic (1H).
('76)

75-77

ENGINES
200 CID 6 (65 HP)(81 HP,'76)
250 " 6 (72 HP)(90 HP,'76)
302 " V8 (122 HP)(134/138 HP,'76)
351 " V8 (143 HP)(152/154 HP,'76)

(1977 ENGINES HAVE 96,98,122 and 135 HP, RESPECTIVELY.)

(52457 BLT.) $4355.
Ghia 4-Door Sedan, Black/Tan Metallic

(1C, 5U)

DASH ('77)

MOONROOF AVAILABLE

$4452. TAN GLOW

(35730 BLT.)
Granada Ghia

$4548.

('77)

('77)

(34166 BLT.)

DARK JADE METALLIC

(STD. MODELS ALSO AVAIL.) 320,683 BLT.)

FORD **GRANADA** 75~77

Ford Granada

$5390.

↑
STD.
GRANADA
250 CID 6 (97 HP)
302 CID V8 (139 HP)
new 255 CID V8 ALSO, 1980

new
2-TONE PAINT AVAIL. ON
1979 GHIA

('79)

2 DR.   **GHIA**

$5556.
('78)

4 DR. $5635.
('78)

note HEAVY
SIDE TRIM ON
GRANADA GHIA

$5878.

('80)

('78)
ESS
('80)
ESS

DASH ('79)

1980 WHEEL
↓ COVERS

78-80

new GRILLE and
ESS MODEL
INTRO. 1978

('80)

note UNIQUE RR.
QUARTER WINDOW
ON _ESS_ CPES.

ESS
('78) SEDAN $5821.

$5936.
('79)

(1980)
ESS
has
THIS
"SPORT"
STEERING
WHEEL
AND
"BLACKOUT"
GRILLE

('79)   TYPE OF ESS COWL LETTERING
DETERMINES YEAR

| 19 | EPA EST. MPG | 28 | EST. HWY. MPG |
| 342 | EST. RANGE | 504 | EST. HWY. RANGE |

1980 GAS MILEAGE

ESS

FORD GRANADA 78~80

FORD MAVERICK · Ford

compact

70 New

(1970-1977 MODELS)

Tartan plaid standard trim comes in three color combinations.

1970 TOTAL = (578,914 BLT.)

Maverick in Anti-Establish Mint, with optional **White Sidewall**

6.00 × 13 TIRES (14" OPT.)

STANDARD DASH

INITIAL (1970) MAVERICK INTRO. APRIL 17, 1969.

For $1995* ... it's a little gas.

(2-DR. ONLY)

$ 2257. (WEST)

For a little more... it's a Grabber.

MAVERICK GRABBER

Here's what you get:
- 200-cubic-inch Six
- Bodyside tape stripes, black-painted hood and grille
- White sidewalls, 14" wheels and trim rings
- Deck lid spoiler, dual racing mirrors
- 3-spoke woodtone steering wheel, black all-vinyl seat trim
- Choice of five hot Grabber colors

STD. SPECS.

103" WB
6 CYL.
170 CID
105 HP @ 4200 RPM
OR
200 CID
120 HP @ 4000 RPM
16-GAL. FUEL TANK

GRILLE EMBLEM

GAS CAP

CARS SOLD ON OR AFTER 9-19-69 ARE THEN CONSIDERED "OFFICIAL" 1970s

GRABBER MODEL ADDED FEB., 1970

FORD MAVERICK 70

Maverick gives you 15 bright new colors,

1. Grabber Blue 2. Medium Green Metallic 3. Platinum
4. Light Gold 5. Medium Yellow Gold 6. Grabber Yellow
7. Grabber Lime 8. White 9. Dark Green Metallic 10. Grabber Green Metallic 11. Grey Gold Metallic 12. Bright Blue Metallic 13. Black 14. Medium Blue Metallic 15. Bright Red

(2-TONES AVAIL.)

ACCENT MAVERICK
If you're a maverick who likes more glitter, the optional Accent Group provides bright window frames and drip moldings, wheel covers and color-keyed carpets.

FORD MAVERICK
new Option
VINYL-COVERED ROOF

MAVERICK
The Simple Machine
VINYL ROOF
A hard-to-resist styling touch that is offered in black, white, and red or gold tweed.

Grabber $2598. ('71)
                 2583. ('72)

STD. 2-DR.
$2419. ('71)
2414. ('72)

new 6.45 x 14"
TIRES
(THROUGH '74)

CHOICE OF
3 SIXES OR
V8 ENGINE
SINCE
MID-1971
SEASON.

(1971 MODELS INTRO. 9-11-70; 1972 MODELS INTRO. 9-24-71)

new GRILLE *and*
HOOD SCOOPS ON
GRABBER

271,897 BLT. 1971

71-72

254,424 BLT. 1972
                    $2479.
new 4-DR.   ('71)
ADDED
                    2469.
                    ('72)

73206 4-DRS. BLT. 1971

TOTAL 1973 PRODUCTION = 291,675.
2-DR. = $2248. UP
DASH (LUXURY DECOR TYPE)

73

$2305.
$2,695.*
WITH *new*
VINYL TOP

new
GRILLE
(110,382
4-DRS.
BLT. 1973)

Maverick is available now with optional 250-six automatic or 302-V8 engines.

FORD MAVERICK
FORD DIVISION *Ford*

MAVERICK

new
BUMPERS

FORD MAVERICK 71~73

426

Ford Maverick

2-Door *(139,818 BLT.)* $2790.

DASHBOARDS IN VARIOUS COLORS (TAN ALSO)

Metallic Glow Paints. Deep lustre finish. Available in glowing Ginger, Silver Blue (Luxury Decor Option only), Green and Tan.

Steel-Belted Radial Ply Tires. Have been tested to give the average driver 40,000 miles of tread life under normal driving conditions. **Other Tires Available.** Wide ovals with raised white lettering make a distinctive addition; enhance ride and handling. Standard on Grabber. Also, non-belted WSW, WSW steel-belted radial ply.

AM RADIO, AIR CONDITIONING, POWER STEERING AVAIL.

Energy absorbing bumper for '74.

4-Door Sedan $2824. *(137,728 BLT.)*

WESTERN PRICES:
2-DR. $3063.
4-DR. 3097.
GRABBER 3196.

note MAVERICK NAME ON DELUXE REAR QUARTER VINYL PANELS

MAVERICK — Grained vinyl roof.

74 TOTAL 1974 PRODUCTION = 301,048

Individual reclining seats in glove soft vinyl.

WITH SHOULDER HARNESSES

Wide Ovals with raised lettering, hub caps and trim rings and new hood and lower body colors. Top car is finished in Pearl White (Code 9C) and Avocado (Code 4B).

Grabber *(23502 BLT.)*

Maverick Grabber for the driver with a little sport in mind. $2923.

Trim Rings/Hub Caps. Standard on Grabber. Tastefully styled for added wheel flair.

GRABBER

MAVERICK

Forged Aluminum Wheels. Light, but strong, for the look of performance.

Lower car in Pearl White (Code 9C) and Orange (Code 5W) with color matching vinyl roof. Also features forged aluminum wheels.

FORD MAVERICK 74

427

Ford Maverick

GRABBER

2-DR.

(64081 BLT.)

$3025.

(8473 BLT. = FINAL GRABBER)

$3282.

2-DR. = 103" WB
4-DR. = 109.9" WB

cushioned bench seats trimmed in random stripe cloth and Vinyl.

In order to achieve the emisssion standards established for 1975, catalytic converters will be installed on all 200 CID engines. On the optional 250 and 302 CID engines, it will not be required.

4-DR.

(63404 BLT.)

$3061.

1975

interior is available in a choice of blue, black, tan or a new light green.

DASH

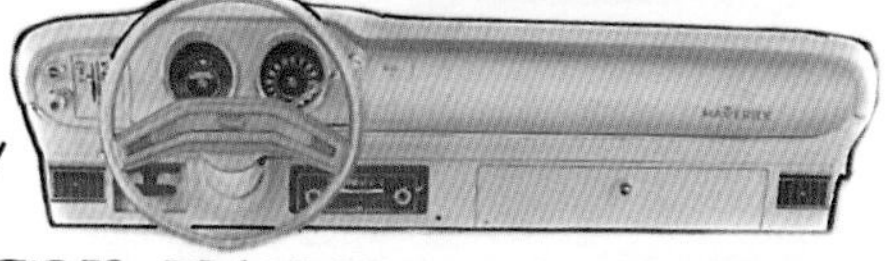

new RADIAL-PLY TIRES BR/CR 78×14 (DR 70×14 - GRABBER)

new 1975 OPTION

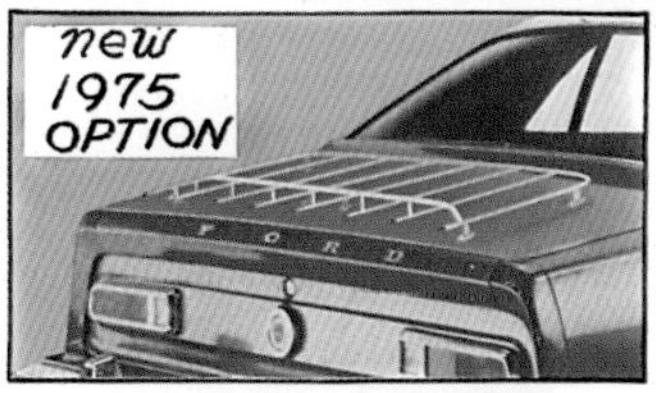

75

TOTAL 1975 PROD. = 135,958

The Ford 200 CID 1V 6-cylinder engine is standard with all 1975 Mavericks. (The 250 CID 6-cylinder engine is standard in California.) This durable engine is designed to provide reliability and economy. The 250 CID Six and the 302 CID V-8 continue as Maverick optional engines.

DECK LID-MOUNTED LUGGAGE RACK.

new POWER FRONT DISC BRAKES OPT.

Maverick 2-Door Sedan with Stallion Group

ABSOLUTELY NO SMOKING

Coca-Cola

OPTIONAL ALPINE PLAID ON SEATS

EPA MPG:
30 HWY.
22 CITY

('76)

MAVERICK DISCONTINUED 1977

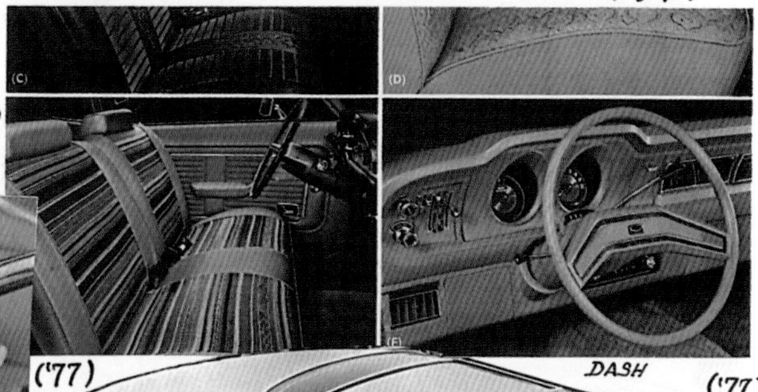

76 -77

MAVERICK "STALLION" PACKAGE

new FLOOR- OPERATED PARKING BRAKE

Dual color-keyed mirrors and distinctive Stallion emblem, below, arc just part of the package's sporty styling accents.

TOTAL. PROD. 1976 = 139 687
" " 1977 = 98 506

P R N D 2 1

AUTOMATIC TRANS. OPT.

('77)

('76)

DASH

('77)

new SPLIT GRILLE

$3189. UP ('76 4-DR.)

('77 2-DR.) $3322. UP

FORD MAVERICK 75~77

428

FORD TORINO
(REPLACES FAIRLANE)

Torino. 14 models

$3506.

TORINO SPORTSROOF

(FINAL FAIRLANE)

250 CID 6
(150 HP)
OR 302 CID V8
(220 HP)

FAIRLANE 500 2-DOOR HARDTOP
(70636 BLT.)

(12490 BLT.)

$3212.

new 117" WB
(114" ON
WAGONS
and
RANCHEROS)

OFFAL PACE CAR

Torino GT Convertible.
The Pace Car for all America.

HOOD
SCOOP ON
GT

GT CVT.
$3968.

(3939
BLT.)

(INTRO. 9-19-69)

Torino GT-

70 A

(TOTALLY
RESTYLED)

WITH HEADLTS. OPEN

GT
has 302,
351
OR
429 CID V8
E78/G78 × 14 TIRES
(F70 × 14, COBRA)

new PROFILE
FOR
SPORTSROOF

TORINO
BROUGHAM
(new) $3762.

(FORMAL
ROOFLINE)

VINYL
TOP

SPOILER
DECK

$3861.

(351 CID
V8
USES
REGULAR GAS)

MOTOR TREND
Car of the Year!

WESTERN PRICES
SHOWN

(CONT'D.
NEXT
PAGE)

FORD TORINO 70~A

TORINO BROUGHAM INTERIOR

TORINO BROUGHAM 4-DOOR HARDTOP

FORD TORINO

LIGHTS CLOSED (BY DAY)

WITH LIGHTS OPEN

WESTERN PRICES FROM $3568.

TORINO 4-DOOR SEDAN

2 COBRA REAR DECK PAINT VARIATIONS

360 HP COBRA (429 CID V8) $3843. (note DUAL PIPES) (7675 BLT.)

RECTANGULAR INSTRUMENTS

WAGON (10613 BLT.) PLAIN TOP, FORMAL ROOFLINE

TORINO COBRA

TORINO 2-DOOR HARDTOP

(49826 BLT.) $3655. WEST

WITH CHROME SIDE TRIM

DELUXE WHEEL CVR.

TORINO SQUIRE

↗ WITH NON-DISAPPEARING HEADLIGHTS

70 B (CONT'D.)

FAIRLANE / TORINO EASTERN PRICES = $2627.~$3379. (FAIRLN. 500 4-DR.) (SQUIRE)

FORD TORINO 70~B

(13166 BLT.)

FORD Torino

GT CVT. (1613 BLT.) $3408.

STD. WAGON

SQUIRE
(15805 BLT.)

250 CID 6 (145 HP)
OR 302 CID V8
(210 HP)

$3660.

GT H/T
(31641 BLT.)

$3150.

WAGON

TORINO 500

(23270 BLT.)

$3170.

$2943.

71
(INTRO. 9-18-70)

WESTERN PRICES
SHOWN

HP RATINGS REDUCED
250 CID 6 (95 HP)
302 CID V8
(140 HP)

(RESTYLED)

(INTRO. 9~24~71)

72 A

The first Gran Torino.

$3883.
(note HOOD SCOOP
ON
SPORT)

4-DR. PILLARED H/T
$3736.

(CONT'D.
NEXT PAGE)

WITH
VINYL TOP

FORD
GRAN
TORINO

SPORT
H/T

(60794 BLT.)

GRAN TOR.
2-DR. H/T
$3756. UP

FORD
TORINO
71-72-A

(132,284 BLT.)

WITH
PLAIN TOP

FORD TORINO —— —71~72-A

new
GRAN
TORINO
has
THIS
new NARROW
GRILLE.

More car than you expected.

FORD TORINO

$2955.

new SHORTER 114" WB
(new 118" WB ON
RANCHERO, WAGONS)

(Standard)
TORINO
has
THIS BROAD GRILLE
(22204 BLT.)

FROM
$3834.
WESTERN PRICE

72 B
(CONT'D.)

DASH
(CIRCULAR
INSTRUMENTS
CONTINUE, AS
IS USUAL
TORINO STYLE.)

FROM
$4275.
WESTERN PRICE

SQUIRE

VIEWS
OF
WOODGRAINED
Gran Torino Wagon

$3486.
(35595 BLT.)

INTERIOR

$3096.
(45212 BLT.)

Gran Torino Wagon
(UNGRAINED)

FORD TORINO 72-B

432

The solid mid-size car.

FORD TORINO

(98404 BLT.)
Gran Torino 4-Door Pillared Hardtop

STD. TORINO has OWN WIDER GRILLE

302, 351, 400 or 429 CID V8s AVAIL. (137 TO 201 HP) 250 CID 6 (92 HP)

3-SEAT SQUIRE $4339.

(40023 BLT.) $3559. UP

114" WB (2-DR.) 118" WB (4-DR.) GRAN TORINO

GRAN TORINO H/T

(138,962 BLT.) $2921. UP

DASH

NOTE new ENERGY~ABSORBING SAFETY BUMPERS

73

new GRILLES (INTRO. FRIDAY, 9-22-72)

(17090 BLT.) Gran Torino Sport 2-Door Hardtop

Gran Torino Sport SportsRoof (51853 BLT.)

The closer you look, the better we look.

22½ GAL. GAS TANK

Gran Torino Brougham Interior in Tobacco cloth and vinyl trim. (Color NZ). Optional Power Side Windows, SelectShift also shown.

STD. WAGON

(15393 BLT.) $3818.

$4300. UP (22837 BLT.)

new 21.2 GAL. GAS TANK

VINYL UPHOLST.

REAR

74.

UNGRAINED WAGON IN STD. SERIES, ALSO AVAIL. IN GRAN TORINO.

V8s 302 CID STD. (400 or 460 CID V8s AVAIL.)

WAGON INTERIOR (VINYL)

GRAN TORINO H/T

Gran Torino Squire $5021. (3-SEAT) [WEST]

$3797. UP (WEST) $3411. UP (EAST)

(76290 BLT.)

(BROUGHAMS ALSO AVAILABLE)

new GRILLES new OPERA WINDOWS IN COUPES

GRAN TORINO ELITE

new (96604 BLT.) ('74½)

DASH

$4437.

$4752. WEST

DUAL OPERA WINDOWS

FORD TORINO 73~74

Ford Torino. Under $4,000.*

with automatic transmission,
power front disc brakes, power steering,
V-8, steel-belted radials

*($3957.)

(22928 BLT.)

new 26½ GAL. GAS TANK

$4883.

GRAN TORINO BROUGHAM
2-DR. H/T

4-DR.

(3183 BLT.)

('76)

75-76

351 CID V8 (148 HP)
G78 x14 TIRES

(400 OR 460 CID V8s OPT. IN ELITE)

TORINO

$4336.

(1329 BLT.)

COMBINED (23951 BLT.)

SQUIRE

GRAN TORINO $4673.

Gran Torino Squire

$4952.

(1975 EXAMPLES SHOWN, UNLESS OTHERWISE INDICATED)

TORINO

('76)

SQUIRE VINYL UPHOLSTERY

UNDER $4200.*

(34518 BLT.)

a lot of car for about $4200.*

For about the same kind of money as a little 4-passenger foreign car
you can choose a 6-passenger '76 Torino with a standard V-8,
automatic transmission, power front disc brakes, power steering,
steel belted radials, solid state ignition, and more.

*($4172.)

('76)

H/T **Torino**

HR 78 x 15 TIRES

▲ The Beautiful Standard Elite Interior.

(146,475 BLT.)
('76)

(ELITES AFTER JAN., 1975 DO NOT
HAVE SEAT-BELT INTERLOCK SYSTEM.)

ELITE WHEEL COVERS

▲ Full Wheel Covers. Standard at no extra cost.

▲ Luxury Wheel Covers. Thunderbird inspired, add a nice dress-up touch.

▲ Wire Wheel Covers. Classic styling in the finest European tradition.

▲ Deep-Dish Aluminum Wheels. A sporty look, with bright chrome lugs.

FORD TORINO (and ELITE) 75~76

ELITE

TORINO/ELITE REPLACED BY 1977 FORD LTD II.

$4879.

('76)

434

FRAZER

(1946—1951)

123½" W.B.
(THROUGH '51)

(REPLACES PRE-WAR GRAHAM.)

47
F-47

EARLY FRAZERS (BLT. 1946) have PAINTED GRILLE.

LATER MODEL, with CHROME GRILLE ➝

EMBLEM

JE SUIS PRET

100 HP @ 3600 RPM (112 HP OPTIONAL IN "MANHATTAN")

7.3 COMPRESS.

6 CYL., L-HEAD CONTINENTAL ENGINES 226.2 CID (USED IN ALL FRAZERS)

F47 = STANDARD SEDAN (36,120 BLT.) – $2295.
F47C = MANHATTAN " (32,655 BLT.) – $2712.

F485(1) = STANDARD SEDAN (29,480 BLT.) – $2483.
F486(1) = MANHATTAN " (18,591 BLT.) – $2746.

SEE ALSO:
KAISER

(SAME ENGS. AS 1947)

3 5/16" × 4 3/8" BORE and STROKE (KAISER SPECS. SIMILAR)

FRAZER REAR VIEW

new = 4 FRONT BUMPER GUARDS

(EARLIEST '48s SOMETIMES CONSIDERED "1947½.")

48 A

F-485 ; (MANHATTAN SEDAN IS NOW F-486)

ILLUSTRATED ON FAMOUS "17-MILE-DRIVE," AT PEBBLE BEACH, CALIF.

ALL FRAZERS ARE 4-DOOR MODELS.

FRAZER 47 ~ 48 (A)

FRAZER

4 8 B
(CONT'D.)

JOSEPH W. FRAZER (left) and HENRY J. KAISER (right,) STANDING BY THE 200,000th CAR (A 1948 FRAZER) TO BE BUILT BY THE KAISER-FRAZER CORP.

J.W. FRAZER

H.J. KAISER

(24,923 TOTAL '49~'50 PROD.)

49-50

112 HP (ALL)

$**2595.**

1949 = F-495 OR F-496 MANHTN.

VAGABOND (HATCHBACK!) PRICED FROM $**2321.**

F-505 and F-506 MANHATTAN are 1950 MODELS.

MANHATTAN SEDAN has HEAVY BAND of SIDE CHROME

new LARGE GRILLE and PARKING LIGHTS

(1950 MODEL ENDS 2-50)

(9950 ? BLT.)

H.P. INCREASED TO 115

(RESTYLED) F-515 OR F-516 MANHATTAN

51

(1951 MODELS START FEB., 1950)

F 515 STANDARD
5151 SEDAN (6931 BLT.?); 5155 VAGABOND (3000 BLT.)
F 516 MANHATTAN
5161 4-DR. H/T (152 BLT.)
5162 4-DR. CONVERTIBLE (131 BLT.)

4-DOOR CVT.
SEDAN

new "MANHATTAN" LOOKS LIKE THE 4-DR. CVT., BUT has STEEL PAINTED OR NYLON-PADDED TOP SECTION. (SAME PRICE AS CVT. SEDAN)

VAGABOND

$**3075.**

$**2399.**

DASH (SIMILAR TO 1949)

$**2359.**

STD. SEDAN
FRAZER 48 (B) ~ 51

436

EXPERIMENTAL SAFETY CAR BLT. 1945 TO 1947 BY
H. GORDON HANSEN,
AT SAN LORENZO, CALIF.

FORD V8
ENGINE

GORDON DIAMOND

156" WB BETWEEN FRONT REAR
SINGLE WHEELS. ANOTHER PAIR OF
WHEELS "AMIDSHIPS."
PURCHASED BY HARRAH'S AUTOMOBILE COLLECTION

GRAHAM (and HUPMOBILE)

6-CYL.
L-HEAD
ENGINES

115"
WB

FORMER CORD
BODY DIES
USED

40-41

'41 GRAHAM:
$895. and up
'40 HUPP:
$1145. and up

GRAHAM "HOLLYWOOD" and
HUPMOBILE "SKYLARK" LOOK ALMOST ALIKE!

GRAHAM (GRAHAM~PAIGE CORP.)
ANCESTRY TO POSTWAR KAISER-FRAZER CORP.

GREGORY

(1949)   (ANOTHER EXPER.
MODEL, 1952)

BEN GREGORY, MFR.,
KANSAS CITY, MO.

4-CYL. Continental
REAR ENGINE
FRONT-WHEEL-
DRIVE

49

PRODUCTION ATTEMPTED

40 HP
94" WB

$1050. (PROPOSED
PRICE)

(1948-1949)

HOPPENSTAND

HOPPENSTAND MOTORS, INC., GREENVILLE, PA.

2-CYL. FLAT, AIR-COOLED, REAR ENG.

48-49

(FULL PRODUCTION NEVER ACHIEVED.)
G and H (MSC.)

HENRY J (KAISER-FRAZER CORP) FOLLOWS ———>

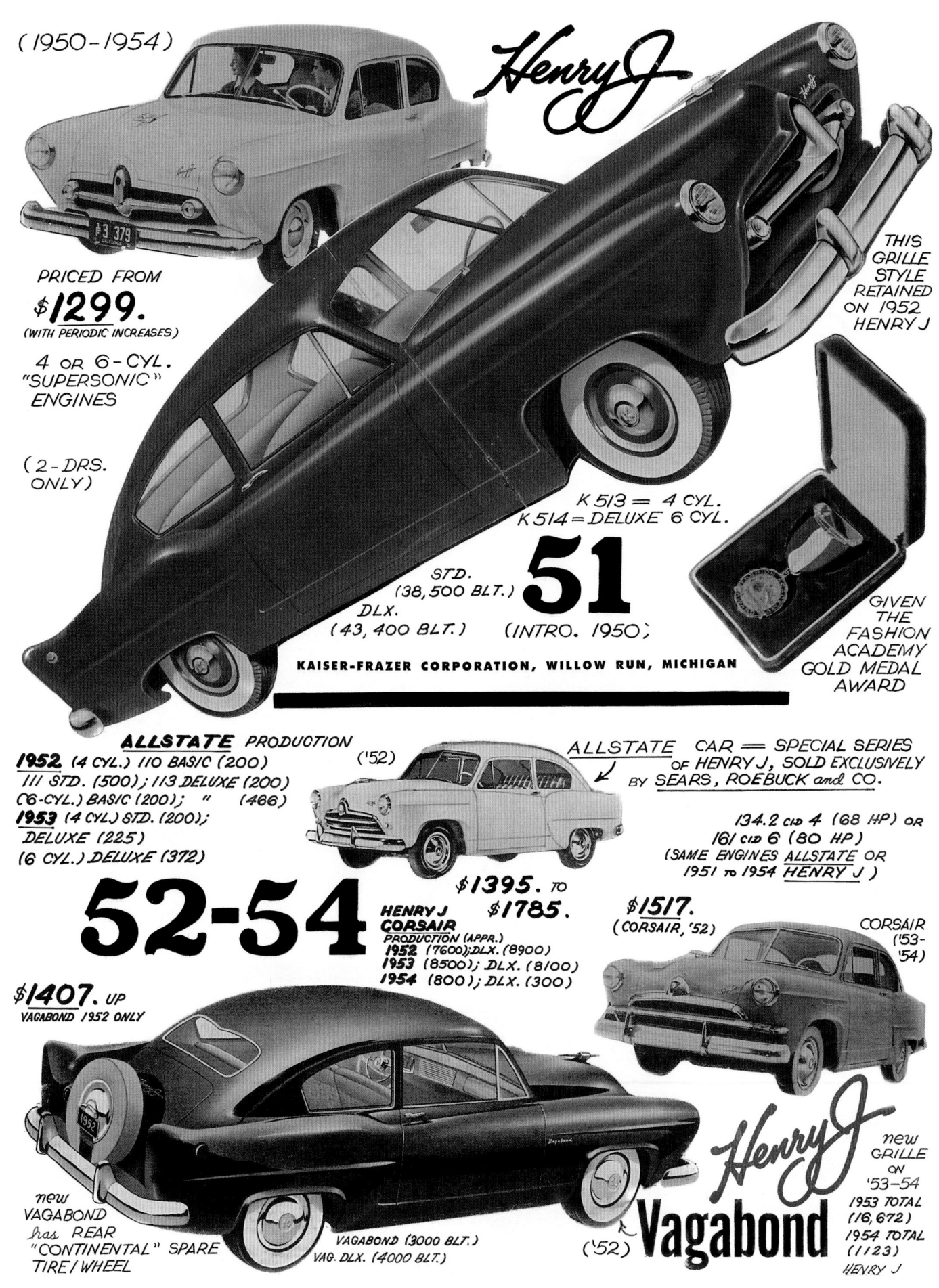

(1950-1954)

Henry J

PRICED FROM
$1299.
(WITH PERIODIC INCREASES)

4 OR 6-CYL.
"SUPERSONIC"
ENGINES

(2-DRS.
ONLY)

THIS
GRILLE
STYLE
RETAINED
ON 1952
HENRY J

K 513 = 4 CYL.
K 514 = DELUXE 6 CYL.

STD.
(38,500 BLT.)
DLX.
(43,400 BLT.)

51
(INTRO. 1950)

GIVEN
THE
FASHION
ACADEMY
GOLD MEDAL
AWARD

KAISER-FRAZER CORPORATION, WILLOW RUN, MICHIGAN

ALLSTATE PRODUCTION
1952 (4 CYL.) 110 BASIC (200)
111 STD. (500); 113 DELUXE (200)
(6-CYL.) BASIC (200); " (466)
1953 (4 CYL.) STD. (200);
DELUXE (225)
(6 CYL.) DELUXE (372)

('52)

ALLSTATE CAR = SPECIAL SERIES
OF HENRY J, SOLD EXCLUSIVELY
BY SEARS, ROEBUCK and CO.

134.2 CID 4 (68 HP) OR
161 CID 6 (80 HP)
(SAME ENGINES ALLSTATE OR
1951 TO 1954 HENRY J)

52-54

$1395. TO
$1785.

HENRY J
CORSAIR
PRODUCTION (APPR.)
1952 (7600); DLX. (8900)
1953 (8500); DLX. (8100)
1954 (800); DLX. (300)

$1517.
(CORSAIR, '52)

CORSAIR
('53-
'54)

$1407. UP
VAGABOND 1952 ONLY

new
VAGABOND
has REAR
"CONTINENTAL" SPARE
TIRE/WHEEL

VAGABOND (3000 BLT.)
VAG. DLX. (4000 BLT.)

('52)

Henry J
Vagabond

new
GRILLE
ON
'53-54
1953 TOTAL
(16,672)
1954 TOTAL
(1123)
HENRY J

70 HORSEPOWER

HORIZON

1978 to 1990
BY PLYMOUTH

WITH VOLKSWAGEN 4 CYL. 104.7 CID ENGINE

99.2" WB
FROM $3981.

155/80 x 13 TIRES

$3706*
38/25†
HWY CITY

*= SALE PRICE

(106,772 BLT.)

GRAIN TRIM (ABOVE)

DODGE OMNI SPECS. SIMILAR

WHEN YOU WANT TO GO ANYWHERE IN COMFORT AND CONFIDENCE.
RELAX. PLYMOUTH HORIZON CAN HANDLE IT.

new 78

THAT'S IMAGINATION. THAT'S PLYMOUTH.

$4469. ('79)
$5526.

99048 BLT., 1979
94740 " 1980

new TC-3 2-DR.
2+2 FASTBACK (HATCHBACK)
$4801. ('79)

79-80

96.7" WB ON 2-DR.

ORIG. TYPE CONT'D. WITH VARIED TRIM and OPTIONS

1980 PRICES:
$5265. (4-DR.)
5611. (2-DR.)
(PRICES VARY)

2-DR. has BODY and GRILLE STYLE UNLIKE 4-DR.
(63715 BLT. 1979; 67738 BLT., 1980)

DASH (TC-3, 1979)

WITH "SPORT APPEARANCE" TRIM

1980 COLORS

HP CUT TO 65 (1980)

HORIZON

COLORS

Frost Blue Metallic
Teal Tropic Green Metallic
Crimson Red Metallic
Burnished Silver Metallic
Spinnaker White
Bright Yellow
Formal Black

Mocha Brown Metallic
Graphic Blue
Graphic Red
Baron Red
Natural Suede Tan
Light Cashmere
Nightwatch Blue

Two-Tone Colors Four-Door
Baron Red/ Natural Suede Tan
Burnished Silver Metallic/ Formal Black
Nightwatch Blue/ Frost Blue Metallic
Light Cashmere/ Natural Suede Tan

TC3
Spinnaker White/ Graphic Red
Frost Blue Metallic/ Nightwatch Blue
Natural Suede Tan/ Mocha Brown Metallic

TC3 Sport Package
Burnished Silver Metallic/ Flat Black
Graphic Red/Flat Black
Bright Yellow/Flat Black
Graphic Blue/Flat Black

439

HUDSON *(1909~1957)*

for 1940...

PRODUCTION
87, 915 (6)
77, 295 (8)

6

$670

New Hudson Six Convertible Sedan, for 6 passengers, $955* (white sidewall tires extra)

$955.

THE ONLY DOUBLE-SAFE BRAKES (PATENTED)!
"Double-safe" because, if hydraulics *should* fail, you just push farther on the same foot pedal, and STOP. Easy-action parking brake gives a *third* braking system. Many authorities say this *complete* braking protection should be required in *all* cars. Today, only Hudson offers it.

NOW! NEW SAFETY VISION... NEW RICHNESS AND BEAUTY!
One of those ideas so simple and practical that nobody ever thought of it before is this new Hudson windshield design, shown below. Clear vision safety glass runs right down to the top of the hood . . . no projecting mouldings to block your view. You see farther up and down, as well as having side-to-side vision already wider than in any other car.

40
A
(RESTYLED)
6 OR 8 CYL.
113, 118 OR
125" WB

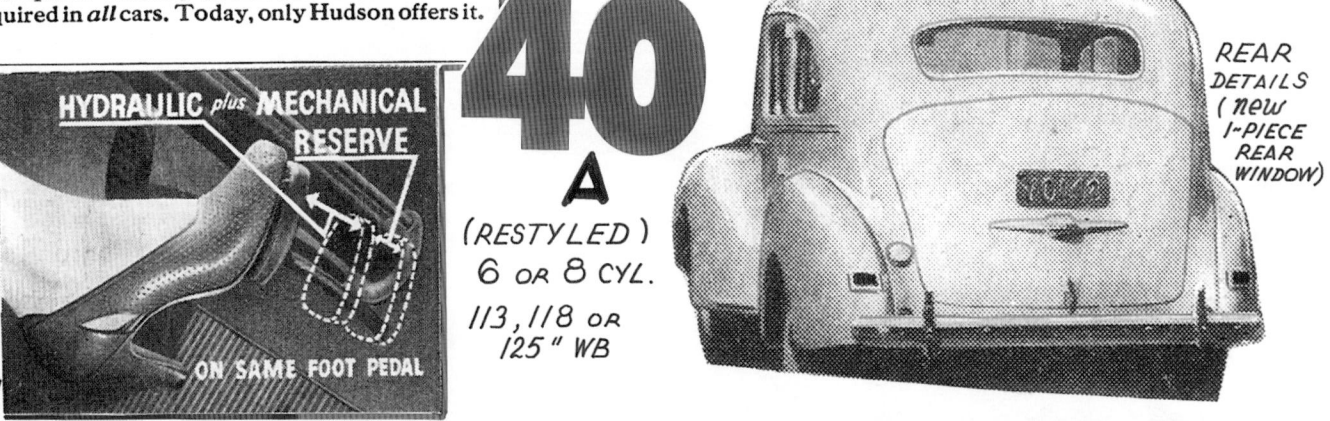

HYDRAULIC *plus* MECHANICAL RESERVE

ON SAME FOOT PEDAL

REAR
DETAILS
(*new*
1-PIECE
REAR
WINDOW)

Safety!

THE   CAR   TO   SEE   WITH   THE   "OTHER   THREE"
Car shown is new Hudson Six Touring Sedan, $763*, delivered in Detroit

L-HEAD 6-CYL.
175 CID 6
92 HP @ 4000 RPM
OR
212 CID 6
102 HP @ 4000 RPM
40 T-TRAVELER
40 P-DELUXE
41 — SUPER 6
43 — COUNTRY CLUB 6

Hudson Six

$763.

(CONT'D. NEXT PAGE) 40 HUDSON (A)

HUDSON

6 WITH OPT. OVERDRIVE →

UP TO **32.66 MILES PER GALLON**

SAFETY HOOD—PLUS THEFT PROTECTION! (OPENS at REAR and LOCKS)

← "COUNTRY CLUB" INTERIOR

NOW! AMAZING ROOMINESS . . . UNMATCHED COMFORT!

AIRFOAM SEAT CUSHIONS! Hudson was first.

AUTO-POISE CONTROL

INDEPENDENT FRONT WHEEL SPRINGING

NOW! THE SMOOTHEST RIDE OF YOUR LIFE!
In every 1940 Hudson, you're pillowed by the finest independent front wheel suspension of the type used only on very costly cars . . . with positive wheel control

for **1940** B *(CONT'D.)*

HUDSON 8 HAS THIS TALL TRIANGULAR EMBLEM HERE.

$952. UP
FOR 8-CYL. 4 DR. SEDANS

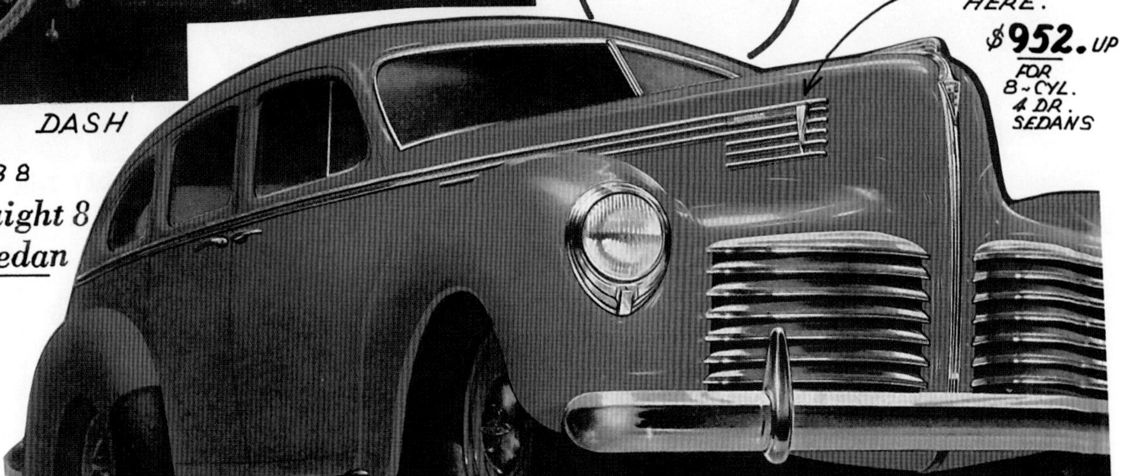

44 – 8
45 – DELUXE 8
47 – COUNTRY CLUB 8

DASH

Straight 8
(Country Club Sedan
HAS LONGER FRONT DOORS)

254.4 CID
STRAIGHT~8
128 HP
@ 4200 RPM
(IN SERIES
44, 45 and 47)

48-"BIG BOY"

40 HUDSON (B)

41 HUDSON

NEW

41

STATION WAGON

$1298. up

new DASH

6 OR 8 CYL.

FORGET THE CLUTCH PEDAL WITH HUDSON'S VACUMOTIVE DRIVE

A WHALE OF A LOT OF CAR FOR MIGHTY LITTLE MONEY

SIX 2-DR.

REAR

DELUXE 6 SEDAN
$846.

new CONCAVE CENTER SECTION

MORE PIECES IN NEW GRILLE

new 116, 121 and 128" WBs

AN INSTANT Tells You the Difference in BEAUTY! Inside, outside, Hudson carries out a *complete* color scheme—in green, tones of blue and gray, or brown and tan! That's the Symphonic Styling you hear so much about. *It doesn't cost one cent extra.*
(SEE ILLUSTR. UPPER LEFT)

A MINUTE in Traffic Tells You the Difference in EASY DRIVING! Go, back up, stop —forget the clutch pedal! Hudson's <u>Vacumotive Drive</u> is the lowest cost feature on the market that *completely* eliminates clutch pedal pushing*. A Hudson's a honey to steer and shift, too—and remember, Overdrive is AVAILABLE.

*-$27.50 EXTRA

EVERY DAY Tells You the Difference in ECONOMY!

$ MORE FOR YOUR MONEY IN *EASY HANDLING!*

AMERICA'S SAFEST CAR

$695 and up
41 HUDSON

HUDSON
SETS THE PACE FOR '42

SUPER 6
CLUB COUPE

$1090.

$946.

DE LUXE 6
2-DR. SEDAN

FROM CAR TO SLEEPING COMPARTMENT IN 5 MINUTES... with the new Hudson Sleeper Kit, a low cost extra. A few simple adjustments of the rear seat, a quick tucking in of sheets and blankets—and you're ready for a real night's rest.

40,661 =
TOTAL PRODUCTION
FOR 1942
MODEL YEAR
(6) 34,069
(8) 6592

LEATHER-TRIMMED FABRIC UPH.
(SUPER 6)

Three buttons on the instrument panel are used in connection with the Hudson Drive-Master. When the right button is depressed, gear shifting and clutch operation are eliminated in second and high

A courtesy light illuminates the running boards when the doors are opened at night

42

new
LOWER GRILLE;
FLARED BODY
SIDES

DRIVE HUDSON MASTER

NEW

COMMODORE 8

The facilities and organization of the automotive industry can be used to great advantage in the nation's defense program. We at Hudson recognize this obligation and have enlisted our services extensively in defense manufacturing.

42 HUDSON

HUDSON 1942

NOW ON DISPLAY... NEW 1942 HUDSON SIX • SUPER-SIX • COMMODORE SERIES (Sixes and Eights)

HUDSON

POSTWAR PRODUCTION RESUMES
8-30-45. 5,005 BLT. 1945;
93,870 BLT. 1946

46

121" WB ON ALL (THROUGH '47)
PRICED FROM
$1481.

SUPER 6

BROUGHAM CVT.
(1035 BLT.)
$1879.

COMM. has
2 VERT.
STRIPS
ON REAR
WINDOW

new GRILLE with RECESSED
CENTER SECTION

COMMODORE (has
HUDSON TRIANGLE EMBLEM AT FRONT END OF CHROME BELT STRIP)

ENGINES (SINCE 1946) =
2/2 CID 6 (102 HP)
OR 254 CID STRAIGHT-8 (128 HP)

SUPER 6 = $1628. up   SUPER 8 = $1855. up
COMMODORE 6 = $1887. up
COMMODORE 8 = $1955. up

$1896.

SUPER 6
SEDAN
$1749.

47

103,310
BLT. 1947

COMMODORE 6
SEDAN

SIMILAR TO 1946, BUT has
HEAVIER CHROME MOULDING MARGIN
AROUND MEDALLION OVER GRILLE.

MODELS = **SUPER 6** (49,388 BLT. '48; 91,333 BLT. '49) 4 DR. SED.; 2 DR. BROUGH.; CPE.; CLUB CPE.; CVT.
COMMODORE 6 (27,159 BLT. '48; 32,715 BLT. '49) 4 DR. SEDAN; CLUB COUPE; CONVERTIBLE
SUPER 8 (5338 BLT. '48; 6365 BLT. '49) 4 DR. SEDAN; CLUB COUPE; ('49 = 2-DR. BROUGHAM)
COMMODORE 8 (35,315 BLT. '48; 28,687 BLT. '49) 4-DR. SEDAN; CLUB COUPE; CONVERTIBLE

144,119 BLT. 1948

142,462 BLT. 1949

CVTS. NOW HAVE MORE
METAL ABOVE WINDSHIELD

new "Step Down" BODIES
SURROUNDED BY FRAME

INTERIOR
('49)

48-49

(TOTALLY
RESTYLED)

new
124" WB ON ALL

" This time it's *Hudson* "

(BIGGEST CHANGE IN HUDSON HISTORY)

WITH "The New Step-Down Ride"

HUDSON 46~49

444

Hudson

new PACEMAKER 6 is LOWER-PRICED SERIES (119" WB)

$1933.

REAR SEAT VIEW

ROAD CLEARANCE

50

INVERTED "V" ON new GRILLE

• NOW—3 GREAT SERIES • LOWER-PRICED PACEMAKER • FAMOUS SUPER • CUSTOM COMMODORE

SEDAN

COMMODORE
$2282. (6)
$2366. (8)

Hudson is the only motor car with a recessed floor ("step-down" design). This results in the lowest-built car of them all, with true streamlining and magnificent beauty. It provides full road clearance and the most room in any automobile at any price! It creates America's lowest center of gravity, which brings you the best and safest ride ever.

124" WB ON ALL MODELS EXCEPT PACEMAKER and PACEMAKER DELUXE

ENGINES :
232 cid 6 (112 HP) (PACEMAKER)
262 cid 6 (123 HP)
254 cid STRAIGHT-8 (128 HP)

143,586 BLT. 1950

(COUPE = $1965.)

92,859 BLT. 1951

51

PACEMAKER 6

$2642. CVT. (430 BLT.)

SUPER 6

$2238.

2-DR. BROUGHAM

COMMODORE 8 CLUB COUPE
$2543.

new GRILLE (HEAVIER and ARCHED)

$2568.

new HORNET 6 = WITH new 308 cid 6 (145 HP) "HORNET" ENGINE. (3 OTHER HUDSON ENGINES CONT'D. FROM '50)

"Monobilt" BODY/FRAME CONSTRUCTION
HUDSON .50~.51

HUDSON
YOUR BEST BUY FOR THE LONG TOMORROW

445

$2264.

PACEMAKER 6   BROUGHAMS

COMMODORE 6

HUDSON WASP TWO-DOOR BROUGHAM $2413.

CVT. (20 BLT.)

new HUDSON WASP with 6-CYL. "H-127" ENG.
Hollywood H/T (new)

$2812.

HOLLYWOOD WASP   (1320 BLT.)

CLUB CPE. $2466.

$3247.

$2742.
HORNET CLUB CPE.

new lower-priced running mate

52

HUDSON HORNET
SEDAN

$2789.

SEDAN

HORNET

equipped with
B-W OVERDRIVE!
(OPTIONAL)

HUDSON   ENGINEERING
B-W PRODUCTION

79,117
BLT. 1952

HYDRA-MATIC DRIVE
available for all '52 Hudsons
at extra cost.

$3342.

COMM. 8 CONVERTIBLE
(ONLY 30 BLT.)

ENGINES :
232 CID 6 (112 HP) (PACEMAKER)
262 CID 6 (127 HP) (WASP, CMDR. 6)
308 CID 6 (145 HP) (HORNET)
254 CID STRAIGHT 8
(128 HP) (COMMODORE 8)

Hudson-Aire Hardtop Styling
at standard sedan and coupe prices

COMMODORE 8

HUDSON 52

FINAL
YEAR FOR
STRAIGHT 8

446

HUDSON

2-DR. SEDAN

53

ENGINES:
232 CID 6 (127 HP) (WASP)
308 CID 6 (145, 160 OR 170 HP)
(HORNET)

HORNET
SEDAN $2769.

SUPER WASP $2413.
119" WB

1953 PRODUCTION:
4C WASP ; 5C SUPER WASP (17,792)
7C HORNET (27,208)

6-CYL.
MODELS ONLY
(THROUGH
1954)

new
HOOD
"AIR-SCOOP"
and new GRILLE
w/o INVERTED "V."

124" WB

(The JETS
SHOWN ON "JET" PAGE)

The WASPS $2466.
in the low-medium
price field

SUPER
WASP

new HIGH
TAIL-LIGHTS

HUDSON DIVISION OF
AMERICAN MOTORS
(RESULT of MERGER WITH NASH,
5-1-54)

new 1-PC.
WINDSHIELD

The HORNET
in the medium price field
$2769.

CLUB COUPES

$2619.

new FRONT END
DESIGN

54A
(RESTYLED)

NEW HORNET SPECIAL
available in Four-Door Sedan, Club Sedan
and Club Coupe—all at new low prices

$2571.

new 262 CID 6 ADDED
(140 HP) SU. WASP

2-DR.
CLUB
SEDAN

HORNET has
160 HP

(170 HP with
"Twin H" Power)

4 DR.
SEDAN

INTERIOR of HOLLYWOOD
(CAR ILLUS. NEXT PAGE)

$2619.

new CHROME PC. ON SIDE

HUDSON

54B
(CONT'D.)

$2988.

HORNET HOLLYWOOD H/T

32,293 HUDSON CARS BLT. 1954

52,688 BLT. 1955 ("HUDSON" NAME also USED on SOME Ramblers and Metropolitans)

CUSTOM WASP SEDAN
$2460.

new SHORTER WHEELBASES
WASP 114.3"
HORNET 121.3"

new ENGINE CHOICES

V8 CHAMPIONSHIP 6

55
(TOTALLY RESTYLED with NASH BODY DESIGN)

HOLLYWOOD H/T

320 CID PACKARD V8 USED

new PEAKS OVER HEADLIGHTS

BIG new DIAMOND-SHAPED GRILLE

22,588 BLT. 1956

HOLLYWOOD H/T

56

SEDAN   DASH

ENGINES: 202 CID 6 (120 or 130 HP) (WASP)
308 CID 6 (165 or 175 HP) (HORNET)
320 CID V8 (208 HP) (HORNET V8, to MARCH, 1956)
250 CID V8 (190 HP) (" ", MARCH, 1956 on)

HUDSON 54~56

WASP SEDAN (2519 BLT.) **HORNET SPECIAL** SED. (1528 BLT.); H/T (229 BLT.); **HORNET** SUPER, CUSTOM SEDANS (3022 BLT.); H/T (358 BLT.) **HORNET V8** SEDAN (1962 BLT.); H/T (1053 BLT.)

$2214. - $3159. PRICE RANGE

HUDSON

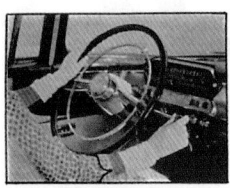

DASH

with new Hydra-Matic

new
SIDE TRIM
MOULDINGS

HORNET
SUPER

Lower outside by 2 full inches

Hornet V-8

121.3" W.B.

IS ONLY AVAIL.
MODEL (SUPER
OR CUSTOM)

327
CID

World's newest V-8 . . . 255 hp

57

new "V" EMBLEM
ON GRILLE

ONLY 1 V8 ENG. AVAIL.
(NO 6-CYL. MODELS)

ONLY 4,080
BLT. 1957 *
(OTHER SOURCES
SAY 3876 BLT.,
OR ONLY 1345)

HORNET HOLLYWOOD H/T
(APPEARS LONGER IN
← PHOTO AT LEFT
THAN IN PHOTO ABOVE)

Slim outside for easy maneuvering

(DISCONTINUED
JUNE 25, 1957)

. . . way up in power, way down in price!

357-1 **HORNET SUPER** SEDAN	**$2821.**
HOLLYWOOD H/T	**$2911.**
357-2 **HORNET CUSTOM** SEDAN	**$3011.**
HOLLYWOOD H/T	**$3101.**

* HIGHER PRODUCTION
FIGURES MAY INCLUDE
"HUDSON" RAMBLERS and
METROPOLITANS.

IMP

INTERNATIONAL MOTOR PRODUCTS
CO., GLENDALE, CALIF.

49-50

FIBERGLASS BODY
63" WB   APPR. 475 lbs.
1-CYL., 7-H.P. GLADDEN engine
HUDSON / IMP

(1949-50)

SOME REPORTS
LIST FINAL DATE AS 1955.

IMPERIAL

54

CUSTOM (C-64)
133½" WB
$4260.

(4324 BLT.)

(EARLIER MODELS ILLUSTRATED WITH CHRYSLER.)

IMPERIAL CONSIDERED A TOP-LINE CHRYSLER SERIES, 1926 to 1954.

331.1 CID V8 (3¹³⁄₁₆ × 3⅝)
235 HP @ 4400 RPM

CROWN (C-66)   145½" WB

7.5 COMPR. (SINCE '51)

| 8-PASS. SEDAN (23 BLT.) | $6922. |
| 8-PASS. LIMOUSINE (77 BLT.) | $7044. |

55

SEDAN (7840 BLT.)
$4483.

$4720.

NEWPORT H/T (3418 BLT.)

new 331 CID V8 (3.81 × 3.63)
250 HP @ 4600 RPM

IMPERIAL (C-69) 130" WB

CROWN IMPERIAL (C-70) 149½" WB (THROUGH '56)

(IMPERIAL CONSIDERED AN INDIVIDUAL MAKE, AS OF 1955.)

new 8.5 COMPRESSION

IMPERIAL (C-73)
new 133" WB
SEDAN (6821 BLT.)
$4832.

354 CID; 280 HP @ 4600 RPM

SOUTHAMPTON H/T (2094 BLT.)

$5094.

56

$7603. UP
CROWN IMPERIAL (C-70)

SOUTHAMPTON 4-DR. H/T ALSO AVAIL. IMPERIAL 54~56

IMPERIAL

(IMI-2) CROWN

$5598. CVT. (1167 BLT.)

new 129" WB (THROUGH '66)

new 392 CID (THROUGH '58)
325 HP @ 4600 RPM
new 9.25 COMPR.

57

new 129" WB (THROUGH '66)

note DIFFERENCES IN NUMBER OF HEADLIGHTS

SEDAN (1729 BLT.)

SEDAN (3642 BLT.)

CROWN (IMI-2) $5406.

LE BARON (IMI-4) $5743.

LYI-L IMPERIAL   SOUTHAMPTON H/T (1801 BLT.); SOUTHAMPTON 4-DR. H/T (3336 BLT.); SEDAN (1926 BLT.)
LYI-M CROWN   "   "   (1939 BLT.);   "   "   " (4146 BLT.);   "   (1240 BLT.);
   CONVERTIBLE (675 BLT.) **LE BARON**   "   "   " (538 BLT.);   "   (501 BLT.)
                           (LYI-H)   **CROWN IMPERIAL** LIMO. (31 BLT.)
                                       ($15,075.)

(538 BLT.)
LE BARON
SOUTHAMPTON

new 10.0 COMPRESSION
345 HP @ 4600 RPM

FENDER-GRILLE DETAILS

LYI SERIES
$5969.

58

IMPERIAL NAME (NON-LE BARONS)

IMPERIAL 57-58

451

IMPERIAL

CUSTOM SOUTHAMPTON (MYI-L)

$6103.

$4910.

(1743 BLT.)

59

LE BARON SOUTHAMPTON (622 BLT.) (MYI-H)

LE BARON

CROWN (MYI-M)
new 413 CID, 10.1 COMPR. (THROUGH '65) 350 HP @ 4600 RPM (THROUGH 61) '65)

(ALSO 392 CID V8 (325 HP) IN CROWN IMPERIAL)

$4910.-$6103. PRICE RANGE

ALSO, 7 CROWN IMPERIAL LIMOS.
AT $15,075. EA.

(PYI-M) CROWN

SEDAN (1594 BLT.)
$5647.

60

(PYI-L) CUSTOM SOUTHAMPTON

$4933.
TO
$6318.
PRICE RANGE

(1498 BLT.)
$4923.

CUSTOM 4-DOOR SOUTHAMPTON (3953 BLT.)

$5029.

new
8.20 × 15 TIRES
(THROUGH '64)

(PY3-H) LE BARON

IMPERIAL 59~60

IMPERIAL

CROWN
(RYI-M)
CVT.
(429 BLT.)

$5774.

129"
WB

SOUTHAMPTON

new "FREE-STANDING HEADLIGHTS (THROUGH '63)

61

$4923. - $6426. PRICE RANGE

9 CRN. IMPL. LIMOS. BLT. $16,500.
(149½" WB)

(RYI- SERIES)

new GRILLE

America's Most Carefully Built Car

H/T
SYI-L CUSTOM #912 SOUTHAMPTON (826 BLT.); #914 SOUTHAMPTON 4-DR. H/T (3587 BLT.)
SYI-M CROWN #922 SOUTHAMPTON H/T (1010 BLT.); SOUTHAMPTON 4-DR. H/T (#924) (6911 BLT.); CVT. (#925) (554 BLT.)
SYI-H LE BARON #934 " 4-DR. H/T (1449 BLT.)

$4920. – $6422. PRICE RANGE

129" WB

$6422.

ORNAMENT at HOOD
FRONT ; new
SPLIT
GRILLE

IMPERIAL LE BARON 4-DR. SOUTHAMPTON (SYI-H)

(CUSTOM
is SYI-L)

CROWN
(SYI-M) $5400.

62

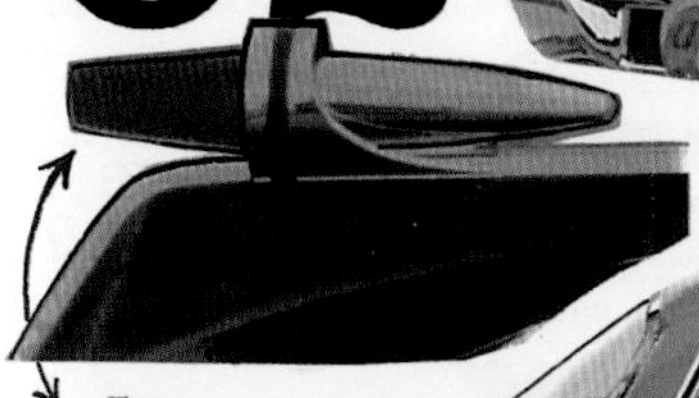

RAISED
TAIL-LIGHTS

HP REDUCED TO
340 @ 4600 RPM
(THROUGH '65)

two-door Southampton

4-DR.
SOUTHAMPTON
$5644.

IMPERIAL 61

453

IMPERIAL

CROWN
(TYI-M)
$5656.

WHEEL COVER

4-DR. H/T (6960 BLT.)

HIGH, NARROW TAIL-LIGHTS

$5058.

(FINAL YEAR FOR "CUSTOM" SERIES.)

(TYI-L) CUSTOM

DASH

63
(TYI SERIES)

(HAND-BUFFED ACRYLIC ENAMELS)

H/T (749 BLT.)

(TYI-H)

IMPERIAL Le BARON

The LeBaron cloisonné crest on the roof makes this the only car on which this federal jewelry excise tax is paid.

FREE-STANDING HEADLIGHTS FOR 3RD AND FINAL YEAR

CLOSE-UP VIEW OF FRONT END   (new GRILLE)

$5058. - $6434. PRICE RANGE

CROWN IMPERIAL LIMOUSINE (13 BLT.)
$18,500.

IMPERIAL 63

454

IMPERIAL

CROWN COUPE (VYI-M)

$5581. (VYI-M)

Imperial Crown 4-Door Hardtop

$5739.

LE BARON (VYI-H)

CROWN CVT. DASH

$5770.

(VYI SERIES)

64

(TOTALLY RESTYLED; new DESIGN SOMEWHAT RESEMBLES LINCOLN CONTINENTAL.)

EAGLE CREST on LE BARON VINYL TOP →

AUTO PILOT (left)
AM/FM RADIO (above)

HEADLIGHTS MOVED INTO new SPLIT GRILLE.

The Incomparable IMPERIAL

VYI-M CROWN H/T (5233 BLT.); 4-DR. H/T (14,181 BLT.); CONVERTIBLE (922 BLT.)
VYI-H LE BARON 4 DR. H/T (2949 BLT.)
CROWN IMPERIAL LIMOUSINE (10 BLT.) $5581. – $6455. PRICE RANGE
       $18,500.   ($5865. to $6740., WEST COAST)

IMPERIAL 64

IMPERIAL

CROWN COUPE (AYI-M)

4-DR. H/T

$5772.

$5930.

REAR DETAILS

CHOICES OF UPH. INCL. REAL LEATHER

65 AYI SERIES

DASH ←

LIGHT FLASHES IF FUEL, OIL, TEMP. GAUGES NEED ATTENTION.

AIR COND. DUCTS (ON DASH)

HEADLIGHTS PAIRED BEHIND GLASS PANELS.

new GRILLE

(LE BARON IS AYI-H)

AYI-M **CROWN**   H/T (3974 BLT.); 4 DR. H/T (11,628 BLT.); CONVERTIBLE (633 BLT.)
AYI-H **LE BARON**   4 DR. H/T (2164 BLT.)

$5772. — $6596. PRICE RANGE

ALSO, 10 **CROWN IMPERIAL** LIMOUSINES, $18,500. EA.

IMPERIAL 65

IMPERIAL

(1926–1975 ; 1981–)

BY CHRYSLER CORPORATION

$5887.

129" WB

(514 BLT.) $6164.

(2373 BLT.)

$6505. (WEST COAST)
CROWN CPE. (H/T)

V8 ENGINE (SINCE '55)
new 440 C.I.D. (350 HP)
9.15 × 15 TIRES

66 BY3

BY3-M
CROWN SERIES
and BY3-H
$7158. LE BARON
4-DR. H/T

new GRILLE

$5733.

CONVERT. AVAIL. AT $6764. (WEST COAST)

(WEST COAST) FR. $6351. (4-DR. H/T)
(8977 BLT.)

THE INCOMPARABLE
IMPERIAL
Finest of the fine cars built
by Chrysler Corporation

(2193 BLT.) $5374.

IMPERIAL NAME SET IN new ALL-HORIZONTAL GRILLE

Imperial '67... the newest prestige automobile in a decade.

← new 4-DR. SEDAN ADDED $5991. (WEST COAST)

new SHORTER 127" WB

67 CYl

(INTRO. 9-29-66)

new CORNER LTS. IN FENDERS

CVT. (577 BLT.)
$6861. (WEST COAST)

IMPERIAL CONVERTIBLE DISCONTINUED AFTER 1968

$6244.

REAR

LE BARON LIMO. (163" WB)
WITH STAGEWAY BODY (6 BLT.) $15,000.

TOTAL 1966 PRODUCTION = 13,742	1966 CALENDAR YEAR : 17,653	
" 1967 " = 14,620	$5733.~6540. 1966 PRICE RANGE	
	5374.~17,000. 1967 " "	

IMPERIAL 66~67

457

IMPERIAL

If you want more than luxury in your luxury car

$6940.

CROWN
COUPE
$5722.
(2656 BLT.)

$6381.
(WEST COAST)

68

(1852 BLT.)

LE BARON
$7599.
(WEST COAST)
(INTRO. 9-14-67)
(FINAL CVT.)

CROWN
4-DR.
H/T
(WEST COAST)
$6774.

440 CID V8 (350 HP)

(360 HP WITH
DUAL EXHAUSTS)

$6115.
(8492 BLT.)

HEADLIGHTS
CONCEALED
IN
new
GRILLE.
"Imperial"
NAME ON GRILLE,
and CREST on
HOOD, REAR DECK.

note
TRIPLE
OPENINGS FOR
SAFETY LT.

440 CID V8 (350 HP)

LE BARON
2-DR. H/T
(new)
$5898.
(4592 BLT.)

VINYL-COVERED
TOP
BEARS
TRADITIONAL
IMPERIAL
EAGLE
MEDALLION

BLOCK-
LETTER
"IMPERIAL" NAME IN CENTER OF REAR
BUMPER

(823 BLT.)

69

(INTRO.
9-19-68)

$5770.

CROWN 4-DR. H/T   IMPERIAL 68-69

LE BARON
4-DR. H/T
$6131. (14,821 BLT.)

TOTALLY
RESTYLED WITH
BULGE-SIDED "FUSELAGE" STYLING

458

IMPERIAL

The LeBaron instrument panel

19 COLORS

Charcoal		
Formal Black		
Platinum	Deep Plum	
	Dark Emerald Metallic	
Jade Green Metallic	Jubilee Blue Metallic	
Bahama Blue Metallic	Navaho Beige	
Satin Tan Metallic	Champagne	
Deep Bronze Metallic	Walnut Metallic	Burgundy Metallic
Spinnaker White	Lime Green Metallic	Mystic Gold Metallic
Citron Gold Metallic	Teal Metallic	

127" WB

TOTAL 1970 PRODUCTION = 11822

REAR

FRONT

EMBLEM ABOVE GRILLE

$5779. ~ $6328.
PRICE RANGE

(6 RARE 163"~W.B. LIMOUSINES ALSO, AT $16500.)

70

9

4~DR. H/T (10116 BLT.) $6778. | HP CUT TO 335 |

1971 Imperial.
The most sophisticated automobile we've ever offered.

71   "YM" LE BARON ONLY (NO "CROWN" OR LIMO.)

(1442 2~DR. H/Ts ALSO BLT., AT $6632.)

← new

note "IMPERIAL" NAME ABOVE THE GRILLE

1971

No other American car offers this 4-wheel Sure-Brake. But the list of exclusive options doesn't stop there.

Imperial is the only luxury car to offer an AM/FM stereo cassette tape player available <u>with a microphone</u>. You can listen. <u>You can record</u>. You can even <u>record directly from the radio</u>.

Another luxury car exclusive — optional headlamp washers that not only rinse the lamps, but also scrub them clean with nylon brushes. *IMPERIAL 70~71*

IMPERIAL (SINCE 1971, REDUCED TO A TOP-LINE MODEL of CHRYSLER, RATHER THAN A SEPARATE MAKE AS SINCE 1955.

72 new GRILLE (INTRO. 9-28-71)

"BUTTERFLY" VENT WINDOWS ELIMINATED

HP CUT TO 225

CHRYSLER Plymouth — Coming through with the kind of car America wants.

2-DR. H/T (2332 BLT.) $6550. ($6795 WEST)

17 BODY COLORS

Silver Frost Metallic | Blue Sky | True Blue Metallic | Regal Blue Metallic | Burnished Red Metallic | Mist Green | Amber Sherwood Metallic | Forest Green Metallic | Sahara Beige | Coral Turquoise Metallic | Chestnut Metallic | Formal Black | Spinnaker White

Sun Fire Yellow | Honey Gold | Golden Haze Metallic | Tahitian Gold Metallic

DASH DIGITAL CLOCK

1:58 30 Chronometer

73

HP CUT TO 215

L84 x 15 TIRES (SINCE '71)

2-DR. H/T (2563 BLT.)

$6829.

IMP'L. PRODUCTION LIMITED ONLY TO LE BARON 2-DR. OR 4-DR. H/Ts, 1971 THRU 1975.

new ENERGY-ABSORBING BUMPERS

$7077. (WEST)

4-DR. H/T (14166 BLT.) $7057. ($7305, WEST)

VERTICAL GUARDS ON IMPROVED BUMPERS

new GRILLE WITH FINER PCS.

'74 PROD. = 14426
1975 PRODUCTION = 8830

HP UP TO 230 (215, 1975)

RESTYLED FOR 1974. (1975 SIMILAR) FEATURING DRAMATIC new NARROW "WATERFALL" GRILLE; new HEADLIGHT

new LR78 x 15 TIRES

4-DR. H/T ('75) $8844.

74 -75

HOOD ORNAMENT ADDED '74

(NO 1976 TO 1980 IMPERIALS)

IMPERIAL '72-75

22,089 JETS BLT. 1953

53 $1858. *and up* **JET** 6 CYLS. (1953-1954)

BY HUDSON

$1954.

SUPER JET   DASH

IN ALL THE WORLD
NO OTHER CAR LIKE THIS!

105" WB (THROUGH '54)

(ALSO 2-DR.
JET FAMILY CLUB SEDAN
and UTILITY SEDAN.)
$1621. UP
JET

$1885. $1858.
(WEST COAST)

54

GRILLE
MODIFIED

4-DR. SED.

5.90 x 15

SUPER-JET

$1933.

ITALIA
DASH

BUCKET SEATS

2-DR. CLUB SEDAN
(4 DR. ALSO AVAIL.)

$4800.

ITALIA

JET-LINER

(ONLY 26
BUILT, ON
SUPER-
JET
CHASSIS)
202 CID 6
(114 HP)
105" WB

$2057.
note
THAT EACH
SERIES IS
QUICKLY
IDENTIFIED
IN '54 BY AMOUNT OF
CHROME SIDE TRIM.

4-DR.
(2-DR. ALSO AVAIL.)

SEE ALSO: Hudson

TOTAL 1954 PRODUCTION =
14,224

1953 and 1954 ENGINE =
202 CID 6 (104 HP, or OPTIONAL 106/114 HP)

JET

461

KAISER

KAISER-FRAZER CORPORATION

● WILLOW RUN, MICHIGAN

(1946–1955)

EARLY MODEL, BUILT 1946

KAISER SPECIAL (65,062 BLT.)

with CORRUGATED BUMPER

SPECIAL = $**1868**.

CUSTOM = $**2547**.

AS IN FRAZER, 6 - CYL., L-HEAD CONTINENTAL ENG. (ON ALL) 226.2 CID
6.50 × 15" TIRES
123½" W.B.
(CUSTOM 5412 BLT.)

EMBLEM

47

KAISER 6

with PLAIN BUMPER

K-100 OR K-101 CUSTOM (112 HP)
(100 HP)

ALL OVER THE MAP — YOU'LL FIND EXPERT KAISER AND FRAZER SERVICE

K-F Distributors and parts warehouses   K-F Dealers, parts and service stations

(EARLIEST '48s SOMETIMES CONSIDERED "1947½.")

48

K-481 OR K-482 CUSTOM

$**1967**.
EARLY PRICES

$**2557**.
new
7.10 × 15" TIRES

SEE ALSO: *FRAZER*

ILLUSTRATED AT CAPE COD, MASS.

KAISER FACTORY-APPROVED PARTS AND **SERVICE** **FRAZER**

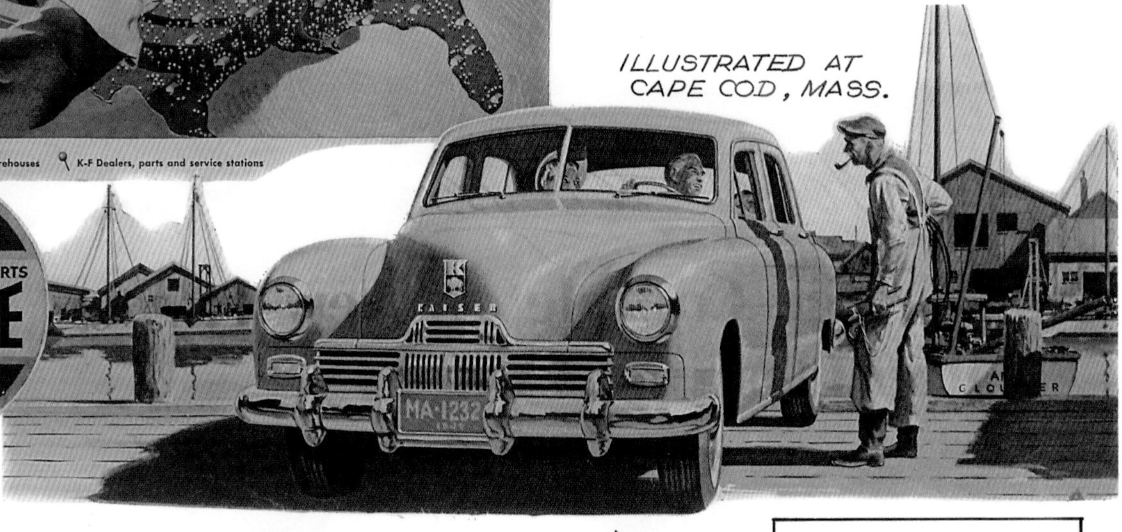

SPECIAL = (90,588 BLT.) $**2244**.

CUSTOM = (1263 BLT.) $**2466**.

1948 PRICES

4-DOOR SEDANS ONLY

226.2 CID 6-CYL. CONTINENTAL ENG. CONTINUES (100 OR 112 HP)

note 4 VERTICAL BUMPER GUARD ARRANGEMENT ('47½ -'48 ONLY)   KAISER 47~48

$3195.

new
4-DOOR
CONVERTIBLE
(54 BLT.)

new GRILLE

49-50

new 112 HP

"TRAVELER"
MODEL NAME
IN SCRIPT

TRAVELER
MODELS
FEATURE
FULL-OPENING
REAR
"HATCHBACK."

2-cars-in-one

$2088*
Kaiser Traveler
(22,000 BLT.)
(new)

$1995.
(SPECIAL)

$2195.
(DELUXE)

SPECIAL (29,000 BLT.)
DE LUXE
(38,250 BLT.)
SEDAN

REAR 3/4 VIEW OF
VIRGINIAN

new
GRILLE

new
VIRGINIAN

4-DOOR
HARDTOP
(946 BLT.)

GEAR RATIOS:
4.09; 3.91; 3.73
(OR 4.27 with OVERDRIVE)

$2995.

new BODY TYPES
(ALL 4-DOOR
MODELS)

KAISER 49~50

1950 MODELS
REPLACED MARCH, 1950
BY TOTALLY RESTYLED
1951 MODELS.

463

Kaiser

$2275.

new 2-door sedan DLX.

SEE ALSO:
"HENRY J"

new HORIZONTAL BLADE GRILLE →

K-511 = SPECIAL
K-512 = DE LUXE

19.51
(TOTALLY RESTYLED)

115 HP @ 3650 RPM

SPECIAL = TRAVELER UTILITY SED. 2 DR. (1500 BLT.); 4 DR. SED. (43,500 BLT.); BUSINESS COUPE (1500 "); 2 DR. SED. (10,000); 4 DR. TRAVELER (2000); CLUB CPE. (1500 BLT.) **DE LUXE** = 2 DR. " (1000 BLT.); 4 DR. SEDAN (70,000 BLT.); 2 DR. SEDAN (11,000 "); TRAVELER 4 DR. UTILITY SEDAN (1000 BLT.); CL. CPE. (6000 BLT.)

new HIGH, ARCHED TOP, WITH HUGE WINDOW AREA!

DELUXE 4-DOOR
$2328.

new 118½" WB

The newest car in America!

Anatomic Design*

$1992.-$2433.
PRICE RANGE

← HOOD ORNAMENT ADDED (ON ALL)

new "GOLDEN DRAGON" (*with* "ALLIGATOR" TYPE UPH., *etc.*)

HUBCAP VARIATION

Hydra-Matic
AUTO. TRANS. OPTIONAL (THROUGH '55; *also* OPT. ON 1951 FRAZER)

Built to Better the Best on the Road!

KAISER 51

464

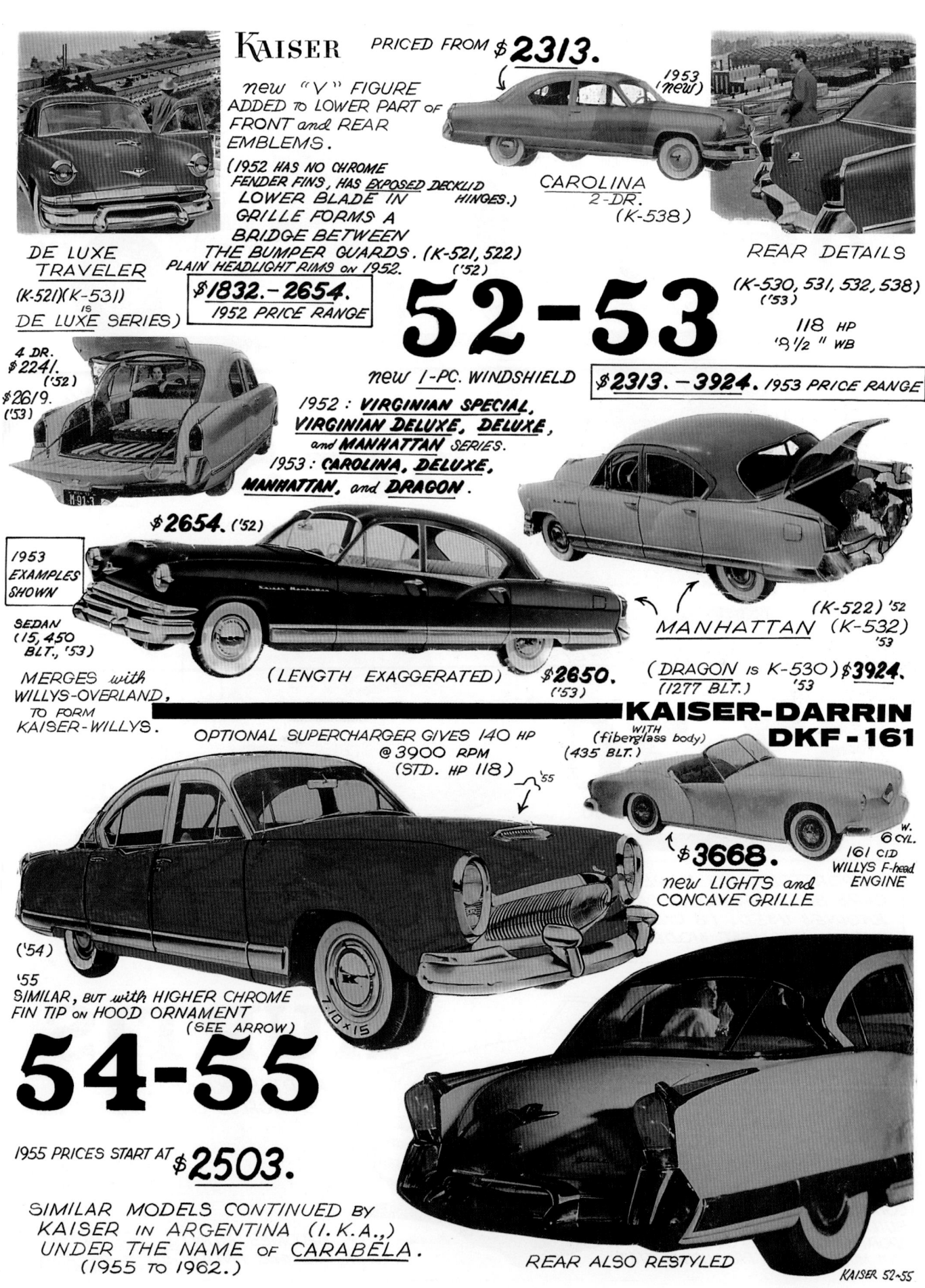

KAISER

PRICED FROM $2313.

new "V" FIGURE ADDED TO LOWER PART OF FRONT and REAR EMBLEMS.

(1952 HAS NO CHROME FENDER FINS, HAS EXPOSED DECKLID HINGES.) LOWER BLADE IN GRILLE FORMS A BRIDGE BETWEEN THE BUMPER GUARDS. (K-521, 522) PLAIN HEADLIGHT RIMS on 1952.

1953 (new)

CAROLINA 2-DR. (K-538)

DE LUXE TRAVELER (K-521)(K-531) IS DE LUXE SERIES)

$1832. - 2654. 1952 PRICE RANGE

('52)

52-53

REAR DETAILS

(K-530, 531, 532, 538) ('53)

118 HP '9 1/2" WB

$2313. - 3924. 1953 PRICE RANGE

4 DR. $2241. ('52) $2619. ('53)

new 1-PC. WINDSHIELD

1952: VIRGINIAN SPECIAL, VIRGINIAN DELUXE, DELUXE, and MANHATTAN SERIES.
1953: CAROLINA, DELUXE, MANHATTAN, and DRAGON.

1953 EXAMPLES SHOWN

$2654. ('52)

SEDAN (15,450 BLT. '53)

MERGES with WILLYS-OVERLAND, TO FORM KAISER-WILLYS.

(LENGTH EXAGGERATED) $2650. ('53)

MANHATTAN (K-522) '52 (K-532) '53

(DRAGON IS K-530) (1277 BLT.) '53 $3924.

KAISER-DARRIN DKF-161

OPTIONAL SUPERCHARGER GIVES 140 HP @ 3900 RPM (STD. HP 118)

WITH (fiberglass body) (435 BLT.)

'55

$3668. new LIGHTS and CONCAVE GRILLE

W. 6 CYL. 161 CID WILLYS F-head ENGINE

('54)

'55 SIMILAR, BUT with HIGHER CHROME FIN TIP on HOOD ORNAMENT (SEE ARROW)

54-55

1955 PRICES START AT $2503.

SIMILAR MODELS CONTINUED BY KAISER IN ARGENTINA (I.K.A.,) UNDER THE NAME OF CARABELA. (1955 TO 1962.)

REAR ALSO RESTYLED

KAISER 52-55

KING MIDGET

(1946-1970)

MIDGET MOTORS
ATHENS, OHIO

I CYL.

SOLD IN KIT FORM
(TO 1948)

(APPROX. **$350.** FOR EARLY KITS)

46-50

76½" WHEELBASE (THROUGH '70)

AVAILABLE FULLY ASSEMBLED, 1949 ON

('55)

EARLY

51-57

(TOTALLY RESTYLED FOR 1951)

I CYL., 7.3 TO 8.5 HP WISCONSIN ENGINE (TO 1966)

APPROXIMATELY 5000 BLT., 1946 ~ 1970

(RESTYLED EARLY '57)

AFTER 1966, 12-HP KOHLER ENG.

LATER

57-70

30% HP INCREASE (TO 12 HP) FOR 1966

DISCONTINUED 1970
$1095. IN '69

REPORTEDLY, NO MORE THAN 50 KURTIS CARS BLT. FORD OR CADILLAC V8 ENGINES USED. (6 CYL. STUDEBAKER ENG. IN EARLIEST MODEL)

FRANK KURTIS, FOUNDER
(ALSO BUILT RACE CARS)

(1949-1950)

CHOICE OF V-8 ENGINES
100" WB

KURTIS

KURTIS-KRAFT, INC.
LOS ANGELES and GLENDALE, CALIF.

KURTIS CONTINUED TO **BUILD OTHER TYPES OF** SPORTS and RACING CARS, AFTER EARL MUNTZ BEGAN PRODUCING "JET" *

* BECOMES MUNTZ JET IN '51, new 116" WB and ENLARGED TO 4-PASS.

KING MIDGET / KURTIS

1961 PRODUCTION: "170" (25,508 BLT.) "770" (49,268 BLT.)

COMPACT

LANCER

CHRYSLER CORPORATION

[DODGE]

Lancer 170 Two-Door Sedan

$2312.

770

WAGON

6 CYL. INCLINED O.H.V. ENGINE
170 CID with
101 HP @ 4400 RPM
or 148 HP @ 5200 RPM

new **61**

RWI-L , RWI-H
170   770

AIR COND.,
POWER STEERING
and POWER BRAKES
AVAIL.

INTERIOR

LARGER 225 CID 6 ALSO AVAIL.,
with 145 HP @ 4000 RPM OR 196 HP @ 5200 RPM

106½" WB

LANCERS BUILT 1961 and 1962 ONLY.
UNITIZED BODY SIMILAR TO PLYMOUTH VALIANT.

H/T
COMPACT DODGE LANCER

1962 MODELS : **170** = (2 DR.; 4-DR.; 4-DR. WAGON) (19,780 BLT.) **$1951.-2306.**
770 = (" " " ") (30,888 BLT.) **$2052.-2408.**
GT = H/T (13,683 BLT.) **$2257.**

LANCER 170 2-DOOR SEDAN 6 $1951.

$2256   (SLI-L) $2011. $2114.   ANCER 770 4-DOOR SEDAN 6

LANCER 170 4-DOOR SEDAN 6   WEST COAST,
$2562.

$2306. $2052.

LANCER 170 6-PASSENGER WAGON 6   LANCER 770 2-DOOR SEDAN 6

new GT

62

SLI

770
(SLI-H)

new GRILLE

$2408.

(SLI-P)

DISCONTINUED
AFTER 1962

$2257.   LANCER

467

LARK BY STUDEBAKER

COMPACT SERIES
(1959 - 1963)

108½" WB
113" WAGONS

2-DR. PLAY WAGON

note LOCATION of GRILLE MEDALLION ON 1959 MODEL

$2296. (6)
$2431. (V8)

PROD.
98,744 6 CYL.
32,334 V8s

1959 LARK CARRIES "STUDEBAKER" NAME

REGAL H/T

$1925. ~ 2590.

59 new!

6 - CYL. OR V8 ENGINES
169.6 CID   259.2 CID
(90 HP)   (180 OR 195 HP)

LUXURY Reclining seats that let all the way down are an optional touch of sublime comfort. Seats are pleated, appointments tasteful. Colors are harmoniously keyed to exteriors.

H/T INTERIOR

DELUXE = 2 DR.; 4-DR.; 2-DR. WAGON; 4 DR. WAGON
REGAL = 4 DR.; H/T; CONVERTIBLE; "   "   (6 OR V8, EITHER SERIES)

60 GRILLE MEDALLION MOVED TO LOWER CENTER

"LOVE THAT *LARK* BY STUDEBAKER"

$1976. ~ 2756. PRICE RANGE

4-DR. WAGON and CONVERT. ARE new IN 1960

REGAL CVT.
$2621. (6) OR **$2756.** (V8)

"LARK" NAME AT REAR END OF FRONT FENDER

LARK 59~60

468

LARK

6 has 112 HP

4 HEADLIGHTS ON new 113" WB CRUISER

180 TO 225 HP

61

GRILLE EMBLEM MOVED; new PARK. LIGHTS; "LARK" NAME MOVED TO FORWARD END OF FR. FENDERS

"You have to drive The Lark to believe it!"

1961 PRODUCTION
6-CYL. = (41,035 BLT.)
V8 = (25,934 ")

$1935. ~ $2689. PRICE RANGE

$1935. ~ $2814. PRICE RANGE

PACE CAR AT 1962 INDY 500 RACE

DAYTONA CVT.

"LARK" IN CAPITAL LETTERS

new ROUND TAIL-LIGHTS

DETAILS OF new GRILLE

VIEWS OF DASH

62

6 CYL. = (54,397 BLT.)
V8 = (38,607 ")

SUNROOF OPTIONAL ON new 225 HP *DAYTONA*

$2308. UP

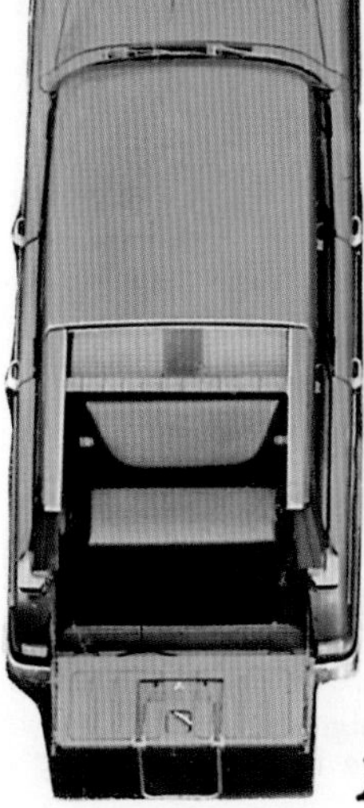

SLIDING REAR ROOF SECTION ON new REGAL LARK WAGONAIRE

STD. WAGONS $2430. UP

LARK NAME USED ONLY 1959-1963

$1935. ~ 2835. PRICE RANGE

63

new GRILLE AGAIN

REGAL LARK $2055. UP

SEE ALSO
Studebaker

REGAL WAGONS FROM 2550.
DAYTONA " " $2700.

74,201 TOTAL 1963 PRODUCTION

LARK 61~63

La Salle V8
A GENERAL MOTORS VALUE

BY

Cadillac

(AVAIL. 1927 TO 1940)

Now there are two LaSalles—the Fifty series in five body styles . . . the completely new Special series in two—both series styled and powered by Cadillac to lead the medium-price field in luxury, performance, comfort and economy.

LaSalle 50 five-passenger four-door convertible sedan

LaSalle 50 two-door

40

LaSalle 50 COUPE $1240.

Convertible coupe on LaSalle 50 chassis

The Chassis

(ABOVE CAR IN NEED OF RESTORATION)

New Series . . .

(NO CHROME BELT TRIM ON SPECIAL)

new BODY STYLE $1440.

THE NEW LASALLE SPECIAL

(SPECIAL COUPE ALSO AVAIL.)

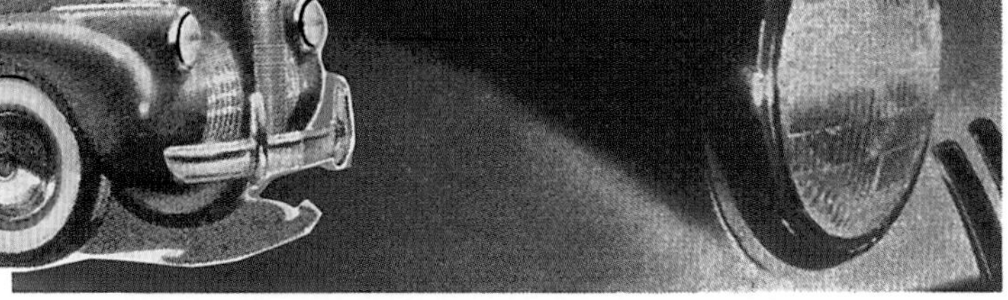

Parking lamps (and front direction signals) are visible from the side as well as the front *LA SALLE*

LINCOLN

40

INTERIOR

$1399. UP

COUPE (1256 BLT.)

new LONGER WIDER BODIES, NO RUNNINGBOARDS (3500 BLT.)

CONVERTIBLE (700 BLT.)

$1818.

WITH VACUUM-POWERED TOP

$1439. UP

New CLUB COUPE

SEDAN (15,764 BLT.)

LINCOLN-ZEPHYR

V·12
125" WB

ENGINE IN ALL LINCOLNS, 1934 THROUGH 1948

292 C/D
new 120 HP (THROUGH '41)

$1439. UP

REAR-MOUNTED SPARE TIRE ON LINCOLN CONTINENTAL

CVT. (54 BLT.) $2916.

SAME GRILLE AS ZEPHYR

The Continental Cabriolet is an ultra smart close-coupled five-passenger car with an over-all height of only 62 inches and a hood which is seven inches longer than on the other models

K→

THE LINCOLN V·12

(150 HP BIG "K" SERIES LINCOLNS with 414 C/D V12 are DISCONTINUED DURING 1940 with ONLY 133 BLT.)

Lincoln Motor Company,

Division of Ford Motor Company.
40 LINCOLN

$2783. CLUB CPE. (350 BLT.) CONTINENTAL

LINCOLN-ZEPHYR V·12

3~WINDOW COUPE
(972 BLT.)
$1478. UP

SEDAN
(14,469 BLT.)
$1541. UP

CONV'T.
(725 BLT.)
$1858.

41

Three Lines Including New
138-Inch Wheelbase Eight-
Passenger Sedan and Limousine

SEDAN INTERIOR

CLUB CPE.
(178 BLT.)

$1541.

DASH

All Lincoln doors are opened from the inside by push-buttons
instead of handles. The Continental models also have push buttons on
the outside.

LINCOLN *Continental*

CONVERTIBLE
(400 BLT.)
$2865.

$2812.
new PUSHBUTTON
DOOR~
OPENERS

CLUB COUPE
(850 BLT.)

$2836.

ELECTRIC WINDOW LIFTS and POWER FR. SEAT IN THE

LINCOLN *Custom*

LIMO.
(295 BLT.) REPLACES "K"

138" WB   41 LINCOLN

472

LINCOLN V-12
Zephyr Continental Custom

$3000. FOR CONTINENT.
CLB. CPE. or CABRIOLET (CVT.)

LINCOLN-CONTINENTAL CABRIOLET (136 BLT.)

(200 CONTINENTAL CLUB COUPES BLT.)

ZEPHYR SEDAN (4418 BLT.)
$1700.~$1795.

FRONT END TOTALLY RESTYLED

PUSHBUTTON DOORS NOW ON ZEPHYR ALSO

42

. **New** Driver's compartment features

LINCOLN-ZEPHYR SEDAN. In the graceful sweep of its modern streamline styling . . . its longer, lower, wider appearance and rich new interior appointments . . . Lincoln designers have given the '42 Lincoln-Zephyr Sedan an all-new type of automotive beauty, while retaining generous size and roominess.

LINCOLN-ZEPHYR V-12

new 305 CID V12 has 130 HP (292 CID V12 RETURNS IN '46)

3~WINDOW COUPE (1236 BLT.)
CLUB COUPE (253 BLT.)
CONVT. (191 BLT.)

new MASCOT

AVAIL. B~W OVERDRIVE, COLUMBIA 2-SPEED REAR AXLE or new LIQUI~MATIC TRANS.

Directional signal and parking lamps are combined with headlamps

Lincoln
CUSTOM
(138" WB)
8~PASS. SEDAN (47 BLT.)
LIMOUSINE (66 BLT.)
$2950.~$3075.
(NOT AVAIL. IN POSTWAR LINE)

with new front fenders, hood, lamps, grilles and bumpers

AG·70-57

42 LINCOLN

Lincoln

(SINCE 1921)
A DIVISION OF FORD MOTOR CO. SINCE 1922
(201 CONTINENTAL CVTS., 265 CLUB CPES.) $4392.
#57

$4474
#56

← CONTINENTAL (PACE CAR AT 1946 INDY 500 RACE)

#77 CLUB COUPE
$2318.

#76
CVT.

$2883.

HEAVIER NAMEPLATE ON SIDES OF 1946 HOOD

46
66-H
292 CID V-12 ENG. (125 HP)
PRICE RANGE:
$2178.
TO
$4205.

#73 SEDAN
$2337.

PUSHBUTTON DOORS ON ALL '46 MODELS

125" WB AS BEFORE, BUT "ZEPHYR" NAME DISCONTINUED.

RAISED HEXAGON AT CENTER OF 1946 HUB CAPS

new HEAVIER GRILLE has BOTH HORIZ. and VERT. PCS.

(16,179 BLT.)

new LARGER BUMPERS

CUSTOM INTERIORS OPTIONAL AT EXTRA COST (THROUGH '48)

CONVENTIONAL DOOR HANDLES RETURN, ON STD. TYPES

$2554. ('48)

"Nothing could be finer"
"Lincoln" NAME IN CHROME ON SIDES OF HOOD and ON new PLAINER HUBCAPS

FINAL LINCOLNS with V-12 ENGINES (1948)

(19,891, 1947 PROD.; 6470, 1948 PROD.)

7-H   8-H
47-48

CONVERTIBLE

CONTINENTALS CONTINUE USE OF BUTTON DOOR OPENERS

1947 (738 BLT.); 1948 (452 BLT.)
CONTINENTAL $4746.

FINAL CONTINENTALS UNTIL 1956 MODEL

luxury car

CLUB COUPE
1947 (831 BLT.); 1948 (847 BLT.)

$4662.

LINCOLN 46~48

LINCOLN

STD. 9EL SERIES (38,384 BLT.)
121" WB

new 2-PC. WINDSHIELD
(ON STANDARD
LINCOLNS ONLY)

$2527.

COUPE

$2575.

COUPE

$3948.

new COSMOPOLITAN
125" WB   (9EH)

$3186.

49

(TOTALLY
RESTYLED)

(35,123 COSMOPOL.
BLT.)

BACK SEAT AREA (COSMO.)

The "custom touch" adds luxury to the 1949 Lincoln Cosmopolitan!

ALL
WITH new
V8 ENGINE
(L-HEAD)
336.7 CID
(152 HP)

$3238.

OEH
COSMOPOLITAN
SPORT SEDAN
(8341 BLT.)
$3240.

121"-WB LINC.
"LIDO" CPE.
IS new
($2721.)

$2529.~3950. PRICE RANGE

new
GRILLE
IS
LOWER **50**

SOME MODELS
PRICED
ONLY $2
HIGHER THAN
LAST
YEAR'S

$2505.~3891. PRICE RANGE

new
FULL-LENGTH CHROME MOULDING ALONG
BODY SIDES OF COSMOPOLITAN MODELS
(AND CONT'D.
ON STD.
LINCOLNS)

121"
WB

LINCOLN SPORT SEDAN

HP INCREASED
TO 154

51

INTRO. DURING 1950,
final   COSMO.
LARGE-SIZED   "CAPRI" CPE.
COSMOPOLITAN   IS new

125"
WB

new
GRILLE

COSMO.
SPORT SEDAN
$3182.

LINCOLN 49~51

LINCOLN

new 123" WB

$3198.

COSMOPOLITAN

H/T
(5681 BLT.)

CAPRI

CVT.
(1191 BLT.) $3665.

COSMO. IS NOW
LOWER-PRICED
SERIES, BELOW CAPRI.

52

(TOTALLY
RESTYLED)

"Lincoln" NAME IN
SCRIPT LETTERING, ABOVE new GRILLE

8.00 × 15" TIRES
TOTAL 1952 PRODUCTION, 31,992
new O.H.V. 317½ CID V8 (160 HP)

$3198.~3665. PRICE RANGE

$3226.

COSMOPOLITAN
SEDAN

COSMOPOLITAN
LETTERING DETAILS

53

(7560 BLT.)

HP INCREASED
TO 205

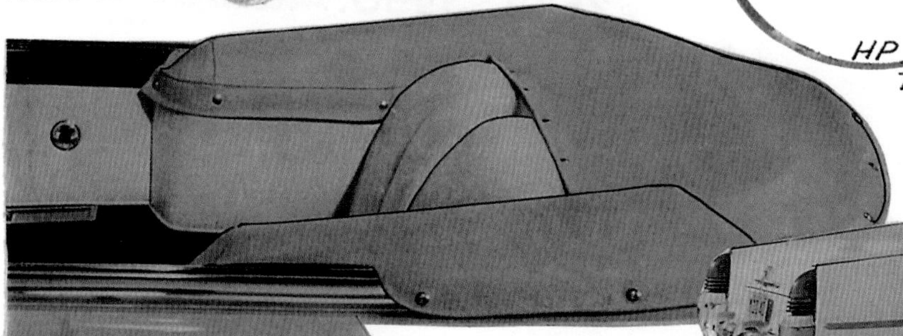

H/T
(12,916 BLT.)

CONV'T. DETAILS

CAPRI
LETTERING
DETAILS

CAPRI $3549.

new BLOCK
"LINCOLN"
LETTERING, ABOVE
GRILLE WHICH
NOW CONTAINS
STYLIZED "V"
and SMALL
EMBLEM

TOTAL 1953 PRODUCTION, 41,962

$3226.~3699.
PRICE RANGE

LINCOLN 52~53

476

LINCOLN

H/T (14,003 BLT.) CAPRI

(1951 BLT.) $4031.

CONV'T.

new FENDER TRIM

54

new GRILLE

$3869.

"LINCOLN" NAME NOW IN SCRIPT, and MOVED TO FRONT FENDER PANELS.

TOTAL 1954 PRODUCTION, 35,733

$3522. ~ 4031. PRICE RANGE

$3563. ~ 4072. PRICE RANGE

new 341 CID V8 (225 HP)

$3752.

TOTAL 1955 PRODUCTION, 41,226

55

CUSTOM IS LOWER-PRICED SERIES, PRICED from $3563.

SEDAN (10,724 BLT.)

CAPRI

H/T (11,462 BLT.)

$3910.

new FENDER TRIM

new GRILLE with ALL HORIZONTAL PIECES

new 126" WB, new 368 CID (285 HP)

56A

new PREMIERE

new PANORAMIC WINDSHIELD

CAPRI H/T

FRENCHED HEADLIGHTS, and new PARK./DIRECTIONAL LIGHTS IN GRILLE

new CHROME SIDE SPEAR

TOTAL 1956 PRODUCTION, 48,995

ALSO, A REVIVED **Continental** (SEE NEXT PAGE)

$4119. ~ 4747. PRICE RANGE   LINCOLN 54~56(A)

LINCOLN

Continental

Mark II

Continental Division · Ford Motor Company

$9538. ('56)

($157. MORE IN 1957.)

368 CID V8 (300 HP)

126" WB

new CONTINENTAL STYLING DIFFERS FROM CAPRI, PREMIERE MODELS (THROUGH '60)

1325 BLT. ('56)
444 BLT. ('57)

56-57
B

1ST CONTINENTAL SINCE 1948.

1957 PRODUCTION 37,870

$4649. ~ 5381. PRICE RANGE

126" WB

NON-CONTINENTAL 1957 TYPES : **CAPRI** PRICED FROM $4649.

(15,185 BLT.)
COUPE (H/T)

$5149.

PREMIERE

(3676 BLT.) CVT.

new LANDAU 4-DR. H/T

$5381.

(11,233 BLT.)
$5294.

new 300 HP IN THESE MODELS

57

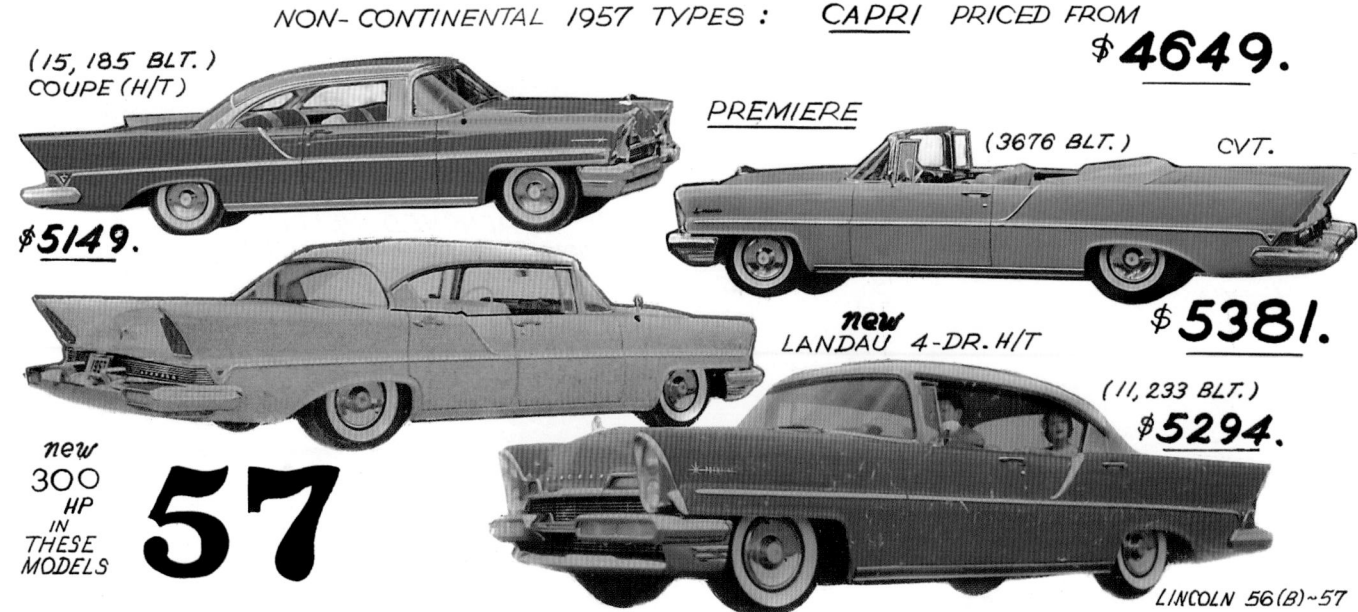

LINCOLN 56(B)~57

478

LINCOLN

CAPRI

new 131" WB (THROUGH '60)

PREMIERE

H/T $4803.

CONTINENTAL MARK III

Unmistakably . . . the finest in the fine car field

58 (TOTALLY RESTYLED)

new 375 HP

CONT'L. HAS new CRISS-CROSS GRILLE PATTERN

CONT'L. NO LONGER HAS "SPARE TIRE BULGE" IN REAR DECK

9.00 × 14 TIRES

$6283. (CVT.)

TOTAL 1958 PRODUCTION, 25,871

(3048 BLT.)

430 CID V8

$4902. ~ 10,230. PRICE RANGE

PREMIERE (CAPRI ALSO AVAIL.)

59 new GRILLE NOW ENCOMPASSES THE CANTED HEADLIGHTS

CUT TO 350 HP

(6604 BLT.)

CONTINENTAL MARK IV

$7056.

9.50 × 14 TIRES

(2195 BLT.)

TOTAL 1959 PRODUCTION, 30,375

LINCOLN 58~59

479

LINCOLN

$5698.

PREMIERE

2-DR. H/T

4-DR.

430 CID V8
HORSEPOWER CUT TO 315 @ 4100 RPM
(new CARBURETOR)
LEAF SPRINGS REPLACE
COILS AT REAR

TYPICAL
UPHOLSTERY
(LEATHER
and
FABRICS)

new HOODED INSTRUMENTS

$5945.

DASH
and
INSIDE
DOOR
HANDLE

60

$6598.

CONTINENTAL MARK V

2-DR. H/T

$5253. TO $10,230.
PRICE RANGE

LANDAU
4-DR. H/T

FINAL YEAR FOR 2-DR.
CONVERTIBLE

$6845.

"TOWN CAR"
FORMAL SEDAN
(136 BLT.)

$7056.

$9208.

LIMOUSINE

$10,230.

(ONLY 34 BLT.)

9.50 × 14 TIRES

1960 PRODUCTION = SEDAN (1093 BLT.); LANDAU 4-DR. H/T (4397 BLT.); H/T (1670 BLT.)
 PREMIERE = SEDAN (1010 BLT.); LANDAU 4-DR. H/T (4200 BLT.); H/T (1365 BLT.)
 CONTINENTAL MARK V = LIMOUSINE (34 BLT.); FORMAL SEDAN (136 BLT.); SEDAN (807 BLT.);
  H/T (1461 BLT.); CONVERTIBLE (2044 BLT.); 4-DR. H/T (6604 BLT.)

LINCOLN 60

LINCOLN CONTINENTAL

new DASH

430 CID V8 CUT TO 300 HP @ 4100 RPM (THROUGH '62)

SLDAN (22307 BLT.) $6067.

SPECIFICATIONS

TRANSMISSION: Twin-range Turbo-Drive automatic torque converter with three-speed planetary gear set.

REAR AXLE: Semi-floating hypoid; gear ratio 2.89 to 1; lubricant capacity 4.8 pints.

WHEEL AND TIRES: Pressed steel disc wheels; Tyrex tire cord, white sidewall standard, 9.00 x 14 on Sedan, 9.50 x 14 on Convertible and Sedan with air conditioning; full wheel covers.

DIMENSIONS: Wheelbase 123"; over-all length 212.4"; maximum width 78.6"; tread—front 62.1, rear 61.0".

LINCOLN-MERCURY DIVISION Ford Motor Company

W.B. REDUCED TO 123" (THROUGH '63)

RADIO

CLOCK

AIR CONDITIONING

21 AVAILABLE COLORS

(TOTALLY RESTYLED)

61

ALL MODELS NOW KNOWN AS Lincoln Continental

Presidential Black

Green Velvet Metallic

Royal Red Metallic

Crystal Green Metallic

Turquoise Mist

Sultana White

Blue Haze

Platinum

Saxon Green Metallic

Executive Gray Metallic

Sunburst Yellow

Sheffield Gray Metallic

Empress Blue Metallic

Columbia Blue Metallic

Honey Beige

DECK LID OPENS WHEN TOP MOVES

Rose Glow Metallic

Summer Rose

Regency Turquoise Metallic

Black Cherry Metallic

Briar Brown Metallic

Desert Frost Metallic

REAR DETAILS

New

Four-Door Convertible

(2857 BLT.)

$6713.

4-DR. CVT. AVAILABLE THRU '67

LINCOLN 61

481

LINCOLN CONTINENTAL

(32/2 BLT.)
$6720.

new THIN WHITE SIDEWALLS
ON TIRES (9.00 × 14")

62

$6074.

(27849 BLT.)

DASH

UPHOLSTERY COLORS

new
GRILLE and
REAR END
OF
HARMONIZING
DESIGN

Royal Red
Metallic

Jamaica Yellow

Oxford Gray
Metallic

Castilian Gold
Metallic

Nocturne Blue
Metallic

Teaberry

Black Cherry
Metallic

Silver Mink
Metallic

Riviera Turquoise
Metallic

Champagne

Scotch Green
Metallic

Powder Blue

Bermuda Blue
Metallic

Velvet Turquoise
Metallic

Desert Frost
Metallic

Highlander Green
Metallic

Platinum

Chestnut
Metallic

Sultana
White

Presidential
Black

BODY COLORS

LINCOLN 62

LINCOLN (CONTINENTAL)

63

DETAIL OF CENTER-OPENING DOORS

new GRILLE

$69/6.

4-DR. CONV'T. with TOP UP

(3138 BLT.)

4-DR. H/T (28,095 BLT.)

new 320 HP (THROUGH '65)

$6270.

The luggage compartment is larger.

LIMOUSINE

4 DR. CVT. $6938. (3328 BLT.)

greater

4 DR. H/T **$6292.**

64

(SLIGHTLY ENLARGED) new 126" WB (THROUGH '69)

interior spaciousness

4 DR. H/T (33,969 BLT.)

3" LONGER THAN BEFORE

4-DR. CONVERTIBLE CONTINUES THROUGH 1967

PRODUCTION:
4 DR. H/T (36,824 BLT.)
4-DR. CONVT. (3356 BLT.)

65

LIMO. ROOFLINE

DASH

CONV. **$6938.**

$6292. →

430 CID V8 (320 HP)

LINCOLN 63~65

new GRILLE with HORIZONTAL MOTIF

LINCOLN Continental
America's most distinguished motorcar.

REAR

LINCOLN CONTINENTAL

Another distinctive touch this year is the Continental emblem hinged to conceal the trunk compartment lock.

1966

$5485.
(15,766 BLT.)

126" WB
new 462 CID V8
(340 HP)
9.15 × 15
TIRES

HOOD ORNAMENT

4-DR.
$5750.

H/T
(new)

↑ $6118. (WEST COAST)

$6383. (35,809 BLT.)
(WEST COAST)

66

(3180 BLT.)

$6383.

(ABOVE)
4-DR. CVT.
$7016.
(WEST COAST)
WITH
(LEATHER
UPH.)

FRONT
END
DETAILS

1966

new DASH

FENDER-TIP LTS.
DISCONTINUED
UNTIL 1968

4 DR. CVT.
(2276 BLT.)

(REAR DETAILS OF
1965 CONT'L.)

67

$6449.

(INTRO. 9-30-66)

2-DR. H/T
(WITHOUT
VINYL TOP)
$6185.
WEST COAST

REAR

1967

$5553.

(11,060 BLT.)

4-DR.
(WITH VINYL
TOP)

GRILLE CH.,
SLIGHTLY
RECESSED,
and EMBLEM
REMOVED
FROM SIDE OF
FRONT FENDER

(33,331 BLT.)

$5795.

4-DR., STD. TOP
$6427. WEST COAST
(VINYL LANDAU
TOP $132. EXTRA)

1967 IS FINAL YEAR FOR THE
4-DOOR CONVERTIBLE.

LINCOLN 66~67

484

new BROAD STEER. WH. HUB, DARKER-COLORED DASH ←

new REAR STYLING

68
(INTRO. 9-22-67)

Wraparound parking lights and taillights

new coupe roof line. → (9415 BLT.)

$5736.

$5970.

$6634.
(WEST COAST)
DETAILS OF
new GRILLE

RAISED HOOD ORNAMENT ELIMINATED (UNTIL 1972)

SEDAN (29,719 BLT.)

EMBLEM REPLACES NAME ABOVE GRILLE, DURING 1968

new SAFETY SIDE LIGHTS

(2 DR. H/T ALSO 9032 BLT. $5830.)

(29 258 BLT.) 4-DR.

2 SERIES NOW AVAIL.

69
new "COMPUTER DESIGNED" 460 CID V8 (365 HP)

(7770 BLT. '68, 23,088 BLT. '69) $6758.

$6063.
Continental
(INTRO. 9-27-68)
new GRILLE WITH CONTINENTAL NAME ABOVE.
(126" WB)

(NO 4-DR. MK. TYPES UNTIL 1980 MK. VI)

LINCOLN 68~69

117.2" WB

Continental Mark III.

MK. III INTRO. 4-5-68

(NEW)

485

LINCOLN CONTINENTAL

H/T = $5976.

70

LONGER and WIDER

new DASH (CONT'L.)

REAR DETAIL

BROCADE and VINYL UPHOLSTERY

117.2" WB

MARK III
(21432 BUILT)
$7281.

new 127" WB
CONTINENTAL
SEDAN (28622 BLT.)
$6211.

(9073 H/Ts)

1971 PRODUCT.
H/T = 8205
SED. = 27346

NEW

Continental: the final step up.

The Town Car. PACKAGE
127" WB

"GOLDEN ANNIVERSARY"
MODELS

VINYL ROOF AVAIL. IN WHITE,
BLACK, DARK GREEN,
DARK BROWN OR DARK BLUE

new NARROWER GRILLE

(INTRO. 9~18~70)
$7016.
and up

71

TOWN CAR

TOWN CAR MODEL
NAME ON LOWER SIDES OF
COWL
(STD.
CONTINENTAL
SIMILAR
STYLING)

MK. III DASH

MARK III

new 118" WB
$8813.
(27091 BLT.)

LINCOLN (CONTINENTAL) 70~71

LINCOLN CONTINENTAL CONTINENTAL MARK IV

72

new GRILLE

(INTRO. 9~17~71)

new 120.4" WB

$8640.

BIG new GRILLE DIPS INTO BUMPER ('72 ONLY)

(48591 BUILT)

$7302.

SEDAN

(35561 BUILT)

2~DR. H/T **$7068.** (10408 BLT.)

new CRISS~CROSS GRILLE PCS.

LC·714

HP CUT TO 224 (212 ON MK. IV)

73

new SAFETY BUMPERS

$7474.

$8984.

(69437 BUILT)

CONTINENTAL MARK IV

SEDAN (45288 BUILT)

Continental

"CONTINENTAL" NAME ABOVE GRILLE

$7230. (13348 BLT.)

2~DR. H/T

HP CUT FURTHER TO 219 (CONT'L.) and 208 (MK. IV) IN SPITE OF SOME REPORTS THAT 1971 FIGURE OF 365 HP RESUMED.

MARK IV DASH

DASH (CONTINENTAL)

REAR DETAILS

LINCOLN (CONTINENTAL) 72~73 MK. IV

CONTINENTAL SEDAN

230 R 15" TIRES

MK. IV
(57316 BLT.)

LINCOLN CONTINENTAL

MARK IV
DASH

$9574.
(10,265. LATER IN YR.)

CONT'L. PRODUCTION
2-DR. = 7316 BLT.
4-DR. = 29351 "

74

new GRILLE (CONTINTL.)

235 x 15" TIRES

Continental

FROM $7727.
($8309. LATER IN YR.)

CONTINENTAL TOWN COUPÉ

"Continental" LETTERING

(21185 BLT.)

FROM $9214.

FROM $9656.
(33513 BLT.)

new GRILLE

75A

CONTINENTAL TOWN CAR

460 CID V8 RATED 206 HP

(CONT'D. ON NEXT PAGE)

TOWN COUPE (UPH.)

MK. IV (UPH.)

MARK IV

LINCOLN 74~75-A

LINCOLN CONTINENTAL

230R15 TIRES (all MODELS)

(120.4" WB=MK. IV 1972~79)

DASH

new WHEEL COVERS

CONTINENTAL MARK IV

75B
(CONT'D.)

new MID-SIDE PROTECTIVE TRIM MOLDING (CONT. and MK. IV)

$11082.

(47145 BLT.)

$11060.

new BAND OVER ROOF (CONTINENTAL TOWN MODELS) TOWN CAR

CLOSER DETAIL OF COACH LAMPS AND TRIM

MARK IV
(56110 BLT.)

76A

CONTINENTAL
(68646 BLT.
2 DR. + 4~DR.)

STD.
2-DR. $9142.
(4-DR.
$9293.)

127.2" WB
(1974~1979)

MERCURY
FORD
LINCOLN

230R15 TIRES

(CONT'D. NEXT PAGE)

LINCOLN 75 (B)~76 (A)

New
Introducing the Mark IV Designer Series

76B (CONT'D)

MK. IV DESIGNER SER. w. SPEC. PAINT and INT. BY DESIGNER FOR WHICH NAMED

PUCCI (BURGUNDY and SILVER)

GIVENCHY (BELOW)

(TURQUOISE and WHITE)

The Givenchy Edition Mark IV

BILL BLASS (BLUE and CREAM)

CARTIER (PEARL GRAY)

FROM $12,560.

(USUAL $11,060 MK. TYPES CONTINUE ALSO)

26½~ GALLON GAS TANK

new MARK V

new 400 CID V8 (173 HP)

PUCCI (BLACK and WHITE)

GIVENCHY (DARK JADE and CHAMOIS)

(DES. = $12,996. UP) (STD. = 11,396.)

BILL BLASS (MIDNIGHT BLUE and PIGSKIN)

77 A (RESTYLED)

CARTIER (DOVE GRAY)

new TRIPLE COWL LOUVRES

(CONT'D. NEXT PAGE)

LINCOLN 76~77(A) (B)

LINCOLN CONTINENTAL
LINCOLN-MERCURY DIVISION *Ford*

$12,529. ('78)
$11,500. ('77)
$13,783. ('79)

'77-79 PROD.=15434; 8931; 21007

VERSAILLES SEDANS ONLY

LINCOLN VERSAILLES
NEW
COMPACT = 110" WB

AVAIL. 1977 TO 1980 WITH FEW CHANGES.

An investment in engineering.
VERSAILLES INTERIOR ('77)

('77)
302 CID V8 IN VERSAILLES (351 CID AVAIL. OUTSIDE CALIF. IN '77)

77-79

STD. CONT'L. NOW USES MARK V-TYPE UPRIGHT GRILLE.

CONTINENTAL

400 OR 460 CID V8 IN '77 AND '78 CONT'L.

1977 Lincoln Continental.

CPE. FROM $9474. 10196. ('78) 11868 ('79)

(FINAL LARGE-SIZED MODELS IN 1979)

Lincoln Continental. A standard by which luxury cars are judged.

('78)
SED. FROM $9636. ('77) 10396. ('78) 12093. ('79)

4 "DESIGNER EDITIONS" CONTINUE, WITH NEW COLORS.
$13,899. ('78)
14,592. ('79)

78-79

MARK V

400 CID V8s ONLY IN 1979 CONT. AND MK. V

SOME CONT. AND MK. V 1979s KNOWN AS "COLLECTOR'S SERIES"

('79)
75939 BLT.

('78)

72602 BLT.

1978 DIAMOND JUBILEE EDITION

Ford 75TH ANNIVERSARY

$12,318. ('78)

LINCOLN 77-79

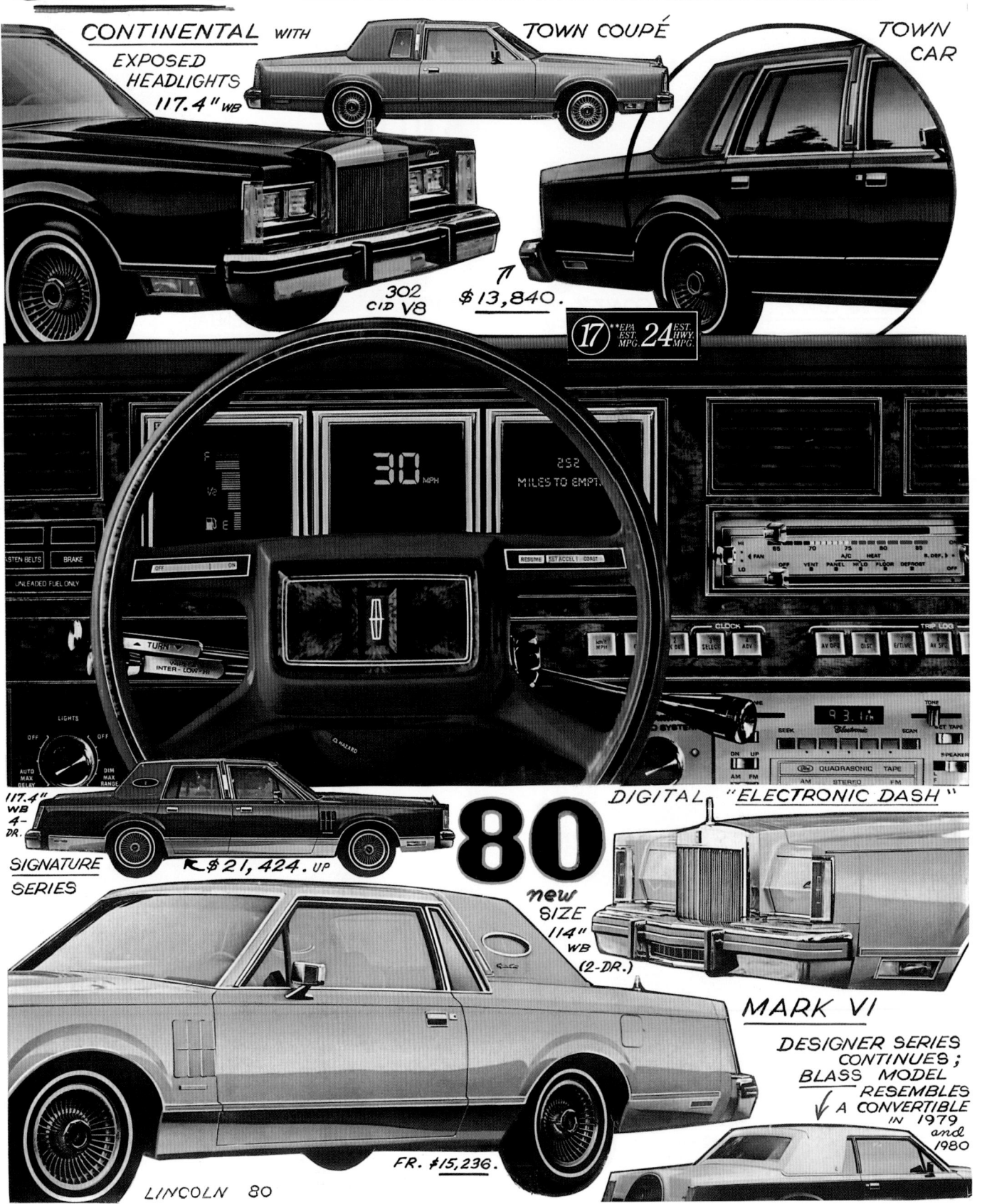

LINCOLN CONTINENTAL
LINCOLN-MERCURY DIVISION

VERSAILLES $15,664. (4784 BLT.)
CONT'L. (2 and 4 DR.) $13,251. up 3122 (31233 BLT.)
MARK VI $16,291. up (38891. BLT.)

(DOWNSIZED)

CONTINENTAL WITH EXPOSED HEADLIGHTS 117.4" WB

TOWN COUPÉ

TOWN CAR

302 CID V8

$13,840.

17 **EPA EST. MPG. 24 EST. HWY. MPG.

30 MPH

252 MILES TO EMPT.

DIGITAL "ELECTRONIC DASH"

117.4" WB 4-DR.

SIGNATURE SERIES

R $21,424. UP

80
new SIZE 114" WB (2-DR.)

MARK VI

DESIGNER SERIES CONTINUES; BLASS MODEL RESEMBLES A CONVERTIBLE IN 1979 and 1980

FR. $15,236.

LINCOLN 80

MERCURY 8
Division of Ford Motor Company.

SINCE 1939

OPTIONAL GRILLE GUARD

CONVERTIBLE SEDAN
(AVAIL. ONLY FOR 1940) $ 1212.

new GRILLE

40

116" WB

4~DR. TOWN SEDAN ↑
$ 987.

2~PC. REAR WINDOW

note CHROME SIDE WINDOW FRAMES ON SEDAN~CPE.
(CLUB COUPE)

1940
REAR DETAILS

ESTIMATED 81,000~PLUS 1940 MERCURYS BUILT.

239 CID V8
95 HP

$ 1079.

White sidewall tires extra

CLUB CONVERTIBLE

2~DR. SEDAN $ 946.

COMPLETE 1940 MERCURY LINE ILLUSTR. ABOVE

PHOTO OF INSTRUMENT PANEL

DASH OF SILVER METAL with BLUE PLASTIC TRIM

new STEERING COLUMN SHIFT

40 MERCURY

493

MERCURY 8 FOR 1941

$946.

THE SEDAN—Body and doors are flared out over semi-concealed running boards to provide more spacious interiors. Generous luggage space in rear deck.

THE SEDAN COUPE—a popular car for business or personal use. Full-width rear seat accommodates three extra passengers.

$977.

● **PARK YOUR BAGGAGE HERE!** Mercury's luggage compartment—with spare tire placed vertically, out of the way—takes big bags, small bags, and then some!

$1100.

THE CLUB CONVERTIBLE—seats five. Automatic top operates at the touch of a button. Leather upholstery in tan, blue or red.

New

RESTYLED
41
new 118" WB

$1141.
WAGON

NEW STATION WAGON—has body of selected maple and birch. Holds up to 8 passengers. Genuine leather upholstery available in your choice of tan, blue or red.

BODY OF REAL WOOD (MAPLE and BIRCH)

$987. 4-DOOR TOWN SEDAN
TRUNK DETAILS

UP TO 20 M.P.G.

new DASH

new GRILLE   41 MERCURY

494

MERCURY 8

WAGON

$1260.

$1215.

new HUB CAPS

$1065.

4~DR. SEDAN   BACK SEAT

42

FRONTAL RESTYLING;
DUAL HORIZONTAL
STRIPS ON FENDERS

$1030.

SPEEDOMETER

CLOCK

2~DR. SEDAN

ESTIMATED NEARLY
23,000 1942 MERC.
CARS BLT (SEPT. '41
TO JAN., 1942)

AY-1180

FUEL

OIL

AMP

TEMP

4113

new GRILLE

42 MERCURY

MERCURY

new SPORTSMAN CONV'T. $2209.

(WOODEN BODY PANELS)

(205 BLT.)

NEW INTERIORS

A WAGON (2797 BLT.)

2-DR. SED. (13,108 BLT.)

46

new GRILLE

RARE CANADIAN MONARCH VARIATION OF 1946-1948, A MERCURY-SIZED CAR SOLD BY CANADA'S FORD DEALERS. (SEE METEOR/ MONARCH FOR MORE!)

$1448.

"COUPE-SEDAN" (24,163 BLT.) $1495.

$1711. ALL-STEEL CONVERTIBLE

new GRILLE

(6044 BLT.)

$1509.

SLOGAN: "STEP OUT WITH MERCURY"

2-DR. SEDAN $1592. (34 BLT. 1947)

STATION WAGON (3558 BLT., 1947; 1889 BLT., 1948)

"MERCURY" NAMEPLATE ABOVE GRILLE NOW HAS BLACK BACKGROUND INSTEAD OF RED AS IN '46.

new BUMPERS

47-48

CHROME

BORDER OF GRILLE IS NOW CHROME-PLATED.

TOLL

$2207.

$1660.

1947 INTERIORS

MERCURY 46~48

More OF EVERYTHING YOU WANT WITH Mercury

496

MERCURY $2716. (8044 BLT.) new 2-DR. WAGON

CONVERTIBLE (16,765 BLT.) $2410.

CLUB CPE.

(120,616 BLT.)

7.10 × 15" TIRES

new 255.4 CID V8 (new 110 HP)

49 TOTALLY RESTYLED

SPORT SEDAN (155,882 BLT.)

BRIER INN.

1949

Make your next car **Mercury**

FROM $1997. (CLUB CPE.)

118" WB

$2031.

(TOTAL 1950 PRODUCTION = 334,081)

new EMBLEMS AT EITHER END

"Better than ever"

50

PACE CAR AT 1950 INDY 500 RACE

$2412. CVT. (8341 BLT.)

$1947. ~ 2530. PRICE RANGE

1950

LARGE PARK. LIGHTS AT ENDS of GRILLE

CLUB COUPE $1980.

4-DR. SPORT SEDAN (157,648 BLT.) $2000.

"MONTEREY" COUPE

CLUB COUPE (ALSO AVAIL. SINCE '50, W. CANVAS OR VINYL TOP COVERING)

$1947.

new GRILLE and new EMBLEMS

Nothing like it on the Road !

B·1592

51 new OPTIONAL **MERC-O-MATIC** AUTO. TRANS.

new 112 HP

AUTO. TRANS.

LARGER BACKLIGHT (REAR WINDOW)

1951

new VERT. TAIL-LIGHTS

for "the buy of your life !"

MERCURY 49~51

497

MERCURY
Merc-O-Matic Drive...or B-W Overdrive

CUSTOM

NEW 125 H.P. HIGH-COMPRESSION V-8

MONTEREY $2225. H/T

hardtop

H/T (24,453 BLT.)

new DASH

255.4 CID

52 (TOTALLY RESTYLED)

1952

118" WB

new HOOD SCOOP

FROM $1987.

new BUMPER-GRILLE

MONTEREY SEDAN

$2115.

7.10 x 15" TIRES, (7.60 x 15" ON '52 CVT. and '53 "MONTEREY" MODELS)

GET THE FACTS — AND YOU'LL GO FOR THE NEW 1953
MERCURY

LOWER-PRICED "CUSTOM" SERIES IN $2004.~2117. PRICE RANGE

MONTEREY

$2133.

DASH

new DECK-LID MEDALLION

POWER STEERING

1953

H/T (76,119 BLT.)

$2244.

new HORIZ. REAR FENDER TRIM

H/T

POWER BRAKES

3 new POWER OPTION CHOICES

53

new GRILLE 118" WB

4-WAY POWER SEAT

MERCURY 52~53

MERCURY

CUSTOM
$2251.

8-PASS. WAGON (11,656 BLT.)
$2776.

TOTAL 1954 PRODUCTION = 256,729

DASH

SEDANS

MONTEREY

new 161-horsepower engine

$2581. →

"SUN VALLEY" (new)

H/T (79,533 BLT.)
$2452.

54

new GRILLE

THE CAR THAT MAKES ANY DRIVING EASY

(9761 BLT.)

TOP-LINE MONTCLAIR SERIES 19 new

55

new 119" WB

new DASH

TOTAL 1955 PRODUCTION 434,911

NEW, EXCLUSIVE POWER LUBRICATION.

new 292 CID O.H.V. V8 ENG.
188 HP (OR 198 HP IN MONTCLAIR)

$2686.

new REAR STYLING →

$2465.

$2844.

(11,968 BLT.)

CUSTOM

$2277.

(69,093 BLT.)

MONTEREY

$2400.

(70,392 BLT.)

new PANORAMIC WINDSHIELD

new SIDE TRIM

7.10 x 15" TIRES

FROM $2218.
(CUSTOM 2-DR.)

$2631.

$2712.

SUN VALLEY

new GRILLE and HOODED HEADLIGHTS

(71,588 BLT.)

MERCURY 54-55

new MONTCLAIR

(1787 BLT.)

MERCURY

For 1956 _ the big move is to THE BIG MERCURY

56

MEDALIST
(new) (1956 ONLY)
(LOWEST-PRICED MODEL)
$2254.

(20,854)

CUSTOM

119" WB

MONTEREY

VOYAGER
(IN Montclair SERIES)

118" WB
ON WAGONS

"PHAETON"
4-DR. HARDTOP
(23,493 BLT.)

$2835.

REAR 3/4 DETAIL

MONTCLAIR

INTERIOR

For 1956 _ the big move is to
THE BIG MERCURY

new
312 CID V8
(210, 225 OR
235 HP)

CONVERTIBLE
(7762 BLT.)
$2900.

MONTCLAIR
H/T (50,562 BLT.)
$2765.

MERCURY .56

CLOSE
VIEW
OF
new
GRILLE

MERCURY

BIG M for '57

HIGH BEAM

LOW OR HIGH BEAM

QUADRI-BEAM HEADLAMPS (LATER MODELS)

MONTEREY

(EARLY) MONTCLAIR

PACE CAR AT 1957 INDY 500 RACE

$3758.

57

with DREAM-CAR DESIGN

(LATER)

(TOTALLY RESTYLED)

new 122" WB 255 HP

CONVENTIONAL STATION WAGON   NEW BIG M STATION WAGON

FRONT ROOF VENTS ON TURNPIKE CR. (290 HP)

MERCURY ELIMINATES THE LIFT GATE, LOWERS THE TAIL GATE

new **TURNPIKE CRUISER**

THERE'S ONLY ONE SIDE PILLAR IN THE NEW MERCURY COMMUTER

VOYAGER   2 and 4-DR. WAGONS

THE OPEN-AIR FEELING OF A HARDTOP -

ONLY 2 HEADLIGHTS ON EARLY MODELS

COLONY PARK

$3677.

6 wagons

BIG new WEDGE TAIL-LIGHTS

CENTER OF BACKLIGHT OPENS, ON TURNPIKE CR.

5-7. NEW MONITOR CONTROL PANEL, TACHOMETER, AVERAGE SPEED COMPUTER

2 V8 ENGINES AVAIL. 312 CID (255 HP); 368 CID (290 HP)
1957 MODELS : MONTEREY = PHAETON 4-DR H/T (22,475 BLT.); SEDAN (53,839 BLT.); PHAETON 2-DR H/T (42,199 BLT.); 2-DR. (33,982 BLT.); PHAETON CONVT. CPE. (5033 BLT.) **MONTCLAIR** = PHAETON 4-DR. H/T (21,567 BLT.); SEDAN (19,836 BLT.); PHAETON 2-DR. H/T (30,111 BLT.); PHAETON CVT. CPE. (4248 BLT.)
TURNPIKE CRUISER = H/T (7291 BLT.); 4-DR. H/T (8305 BLT.); CONVT. (1265 BLT.) **WAGONS** = COMMUTER 2-DR. (4885 BLT.); VOYAGER 2-DR. (2283 BLT.); COMMUTER 4-DR. (11,990 BLT.); COLONY PARK, 4 DR., 9-PASS. (7386 BLT.); COMMUTER, 4 DR., 9-PASS. (5752); VOYAGER, 4-DR., 9-PASS. (3716 BLT.)

MERCURY 57

MERCURY

PRICED FROM **$2547.** TO **4118.**

THE ALL-NEW **PARK LANE**

(LOW PRICED *MEDALIST* RETURNS FOR 1 MORE YEAR.)

$3944.

WHEEL COVER

58

ENGINES :
312 CID V8 (235 HP)
383 CID V8 (312 OR 330 HP)
NEW 430 CID V8 (360 HP)

122" WB (126" ON PARK LANE)
PARK LANE REPLACES TURNPIKE CRUISER

TOTAL 1959 PRODUCTION = 156,756
$2768. ~ 4206. PRICE RANGE
(MONTEREY 2-DR.) (PARK LANE CVT.)

ENGINES :
312 CID V8 (210 OR 280 HP)
383 CID V8 (280 OR 322 HP)
430 CID V8 (345 HP)

20th ANNIVERSARY
'59 MERCURY

MONTEREY 4-DR. H/T (11,355 BLT.)

"BUILT TO LEAD — BUILT TO LAST" $2918.

59A ENGINE

new ENLARGED WINDSHIELD AREA

new GRILLE VARIES IN APPEARANCE, DEPENDING ON ANGLE FROM WHICH IT IS VIEWED (SEE ALSO NEXT PG.)

(CONT'D.)
MERCURY 58~59(A)

502

MERCURY

MONTEREY SEDAN

$3357. (7375 QLT.)

(28,892 BLT.)
$2721.

MONTCLAIR

59B
(CONT'D.)

1959

FANCIER REAR STYLING
ON MONTCLAIR

(7206 BLT.)
$4031.

(15,122 BLT.)
COMMUTER 4-DR.
6-PASS. WAGON
$3215.

VOYAGER 4-DR., 6-PASS.
(2496 BLT.)   WAGON
$3793.

VOYAGER

PARK LANE
4-DR. H/T
CRUISER
(ABOVE)
has SPECIAL
REAR SIDE
TRIM

COMMUTER

WHEEL
COVER

126" WB
(128"
ON
Park Lane)

COLONY PARK
$3932.
(6-PASS.)

WAGON DETAILS

SLIP THE THIRD SEAT UNDER THE FLOOR

$3330. (9-PASS.)

COMMUTER
MERCURY 59(B)

MERCURY

$2631.

2-DR. H/T (MONTEREY)

MONTCLAIR

2 DR. MONTEREY (21,557 BLT.)

CVT.

(6062 BLT.)

$3077.

(RESTYLED) **60**

4-DR H/T

(MONTEREY)

9-PASS. COMMUTER
$3240.

COLONY PARK
$3950.
(7411 BLT.)

9-PASS.

$3858.

$4018.

PARK LANE
4-DR. H/T "CRUISER"
(5788 BLT.)

126" WB ON ALL MERCURYS (1960 ONLY)

PARK LANE CVT.
(1525 BLT.)

5 VERTICAL CHROME PCS. IDENTIFY PARK LANE. COLONY PARK has 6 PCS, and MONTCLAIR has 3.

1960 PRICE RANGE = $2631. ~ 4018.

(ONLY 2 STATION WAGON MODELS AVAIL. 1960, EACH ILLUSTRATED ON THIS PAGE.)

ENGINES: 312 CID V8 (205 HP) 383 CID V8 (280 HP) OR 430 CID V8 (310 HP)

TOTAL 1960 PRODUCTION = 161,787   MERCURY 60

MERCURY

the better low-price cars

61

METEOR 600
new series
V8 OR new 6

METEOR 800

H/T $2774.

MODEL NAME AT FRONT END OF DOOR →

Meteor 800

4-DR. H/T (9252 BLT.)
MONTEREY

$2878.

MONTEREY

$2924.
COMMUTER

COLONY PARK

(7887) BLT.

$3120. UP

MODEL SERIES : METEOR 600 = $2535. 2589. (18,117 BLT.)
METEOR 800 = $2713. 2839.   MONTEREY = $2871. 3128.
4 DR. STATION WAGONS = $2924. ~ 3191.   4 DR. (22,881 BLT.)
    COMMUTER (8945 BLT.)   H/T (10,942 BLT.)
    COLONY PARK (9-PASS.) } (7887 BLT.)   4 DR. H/T (9252 BLT.)
    COMMUTER (" ") (6 BLT.)   CONVERTIBLE (7053 BLT.)

125,792
TOTAL 1961 PRODUCTION

$2278. ~ 3738.
PRICE RANGE

MERCURY METEOR
116½" WB

62

S-33 DASH

TOTAL 1962 PRODUCTION = 190,560

METEOR

MONTEREY CUSTOM

new GRILLES

S-33 WHEEL COVER

(18,975 BLT.)

MONTEREY
$2672.
new TAIL-LIGHTS AT TOP OF FENDERS
MERCURY 61~62

6 OR V8 (101 TO 330 HP)

BA-9536

(S-55 MODELS ALSO)

"BEST-LOOKING BUYS...NOW IN EACH SIZE"

MERCURY

(4865 BLT.) $2628. **METEOR** $2278. *and up*

FINAL METEOR. 6-CYL.
MERC. ENG. ONLY IN COMET AFTER '63.

METEOR S-33

MONTEREY
$2930.

new OPENING "BREEZEWAY" BACKLIGHT →

H/T (3879 BLT.)

$2995.
4-DR
H/T

CONSOLE (S-55)

(1692 BLT.)

63

S-55 CONVERTIBLE and INTERIOR ↔

MONTEREY CUSTOM

(1379 BLT.)
$3900.

ENGINES:
170 CID 6 (101 HP)
221 CID V8 (145 HP)
260 CID V8 (164 HP)
390 CID V8 (250, 300 OR 330 HP)
406 CID V8 (385 OR 405 HP)

TOTAL 1963 PRODUCTION = 141,392

$3083.
MONTRY. CUSTOM MARAUDER ('63½)

(7298 BLT.)

$2719.

METEOR CUSTOM (3636 BLT.)

COUNTRY CRUISER

(13,936 BLT.)

COLONY PARK and INTERIOR

MERCURY 63

506

MERCURY

V8s ONLY

No finer car in the medium-price field

$3236. UP

COMMUTER WAGON

Commuter station wagon

2-DR. H/T

$3434. UP
COLONY PARK

MONTEREY
FROM $3202.
WEST COAST
120" WB
(ALL MOD.)

250 HP
V8

64

4-DR. MARAUDER
H/T $3413.

$3567.
WEST COAST

MONTCLAIR

MARAUDER
SO-CALLED "FASTBACK"-STYLE H/T
(6459 BLT.)

$3127.

$3127.

2-DR. H/T
(BREEZEWAY ROOFLINE)
(2329 BLT.)

CLOSE-UP OF DOOR
(PARK LANE) SHOWN ABOVE

WEST COAST
$3799.
EASTERN
$3413.
4-DR. MARAUDER H/T

PARK LANE (300 HP)
INTERIOR →

$3359.

2-DR.
H/T
(BREEZEWAY ROOFLINE)
(1786 BLT.)

DASH

1964 ENGINES: 390 CID V8 (250, 266, 300 OR 330 HP)
427 CID V8 (410 OR 425 HP)

1964 PRICE RANGE =
$2819. ~ 3549.

NOTE THE DIFFERING ROOFLINE STYLES,
AS ILLUSTRATED

MERCURY 64

MERCURY

Automatic Headlamp Dimmer—
low fuel warning light AVAIL.

• Multi-Drive Merc-O-Matic transmission •

1965 Mercury
$3434. UP

Station wagon

COLONY PARK
(15294 BLT.)
(8081 BLT.)

REAR

PARK LANL CVT. (3006 BLT.)

DASH

$3599.

65

TOTALLY RESTYLED

COMMUTER UNGRAINED WAGON $3235. UP

H/T

SEDAN

MONTCLAIR SIDE TRIM

4~DR. H/T

$2904.

(19569 BLT.)

AVAIL. emergency flasher

MONTEREY SEDAN WITH OPENING "BREEZEWAY" REAR WINDOW $3442. (14211 BLT.)

4~DR. HARDTOP

PARK LANE

FORWARD SIDE TRIM

PARK LANE

$2767.~3599.
PRICE RANGE

MERCURY

1965

TOTAL 1965 PROD.= 346,751

NOW IN THE LINCOLN CONTINENTAL TRADITION

Colony Park all-vinyl interiors are available in blue, red, turquoise, ivy gold and palomino. Cloth and vinyl, palomino only.

REAR DETAILS

—IMPROVED MARAUDER ENGINES	Adv hp @ rpm	CAR SERIES				
		Park Lane	Montclair	Monterey	Colony Park	Commuter
390 V-8	250 @ 4400	N.A.	Standard	Standard	Standard	Standard
390 V-8	266 @ 4400	N.A.	Standard‡	N.A.	Standard‡	N.A.
Super 390 V-8†	300 @ 4600	Standard	Optional	Optional	Optional	Optional
Interceptor 390 V-8*	330 @ 5000	Optional	Optional	Optional	Optional	Optional
Super 427 V-8*	425 @ 6000	Optional	Optional	Optional	N.A.	N.A.

seat belt warning light, door ajar warning light AVAIL.   power door locks AVAIL.   MERCURY 65

Mercury

390 CID V8 (265 or 275 HP)
410 CID V8 (330 HP)
428 CID V8 (345 HP)

Dual-Action Tailgate. Swings down like a regular tailgate for cargo. Or swings aside like a door for people.

COLONY PARK WAGON

119" WB (WAGONS)

walnut-toned paneling.

2-SEAT=$3893.; 3-SEAT=$3988.
(UNGRAINED COMMUTER
WAGONS
ALSO
AVAIL.)

66

MONTEREY, MONTCLAIR,
PARK LANE, S-55
MODELS

123" WB
(343,149 BLT.)

new BROUGHAM and MARQUIS MODELS

new SIDE TRIM on COLONY PK. WAGON (18,690 BLT.)

MONTEREY

67

(INTRO. 9-30-66)

$3657. UP

new PROTRUDING CENTER SECTION OF FRONT END

STD. 390 CID V8 has new 270 HP
(S-55 DISCONTINUED)

(354,923 BLT.)

FRONT DETAIL

ENGINES:
390 CID V8
(265, 280 or 315 HP)
428 CID V8
(340 HP)

(INTRO. 9-22-67)

new FRONT CORNERING and REAR SIDE LTS.

new SWEPT-BACK ROOFLINE

First hardtop with yacht-deck vinyl paneling.

PARK LANE $3575.

68

360,467 BLT.

BROUGHAM 4-DR. H/T
BROUGHAM OPTION $272. EXTRA

new GRILLE

MERCURY 66~68

Mercury

$3237. MONTEREY H/T CVT.

(9865 BLT.)

Monterey cloth-and-vinyl interior

$3757. MONT. CUSTOM station wagon

(1920 BLT.)

1969

(1297 BLT.)

$3540.

TOTAL 1969 PROD.: 398,262

69 (INTRO. 9~27~68)

new 124" WB

MARQUIS CVT.

$4124. (2319 BLT.)

new CONCEALED HDLTS. on MARQUIS, MARAUDER)

4~DR. H/T

$4262.

(14966 BLT.)

Marquis:

$3857.

(16787 BLT.)

(new) Marquis Brougham:

H/T

$4191.

(8395 BLT.)

STD.
390 CID V8
(265 OR 280 HP)
429 CID V8 (320 HP)

(25604 BLT.)

Marquis Colony Park

WAGON

$3895.

INTERIOR

H/T

Marauder:
(OWN 121" WB)
(121 on WAGONS ALSO)

(9031 BLT.)

$3368.

$4091.

new
Marauder X-100. In case just luxury isn't enough

429 CID V8
(360 HP)

(5635 BLT.)

MARQUIS BRM. DASH

UPHOLSTERY (X-100)

$3158.~4262.
PRICE RANGE

MERCURY 69

510

STATION WAGON 121" WB
(2388 BLT.)

(5164 BLT.)
MONTEREY $3682. UP
$3930. UP
MARQUIS

Twin Comfort lounge seats optional in Colony Park

Marquis Colony Park
(19204 BLT.)
$4123. UP

Mercury

(SAME V8 ENGINES and HP AS IN 1969)

(DASHBOARDS GENERALLY SIMILAR TO 1969)

$3600. H/T

G78 × 15 TIRES
H78 × 15, WAGONS

$3668.

MONTEREY CUSTOM

(1357 BLT.)

CVT. (581 BLT.)
MONTEREY 124" WB

REAR INSIGNIA and WHEEL DETAILS

(1194 BLT.. 4~DR. H/T

MARQ. 4-DR. H/T INT.

$4113. H/T

$3676.

70

NO MORE HORN RINGS ON STEER. WHEELS

(6229 BLT.)

Marquis
124" WB

(INTRO. 9-19-69)

MARAUDER
$3503.

(ON MARQ., MARAUDER)
VERTICAL PCS ADDED TO GRILLE

H/T (3397 BLT.)

121" WB

4-DR. H/T (11623 BLT.)
(MARQUIS CVT. ALSO)
(1233 BLT.)

MARQUIS BROUGHAM $4500.

TOTAL 1970 PRODUCTION = 324,716
(8TH PLACE IN SALES, 1965 TO 1973)

(2646 BLT.)
MARAUDER
X~100 H/T $4136.

(FINAL FULL-SIZED MERCURY CONVERTIBLES)

MERCURY 70

MERCURY $3968.

4-DR. H/T MONTEREY
(2483 BLT.)

H/T

(9099 BLT.)

$3900.

$4283. UP

(4160 BLT.) MONTEREY

WAGON

DASH (22744 BLT.)

SEDAN $3858.

(INTRO. 9-18-70)

71

MARQ. BRGH. UPHOL.

new GRILLES, ENTIRELY ABOVE BUMPER

MARQUIS

WAGON

TOTAL 1971 PROD.= 365,310

MONTEREY CUSTOM H/T (4508 BLT.)

FROM $4547. (2158 BLT.)

new 351 CID V8 (240 HP)
new 400 CID V8 (260 HP)
429 CID V8 (320/360 HP)

$4113.
Marquis

MARQUIS INTERIOR

(5491 BLT.) $4624.

(13781 BLT.) MARQUIS BROUGHAM

4-DR. H/T

4-DR. H/T

$5033.

SEDAN $4880.

(25790 BLT.)

MARQUIS, MARQUIS BROUGH. and COLONY PARK GRILLE and DASH

IMITATION CHERRYWOOD TRIM
MERCURY 71

Better ideas make better cars.

512

Mercury

$3896. (1416 BLT.)

MONTEREY
4-DR. H/T $4391. (WEST)

DASH (MONTEREY CUSTOM) (5910 BLT.)

note SMALL HUB CAPS

$4035.
MONTEREY H/T
CUSTOM $4530.
(has CHROME STRIP ALONG MID-SIDE)
WESTERN PRICE

VARIOUS MONTEREY TYPES have EXPOSED HEADLIGHTS

H.P. CUT:
351 CID V8 (163 HP)
400 CID V8 (172 HP)
429 CID V8 (208 HP)

REAR (MONTEREY)

TOTAL 1972 PROD.:
441,964

(20192 BLT.)

72

new "WAFFLE" GRILLE PATTERN

$4550.
COLONY PARK
($5045. (2-SEAT)
5167. (4-SEAT)

(INTRO. 9-17-71)

OPT. SUNROOF

Better ideas make better cars:

Marquis
4-DR. H/T
$5132. (WEST)

$4637.
(1583 BLT.)

Mercury's ride rated better than a $34,000 limousine by 36 out of 50 professional chauffeurs.

$4890. (38242 BLT.)

DASH (MARQUIS BROUGHAM)

$5400. (WEST)
MARQUIS BROUGHAM
PILLARED
4-DR. H/T (SEDAN)

MARQUIS BROUGHAM INTERIOR

(2085 BLT.)
MARQUIS WAGON

MERCURY LINCOLN

MONTEREY INTERIOR

INTERIOR $4445. MERCURY ~ 72

Mercury

MTY. / MTY. CUSTOM (MARQUIS DASH. SIMILAR, BUT T-SHAPED ST. WH. SPOKES)
DASH

MARQUIS BROUGHAM

MARQUIS

MONTEREY CUSTOM

new FINER GRILLE PCS.; CORNER LTS. on FRONT FENDERS FOR 1ST TIME SINCE 1968.

new ENERGY-ABSORBING SAFETY BUMPERS

73
Built better to ride better.

TOTAL 1973 PROD. = 486,470

"MONTEREY" SERIES STOPS DURING 1974.

MARQUIS INTERIOR

74

"MERCURY" NAME ABOVE new GRILLE (1974 ONLY) (194

new 250 cid 6 (91 HP) 400 cid V8 (170 HP) 460 cid V8 (175 HP)

TOTAL 1974 PRODUCTION = 403,977

('75) DASH (MARQUIS)

MARQUIS WAGON

MARQUIS

HOOD ORNAMENT NOW UPRIGHT

new HEADLIGHT COVERS, new GRILLE, HIGHER CORNER LIGHTS

75-78 A

1978 MARQUIS has SIDE TRIM LIKE GRAND MARQUIS

(CONT'D. NEXT PAGE)

H/T

Mercury Marquis Brougham

MERCURY 75-78 (A)

Mercury

GRAND MARQUIS

DETAILS OF *new* UPRIGHT HOOD ORNAMENT INTRO. 1975

GRAND MARQUIS DASH *has* SWIRLED WOOD-GRAIN VINYL TRIM

75-78 (CONT'D.) B

'RIDE-ENGINEERED *by* LINCOLN *&* MERCURY
DASH PLAQUE ('77)

PRODUCTION/PRICE RANGE

Year	Production	Price Range
1975	404,650	$5049.~6469.
1976	480,361	5063.~6528.
1977	521,909	5496.~6975.
1978	635,051	5897.~7399.

COLONY PARK

ENGINES
1975- FINAL 250 CID 6
351 CID V8 (144/145 HP) (1978)
400 CID V8 (170 HP, 1974) (158 HP, 1975)
(180 HP, 1976) (173 HP, 1977) (160 HP, 1978)
460 CID V8 (195 HP, 1974) (216 HP, 1975)
(202 HP, 1976) (197 HP, 1977) (460 HP, 1978)

DASH

Marquis 2-door sedan

GRAND MARQUIS RECOGNIZED BY THIS

Marquis Colony Park

MARQUIS BROUGHAM. $6986.

302 CID V8 (129 HP)
351 CID V8 (138 HP)

(10627 BLT.)

MARQUIS SEDAN (32289 BLT.)

(13758 BLT.) $7495. UP

(5994 BLT.) Marquis Wagon

79

RESTYLED and DOWNSIZED $6701. UP 114.3" WB

Color swatches: 1C, 9C, 1G, 2J, 3F, 3L, 2H, 3H, 8J, 75, 1N, 5P, 8N, 62, 76, 4D

MARQUIS EXTERIOR COLORS.

Standard Colors
1C Black
9C White
1G Silver Met.
2J Dark Maroon
3F Lt. Med. Blue
3L Dark Blue Met.
4D Dark Pine Met.
76 Lt. Med. Pine

62 Antique Cream
8N Dark Cordovan Met.
5P Pastel Chamois
1N Dove Grey
Optional Glamour Paints
2H Med. Red Met.
3H Med. Blue Met.
75 Med. Pine Met.
8J Med. Tan Met.

Optional Tu-Tone accent

1979 PROD. 669,138

MERCURY 75(B)~79

515

Mercury

LUXURY WHEEL COVER

MARQUIS $7185.

SEDAN (13018 BLT.)

DASH

$8477. UP

COLONY PARK

15" FULL WHEEL COVER

302 c/d V8 (130 HP)
351 c/d V8 (140 HP)

REAR DETAILS

(5781 BLT.)

UNGRAINED MARQUIS STATION WAGON
SIMILAR TO 1979 ILLUSTRATION.

MINOR TRIM CHANGES IN SOME TYPES, new AUTOMATIC OVERDRIVE TRANS. AVAIL.

GRAND MARQUIS TWO-DOOR.

80

P205/75 R x 14 TIRES (P215/75R x 14, WAGONS)

(3434 BLT.) $8631.

CAST ALUMINUM TURBINE SPOKE WHEELS

WIRE WHEEL COVERS

RED CENTER ON '79 TYPE, BLACK ON '80 (PERTAINS TO WIRE ONLY)

4-DR. $8846. (WEST)

INTERIOR

note COURTESY LT. and BAND OVER ROOF

$8824.

GRAND MARQUIS.. SEDAN (15995 BLT.)

FRONT DETAILS

"RESUME" SWITCH AVAIL. SINCE 1979

MARQUIS EXTERIOR COLORS

Standard Colors
1C Black
9D White
1G Silver Metallic
2H Med. Red Metallic
3F Lt. Medium Blue
3D Dark Blue Metallic
4D Dark Pine Metallic
2K Candy Apple Red
8N Dk. Cordovan Metallic

5P Pastel Sand
1N Light Grey
1P Med. Grey Metallic

Optional Glamour Paints
4E Pastel Pine Metallic
3H Med. Blue Metallic
6B Sand Metallic
8D Med. Bittersweet Met.

1C	9D	1G	2H	3F	3D	4E	3H
4D	2K	8N	5P	1N	1P	6B	8D

MERCURY 80

MERCURY Bobcat
(1975-1980)

140 CID 4 (92 HP) (ALSO AVAIL., STARTING '76 171 CID V6, 100 HP)

94½" WB (WAGON 94.8")

3-DOOR RUNABOUT
$3189. ('75)
(20651 BLT. '75)

(QUITE SIMILAR TO FORD PINTO, BUT SCARCER.)

24 TO 29 MPG HWY.
17 TO 19 MPG CITY ('75)

3-DR. FROM $3456. (WEST) ('75)

('75)

DASH

('75)

FROM $3748. ('75) (WEST)

$3481. (13583 BLT. '75)

VILLAGER WAGON

75-78

REAR

1976 = IMITATION CHERRY WOODGRAIN OPT. ON RUNABOUT, AT $3809.

1977 = new EXTRUDED ALUMINUM BUMPERS; new ALL-GLASS HATCHBACK DOOR, MOON-ROOF, 4-WAY ADJUSTABLE DRIVER'S SEAT ARE OPTIONAL

(23428 BLT., 1978)

UNGRAINED WAGON ALSO AVAIL. SINCE 1977.

Bobcat wagons come with all the same standard features.

1978 is the year to LOVE THAT BOBCAT. More standard features than last year for a lower sticker price.*

a. Steel-belted radials now standard.
b. Styled-steel wheels with trim rings now standard.
c. Power front-disc brakes now standard.
d. Tinted glass now standard.
e. Front stabilizer bar now standard.

('78)

$3830. ('78)

BOBCAT RUNABOUT

WITH WOODGRAIN OPTION ('76)

VINYL INTERIOR TRIM OPTION ('76)

STANDARD CLOTH ~ AND ~ VINYL INTERIOR ('76)

MERCURY BOBCAT 75~78

MERCURY BOBCAT

('79)
$4104.
UP

WHEEL
and
WHEEL
COVER
CHOICES →

STANDARD
3-DOOR RUNABOUT
$4104. ('79)
4764. ('80)

w.
SPORTS
ACCENT
GROUP
('80)

WITH SPORTS
PACKAGE OPTION ('79)

new GRILLE **79-80**

WITH
SPORT OPTION
and BLACK GRILLE ('80)

140 CID 4 OR 171 CID V6
BR 78 × 13 TIRES

OPTIONAL SPORTS
INSTRUMENTATION DASH

STD. VINYL INT. ('80)

RECTANGLE
DASH
CLUSTER

('80)

$4410. ('79)
5070. ('80)

BOBCAT AND
VILLAGER WAGONS

$4523. ('79)
5183. ('80)

('79)

ROSEWOOD~TONE and
WOODTONE GRAIN
VILLAGER
$4519. ('79)
4950. ('80)
(REPLACED BY
1981 LYNX)

12 COLOR CHOICES ('80)

Silver Metallic 1G
All Models

Bright Blue 3J
Capri-Bobcat

Bright Yellow 6N
Capri-Bobcat

Bright Red 27
Capri-Bobcat

Light Medium Blue 3F
All Models except Cougar XR-7

Dark Pine Metallic 7M
All Models except Monarch
and Capri

Dark Cordovan Met. 8N
All Models

Dark Chamois Metallic 8A
All Models except Marquis

OPTIONAL EXTERIOR COLOR

Bright Bittersweet 2G
Capri-Bobcat

Bright Caramel 5T
Capri-Bobcat

White 9D
All Models

Medium Red Metallic 2H
All Models except Monarch
and Capri

MERCURY
BOBCAT 79~80

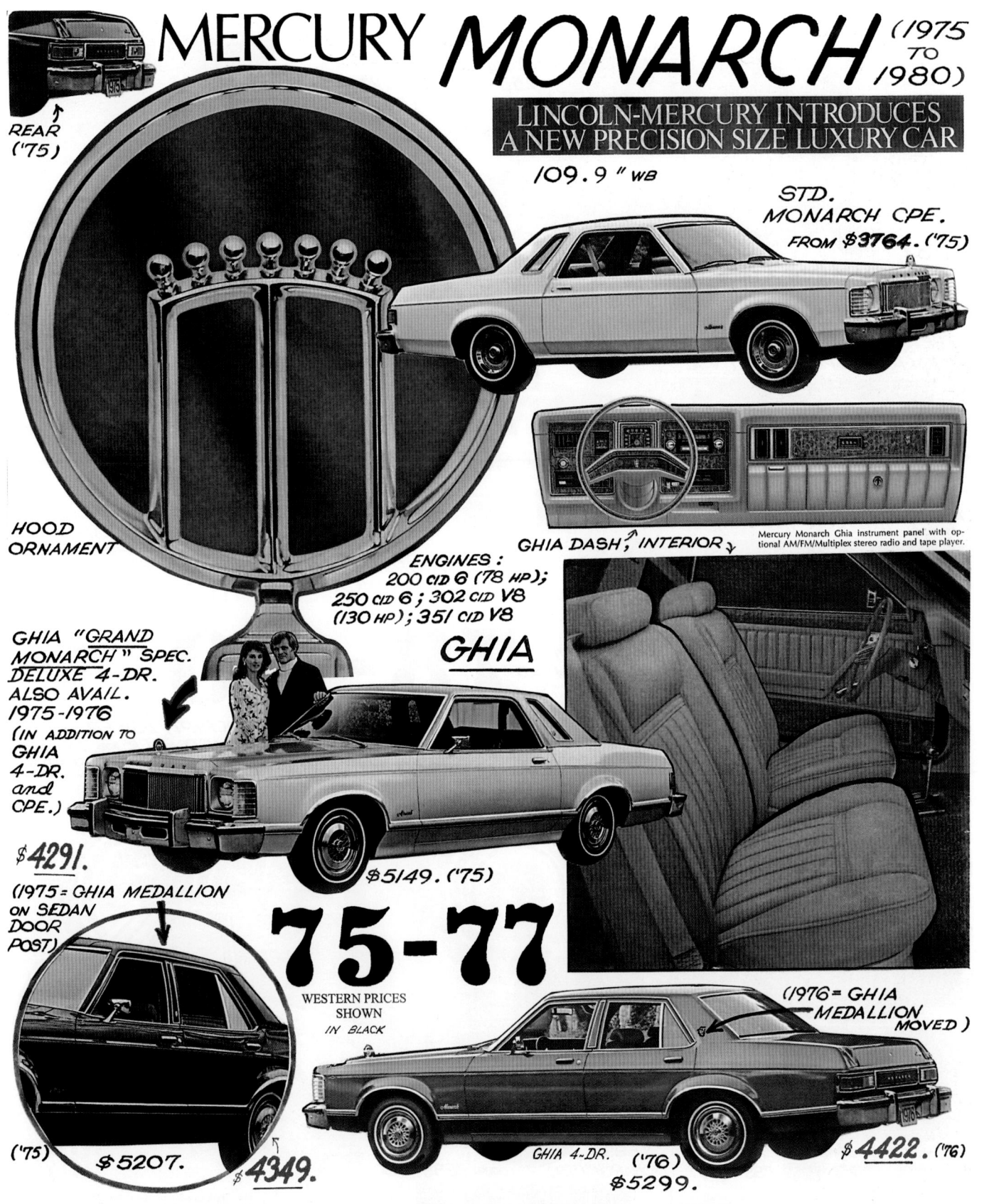

MERCURY *MONARCH* (1975 TO 1980)

REAR ('75)

LINCOLN-MERCURY INTRODUCES A NEW PRECISION SIZE LUXURY CAR

109.9" WB

STD. MONARCH CPE. FROM $3764. ('75)

HOOD ORNAMENT

GHIA DASH, INTERIOR

Mercury Monarch Ghia instrument panel with optional AM/FM/Multiplex stereo radio and tape player.

ENGINES: 200 CID 6 (78 HP); 250 CID 6; 302 CID V8 (130 HP); 351 CID V8

GHIA

GHIA "GRAND MONARCH" SPEC. DELUXE 4-DR. ALSO AVAIL. 1975-1976 (IN ADDITION TO GHIA 4-DR. and CPE.)

$4291.

(1975 = GHIA MEDALLION ON SEDAN DOOR POST)

$5149. ('75)

75-77

WESTERN PRICES SHOWN IN BLACK

(1976 = GHIA MEDALLION MOVED)

('75) $5207.

$4349.

GHIA 4-DR. ('76) $5299.

$4422. ('76)

PRICE RANGE (EAST)	PRODUCTION BY MODEL (YEARLY)			
	2-DR.	4 DR.	GHIA 2-DR.	GHIA/GRAND 4-DR.
1975 = $3764. ~ 5375.	(29151);	(34307);	(17755);	(22723)
1976 = 3773. ~ 5740.	" (47466)	" (56351)	" (14950)	" " (27056)
1977 = 4076. ~ 4722.	" (44509)	" (55952)	" (11051);	GHIA 4~DR. (16545)

MERCURY MONARCH 75~77

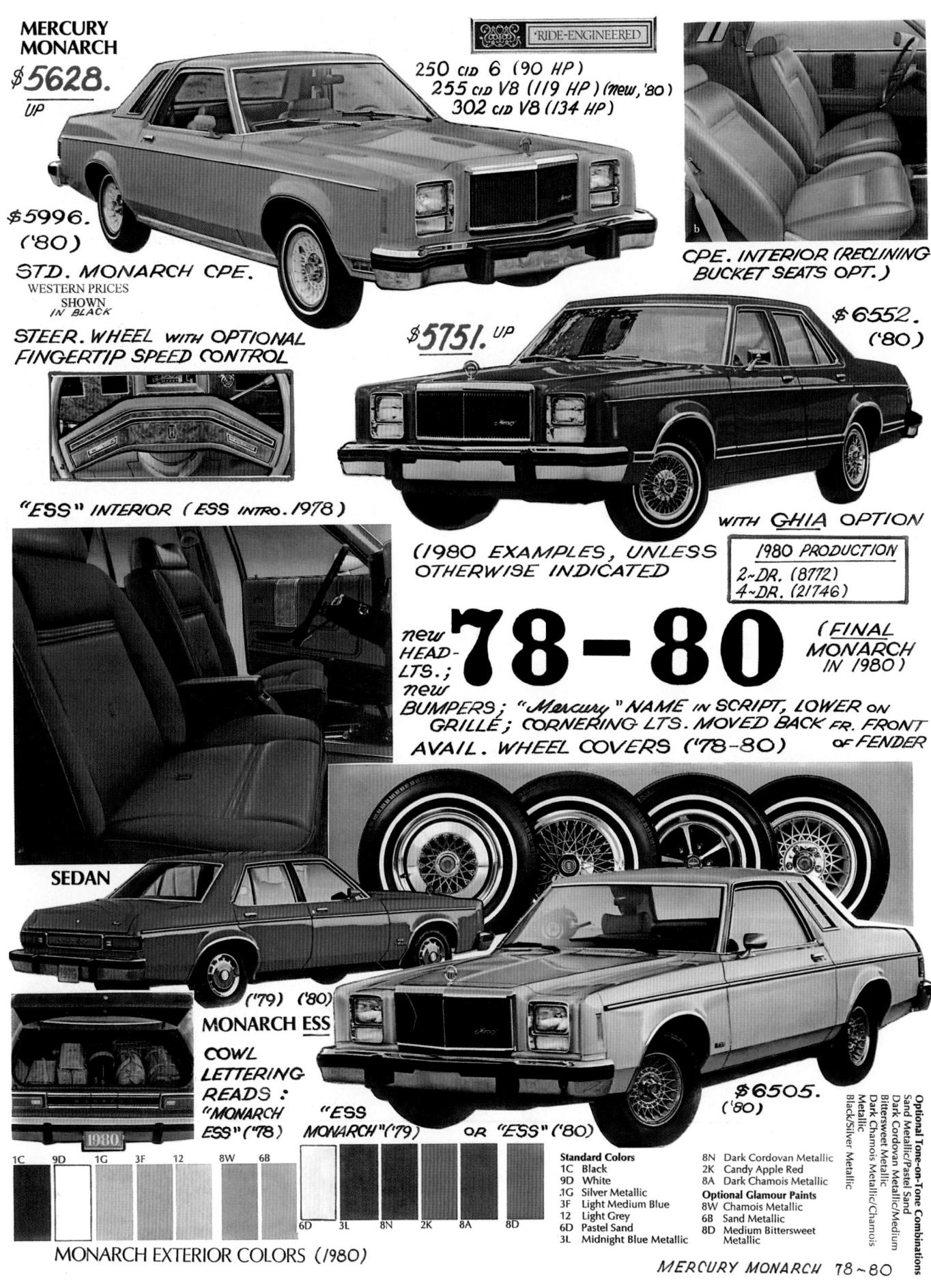

MERCURY MONARCH

$5628. UP

$5996. ('80)
STD. MONARCH CPE.
WESTERN PRICES SHOWN IN BLACK

·RIDE-ENGINEERED·

250 CID 6 (90 HP)
255 CID V8 (119 HP) (new, '80)
302 CID V8 (134 HP)

CPE. INTERIOR (RECLINING BUCKET SEATS OPT.)

STEER. WHEEL WITH OPTIONAL FINGERTIP SPEED CONTROL

$5751. UP

$6552. ('80)

WITH GHIA OPTION

"ESS" INTERIOR (ESS INTRO. 1978)

(1980 EXAMPLES, UNLESS OTHERWISE INDICATED

1980 PRODUCTION
2~DR. (8772)
4~DR. (21746)

new HEAD-LTS.; new **78-80** (FINAL MONARCH IN 1980)
BUMPERS; "Mercury" NAME IN SCRIPT, LOWER ON GRILLE; CORNERING LTS. MOVED BACK FR. FRONT OF FENDER
AVAIL. WHEEL COVERS ('78-80)

SEDAN

('79) ('80)

MONARCH ESS

COWL LETTERING READS: "MONARCH ESS" ('78)

"ESS MONARCH" ('79)

OR "ESS" ('80)

$6505. ('80)

1980

MONARCH EXTERIOR COLORS (1980)

1C 9D 1G 3F 12 8W 6B
6D 3L 8N 2K 8A 8D

Standard Colors
1C   Black
9D   White
1G   Silver Metallic
3F   Light Medium Blue
12   Light Grey
6D   Pastel Sand
3L   Midnight Blue Metallic

8N   Dark Cordovan Metallic
2K   Candy Apple Red
8A   Dark Chamois Metallic
Optional Glamour Paints
8W   Chamois Metallic
6B   Sand Metallic
8D   Medium Bittersweet Metallic

Optional Tone-on-Tone Combinations
Sand Metallic/Pastel Sand
Dark Cordovan Metallic/Medium
Bittersweet Metallic
Dark Chamois Metallic/Chamois Metallic
Black/Silver Metallic

MERCURY MONARCH 78~80

MERCURY ZEPHYR (STARTS 1978)

(QUITE SIMILAR TO FORD FAIRMONT)

WAGONS

STD. ROUND-HUB STEER. WH.

LOWER DASH IS ↑ OPTIONAL SPORTS INSTRUMENTATION GROUP

REAR WIPER AVAIL. FOR WAGON

1978 WHEEL CVR. →

1979-1980 WHEELS and COVERS

2-DR.

AVAIL. WITH GHIA OPTION

4-DR.

78-80

ENERGY ENGINEERED FOR MILEAGE: EPA EST.
33 HWY. **23** CITY

140.3 CID 4 (89 HP), 200 CID 6 (96 HP), 302 CID V8 (130 HP) (255 CID V8 AVAIL. '80)

(105½" WB)
1980 EXAMPLES ILLUSTRATED

Z-7 SPORT COUPE.

SPECIAL HOOD and WHEELS WITH **TURBO OPTION**

"ES" OPTION ('78-79) has BLACK AREAS AROUND SIDE WINDOWS

$5944. ('80)

ORIG. 1978 PRICES $4700. and UP

RIDE-ENGINEERED

1978 = $3777. ~ 4216.
1979 = 4253. ~ 4647.
1980 = 5041. ~ 5364.
EASTERN PRICE RANGES ABOVE

PRODUCTION BY MODEL (YEARLY)
2-DR. (27673); 4-DR. (47334); Z-7 SPT. CPE. (44569); WAGON (32596)
(15920) " (41316) " (42923) " (25218)
(10977) " (40399) " (19486) " (20341)

MERCURY ZEPHYR 78~80

METEOR (STARTS 1949)

FORD-SIZED CAR SOLD BY CANADIAN LINCOLN-MERCURY DEALERS

49

NEW!

INTRODUCED 1949 $1882. UP 239.4 CID V8 (100 HP) 114" WB

23,027 BLT.

$1837. UP

26,075 BLT.

50

114" WB

METEOR

239.4 CID V8 (100 HP)

114" WB

1951

$2170. UP

23,138 BLT.

DASH

$2155. UP "MAINLINE" SERIES

52

20,709 BLT.

NEW 115" WB

NEW L-HEAD 239 CID V8 (110 HP)

"CUSTOMLINE" HAS 255 CID V8, MERCURY-STYLE DASH. 120 HP

115" WB $2157. UP

DASH

40,115 BLT. (FINAL MAINLINE and CUSTOMLINE 1954)

SAME WB, ENGS. AS METEOR 1952

REAR DECK INSIGNIA

more than ever—miles ahead **'53 Meteor**

L HEAD V8s = 239 CID (110 HP) OR 255.4 CID (125 HP) $2157. UP

115" WB 6.70 OR 7.10 x 15 TIRES

new METEOR, NIAGARA and RIDEAU SERIES

1954

27,269 BLT.

'54 Meteor

MONARCH **MERCURY**-SIZED CAR SOLD BY CANADIAN FORD DEALERS. (STARTS 1946.) (ALSO SEE MERCURY, 1946.)

$2595. UP

49

118" WB (THRU IN '54) 11,317 BLT.

$2481. UP

1950 Monarch

Ride like a King in a **Monarch**

6056 BLT.

$2924. UP **51**

7682 BLT.

1951 451 **MONARCH**

255.4 CID V8 (125 HP)

1952 Monarch

(DLX.) MONTEREY SERIES is new

$2793. UP

4529 BLT.

MONARCH $2812. UP

53 255.4 CID V8 (125 HP)

7A52 BLT.

NEW 256 CID V8 (161 HP) $2814. UP 8566 BLT.

54 *new CUSTOM and LUCERNE SERIES*

DASH

METEOR/MONARCH '49-'54

MONARCH

Meteor

55 23,590 BLT.
$2172. UP
272 CID V8 (162 HP)
(175 HP AVAIL.)

56 38,397 BLT.
new 115 1/2" WB
new 6 CYL. AVAIL. ALSO (223 CID, 137 HP)
$2327. UP
METEOR, NIAGARA and RIDEAU SERIES
272 CID V8 (173 OR 176 HP) OR
292 CID V8 (200 OR 202 HP);
6.70 OR 7.10 x 15 TIRES

57
223 CID 6 (144 HP)
272 CID V8 (190 HP)
292 V8 (212 HP)
312 CID V8 (245 HP)
new 116 OR 118" WB
new 7.50 x 14 TIRES
34,164 BLT.
$2434. UP

58
23,933 BLT.
4 HEADLIGHTS
6 OR 3 V8s (145-303 HP)
116" WB NIAGARA OR 118" WB RIDEAU MODELS
DASH

59 33,710 BLT. METEOR
223 CID 6 (145 HP)
332 CID V8 OR
361 CID V8 (303 HP)
$2684. UP
1959
118" WB

60
new 119" WB
19,356 BLT.
223 CID 6 (145 HP)
$2744. UP
CX 0000
332 CID V8 (225 HP)
352 CID V8 (300 HP)
METEOR GRILLE

61
14,189 BLT.
$2744. UP
M-1961
119" WB
METEOR

Monarch **55**
6151 BLT.
$2783. UP
INTERIOR LUCERNE and RICHELIEU SERIES

56
MONARCH
10,156 BLT.
119" WB
1956
DASH

57
MONARCH
8468 BLT.
$3291. UP
57
312 CID V8 (255 HP)
All-new instrument panel centralizes controls for unprecedented driving ease!

1957 MONARCH INTERIOR →
RICHELIEU SERIES

FOR '58 ONLY, EDSEL REPLACES MONARCH
↓
'58 UNAVAILABLE

59 MONARCH
$3531. UP
4979 b-J.

60 FRONTENAC
$2360. UP
(REAR)
FALCON-SIZED, AVAIL. 1960 ONLY
144 CID 6 (90 HP)
109 1/2" WB
19-60

60 MONARCH
4494 BLT.
9536 BLT.
V8s 280 OR 310 HP
3723 BLT.
$4109. UP

61
V8s 352 OR 390 CID (220 OR 300 HP)
METEOR/MONARCH SS~61
120" WB
MONARCH

ASSEMBLED IN ENGLAND BY AUSTIN, FOR U.S. MARKET

Metropolitan (1954~1961)

85" WB ON ALL

UP TO 40 MILES A GALLON!

YEARLY PRODUCTION:
1954 = 13,095	1955 = 6096
1956 = 9068	1957 = 15,317
1958 = 13,128	1959 22,309
1960 = 13,103	1961 853
1962 = 412	

(1961 and 1962 MODELS WERE ACTUALLY 1960 LEFTOVERS.)

542 COUPE

1445.

4 CYL. O.H.V. AUSTIN ENGINE 73.8 CID (42 HP)

Nash OR HUDSON NAMEPLATE UNTIL '57.

54-55   "1200" SERIES 54

PULL~KNOB STARTER CONTROL AND OPEN GLOVE BOX BEFORE '56.   DASH

541 CONVERTIBLE 1469.

WITH TOP UP

$1697. CONVERTIBLE ('60)

DASH

BEFORE '59 THE ONLY ACCESS TO TRUNK WAS TO SWING REAR SEATBACK FORWARD.

90.4 CID 4 (52 HP)

DURING 1959, OUTSIDE DECK LID ADDED, ALSO VENT WINDOW~ WINGS.

56-*61   "1500" SERIES 56

NEW GRILLE and SIDE TRIM
2-TONE COLORS
GRILLE CLOSE-UP

DOOR HANDLE DETAIL

AT YOUR
RAMBLER-METROPOLITAN DEALER

$1673. COUPE ('60)

METROPOLITAN

MUSTANG

ROY C. McCARTHY,
MUSTANG ENGINEERING CO.,
SEATTLE AND RENTON, WASH.

(1947-1949)

49

4-CYL. HERCULES ENGINE
59 H.P.   65 M.P.H.
NO DEALERSHIPS; FACTORY ORDERS ONLY

ALUMINUM BODY
102" W.B.
5.50 × 15" TIRES

TUBULAR CHASSIS FRAME

THIS MUSTANG NOT AFFILIATED WITH
FORD MOTOR COMPANY.

$1235.

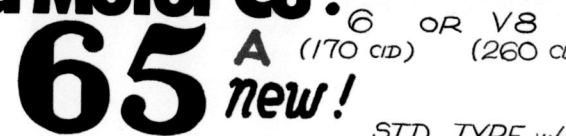

MUSTANG *Ford*   BY **Ford Motor Co.** 6 OR V8
(170 CID) (260 CID)

65 new!

(STARTS APRIL, 1964)

STD. TYPE w/o
GRILLE LIGHTS �

standard-equipment

(bucket seats, full carpeting, vinyl interior,
floor-mounted transmission)

Surprisingly spacious trunk

REAR

CVT. IS PACE CAR AT
1964 INDY 500
RACE.

WHEEL
COVER

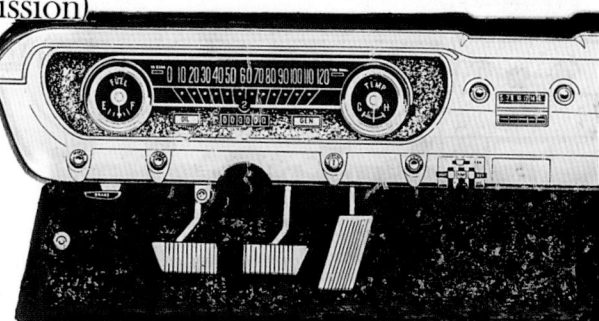

STD. DASH

ALL CIRCULAR GAUGES ON
DE LUXE DASH
(BELOW)

$2368* f.o.b.
Detroit
— AND UP —

INTRO.
PRICE

108" WB
(THROUGH 1970)

options *INCLUDE:*

a 289 cu. in. V-8. Four-on-the-floor. Tachometer and clock
combo. Special handling package. Front disc brakes—

New luxury instrument panel

STANDARD
SIDE
EMBLEM
→

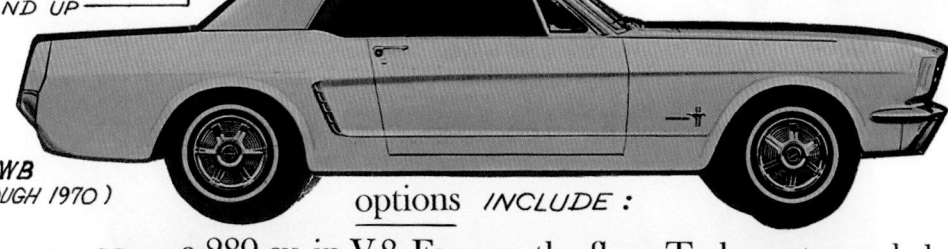

NOTE
MESH
GRILLE
ON '65.

(SOME COLLECTORS CONSIDER EARLY MODELS "1964½") (CONT'D. NEXT PAGE)

MUSTANG~49 / MUSTANG 65(A)

MUSTANG

Unique Ford GT stripe — badge of America's greatest total performance cars!

"2 + 2" BACK SEAT

New integral arm rests — courtesy lights

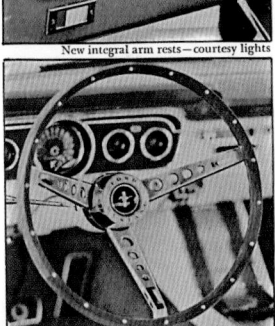

INTERIOR VIEWS (ABOVE) $2372.

"2 + 2" FASTBACK $2589.

NOTCHBACK HARDTOP

Mustang GT

CONVERTIBLE $2614.

65 B (CONT'D.)

ENGINES

170 CID 6 (101 HP) ●
200 " 6 (120 HP)
260 " V8 (164 HP) ●
289 " V8 (200 HP)
289 " V8 (225/271 HP)

● = STD. UNTIL 9~24~64

EXTRA (FOG) LIGHTS IN GT GRILLE

IDENTIFYING RACING STRIPES ON GT

MUSTANG

1965 PRODUCTION (SINCE APRIL, 1964)
#07 2-DR. H/T (NOTCHBACK) (501,965 BLT.)
#08 CONVERTIBLE (101,945 BLT.) = $2614. UP
#09 FASTBACK COUPE (77,079 BLT.)

(303,408 MUSTANGS BLT. BEFORE 1965 CALENDAR YEAR)

ENGINES: 170 CID 6 (101 HP) (TO 9-25-64)
200 CID 6 (120 HP) (9-25-64 ON)
260 CID V8 (164 HP) (TO 9-25-64)
289 CID V8 (200 HP) (9-25-64 ON)
(225 OR 271 HP OPTIONAL ON ALL 289 CID V8s)
(VINYL-COVERED ROOF AVAIL.)
(2 DR. H/T)
MUSTANG 65~B

526

YOU'RE AHEAD IN A FORD ALL THE WAY!

MUSTANG

Ford

COWL EMBLEM

Mustang's new instrument panel groups five easy-to-read dials

2+2 $2607. (35698 BLT.)

GT

↑ FENDER BADGE ON GT

Cruise-O-Matic AVAIL. behind the 271 solid-lifter V-8 $2653.

CVT. (72119 BLT.)

66

REAR $2416. H/T

VARIATION

HORSE EMBLEM

GT has EXHAUST PIPE EXTENSIONS

America's Favorite Fun Car
MUSTANG
MUSTANG
MUSTANG

(499,751 BLT.)

new GRILLE WITH HORIZONTAL PIECES

1966 PROD. = 607,568

(44808 CVTS. BLT '67) $2653. new DASH

new GRILLE

120 MPH SPEEDO.

Select Shift

GT REAR (CORRUGATED)

(SMOOTH REAR PANEL)
2+2 ↓

$2592.

67
A

ENGINES = 200 CID 6 (120 HP)
289 CID V8 (200, 225 or 271 HP)
new 390 CID V8 (320 HP)

SHELBY G.T. ('67½)

1967 PROD. = 472,121

(71042 BLT.)

350 and 500 The Road Cars

take the MUSTANG PLEDGE!

SHELBY CONT'D. NEXT PAGE

Ford ...has a better idea

(356,271 H/Ts BLT.) $2461.

MUSTANG 66~67(A)

527

MUSTANG

$3995.

Carroll Shelby Presents _The Road Cars..._
G.T. 350 and G.T. 500 **for 1967**

500

289 CID V8 (306 HP)

SHELBY G.T.
350 (1175 BLT.)

$67\frac{1}{2}$

428 CID V8 (400 HP)

(2050 BLT.)

MODIFIED (SHELBY TYPES)

$4195.

$4317.

Shelby Cobra

SHELBY COBRA

SHELBY COBRA DASH

← GT-500

(1140 BLT. PLUS 402 CONV.)
(GT-350 = 1253 BLT. PLUS 404 CVTS.)

new SIDE TRIM

MUSTANG
GT

H/T

6.95 x 14 TIRES

(42581 2+2s BLT.)

CLOCK

SPEEDOMETER

SPORT DASH (OPT.)

TACHOMETER (TO 8000 RPM)

S T

OPTIONAL POWER FRONT DISC BRAKES

68A

new GRILLES

OPTIONAL STRIPES

CONT'D. NEXT PAGE
MUSTANG 67½ ~ 68(A)

MUSTANG

$2712. 2+

Mustang's five dial instrument cluster and padded instrument panel

STANDARD INTERIOR

CONVERTIBLE

68
(CONT'D.)
B

H/T $2602. (249,447 BLT.)

new 302 cid V8

TOTAL 1968 PRODUCTION = 317,404

$2814.
(25376 BLT.)

230 HP

(new 427 cid V8, 390 HP)

OPT. CONSOLE

COLLAPSIBLE SPARE TIRE

INFLATABLE WITH PRESSURE CAN

A   B

AVAIL. WHEEL COVERS

California made it happen!

$3500.~ PLUS, INCLUDING SOME EXTRAS

68½

GT/CS

VARIOUS V8s

(6 ALSO AVAIL.)

THE ALL NEW G.T. CALIFORNIA SPECIAL
(4800+ BLT. AT MILPITAS CALIF. FORD PLANT)

We lit it up.
Mustang GT/CS standard features include rectangular fog lamps set in a wild blackout grille.

We scooped it.
Wicked-looking side scoops and special GT/CS stripes are also standard on every Mustang GT/CS. So is the functional louvered hood with integral turn signals — and competition-type hood locks.

And we added a spoiler.
Inspired by the famous Shelby GT, the spoiler and the horizontal taillights are both standard equipment. Plus pop-open gas cap. You get it all at a low Mustang price. There's a lot more to the Mustang GT/CS story, including a list of options that practically let you create your own personal custom car.

H/T

MUSTANG GT/CS
"CALIFORNIA SPECIAL"

The most exciting Mustang since Mustang

MUSTANG 68 (B) ~ 68½

529

MUSTANG

FORD DIVISION *Ford*

69 *new* GRILLE

MACH 1 SPORTSROOF

GT H/T — $3129.

Ford's Exclusive "Shaker" scoop actually protrudes through the hood—rams air directly into the carburetor under full throttle.

MACH 1 — $3480.

1969

(MUSTANG "E" SPORTSROOF IS $3078 WITH 250 CID 6, 155 HP)

MACH 1 ENGINE: 351 CID V8 (250 HP)

GT SPORTSROOF (FASTBACK)

GRANDE

$3329 GRANDE has LOW REAR-FACING "SCOOP" LIKE GT MODELS.

STD. ENGINES: 200 CID 6 (115 HP) 302 CID V8 (220 HP)

SHELBY CARS STILL CUSTOM-CRAFTED WITH FORD PARTS, BUT NO LONGER BEAR A CLOSE RESEMBLANCE TO MUSTANG.

GT CVT. $3343. (WEST COAST)

(WEST COAST PRICES IN SMALLER PRINT, ABOVE)

STANDARD PRICES, PRODUCTION FIGURES FOR 1969: H/T (128,458 BLT.) $2635.
FASTBACK (60,046 BLT.) $2635.; BOSS 302 V8 FASTBACK (1934 BLT.); CVT. (14,746 BLT.) $2849.
GRANDE H/T (22,182 BLT.) $2866. $3588.
MACH 1 FASTBACK
(40,970 BLT.) $3271.   MUSTANG 69

530

MUSTANG

200 CID 1V Six—120 hp; 3.68" bore x 3.13" stroke; 8.8 to 1 comp. ratio; 7 main bearings; reg. fuel.

250 CID 1V Six—155 hp; 3.68" bore x 3.91" stroke; 9.0 to 1 comp. ratio; 7 main bearings; reg. fuel.

CVT. (7673 BLT.)

$ 3025.

GRANDE (13582 BLT.)

(40970 BLT.)

(82569 STD. H/Ts BUILT, AT $ 2721.)

$ 2926. $ 3283. (WEST)

$ 3876. (WEST)

MACH 1

WITH 428 COBRA JET V-8 (E70×14 TIRES)

$ 3271.

$ 3628. (WEST)

SHAKER HOOD SCOOP (ALSO AVAIL. on BOSS 302)

Cobra VII

$ 3720.

Boss 302

(63/9 BLT.)

302 CID 2V V-8—220 hp; 4.00" bore x 3.00" stroke; 9.5 to 1 comp. ratio; regular fuel.

302 CID 4V "Boss" V-8—290 hp; 4.00" bore x 3.00" stroke; 10.6 to 1 comp. ratio; premium fuel.

351 CID 2V V-8—250 hp; 4.00" bore x 3.50" stroke; 9.5 to 1 comp. ratio; regular fuel.

351 CID 4V V-8—300 hp; 4.00" bore x 3.50" stroke; 11.0 to 1 comp. ratio; premium fuel.

428 CID 4V Cobra V-8—335 hp; 4.13" bore x 3.98" stroke; 10.6 to 1 comp. ratio; premium fuel.

428 CID Cobra Jet Ram-Air 4V V-8*—335 hp; 4.13" bore x 3.98" stroke; 10.6 to 1 compression ratio; premium fuel.

429 CID 4V "Boss" V-8—375 hp; 4.36" bore x 3.60" stroke; 10.5 to 1 comp. ratio; premium fuel.

70
new GRILLE

FRONT SPOILER

(39316 BLT.)

BOSS 302 WHEEL COVER

BOSS 302 USES 302 CID, 290-H.P. V-8, F60 × 15 TIRES. (new E78×14, MOST OTHER MODELS)

$ 2771.

MUSTANG 70

531

MUSTANG $3227.
(6/21 BLT.)
MUSTANG CONVERTIBLE

new 109" WB
(RESTYLED)
FULL LINE ILLUSTRATED

DASH

STD.
HARDTOP
(65696 BLT.)
$2911.
$3783.
(WEST)

71

WEST,
($3989.)
$3117.

MUSTANG GRANDE
(17406 BLT.)
VINYL-COVERED TOP

"DUAL RAM INDUCTION"

(36499 BLT.)
MUSTANG MACH 1

BOSS 351
MUSTANG BOSS 351 $4124.
(23956 BLT.)

WHEEL DETAIL (MACH I)

MACH I

$2973.
MUSTANG SPORTSROOF

REAR WINDOW DEFROSTER AVAIL.

REAR DETAILS

$3268.

OPTIONAL V8s
302
351
429

MACH I GRILLE

Engines*:
250 CID 1V Six—145 hp; 3.68" bore x 3.91" stroke; 9.0 to 1 comp. ratio; 7 main bearings; regular fuel.
302 CID 2V V-8—210 hp; 4.00" bore x 3.00" stroke; 9.0 to 1 comp. ratio; regular fuel.
351 CID 2V V-8—240 hp; 4.00" bore x 3.50" stroke; 9.0 to 1 comp. ratio; regular fuel.
351 CID 4V V-8—285 hp; 4.00" bore x 3.50" stroke; 10.7 to 1 comp. ratio; premium fuel.
351 CID 4V H.O. (Dual Ram Induction) V-8—330 hp; 4.00" bore x 3.00" stroke; 11.7 to 1 comp. ratio; premium fuel.
429 CID 4V CJ V-8*—370 hp; 4.13" bore x 3.98" stroke; 11.3 to 1 comp. ratio; premium fuel.
429 CID 4V CJ-R (Dual Ram Induction) V-8**—370 hp; 4.13" bore x 3.98" stroke; 11.3 to 1 comp. ratio; premium fuel.

20~GAL. GAS TANK

$4046. (WEST)

For Spring Only. A Mustang of a New Stripe.
A New Mustang Hardtop. It's a Special Spring Value at your Ford Dealer's. Now.

STYLED LIKE MACH I, BUT has BLACK VINYL-COVERED TOP, BLACK SIDE STRIPES; BODY, BUMPERS ARE RED.

71½

MUSTANG 71~71½

532

MUSTANG

Mustang Grandé Instrument Panel with Personalized Designer Options

Mustang Grandé in Light Pewter with Black Vinyl Roof

GRANDE
(18045 BLT.)

$2915.

Safety Feature
UNI-LOCK HARNESS →

MACH I
$3737.
(WEST)

(27675 BLT.)
SAFETY-DESIGN INTERIOR DOOR HANDLE UNDER ARMREST

SPORTSROOF

$3053.

72

TYPICAL INTERIOR

STRIPES OPTIONAL ↓ ↓

$3686.
(WEST)

BOSS 351 DISCONTINUED

$2729.
H/T

$3500.
(WEST)
(57350 BLT.)

STD. GRILLE (H/T)

CVT. $3785. WEST

$3015.
(6401 BLT.)

AVAILABLE

$2786.

HORSEPOWER CUTS

302 CID V8 (99 HP)
351 CID V8 (141 HP)
(177, 266 OR 275 HP)

FORD PREFIX ADDED IN MUSTANG ADVERTISING, 1972.

$3557.
(WEST)

Control and balance
Mustang. The Driving Machine.

(15622 BLT.)

Mustang SportsRoof.

MUSTANG 72

533

MUSTANG

DASH

LAST "BIG" 109" W.B. MODELS
(OPT. VINYL TOP)

(51480 BLT.) ↓

Hardtop

$2760.

73
new GRILLES

$2820.

$3500.
PLAIN ROOF
Hardtop

MUSTANG SPORTSROOF
(10820 BLT.)

SPORTS WHEEL COVER →

E70x14 TIRES

MACH I

(35440 BLT.)

Mach I

Personal Sporty Styling. Mustang for 1973 highlights a new front appearance and a new grille, color-keyed urethane front bumper, *ON MACH I, GRANDE and CVT.*

CONVT. INTERIOR

$3102.

LAST MUSTANG CVT. UNTIL 1982.
(11853 BLT.)

Mustang Convertible with exciting new front

color-keyed hood and fender moldings plus new exterior and interior colors. Mustang offers more styling than any other car of its kind. <u>Five models.</u> And the lowest priced U.S.-built convertible in the personal sporty car field.

$3088.

(<u>ALL</u> MODELS SHOWN)
250 CID 6 (95 HP)
302 CID V8 (136 HP)
351 CID V8 (154/156 HP)

GRANDE FRONT DETAILS

CLOSER DETAIL OF GRILLE CENTER

GRANDE
(25674 BLT.)
$2946.

note new SHOULDER HARNESS IN THIS CAR.

MUSTANG 73

Ford Mustang II. A new class of small car: First Class.

DASH

HATCH-BACK

B78/BR78/BR70×13 TIRES (new)

Mach 1.
$4444.
(WEST)
(44046 BLT.)

$3674.

$4327.
(WEST)

3-Door 2+2.
(74799 BLT.)

$3328.

FRONT CLOSE-UP (GHIA)

DOWNSIZED

WINDOW DEFR.

74

88 HP, 139 CID
4-CYL.
OR
V-6
(169 CID)
105 HP

ALL - NEW
SMALLER THAN
PREVIOUS
MUSTANGS
(96.2" WB)

Ghia
$4479.
(WEST)

Hardtop.
$4133.
(WEST)

ON GHIA, THIS MEDALLION USUALLY SEEN

smart Ghia interiors...

STD. H/T
(177,671 BLT.)
$3134.

DIGITAL CLOCK AVAIL.

"CITY/COUNTRY"*
HORN FOR CARS
SOLD IN N.Y.

* SOFTER TONE
FOR CITY

(89477 BLT.)=GHIA CPE.
$3480.

MUSTANG (II)~74

535

MUSTANG II

The closer you look, the better we look

GHIA '75 MODELS have new ROOFLINE and new UPRIGHT RADIATOR ORNAMENT

Silver Ghia. (new)

(89477 BLT.)

GHIA FR. $4514.

new 1975 STEERING WHEEL WITH DOWNWARD-CURVED SPOKE

(85155 BLT.)

STD. TYPE H/T

75

(30038 BLT.)

$4105.

new HUB CAPS

BR 78 × 13 TIRES
139 CID 4 (83 HP)
169 CID 6 (97 HP)

(44046 BLT.)

3-Door 2+2.
$4394.

CARS WITH new CATALYTIC CONVERTER HAVE UNLEADED FUEL WARNING DECAL OVER GAS FILLER CAP.
("UNLEADED FUEL ONLY")

Mach 1. $4492.

302 CID V-8 JOINS 4-CYL. and V-6.

LATE IN 1975 MODEL YEAR, SIMPLIFIED MPG MODELS JOIN OTHERS, AS LOW-PRICED ECONOMY LEADERS.

$3529.

(SALE PRICE)

Official U.S. Government Environmental Protection Agency tests:
28mpg (4-speed manual) highway...18mpg city.
26mpg (automatic) highway...18mpg city.
New Mustang II MPG

WESTERN PRICES SHOWN ABOVE, IN BLACK

GHIA MPG

75½

NO HOOD ORNAMENT, new HUB CAPS, FEWER "FRILLS."

EASTERN PRICES BELOW

Mustang II MPG $3,529*

cpe 2d – $3,529.

Ghia – $3,938.

htchbk – $3,818.

Mach 1 – $4,188.

MUSTANG (II)-75-75½

536

MUSTANG II

MPG

2-DOOR

STALLION (new)

AVAIL. AS 2+2 OR H/T, with BLACK GRILLE and WINDOW MOLDINGS. STALLION DECAL ON COWL

3-DOOR

(78508 BLT.)

2+2
(37515 BLT.)

EPA estimates: Mustang II MPG.
34 mpg highway **24** mpg city

$4519.

MACH I
(9232 BLT.)

FROM $4101.

DASH

(INCLUDES TACHOMETER)

COBRA II

76

new AIR-SCOOP UNDERNEATH FRONT BUMPER.

140 CID 4 (new 92 HP)
new 171 CID V6 (100 HP)
302 CID V8 (134 HP)

The score for '76:

HATCHBACK (62312 BLT.)

COBRA II

Mustang II. Boredom Zero.

MACH I

(6719 BLT.)

(67783 BLT.)
H/T (SPECIAL PAINT OR DECALS OPTIONAL)

GEAR RATIO 3.18
WITH 4 CYL.; OTHERWISE 3.0

$4645.

16½-GAL. FUEL TANK

VINYL TOP AVAIL. (H/T)

$4496.
(49161 BLT.)

3-DOOR
2+2

77
(HP CUTS)

GHIA (29510 BLT.)

SUPER COUPE
COBRA II

ENGINES =
89 HP
4-CYL. (140 CID)
V-6 (170.8 CID)(93 HP)
V-8 (302 CID)(139 HP)

SPORT DASH

Mustang II options.

MUSTANG (II) ~76~77

GHIA 2-DR.
$4538.

DASH

140 CID 4 (88 HP)
171 CID V6 (90 HP)
302 CID V8
(139 HP)

MUSTANG II

78 FINAL "MUSTANG II" STD. H/T FROM $4121.

COBRA
(COBRA FIG. ON GRILLE)

MUSTANG '79 "THE NEW BREED"

RUNNING LAMP   HEADLAMP   QUARTZ   4:48
LOW FUEL
BRAKE LAMP   WASHER FLUID   DATE   E/T   TIME

GRAPHIC WARNING MODULE

DASH

79 -80

(156,666 BLT.)
Mustang 2-Door, Medium Vaquero Glow (5W)

(36384 BLT.)
Mustang Ghia 3-Door, Light Chamois (83)

(120,535 BLT.)
Mustang 3-Door, Medium Blue Glow (3H)

$4494.

Mustang 2-Door with Exterior Accent Group*
Light Medium Blue (3F)

FORD MUSTANG
CHOICES

COBRA

Cobra 3-Door,* Yellow (64)

TOTALLY RESTYLED and
ENLARGED   104.4" WB

"COBRA" UPHOLSTERY

Mustang 2-Door with Sport Option,*
Tangerine (85)

('80)

Mustang Cobra 3-Door,* Black (1C)   ('80)
302 CID V8 (140 HP)
170 CID V6 (109 HP)
('79 ONLY)
255 CID V8
(118 HP)
('80 ONLY)
200 CID 6
(91 HP)('79 + '80)

$5338.

(128,893 BLT.)
Mustang 2-Door, Bittersweet Glow (8D)

$5064.

(56351 BLT.)
Mustang Ghia 2-Door, Medium Grey Metallic
(1P)

('80)

(98497 BLT.)
Mustang 3-Door, Dark Cordovan Metallic (8N)
('80)

Mustang 2-Door with Sport Option,
new Carriage Roof and Turbocharged Engine

$5616.

3-DR.

☐ ATMOSPHERIC AIR
☐ ATMOSPHERIC AIR AND FUEL MIXTURE
☐ PRESSURIZED AIR AND FUEL MIXTURE
☐ EXHAUST TO TURBO
☐ EXHAUST FROM TURBO TO MUFFLER

('80)

140 CID 4 w. TURBO
DETAILS
(140 HP)

TURBO HOOD SCOOP

('79)

1979, UNLESS
LABELED OTHERWISE

2-DR.

COBRA $7474.
(WEST)
('80)

('80)

140 CID 4 (88 HP w/o TURBO)
MUSTANG 78~80

538

NASH

(1917~1957)

TOTAL 1940 PRODUCTION 62,131

DASH

O.H.V. ENGINES IN AMBASS. 6 and 8

Nash LaFayette 6, 4018 $875.
(117" WB)

Nash Ambassador 6, 4028 $985.

40

121" WB AMBASSADOR
(1937 THRU 1951)
STRAIGHT~8 260.8 CID (115 HP)
6 CYL. 234.8 CID (105 HP AMBASSADOR)
(99 HP LAFAYETTE)

LARGER FLANKING GRILLES;
SEALED~BEAM HEADLIGHTS

$1135.
#4085 AMBASSADOR 8
BUSINESS COUPE

AVAILABLE: FRONT-
and BACK SEATS THAT
FOLD, TO FORM A BED
(SINCE 1935)

Nash Ambassador 8, 4088 $1195.

LOW SIDE DOORS ON
CUSTOM AMBASSADOR CVT.

FIRST 2 DIGITS OF
4~DIGIT MODEL #
DENOTES YEAR
OF CAR.
(FROM 1935 TO
1957)

40 NASH

AMBASSADOR
"ALL~PURPOSE" CABRIOLET
6~CYL. #4021 = $1085.
8 " 4081 = 1295.

"WEATHER EYE" HEATER/VENTILATOR (SINCE 1938)

You'll be Happier in a NASH

1941 PRODUCTION = 84,007

Go NASH
AND SAVE MONEY EVERY MILE

X-RAY VIEW

Nash "600" 6, 4140 DASH

New

UNITIZED BODY~ FRAME CONSTRUCTION
"600"

$880.

41 A
RESTYLED

FINAL YEAR FOR "TWIN IGNITION"

#4140 DELUXE T/B

LOW~PRICED LAFAYETTE SERIES REPLACED BY new "600" 112" WB

NEW NASH PRICES AS LOW AS $710

*Sedan, illustrated above, $745 delivered at factory, including standard equipment and federal tax. The White Side Wall Tires, Two-tone Paint, Convertible Bed, Deluxe Bumper Guards, Weather Eye Conditioned Air System, Fourth Speed Forward are optional extras. See Nash's Ambassador "6" and "8" Series—each the outstanding value in its own price class!

* REGULARLY $730. (COUPE)
new SMALLER (172.6 cu.) L~HEAD 6 IN "600" (75 HP @ 3600 RPM)

4149 DELUXE "600" 2 DR. FASTBACK

$797.

"600" HAS LOW~CUT REAR FENDER OPENING.

"AMBASSADOR" HAS FULL REAR FENDER OPENING. (SKIRTS AVAIL.) 6.50 x 16 TIRES

4.1 GEAR RATIO (ALL SERIES)

AMBASSADOR 6

AMBASSADOR 8 #4187
"SPECIAL" FASTBACK SED.
$1091.

#4161 ALL~PURPOSE CABRIOLET (CVT.)
$1130.

(CONT'D. NEXT PAGE)
41 NASH (A)

Nash

AMBASSADOR 6 INSTRUMENT PANEL

four coil springs suspension (600)

ENGINE
172.6 CID
6 CYL. L~HEAD ENGINE IN "600" MODELS (75 HP @ 3600 RPM) (ILLUSTRATED)

4160

Ambassador 8 Similar

REMOVABLE REAR FENDER SKIRTS ON AMBASSADOR 6, 8

41ᴮ (CONT'D.)

New Grille Treatment and Styling

42

PRICE RANGE = $843. ~ $1119.

CLUB COUPE

WITH PAINTED "BLACKOUT" TRIM (FINAL NASH STRAIGHT-8s IN 1942)

RUNNINGBOARDS CONCEALED BY FLARED SIDE DOORS

$893.

HEATER~VENTILATOR BEHIND DASHBOARD

"600" FASTBACK SEDAN

Nash Conditioned Air

COWL VENT IS AN ALWAYS~OPEN AIR SCOOP (new)

TRUNK~BACK SEDAN $9/8. "600"

Imagine—this big 1942 Nash goes 25 to 30 Miles on a Gallon of Gasoline at Highway Speed!

SEDANS AVAIL. IN BOTH "FASTBACK" OR "BUSTLEBACK" (TRUNK-BACK) STYLE.
1942 PRODUCTION = 31,780

MACHINE~TURNED INSTRUMENT PANEL   41/42 NASH

NASH

(1917~1957)

FIRST 2 DIGITS IN MODEL NUMBER ARE THE YEAR MODEL

NOW 6-CYL. ONLY (THROUGH '54)

600 DLX.

112" WB L-HEAD ENG.
$1342.

4640

121" WB
112 HP OHV

4663

$1453.

new MEDALLION and PK. LITES

46

AMBASSADOR
PROD. 6148 (LATER '45)
98,769 (DURING '46)
$1929.

MODEL 4664 AMB. SUBURBAN SEDAN with WOODEN PANELING (272 BLT. '46; 595 BLT. '47)

new GRILLE

AMBASS. SEDAN IS PACE CAR AT 1947 INDY 500 RACE

EL SEGUNDO, CALIF. and TORONTO, ONT. BRANCH PLANTS PURCHASED THE PRECEDING YR.
MEXICO CITY PLANT OPENS 6-18-47.

4740 (600)
4760 (AMB.)
$1809.

"You'll be Ahead with Nash"

47

new CHROMED EXTENSIONS AT EITHER SIDE OF UPPER GRILLE PORTION

4748 (fastback)
4740 (bustle-back)

PROD.: 113,315

600

4842
$1874.

48A

EXCEPT ON "600," new HIGHER BELT LINE CHROME FOR 1948
$2345.

COUPE (BROUGHAM)
$1478.

AMBASSADOR SUPER

"FASTBACK" SEDAN

4868

new CVT. (1,000 BLT.) AMBASSADOR
4871

600

"BUSTLE BACK" SEDAN

4840

$1587.

TO $2047
(COUPE)

AMB. 4863 OR 4843 600

DASH (MORE DETAILS NEXT PAGE

TO $2047. (AMB. CUSTOM 4873

600 = DELUXE BUSINESS CPE.; SUPER TRUNK-BACK 4-DR.; 2-DR. BROUGHAM; FASTBACK 4-DR.
CUSTOM TRUNK-BACK 4-DR.; 2-DR. BROUGHAM; FASTBACK 4-DR. AMBASSADOR = SIMILAR SUPER and
CUSTOM MODELS, ALSO SUPER SUBURBAN (130 BLT.) and CUSTOM CONVT. (1000 BLT.)

(CONT'D. NEXT PAGE) NASH 46~48(A)

NASH

48 B (CONT'D.)

118,621 BLT.

FULL VIEW OF INTERIOR

You'll be Ahead with **Nash**

Great Cars Since 1902

$1916.

"SUPER" and "CUSTOM" are new

AMB. SUPER (MODEL NAME ON SIDE OF HOOD.)

7.10 x 15

4860

600 SUPER 2-DR. 4949

82 HP

EL SEGUNDO, CALIF. PLANT OPENS 10-48

Has "600" IN CHROME, ON FRONT FENDER PANEL.

$1786.

PHANTOM VIEW

49 TOTALLY RESTYLED new *Airflyte* MODELS (NO CVTS.)

ONE SINGLE WELDED UNIT!

with Girder-built Unitized Body and Frame ...Airliner-styled interiors... Cockpit Control...Uniscope... Matched Coil Springs on all Four Wheels...Twin Beds... Uniflo-Jet Carb

AMBASSADOR 112 HP
$2195. UP

7.10 x 15

1949 PRODUCTION: 142,592	600 OR AMBASSADOR, AVAIL. IN SPECIAL, SUPER SPECIAL OR CUSTOM MODELS
ENGINES = 172.6 CID 6 (82 HP) "600" 234.8 CID 6 (112 HP) AMBASSADOR	$1786. ~ 2363. PRICE RANGE

NASH 48 (B) ~ 49

NASH

WITH *HYDRA-MATIC DRIVE*

BACKLIGHTS ENLARGED

The Statesman 85 HP

(REPLACES 600)

5078
$2223.
191,865 BLT.

The Ambassador Custom 115 HP

50
...NEW SUPER-POWER ENGINES!

new SLIDING GLOVE DRAWER
THICKER BUMPER GUARDS

new **Rambler** *also avail.* AT NASH DEALERS

(SEE **RAMBLER** SECTION)

$1633. ~ 2223. PRICE RANGE

2 DR. BROUGHAMS, 2 DR. SEDANS
and 4 DR. SEDANS, IN
SUPER, SUPER SPECIAL, CUSTOM
MODELS (STATESMAN OR AMBASSADOR)

Airflytes for 1951

SUPER SEDAN 5148
$1955.

STATESMAN

$2099.

5159
CUSTOM 2-DR.

51

new GRILLE
with ALL-VERTICAL
PIECES

note PROTRUDING
BUMPER
GUARDS ON
AMBASSADOR's

— new BUMPERS.

new GRILLE
with VERTICAL
PCS.

New sky-flow fenders

TRUNK DETAILS

$2304.
5169

AMBASSADOR
SUPER
$2330

5168

RECLINING SEATS
(*with* BODY CENTERPOST
NOT SHOWN, IN ORDER THAT
SEAT DETAIL CAN BE SEEN.)

new
PARKING LIGHTS

103,585 BLT.

NASH 50~51

544

NASH

(TOTALLY RESTYLED FOR 1952)

Golden Airflytes 50TH ANNIVERSARY (OF RAMBLERS)

Pinin Farina, STYLIST

$2332. 5255 ('52)

new 88 HP

new 114¼" WB
STATESMAN CUSTOM
AMBASSADOR CUSTOM
← 120 HP

5275 $2716.

new 121¼" WB

'53 has CHROMED HORIZ. SPACERS ON COWL AIR SCOOP)

$2332.

*= INCL. RMBLR.

5355

52-53

152,141 BLT. *   153,753 BLT. *

('53) 100 HP

DASH ('53)

'53 with new STRIPS OF CHROME ON VENT

O.H.V. AMBASSADOR ENG.

('53)
AMBASSADOR COUNTRY CLUB
$2829.   5377

Ambassador Country Club

MODELS : STATESMAN=#5445 SUPER 4-DR. SEDAN; #5446 SUPER 2-DR. SEDAN;
#5455 CUSTOM 4-DR. SEDAN; #5457 CUSTOM COUNTRY CLUB H/T
AMBASSADOR = 5475 " " " " ; 5477 " " " "
#5465 SUPER 4-DR. SEDAN; #5466 SUPER 2-DR. SEDAN

$2110. ~ 2735. PRICE RANGE

$2417.

67,192 BLT.

STATESMAN SUPER

$2110.
5446

54

GRILLE MODIFIED (NOW CONCAVE)
5475

new BORDERS AROUND MODIFIED GRILLE

AMBASSADOR SUPER
5465

ST. OR AM. CUST. MODELS have REAR-MOUNTED "CONTINENTAL" SPARE TIRE.

AMERICAN MOTORS CORP. FORMED BY MAY 1, 1954 NASH-HUDSON MERGER.

$2600.

AMBASSADOR CUSTOM

NASH 52~54

STATESMAN = 195.6 CID 6 (110 HP)

AMBASSADOR=252.6 CID 6 (130 OR 140 HP)

'55 NASH
(6 or V8)

STATESMAN 6 = $2215.~2495.
AMBASSADOR 6 = $2480.~2795.
AMBASSADOR V8 = $2775.~3095.

6 CYL. ENGS. CONTINUE;
new 320 CID V8 (208 HP)
AVAIL. IN AMBASSADOR

$2215.   STATESMAN SUPER
5545-1

$2495.   CNTRY. CLUB 5547-2

(RESTYLED) Scena-Ramic WINDSH.

$2775.
5585-1

AMBASSADOR SUPER

new "INBOARD" HEADLIGHTS

5585-2
$2965.

57,619 BLT.

AMB. CUSTOM
208-HP V8
PACKARD ENG. OPTIONAL

(THE ONLY STATESMAN 1956)
STATESMAN SUPER
5645-1

new Ambassador Special
(LOWER PRICED THAN AMB.)
121.3" WB

$2355. UP

130 HP

$2139.   114½" WB

14,352 (OR 17,841) BLT.

56 A
(6 or V8)

5665-1 (6)
↙ $2425.

AMBASSADOR SUPER 6
121.3" WB

$2939.
AMBASSADOR CUSTOM V8

5657-1

5685-2

Torque-Flo V-8

COUNTRY CLUB H/T

THE NEW
Ambassador Special
WITH new A.M.C.- BUILT V8
190 HP
250 CID
114½" WB
(INTRO. 4-56)

NASH 55~56 (A)

$2462.

(CONT'D. NEXT PAGE)

NASH

AMBASSADOR
COUNTRY CLUB

56B $3072.
(CONT'D.)

DELUXE, SUPER, OR CUSTOM 6
REPLACE
STATESMAN 6
MODELS

AMBASSADOR SUPER
$2586.

327 CID
V·8

5785-1

new GRILLE *and* SIDE TRIM

57

255 HP
$2847.

THE
FINAL
NASH
(3561 BLT.)

5787-2

AMBASSADOR CUSTOM

121½" WB

note
2-TONE
SIDE TRIM

• New wider front tread for surer footing
• New sharper, easier turning
• Airliner Reclining Seats
• All-Season Air Conditioning
• Choice of Hydramatic, Overdrive or Standard
• Twin Travel Beds

5785-2

$2763.

SUPERSEDED BY
RAMBLER

JOIN THE SWING TO THE TRAVEL KING
'57 *Nash*
World's Finest Travel Car

new
STACKED HEADLIGHTS

DURING 1957,
V8 **ONLY** IN NASH. (6-CYL. AVAIL. IN RAMBLER)

SEE **RAMBLER** SECTION

NASH 56 (B) - 57

547

OLDSMOBILE

AMERICA'S BIGGEST MONEY'S WORTH

"BEST LOOKING CAR ON THE ROAD!"

ONLY CAR OFFERING HYDRA-MATIC DRIVE !

NO GEARS TO SHIFT !

NO CLUTCH TO PRESS !

The most sensational feature of the year is offered only in Olds. No clutch! No shift! Cuts driving effort in half. Saves money on gas. Steps up performance to a thrilling new peak. Optional on all 1940 models at slight extra cost.

STATION WAGON AVAILABLE ONLY IN 60 SER. (633 BLT.) **$1042.**

40 A

SEDAN (24422 BLT.) **$899.**

NEW 95-HORSEPOWER OLDS SIXTY
WITH NEW STREAMLINED BODY BY FISHER—116" WHEELBASE

60 SERIES
(F~40)
116" WB

229.7 C/D
6 CYL.
95 HP

Oldsmobile 6, 60 (REAR)

"ALLIGATOR" FRONT OPENING HOOD

Charges Batteries, in the car, on an average of **27 minutes**

SOLD BY LEADING JOBBERS

(ABOVE) CLUB COUPE (7664 BLT.) **$848.**

(MODELS 70, 90 ON NEXT PAGE)

40 OLDSMOBILE (A)

OLDSMOBILE

"BEST LOOKING CAR ON THE ROAD!"

NEW 95-HORSEPOWER OLDS SEVENTY
WITH NEW OBSERVATION BODY BY FISHER—120" WHEELBASE

SLDAN
(41467 BLT.) $963.

(G~40)
70 SERIES
120" WB
(SAMI 6~CYL.
INGINI AS
IN 60 SIRIIS)

Oldsmobile 6, 70

THE NEW *Styleader*

BIGGER AND BETTER TO LOOK AT

Stirring in Action!
Everything New!

CONVERTIBLES IN ALL 3 SERIES
60	(1347 BLT.)	$1021.
70	(1045 BLT.)	1045.
90	(290 BLT.)	1222.

40 **90 SERIES**
(L~40)
B

124" WB
257.1 CID
SIRNICIII~8
110 HP

Oldsmobile 8, 90

It's a Thrill on a Hill!
AND A SWIFT, SMOOTH STEPPER ON THE LEVEL!

NEW 110-HORSEPOWER OLDS CUSTOM "8" CRUISER
WITH NEW LUXURY BODY BY FISHER—124" WHEELBASE

40 OLDSMOBILE (B)

$852

THE NEW OLDS "SPECIAL" IS DOWN IN THE LOW-PRICE FIELD!

OLDSMOBILE

NEW OLDS SPECIAL (*shown in yellow*) 119-inch wheelbase. Six body types. Six or eight-cylinder power. Low price.

So many people think Oldsmobile is higher priced than it is. Perhaps, after all, that's not so unusual. whether you choose the economical 100 H. P. Six or the 110 H. P. Straight-Eight Engine.

Coupe prices begin at $852, Sedan prices start at $898, *delivered at Lansing, Mich. State tax, optional

6 NEW LINES FOR '41
3 SIXES 3 EIGHTS

ALL offering HYDRA-MATIC DRIVE

NO CLUTCH NO SHIFT!

Crowning all Oldsmobile advancements for 1941 is Hydra-Matic Drive—Olds' exclusive combination of fluid coupling and completely automatic transmission. With *no clutch* and *no shift*, it simplifies driving, steps up performance, saves gas. It's optional at extra cost. Try it *now!*

(STATION WAGON IN SPECIAL SERIES ONLY)

CVT. AVAIL. IN SPECIAL OR CUSTOM CRUISER SERIES

$1048. UP

new MODEL NAMES

41 A

(DYNAMIC CRUISER and CUSTOM CRUISER, NEXT PAGE)

100 H.P. ECONO-MASTER ENGINE
new 238.1 CID   6 CYL.

new GRILLE and SUNKEN HEADLIGHTS

HYDRA-MATIC

THE CAR *Ahead!* IT'S OLDS

41 OLDSMOBILE (A)

550

OLDSMOBILE

NEW DYNAMIC CRUISER *(shown in red)* 125-inch wheelbase. Two body types. Six or eight-cylinder power. Popular price.

4~DR. DYNAMIC CRUISER
(6~76) (40719 BLT.) — **$1010.**
(6~78) (15580 BLT.) — **$1045.**

Three Sixes! Three Eights! Three different versions of streamline style. That's what Olds offers for 1941—six and eight cylinder models of the magnificent Custom Cruiser, the stunning Dynamic Cruiser and the big, low-priced Olds Special!

DYNAMIC CRUISER
2~DR. CLUB SEDAN
(6~76) (46885 BLT.) **$954.**

(8~78) (13598 BLT.) **$989.**

BUSINESS COUPE
(6~76) (353 BLT.)
$908.
(6~78) (ONLY 51 BLT.)
$944.

Car illustrated: Dynamic Cruiser Club Sedan — available as either a Six or an Eight

HYDRA-MATIC DRIVE

NO CLUTCH!

NO SHIFT!

offered in the
BIGGEST LINE OF CARS IN OLDSMOBILE HISTORY!
★**Hydra-Matic Drive Optional at Extra Cost on All Olds**

RARE!! THE 119 4~DR. CONVT'S BLT. (8~CYL. ONLY) PRICED AT **$1575.**

41 B
(CONT'D.)

CUSTOM CRUISERS PRICED FROM **$1043.**

NEW CUSTOM CRUISER *(shown in blue)* 125-inch wheelbase. Four body types. Six or eight-cylinder power. Medium price.

Oldsmobile Custom 96 & 98 (6 & 8)

8~98 4~DR. (22081 BLT.) **$1135.**   41 OLDSMOBILE (B)

YOU CAN ALWAYS COUNT ON

OLDSMOBILE 1944

BETTER LOOKING, BETTER
LASTING, BETTER BUILT!

IT'S QUALITY-BUILT TO LAST!

Series 60, 6 or 8
4-Door Sedan
$1005. UP

Series 70, 6 or 8
4-Door Sedan
$1065. UP

HYDRA-MATIC

**GENERAL MOTORS' CONTRIBUTION
TO SIMPLER, SAFER, THRIFTIER DRIVING!**

Hydra-Matic not only provides simpler and safer driving, but it reduces gasoline consumption by 10 to 15 per cent. No other drive can match it.

*Optional at Extra Cost

42
new GRILLE

NO CLUTCH
TO PRESS!

68
CLUB
COUPE
$995.

Only **HYDRA-MATIC** *is*
Completely Automatic!

INTERIOR

DEFENSE
FIRST
WITH
OLDSMOBILE

CLUB SEDAN
(1771 BLT.)
$1220.

WITH FULL CHROME TRIM

98
4-DR. SED.
(4672 BLT.)

60 SERIES (119" WB)
66 (6 CYL.)
68 (STR.-8)
70 SERIES (125" WB)
76 (6 CYL.)
78 (STR.-8)
90 SERIES (127" WB)
98 (STRAIGHT-8 ONLY)

PRODUCTION
66 (3021/9)   68 (4089)
76 (1901/3)   78 (7803)
98 (6659)

$1275. (PRICE NOT REDUCED FOR THIS PLAIN WARTIME BLACKOUT MODEL.)

(JAN., 1942 "BLACKOUT" MODEL W/O CHROME) 42 OLDSMOBILE

OLDSMOBILE (SINCE 1897)

A DIVISION OF GENERAL MOTORS CORP.

MODELS: F46 SPECIAL 66; G46 DYNAMIC CRUISER 76=238.1 c.i.d 6 (100 HP)
J46 DYNAMIC CRUISER 78; L46 CUSTOM CRUISER 98=257.1 c.i.d STRAIGHT-8 (110 HP)

1946 PRODUCTION: 114,674

SEDAN $1568. UP   76

A NEW AND FINER AUTOMATIC TRANSMISSION

GM GENERAL MOTORS   HYDRA-MATIC DRIVE

INTERIOR   66

$1433. (11,721 BLT.)

98

125"WB SEDAN (11,031 BLT.) $1812.

CLUB SEDAN   119"WB

46

$1407. and up, f.o.b. (66 CL. CPE.)

($81. MORE IN '47)

(968 BLT.)   66

ENGINE SPECS. (6 and 8) AS SINCE '41

(1409 BLT.)   66

$2456.   STATION WAGON

CVT. $1681.

98 CUSTOM $2307. CRUISER CVT.

(3940 BLT.)

119", 125" OR 127" WB (THROUGH '48)

LONGER RED SECTION AROUND "OLDSMOBILE" NAME IN FRONT FENDER CHROME STRIP

47

It's *Smart* to own an Olds

CENTER SECTION OF BUMPER NO LONGER GROOVED AT TOP

1947 PRODUCTION: 191,454

OLDSMOBILE 46-47

553

OLDSMOBILE

$1609.
and up, f.o.b.
(66 CL. CPE.
OR 2-DR.)

DELUXE SEDAN
$1947.

76 (6-CYL.)

119" OR 125" WB ON OLD-STYLED 6 and 8

48

RETAINS 1947-STYLE BODY, BUT *has* "OLDSMOBILE" NAME *and* *new* CIRCLE EMBLEM ABOVE GRILLE, *and* NEW-STYLE CHROME SIDE TRIM.

new FUTURAMIC

"98" MODELS TOTALLY RESTYLED
DELUXE SEDAN

$2256.   127" WB

98 (OLDSMOBILE'S FINAL CARS *with* STRAIGHT-8 ENGINE)

"FUTURAMIC" NAME BEGINS WITH *the* 8-CYL. RESTYLED 1948 OLDSMOBILES, AND IS USED FOR A FEW YEARS AFTERWARDS.

CVT. (12,914 BLT.)

2-DR. CLUB SEDAN

$2078.

$2624.

98 CONVERTIBLE *has* *new* HYDRAULICALLY OPERATED POWER SIDE WINDOWS *and* AUTOMATIC FRONT SEAT ADJUSTER

F U T U R A M I C

MODELS :				PRICE RANGE	PRODUCTION
DYNAMIC	66	(6 CYL.)		$1609. ~ 2739.	(41,993)
"	68	8	"	1667. ~ 2797.	(16,614)
"	76	6	"	1726. ~ 1947.	(29,167)
"	78	8	"	1785. ~ 2005.	(20,651)
FUTURAMIC	98	8	"	2078. ~ 2624.	(65,335)

(*EARLIEST* 98s "DYNAMIC" MODELS *with* '46~47 STYLING)

ENGINES :	IN MODELS :
6 CYL. (100 HP)	66, 76
STRAIGHT-8 (110 HP)	68, 78
" " (115 HP)	98

OLDSMOBILE 48

OLDSMOBILE

$1732., and up, f.o.b.
(76 CL. CP.)

76

New

NEW *ROCKET* ENGINE!
(O.H.V **V8**)
303 CID
135 HP
(TO '52)
IN
88 and 98
MODELS

new 105 HP
119½" WB
6

(282,885 BLT.) **49**

.new AIR SCOOPS BELOW HEADLIGHTS

98
(125" WB)

You've got to drive it to believe it!

new "HOLIDAY" H/T $2973.

ALL MODELS NOW HAVE "FUTURAMIC" BODIES:

6 - CYL. "76" = $1732. ~ 2895.
V8   "88" = $2143. ~ 3296.
V8   "98" = $2426. ~ 2973.

DELUXE STATION WAGON IS HIGHEST-PRICED MODEL IN 76, 88 SERIES.

"88" DESIGNATION USUALLY ON REAR FENDER

DELUXE CLUB SEDAN
(11,820 BLT.)

$2301.

UNLIKE "98," THE *new* '49½ "88" *has* CURVED LOWER EDGES OF WINDSHIELD.

NEW "**88**" (49½ INTRO. AFTER SEASON UNDER WAY)

LOWEST-PRICED CAR WITH "ROCKET" ENGINE
$2375.

"The New Thrill"

88 DLX. SEDAN

THIS IDENTIFIES V8 MODELS

119½" WB

"**88**"

CVT. IS PACE CAR AT 1949 INDY 500 RACE

OLDSMOBILE 49

OLDSMOBILE ROCKETS AHEAD

FINAL 6-CYL. "76" has NO CHROME STRIP ON FRONT FENDER

$1719.
and up, f.o.b. ("76" CL. CPE.)

88

OLDSMOBILE "88"

50

new 1-PC. WINDSHIELD

Make a Date with a "Rocket 8"!

88 CVT.
$2294., f.o.b.

98

8.20 x 15 TIRES ON 98 CVT.

note: "98" BODY STYLE DIFFERS FROM "76" and "88."

FINAL OLDSMOBILE STATION WAGONS UNTIL 1957

$1719. ~ 2772. 1950 PRICE RANGE
35 DIFF. MODELS!   PROD.: 407,889

NEW! SUPER "88"

51 A

135 HP

7.60 x 15 TIRES (88, SU-88)

V8s ONLY

(119½" WB ON 88 ONLY)

SUPER 88 SEDAN (90,131 BLT.)

$2328.

$2558.

HOLIDAY H/T (14,180 BLT.)

$2049. and up (88 2-DR.)

(CONT'D.) 50+ OLDSMOBILE 51/4

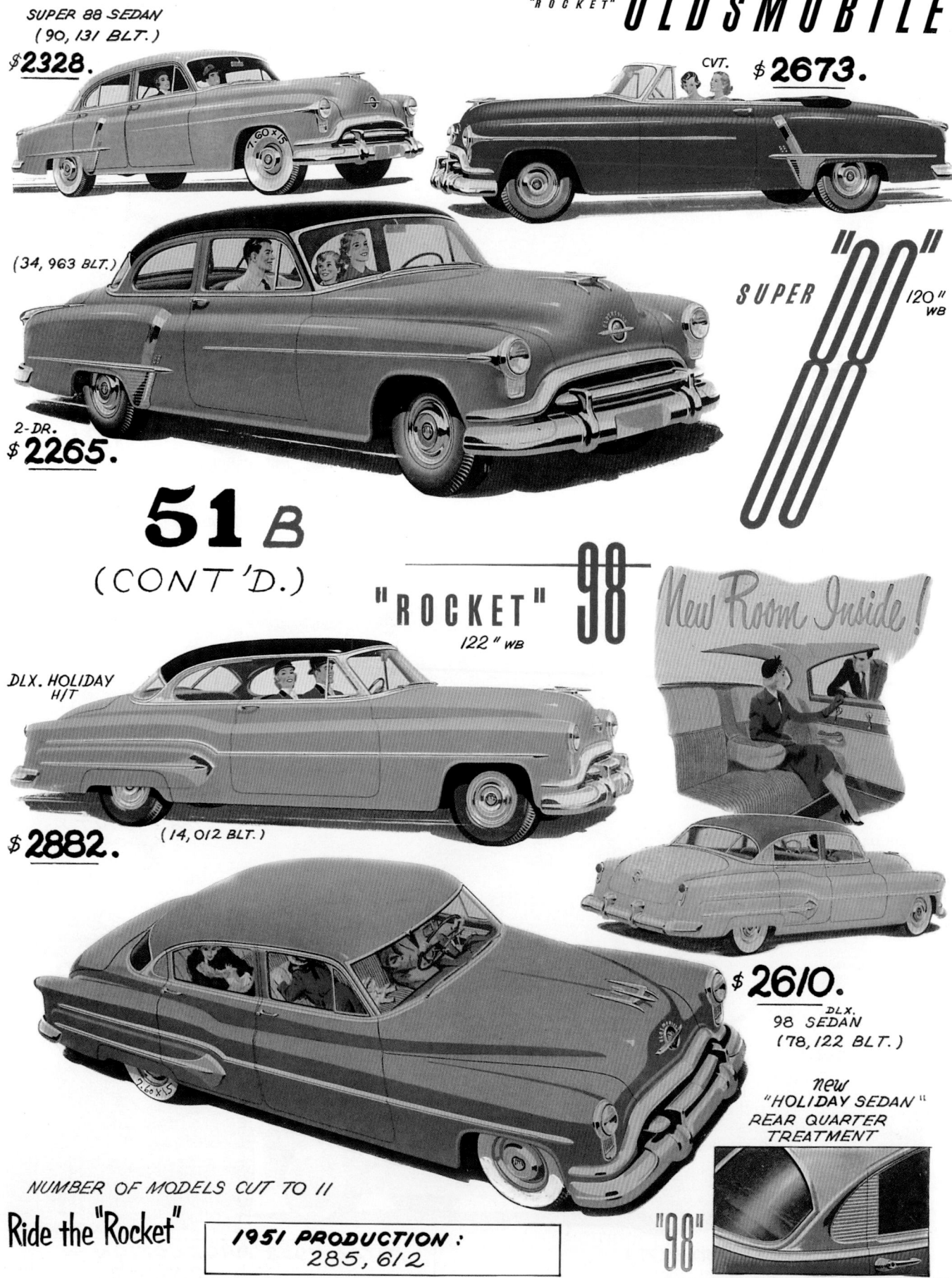

"ROCKET" OLDSMOBILE

SUPER 88 SEDAN
(90, 131 BLT.)
$2328.

CVT. $2673.

(34, 963 BLT.)

SUPER "88" 120" WB

2-DR.
$2265.

51 B
(CONT'D.)

"ROCKET" 98
122" WB

New Room Inside!

DLX. HOLIDAY
H/T

$2882. (14,012 BLT.)

$2610.
DLX.
98 SEDAN
(78,122 BLT.)

new
"HOLIDAY SEDAN"
REAR QUARTER
TREATMENT

NUMBER OF MODELS CUT TO 11

Ride the "Rocket"

1951 PRODUCTION:
285,612

"98"

OLDSMOBILE 51 (B)

557

OLDSMOBILE

(6402 BLT.)   88

$2262.   2-DR.   120" WB

$2462.   SU-88 SEDAN

(70,606 BLT.)

The "Rocket" Oldsmobile's New Power Steering* makes driving so easy you can...

Park with just 1 finger!

$2673.

SU-88 H/T

(15,777 BLT.)

HORIZ. GROOVES ON SU-88 FENDER PAD; VERTICAL GROOVES ON 98.

new VERTICAL "TOOTH" AT CENTER OF GRILLE

SUPER 88

52

new SIDE TRIM (SEE DETAILS)

98 TAIL-LIGHT

Ninety-Eight

(58,550 BLT.)   SEDAN $2786.

(58,550 BLT.)

124" WB   160 HP

new "SUPER" RANGE IN Hydra-Matic

$3229.   CVT.

Ninety Eight

REAR QUARTER DETAILS (SEDAN)   98

new SIDE TRIM DESIGN IDENTIFIES '52

H/T

HOLIDAY H/T (14,150 BLT.)
$3022.

TOTAL 1952 PRODUCTION = 228,452

OLDSMOBILE 52

OLDSMOBILE

88
2-DR.

88 has 150 HP @ 3600 RPM
$2262.

(12,400 BLT.)

FINAL YR. FOR 303 CID V8s

53

HOLIDAY H/T
(36,881 BLT.)

$2673.

DETAILS OF SUPER 88 HOLIDAY H/T

DETAILS OF THE 1953 ENGINE

SUPER 88
$2462.

7.60 X 15

SEDAN (119,317 BLT.)

SU-88, 98 have 165 HP @ 3600 RPM

98 CVT.
3229.

(7521 BLT.)

Ninety-Eight

AIR COND. AVAIL.

Holiday
H/T

$3022.

(27,920 BLT.)

458 98 "FIESTA" SPECIAL CONVERTIBLES ALSO BUILT, AT $5717. EACH

INTERIOR OF "98" CONVERTIBLE

POWER BRAKES and POWER STEERING ORDERED with MOST UNITS.

1953 PRODUCTION: 334,462

OLDSMOBILE 53

OLDSMOBILE

$ **2237.**, and up, f.o.b. (88 2-DR.)

88

$ **2337.**

new PANORAMIC WINDSHIELDS ON ALL

$ **2410.**

7.60 x 15

SUPER 88

7.60 x 15

DLX. HOLIDAY COUPÉ

$ **2688.**

$ **2826.** up

170 HP @ 4000 (88)

185 HP @ 4000 (SU-88, 98)

ALL with new 324 CID V8s. (THROUGH '56)

54 (RESTYLED)

98

122" WB (88, SU-88)
126" WB (98)

8.00 x 15

Ninety-Eight

REAR DETAILS (98)

98 STARFIRE CVT.

$ **3248.**

INTERIOR OF NEW "Starfire"
185 HP

LARGE, BOXY DECK AREA

1954

1954 PRODUCTION : **88** = 4-DR. (29,028 BLT.); 2-DR. (18,013); HOLIDAY H/T (25,820)
SUPER 88 = 4 DR. (111,326); 2-DR. (27,882); CONVERTIBLE (6452); DELUXE HOLIDAY H/T (42,155)
98 = 4-DR. (47,972); HOLIDAY H/T (8865); DELUXE HOLIDAY H/T (29,688); STARFIRE CVT. (6800)

$ **2237.** ~ **3248.** PRICE RANGE   **TOTAL 1954 PROD.** : 354,001

OLDSMOBILE 54

560

OLDSMOBILE

(*new* 4-DR. HARDTOPS JOIN
EXISTING LINE OF 2-DR. H/Ts IN ALL 3
MODEL SERIES = 88, SU. 88, and 98.)

TOTAL 1955 PROD. : 583,179

$2297. ~ 3276. PRICE RANGE

"OLDSMOBILE" NAME
ATOP CENTER
BLADE of GRILLE

55

HOLIDAY H/T
(85,767 BLT.)

$2474.

$2362., f.o.b.
SEDAN

88

88
185 HP
INT.

OLDSMOBILE'S
ENTIRELY NEW

(29,028 BLT.)

new
98 4 DR. H/T
(31,267 BLT.)
$3140.

SUPER 88
2-DR.
(11,950 BLT.)

7.60x15

$2436.

Holiday Sedan

A HARDTOP...WITH 4 DOORS!

IT'S A HOLIDAY...with Sedan convenience!
IT'S A SEDAN...with Holiday smartness!

Ninety Eight

NEW!
NEW!

ALL-AROUND
new
202 HP
ENG.
(SU-88, 98)

$3069.

DLX. HOLIDAY H/T   (38,363 BLT.)

REAR

56 A
88

FINAL
YR. FOR
324 CID V8
(230 OR 240 HP @ 4400 RPM)

INTERIOR

88
H/T
(74,739 BLT.)
$2599.

"Holiday"

OLDSMOBILE 55~56 (A)

new
BISECTED
GRILLE W.
SMALL HORIZONTAL PCS.

$2422.

88
2-DR.
(31,949 BLT.)

(CONT'D.)

OLDSMOBILE
SUPER 88

$2484., f.o.b.
SU-88 2-DR.

INCREASED TO
$2574.

98 4-DR. H/T
DLX. HOLIDAY
H/T SEDAN

56 B
(CONT'D.)

(42,320 BLT.)

$3456.,
INCREASED TO
$3551.

$2422. ~ 3740. PRICE RANGE

TOTAL 1956 PRODUCTION : 432,903 (OR 485,458)

GOLDEN
ROCKET
88 CVT. (6423 BLT.)

$3182.

GOLDEN
ROCKET

f.o.b.
f.o.b. PRICES START AT
$2691. (88 2-DR.)
277 HP @ 4400
RPM
WITH new
371 CID
V8
(371 CID AVAIL.
THROUGH '60)

57
(RESTYLED)

new
TAIL-LIGHTS and
SIDE TRIM

WAGONS
RETURN!

8.50 x 14
TIRES

new
SUPER 88 FIESTA

$3541.

SUPER 88

new GRILLE

122" WB (126" ON 98)

(8981 BLT.)

SUPER 88

$3887.,*
f.o.b.

note 3-PC.
BACKLIGHT ON
H/T (new)

new
Starfire 98

(17,791 BLT.) H/T

4 DR.
H/T
(39,162 BLT.)

$3257. OLDSMOBILE 56(b)-57

*INCREASED TO $3937.

TOTAL 1957 PRODUCTION : 390,091

OLDSMOBILE

88 FIESTA WAGON
(3249 BLT.)
$3284

HOLIDAY H/T
(53,036 BLT.)

88

$2893.

FIESTA

88

| DYNAMIC 88 |
| SUPER 88 |
| NINETY-EIGHT |
| 16 models to choose from! |

(TOTALLY RESTYLED)

88 CVT.

122½" WB

$3221. ↗

$3262.

(4456 BLT.)

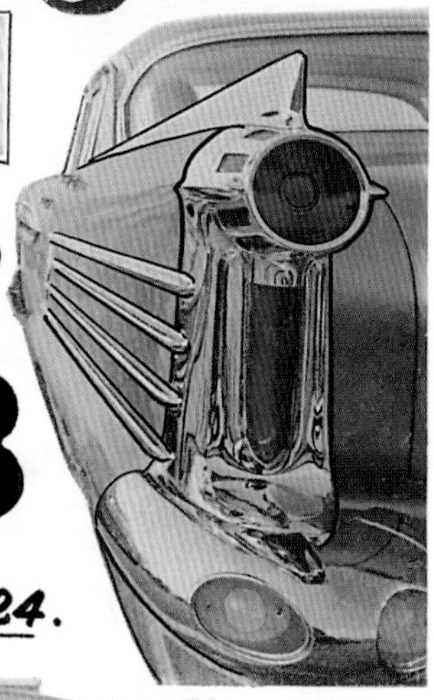

265, 305 OR 312 HP
(88) (SU 88, 98)

58

98 SEDAN (16,595 BLT.)

$3824.

SUPER 88

122½" WB

(18,653 BLT.)

BADGE ON SU-88 and 98

98

for '58

126½" WB ON 98

THE "CHROME KING" OF ALL CARS! *

New Rocket Engine is more powerful, gives greater performance than ever before. In addition, carburetion advances provide you with an opportunity for improved fuel savings, as much as 20%!

"OLDSmobility"

4 HEADLTS. ABOVE new GRILLE

DASH DETAILS →

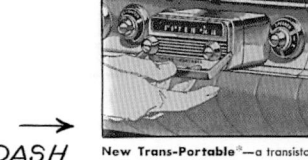

New Trans-Portable—a transistor radio that serves as your regular car radio, operating on car's built-in circuit, can also be unlocked and carried from car as a compact, lightweight portable.

New Safety-Vee Steering Wheel, with modern two-spoke, safety recessed design, allows unobstructed view of vital instrument panel gauges. New twin horn buttons are located within easy reach.

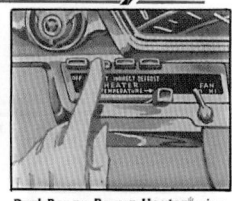

Dual-Range Power Heater gives the exact amount of heat or ventilation exactly where you want it . . . when you want it. You merely touch a button . . . power does all the work for you!

*Optional at extra cost.

$2772. ~ 4300. PRICE RANGE

TOTAL 1958 PRODUCTION: 310,795

(ON ALL MODELS)
*LAVISH USE OF CHROME TRIM ON 1958 OLDSMOBILES

---

new "LINEAR" LOOK

LTS. SEPERATED WITHIN new GRILLE

371 CID (270 HP @ 4600)
OR
new 394 CID
(315 HP @ 4600)

59A

(TOTALLY RESTYLED AGAIN)

$2837., and up, f.o.b.

(CONT'D.) 58+
OLDSMOBILE 59/1

OLDSMOBILE

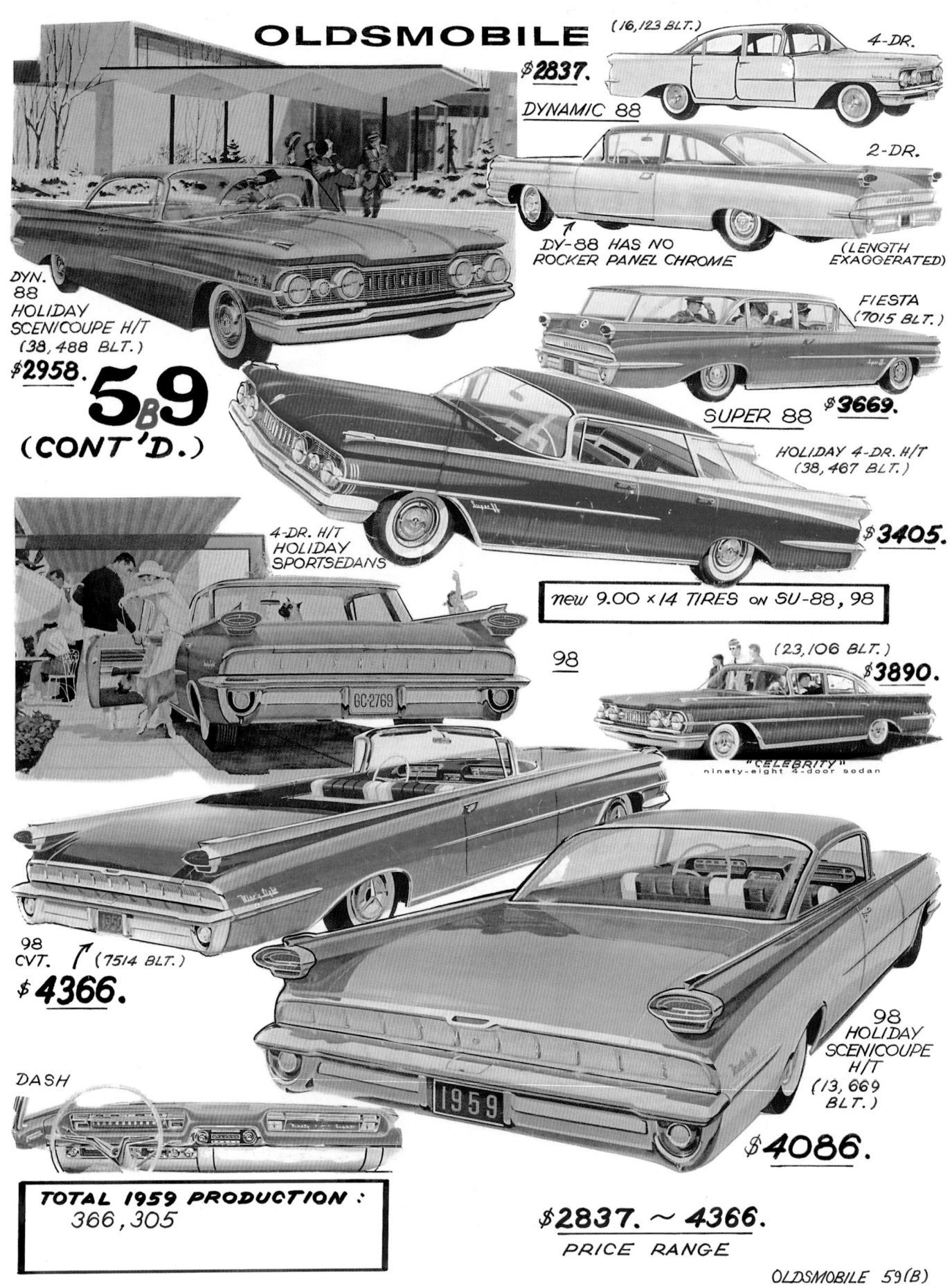

(16,123 BLT.)

$2837.

4-DR.

DYNAMIC 88

2-DR.

DY-88 HAS NO
ROCKER PANEL CHROME

(LENGTH
EXAGGERATED)

DYN.
88
HOLIDAY
SCEN/COUPE H/T
(38,488 BLT.)

$2958.

5 B 9
(CONT'D.)

FIESTA
(7015 BLT.)

SUPER 88 $3669.

HOLIDAY 4-DR. H/T
(38,467 BLT.)

$3405.

4-DR. H/T
HOLIDAY
SPORTSEDANS

new 9.00 x 14 TIRES on SU-88, 98

98

(23,106 BLT.)
$3890.

6C-2769

"CELEBRITY"
ninety-eight 4-door sedan

98
CVT. (7514 BLT.)

$4366.

98
HOLIDAY
SCEN/COUPE
H/T
(13,669
BLT.)

$4086.

DASH

1959

TOTAL 1959 PRODUCTION :
366,305

$2837. ~ 4366.
PRICE RANGE

OLDSMOBILE 59(B)

564

OLDSMOBILE

$ **2900**., f.o.b.

88 CELEBRITY 4-DR. SEDAN

(76,377 BLT.)

FIESTA WAGON

SUPER 88 →

H/T (16,464 BLT.)

$3325.

H/T (29,368 BLT.) $2956.

DYNAMIC 88

4-DR. H/T (43,761 BLT.)

$3034.

60

PACE CAR AT 1960 INDY 500 RACE

new SEGMENTED GRILLE, REAR END RESTYLED

$ **2835.** ~ **4362.**
PRICE RANGE

SUPER 88

CVT. (5830 BLT.)

$ **3592.**

$4083.

H/T (7635 BLT.)

98

with *Roto-Matic Power Steering*

240 or 315 HP @ 4600 RPM
(FINAL YR. FOR SMALLER (371) V8)

GO OLDS '60!

DASH

SU-88 FIESTA WAGON

$ **3665.** UP   (7240 BLT.)

TOTAL 1960 PRODUCTION: 362,681

OLDSMOBILE 60

565

OLDSMOBILE

HOLIDAY H/T (19,878 BLT.)

$2956.

power features
and accessories
for your
driving pleasure

WINDOW SWITCHES

RADIO

WONDER BAR

POWER HEATER

MANUAL HEATER

Other Oldsmobile Options include such convenience features as: Guide-Matic Power Headlight Control, Safety Sentinel, Swivel Dome and Reading Lamp, Deck Lid Power Lock Release, Electric Ventipanes, De Luxe Wheel Discs, Trim Rings and Air Conditioning.

Starglo Moracceen interiors—optional at no extra cost in both Dynamic 88 Holiday Sedans and Holiday Coupes. And this long-wearing, easy-to-clean all-vinyl trim is as handsome as it is durable.

THIS REAR-END STYLING IN 1961 ONLY

2-DR. DYNAMIC 88 123" WB 250 HP
(4920 BLT.)
$2835.

POWER ANTENNA

REAR QUARTER DETAIL

CLASSIC 98 HOLIDAY SEDAN

98

CVT. (9049 BLT.)
$3284.

61
(TOTALLY RESTYLED)

DYNAMIC 88 FIESTA (AVAILABLE IN 2 AND 3-SEAT MODELS)

(9387 BLT.) (ABOVE)
$3363. OR 4013.

(2 DR. 88 SEDAN)
$2835.)

394 CID V8

CLASSIC 98 TOWN SEDAN

COSTLIEST '61 OLDS
$4647.

STARFIRE CVT. (7600 BLT.)

Super 88

TWIN TRIANGLE STABILITY KEEPS YOU ON THE LEVEL!

DISTINGUISHED...
DISTINCTIVE...
DECIDEDLY NEW!

CVT. (2624 BLT.)
$3592.

OLDSMOBILE 123" WB

Skyrocket PERFORMANCE!

new "Skyrocket"

ENGINE (394 CID V8)
325 HP @ 4600 RPM
10 TO 1 COMPRESSION
(USED IN SU-88, 98;
OPTIONAL IN DY-88)

DASH

H/T (7009 BLT.)

S-88-61

"OLDSMOBILE" NAME BELOW new GRILLE (ON 88s)

$3325.

Foam-padded pattern cloth—handsomely accented with lustrous Jeweltone Moracceen, adds brilliant new sparkle to this Super 88 Holiday Sedan. Five harmonizing color choices are available.

TOTAL 1961 PRODUCTION: 253,944
OLDSMOBILE 61

566

#3247 HOLIDAY H/T (39,676 BLT.)

(LENGTH EXAGGERATED)

$3054. H/T

DYNAMIC 88

$3131.

(53,438 BLT.)

HOLIDAY 4-DR. H/T

WAGON has UNIQUE REAR FENDER DESIGN

$2997.~ 4744. PRICE RANGE

WEST COAST, $3404., and up, f.o.b.

260 to 345 HP (THROUGH '63)

1962 PRODUCTION: 356,058

new UPRIGHT GRILLE with "OLDSMOBILE" NAME ABOVE

62 (RESTYLED)

new SIDE SCULPTURING

#3269 CELEBRITY SEDAN (68,467 BLT.)

$2997.

#3569 CELEBRITY SEDAN (24,125 BLT.)

SUPER 88

#3535 FIESTA WAGON (3837 BLT.)

$3762.

$3273.

$4744.

98 TOWN SEDAN (12,167 BLT.)

HOLIDAY SPORTS SED. (98)

(33,095 BLT.)

(7149 BLT.) STARFIRE

$3984.

$4256.

98 and STARFIRE have 4 TAILLIGHTS.

98 WHEEL COVERS

$4131.

(34,839 BLT.)

new HARDTOP CPE. IN STARFIRE SERIES

OLDSMOBILE

MODIFIED GRILLES,
ALL-new TAILLIGHTS,
new SIDE TRIM

63

DYNAMIC 88
HOLIDAY H/T
(39,071 BLT.)
$3052.

SU-88 GRILLE LIKE
DYNAMIC 88
$3408.

HOLIDAY H/T
SUPER 88
(8930 BLT.)

STARFIRE
H/T
(21,148 BLT.)
$4129.

REAR
ROOFLINE

SU-88 FIESTA
$3748.
(3878 BLT.)

98 TOWN SEDAN
(11,053 BLT.)

$4742.
(4401 BLT.)
STARFIRE

REAR

STARFIRE
WHEEL
COVER

$3982.

98-LS
(LUXURY SEDAN)
4332.
(19,252 BLT.)

(98 DETAILS)

(23,330 BLT.)
4-DR. H/T
(SPORT SEDAN) $4238.
(INCREASED TO
$4258.)

TOTAL 1963 PRODUCTION: 371,033

WEST COAST
$3391.

Jetstar 88

"New full-size '88' series at a new lower price!"
new 330-cubic-inch Jetfire Rocket
V-8

$2992.

'64 OLDS →
WHERE THE ACTION IS!
(14,663 BLT.) H/T

JETSTAR 88 CELEBRITY SEDAN
$2935.

JETSTAR 88 HOLIDAY SEDAN
(19,325 BLT.)

$3069.
(32,369 BLT.)
$3062.

$3318. Jetstar 88

DYNAMIC 88 HOLIDAY COUPE

$3468.
UP

FIESTA STATION WAGON (2- or 3-seat)

CELEBRITY SEDAN

DYNAMIC 88

SUPER 88

#3457
JETSTAR I H/T
(16,084 BLT.)

394-cubic-inch
Starfire V-8 Engine

CVT.
(10,042 BLT.)
$3389.

Brilliant new sports coupe in the medium-price class! *Jetstar I*

1964

TOWN SEDAN

#3667 CVT.
(2410 BLT.)

(11,380 BLT.) 98

64

Starfire

NINETY-EIGHT

1964

(13,753 BLT.) H/T

REAR
FENDER
(98)

MODELS: JETSTAR 88 = **$2935.** ~ **3318.**
DYNAMIC 88 = **$3005.** ~ **3603.**
SUPER 88 = **$3256.** (CELEBRITY SEDAN); **$3486.** (HOLIDAY 4-DR. H/T)
STARFIRE = **$4138.** (H/T); **$4753.** (CONVERTIBLE)
98 = **$3993.** ~ **4468.**

ENGINES: 330 CID V8 (230, 245 or 290 HP)
394 " " (280, 330 or 345 HP)

TOTAL
1964
PRODUCTION:
335,637

OLDSMOBILE

$3072.
JETSTAR 88
HOLIDAY 4 DR. H/T
(15,922 BLT.)

330 CID V8   260 HP   123" WB
7.75 × 14 TIRES
Jetstar 88

DYNAMIC 88 LINE
JOINED BY
new DELTA 88

← new STYLING!

(22,725 BLT.) $2938.

(24,746 BLT.) $3065.

DYNAMIC
88
H/T

123"
WB

Delta 88.

(23,194 BLT.)
$3253.

8.25 × 14
TIRES

425 CID
SUPER
ROCKET
V8
360 HP
(TO 370 IN DELTA
88)

new GRILLE

GC·5580

DELTA 88 DASH

330 CID V8
(260 HP)

425 CID V8
(310, 360
OR 370 HP)

65

TOTAL 1965
PRODUCTION:
400,664

$2938. ∼ 4778.
PRICE RANGE

note THAT STARFIRE and 98
have OWN GRILLE
DESIGNS

(2238 BLT.)   CVT.

370 HP
STARFIRE →   (13,024 BLT.)

$4761.

H/T

98 (126" WB)

98
LUXURY
SEDAN

$4334.,
f.o.b.

$4138.   WEST
COAST $4237.

Ninety-Eight

$4273.

HOLIDAY
SPORT
SEDAN
(28,480 BLT.)

WITH
VINYL
TOP

8.55 × 14 TIRES

NINETY-EIGHT

98 DASH

'65 OLDSMOBILE
The Rocket Action Car!

CUTLASS, F-85 and TORONADO MODELS ILLUSTRATED SEPARATELY.

Oldsmobile $2927. ~ 4443. PRICE RANGE
(WEST COAST PRICES IN SMALL PRINT)

GM GENERAL MOTORS

JETSTAR 88 FROM $3314.
DYNAMIC 88 FROM $3442.

123" WB

88

$3328.

4-DR. H/T HOLIDAY SEDAN $3757.

(33,326 BLT.)

DELTA **88**

$3253.

66

2-DR. H/T HOLIDAY CPE. $3682.

(20,857 BLT.)

425 CID V8 (310 HP) STD.
(JETSTAR 88 has 330 CID V8 (260 HP)
(13,019 BLT.)

123" WB
425 CID V8 (365 HP)

Starfire:

$3564.

(STARFIRE IS LUXURY H/T WITH BIG V8. NOT TO BE CONFUSED WITH SMALL CAR OF 1975 ON, WITH SAME NAME.)

Ninety-Eight:

126" WB
(THROUGH '68)

98 SEDANS FROM $4592.

98 has CRISS-CROSS GRILLE PCS.

$3966.

STEP OUT FRONT IN '66 ... in a Rocket Action Olds!

365 HP (98)

ENGINES : 330 CID V8 (250 OR 260 HP) ;(JETSTAR 88)
330 CID V8 (320 HP) (OPT. IN JETSTAR 88)
425 CID V8 (300, 310, 365 OR 375 HP) (DYNAMIC 88, DELTA 88, STARFIRE OR 98)

1966 PRODUCTION :
318,667 (88s, 98s)
(578,385, INCL. F-85, CUTLASS, TORONADO)

OLDSMOBILE 66

Oldsmobile

(new DELMONT 88 REPLACES FORMER JETSTAR 88)

330 OR 425 CID V8 s (250 TO 375 HP)

TOWN SED. $3543. (WEST)

4-DR. H/T $3675. (WEST)

$3008. UP

IN "330" OR "425 SERIES:

DELMONT 88
Brand-new 88 series!
Goes to show what Olds can do
with a modest price tag . . .
and a lot of Toronado inspiration.

Has DELMONT 88 NAME OVER COWL

8.55 x 14 TIRES

DELMONT 88 DASH

CVT. (3525 BLT.) (ONLY AVAIL. IN "425" SERIES)

$3462.

$3912. (WEST)

1967 PRODUCTION: 277, 910 (88s and 98s)

67 A

new GRILLES

$3008. ~ 4498.
PRICE RANGE

The Rocket Action Cars are out front again!

(21,909 BLT.) (STD.)

3386.

(INTRO. 9-29-66)

Engineered for excitement . . . Toronado-style!
'67 OLDSMOBILE

$3646.

(2447 BLT.)

DELTA 88 CVT.

DELTA 88 4-DR. H/T HOLIDAY SEDAN $3954. (WEST)

REAR

(CUSTOM 2 and 4 DR. H/Ts ALSO)

$3218. DELTA 88 (WEST) $3786.

DELTA 88 HOLIDAY COUPE (2-DR. H/T) $3878. (WEST)

$3310 STD.

(22,770 BLT.)

TOWN SEDAN

(CONT'D. NEXT PAGE)

STD. (14,471 BLT.)

OLDSMOBILE 67(A)

Oldsmobile

DELTA 88 CUSTOM MODELS DIFFER THUS FROM STANDARD DELTA 88s: CUSTOM MODELS' SIDE TRIM

How do you top a line of cars as luxurious as the Olds Delta 88 for 1967?

Bring on an all-new, ultra-luxurious Delta 88 Custom.

HOLIDAY H/T $3522.

(12,192 BLT.)

↗ CLOSE VIEW OF SIDE TRIM LOUVRES

(14,306 BLT.)

425 CID V8

DELTA 88 CUSTOM
Two all-new Custom hardtops highlight the Delta 88 line.

1967

CUSTOM 4 DR. H/T

$4011. (WEST)

$3582.

67 B (CONT'D.)

Ninety-Eight:
HOLIDAY CPE. (H/T)

$4736. (WEST)

$4214. (10,476 BLT.)

98 LUXURY SEDAN (35,511 BLT.)

$4351.

$4873. (WEST)

$4498.

98

365 HP

note VERTICAL TAIL LTS. →

CLOSE-UP (REAR)

(98)

$5020. (WEST)

CVT. (3769 BLT.)

$4798. (WEST)

8.85 × 14 TIRES

98 DASH

HOLIDAY H/T SEDAN

(17,533 BLT.)

$4276.

OLDSMOBILE 67 (B)

573

Oldsmobile

FINAL YEAR FOR
DELMONT
88 ↘

(INTRO. 9-21-67)

Drive a youngmobile from Oldsmobile

68

V8s UP TO
455 CID

new
SPLIT
GRILLES

98

(DELTA
GRILLE
SAME)

$4497.

H/T
(18,391 BLT.)

$3202. ↗

Tilt & Telescope
steering wheel"

LUXURY
SEDAN
(40,755
BLT.)

$3146. ~ 4618. PRICE RANGE

ENGINES: 330 CID V8
(250, 260 OR 320 HP)
425 CID (300, 310,
365 OR 375 HP)

1968 PRODUCTION:
331,566 (88s and 98s)
627,533 (ALL MODELS)

Escape from the ordinary in Olds

DELTA 88 has
350 CID V8
(250 HP)

Delta 88 Royale

(new 124" WB) ⟶

(INTRO. 9-26-68)

(310 HP)
455 CID
V8

REAR

69

new
GRILLES

8.55
x 15
TIRES

**Delta 88
Royale**

OLDSMOBILE
NOW SHOWING
YOUNGMOBILE
THINKING 1969

note
SIDE
LOUVRES

98
REAR

Olds Ninety-Eight

(new 127" WB)

HOLIDAY H/T

(27,041 BLT.)

$4461.

(BRIGHTWORK ON ROCKER PANELS)

$3222. ~ 4719. PRICE RANGE

1969 PROD.:
368,045 (88s and 98s); 635,241 (ALL MODELS)

OLDSMOBILE
68~69

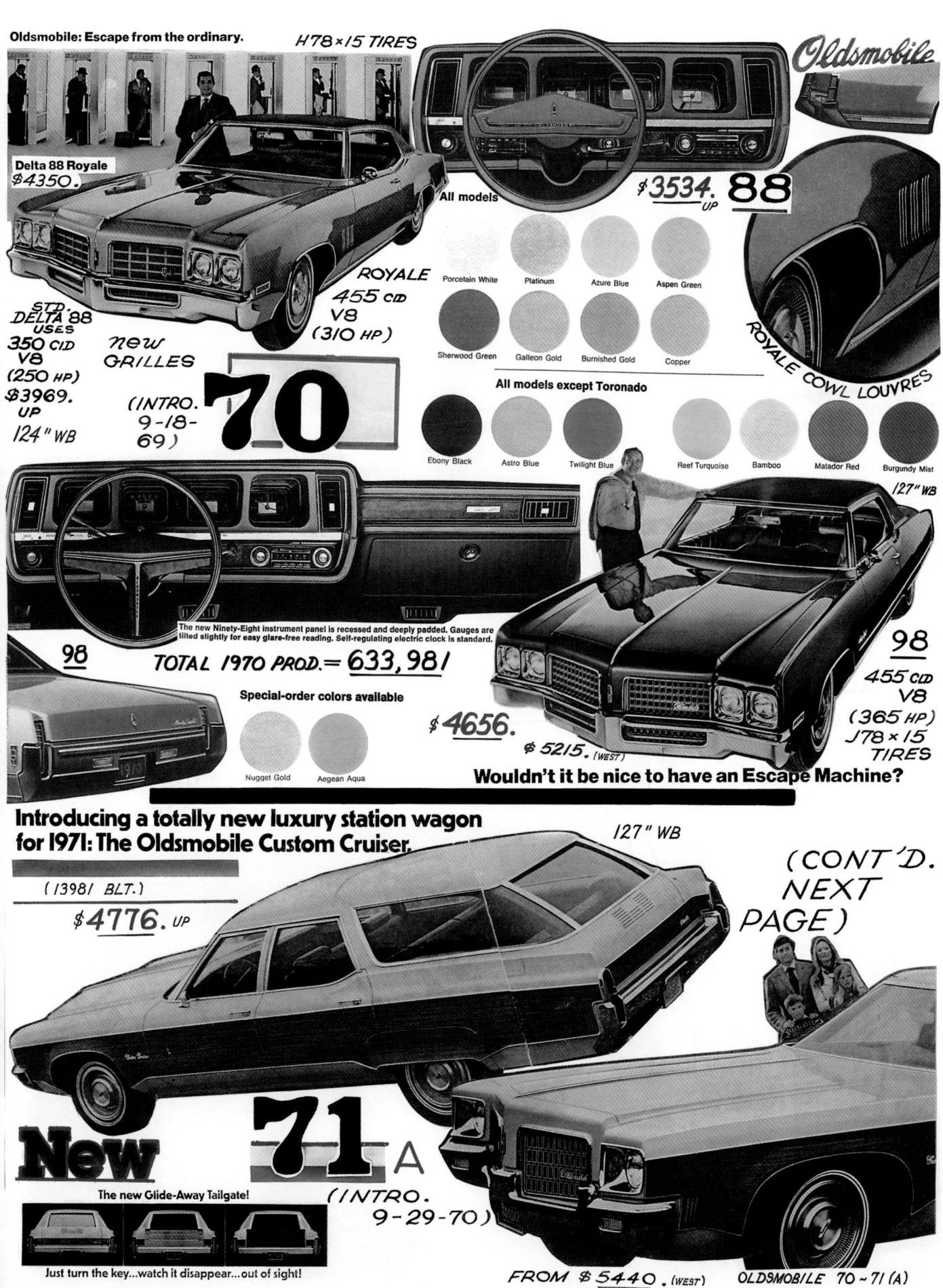

Oldsmobile: Escape from the ordinary.

H78×15 TIRES

Oldsmobile

Delta 88 Royale
$4350.

$3534. UP **88**

ROYALE COWL LOUVRES

ROYALE 455 CID V8 (310 HP)

STD. DELTA 88 USES 350 CID V8 (250 HP) $3969. UP 124" WB

new GRILLES

(INTRO. 9-18-69)

70

All models

Porcelain White · Platinum · Azure Blue · Aspen Green

Sherwood Green · Galleon Gold · Burnished Gold · Copper

All models except Toronado

Ebony Black · Astro Blue · Twilight Blue · Reef Turquoise · Bamboo · Matador Red · Burgundy Mist

127" WB

The new Ninety-Eight instrument panel is recessed and deeply padded. Gauges are tilted slightly for easy glare-free reading. Self-regulating electric clock is standard.

98

TOTAL 1970 PROD. = 633,981

Special-order colors available

Nugget Gold · Aegean Aqua

$4656.

$5215. (WEST)

98
455 CID V8 (365 HP) J78×15 TIRES

Wouldn't it be nice to have an Escape Machine?

Introducing a totally new luxury station wagon for 1971: The Oldsmobile Custom Cruiser.

127" WB

(13981 BLT.)

$4776. UP

(CONT'D. NEXT PAGE)

New 71 A

(INTRO. 9-29-70)

The new Glide-Away Tailgate!

Just turn the key...watch it disappear...out of sight!

FROM $5440. (WEST) *OLDSMOBILE 70~71 (A)*

Oldsmobile H/T (2703J BLT.) $3826.

DELTA 88 TOWN SEDAN (38298 BLT.) $3770.

THIS TOWN SEDAN IS ONLY DELTA 88 CSTM. WITH CHROME STRIP SHOWN HERE (22209 BLT.)

DELTA 88 CUSTOM $3966.

$4516. (WEST)

DELTA 88 and DELTA 88 CUSTOM GRILLE →

DELTA (4~DR.) H/T ROOFLINES

ROYALE (2~DR.)

new DASH DELTA 88

$4317. H/T (8397 BLT.)

DELTA 88 ROYALE $4325. CVT.

Bumper Guards, Front and Rear— Feature rubber inserts to reduce dings, dents and help protect your investment. →

1971 Exterior Colors
Available on all Olds models

Cameo White · Sterling Silver · Oxford Gray* · Ebony Black** · Nordic Blue · Monarch Blue† · Casol Aqua* · Palm Green · Antique Jade · Galleon Gold† · Sundstwood · Sienna** · Sable Brown · Matador Red** · Antique Beige**

*N.A. on Toronado or Cutlass/F-85
**N.A. on Toronado

CHILD and BABY SEATS AVAIL. (STRAP~ON TYPE)

(2883 BLT.)

TOTAL 1971 PROD. = 567,891

71ᴮ (CONT'D.)

98s PRICED FROM $5454. 455 CID V8 (320 HP)

new 98 DASH ←

$5103.

98 LUXURY 4~DR. H/T (BELOW)

MFRS. SUGGESTED RETAIL PRICES ON THIS PAGE. (IN RED)

NINETY-EIGHT LUXURY COUPE (14876 BLT.)

98 REAR DETAIL

Oldsmobile ALWAYS A STEP AHEAD

(98 CONVERTIBLE NO LONGER AVAIL.) STD. 98s PRICED FROM $4828.

(45055 BLT.) $5197. $5690. (WEST)

OLDSMOBILE 71 (B)

Oldsmobile

Pinehurst Green Silver Pewter Nordic Blue

Matador Red Covert Beige Sequoia Green

Bamboo Cameo White Baroque Gold

▲ AVAILABLE ON ALL OLDS MODELS

Sovereign Gold Saddle Tan Nutmeg

Royal Blue Antique Pewter Ebony Black

▲ AVAILABLE ON FULL-SIZE MODELS ONLY

$3948.

DELTA 88 TOWN SEDAN
(46092 BLT.)

350 CID V8
(160 HP)

Delta 88
H/T

$4517.

(32036 BLT.)

$4001.
WESTERN PRICES
SHOWN
IN BLACK

Delta 88 Royale
Not just another pretty car.

$4238.

$4754.

$4179.

(34345 BLT.)
DELTA 88 ROYALE HARDTOP COUPE
4695.

$4101.

(34150 BLT.)
DELTA 88 ROYALE TOWN SEDAN
4617.

$4387.

DELTA 88 ROYALE CONVERTIBLE
(3900 BLT.)
4903.

(INTRO. 9-23-71)

72

An exceptional new bumper

It gives a little.
Mounted on steel springs, it
flexes, then returns to position, to
help absorb minor impacts.

4~DR.
H/T

(42606 BLT.)
new GRILLES

TOTAL
1972 PROD.=
762,199

98
REAR

Ninety-Eight

A responsive 455-cubic-inch
Rocket V-8 engine that runs
efficiently on regular, no-lead or
low-lead gasolines.

$4748.
UP

TIFFANY CLOCK

The Limited-Edition Regency.
A very special Ninety-Eight with the Tiffany touch
to mark Oldsmobile's 75th Anniversary.

98
REGENCY
INTERIOR

(225 HP)

$5393.

Custom Cruiser

FROM
$5391.

$4700.
UP

OLDSMOBILE
ALWAYS A STEP AHEAD

2-SEAT (6907 BLT.)
3-SEAT (18087 BLT.)

OLDSMOBILE 72

Oldsmobile

$4517. Delta 88 Royale. 124" WB

$4221. Not just another pretty car.

H/T (27096 BLT.)

88 REAR

98 REAR

73 (RESTYLED)

$5452.

Ninety-Eight
DASH

Custom-Cruiser. FROM $5356.

127" WB
455 CID V8
(225 HP)

98 $4860. UP

$4785. OR $4924.
2 SEATS (7/42 BLT.) 3 SEATS (19/63 BLT.)
922,771 TOTAL 1973 PROD.

1973 COLORS

Ebony Black | Tamarack | Honey Beige ALL MODELS BUT OMEGA | Cameo White | Chamois Gold | Crystal Green | Moss Gold | Zodiac Blue | Cranberry Red | Brewster Green | Mayan Gold | Emerald Green | Wedgewood Blue | Chestnut | Eclipse Blue | Silver Taupe ALL MODELS

WESTERN PRICES SHOWN IN BLACK

$4490. $5049. DELTA 88 $4988 new COUPE STYLING $4429.

DELTA 88 GRILLE

TOTAL 1974 PROD. = 581,195

74 A
new GRILLES, "WATERFALL" STYLE

$5683. UP
CUSTOM CRUISER (4009 BLT.)
(CONT'D. NEXT PAGE)

$4981.

Front and rear bumpers are mounted on hydraulic cylinders which cushion minor impacts. '74 Oldsmobile Delta 88.

OLDSMOBILE 73~74(A)

Oldsmobile

98s FROM $6003. $5303.

4-DR. H/T

instrument panel is now redesigned to provide a new message center which monitors the car and signals you when something is wrong.

(4395 BLT.)

NINETY-EIGHT

HOOD ORNAMENT ADDED

$6334.
WESTERN PRICE

98 REGENCY.

455 CID V8 (210 HP)
J/L 78 × 15 TIRES

(10719 BLT.) $5776.

74 (CONT'D.)
B

DELTA 88 ROYALE

FINAL CVT. (DELTA 88 ROYALE) $5772.

124" WB 350 CID V8 (170 HP)

98 REGENCY

$6925.

SLOGAN "IT'S A GOOD FEELING TO HAVE AN OLDS AROUND YOU."

$5623.

Delta 88 Royale

75 new GRILLES

98 REGENCY $6784.

CUSTOM CRUISER

TOTAL 1975 PROD. = 631,795

98: 127" WB 455 CID V8 (190 HP)

98 GRILLE DETAILS and DASH

FROM $6134.

98 INTERIORS

OLDSMOBILE 74(B)-75

579

Oldsmobile
Can we build one for you?
(17115 BLT.)

DELTA 88

4-DR. H/T
$5641.

TOWN
SEDAN
$5521.

$4918.

$5078.

(33268 BLT.)

"MESSAGE CENTER"

TOWN
SEDAN
$5681.

DELTA 88 ROYALE

WITH CROWN LANDAU
OPTION →

DASH

350 CID V8
170 HP
HR 78 × 15 TIRES

(33364 BLT.)

H/T
$5749.

1976
PRODUCTION
TOTAL =
891,368

DELTA
88 ROYALE
(REAR)

$5146. ↗
(98 ON
NEXT
PAGE)

HJK·943

76 A
new
GRILLES

$5563. UP
(UNGRAINED)

$5719. UP

127" WB

(6198 BLT.)

455 CID V8
190 HP
FROM
$6326.

MMK·357

CUSTOM CRUISER

(WITH GRAIN)

(16118 BLT.)

AVAIL. WHEEL COVERS

A/R
BAGS
AVAIL. →

MIN   MAX
FUEL ECONOMY

FUEL ECONOMY GA.

OLDSMOBILE 76 (A)

580

Oldsmobile
Can we build one for you?

RADIO

98

(6056 BLT.)

$6271.

LS COUPE

$669l.
$7294.
(55339 BLT.)

$6544.
$7147.
(WEST)

REGENCY SEDAN

(26282 BLT.)

76ᴮ
(CONT'D.)

AVAILABLE DIGITAL CLOCK

98 REGENCY CPE.

PYH·722

Delta 88 Can we build one for you?

$5145. UP

IMPROVED RADIOS and STEREO

new DASH

$5205. UP

EPA MPG 22 HWY. 17 CITY WITH AVAIL. 260 CID V8 (110 HP)

Delta 88

The 1977 Delta 88.

new 116" WB

$6109.
231 CID V6 (105 HP) ALSO AVAIL.

DELTA 88

98 Regency Coupé

new 119" WB

98 REG.

DOWNSIZED, new GRILLES

98 (REAR)

REAR QUARTERS

$7764.

(WAGON ON NEXT PAGE)

77
A
98 Regency
Can we build one for you?

KMN·204

1977 BUICK and CADILLAC EACH OFFERED A COLOR SCHEME SIMILAR TO THIS.

new DASH (SWIRLED WALNUT IMITATION GRAIN)

98 "LS" COUPE and 98 DASH
(5058 BLT.)

$6609.

TOTAL 1977 PROD. = 1,135,803
OLDSMOBILE 76(B)-77(A)

Oldsmobile

NOW *has* GRILLE LIKE 88 →

FROM $6725.

(32827 BLT.)

CUSTOM CRUISER $5923. UP

77 B (CONT'D.)

NOW ON 116" WB, LIKE 88 SERIES

WESTERN PRICES SHOWN IN BLACK

(*new* REAR-FACING 3RD SEAT AVAIL.)

$6419. UP

Custom Cruiser (34191 BLT.)
27 mpg HWY. 19 mpg CITY 22 mpg Composite
FROM $7191.

There's a lot of News in Olds today.

Introducing the world's first passenger cars with a diesel V8.
TOTAL 1978 PROD. = 1,015,805

78

OLDSMOBILE NAME MOVED LOWER

$7918.

Ninety-Eight
30 mpg HWY. 21 mpg CITY 24 mpg Composite

Delta 88
30 mpg HWY. 21 mpg CITY 24 mpg Composite

HOOD EMBLEM ON DIESELS

(new) Oldsmobile
Holiday 88 Coupe
Can we build one for you?

"OLDSMOBILE" NAME MOVED TO LOWER PORTION OF GRILLES IN 1978.

$6311.

DELTA 88
Can we build one for you?

note: CUSTOM CRUISER *has* OWN UNIQUE GRILLE IN 1979

$7201. UP

Custom Cruiser
Have one built for you.

FROM $7651. (WEST)
(36648 BLT.)

GRAINED

79 A

UNGRAINED

2~WAY TAILGATE ←

Egg

DELTA 88 DASH →

OLDSMOBILE 77(B) ~ 79(A)

Oldsmobile

231 CID V6 (115 HP)
260 CID V8 (105 HP)

DELTA 88

88 Holiday Coupe
Have one built for you.

$ 6626.

$ 6212. (25424 BLT.) $ 6726.

DIESEL HOOD EMBLEM

$ 6524.
Delta 88 Royale

Royale

(152,526 BLT.)

$ 6998. (WEST)

Have one built for you.

DELTA 88 ROYALE (REAR)

79 B
TOTAL 1979 PRODUCTION=
(CONT'D.) 1,068,154

98 LS

$ 8795.

98 DASH

SEDAN (6720 BLT.)

98 REGENCY SEDAN REAR QUARTER PANEL

$ 8377.

Regency

98 Regency
Have one built for you.

$ 8579.

350 CID V8

ENGINES
GAS—160 HP
DIESEL—125 HP

8 TRACK STEREO AVAIL.

EPA MPG:

GAS
21 HWY.
15 CITY
DIESEL
29 HWY.
21 CITY

GRILLE EMBLEM WITH ANTIQUE OLDS~MOBILE LOGO

79 OLDSMOBILE EXTERIOR COLORS ON ALL

Oldsmobile

ALL MODELS EXCEPT STARFIRE AND OMEGA

VOLUME SELECTOR

CB RADIO OPTIONAL

WHITE | SILVER METALLIC | BLACK | LIGHT BLUE METALLIC | DARK BLUE METALLIC | PASTEL GREEN | MEDIUM GREEN METALLIC | MEDIUM BEIGE | CAMEL METALLIC | DARK BROWN METALLIC | CARMINE RED METALLIC | PASTEL BLUE | PASTEL YELLOW | DARK CARMINE METALLIC

OLDSMOBILE 79 (B)

583

Oldsmobile

WE'VE HAD ONE BUILT FOR YOU.

diesel Delta 88.

22	594
EPA EST MPG	EST DRIVING RANGE
34	**918**
HWY. EST	EST HIGHWAY RANGE

DELTA 88 (GAS) PRICES START AT $7382.

(15285 BLT.)

HOLIDAY COUPE

DELTA 88

BR-8250

ROYALE

$7641.

(39303 BLT.)

DELTA 88 DASH AND STEERING WHEEL

(1239] BLT.)

98 REGENCY

$10149.
$9741.

(58603 BLT.)

$9619.

98 MILEAGE

17	425
EPA EST MPG	EST DRIVING RANGE
25	**625**
HWY EST MPG	EST HIGHWAY RANGE

$10035.

80

(RESTYLED)

Custom Cruiser Diesel

21	462	31	682
EPA MPG	EPA Est Range	Hwy Est	Hwy Range

$7820. UP

UNGRAINED
WOODGRAINED

Custom Cruiser. FROM $8410.
(WEST)

98

88-STYLE GRILLE RESUMES

88~ STYLE GRILLE RESUMES

(17067 BLT.)

1980 OLDSMOBILE EXTERIOR COLORS ON ALL MODELS

ALL MODELS EXCEPT STARFIRE AND OMEGA

NINETY-EIGHT AND TORONADO MODELS ONLY

WHITE · SILVER METALLIC · BLACK · LIGHT BLUE METALLIC · DARK BLUE METALLIC · DARK GREEN METALLIC · YELLOW · PASTEL BEIGE · LIGHT CAMEL METALLIC · MEDIUM CAMEL METALLIC · DARK CLARET METALLIC · CINNABAR · LIGHT GRAY · CLARET METALLIC · MEDIUM BROWN FIREMIST · CHARCOAL FIREMIST · DARK BROWN FIREMIST

Printed colors are approximates only, and may vary from actual car

TOTAL 1980 PRODUCTION = 910,306

OLDSMOBILE 80

584

OLDS **F-85**
BY
OLDSMOBILE
(COMPACT)

(CUTLASS)
NEW

(STARTS 1961)

ENTIRE REAR DOOR
RAISES, ON WAGON

WAGONS FROM
$2681.

61

$2621.

112" WB
6.50 x 13 TIRES
3.36 GEAR RATIO

(9935 BLT.)

INTERIOR

F-85 *Cutlass*

Above: F-85 Cutlass Sports Coupe. Also available: new F-85 Club Coupe . . .

new
ROCKETTE 185 Engine
(ALUMINUM BLOCK)
(155 OR) 185 HP V8
(215 CID)

TO 10.25 COMPR.
4 BBL. CARB.

$2519.

F-85 SEDAN (4-DR.) DE LUXE
$2713.
WESTERN PRICE

F-85-61

IN MANY WAYS COMPARABLE TO BUICK'S *new* REVIVED "SPECIAL" COMPACT SERIES, ALSO STARTING 1961.

PRODUCTION:

F 85		F 85 DE LUXE	
#3019 4-DR. (19,765 BLT.)		#3117 CUTLASS SPT. CPE. (9935)	
3027 CLUB CPE. (2336)		3119 4 DR. (26,311)	
3035 4-DR. WAGON, 6~PASS. (6677)		3135 4 DR. WAGON, 6 PASS. (526)	
3045 8~PASS. (10,087)		3145 " " " 8 PASS. (757)	

$2330. ~ 2897.
PRICE RANGE

OLDSMOBILE CUTLASS 61

"...it's every inch an
OLDSMOBILE "

585

OLDS F-85

(7909 BLT.)   F-85 CL. COUPE

$2403.

$2754. UP (10065 BLT.~ STD. and DELUXE)

(32,461 BLT.)

CUTLASS COUPE (SPORT)   CUTLASS

$2949. (WEST COAST)

(SAME PRICE AS LAST YEAR)

62

new GRILLE with "OLDSMOBILE" NAME ABOVE

CUTLASS SPORT COUPE (32461 BLT.)

$2694.

2 CONVERTIBLES ADDED TO LINE : #3067 CVT. (3660 BLT.) $2760.
F85 DLX. #3167 CUTLASS CVT. (9893 BLT.) $2971.
ALSO new : F85 DELUXE JETFIRE #3147 SPT. CPE. (3765 BLT.) $3049.

$2403. ~ 3049. PRICE RANGE   215 CID V8 (155, 185 or 215 HP)

TOTAL 1962 PRODUCTION : 102,301

F-85 COUPE (11,276 BLT.)

TOTAL 1963 PRODUCTION : 133,522

CUTLASS   (41,343 BLT.) H/T

$2694.

$2971.   CVT. (12,149 BLT.)

$2403.

DELUXE WAGON

$3048.   (5842 BLT.)

JETFIRE H/T (note HEAVIER SIDE TRIM)

new SHAPE OF TAIL-LIGHT

(6647 BLT.)

$2889.

TO 195 HP with ALUMINUM V8

DELUXE SEDAN (29,269 BLT.)

$2592.

63

new GRILLE with "OLDSMOBILE" NAME ACROSS CENTER STRIP

OLDSMOBILE CUTLASS 62~63

OLDS F-85

There's 'Something Extra' about owning an OLDSMOBILE!

$2797.

WAGON (DLX.) (909 BLT.)

$2537.

OLDS F-85

CUTLASS

new 230 HP

F-85 V-6 SPORTS COUPE (6594 BLT.)

VISTA-CRS. 120" WB

$2938. UP

WHERE THE ACTION IS!

64

V8 OR V6

new VISTA-CRUISER WAGON has ROOF WINDOWS

(3394 BLT.)

WIRE WH. COVERS AVAIL.

OLDSMOBILE

F-85-64

CVT.

115" WB

new GRILLE

an all-new transmission

new V6

ECON-O-WAY V-6 225 CID (155 HP)

SEDAN PROFILE

F-1964-C

JETAWAY DRIVE

JETFIRE ROCKET V-8

TOTAL 1965 PRODUCTION: 233,154

$2937. UP

ENGINES: 225 CID V6 (155 HP)
330 CID V8 (250, 260, 315 HP)
new 400 CID V8 (320 HP)

Vista-Cruiser

(5445 BLT.)

(26,441 BLT.)

$2643.

AC 207

CUTLASS

65

AA 9719

4-4-2 has 400 CID V8

442

new GRILLE; OLDSMOBILE NAME RETURNS TO CENTER

1965

The Rocket Action Car!

CUTLASS $2643. UP

VISTA-CRUISER has FOLDING, FORWARD-FACING 3RD SEAT
Roomy cargo area—holds over 100 cubic feet!

OLDSMOBILE CUTLASS 64~65

587

Oldsmobile CUTLASS

with 12 windows.

115" WB (EXCEPT ON VISTA CRUISER)

F-85 HAS NO SIDE CHROME, PRICED FROM $2348. (6 CYL.) V8 AVAILABLE

VISTA-CRUISER
V8 120" WB

(26603 BLT.) $2935. UP

250 cid 6 (155 HP);
330 cid V8 (250, 310 or 320 HP);
400 cid (350 HP)

(13518 BLT.) SPORTS CPE.
$2633.

new GRILLE WITH "OLDSMOBILE" NAME NOW ON UPPER BORDER

66

new REAR

$2348. ~ 3278. PRICE RANGE

FINAL YR. FOR 330 cid V8 (260, 310 or 320 HP)

VISTA~CRUISER
$3136. UP
(27554 BLT.)

4-4-2 REAR

DASH

$2900.

CUTLASS SUPREME
4 DR. H/T

(22571 BLT.)

67 new GRILLE AUX. LIGHTS BETWEEN EA. PAIR OF HEADLIGHTS

(36143 BLT.) VISTA~ CRUISER

new 112" WB (2-DR.)
116" WB (4-DR.)
121" WB (WAGONS)

CUTLASS "S" COUPE

Drive a youngmobile from Oldsmobile

$3367. UP

68 RESTYLED

$2561. ~ 3600. PRICE RANGE

CUTLASS SUPREME 4-DR. H/T
(8714 BLT.)

W-31 ENGINES:
250 cid 6 (155 HP); 350 cid V8 (250, 310 or 325 HP);
400 cid V8 (325, 350 or 360 HP)

69 GRILLES NOW SPLIT. AUX. LIGHTS NOW IN FRONT BUMPER

$3111.

OLDSMOBILE CUTLASS 66~69

Oldsmobile
CUTLASS
F-85

Olds Vista-Cruiser: **The all-family Escape Machine.**

"S" DASH ←

ROOF DETAILS

(11116 BLT.) SPT. CPE. ONLY
$2676. UP

(34094 VISTA~CRUISER WAGONS BLT.)
PRICED FROM
$3636.

CUTLASS "S" H/T ↘

(99255 BLT.)

CUTLASS SUPREME (FRONT)

↗ **$2907.** UP

70
(RESTYLED)

150 CID 6 (155 HP)
350 CID V8 (250 HP)

"DR. OLDSMOBILE" and HIS ODDBALL ASSISTANT CREW

$3151

Cutlass Supreme Convertible ↗

Cutlass Supreme—
Wouldn't it be nice to have an Escape Machine?

new 2-DR. H/T
$3532.

W-30 H/T (4-4-2)
455 CID V8
370 HP @
5200 RPM
↓ 3.42 G.R.
G70 x 14 TIRES

RALLYE 350 ↑

4-4-2

443

SPLIT GRILLES
$3312. UP

note "442" AT CENTER

(4-4-2 CVT. AVAIL.~2933 BLT.)
(**$3567.**)

OLDSMOBILE CUTLASS 70

F-85
SEDAN
$3789.
(WEST)

250 CID 6
(145 HP)
(769 6s; 3650 V8s)

350 CID
V8s
(240 OR
260
HP)

$2885. UP

$4291.
(WEST)

Oldsmobile
CUTLASS

(10522
CUTL. SUPR.
CVTS.)
$3507.

71

$3454.
UP

6 CYL. (ONLY
47 BLT.)
(6742 V8s)

112" WB (2-DR.)
116" (4-DR.)

Oldsmobile
ALWAYS A STEP AHEAD

6 CYL. (113 BLT.)
(4339 V8s)

$3866. UP
(26546
BLT.)

CUTLASS
CRUISER
$4358.
(WEST)

VISTA ~ CRUISER
$4922.
(3-SEAT)

CUTLASS
"S"

$3862.
(WEST)

CUTLASS
SUPREME
REAR
ROOFLINE

(ALSO AVAIL. ON
F-85 and CUTLASS)
4 new
4-4-2 COLORS

VIKING BLUE

LIME GREEN

$2958.

4-4-2 OPTIONAL HOOD WITH
DUAL AIR SCOOPS

15 COLORS OF
SUPER STOCK WHEELS AVAIL.

BITTERSWEET

SATURN GOLD

$3552.
CUTLASS
SUPR.
INTERIOR

4-4-2 SPECIAL
STEERING
WHEEL

DASH

4-4-2
H/T (6285 BLT.)
(ALSO 1304 CVTS.)

455 CID V8 (340 OR 320 HP)
OLDSMOBILE CUTLASS 71!

Oldsmobile

CUTLASS

WAGONS FOR 1972

GM MARK OF EXCELLENCE

$3908. (3-SEAT) $4706. (WEST)

$3498.

(ABOVE) CUTLASS CRUISER (7979 BLT.)

$4296. (WEST)

FINAL 121" WB V.C. WITH RAISED ROOF WINDOW SECT. (GRILLE LIKE CUTL. SUPR.)

CUTLASS 350 CID V8 (160 HP)

H/T

$2973. (37790 BLT.)

new GRILLES

F-85 DASH

F 85 TOWN SEDAN $3756. (WEST) (3792 BLT.)

$2958.

Cutlass Supreme

350 CID V8 (180 HP) H/T

Cutlass Supreme Hardtop Coupe.

4-4-2 DASH

$4046. (WEST) (105,087 BLT.)

$3258.

4-4-2

new 6-SEGMENT TAIL LTS. (ON ALL BUT WAGONS)

72

442 *has* DUAL EXHAUST PIPES

4-4-2

CUTLASS S

$3825. (WEST) HOLIDAY H/T (78461 BLT.)

$3087.

now in 4 types: 4-4-2 AVAIL. W. 350 CID OR 455 CID V8

Meet the 1972 Olds 4·4·2, 4·4·2, 4·4·2, 4·4·2!

1972 OLDSMOBILE ALWAYS A STEP AHEAD

CUTLASS SUPREME DASH and INTERIOR

IMITATION LEATHER "MADRID and ELK ~ GRAIN MOROCCEEN VINYL" SEAT UPHOL.

OLDSMOBILE CUTLASS 72

591

Oldsmobile **CUTLASS**

4~DR. (COLONNADE (35578 BLT.) $3137. $3885. (WEST)

2~DR. COLONNADE (22022 BLT.) $3049.

350 CID V8 (180 HP) (THROUGH '74)

The brand-new '73 Olds Vista-Cruiser. If you don't see the 9th window right away...

new 116" WB

... look in the roof.

73

VISTA~CRUISER 2 SEAT (10894 BLT.) $3789. 3~SEAT (13531 BLT.) $4634. (WEST) $3902.

TOTALLY RESTYLED new "COLONNADE" ROOFS ON 2 and 4~DR. H/Ts

G70 x 14 or G78 x 14 TIRES

Cutlass Salon. A new Olds in the grand touring tradition.

$5230. (WITH EXTRAS)

$3755.60 (WITHOUT EXTRAS) ($4496. (WEST))

(DASH SAME AS "S" AT BOTTOM OF PAGE)

Cutlass Salon

new

SALON

REAR DETAILS

SUPREME 2~DR.

new OPERA WINDOWS

4-4-2 PACKAGE

(W~29)

Cutlass Supreme

2~DR.

GR 70 x 15 TIRES

219,857 BLT.

$4064. (WEST)

$3324.

CUTLASS "S" 77558 BLT.

"SOFT-SELL" SALES CAMPAIGN BY

(SUPREME 4~DR. ALSO, 26099 BLT.) $3395.

The Quiet Men of Olds

We give you a great deal more than just a great deal.

DASH ("S")

$3159.

OLDSMOBILE CUTLASS 73

592

Oldsmobile CUTLASS

"S" COUPE

H78 × 14 TIRES

(50860 BLT.)

Whatever happens with gasoline, the important thing to you is the car you put the gasoline in.

OLDSMOBILE

$3890.

SUPREME CRUISER

(NO WOOD-GRAIN)
2-SEAT
(3437 BLT.) $4289.

3-SEAT
(3101 BLT.) $4481.
$4402. (WEST)

SUPREME

COUPE
(172,360 BLT.)

$4085.

Recent Proving Ground tests show 17.6 mpg average at 55 mph.

'74

ENERGY-ABSORBING HYDRAULIC SHOCK-ABSORBING BUMPER SYSTEM, SWING-BACK GRILLES

FROM $4143. (WEST)

$4499. UP

VISTA-CRUISER

2-SEAT – 4191 BLT.
3-SEAT – 7013 BLT.

3-SEAT: $4691. (WEST)

IMPROVED PADDED SOFT-GRIP STEERING WHEEL

DASH (CUTLASS SALON)

SEDAN

4-4-2 PACKAGE

SALON COUPE IS new

SALON

CUTLASS SALON

Built in the Grand Touring tradition.

INTERIOR ("S")

new AUX. LTS. QUICKLY IDENTIFY A 1974 MODEL (EXCEPT 4-4-2)

OLDSMOBILE CUTLASS

74

Oldsmobile **CUTLASS** $3756.*

250 CID 6
(105 HP)

*-$4583. WEST

16 MPG CITY
21 MPG HWY.

new GRILLES **75**

new TAIL LTS.

$3818.

CUTLASS SEDAN

FR 78 x 15 TIRES

SUPREME GRILLE

$4291. UP

SUPREME and SALON have NEW HOOD ORNAMENT.

$4890.

260 CID V8
(110 HP)

350 CID V8
(170 HP)

SALON has VERTICALLY~ SPLIT TAIL LTS.

Cutlass S:
$3840.

(42921 BLT.)

Cutlass Salon

(4~4~2 has HOOD STRIPES and SLOTS; CHROME IN PLACE OF AUX. LIGHTS)

It's a good feeling to have an Olds around you.

SALON

CUTLASS S
FROM $4905. (WEST)

"S" WITH 4~4~2 PACKAGE

442

(59179 BLT.) $3999. UP

76 A

new "WATERFALL" GRILLES

(13964 BLT.)

Can we build one for you?

VISTA~CRUISER
(20560 BLT.)

$5041. UP

3~SEAT:
$5728.
(WEST)

CUTLASS SUPREME CRUISER

$4923. UP

3~ SEAT:
$5610.
(WEST)

(CONT'D. NEXT PAGE)

OLDSMOBILE CUTLASS 75 ~ 76 (A)

Oldsmobile
CUTLASS

231 CID V6 (105 HP)

Cutlass Salon

4033. ROCKET 260 CID V8 STD. (110 HP)

76 (CONT'D.) $4965.↗
B

S

$3999.

(34994 BLT.)

$4033.

350 CID V8s AVAILABLE (170 HP)

$4291. (SUPREME COUPE)

New
Cutlass S Sedan

3. Sporty 5-speed manual transmission available. The 5th gear is overdrive for efficiency.

S DASH

$5486. (WEST)

Cutlass Supreme Brougham

$4580.

(91312 BLT.)

T~BAR ROOF AVAIL. (SALON and SUPREME 2-DR.)

DASH

S

(42993 BLT.)

$4387.

FINAL VISTA~CRUISERS

PLAIN SIDES

$5395. UP

(25816 BLT.)

GRAINED

$4351. (70155 BLT.)

new GRILLES

77

4~4~2

25 MPG HWY.
17 CITY
STD. 231 CID V6

CUTLASS SUPREME BROUGHAM COUPE

$4969.

ALL MODELS EXCEPT STARFIRE AND OMEGA

YELLOW   RED   DARK GREEN METALLIC

Printed colors are approximate only

1977 OLDSMOBILE EXTERIOR COLORS ON ALL MODELS

SILVER METALLIC | LIGHT BLUE METALLIC | DARK BLUE METALLIC | BROWN METALLIC | FIRETHORN RED METALLIC | BUCKSKIN METALLIC | LIGHT BUCKSKIN | MANDARIN ORANGE MET. | WHITE | MED. GREEN METALLIC | BLACK

Can we build one for you?

(124,712 BLT.)

OLDSMOBILE CUTLASS 76(B)~77

Oldsmobile **CUTLASS** (29509 BLT.)

FASTBACK $4543.

23	MPG HIGHWAY
16	MPG CITY
18	MPG COMBINED

All new bi-level instrument panel.

CUTLASS S

THE NEW CUTLASS SALON.
A CARFULL OF NEW IDEAS
78

Cutlass Cruiser (44617 BLT.) (new 2-PIECE TAILGATE) $5287.

DOWNSIZED 108" WB
new FASTBACK MODELS

CUTLASS SUPREME

Color-coordinated dual mirrors add eye-catching sportiness.

Special paint scheme: White w choice of metallic Carmine, Camel Tan, Blue or Green.

Super-stock wheels to give an added flash of color.

DASH (240,917 BLT.) $4873.

SUPREME

Cutlass Supreme

Supreme Brougham (117,880 BLT.)

$5287.

T-TOP AVAIL.

Cutlass Supreme

CALAIS AND SALON INSTRUMENT PANEL

27 MPG HWY., 19 CITY WITH AVAIL. 260 CID V8 (110 HP)

ALSO 305 CID V8s (145 OR 165 HP)
350 CID V8 (170 HP)

CUTLASS SUPREME UPHOLSTERY

new Cutlass Calais V6

Available 5-speed manual overdrive

4~4~2

231 CID V6 (105 HP)

new FASTBACK STYLING

OPT. IN CALAIS, SALON

(40842 BLT.) $5231.

Can we build one for you?

OLDSMOBILE CUTLASS 78

596

Oldsmobile **CUTLASS**

2-DR. SALON

$4938.

(20266 BLT.) $5038.

Cutlass Salon
Have one built for you.

$6085. (WEST)

$6269. (WEST)

$5227.

There's a lot of news in Olds today.

(8399 BLT.) $5985. (WEST)

new 90 HP DIESEL V8 (260 CID) AVAIL., 32 MPG HWY., 24 MPG CITY
ALSO 231 CID V6 (115 HP) OR 260 CID V8 (105 HP)

$6394. (WEST)

(18714 BUILT) $5352.

SALON BROUGHAM (36/7 BLT.)

5.7-litre, 350 CID V8s ALSO AVAIL. (GAS OR DIESEL, 125 HP)

(43780 BLT.)

CUTLASS CALAIS $5828.

$6853. (WEST)

(277,944 BLT.)

$6425. (WEST)

CUTLASS SUPREME COUPE $5390.

OPT. T-BAR ROOF

CALAIS DASH and STEERING WHEEL

79
new GRILLES

4-4-2

UNIQUE GRILLE

CUTLASS SUPREME BROUGHAM

(137,323 BLT.)

$5829.

$6854. (WEST)

"TAHOE" UPH. (SALON BROUGH.)

CUTLASS CRUISERS (2-SEAT ONLY)

"MOJAVE" INTERIOR AVAIL. IN BROUGHAM

(10755 BLT.) CUTLASS CRUISER $5223.

CRUISER BROUGHAM (WOODGRAIN OPTIONAL) (42953 BLT.)
$5775. $6468. (WEST)

350 CID DIESEL V8 (125 HP) AVAILABLE

OLDSMOBILE CUTLASS 79

597

Oldsmobile
CUTLASS

GRILLE DETAIL

80 A

SALON

SALON BROUGH. $6054.

$7168. (WEST) (ONLY 965 BLT.)

new GRILLES

ENGINE CHOICES:
231 CID V6 (110 HP)
260 CID V8 (105 HP)
305 CID V8
350 CID DIESEL V8 (105 HP)

DASH

$6780

(36923 BLT.) 6/24.

CUTLASS 4-DOOR

CUTLASS LS SEDAN:
(86868 BLT.) $7327. (WEST)

Cutlass Brougham Sedan.

AVAIL. PADDED-GRIP CUSTOM SPORT STEER. WHEEL

$7219. (52462 BLT.) $7653. (WEST)

(STD. EQUIP. ON CALAIS)

$7119. **CALAIS**
$7690. (WEST)

Available instrumentation—with voltmeter, temperature and oil pressure gages, plus trip odometer. Standard on Calais.

Pick from five available wheel covers and wheels. Including (A) special cast aluminum wheel, (B) wheel cover with matching body color, (C) Super-Stock wheel with matching body color, (D) simulated wire wheel disc and (E) deluxe wheel disc.

(26269 BLT.)

ALL MODELS EXCEPT STARFIRE AND OMEGA

1980 OLDSMOBILE EXTERIOR COLORS ON ALL MODELS

20 EPA EST MPG **360** EST DRIVING RANGE

27 HWY EST MPG **486** EST HIGHWAY RANGE

(CONT'D. NEXT PAGE)

WHITE | SILVER METALLIC | BLACK | LIGHT BLUE METALLIC | DARK BLUE METALLIC | DARK GREEN METALLIC | YELLOW | PASTEL BEIGE | LIGHT CAMEL METALLIC | MEDIUM CAMEL METALLIC | DARK CLARET METALLIC | CINNABAR | LIGHT GRAY | CLARET METALLIC

Printed colors are approximates only.

OLDSMOBILE CUTLASS 80 (A)

Oldsmobile **CUTLASS**

REAR DETAILS

$6655.

(169,597 BLT.)

$7226. (WEST)

CUTLASS SUPREME

| 20 EPA EST. MPG | 360 EST. DRIVING RANGE |
| 27 HWY. EST. MPG | 486 EST. HIGHWAY RANGE |

T-BAR ROOF OPTION

SUNROOF OPT.

80B (CONT'D.)

For special distinction, a new "Renaissance" interior trim, available exclusively on Cutlass Supreme Brougham models. Features complementary shades of blue and camel in a bold, contemporary pattern of rich velour.

AVAILABLE INTERIOR

(BELOW)

SUPREME BROUGHAM
COUPE (77875 BLT.)
$7094.

AVAILABLE 5.7~litre (350 CID) DIESEL V8 ENGINE ($960. EXTRA)

(WEST) $7568

CUTLASS CRUISER

$6572.
(7815 BLT.)
$7029. (WEST)
(V-6 OR DIESEL V8 OPT.)

wagon

Cutlass Cruiser Diesel
| 22 EPA Est. MPG | 400 EPA Est. Range | 34 Hwy. Est. | 618 Hwy. Range |

2~SEAT MODELS ONLY

N. KANARIS

CRUISER BROUGHAM

(22791 BLT.)

$7524. (WEST)

$6809.

INTERIOR

| EPA MPG 20 EST. MPG | 362 EST. DRIVING RANGE |
| 27 HWY. | 488 EST. HIGHWAY RANGE |

$7254. (WEST)

Oldsmobile

WE'VE HAD ONE BUILT FOR YOU.

OLDSMOBILE CUTLASS 80 (B)

599

Meet the new Compact Olds— at a compact price.

OLDS OMEGA

(1973~1984)

A glove compartment with a door and a lock. Rear windows that roll down.

4-door sedan.
TOWN SEDAN
(12804 BLT.)
$2641.

3-door hatchback.
(21433 BLT.)
$2762.

2-door coupe.
(26/26 BLT.)

Omega Yellow
Omega Orange
Omega Red
OMEGA ONLY

Silver Taupe ALL MODELS · Eclipse Blue · Chestnut · Wedgewood Blue · Emerald Green · Mayan Gold · Brewster Green · Cranberry Red · Zodiac Blue · Moss Gold · Crystal Gold · Chamois Gold · Cameo White

1973 EXTERIOR COLORS

Deluxe interior with new "wet-look" vinyl trim. Full carpeting. Vinyl-grip steering wheel. Chrome trim around the windows and wheel openings.

GM

COUPE
FROM $2612.70
(SALE)

250 CID 6
(100 HP)

Omega

73 New

Your choice of 2, 3 or 4 doors.

$3334.
(WEST)
111" WB
(THROUGH '79)

LESS BRIGHTWORK ON new DASH

The soft grip steering wheel is wrapped in vinyl, and feels good underhand. The instrument panel has a good-looking quality to it, too, right down to the grained inlays. Air conditioning is available also.

FROM $3043.
$3867. (WEST)

350 CID V8 (180 HP) ALSO AVAIL. (INTRO. '73 SEASON)

74 new GRILLE

$4814. (WEST)

It's a good feeling to have a little Olds around you.

new GRILLE

$3463.05
4~DR.

'75 STD. INT.

2~DR.

"Omega Salon"

new SALON MODELS
new TAIL~ LTS.

new DASH

75

SALONS FROM $4148.

HGJ·249

OLDSMOBILE OMEGA 73~75

600

Olds Omega C.PE.

DASH

(15347 BLT.)

new GRILLE

$3485.

OMEGA $4409. (WEST)

76

$3390. (3918 BLT.)

Omega F-85 (INTRO. DURING 1975 SEASON)

Can we build one for you?

(LITTLE CHROME ON F-85)

$4314. (WEST)

F85 INTERIOR IN "RACINE FABRIC"

Omega SX HATCHBACK

(5682 HATCHBACKS BLT.) $3627. UP

250 CID 6 (105 HP)
260 CID V8 (110 HP)
350 CID V8 (140/155 HP)

$3514.

COUPE (HATCHBACK, 4-DR. BROUGHAM ALSO)

BROUGHAM

$3675. (5363 BLT.)

$4599. (WEST)

20221 OMEGA SEDANS BLT.

STARFIRE AND OMEGA COLORS ONLY

BRIGHT RED | BRIGHT YELLOW | DARK AQUA METALLIC

77 OLDSMOBILE EXTERIOR COLORS ON ALL MODELS

SILVER METALLIC | LIGHT BLUE METALLIC | DARK BLUE METALLIC | BROWN METALLIC | FIRETHORN RED METALLIC | BUCKSKIN METALLIC | LIGHT BUCKSKIN | MANDARIN ORANGE MET. | WHITE | MED. GREEN METALLIC | BLACK

SX

$3905. UP (4739 HATCHBKS.)

(2241 BLT.) 3653.

OMEGA F-85 COUPE

CPE.

BROUGHAM 3934.

(6478 BLT.)

new TAIL-LIGHTS new GRILLE

77

3740.

OMEGA (18611 CPES.) (21723 SEDANS.) 3797.

BROUGHAM SEDAN (9003 BLT.) 3994.

new DASH

OLDSMOBILE OMEGA 76~77

Olds Omega

WITH SX SPORT TRIM

28 MPG HWY.
16 MPG CITY (V6)

Oldsmobile Omega Brougham
Can we build one for you?

78

new GRILLE

$4482. (7125 BLT.)

$5300. (WEST) INTERIOR

OMEGA

OMEGA BROUGHAM COUPE

$4215. ↑ (3798 BLT.)

STARFIRE AND OMEGA COLORS ONLY

BRIGHT RED   BRIGHT YELLOW   BRIGHT BLUE METALLIC   DARK GREEN METALLIC

SOME OTHER OLDSMOBILE COLORS ALSO AVAILABLE.

Oldsmobile
Omega Hatchback '78
Can we build one for you?

$4173. UP (4084 BLT.)

---

231 CID V6 (115 HP) OR 305 CID V8 (130 HP)
(OMEGA's FINAL V8)

1078 BLT.

$4387.

BROUGHAM

$4345. UP
HATCHBACK (SX PACKAGE)

(ONLY 956 BLT.)

79

Oldsmobile
Omega
Have one built for you.

BROUGHAM (2145 BLT.) SEDAN

$4487.
$5672. (WEST)

new GRILLE WITH ALL-VERTICAL PCS.

CPE.

BROUGHAM SEDAN
$5858.

(21595 BLT.)

(42289 BLT.)

$6455. (WEST)

new 105" (104.9") WB
(42172 BLT.)

new DASH
SEDAN $5672.

new 151 CID 4 (90 HP) OR 173 CID V6 (115 HP)

OMEGA

SX

COUPE (28267 BLT.)
$5501.

TOTALLY RESTYLED and DOWNSIZED. "WATERFALL" GRILLE

80

$5501. ~ 6013.
PRICE RANGE

SX GRILLE and TRIM ARE BLACK.

Oldsmobile Omega. 78 ~ 80

602

Oldsmobile Starfire (1975-1980)

INTERIOR

FROM $4171. ('75)

FULL INSTRUMENTS STD.

1975 DASH

1975 DASH

97" WB

231 CID V6 OR 140 CID 4

2.56 GEAR RATIO

STD. TYPE ('76)

('75)

B78 x 13 TIRES
18½-GAL. FUEL TANK

75-76

GT ('76)

(SX MODEL has THINNER SIDE STRIPE THAN GT)

new DASH, 1976, LOOKS SAME AS '77 and FOLLOWING YRS.

JERRY'S BURGERS

ORANGE

FROM $4261. ('77) (WEST)

SUBMARINE SAND.

OPEN

140 CID 4 *
(84 HP) OR
231 CID V6 (105 HP)
(145 HP, 305 CID
V8 AVAIL. '78)

('77)

new GRILLE

77-78

GT '77

$3942. UP ('77)

SX
$4306.
(9265 BLT.)

18½-GAL. GAS TANK

* = 151 CID 4 (85 HP) AVAIL. 1978

('78)

('78)

OLDSMOBILE STARFIRE 75~78

Oldsmobile Starfire

$4095.⁰⁰
(SALE PRICE)

FIRENZA

GT

NO SIDE-STRIPING ON STD. STARFIRE

SPT. STEER. WH.

79

new GRILLE and SINGLE HEAD-LIGHTS

151 CID 4, 231 CID V6, OR 305 CID V8 (130 HP)

REAR VIEW

$4275. and up
(REGULAR PRICE)

There's a lot of news in Olds today.

WHEEL

INTERIOR   (20299 BLT.)

A 78 x 13 TIRES
151 CID 4 (90 HP)

231 CID V6 (110 HP; DOWN FROM 115)

(8237 BLT.)

STD. STARFIRE
$5294.
(WEST)

TYPICAL 1980 STARFIRE INTERIOR SAME AS 1979 SHOWN ABOVE
$4750. UP

Dual sport mirrors

FIRENZA $5721.
(WEST)

(ORIG. INTRO. DURING '78 MODEL YEAR)
(has REAR SPOILER)

GT
$5495. (SX)

(THE FINAL STARFIRE)

new GRILLE WITH MOSTLY HORIZONTAL PCS.

80

STARFIRE
Nifty little road machines built for the long and winding.

Delco AM radio, standard.

Contour, high-back bucket seats, standard.

4-speed manual, standard.

Sport steering wheel, standard.

OLDSMOBILE STARFIRE 79~80

604

Oldsmobile TORONADO

(SINCE 1966)

Front-wheel drive

$4617. UP

$5125. UP (WEST COAST)

NEW
66

119" WB (THROUGH '70)

(40,963 BLT.)

V8 ENGINE (ON ALL)
425 CID
385 HP (21,790 BLT.)

$4674. UP

new WHEEL COVERS

new GRILLE

Drum speedometer, needle gauges

$5182. UP (WEST COAST)

$4674. UP

$4750. UP

$5258. (WEST COAST)

(26,454 BLT.)
new 455 CID V8 (375 HP)

DASH

68

HEADLTS. OPEN →

Toronado. Test drive the front-wheel-drive "youngmobile" from Oldsmobile.

REAR

new GRILLE

OLDSMOBILE NOW SHOWING YOUNGMOBILE THINKING 1969

Escape from the ordinary

(28,494 BLT.)
$4835.

69

new REAR DECK

MODIFIED GRILLE

AS BEFORE, 8.85 x 15 TIRES

OLDSMOBILE TORONADO 66~69

CUSTOM = $5030.

$5344. (WEST COAST)

Oldsmobile
Toronado

455 C/D V8 (375 OR 400 HP)
119" WB

Toronado Exclusively

Oxford Gray   Viking Blue   Ming Jade   Sandalwood

The elegant new Toronado control center. Even the rich inlays cannot mask the precision and purposefulness of its instruments and controls. For the ultimate in driving comfort, the Tilt-and-Telescope Steering Wheel may be ordered.

Wouldn't it be nice to have an Escape Machine?

Cinnamon Bronze   Grenadier Red   Regency Rose

PREMIUM

$5023. (STD.)

REAR 3/4 VIEW

70

CLOSE DETAIL

CLOSE REAR VIEW ←

PROD. = STD. - 2351
CUSTOM - 23082

new FRONT STYLING

CUSTOM = $5216.

Oldsmobile
ALWAYS A STEP AHEAD

new ROOFLINE

new WRAP-AROUND "CONTROL CENTER" DASH
$5457. UP

CUSTOM H/T $5988. (WEST)

(28980 BLT.)

new DOOR HANDLES

(RESTYLED)

71

new TWO-LEVEL TAIL LTS.
(15 YRS. AHEAD OF ITS TIME!)

new GRILLE OPENINGS BELOW LTS.
350 HP

new 122.3" WB

1971 Toronado
The Unmistakable One, from Oldsmobile.

OLDSMOBILE TORONADO 70~71

606

1972 TORONADO.
THERE'S NOTHING COMMON ABOUT IT.

CARPETING

DASH

2-LEVEL
TAIL-LIGHTS
CONTINUE

$5341.

(48900 BLT.)
HP CUT
TO 250

WILL RUN ON
EITHER LEADED
OR UNLEADED GAS
(SINCE '71)

72

CUSTOM
$5986.
BROUGHAM
$6140.

WESTERN PRICES

ALL-VERTICAL
GRILLE OPENINGS

OLDSMOBILE
ALWAYS A STEP AHEAD

DASH

INTERIOR

$5441.

73

(55921 BLT.)

REAR

new
GRILLE SLOTS ATOP
FR. BUMPER

WESTERN
PRICES AS IN 1972

OLDSMOBILE   TORONADO 72-73

DIGITAL CLOCK STANDARD in TORONADO and 98.

7:00 TORONADO

Oldsmobile's message center is arranged in two panels flanking the Hydra-matic quadrant, signals you when any one of many functions requires your attention.

GEN	OIL	PARK R N D S L	FASTEN SEAT BELTS	
BRAKE			HOT	LOW FUEL
LIGHTS ON			EXTERNAL LAMP	

Oldsmobile
Toronado

$5933.

new DASH (new "MESSAGE CENTER" WARNING LTS.)

HOOD ORNAMENT ADDED

74

(27582 BLT.)

WITH OPERA ROOF

New steel-belted radial tires, designed to meet GM performance specifications, are available for all Oldsmobile models.

HP CUT TO 230

CUSTOM $6634.

BROUGHAM $6798.

CUSTOM (4419 BLT.)
BROUGHAM (18882 BLT.)

CUSTOM $7095.

BROUGHAM $7325.

new SQUARE LTS.

75

HP CUT TO 215

A new touch of distinction: Toronado's T-crest hood ornament. Another, the opera roof you can order (seen below).

ORNAMENT

note TOP COVER VARIATIONS

It's a good feeling to have an Olds around you.

$6523. ~ 6753.
CUSTOM   BROUGHAM

608

X~RAY VIEW, SHOWING DETAILS OF CONSTRUCTION

Oldsmobile
Toronado

R.1 REAR VIEW

CLOSER DETAILS

DETAILS OF "MESSAGE CENTER" SECTIONS BELOW SPEEDO.

CUSTOM = $**6891.**

BROUGHAM = $**7137.**

new STRIP ON REAR FENDER, and HEAVIER SIDE TRIM STRIPS, ARE THE MOST OBVIOUS MEANS OF DISTINGUISHING THE 1976 FROM PREVIOUS TORONADO.

1976 PROD.

CUSTOM (2555)
BROUGHAM (21749)

CUSTOM $7494.

BROUGHAM $7740.

WESTERN PRICES SHOWN

76

BACK SEAT

ALL MODELS EXCEPT STARFIRE AND OMEGA

LIME METALLIC   CREAM   BLACK   YELLOW   RED
Printed colors are approximate only and may vary

OTHER UPH. STYLES ALSO AVAIL.

FRONT COMPARTMENT

1976 OLDSMOBILE EXTERIOR COLORS ON ALL MODELS

BUCKSKIN
WHITE
DARK GREEN METALLIC
SADDLE METALLIC
MAHOGANY METALLIC
RED METALLIC
DARK BLUE METALLIC
LIGHT BLUE METALLIC
SILVER METALLIC

OLDSMOBILE TORONADO 76

Oldsmobile **Toronado**

new SMALLER 403 CID V8 (200 HP)

DASH

BROUGHAM $8287.

BROUGHAM (3/371 BLT.)

Printed colors are approximate only

1977 OLDSMOBILE EXTERIOR COLORS ON ALL MODELS

SILVER METALLIC | LIGHT BLUE METALLIC | DARK BLUE METALLIC | BROWN METALLIC | FIRETHORN RED METALLIC

77

NEW

XSR has WRAP-AROUND REAR WINDOW w. CREASED CORNERS AT EACH SIDE!

NEW Toronado XSR
Can we build one for you?

XSR (2714 BLT.) $11132.

ALL MODELS EXCEPT STARFIRE AND OMEGA

YELLOW | RED | DARK GREEN METALLIC

T-BAR ROOF OPT.
XS-$10837.
XSR-$11285.

WESTERN PRICES

new GRILLE

BUCKSKIN METALLIC | LIGHT BUCKSKIN | MANDARIN ORANGE MET. | WHITE | MED. GREEN METALLIC | BLACK

Oldsmobile

78
HP CUT TO 190

Can we build one for you?
XS (XSC) (2453 BLT.) $11599.

new GRILLE WITH ALL VERTICAL PCS.

FINAL TORONADO WITH THIS TYPE BODY, BEFORE MAJOR RESTYLING

XS

BROUGHAM

1978 Olds Toronado...

1978 OLDSMOBILE EXTERIOR COLORS ON ALL MODELS

SILVER METALLIC | LIGHT BLUE METALLIC | CARMINE RED METALLIC | LIGHT CAMEL BEIGE | MEDIUM CAMEL METALLIC | DARK CAMEL METALLIC | RUSSET METALLIC | LIGHT GREEN METALLIC | WHITE | BLACK

ALL MODELS EXCEPT STARFIRE AND OMEGA

PASTEL BLUE | DARK BLUE METALLIC | MED. GREEN METALLIC | DARK CARMINE RED METALLIC

(22362 BLT.) $9412. UP

SALE: $8899.
(BROUGHAM)

OLDSMOBILE TORONADO 77-78

Oldsmobile
Toronado
Have one built for you.

Announcing the all-new 1979 Toronado...

new SMALLER 350 cid V8 (HP CUT TO 165)

new DASH

new FORMAL ROOFLINE

79

TOTALLY RESTYLED and DOWNSIZED (new 114" WB)   (50056 BLT.)

$10709.

SALE: $10112. (WEST)

"Oldsmobile" (IN LOWER-CASE LETTERS)

XSC SPORT COUPE
(WITH SPECIAL DECOR)

new STEERING WHEEL DESIGN

BROUGHAM

new GRILLE

$11934. UP
(43440 TOTAL 1980 PROD.)

GM

GAS OR DIESEL V8s

80

1980 OLDSMOBILE EXTERIOR COLORS ON ALL MODELS

| WHITE | SILVER METALLIC | BLACK | LIGHT BLUE METALLIC | DARK BLUE METALLIC | DARK GREEN METALLIC | YELLOW | PASTEL BEIGE | LIGHT CAMEL METALLIC | MEDIUM CAMEL METALLIC | DARK CLARET METALLIC |

SALE: $11360. (WEST)

2.41 GEAR RATIO

ALL MODELS EXCEPT STARFIRE AND OMEGA

NINETY-EIGHT AND TORONADO MODELS ONLY

| CINNABAR | LIGHT GRAY | CLARET METALLIC | MEDIUM BROWN FIREMIST | CHARCOAL FIREMIST | DARK BROWN FIREMIST |

Printed colors are approximates only, and may vary from actual car paint colors

Printed in U.S.A. 8-79

ENGINES
GAS = 307 cid V8 (new) (150 HP)
350 cid V8 (160 HP)
DIESEL = 350 cid V8 (105 HP)

OLDSMOBILE TORONADO 79~80

PACKARD
ASK THE MAN WHO OWNS ONE

Station Wagon $1200.

6 CYL.
245.3 CID
100 HP
(THRU '41)
110
122" WB

CLUB COUPE

$940.

$990.

TOTAL OF 62300 110 SERIES BLT.

Packard 110, 1800

"110" TOURING SEDAN

9 HOOD VENT SLOTS "110"
10 " " " "120"

40

A
new FENDER GRILLES FLANK CENTER GRILLE

$1161.
"120" TOURING SEDAN
127" WB

AIR~CONDITIONING
Packard makes possible this long-awaited motoring comfort for summer's sweltering heat —the first mechanically refrigerated air-cooling system ever offered to motor car owners.

120
120 HP
282 CID
STRAIGHT~8
(THRU '47)
127" WB

2~DR. FAMILY SEDAN

$1130.

Illustrated: Packard One-Twenty Family Sedan, $1130* (white sidewall tires extra)

TOTAL OF 28136 120 SERIES BLT. 127" WB

U 28995

$1277.

Limitless possibilities! Just picture any 1940 Packard . . . Any place . . . Any situation

(CONT'D. NEXT PAGE)

40 Packard 120. 1801   (A)

PACKARD 160, 180

NEW ENGINE

356 c/d STR.~ 8
160 HP (THRU 1950)

160 SUPER-8
TOURING SEDAN

1632.

Model illustrated is Packard Super-8 One-Sixty Touring Sedan $1632* (white sidewall tires extra)

(TOTAL OF 5662 160 SERIES BUILT)

138" WB
$2464.

HERE IS A CAR SO FAR AHEAD THAT ANYTHING ELSE SEEMS YEARS BEHIND!

PACKARD ONE-EIGHTY

Illustrated — the five-passenger long-wheelbase Touring Sedan, $2464* (white sidewall tires extra)

40 B (CONT'D.)

SUPER 180

DASH

FORMAL SEDAN (LEATHER BACK AND ROOF)

Seven-passenger sedan on 180 chassis

CUSTOM ONE-EIGHTY

CLUB SEDAN $2297.

$2894.

One-Eighty

Darrin-designed

ACTUAL PHOTO
(NOTE CUT-DOWN SIDE DOORS!) (AD)
(AVAIL. THRU '42 SEASON)

PACKARD

$4593.

(TOTAL OF 1900 180 SERIES BUILT)

Darrin-designed
One-Eighty

$6100.

CUSTOM SPORT SEDAN (AD)

For a Fortunate Few

ACTUAL PHOTO →

(AVAIL. THRU 1941)

INTERIOR

40 PACKARD (B)

PACKARD

TOTAL OF 34700 "110s" BLT.

1941 PACKARD 110

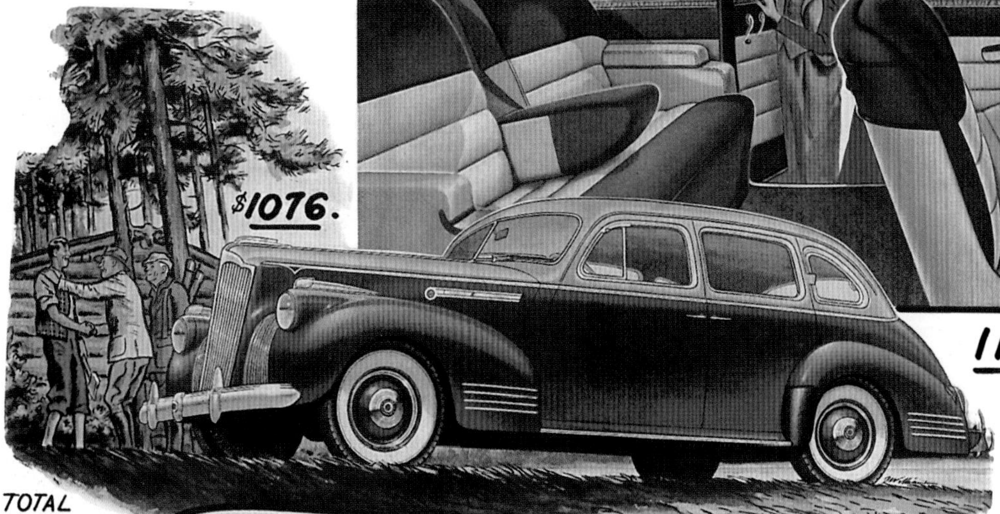

$1076.

_110_ INTERIOR $1420.

"FADE-AWAY" FENDERS

41½

CLIPPER

(16600 BLT.) 127" WB

TOTAL OF 17000 "120s" BLT.

Illustrated: *the new Packard One-Ten Deluxe Touring Sed.*
(ABOVE)

$1291.
_120_
127-INCH WHEELBASE
120 HP

$1407.

New

41 125 HP IN CLIPPER (STR.~8) 282 CID

the Class of '41

One Eighty Formal Sedan

TOTAL OF 3525 "160s" BLT. (127, 138 or 148" WB)

138" WB

Aero-Drive* boosts your savings still more—one free mile in five! Try Air Conditioning* (a Packard *first*) with *real* refrigeration. Try the smoother, mellower Air-Glide ride. All these—and 59 more important new improvements—are yours in this value of values! See it now! *Ask the man who owns one.*

* *Available at extra cost.*

$3090.

(SAME 3 WBs AS 160)

TOTAL OF 930 "180s" BLT.

CONV'T. SEDAN

Just a few of the stunning new upholstery trims—122 offered at no extra cost

DARRIN, ROLLSTON OR LE BARON BODIES AVAIL.

1941 PACKARD

PACKARD

Clipper

WBs:
120
122
127
138 or
148"

ELECTROMATIC DRIVE

SIMPLIFIED DRIVING WITH
NO JERK · NO SLIP · NO CREEP

Here's the last *PACKARD*
'Til we win the war—
It's 'all out' on *ENGINES*
To even the score!

11325 "110s" BLT.

PRICES START AT **$1166.**

19199 "120s" BLT.

$1308.

Six and Eight Custom Clipper Club Sedan

"*Clipper*" NAME ON DOOR

CLIPPER

HOOD OPENS AT LEFT SIDE

Wartime

42

2580 "160s" BLT.
672 "180s" "

$2099.

Clipper six-passenger 180 Custom Club Sedan

1942 Packard Formal Sedan, Super 8
Custom 180 138"WB
$3011.

OLD~STYLE
SENIOR PACKARDS
ADOPT HORIZ.
PCS. FLANKING
VERTICAL~BAR
CENTER GRILLE.

1942 PACKARD 180

Series 2007

PACKARD MOTOR CAR CO., DETROIT
(STUDEBAKER-PACKARD CORP.,
1954~1958)

PACKARD

(1899 TO 1958)

new CLIPPER 8 CYL.
(STARTS 4-41)

41½
(OR EARLY '42)

(1951 SERIES)
$1375.

OTHER 1941 MODELS CONTINUE ALSO

Clipper

←*new* 2-DR. CLIPPERS NOW ALSO AVAIL.

110

180

INTERIOR

LOOKING AHEAD?
SKIPPER THE CLIPPER

42-45
new CHOICE of 6 or 8-CYL. CLIPPERS

(2000 SERIES)
6776 BLT. '42.
2652 AVAIL. 1943
TO 1945 FOR
MILITARY STAFF

ELECTROMATIC DRIVE
SIMPLIFIED DRIVING WITH
NO JERK·NO SLIP·NO CREEP

CUSTOM SUPER CLIPPER

SUPER 8 *has* 148" WB

$1746.
DELUXE CLIPPER

46-
47
(2100 SERIES)

(BIG-CITY
PACKARD SHOWROOMS
MORE LUXURIOUS THAN THIS RURAL OUTLET)

42,102 BLT. 1946

55,477 BLT. 1947
PACKARD 41½~47

616

PACKARD

NEW

$3161.

STATION SEDAN

ALL "CLIPPER" MODEL NAMES DISCONTINUED UNTIL 1953.

EIGHT 120" WB

2-DR. CLUB SEDAN $2250.

NEW SMOOTH SIDE BODIES

SUPER-8 CVT. IS FIRST OF 1948 PACKARDS TO BE INTRODUCED.

$2990.

SUPER 8 130 HP

$2529.

2-DR. CLUB SEDANS, LIMOS. ALSO AVAIL.

EARLY
48-49
(RESTYLED) (2200 SERIES)

$3461. CUSTOM 8 160 HP

127" OR 148" WB ON CUSTOM 8 CLOSED MODELS.

127" WB CVT.
$3866.
(1318 BLT.)

1948 - EARLY '49 DASH ILLUSTR. ON NEXT PAGE

CUSTOM 8 *has* CRISS-CROSS PIECES IN GRILLE, MATCHING TRIM BELOW REAR DECK LID.

CREST

ASK THE MAN WHO OWNS ONE

3 DIFF. STRAIGHT-8 ENGINES : 288 CID (130 HP) = 8, DELUXE 8
327 CID (145 HP) = SUPER 8
356 CID (160 HP) = CUSTOM 8

98,897 BLT. (1948)
104,593 " (1949)

PACKARD 48-49

PACKARD

CLOSE-UP VIEW OF DASH

(2200 SERIES)

135 HP (8)
150 HP (SU.8)
160 HP (CUST. 8)

$2383. ('50)

DELUXE 8

CLUB SEDAN

$2224. UP (LOWEST-PRICED MODEL)

EIGHT (120" WB)

SUPER 8
new 127" WB

$2633.

DASH and BACKLIGHT DETAILS

Ultramatic Drive AVAIL.

"Golden Anniversary" MODELS   new LARGER BACKLIGHTS ON 4-DOOR SEDANS

49½-50

(2300 SERIES)
77 MAJOR IMPROVEMENTS

CUSTOM 8
127" WB

STATION SEDAN (WAGON) STILL AVAIL. (THROUGH '50)

#2333   CONVERTIBLE   (68 BLT. '49½ ; 77 BLT. '50)
$4295. (1949½) $4520. (1950)
(HIGHEST-PRICED MODEL)

new : SIDE TRIM ADDED :
HORIZONTAL CHROME STRIP and "PACKARD" NAME

FINAL 356 CID STR. 8 (CUSTOM 8)
(288 and 327 CID 8s CONTINUED THROUGH 1954.)

TOTAL 1950 PRODUCTION : 72,138

PACKARD 49½-50

618

PACKARD
200 CLUB SEDAN **$2366.** UP

250 (CVT. and H/T) (4640 BLT. '51; 5201 BLT. '52)

Prestige car of the medium-priced field: Packard '200' Club Sedan—$2366
—one of nine exciting new models for '51

122" WB

"NEW, ALL-NEW"

CVT. ('51)
$3391.
CVT. ('52)
$3476.

250 CVT.

$3234. UP

51-52
(2500 SER.)

(TOTALLY
RESTYLED
2400 SERIES)

300

250 MAYFAIR

$3034. UP
REAR SIDE
DETAILS

(15,309 BLT. '51; 6705 BLT. '52)

1952 MODEL
(left) SIMILAR,
BUT has new
HOOD ORNAMENT
and MEDALLION ON
GRILLE

Ultramatic

400 PATRICIAN

(9001 BLT. '51)
(3975 BLT. '52)

COSTLY MODELS CONTINUE
CORMORANT FIGURE
AS 1951 ORNAMENT

1951 MODELS
have "PACKARD"
NAME ABOVE
GRILLE

New Armor-rib body construction!
New Tele-glance instrument panel!
New Safeti-set brake!

—the one for '51!

$2302. ~ 3662. (1951 PRICE RANGE)
$2494. ~ 3797. (1952)
(200)   (400 PATRICIAN)

ENGINES: (STRAIGHT-8)
288 CID (135 HP)
327 CID (150 OR
155 HP)

76,075 BLT. 1951
62,988 BLT. 1952
PACKARD 51-52

PACKARD

(STANDARD) CLIPPER PRICED FROM $2544. (2-DR. CLUB SEDAN) (6370 BLT.) #2695

$2588. SEDAN (26,027 BLT.)
(INCR. TO $2745.)
CLIPPER DELUXE
122" WB
#2662

#2665 CLUB SEDAN (4678 BLT.) $2691.

New Packard CLIPPER

new HOOD ORNAMENT and SMOOTH HORIZONTAL GRILLE PIECE (ON CLIPPER ONLY)

160 HP

53 (2600 SERIES)

CLIPPER SERIES RETURNS (PREVIOUSLY AVAIL. 1941 – 1947)

new CAVALIER
127" WB
(10,799 BLT.)
#2672
$3234.

#2679
CVT. (1518 BLT.)
$3486.
MAYFAIR 122" WB

MAYFAIR H/T ALSO, (5150 BLT.), W/O 3 CHROME REAR FENDER PLAQUES SEEN ON ABOVE CVT.

400 PATRICIAN SEDAN #2652
(7456 BLT.)
127" WB

(25 CUSTOM BLT. #2653 DERHAM SEDANS AT $6539.) $3740.

(150 LIMOS., 8 PASS. EXECUTIVE SEDANS, on 149" WB)

new GROOVES IN HORIZONTAL GRILLE PIECE (EXCEPT ON CLIPPER)

note "CONTINENTAL" REAR SPARE TIRE and COVER

new CARIBBEAN #2678

$5209.
(750 BLT.)

STRAIGHT-8
ENGINES: 288 CID (150 HP) (CLIPPER)
327 CID (160 HP) (" DELUXE)
327 CID (180 HP) (CAVALIER, MAYFAIR, CARIBBEAN)
(9-MAIN-BEARING 327 CID ENG. IN PATRICIAN, LIMOUSINES)

TOTAL 1953 PRODUCTION: 80,371

PACKARD 53

620

PACKARD

RARE CLIPPER SPECIAL (970 SEDANS, 912 CLUB SEDANS BLT.)
$2594. $2544.

$3125. (3618 BLT.)

#5467 → PANAMA

CLIPPER DELUXE
$2645. UP

SUPER CLIPPER

122", 127" OR 149" WB
150, 165, 185 OR 212 HP

54
(5400 SERIES)

SEDAN (6270 BLT.)
$2815.

$3344.

DASH

CAVALIER
127" WB

#5472 SEDAN (2580 BLT.)

PATRICIAN 127" WB

(7456 BLT.)

TOTAL 1954 PRODUCTION: 27,307
FINAL STRAIGHT-8 ENGINES
(288, 327 OR 359 CID)

$3740.

STUDEBAKER-PACKARD MERGER

122" WB

CLIPPER

WITH (FINE VERTICAL GRILLE PCS.)

FIRST MAJOR RESTYLING SINCE 1951

PATRICIAN

PRICE RANGE:
$2586. TO $5932.

TOTAL 1955 PRODUCTION:
68,674 EST.

new 12-VOLT ELECTRICAL SYSTEM

CARIBBEAN CONVT. (APPROX. 490 BLT.)

127" WB
$3740.

400

5500 SERIES

55
TOTALLY RESTYLED

$5932.

new V8 O.H.V. ENGINES! (4600 RPM)
320 CID (225 HP) (CLIPPER DLX., SUPER)
352 CID (245 HP, CLIPPER CUSTOM)
(260 HP, PACKARDS)
(275 HP, CARIB.)

621

PACKARD

2731. #5622 SEDAN

CLIPPER DELUXE

(5715 BLT.)

(CLIPPER TREATED AS A SEPARATE MAKE FROM PACKARD IN 1956.)

CLIPPER SUPER *also avail.* #5642, 5647

$3069. ← #5662 SEDAN (2129 BLT.)

(SUPER SEDAN, H/T ALSO) $2866., $2916.

CUSTOM CLIPPER

MEMBERS OF CLIPPER GRILLE NOW HORIZONTAL.

CUSTOM CLIPPER CONSTELLATION H/T → #5667

$3164. (1466 BLT.)

122" WB (CLIPPERS) OTHERS, 127" WB

PACKARD MODELS

56 *new* GRILLES

(5600 SERIES)

new DISPLACEMENT OF 374 CID ON ALL PACKARD V8 ENGINES. ALL BUT CARIBBEAN *have* 290 HP @ 4600 RPM.

$3483. (1784 BLT.)

122" WB

EXECUTIVE

H/T (1031 BLT.)

$3658.

127" WB

PATRICIAN

(3775 BLT.)

$4160.

WIDER-SPACED GRILLE PIECES *with* MESH BACKGROUND

$4190.

400 H/T

(3224 BLT.)

"ASK THE MAN WHO OWNS *the New* ONE"

$5995.

(276 BLT.)

CARIBBEAN *has* 310 HP @ 4600 RPM

263 CARIBBEAN H/Ts ALSO, **$5495.** (A SMALL NO. OF '55 H/Ts DISCOVERED!)

1956 PRICE RANGES =
$2731. ~ 3164. (CLIPPER)
3465. ~ 5995. (PACKARD)

PACKARD 56

TOTAL 1956 PRODUCTION : 13,432, PLUS 18,482 CLIPPERS.

57-L

PACKARD

57

(57-L SERIES) new 120½" WB

$3212.

new SMALLER V8 DISPLACEMENT OF 289 CID

HP REDUCED TO 275 @ 4800 RPM

Y8 SEDAN

CLIPPER

SEDAN and WAGON are ONLY CHOICES LISTED DURING 1957.

new 116½" WB BODIES LIKE STUDEBAKER (THROUGH '58)

P8

275 HP (THROUGH '58)

(3940 BLT.)

#P8 WAGON (159 BLT.)

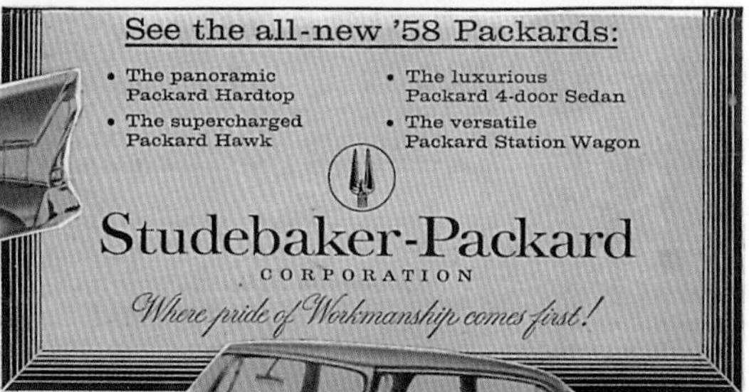

See the all-new '58 Packards:

- The panoramic Packard Hardtop
- The supercharged Packard Hawk
- The luxurious Packard 4-door Sedan
- The versatile Packard Station Wagon

Studebaker-Packard

CORPORATION

Where pride of Workmanship comes first!

$3384. (AS IN '57)

58-L

58

(58-L SERIES)

$3212.

ENG. SPECS. AS IN 1957. 210 HP, BUT 275 HP IN new #K9 HAWK H/T (ILLUSTRATED)

THE FINAL PACKARDS

SEDAN #J8 (1200 BLT.)

4 HEADLIGHTS (EXCEPT ON HAWK)

FRONT END DETAILS

$3995. (588 BLT.)

HAWK has 2 HEADLIGHTS, and A LOWER GRILLE

non-HAWK H/T ALSO (675 BLT.) $3262.

TOTAL PRODUCTION, (1957 = 5495) (1958 = 1745) (ONLY 4 MODELS IN 1958)

(PACKARD DISCONTINUED 1958)

48 HP with 133 CID HERCULES ENGINE OR 40 HP with 91 CID CONT. ENG.

STEEL RETRACTABLE TOP

97 BLT. 4 CYL.

PLAYBOY

PLAYBOY MOTOR CAR CORP., BUFFALO, N.Y. (1946-1951)

48

3.73 OR 4.1 GEAR RATIO 90" W.B.

INTER.

$985.

(1971–1980)

Pinto
Ford Motor Co.

94" WB, 4 CYL.
$1919.

Hello world.

$2062. $2298.

(63796 BLT.)

3-DOOR HATCHBACK

97.6 CID (75 HP @ 5000 RPM) OR 122 CID (100 HP @ 5600)

2-DR. $2155. (WEST) (288,606 BLT.)

The OHC Four 2000 cc.:
Carburetor 2V
Horsepower @ RPM ....100 @ 5600
Torque @ RPM ....120 @ 3600
Compression ratio ....9 to 1
Bore and stroke ....3.58 x 3.03
Fuel ....Regular
Transmission ...4-Speed Manual,* Floor-Mounted
*Optional SelectShift Cruise-O-Matic also available.

new 71 (INTRO. 9-11-70)

Luxury Decor Group.

Air Conditioning. The SelectAire unit (requires 2000-cc. engine) gives all-season comfort. Heats, defrosts, cools. (OPT.)

MULTI-PURPOSE KEY

Do it yourself and save. Pinto is designed to be so simple you can do most servicing yourself. The owner's manual shows you how. And the free Do-It-Yourself Key (above) helps you do everything from gauge the spark-plug gap to adjust the headlight beam.

Put a little kick in your life.   TOTAL = 352,402

6.00 × 13 TIRES

BLACK OR WHITE VINYL TOP AVAIL.

$2494. (WEST)

$2265.

ALSO AVAIL. W/O GRAIN PANELS

new SPORTS ACCENT TRIM

122 CID 4 CUT TO 86 HP

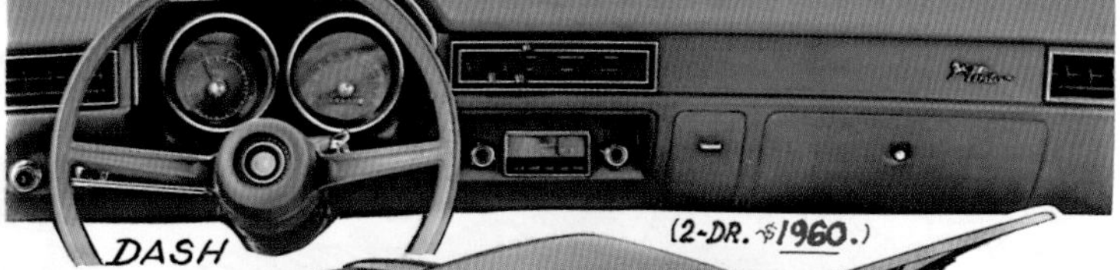

new **Wagon**   (101,483 BLT.)

$2708. (WEST)

72 (INTRO. 9-24-71)

DASH   (2-DR. $1960.)

3-DOOR HATCHBACK (197290 SOLD)

new SPRINT DECOR IN WHITE and BLUE WITH RED STRIPING

(OPTIONAL *new* SUNROOF) TOTAL 1972 PROD. = 479,775

$2078.

$2355. WEST,   PINTO 71~72

When you get back to basics, you get back to Ford.

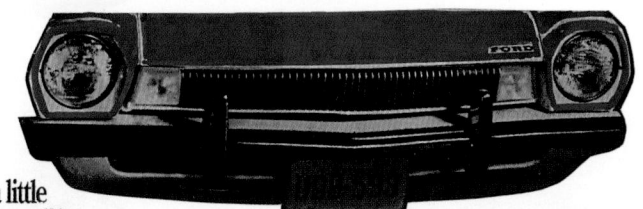

PINTO

$2343.
$2572. (WEST)

WAGON

(217,763 BLT.)

3-DR. (150,603 BLT.)

$2144.
$2422. (WEST)

DELUXE BUMPER HAS VERTICAL GUARDS and PROTECTIVE BLACK VINYL STRIP

2-DR. (116,146 BLT.)

$2021.

SQUIRE WAGON $2809. (WEST)

OPT. VINYL~ COVERED TOP and SUNROOF

6.00 x 13 / A 78 x 13 TIRES

2-DR.

98.6 CID 4 (54 HP) OR 122 CID 4 (83 HP)

73

Listening better.
Building better.
That's Ford.

$2299.
WESTERN PRICE

new ENERGY-ABSORBING BUMPERS

2-DR. (132,061 BLT.)

$2527.

SQUIRE WAGON $3337., WEST

Outsells all other Wagons, big or small. (237,394 WAGONS BLT.)

$2676.

3-DR. (174,754 BLT.)

$2852. (WEST)

$2771. UP

74

UNGRAINED WAGON INTERIOR

DASH AVAIL. IN VARIOUS COLORS.

PINTO 73~74

PINTO $2769. UP (6408/ BLT.)

new BR 78 x 13" TIRES

VINYL TOP OPTIONAL

2-Door Sedan

Pinto Wagon

Pinto Wagon With Squire Option

(A) Trim Rings/Hub Caps. Add more flair. Shown with raised white letter wide-oval steel-belted tires. (B) Wheel Covers. For that beautiful finishing touch. (C) Styled Steel Wheels. Smart styling distinction. Adding trim rings recommended, as shown. (D) Aluminum Wheels. Rugged, sporty look. For extra dash, add optional white sidewall or raised white letter tires.

A   B

C   D

(90763 WAGONS BLT.) $3153. UP

Pinto 3-Door Runabout

WITH OPTIONAL SUNROOF

75

SOME INTERIORS HARMONIZE WITH EXTERIOR COLORS.

THE CLOSER YOU LOOK BOOK 1975

Sports Accent Group Interior complements the sporty exterior illustrated above.

(689/9 BLT.) $2984.

DASH

3-Door Runabout

$3700.

(1975 139 CID 4 RATED AT 83 HP)

WESTERN PRICES SHOWN

75½

New Ford Pinto MPG 28mpg. $2,769. (SALE)

REG. FR. $3329.

MPG WITH DLX. BUMPERS EXTERIOR DECOR TRIM STRIP

2-Door Sedan 1975 Pinto

PINTO

NEW

New Pinto 3-Door
Stallion Runabout

New

Pinto Pony MPG
$2,895

$2966.
(WEST)

38 MPG highway, 25 city).

new
PONY MPG Pinto Pony MPG. More car for the money.

(ABOVE) has A MINIMUM
OF CHROME TRIM,
AND PLAIN HUBCAPS (LOWEST-PRICED MODEL)

76

CRISS-CROSS PCS.

new
GRILLE
WITH

PINTO

COWL DECAL

(VARIOUS OTHER MODELS
CONTINUE.)

WITH
PLAIN
SIDES

WAGON	
33 mpg highway	23 mpg city
HWY.	CITY

$4075.
('78)

A 78 x 13
TIRES

the best sellers in their class

Wagons

Critical areas
around lights and
grille are dent,
chip and scratch
resistant...and
absolutely
rustproof!

6.
Woodgrain
vinyl
paneling.

DuraSpark ignition.
No points or
condenser to
replace.

7.
Roomy cargo
area (cargo
volume index
57.2 cubic feet).

8.
Flipper rear side
windows.

FRONT
END
RESTYLED ('77)

2-DR.
$3550. ('77)
3617. ('78)
2-DR. PONY =
$3164. ('77)
$3341. ('78)

1977:
140 CID 4
(89 HP)
171 CID V6
(93 HP)
RESPECTIVE
HP CUT TO
88 AND 90
IN 1978.

15.
Larger standard
engine (2.3 litre,
4-cylinder cast
iron) than Datsun
F-10 Sportswagon,
Toyota Corolla
and Corona

14.
Power front
disc brakes.

13.
Precise rack and
pinion steering.

12.
4-speed
floor-mounted
transmission
(standard).
SelectShift
automatic (optional).

11.
Sporty suspension
system.

9.
Low sticker price.

10.
Electro-dip
corrosion
protection

STANDARD
HATCHBACK
DOOR

77-78

SQUIRE
WAGON
$4207. ('77)

WESTERN PRICES
SHOWN

3-DR.

$3666.
('77)
$3861.
('77)

DASH
('77)

NEW
"ALL-GLASS"
HATCHBACK
DOOR
VARIATION
('77)

mileage.

39 mpg highway	27 mpg city

PINTO 77~78

627

PINTO

PONY wagon

$4627.

$5004.

STD. WAGON

SPORT STEERING WHEELS

('79)

NEW Design up here

CRUISING (PANEL/VAN) WAGON

THIS TYPE INTRO. 1977

FRONT, REAR CHANGES

1979

NEW Design back here

NEW Design in here

A78×13 ('79)
TIRES   BR78×13 ('80)

$5320.

('80)
SQUIRE

OLD-STYLE DUAL-CLUSTER ALSO CONT'D.

3~DR.

1980

199,018 = PROD. = 185,054

79-80

new FRONT END, new TAIL-LIGHTS

$4717.

3~DR.

note 3 STYLES of REAR WINDOW

PONY FROM
$3571. ('79)
$4121. ('80)

NEW UP FRONT

WESTERN PRICES SHOWN IN BLACK

WITH
RALLYE
TRIM

SPOILER

Pinto 3-Door Runabout with Rallye Pack,* Silver Metallic (1G)

RALLYE

Pinto Wagon with Rallye Pack,* Bright Bittersweet (2G)

PINTO 79-80

FINAL PINTO, 1980
2-DR.
$4643. ('80)

1980

$4605.

1980 EASTERN PRICES IN RED

1980 DASH

PLYMOUTH

STARTS SUMMER, '28 ('29 "Q")

PLYMOUTH DIVISION OF   CHRYSLER CORPORATION

Plymouth DeLuxe 6, P10

Plymouth Roadking 6, P9

Plymouth DeLuxe 6, P10

Longer, Lower, Larger Bodies

P~9 ROADKING $645. UP

P~10 DELUXE $725. UP

(BUSINESS COUPES)

NEW DESIGNING—BIGGER DIMENSIONS—have made this Plymouth 4-Passenger Coupe the roomiest in the low-price field...and the most beautiful! You'll find auxiliary, drop-type seats...a roomy rear deck luggage compartment...and the great Luxury Ride!

auxiliary seats fold out of the way when not in use

Luggage space has been enlarged by raising the curve of the rear deck and by standing the spare tire up at one side

new 137" WB ON 7~PASS SEDAN and LIMOUSINE (THRU 1941)

40 A
RESTYLED

(CONT'D. NEXT PAGE)

new 117" WB (THRU 1948)

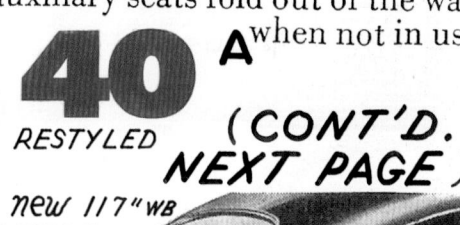

REAR DETAILS

Plymouth DeLuxe P10. Roadking 6, P9*

RUNNING~ BOARDS OPTIONAL

SEALED~BEAM HEADLTS. (new)

Red warning discs below the four instrument dials call the driver's attention to impending difficulty. The illuminated safety speedometer hand is also shown

40 PLYMOUTH (A)

Steering Post Gear Shift standard <u>on</u> <u>all</u> <u>models</u>!

Plymouth has coil springs of Amola Steel.

Plymouth Builds Great Cars

P9 Roadking			
bus cpe	$ 645.	26,745	BLT.
sdn 2d	699.	55,092	
sdn 4d	740.	20,076	
util sdn	699.	589	
club cpe	699.	360	
wgn 4d	925.	80	
chassis		907	*

P10 DeLuxe			
bus cpe	725.	32,244	
sdn 2d	775.	76,781	
sdn 4d	805.	173,351	
util sdn	775.	4	
club cpe	770.	22,174	
conv cpe	950.	6,986	
wgn 4d	970.	3,126	
137" WB { sdn 4d 7P	1,005.	1,179	
limo 7P	1,080.	68	#
chassis		503	#

40 B

* = ON SPECIAL ORDER

(CONT'D.)

CONVERTIBLE $950.

(ABOVE)
Roadking 6, P9

DELUXE 6, P10

WINDWING

PLYMOUTH'S THRILLING NEW "SPORTSMEN"

WAGONS FROM $925.

40 PLYMOUTH (B)

630

P~11 DELUXE
P~12 SPECIAL DELUXE

PLYMOUTH

NEW PLYMOUTH SPECIAL DE LUXE
SERIES

41

power-operated top

COMPARE PRICES OF "ALL 3"

FINAL YEAR FOR 137" WB 7~PASS. SEDANS and LIMOS.

Special DeLuxe P12

CLUB COUPE W. SMALL AUX. BACK SEAT

PLYMOUTH THE "ONE" FOR 41

new GRILLE

DRIVE THE POWERMATIC WAY—vast reduction in driving effort—and, with Plymouth's new transmission, actual elimination of certain shifting motions in normal driving.

41 PLYMOUTH

PLYMOUTH

P~14
S~DELUXE
C~SPC. DLX.

CHRYSLER CORPORATION'S NO. 1 CAR _ THE QUALITY CAR WITH ECONOMY

$935.

S~11973   C~68924   FOUR-DOOR SEDAN.

$895.

S~9350   C~24142   TWO-DOOR SEDAN

$1078.

C~2806   CONVERTIBLE

NEW
4~DOOR
TOWN
SEDAN
C~5821
BLT.
(AVAIL.
1942
ONLY)

$980.

AVAIL. ONLY AS SPECIAL DE LUXE

$1145.

PRICED
FROM
$812.
(S~DLX.
BUS. CPE.)

STATION WAGON
C~1136 BLT.

new
217.8 CID 6
(95 HP
THRU '48)

RESTYLED

42

BUS.
COUPE
S~3783 C~7258
$855.

*Buy Wisely_*
BUY PLYMOUTH

New
CONCEALED
RUNNING~
BOARDS ➤

CLUB COUPE

new
LONG
CAB

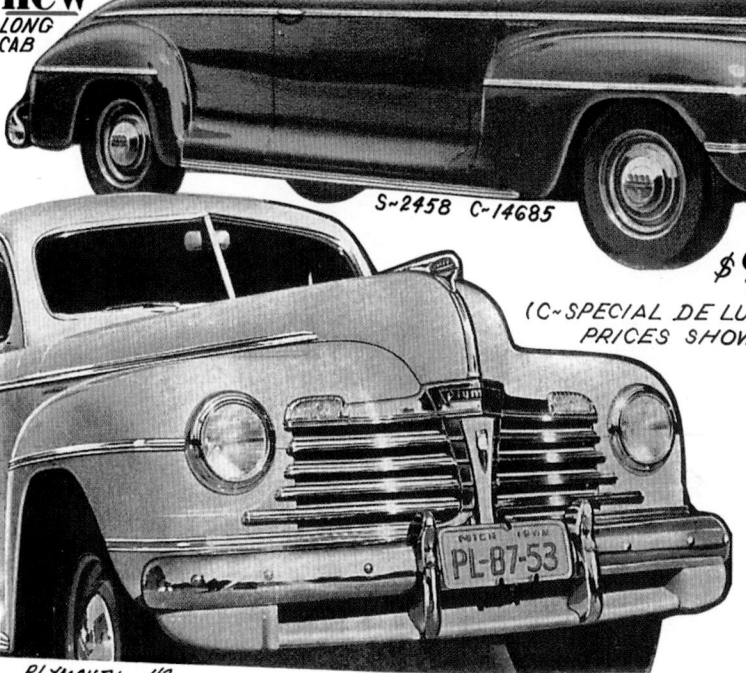

S~245B C~14685

$928.
(C~SPECIAL DE LUXE
PRICES SHOWN)

PLYMOUTH 42

New At night, the entire speedometer face glows green up to 30 mph, turns to orange from 30 to 50 and is red above 50.

Plymouth (A DIVISION OF CHRYSLER CORP.) (SINCE MID ~1928)

1946 MODELS HAVE 16" WHEELS PAINTED BODY COLOR WITH CONTRASTING STRIPING.

3-YEAR BODY TYPE PROD. FIGS.: (49,918 DLX.; 125,704 SPL. DLX.)

2 DR. SEDAN

STATION WAGON (WOODEN BODY) (12,913)

SPECIAL DE LUXE *has* CHROME EFFECT on WINDSHIELD FRAME

CVT. (15,295)

4 DR. SEDAN (120,757 DLX.; 514,986 SPL. DLX.)

1946 *has* FLAT BUTTON TYPE DOOR LOCK COVERS.

1948 *has* new 7.50 × 15 LOW-PRESSURE TIRES.

46-48*

P-15S DLX. OR P-15C SPECIAL DLX.

* = CONT'D. TO 2-49

95 HP @ 3600 RPM

WHITE BEAUTY RINGS ADDED 1947, DURING MODEL YR.

(10,400 DLX.; 156,629 SPL. DLX.)

REAR (SEDAN)

CLUB COUPE

$1075. TO $2068. (PRICE RANGE, 1946 TO EARLY 1949)

CONVERTIBLE DASH IS PAINTED in BODY COLOR, INSTEAD of BEING WOODGRAINED.

SEDAN INTERIOR

(3-PASS. BUSINESS COUPE ALSO AVAIL., *with* SMALLER REAR QUARTER WINDOWS *and* SHORTER CAB THAN CLUB COUPE.) (16,117 DLX.; 31,399 SPL. DLX.)

SPECIAL DE LUXE *has* RADIO GRILLE

DE LUXE

P-15 PLYMOUTH PRODUCTION : 1945 (YEAR'S END) = 749
1946 = 241,656
1947 = 347,946
1948 = 381,139 PLYMOUTH 46-48

Plymouth

$1629.

SPEC. DLX. SEDAN + INTERIOR

new ALL-METAL 2-DR. SUBURBAN WAGON $1840.

P-17

SEDAN REAR DOORS NOW FRONT-HINGED

6.40 × 15 OR 6.70 × 15 TIRES (THROUGH '52)

SPECIAL DELUXE 4-DOOR WAGON has WOODEN PANELS.

P-18 $2372.

$1982.

new 97 HP @ 3600 RPM (THROUGH '52)

SPEC. DLX. CLUB COUPE

$1603.

new "Double-Size" CVT. BACKLIGHT has REMOVABLE, ZIPPERED CENTER SECTION

3-WINDOW BUSINESS CPE. AVAIL., $1371.

49

P-17 (111" WB)
P-18 (118½" WB)

(TOTALLY RESTYLED)

HORIZONTAL CREASES ON BUMPERS ('49 ONLY)

new SWITCH-KEY STARTING

SLOGAN: "The car that likes to be compared"

PRODUCTION: P17 DELUXE = BUSINESS CPE. (15,715); 2-DR. (28,516); 2 DR. SUBURBAN WAGON (19,220);
P18 DELUXE = CLUB CPE. (25,687); 4-DR. SEDAN (61,021)
P18 SPECIAL DELUXE = CLUB CPE. (99,361); 4-DR. SEDAN (234,084); CONVERTIBLE (12,697);
4 DR. WAGON (2059)

PRODUCTION = MODEL YEAR 498,360; CALENDAR YEAR 569,260

PLYMOUTH 49

Plymouth

2-DR. (67,584 BLT.) **$1371.**

DE LUXE

3-WINDOW BUSINESS COUPE

(16,861 BLT.)

$1492.

SUBURBAN

CLUB CPE. (99,361 BLT.)

4 DR. WAGON

SPECIAL DE LUXE

$1603.

$1629. (234,084)

PRICE RANGE: **$1371.** TO **$2372.**

(12,697 BLT.)

$1982.

P-19 DE LUXE (111" WB)

P-20 DE LUXE; SPEC. DLX. (118½" WB)

50

new EMBLEM

PLYMOUTH

DASH

new SMOOTH BUMPER SURFACE

new GRILLE has FEWER PIECES.

MODEL LINE-UP CONTINUES AS IN 1949, BUT SUBURBAN 2-DR. ($1840.) IS JOINED BY new SUBURBAN 2-DR. SPECIAL ($1946.) TOTAL NUMBER PRODUCED OF BOTH IS 34,457. ALSO, 2059 4-DR. WOOD-PANELED WAGONS BUILT (AT $2372.)

TOTAL 1950 PRODUCTION = 567,381

PLYMOUTH 50

Plymouth (76,250)

P-22 CONCORD

(49,139) 111" WB
2-DR.

$1537. ~ 2222.
1951 PRICE RANGE

(14,255)
3-WINDOW COUPE

(388,785)

(15,650)

REAR DETAILS 1951

1951 MODELS ILLUSTRATED UNLESS OTHERWISE NOTED.

1951 BELVEDERE IS new H/T. $2114.

SHIELD BADGE REPLACED BY CIRCLE ON '52.

'52

(51,266)

51-52

new CONCORD, CAMBRIDGE, CRANBROOK MODEL NAMES

DASH

MODEL NAME IN SCRIPT ON 1952 FRONT FENDER

('51)

P-23 CAMBRIDGE and CRANBRK. have 118½" WB
$1610. ~ 2329.
1952 PRICE RANGE

'50 PLYMOUTH TAXI

1952 BELVEDERE (BELOW) has new REAR COLOR SWEEP

('52)

TOTAL PLYMOUTH PRODUCTION,	1951	= 607,691
" " "	1952	= 466,289

$2216.

PLYMOUTH 51~52

Plymouth

new 100 HP @ 3600 RPM

new SPORT WIRE WHEELS OPTIONAL

SAVOY WAGON

CRANBROOK BELVEDERE

P-21769

53
(TOTALLY RESTYLED)
P-24-1 CAMBRIDGE
P-24-2 CRANBR.

CRANBROOK

Cranbrook

new 114" WB (THROUGH '54)

6.70 x 15 TIRES (TO '56)

$1618. ~ 2220. PRICE RANGE

TOTAL 1953 PRODUCTION = 654,414

P-25-3 BELVEDERE

P-25-1 PLAZA

DASH

LATE '54 has new 230.2 CID and 110 HP @ 3600 RPM

P-25-2 SAVOY

$1618. UP

54

EARLY 1954 BELVEDERE H/T DOES NOT HAVE THIS COLOR BAND ON SIDE

BELVEDERE

(25,592 BLT.)

$1618. ~ 2301. PRICE RANGE

TOTAL 1954 PRODUCTION = 396,702

PLYMOUTH 53~54

637

Plymouth

230 CID 6 CYL. OR NEW 241 CID OR 260 CID V8s. $2077. UP 2 DR. WAGON

new AUTOMATIC TRANSMISSION CONTROL ON DASH →

2-DR. and 4 DR. WAGONS IN PLAZA SERIES.

PLAZA $1738. UP

SAVOY $1880. UP (NO SAVOY WAGONS)

55
(TOTALLY RESTYLED with new "FORWARD LOOK")
new 115" WB (THROUGH '56)

| 6 = 117 HP @ 4000 RPM |
| V8 = 157 or 167 HP @ 4400 RPM |

CLUB COUPE

new PANORAMIC WINDSHIELD $1738. ~ $2425. PRICE RANGE

$2322. UP

(41,645 BLT.)
6 CYL. = $1936.
V8 = $2039.

BELVEDERE 6 OR V8 IN ALL MODEL SERIES

4 DR. WAGON ONLY IN BELVEDERE SERIES

BELVEDERE SUBURBAN WAGON (18,488 BLT.)

BELVEDERE H/T (47,375 BLT.)

1955 PRODUCTION: 746,361

$2113. UP

REAR VIEW

6-CYL. has STRAIGHT EMBLEM ABOVE GRILLE →

new FRENCHED HEADLIGHTS

1955

V8 has ABOVE TYPE OF EMBLEM

PLYMOUTH 55

Plymouth $2196. (23,866 BLT.) $2314. (33,333 BLT.)

SUBURBAN
DE LUXE 2-DR. WAGON

6.70 × 15 TIRES
(ALL BUT
new FURY)

$2267. CUSTOM SUBURBAN 4 DR. 2 DR.

(9489 BLT.)

PLAZA

$1784. UP

$2109. BELVEDERE $2484. SPORT SUBURBAN (15,104 BLT.)
(84,218 BLT.) SEDAN
(ABOVE)

SAVOY
$2130. (16,473 BLT.) H/T

56
P-28 (6)
P-29 (V8)

PUSHBUTTON POWERFLITE:

new BELVEDERE
4-DR. H/T
(BELOW)

(17,515 BLT.)

ENGINES :
230.2 CID 6 (125 OR 131 HP)
270 CID V8 (180 HP) (1956 ONLY)
277 CID V8 (187 OR 200 HP)
(*new* FURY has OWN 303 CID V8)

TOTAL 1956 PRODUCTION :
552,577

$2287.

new **Fury** 240 OR 270 HP
(WITH *new*
303 CID V8)
7.10 × 15 TIRES)

$2866. (4485 BLT.)

new
SHARPLY-
PEAKED
TAIL FINS

H/T

new MESH AT GRILLE CENTER

1956

PLYMOUTH 56

Plymouth

PLAZA — $2009.

EARLY '57 (6 OPEN SLOTS BELOW BUMPERS) ↗

2 DR. (49,137 BLT.)

BELVEDERE

$2229.

H/T (31,373 BLT.)

SAVOY

BELVEDERE

H/T — $2349. ↗

(67,268 BLT.)

4 DR. H/T — $2419.

318 CID V8 IN FURY (7438 BLT.) ↘

LATE '57 (EXTRA VERTICAL MEMBERS BELOW BUMPERS) ↘

new 118" WB (122" WB ON WAGONS) (THROUGH '61)

new 8.00 x 14 TIRES ON FURY H/T $2925.

SPORT SDN. (BELV.)

TAILGATE WINDOW DETAILS

SECRET LUGGAGE COMPARTMENT. Almost 10 cubic feet of locked space for safe, out-of-sight storage of luggage, cameras and other valuables. On all 6-pass. models.

$2622. UP (23,402 BLT.)

new 7.50 x 14 TIRES (ALL BUT FURY)

57 (TOTALLY RESTYLED)

P-30 (6)
P-31 (V8)

EARLY '57 FRONT END CLOSE-UP

DASH

$1899. ~ 2777. PRICE RANGE

TOTAL 1957 PRODUCTION: 655,006
SLOGAN: "SUDDENLY IT'S 1960!"

ENGINES: 230.2 CID 6 (132 HP)
277 CID V8 (197 OR 235 HP)
301 CID V8 (215 OR 235 HP)
318 CID V8 (290 HP) (FURY)

PLYMOUTH 57

Plymouth

SUBURBAN

$2432.

(15,625 BLT.) The De Luxe Suburban—2-door, 6-passenger

$2553.

(5925 BLT.) The Custom Suburban—2-door, 6-passenger

The Custom Suburban—4-door, 9- or 6-passenger

SPORT SUBURBAN

(23,170 BLT.) $2760. UP

✳ Star of the Forward Look

58 new GRILLE

LP-1 (6)
LP-2 (V8)

$2028.~2900.
PRICE RANGE
TOTAL 1958 PRODUCTION:
366,758

INSTRUMENT CLUSTER

PLAZA $2028.

(1958 IS FINAL YEAR FOR PLAZA SERIES.)

The Plaza 2-door Business Coupe
(1472 BLT.)

SAVOY
$2305.

(67,923 BLT.)

The Savoy 4-door Sedan

$2400.   The Savoy 4-door Hardtop
(5060 BLT.)

(49,124 BLT.)

$2440.

BELVEDERE

$2762. →   The Belvedere 4-door Sedan

$2457.

The Belvedere Convertible
(9941 BLT.)

(36,043 BLT.)

7.50 × 14 TIRES
BELVEDERE

(8.00 × 14 ON
9- PASS. WAGONS
and FURY H/T)

← FURY

$3067.
230 CID 6 (132 HP @ 3600)
318 CID V8
(225 or 250 HP @ 4400)
350 CID V8
(305 or 315 HP
@ 5000 RPM)

(5303 BLT.)

4 HEADLIGHTS

newest engine—"Golden Commando V-8"
(WITH ELECTRONIC FUEL INJECTION)

SILVER SPECIAL (RARE!)
(PLAZA)

PLYMOUTH 58   NOTE SPECIAL SIDE TRIM

Plymouth

CUSTOM SUBURBAN

SAVOY

BELVEDERE

4-door Sedan, V-8 or 6

2-door Sedan, V-8 or 6

$2881. UP

OPTIONAL *new* SWIVEL SEATS (STD. IN SPORT FURY)

59

MP-1 (6)
MP-2 (V8)

7.50 × 14 TIRES

DASH

SPORT SUBURBAN

(2-DR. and 4-DR. WAGONS IN DE LUXE and CUSTOM SUBURBAN SERIES.)

6 PASSENGER (7224 BLT.) = $3021.
9 " (9549 ") = $3131.

(NO MORE LOW-PRICED **PLAZA** SERIES.)

$2143. ~ 3131.
PRICE RANGE

TOTAL 1959 PRODUCTION : 393,213

new DECORATIVE "SPARE TIRE COVER" ON DECK LID OF SPORT FURY

$2927.

new GRILLE

new SPORT FURY H/T
(17,867 BLT.)

FINAL USE OF L-HEAD DESIGN IN PLYMOUTH SIX

new TAIL FINS

CVT. (5990 BLT.)

SPORT FURY CONVERTIBLE

ENGINES :
230 CID 6 (132 HP @ 3600)
318 CID V8 (230 or 260 HP @ 4400 RPM)
361 CID V8 (305 HP @ 4600 RPM)

PLYMOUTH 59

Plymouth

SEDAN $2439.

← BELVEDERE

H/T $2641.

SAVOY

V8s have 318, 361, OR 383 CID (230, 260, 305, 310, 325 OR 330 HP)

new SLANTING O.H.V. 225 CID 6 (145 HP @ 4000 RPM) (TO '71)

note THE REAR FENDER ORNAMENTS WHICH IDENTIFY EACH INDIVIDUAL MODEL SERIES.

CUSTOM SUBURBAN $2880. UP

(9036 BLT.) $2656. FURY →

4-DR. H/T

2-DR. H/T

WITH SEMI-RECTANGULAR STEERING WHEEL

WITHOUT GRILLE GUARD

WITH GRILLE GUARD

new GRILLE

60

PP-1 (6 CYL.)
PP-2 (V8)

SHOWN *with* ROUND STEERING WHEEL

DASH

CLOSER DETAILS OF WAGON

7.50 x 14" TIRES

VALIANT COMPACT SERIES INTRO.

TOTAL 1960 PRODUCTION: 447,724
(252,453 FULL-SIZED PLYMOUTHS)

SEE ALSO: **VALIANT**

$2260. ~ 3134. PRICE RANGE

FROM 1960 ON, *VALIANT* PRODUCTION FIGURES LISTED SEPARATELY.

PLYMOUTH 60

Plymouth

Battery-saving Alternator keeps battery charged when generators can't. Many police and taxi fleets pay extra to get special Alternator installations. Yet the amazing new Alternator is standard equipment on all 1961 Chrysler Corporation cars.

7.00 × 14 TIRES (6)
7.50 × 14 ON 6-CYL. WAGONS *and* V8s.
8.00 × 14 ON 9-PASS. V8 WAGON

1961

9-PASS. V8 IS COSTLIEST MODEL, AT $3134.

ALTERNATOR TEST DETROIT to CHICAGO

PLYMOUTH—This car traveled 328 miles without a battery. Alternator, standard on 1961 Chrysler Corporation cars, provided all necessary electrical energy.

61 RP-1 (6)
RP-2 (V8)

1961

SPORT SUBURBAN

SUBURBAN 2 *and* 4 DR. WAGONS
$2602. UP

FURY 4-DR. H/T
(8507 BLT.)
$2656. (6)
$2775. (V8)

TOTAL 1961 PRODUCTION:
188,170 (FULL-SIZED)

LOWEST-PRICED SAVOY 2-DR.
$2260. OR 2379.
(6)   (V8)

ENGINES:
225 CID SLANT-6 (145 HP)
318 CID V8 (230 OR 260 HP)
361 CID V8 (305 HP)
383 CID V8 (330 HP)
ALSO,
LARGEST OF 4
PLYMOUTH V8s
IS *new*
413 CID
ENGINE (UP TO
375 HP
@ 5200
RPM)

$2967. **FURY**
CONVERTIBLE
(6948 BLT.)

118" WB (WAGONS 122")

GRILLE GUARD AVAIL. ON SOME 1961 MODELS

new GRILLE

...SOLID BEAUTY
PLYMOUTH 61

Plymouth

SAVOY

Look at Plymouth now!

WEST COAST PRICED FROM $2531.

$2609. UP

SAVOY $2262. UP

6 = 6.50 × 14 TIRES
V8 = 7.00 × 14

"PLYMOUTH" NAME ON DOOR OF SAVOY

"BELVEDERE" NAME ON DOOR OF BELVEDERE

$2342. UP

Plymouth Belvedere 2-dr Sedan
(3128 BLT.)

62
(TOTALLY RESTYLED)

SP-1 (6)
SP-2 (V8)

new 116" WB

FROM $2563.

(ABOVE) FURY SEDAN (17,531 BLT.)

New Forward Flair Design

FURY

FURY
4 DR. H/T
(5995 BLT.)

FURY
CONVERTIBLE
$2924.
(4349 BLT.)

$2742.

FURY TURBO-

FURY (SPECIAL)
$2851.

SPT. FURY
H/T
(4039 BLT.)

NEW SPORT FURY

CONVERTIBLE (1516 BLT.)

Special red, white and blue insignia, new wheel covers and new rear deck design tell you that this one is the real thing! There is no mistaking a new Sport Fury—hardtop or convertible.

Action! Fly to 60 mph in 8.5 secs. with optional 305-hp Golden Commando V-8 engine.

$3082.

TOTAL 1962 PRODUCTION:
177,651

$2206. ~ 3082.
PRICE RANGE

ENGINES   225 CID 6 (145 HP)
318 CID V8 (230 or 260 HP)
361 CID V8 (305 HP)

PLYMOUTH 62

Plymouth $2609. UP

SAVOY WAGON (17,216 BLT.)

BELVEDERE $2342. UP
2-DR. (6218 BLT.)

H/T (13,832 BLT.)

FURY

$2585. UP FURY

V8 OPTIONS
318 CID (230 HP @ 4400)
361 CID (265 HP @ 4400)
383 CID (320 to 330 HP)
426 CID (370 HP @ 4600 to 425 HP @ 5600 RPM)

$2924. CVT. (5221 BLT.)

1963 is ONLY YEAR with UNUSUAL FRONT CORNER PARK./DIRECTIONAL LIGHTS

FURY 4-DR. H/T (11,887 BLT.)

with a 5-year or 50,000-mile warranty

63

7.00 x 14 TIRES

TP-1 (6 CYL.)
TP-2 (V8)

new GRILLE
new TAIL-LIGHTS
new FULL-LENGTH SIDE TRIM

Get up and go Plymouth!

$2742.

new 426 CID V8 ENGINE KNOWN AS "Super Stock"

TOTAL 1963 PRODUCTION:
274,735

$2206. ~ 3082.
PRICE RANGE

MOST POPULAR MODELS:
SAVOY 4 DR. SEDANS (56,313 BLT.)
BELVEDERE 4 DR. " (54,929 BLT.)
(BOTH SIXES and V8s)

DASH

$2851.
H/T (11,483 BLT.)

A Transmission Drive Selector (optional)
B Transmission Parking Lock
C Clock (optional)
D Turn Signal Indicator
E Heater Controls (optional)
F Headlights and Panel Lights
G Defroster Outlets
H Windshield Wiper Control
I Ignition Switch
J Cigarette Lighter
K Ash Receiver
L Glove Compartment Lock
M Radio (optional)

PLYMOUTH 63

PLYMOUTH'S ON THE MOVE

SPORT FURY (3836 CVTS. ALSO)

Plymouth

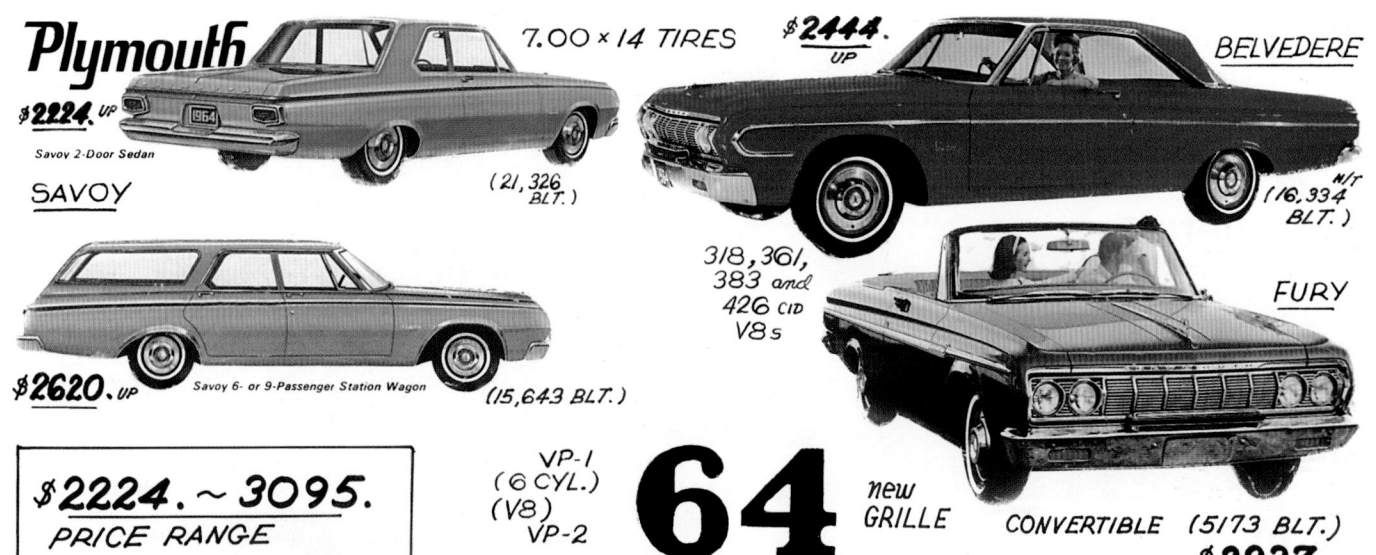

$2224. UP
Savoy 2-Door Sedan

SAVOY

$2620. UP   Savoy 6- or 9-Passenger Station Wagon

7.00 × 14 TIRES

(21,326 BLT.)

(15,643 BLT.)

$2444. UP

BELVEDERE

N/T
(16,334 BLT.)

318, 361, 383 and 426 CID V8s

FURY

CONVERTIBLE (5173 BLT.)
$2937.

new GRILLE

$2224. ~ 3095.
PRICE RANGE

VP-1 (6 CYL.)
(V8)
VP-2

64

230 TO 425 HP

TOTAL 1964 PRODUCTION:
571,339
(INCL. BARRACUDA)

BELV.

$2981. UP

FURY wagon
(8/28 BLT.)

$2864.

H/T (23,695 BLT.)

REAR OF FURY WAGON

$3/95.
(WEST COAST)

SPORT FURY

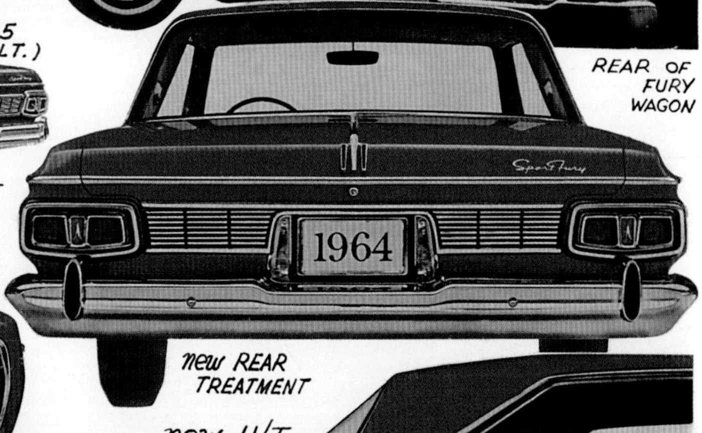

1964

new REAR TREATMENT

new H/T ROOFLINE

new CONVEX GRILLE CLOSE UP

COWL TRIM

647

Plymouth

BELVEDERE II
116" WB

Belvedere
Satellite

Belvedere I

SEDAN (35,968 BLT.)

$2265.

new
BELVEDERE
SATELLITE
IS AVAIL. WITH
TOP-OF-LINE
426 CID V8
WITH
425 HP @
6000
RPM.

BELV. has
7.35 × 14
TIRES (EXC.
WAGON)

Fury I
2 DR.
(17,294
BLT.)

$2376.

$3209.

(6272
BLT.)

273 CID
BARRACUDA V8 ENG.
NOW AVAIL. IN BELVEDERE I
(180 HP @ 4200 RPM)

PACE CAR AT 1965
INDY 500 RACE

SPORT
FURY

Fury
II

$2478.

DASH

Fury
III

7.75 × 14 TIRES
8.55 × 14 (FURY WAGON)

FURY
III
H/T

65
RESTYLED

AR-1 (6-CYL.)
AR-2 (V8)

ALL FURY TYPES
GET new 119" WB
(WAGONS 121")

Fury III 4-Door Hardtop

(43,251
BLT.)

THE ROARING '65s

(21,367 BLT.)

$2863.

MORE MODEL SERIES FOR 1965 :
BELVEDERE I, BELVEDERE II, SATELLITE ($2649. UP)
FURY I, FURY II, FURY III, SPORT FURY (119"WB)
($2376. UP)($2478. UP)($2684. UP) ($2960. UP)

$2226. ~ 4671. (BELV. I SUPER STOCK H/T)
(115" WB)

ENGINES :
225 CID 6 (145 HP)
273 CID V8 (180 HP)
318 CID V8 (230 HP)
361 CID V8 (265 HP)
383 CID V8 (270 OR 330 HP)
426 CID V8 (365 OR 425 HP)

TOTAL
1965
PROD. =
721,234

PLYMOUTH 65

The new 2-d hardtop VIP.

Plymouth

$3069.

DASH

66 ½

(INTRO. 1-66)

2-DR. VIP $3429. (WEST)

$2318. ~ 3279. PRICE RANGE

DASH $2747.

7.35 x 14" TIRES

(30,328 BLT.)

BELVEDERE ; BELVEDERE I ; BELV. II ;
SATELLITE ; " GTX ;
FURY I ; FURY II ; FURY III ;
SPORT FURY ; VIP
MODELS AVAIL. 1967

(WEST) $3101.

Belvedere
(SATELLITE)

67
A
new GRILLES

(INTRO. 9-29-66)

$3178.

REAR DECK DETAILS (GTX)

Belvedere GTX (new)

WITH
440 CID V8 (375 HP)
PLYMOUTH 66½ ~ 67(A)

GTX H/T $3330. (WEST)

(CONT'D. NEXT PAGE)

'67 Plymouth $2872. FURY III H/T

(37,448 BLT.)

Plymouth is out to win you over this year. $3033.

SPORT Fury

Fury

SPORT FURY CVT.

Sport Fury
COWL INSIGNIA

new "FAST TOP"

FURY III $2922.

$3279.

FURY 4 DR. H/T III DETAIL

67 B
(CONT'D.)

$3062.
crew-size Fury wagon

(43,614 BLT.)

FURY III

$3144.

(21,803 BLT.)

REAR FACING SEAT

eng.,
drive tr.
5-year/50,000-mile
warranty

DASH

Fury

WHEEL CVR.

FURY I, FURY II, FURY III and SPORT FURY MODELS (SINCE '65)

'67 Plymouth VIP

H/T
(7912 BLT.)

$3182.

PLYMOUTH 67 (B)

651

Plymouth

(**GTX** has ALL HORIZONTAL GRILLE P(S.)

SATELLITE

$2594.
H/T $3047. (WEST)
(46,539 BLT.)

7.75 x 14" or 8.55 x 14" TIRES

3-SEAT $3602.

Satellite Sport Wagon

(15,539 BLT.)

SPT. SATELLITE SERIES has 318 CID V8 (230 HP)

(INTRO. 9-14-67)

68

new CIRCULAR SIDE SAFETY LIGHTS AT EITHER END ←

ROAD-RUNNER (new) WITH 383 CID V8 (335 HP) (426 CID V8 OPT.)

F70 x 14" TIRES

H/T $3034. $3229. (WEST)

SPT. SUBURBAN FROM $3805. (WEST)

(FURY) SPORT SUBURBAN

$3442. UP

FURY III 4-DR. H/T $3430. (WEST)

SATELLITE WAGON (FRONT) 8.25 x 14" TIRES

(new 8-TRACK STEREO TAPE OPT.)

$3206. ↓ UP

Fury

$3623. (WEST)

1968

VIP

...the Plymouth win-you-over beat goes on ♥

(BODY/FRAME WELDED INTO 1 UNIT)

SPORT FURY FROM $3569. (WEST) (2 ROOFLINES AVAIL.)

LARGEST-SELLING MODEL: **FURY III** SEDAN (57,899 BLT.) $2890.
SCARCEST PRODUCED: **GTX** CVT. (1026 BLT.) $3590.
LOWEST-PRICED: **BELVEDERE** CL. COUPE (15,702 BLT.) $2444.
HIGHEST-PRICED: **SPORT SUBURBAN** 9-PASS. WAGON (13,224 BLT.) $3543. ($3906., WEST COAST)

PLYMOUTH 68

1968 PROD.: 591,030

ENGINES: 225 CID SLANT-6 (145 HP); 273 CID V8 (new 190 HP); 318 CID V8 (230 HP); 383 CID V8 (300, 330 or 335 HP); 426 CID V8 (425 HP); 440 CID V8 (350 or 375 HP)

652

Belvedere
$2509.

Plymouth

CPE. $2967.
(7063 BLT.) (WEST)

2883. BELVEDERE
SPORT SATELLITE
H/T (15,807 BLT.)

(WEST)
$3251.

new
AIR VANE VENTILATION
FOR WAGON

(RESTYLED)

69

(INTRO.
9-19-68)

Road Runner

$3083.

$3284.
H/T (WEST)
(48,549 BLT.)

$3303. FORMAL H/T

SPORT FURY
$3671.
(WEST)

Sport Suburban

(OTHER
VIEW
ABOVE)

A completely new Fury
for 1969.

(2169 BLT.)

$3718.

VIP
GRILLE

$4086. (WEST)
(3-SEAT)

DASH
(FURY)

STARTING
1969,
PLYMOUTH
SIDE
LIGHTS
ARE
RECTANGULAR.

VIP FROM
$3382.

Look what Plymouth's up to now:

$2509. ~ 3718.
PRICE RANGE

MODELS: RL BELVEDERE ; RH SATELLITE ; RP SPT. SATELLITE ;
RM ROAD RUNNER ; RS GTX ; PE FURY I ; PL FURY II ;
PM FURY III ; PH SPORT FURY ; PP VIP ; EP SUBURBAN WAGONS

1969 PRODUCTION: 581,004
PLYMOUTH 69

Plymouth

CHRYSLER MOTORS CORPORATION

225 CID 6 (145 HP); 318 CID V8 (230 HP); 383 CID V8 (290 330 OR 335 HP); 426 CID V8 (425 HP); 440 CID V8 (350, 375 OR 390 HP)

AVAIL. COLORS

	Code	RR & GTX	'Cuda & Duster	Fury GT			Code	RR & GTX	'Cuda & Duster	Fury GT
1. Citron Gold Metallic	FY6	*	*	•	14. Burnt Orange Metallic	FK3	*	*	•
2. Citron Mist Metallic	FY4			•	15. Vitamin C†	EK2	•	•	•
3. Yellow Gold	DY3	*	*	•	16. Lime Light†	FJ5	•	•	•
4. Sunfire Yellow	DY2	*	*	*	17. Ivy Green Metallic	EF8	•	•	•
5. Lemon Twist†	FY1	*	*	*	18. Lime Green Metallic	FF4	•	•	•
6. Black Velvet	TX9	•	•	•	19. Rallye Red	FE5	•	•	•
7. Tor-Red†	EV2	•	•	•	20. In Violet Metallic†	FC7	*	*	•
8. Burnt Tan Metallic	FT6	*	*	•	21. Jamaica Blue Metallic	EB7	•	•	•
9. Sahara Tan Metallic	FT3	*	*	•	22. Blue Fire Metallic	EB5	•	•	•
10. Scorch Red	ER6	*	*	•	23. Ice Blue Metallic	EB3	•	•	•
11. Frosted Teal Metallic	FP6	*	*	•	24. Silver Metallic	EA4	*	*	•
12. Sandpebble Beige	BL1			•	25. Alpine White	EW1	•	•	•
13. Deep Burnt Orange	FK5			•					

• Available   * Not Available   † Extra Cost

$2603.

Owning your own Belvedere makes it.

BELVEDERE (116" WB)
COUPE (4717 BLT.)

Belvedere $2641.

SEDAN (13945 BLT.)

$3006.   (701 BLT.) CVT.

SATELLITE (116" WB)

SEDAN (30377 BLT.)

$2988.

SPORT SATELLITE H/T (8749 BLT.)

70 A

TOTAL 1970 PRODUCTION: 684,975

$2741.

WAGON REAR WIND DEFLECTOR AVAILABLE

Fury & Belvedere Wagons

$3345. UP

SPORT SATELLITE WAGON 117" WB (4136 BLT.)

$3535.

SPORT SUBURBAN 122" WB (13573 BLT.)

SPORT FURY GT H/T 120" WB

440 CID V8 (350 HP)

$3898.

Plymouth makes it!

GTX H/T

440 CID V8 STD. (375 HP) 116" WB (7748 BLT.)

1970

PLYMOUTH 70 (A)

654

Plymouth

NOBODY MAKES IT LIKE
Plymouth
makes it ♥

ROAD RUNNER H/T (24944 BLT.) $3034.

ROAD RUNNER BIRD FIGURE NOT AVAILABLE. (USED ONLY IN ADVERTISING TO IDENTIFY ROAD RUNNER.) BELVEDERE GRILLES SIMILAR, BUT WITHOUT BRIGHT VERTICAL PCS. (INTRO. 9-23-69)

REAR

70 B

ANTI-THEFT LOCK ON STEERING COLUMN.

SUPERBIRD (1920 BLT.) $4298.

(21316 BLT.)

FURY II
2-DR.
$3381.
(WEST)
$2903.
(EAST)

Fury I

SEDAN $3303.
(EAST)

FURY GRAN COUPE

new FULL-LOOP FURY BUMPERS ENCIRCLE LTS. FRONT and REAR.

(14813 BLT.)
$2825.

$3833.

NOTE new CONCEALED HEADLIGHT FEATURE (ALSO ON SPORT FURY)*

RAPID TRANSIT SYSTEM
Plymouth makes it

TACHOMETER~ CLOCK (OPT.)

* NEXT PAGE

$3415. (1952 BLT.)
FURY III CONVERTIBLE
$3788.
(WEST)

SPORT FURY S/23 H/T
$3379.

PLYMOUTH 70 (B)

655

Plymouth

$3535.

SATELLITE TYPES WITH new 3-PC. SIDE LTS.

CHRYSLER Plymouth Coming Through.

Satellite

new 115" WB (2-DR.)
117" WB (4-DR.)

↙ SAT. CUSTOM, BROUGHAM have EXTRA LTS. IN GRILLE

(RESTYLED)

1971

71A

new GRILLES, ETC.

new **Sebring**
(CPE., DASH BELOW)

$3930.
SEBRING PLUS

$4268.

GTX ↗

WITH 440 CID V8 (370 HP)
(note UNIQUE STRIPING, TRIM ON THESE SPECIALTY CPÉS.)

ROAD RUNNER ↘

DASH (GTX, ROAD RUNNER)

SOME ROAD RUNNERS ADVERTISED WITH CHROME AROUND GRILLE
(RR 383 CID V8 has 300 HP)

$3918.

COLORS. The key is to color-key. Check salesman to see how you can match protective vinyl side moldings on some models.

Slate Gray Metallic*	Glacial Blue Metallic	Evening Blue Metallic	Winchester Gray Metallic†	True Blue Metallic†	Mood Indigo Metallic*	Burnished Red Metallic*	Amber Sherwood Metallic	
Sherwood Green Metallic	April Green Metallic*	Autumn Bronze Metallic	In-Violet Metallic†	Sassy Grass Green‡	Sandstwood Beige	Coral Turquoise Metallic*	Tahitian Walnut Metallic*	
Tor-Red‡	Spinnaker White*	Formal Black	Bahama Yellow†‡ / Sno White†	Tunisian Tan Metallic† / Rallye Red‡	Curious Yellow‡	Gold Leaf Metallic	Tawny Gold Metallic	

*Fury only. †Satellite only. ‡Optional at extra cost.

FURY CUSTOM SUBURBAN

PLYMOUTH 71 (A)

656

Plymouth

FURY I HAS LESS SIDE CHROME $3676.

Fury II
$3824.

Fury Gran Coupe ■ Fury III ■ Fury II ■ Fury I

FURY II and III GRILLE

Fury III Interior

Fury III

ALTERNATOR, TEMP. GAS GAUGES SET ABOVE

$3998.

71ᴮ
(CONT'D.)

1971 PLYMOUTHS INTRO. 10~6~70

$4030.

2-DR. FORMAL HARDTOPS

FURY III

Sport Fury

120-MPH SPEEDO.

$4086.

$4140.

Sport Fury

(FROM $4494.) SPORT SUBURBAN

GRAN CPE.

3 CHROME TABS ATOP FR. FENDERS OF
Sport Fury GT

1971 Plymouth Station Wagons

SATELLITE CUSTOM (SIDE CHROME)

SATELLITE REGENT

PLYMOUTH 71 (B)   SATELLITE (NO SIDE CHROME)

Plymouth

Coming through with the kind of car America wants.

$2678.

$3553. (WEST)

SATELLITE $2609. $3484. (WEST)

SATELLITE DASH

SEBRING has CHROME SIDE

SATELLITE CUSTOM $3723.

(34973 BLT.)

(INTRO. 9-28-71)

(10507 BLT.)

72

TOTAL 1972 PROD. = 756,605

ROAD RUNNER

$3863.

RR 400 CID V8 (255 HP)

THIS GRILLE ALSO USED BY SATELLITE REGENT WAGON

1972

FURY I $3915.

STD. 318 CID V8 CUT TO 150 HP 225 CID 6 = 110 " 360 400 and 440 CID V8s ALSO

FURY III $4214.

FURY GRAN HIT SEDAN

H/T CPE.

2-DR. H/T and FORMAL H/T AVAIL.

(20599 BLT.)

$4389. UP

(17551 BLT.) $3987. (4438., WEST)

FORMAL H/T (FURY III)

new GRILLE

FURY SPORT SUBURBAN FR. $4840.

FURY II FURY III GRILLE

(OPT.)

FURY DASH

PLYMOUTH 72

658

Plymouth 73

A

STD. 225 CID 6 (105 HP)
318 CID V8 (150 HP)

Satellite Wagon

$3272. (6906 BLT.)

SATELLITE, CUSTOM, REGENT WAGONS IN SAT. SERIES

Satellite

(14716 BLT.)

FRONT RESTYLED

TOTAL 1973 PROD.: 882,196

SEDAN

$2824.

(7567 BLT.)

DIFFERING TAIL LIGHT DESIGN

SATELLITE REGENT WAGON (SAME GRILLE AS SATELLITE CUSTOM)

$3621. UP

$2755. (13570 BLT.)

Satellite Coupe

E/F/H78; F70×14 TIRES (ON VARIOUS SAT. TYPES)

SATELLITE DASH

SATELLITE SEBRING

ROAD RUNNER

Road Runner (19056 BLT.)

$3115.

FURY ON NEXT PAGE

PLYMOUTH 73(A)

Plymouth
FURY

$4323. (WEST)

F78×15 TIRES

Fury I 4-Door Sedan

$4032. (WEST)

Fury III

four-door
73 B
(CONT'D.)

1973

Fury II
SEDAN
(21,646 BLT.)

360 CID
V8
(170 HP)
ENGINE IN
SUBURBAN,
CUSTOM SUBURBAN,
and SPT. SUB.
WAGONS have
(FURY SERIES)

$3694.

SPORT SUBURBAN
has GRAB
IRONS
$5056. WEST
(3-SEAT)

$4599.

FR.
$4521. (WEST)

FURY
GRAN
note EMBLEMS

(20,512
BLT.)

wagon

CUSTOM
SUBURBAN

$4246. UP
(25,559 BLT.)

1973

DASH

FR. $4703. (WEST)
CUSTOM SUBURBAN

AVAILABLE
1973 COLORS

Silver Frost Metallic | Blue Sky | True Blue Metallic | Basin Street Blue¹ | Regal Blue Metall

Rallye Red | Mist Green | Amber Sherwood Metallic | Forest Green Metallic | Autumn Bronze Metallic¹

Sahara Beige | Coral Turquoise Metallic² | Mojave Tan Metallic¹ | Chestnut Metallic² | Lemon Twist¹*

Sun Fire Yellow² | Honey Gold | Golden Haze Metallic | Tahitian Gold Metallic | Formal Black

Spinnaker White

¹ Satellite only ² Fury only *Optional at extra cost

PLYMOUTH 73 (B)

Plymouth

(SATELLITE SERIES ENDS DURING 1974)

(FINAL) **SATELLITE**

SLDAN (12726 BLT.) $3226.

360 CID V8 (180 HP)

Fury

FURY DASH
FURY III H/T $4418.

SATELLITE WAGONS
CUSTOM $3839. UP

SATELLITE REGENT
(SATELLITE CUSTOM SED. has SAME new GRILLE DESIGN)

$4767. UP

FURY II $4223.

74
TOTAL 1974 PROD.: 739,894.

FURY III $4400.

OPTIONAL

PLYMOUTH FURY WAGONS

CUSTOM SUBURBAN (6505 BLT.)

SPT. SUBURBAN FR. $5065.

400 CID V8 (185/205 HP) IN GRAN FURY, WAGONS.

HORN RING STILL AVAILABLE! (OPTIONAL)

Deluxe Steering Wheel

GRAN FURY $4675.

WAGONS INCLUDE:
Fury Sport Suburban ■ Custom Suburban ■ Suburban
Satellite Regent ■ Satellite Custom ■ Satellite

1974 PLYMOUTH FURY EXTERIOR COLORS

Silver Frost Metallic	Dark Moonstone Metallic
Powder Blue	Sienna Metallic
Lucerne Blue Metallic	Dark Chestnut Metallic
Starlight Blue Metallic	Spinnaker White
Rallye Red	Formal Black
Frosty Green Metallic	Sun Fire Yellow
Deep Sherwood Metallic	Golden Fawn
Avocado Gold Metallic	Golden Haze Metallic
Sahara Beige	Tahitian Gold Metallic

B-100 B-200 OR B-300 SERIES

109" WB and up

VOYAGER
new
SIMILAR: DODGE VAN   PLYMOUTH 74 $4060.

NOTE: Due to occasional printing irregularities, the above colors may vary slightly from actual hues. See your Plymouth Dealer for accurate color chips.

Plymouth

**FURY, GRAN FURY
ROAD RUNNER**

ENGINES AVAIL:
225 CID 6 (95 HP)
318 " V8 (135 HP OR 150)
360 " " (180 HP " 190)
400 " " (165/185 HP)
" " " (175 HP)
" " " (190/235 HP)
" " " (195 HP OR 215)

1975 PLYMOUTH FURY EXTERIOR COLORS

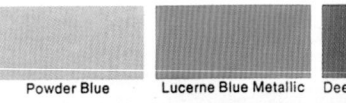
Powder Blue

Lucerne Blue Metallic

Deep Sherwood Metallic

Avocado Gold Metallic

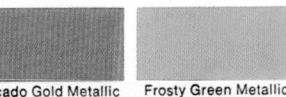
Frosty Green Metallic

Yellow Blaze

Golden Fawn

Sienna Metallic

Bittersweet Metallic

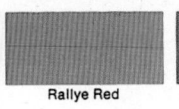
Rallye Red

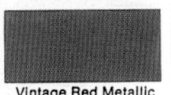
Vintage Red Metallic

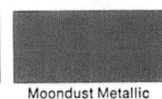
Moondust Metallic

Inca Gold Metallic

Spanish Gold Metallic

Aztec Gold Metallic

Spinnaker White

Silver Cloud Metallic

Formal Black

Plymouth Fury

For Release: 6 A.M., EDT, Thurs., Sept. 12, 1974.

NOTE: Due to occasional printing irregularities, the above colors may vary slightly from actual hues. See your Plymouth Dealer for accurate color chips.

from Plymouth for 1975
The Small Fury

new SHORTER 117½" WB (115" on COUPES)

4105.

(17782 BLT.)

FURY *SPORT*

75 A

DASH

Handsome, readable Fury instrument panel with standard steering wheel.

SEDAN (31080 BLT.)

$3704.

FURY CUSTOM

$3711.
(27486 BLT.)

124" WB

117½" WB

FURY SALON
A new level of luxury at a modest price.

FROM $4309. TO $5573.

new

FURY WAGONS

(CONT'D. NEXT PAGE) PLYMOUTH 75 (A)

Plymouth

$5067.

Fury Brougham 4-Door Hardtop

GRAN FURY BROUGHAM
(552I BLT.)

$5146.
(652I BLT.)

REAR DETAILS

GRAN FURY INSTRUMENT PANEL *has* RECTANGULAR SPEEDOMETER

121½" WB GRAN FURY

The beautifully finished instrument panel is as easy to use as it is to look at.

Optional Auto Speed Control—helps maintain road speed and avoid wasting fuel.

3

GRAN FURY UPHOLSTERY OPTION

75 B (CONT'D.)

ROAD RUNNER

(BELOW)

Colorful Sundance cloth-and-vinyl bucket seats are available on the Road Runner.

ROAD RUNNER

1975 Plymouth Gran Fury Exterior Colors

Silver Cloud Metallic	Platinum Metallic	Powder Blue	Astral Blue Metallic	Starlight Blue Met.
Vintage Red	Frosty Green Metallic	Deep Sherwood Metallic	Avocado Gold Metallic	Sahara Beige
Moondust Metallic	Sienna Metallic	Dark Chestnut Metallic	Spinnaker White	Formal Black
Golden Fawn	Bittersweet	Inca Gold Metallic	Spanish Gold Metallic	

NOTE: Due to occasional printing irregularities, the above colors may vary slightly from actual hues.

ROAD RUNNER DASH

Road Runner instrument panel features optional tachometer and sporty "Tuff" steering wheel.

(ROAD-RUNNER MOVED TO FURY SERIES, 1975)

note DECAL on REAR DECK.

POLYGLAS - E70-14

14" Rallye wheel.

ROAD~RUNNER *has* OWN GRILLE.
WITH 318, 360 OR 400 CID V8

HAS "BEEP~BEEP" HORN

G70 x 14" TIRES ON RALLYE WHEELS

New 15" polycast urethane road wheel.

PLYMOUTH 75 (B)

ROAD RUNNER
The others haven't caught up with it yet.

663

Plymouth FURY H/T 115" WB **$3699.** (16415 BLT.)

$3988. (28851 BLT.)

FURY SPORT COUPE

FURY SEDAN 117½" WB

(22654 BLT.) **$3733.**

(5657 BLT.) **$4986.** UP

FURY SPORT SUBURBAN

(new) *Fury Salon*

ENGINES

225 c/d 6 (100 HP)
318 c/d V8 (150 ")
360 c/d V8 (170 ")

(20234 BLT.) **$4022.**

400 c/d V8 ALSO AVAIL. (175, 200 OR 210 HP)

Optional 60/40 Boca Raton split-bench seat in rich woven cloth and grained vinyl with center armrest and dual reclining seat-backs.

OPTIONAL "BOCA RATON" CLOTH/VINYL 60/40 SPLIT~BENCH SEATS IN FURY SPORT

"MODULAR" DASH

FURY SALON

76

$5761.

(2484 BLT.) 124" WB Gran Fury Sport Suburban.

FURY

(NO 121½" 124" WB GRAN FURY TYPES AFTER 1977)
ROAD~RUNNLR RE~APPLARS AS A 1977 VOLARE MODEL.

SINCE 1975, NUMBER OF FULL-SIZE PLYMOUTH MODELS REDUCED

FURY H/T (16410 BLT.) **$3893.**

new GRILLE '77

77-78

FURY H/T '78 (13276 BLT.) **$4236.**

FINAL 400 c/d V8 (190 HP) (OTHER ENGINES CONTINUED) PLYMOUTH 76~78

Plymouth

DASH

SPEED and WIPER CONTROL STALK

RADIO and HEATER CONTROLS

GRAN FURY ONLY, IN 1980

COLORS

Light Heather Gray Metallic*

Frost Blue Metallic

Teal Frost Metallic

Crimson Red Metallic*

Light Cashmere

Mocha Brown Metallic

Formal Black

Light Heather Gray*

Nightwatch Blue*

Teal Tropic Green Metallic

Baron Red*

Natural Suede Tan

Spinnaker White

*Salon model only.

INTERIOR
(SAXONY CLOTH and VINYL)

$7116.

1980 PLYMOUTH GRAN FURY.
A MATTER OF FAMILY PRIDE.

TOTALLY RESTYLED and DOWNSIZED,
1980 GRAN FURY RETURNS
(WITH 118½" WB)

SALON SEDAN
(3255 BLT.)
DELUXE SIDE TRIM
(VINYL~COVERED ROOF AVAIL.,
AS ILLUSTRATED)

2.9:1 Six (2.4:1 V-8)	
Front—Disc, power Rear—Drum, power	
Battery—370-amp (Six) Alternator—65-amp	
P195/75R15 glass-belted radial white sidewall	

21~GALLON GAS TANK

$6741.

4~DR. SEDANS ONLY

(STD.) SEDAN
(15469 BLT.)
(MINIMUM OF DECOR~ATIVE TRIM)

CHRYSLER CORPORATION'S PROTECTION PLAN

Two-Tone Paint Package (Salon)
(Upper/Lower)

Lt. Heather Gray / Lt. Heather Gray Metallic

Lt. Heather Gray / Baron Red

Frost Blue Metallic / Nightwatch Blue

Teal Frost Metallic / Teal Tropic Green Metallic

Natural Suede Tan / Mocha Brown Metallic

engine features
Net Horsepower

90 @ 3,600 rpm

90 HP
Standard 3.7-liter (225 CID) Slant Six.

120 HP
Optional 5.2-liter (318 CID) V-8.

130 HP
5.9-liter (360 CID) 4-bbl V-8

PLYMOUTH 80

Pontiac
AMERICA'S FINEST LOW-PRICED CAR

E. STANDS FOR ECONOMY—*and so does Pontiac!* Owners report 18 to 24 miles per gallon of gasoline . . . say Pontiac is just as economical to own as small cars! Amazingly trouble-free, too, because Pontiac is built to last 100,000 miles!

6 CYL. OR STRAIGHT~8

40 A
RESTYLED

DECORATIVE CHROME
PARALLEL STRIPS ALONG
CENTER OF HOOD AND DECK
(SINCE 1935.)

5 BIG WEEKLY CONTESTS
THESE PRIZES EACH WEEK
TEN 1940 PONTIAC 4-DOOR SEDANS
EACH WITH 1000 GALLONS OF TEXACO
FIRE-CHIEF GASOLINE
PLUS $100 VACATION MONEY
TO EACH PONTIAC WINNER
and also Each Week
100 CASH PRIZES OF $10 EACH

THE PONTIAC SPECIAL "6"
A big, luxurious, "power-packed" beauty. 5½ inches longer and 4 inches wider at the front seat, than last year's Pontiac. Famous for engine quietness, economy, for its "Triple-Cushioned" ride. Your choice of 10 standard colors.

4~DR. **$876.**
Pontiac Special 6, 40-25
117" WB

4 New Lines of Pontiacs in 4 Price Ranges
17 Models Ranging from Low-Priced Sixes to Luxury Eight

DASH

Special Six
TWO-DOOR SEDAN
$830.

6 CYL.
222.7 CID
(SINCE '37)
new 87 HP

SERIAL # PREFIX INDICATES WHERE
CAR WAS BUILT: P = PONTIAC, MI.;
L = NEW JERSEY;
C = CALIFORNIA

1940 PRODUCTION
SPECIAL 6 — 106,892
DE LUXE 6 — 58,452
DE LUXE 8 — 20,433
TORPEDO 8 — 31,224

6.00 x 16" TIRES
4.3 GEAR RATIO
(SPEC. 6)

REAR VIEW

ONLY $783*
FOR THE SPECIAL SIX BUSINESS COUPE
OTHER MODELS SLIGHTLY HIGHER
PONTIAC FOR PRIDE AND PERFORMANCE

Special Six Business Coupe, $783*

4~PASS. SPORT COUPE = $819.

A-11214
1940

Special 6, 40-25 (4~DR.)

(CONT'D. NEXT PAGE)

40 PONTIAC (A)

Pontiac

$1015.

Instruments and clock
DELUXE 6

DE LUXE 6

(ABOVE) SPECIAL 6 WAGON

$876.

De Luxe Six Business Coupe, $835*
(Pontiac also builds the Business Coupe on the De Luxe Eight chassis)

DE LUXE SIX SPORT COUPE $876*—Exceptionally spacious, wide-visioned body. Full-width auxiliary seat makes
it a five or six-passenger car. Two upholstery options. (De Luxe Eight model also available.)

$1003.

DE LUXE SIX CABRIOLET $1003*—Nine different upholstery combinations featuring colored Spanish leather. Three
top colors. Full-width auxiliary seat. Extra large luggage space. (De Luxe Eight model also available.)

40 B
(CONT'D.)

$919.

$970.
DE LUXE 8 4~DR.

De Luxe Six
FOUR-DOOR SEDAN
$932.

120" WB ON
DLX. 6 and 8

248.9 CID STR.~8
(SINCE '37)
100 HP (SINCE
'37)

De Luxe Eight
TWO-DOOR SEDAN

Torpedo Eight
new!

DeLuxe 8, 40-28. 40-26*

6.50 x 16" TIRES
ON ALL 8~CYL.
MODELS

Pontiac Torpedo 8, 40-29

SHELL

"Torpedo" Eight Sport Coupe, $1026*

122" WB

Pontiac Torpedo 8, 40-29

"Torpedo" Eight 4-Door Touring Sedan, $1092*

103 HP WITH
DUAL CARB.

40 PONTIAC (B)

667

Pontiac

PONTIAC PRICES BEGIN AT **$828**
★ FOR THE DE LUXE "TORPEDO" SIX BUSINESS COUPE

DE LUXE "TORPEDO" SIX BUSINESS COUPE $828*
(white sidewall tires extra)

$864.

DE LUXE "TORPEDO" SIX SEDAN COUPE $864*
(white sidewall tires and two-tone colors extra)

$995.

CUSTOM "TORPEDO" SIX SEDAN COUPE $995*
(white sidewall tires extra)

Pontiac Custom 24 & 29 (6 & 8)

DeLuxe 25 & 27   and Streamliner 26 & 28

"TORPEDO" SIX

$1175.

CUSTOM "TORPEDO" SIX STATION WAGON $1175*
(white sidewall tires extra)

(VARIATIONS IN WOOD and BODY COLORS)

Custom "Torpedo" Six Station Wagon, $1175*

DECORATIVE PARALLEL STRIPS ALSO ON FRONT and REAR FENDERS

41ᴬ

De Luxe "Torpedo" Six Convertible Sedan Coupe $1023*
(white sidewall tires extra)

$1023.

Pontiac Custom 24 & 29 (6 & 8)

New GRILLE

(SEDANS ON NEXT PAGE)

41 PONTIAC (A)

668

Pontiac

Why not visit your Pontiac dealer today and pick out your new "Torpedo"? You may have any model in either the Six or the Eight with the Eight costing only $25 more.

DE LUXE "TORPEDO" SIX
TWO-DOOR SEDAN $874*

(white sidewall tires extra)

DE LUXE "TORPEDO" SIX FOUR-DOOR SEDAN $921*

NEW!

*Streamliner "Torpedo" Six Sedan Coupe, $923**

Eleven beautiful "Torpedo" models

41^B

(CONT'D.)

NEW

STREAMLINER "TORPEDO" EIGHT
FOUR-DOOR SEDAN $1005*

This four-door, four-window sedan, with original Custom "Torpedo" styling, offers more pronounced streamlining and greater rear seat privacy than the conventional six-window sedan.

METROPOLITAN
"TORPEDO" SIX FOUR-DOOR SEDAN $921*

CUSTOM
"TORPEDO" EIGHT
FOUR-DOOR SEDAN $1077*

(white sidewall tires and two-tone colors extra)

41 PONTIAC (B)

Pontiac

6 CYL. OR STRAIGHT~8 IN ANY MODEL

Instruments and clock have edge-lighted plastic numerals. Burma copper finish is used with chrome trim. The panel is finished in a brown mahogany swirl

$935.

Torpedo Sport Coupe

$940

Torpedo Two-Door Sedan

$985. FOR EITHER

Torpedo Four-Door Sedan

Torpedo Metropolitan Four-Door Sedan

$1165.

Torpedo Convertible Sedan Coupe

Several Chassis Improvements $895.

Torpedo Business Coupe $1035.

THE *FINE CAR* WITH THE *LOW PRICE*

42

6-CYL. PRICES SHOWN

new "FADEAWAY" FENDERS

85,555 1942 PONTIACS BUILT

Streamliner Four-Door Sedan

$980.

Streamliner Sedan Coupe

Streamliner Station Wagon $1265.

TORPEDO SEDAN COUPE $950.

new GRILLE

Torpedo

Pontiac **for** 1942

Pontiac

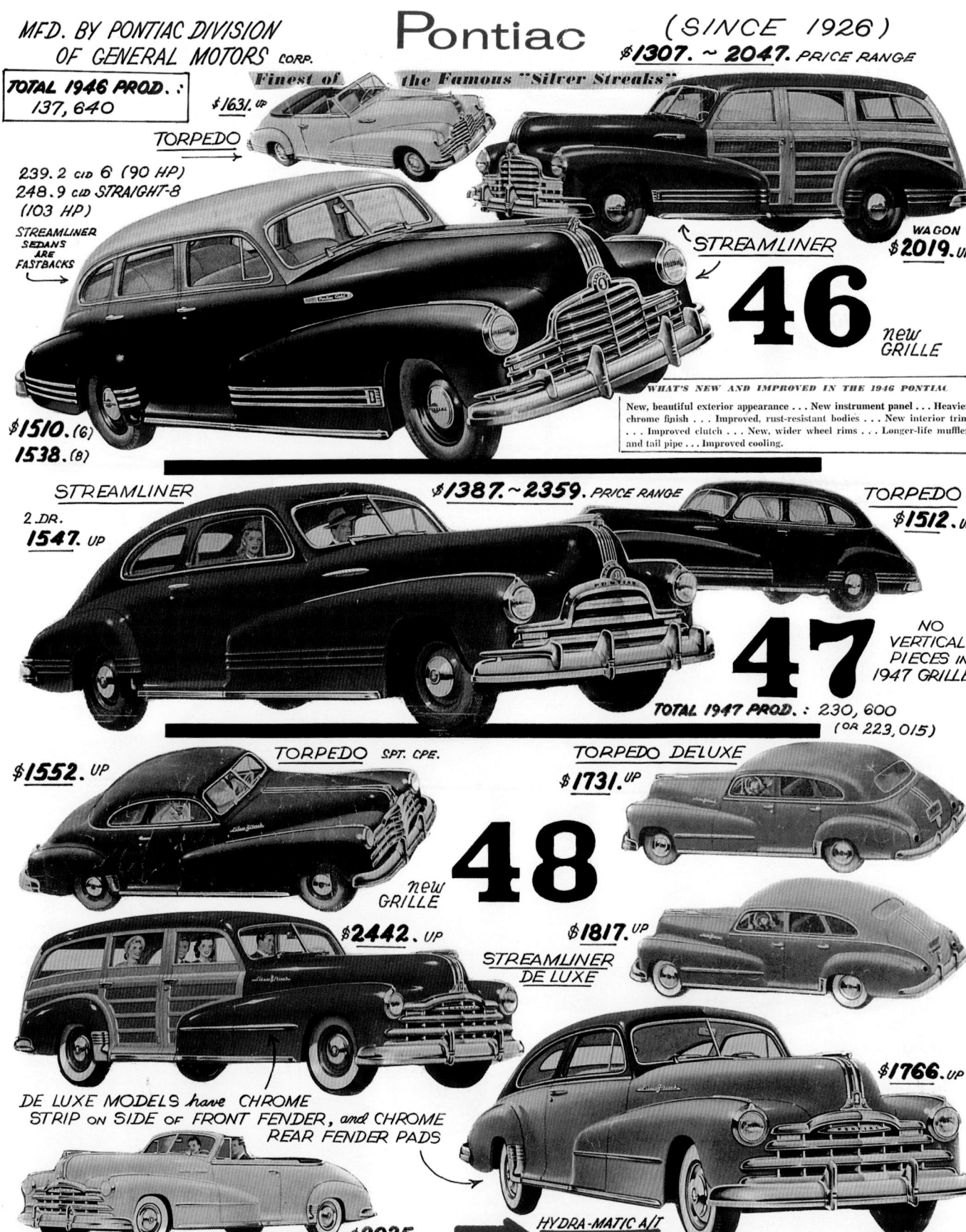

MFD. BY PONTIAC DIVISION OF GENERAL MOTORS CORP.

(SINCE 1926)
$1307. ~ 2047. PRICE RANGE

TOTAL 1946 PROD.: 137,640

Finest of the Famous "Silver Streaks"

$1631. UP

TORPEDO →

239.2 CID 6 (90 HP)
248.9 CID STRAIGHT-8 (103 HP)

STREAMLINER SEDANS ARE FASTBACKS →

STREAMLINER

WAGON $2019. UP

46

new GRILLE

$1510. (6)
1538. (8)

WHAT'S NEW AND IMPROVED IN THE 1946 PONTIAC
New, beautiful exterior appearance . . . New instrument panel . . . Heavier chrome finish . . . Improved, rust-resistant bodies . . . New interior trim . . . Improved clutch . . . New, wider wheel rims . . . Longer-life muffler and tail pipe . . . Improved cooling.

STREAMLINER

2 DR. 1547. UP

$1387. ~ 2359. PRICE RANGE

TORPEDO $1512. UP

47

NO VERTICAL PIECES IN 1947 GRILLE

TOTAL 1947 PROD.: 230,600
(OR 223,015)

$1552. UP

TORPEDO SPT. CPE.

TORPEDO DELUXE

$1731. UP

48

new GRILLE

$2442. UP

$1817. UP

STREAMLINER DE LUXE

DE LUXE MODELS have CHROME STRIP ON SIDE OF FRONT FENDER, and CHROME REAR FENDER PADS

$1766. UP

HYDRA-MATIC A/T NOW AVAILABLE

TORPEDO DELUXE CVT. $2025.

NEW 104 HP IN STRAIGHT-8
PONTIAC 46-48

$1500. ~ 2490. PRICE RANGE

TOTAL 1948 PRODUCTION: 235,419
(OR 253,469)

PONTIAC

CHIEFTAN CVT.
$2138. →
UP

STREAMLINER

STREAMLINER
(FASTBACK)

TOTAL 1949 PROD.
333,957

$1740. (6)
1808. (8)

CHOICE OF
METAL OR WOOD-BODY
WAGONS IN 1949
$2622. $2690.
(6)   (8)

49

(TOTALLY RESTYLED)

models
STREAMLINER 6 OR 8
CHIEFTAN 6 OR 8 (REPLACES "TORPEDO")
ENGINES = 239.2 CID 6 (90 OR 93 HP); 248.9 CID STRAIGHT-8 (104 OR 106 HP)
7.10 x 15" TIRES

120" W.B. (THROUGH '52)

CHIEFTAN
SEDAN $1761. (6)
1829. (8)

90 HP 6 OR
108 HP (268.4 CID) 8

TOTAL 1950 PRODUCTION : 467,655 (OR 446,429)

$1673. ~ 2411. PRICE RANGE

STREAMLINER

$2343. UP

CHIEFTAN
CLUB COUPE
$1694. UP

DELUXE
ALL-
STEEL
WAGON

CHIEFTAN

1950

50

VERTICAL
"TEETH" NOW
ADDED TO
UPPER SECTION
OF GRILLE

SUPER
CATALINA H/T (NEW)
$2058. UP

WHEEL
COVER

CHIEFTAN
SEDAN
$1745.

PONTIAC 49-50

CHIEFTAN (RUBBER REAR FENDER GUARDS IDENTIFY STD. MODELS) WAGON STREAMLINER
STD. $1977. DLX. $2081. DLX. $2629.
(8) (8)

DLX. SEDAN

REAR FENDER PAD DETAILS (CHROMED ON DELUXE)

TAILLIGHTS SLIGHTLY ENLARGED

"Pontiac Eight" ABOVE TRIM

$1713. ~ 2629. PRICE RANGE

TOTAL 1951 PRODUCTION: 343,795

51 new GRILLE

new 102 HP (6) OR 122 HP (8)

L-HEAD 6 CYL. and STRAIGHT-8 ENGINES CONTINUE (THROUGH '54)

('52) LESS SIDE CHROME on STANDARD MODELS.

Dollar for Dollar you can't beat a **Pontiac**

CHIEFTAN

CVT. $2388. (8)

PONTIAC NAME OVER GRILLE IS IN Cursive SCRIPT AS PREVIOUSLY

New High-Performance Economy Axle

new 1952 WHEEL COVER

52

SIDE VIEW OF MASCOT FOR 1952

4 new "SLOTS" BELOW PONTIAC NAME (NOW IN CAPITALS)

More Power

PONTIAC

new SIDE TRIM

New **Dual-Range** Hydra-Matic Drive* (IMPROVED AUTOMATIC TRANSMISSION)

TOTAL 1952 PRODUCTION: 277,156

(SAME ENGINES and HP AS IN '51)

CHIEFTAN MODELS ONLY (THROUGH '53)

$1956. ~ 2772. PRICE RANGE

PONTIAC .51~52.

PONTIAC
CHIEFTAN DELUXE
$2119. UP

LOWEST PRICED MODEL, AT
$1956.

CHIEFTAN SPECIAL

$2060. UP

new "DUAL STREAK" RESTYLING
FEATURES TWIN GROUPS of
CHROME BANDS ALONG HOOD
and DECK, with new BODIES

53
new
1-PIECE
WINDSHIELD

CHIEFTAN DELUXE

TOTAL 1953 PRODUCTION:
414,011

new 122" WB

$1956.

$2774.
PRICE
RANGE

WAGONS with GRAIN-DECORATED
UPPER PANELS (ABOVE) ARE PRICED
$80. ABOVE SIMILAR WAGONS
of ONE SOLID COLOR ONLY.

WOODGRAINED
DLX. WAGON
(8) IS
COSTLIEST
MODEL
AT
2744.

ENGINES:
115 or 118 HP 6
118 or 122 HP STRAIGHT 8

The experimental Parisienne stands only
56 inches high. Inside and out it is a
designer's dream of how one "car of the
future" might be styled and equipped.

PARISIENNE
(SHOW CAR)
PUBLICLY DISPLAYED, BUT
NOT A PRODUCTION BODY
TYPE

De Luxe Catalina

CHIEFTAN DLX.
8
SEDAN
$2194.

DELUXE CATALINA 6 H/T $2304.
CUSTOM   "   "   2370.
DELUXE   "   8   2380.
CUSTOM   "   "   2446.

DOLLAR FOR DOLLAR YOU CAN'T
beat a
Pontiac

PONTIAC 53

674

PONTIAC

$1968. ~ 2630.
PRICE RANGE

ENGINES:
239.2 cid 6 (115 or 118 HP)
268.4 cid STRAIGHT-8 (122 or 127 HP)

CHIEFTAN DELUXE
(6 OR 8 CYL.)
2 DR.
6 CYL. SEDAN
$2131.

122" WB

CHIEFTAN SPECIAL 6
(ALSO AVAIL. as 8)
$2027.
(8 CYL., 2102.)

A BRIEF (1 YR.) RETURN TO SINGLE GROUP OF CHROME STRIPS ON HOOD and DECK

new GRILLE with EMBLEM PLACED ABOVE

54

6-Z or 8-Z

DELUXE (ABOVE) HAS MORE SIDE TRIM THAN SPECIAL (TOP)

WAGON INTERIOR

The rear seat in this handsome 6-passenger interior, in green or red Morrokide with ivory trim, folds forward to provide almost six feet of cargo space—eight feet with tail gate open.

122" WB

CHIEFTAN DELUXE STATION WAGON

$2504.(6); 2579.(8)

STAR CHIEF DE LUXE 8 (BELOW) COSTS LESS THAN CUSTOM 8.

CONVERTIBLE
$2630.

124" WB

STAR CHIEF CUSTOM 8
(AT RIGHT and BELOW)
(115,088 STAR CHIEF DLX. and CUSTOM MODELS BLT.)

Dollar for Dollar

You Can't Beat a

PONTIAC

$2394.

THE NEW *Star Chief*

8-CYL.   124" WB
SERIES "8-Z" IDENTIFIED BY THESE "STARS" ON SIDE OF REAR FENDER

TOTAL 1954 PRODUCTION:
370,887 (or 287,744, DEPENDING ON VARYING REPORTS)
PONTIAC 54

PONTIAC

2 DR. (58,654 BLT.)

CHIEFTAN 860

$2105.

(TOTALLY RESTYLED)

55

4 DR. WAGON (19,439 BLT.) $2603.

2 OR 4 DR. 860 WAGONS

new PANORAMIC WINDSHIELD

Pontiac leads in station wagon value with four models —the beautiful 860, left, in two- and four-door models, the spectacular 870 four-door and the fabulous Safari.

CHIEFTAN 870

$2105. TO $2962. PRICE RANGE

(91,187 BLT.) $2268.

CHIEFTAN = 122" WB

STAR CHIEF = 124" WB

new DASH

CHIEFTAN 870 CATALINA H/T (2 VIEWS)

$2335. (72,608 BLT.)

STAR CHIEF CONVERTIBLE (19,762 BLT.)

STAR CHIEF CUSTOM CATALINA

$2691.

ALL MODELS *with* new "STRATO-STREAK" O.H.V. V8 ENGINE → 180 OR 200 HP (287.2 CID)

$2499. (99,629 BLT.)

FRONT DETAILS CLOSE UP

new STAR CHIEF CUST. SAFARI 2 DR. LUXURY WAGON

Pontiac's flair for years ahead styling was never more evident than in the fabulous all-new Safari.

(3760 BLT.) $2962. (SAFARI SIMILAR TO CHEVROLET NOMAD WAGON)

PONTIAC .55

REAR 3/4 VIEW OF CHIEFTAN 870 STATION WAGON

TOTAL 1955 PRODUCTION: 581,860

new 12-VOLT ELECTRICAL SYSTEM

BUMPER GUARDS AVAILABLE (RARE)

2-DR. WAGON
CHIEFTAN

(8620 BLT.)

SAFARI

(4042 BLT.)

STAR CHIEF

new
4-DR. H/T

$3129.

CHIEFTAN 860
8-PASS. WAGON
$2613.

(12,702 BLT.)

PLASTIC "JR. STAR CHIEF" CHILD'S ELECTRIC CARS ALSO, FOR DEALER PROMOTIONAL PURPOSES

56 Pontiac

STAR CHIEF
Custom Convertible

(19,762 BLT.)

$2691.

new GRILLE with MORE CHROME

REAR DETAILS

ENLARGED new 316.6 cid V8 (205 or 227 HP)

$2240. ~ 3129.
PRICE RANGE

TOTAL 1956 PRODUCTION:
332,268

PONTIAC 56

677

PONTIAC

CHIEFTAN 252 HP

$2527. (35,671 BLT.)

new 4-DR. "SAFARI" (14,095 BLT.)

SUPER CHIEF 270 HP

$3021.

8.50 x 14 TIRES ON WAGONS

SU. CHIEF WAGON DOOR

PONTIAC 1957

57 RESTYLED

STAR CHIEF 270 HP CUSTOM CATALINA 4-DR. H/T

$3481. CUSTOM SAFARI WAGON (1292 BLT.)

$2975.

(44,283 BLT.)

$5782. **BONNEVILLE** (new)

(630 BLT.) (LIMITED PRODUCTION)

$3105. 12,789 BLT.

STAR CHIEF has HEAVY CHROME BAND PLACED WITHIN COLOR CONTRAST PANEL on REAR FENDER

AMERICA'S NUMBER ① ROAD CAR!

new FRONT END (NO LONGER USES "SILVER STREAK" CHROME BANDS)

new 8.00 x 14" TIRES (7.50 x 14 CHIEFTAN)

STAR CH. 2-DR. H/T (CUSTOM CATALINA) (32,864 BLT.) $2901.

ENGINES :
347 CID V8
(252, 270 OR 290 HP)
370 CID (BONNEVILLE)
(300 HP w. FUEL INJECTION)

IN 1957, ALL PONTIAC STATION WAGONS (2 OR 4 DR.) CARRIED THE "SAFARI" NAME. BUT ONLY THE 2-DR. CUSTOM SAFARI (1955~1957) IS THE "CLASSIC" MODEL SO DESIRED BY COLLECTORS.

$2463. ~ 5782. PRICE RANGE

TOTAL 1957 PRODUCTION : 343,298

PONTIAC 57

PONTIAC — CHIEFTAN — DASH

CATALINA 4-DR. H/T
(17,946 BLT.)
$2792.

3 STAR-LIKE FIGS. ON REAR FENDER OF CHIEFTAN ; 4 ON SUPER CHIEF. (EACH MODEL CAN BE IDENTIFIED BY FENDER DECOR., AS ILLUS. BELOW)

370 CID V8 (240, 255, 270, 285, 300 OR 310 HP)

SUPER CHIEF

H/T
(7236 BLT.)
$2880.

58
(RESTYLED)

STAR CHIEF H/T

BOLDEST ADVANCE IN 50 YEARS

BOLD NEW Bonneville BY PONTIAC
$3586. (3096 BLT.)

PACE CAR AT 1958 INDY 500 RACE

3122.
(13,888 BLT.)

$3481.

CVT.

BONNEVILLE H/T

(9144 BLT.)

models

		PRICE RANGE	
CHIEFTAN	122" WB =========	$2573. ~ 3088.	
SUPER CHIEF	124" WB =========	2834. ~ 2961.	" "
STAR CHIEF (CUSTOM)	124" WB =======	3071. ~ 3350.	" "
BONNEVILLE (CUSTOM)	122" WB ====	3481. (H/T); 3586. (CVT.)	

MODEL MOST PRODUCED = CHIEFTAN 4-DR. (44,999)
LEAST = STAR CHIEF CUST. SAFARI WAG. (2905)

TOTAL 1958 PRODUCTION :
219, 823

PONTIAC 58

PONTIAC

$3333.

new BONNEVILLE VISTA (38,696 BLT.) 4-DR. H/T

"BONNEVILLE" NAME on BONNEVL. GRILLE (ABOVE)

"PONTIAC" NAME ON GRILLE OF CATALINA and STAR CHIEF. STAR CHIEF has STAR-LIKE FIGURES ALONG SIDE OF REAR FENDER.

DASH

CATALINA SEDAN (72,377 BLT.) $2702.

new "WIDE-TRACK"

59
(TOTALLY RESTYLED)

122" WB (CATALINA SERIES and on BONNEVL. WAGON) 124" WB on OTHERS

CATALINA SAFARI WAGON

CATALINA → WAGON (14,084 BLT.) (9 PASS.) (21,162 6 PASS.)

BONNEVILLE H/T (27,769 BLT.)

3207. (9-PASS.)

(WIDTH EXAGGERATED)

8.00 × 14 TIRES

$3257.
245 HP (280 w. Hydra Matic) BONNEVL. has 260 HP (300 w. Hyd.)

new 389 c.i.d. V8 ENGINE (in ALL MODELS) (215, 245, 260, 280, 300 or 310 HP)

models		
CATALINA 122" WB	$2633. ~ 3209.	
STAR CHIEF 124" WB	2934. ~ 3138.	
BONNEVILLE (and "CUSTOM SAFARI") 124" WB 122" WB	3257. ~ 3532.	

TOTAL 1959 PRODUCTION :
388,856

PONTIAC 59

680

PONTIAC 1960

TOTAL 1960 PRODUCTION : 418,154

STAR CHIEF — SEDAN (23,038 BLT.) — THE ONLY CAR WITH WIDE·TRACK WHEELS — $3003.

WAGON AND VISTA DETAILS

CVT. (17,062 BLT.) $3476. BONNEVILLE

$2971.

60

new GRILLE WITH HORIZONTAL PCS.

VENTURA H/T (new) (27,577 BLT.)

389 CID V8 (215, 245, 260, 283, 303 OR 318 HP)

H/T (24,015 BLT.) $3255.

389 CID V8 (215, 230, 235, 267, 283, 287, 303 OR 318 HP)

61 A (RESTYLED)

PRODUCTION: (FULL-SIZED) 244,391

$2631. ~ 3530. PRICE RANGE

➤ new PONTIAC TEMPEST COMPACT SERIES (SHOWN SEPARATELY)

$2631. ↙ CATALINA 2-DR. SPT. SEDAN

(9846 BLT.)

SAFARI

models
CATALINA
VENTURA
STAR CHIEF
BONNEVILLE

BONNEVILLE H/T (STAR CHF. TAILLIGHTS SIMILAR) (16,906 BLT.)
$3255.

PONTIAC 60~61 (A)

TOTAL 1961 PRODUCTION: 244,391

(CONT'D. NEXT PAGE)

PONTIAC

STAR CHIEF
VISTA
4 DR. H/T
(13,559 BLT.)
3136.

61B
CONT'D.

BONNEVILLE
OFTEN *has*
"BONNEVILLE"
NAME ON GRILLE
AS ILLUSTR.

VISTA 4 DOOR HARDTOPS

VISTA
4 DR. H/T

(30,830 BLT.)   **$3331.**

$3230.

STAR CHIEF (13,882 BLT.)

STAR CHIEF VISTA

Wide-Track Pontiac
WIDEST STANCE ON THE ROAD

62A

new
GRILLES
and TAIL LIGHTS

SPORT
H/T
(31,629 BLT.)
$3349.

Bonneville

CATALINA
9-PASS. SAFARI WAG.   (10,716 BLT.)
$3301.

CATALINA 9-PASSENGER SAFARI

389 CID V8
(215, 230, 235, 267, 283,
303, 318, 333 OR 345 HP)

CLOSE-UP
OF
FRONT
END

(CONT'D. NEXT PAGE)

1962 PRODUCTION: 401,674

PONTIAC 61 (B) ~ 62 (A)

PONTIAC

STRATO - CHIEF
(SOLD ONLY IN CANADA)

WAGONS

LAURENTIAN
2 - DOOR

PONTIAC

LAURENTIAN
(SOLD ONLY IN
CANADA)

62ᵦ
(CONT'D.)

SPORT COUPE

SPORT COUPES

PARISIENNE
(SOLD ONLY IN CANADA)

SEDAN

GRAND PRIX (REAR)

GP

AMERICAN
GRAND PRIX
New   H/T →

MANUAL
SHIFT
CONSOLE

BUCKET
SEATS

AUTO.
SHIFT
CONSOLE

TACH.

GRAND PRIX (GP) DETAILS (ABOVE)

$3490.
303 HP

4 BBL. CARB.

$3917. (WEST COAST)

2-DR. GP H/T ONLY

(30,195 BLT.)

$2725. ~ 3624. PRICE RANGE

PONTIAC 62 (B)

683

PONTIAC $3300.

CATALINA

9-PASSENGER SAFARI

(11,751 BLT.)

$2795.
CATALINA SEDAN
(79,961 BLT.)

$3096.

(28,309 BLT.)

STAR CHIEF 4-DOOR SEDAN

← BEST-SELLING 1963 PONTIAC

(30,955 BLT.)

$3348.

(14,091 BLT.)

$2725.
CATALINA SPORTS SEDAN

BONNEVILLE SPORTS COUPE

BONNEVILLE VISTA

$3423.

(49,929 BLT.)

CATALINA / ST. CHIEF

2367

CATALINA
SPORT H/T
(60,795 BLT.)
$2859.

BONNEVILLE
CVT. (23,459 BLT.)
$3568.

63 new GRILLE
$2725. ~ 3623.
PRICE RANGE

ENGINES (V8s)
389 CID (215, 230, 235, 267, 283, 303 OR 318 HP)
new 421 CID (353 OR 370 HP)

2 VIEWS OF G.P.

GP
PONTIAC GRAND PRIX

SPORT H/T
(72,959 BLT.)

$3489.

'63 WIDE-TRACK PONTIAC

TOTAL 1963 PRODUCTION:
481,652
PONTIAC 63

684

PONTIAC 120" WB CATALINA
(12,480 BLT.)

$2735.

STAR CHIEF
(FRONT SIMILAR TO
CATALINA)
123" WB
235 HP

$3203. UP

(26,453 BLT.) $3107.

$2735. ~ 3633. PRICE RANGE

$3433.

64 new GRILLES

CATALINA SEDAN
(84,457 BLT.)

$2806.

4-DR.
H/T
(57,630
BLT.)

BONNEVILLE

$3578.

BONNEVILLE

123" WB

WHEEL COVER

BONN. BROUGHAM
w. VINYL TOP (BELOW)

INTERIOR

64-100

WEST COAST
$3995.
(CVT.)
(22,016 BLT.)
306 HP

PRESTON CLOTH-and-MORROKIDE INTERIOR

G.P.

WAGON
(BONNEVILLE)

120" WB
(63,810 BLT.)
$3499.

SAFARI 4 DR. (5844 BLT.)
$3633.

ENGINES: 389 CID (230 TO 330 HP)
421 CID (350 OR 370 CID

TOTAL 1964 PRODUCTION: 443,306

PONTIAC 64

685

PONTIAC

CATALINA
12.1" WB

CATALINA 2+2

note
LOUVRES
ON
COWL OF
2+2

BON. BROUGHAM
INTERIOR

(21,050 BLT.)

$3594.

CVT.   BONNEVILLE

DASH

ENGINES:
389 CID V8
(256, 290,
325 or 333 HP)
421 CID V8
(338, 356
or 376 HP)

$2734.~3632.
PRICE RANGE

TOTAL 1965
PRODUCTION:
534,633
(FULL-SIZED)

(62,480 BLT.)

BONNEVILLE   (325 HP)
BROUGHAM 4-DR. H/T

$3433.

new GRILLES and
PROTRUDING CENTER
"NOSE"

$3433.

65

(57,881 BLT.)
$3498.

G.P.

CAT. 2+2 INTERIOR

Pontiac for 1965
The year of the Quick Wide-Tracks

new GRILLE

Grand Prix

PONTIAC 65

686

PONTIAC

GM MARK OF EXCELLENCE

full-sized cars

$3219. CVT.
(14,837 BLT.)
$3628. (WEST)

V-8 ENGINES (SINCE 1955)

CATALINA SCRIPT; COWL LETTERING IN OTHER MODELS WITH NAMES IN BLOCK LETTERS

Catalina

252

389 CID V8 (290 HP) 121" WB

← $3240.

$3217. UP

66 A

new GRILLES

ENGINES (V8s)
389 CID (256, 290, 325, or 333 HP)
421 CID (338, 356 or 376 HP)

Wide-Track Pontiac/'66
"2+2" LETTERING

CATALINA WAGONS FROM $4164. (WEST)

DASH

1966 PRODUCTION: 481,591

$3602.
$4011. (WEST)

254
2+2
421 CID V8
(338 HP) (356 or 376 HP AVAIL.)
121" WB

Ventura

Star Chief Executive

256

389 CID V8 (290 HP)

124" WB

REAR FENDER TRIM

H/T (new) $3590. (WEST)

$3170. (BASE PRICE)

INTERIOR (EXEC.)

H/T (10,140 BLT.)

(CONT'D. NEXT PAGE)

PONTIAC 66 (A)

687

PONTIAC

$4385.

WAGONS : 121" WB

Wide-Track Pontiac/'66

"BONNEVILLE" NAME ALSO SEEN ON GRILLE OF

Bonneville 262

124" WB

$4543. (WEST)

STAINLESS STEEL LOWER SIDE TRIM (BNVL., GP)

BONNEVILLE CVT. (16,299 BLT.) $3586. (BASE PRICE)

BONNEVILLE WAGON $4704.

(8452 BLT.) $3747. (BASE PRICE)

$2762.~3747. PRICE RANGE

GRAND PRIX H/T (36,757 BLT.) $3492.

66 B (CONT'D.)

389 C/D V8 IN BON., GP (333 HP)

BONNEVILLE BROUGHAM OPTION

GRAND PRIX has OWN REAR STYLING, 121" WB

Grand Prix 266

$4449.

AVAIL. ONLY AS A 2-DR. H/T

GRAND PRIX has "GP" and RALLY LTS. ON GRILLE

(2-DR. H/Ts ONLY, IN GP SERIES, UNTIL 1967.)

SIDE DETAILS

UP TO 376 HP AVAIL. (GP)

GRAND PRIX has OWN GRILLE

WOOD-GRAIN ON GRAND PRIX DASH

PONTIAC ·66 (B)

688

Pontiac/67

new 400 CID V8 (290 HP)
(265 325 333 and 350 HP ALSO)

new 8-TRACK STEREO TAPE SYSTEM OPTIONAL

new 428 CID V8 ALSO (360 or 376 HP)

Where did they hide the windshield wipers * on the 1967 Pontiacs?

Only your Pontiac dealer knows.
And he's not talking until September 29.

CVT. (10,033 BLT.)

Catalina

"PONTIAC" NAME ON GRILLE

1967 CA

$3276.
TOTAL 1967 FULL-SIZE PRODUCTION: 445,950

(new) EXECUTIVE SAFARI WAGON

(WEST) $3274.
$2866. BASE PRICE

(5903 - 6 PASS.)
(5593 BLT., 9 PASS.)
$3600. UP

* = new WIPERS CONCEALED BELOW REAR END OF HOOD

FR. $4557.

new ENERGY-ABSORBING STEERING COLUMN; new 4-WAY HAZARD FLASHER, DUAL MASTER CYLINDER BRAKE SYSTEM

BONNEVILLE H/T 400 CID V8 (325 HP)

UP TO 376 HP WITH new 400, 428 CID V8s.

new GRILLES

67

8.55 x 14 TIRES

Bonneville

(INTRO. 9-29-66)

(31,016 BLT.)
"BONNEVILLE" NAME ABOVE GRILLE

$3448.
$4405. (WEST)

BONNEVILLE H/T (REAR QUARTERS)

new FRONT DISC BRAKE OPTION

'67 Grand Prix (GP)

(5856 CVTS. BLT.)

GP $4770.
CONVERTIBLE ADDED TO LINE (1967 ONLY)

GP 400 CID V8 has 350 HP

67-108

new CONCEALED HEADLIGHTS (ONLY ON GRAND PRIX)
(37,125 GP H/Ts ALSO BLT.)

GP

Pontiac 67/Ride the Wide-Track Winning Streak

PONTIAC 67

689

PONTIAC

CATALINA, VENTURA, EXECUTIVE
400 CID V8 STD.
(265 OR 290 HP)
(428 CID V8 OPT.)

CATALINA
H/T (92,217 BLT.)
$3518.
(WEST)

$3744.
UP

FROM $4723.
(WEST)

(INTRO. 9-21-67)

68

METAL "NOSE" MORE PRONOUNCED THAN BEFORE.

3089. (BASE PRICE)
VENTURA
4-DR. H/T

new GRILLES, TAIL LTS.

EXECUTIVE SAFARI WAGON

"MORROKIDE" (IMITATION LEATHER) and CLOTH UPHOLSTERY AVAIL.

(41,727 BLT.)
(CATALINA SERIES, VENTURA PACKAGE OPTIONAL)

$3158. W/O VENTURA OPTION

$3592.

$4571.
(WEST)

DASH
(BONNEVILLE BROUGHAM)

400 CID V8
(340 HP)

124" WB
BONNEVILLE
H/T (WITH TAIL LIGHT DETAILS ABOVE)
(57,055 BLT.)

$3697.
(31,701 BLT.)

8.55 x 14"
TIRES STD.

GP
400 CID
V8
(350 HP)

GRAND
PRIX
H/T
$4676.
(WEST)

WAGONS have
400 CID V8
(265, 290 OR 340 HP)

(GP CVT. DISCONTINUED)

$2945.~3987.
PRICE RANGE

ENGINES: 400 CID V8 (265, 290, 340, OR 350 HP)
428 CID V8 (375 OR 390 HP)

TOTAL 1968 FULL-SIZE PRODUCTION:
484,849 (910,482=ALL SIZES)

PONTIAC 68

Pontiac
announces
the
great
break away!

Pontiac Station Wagons

$3519. UP
$4496. UP (WEST)
CATALINA

$4104.
$5081. (WEST)
BONNEVILLE

$3872. UP

EXECUTIVE
SAFARI

FROM
$4849.
(WEST)

CATALINA,
VENTURA, EXECUTIVE
have THIS GRILLE

new
GRILLES
69
(INTRO. 9-26-68)

RECTANGULAR-CLUSTER
NON-GP
DASH

4 DR.
H/T
$3756.

BONNEVILLE $4733.
(WEST)

new
125"
WB

(50,817 BLT.)

428 CID V8 (360 HP)
BONNEVILLE

TYPICAL
PONTIAC
MEDALLION

GRAND PRIX

new
118" WB

GP NOW has
UN-SHROUDED
INDIVIDUALLY-
SET
HEADLIGHTS

GP new
"WRAP-AROUND"
DASH
$3866.

$4853.
(WEST)

400 CID V8
(350 HP)

(112,486 BLT.)

GP IS BEST-SELLING '69 PONTIAC

400 CID V8 USED IN MOST FULL-SIZED 1969 PONTIACS,
EXCEPT BONNEVILLES.

$3090.~4104. PRICE RANGE

PONTIAC 69

TOTAL 1969 PRODUCTION, FULL-SIZE:
493,453
(870,081=ALL SIZES)

4-DR. SEDAN (13061 BLT.) $3538.

4-DR. H/T (5376 BLT.)

PONTIAC $3669.

EXECUTIVE

125" WB (122" ON WAGON) $4168.

$4034. (WEST)

(5629 BLT.) EXECUTIVE 3-SEAT WAGON $5178. (WEST)

$3604.

70

new GRILLES (INTRO. 9-18-69) TOTAL 1970 PROD. = 690,953 (3686 BLT.)

122" WB (SINCE '69) CATALINA CONVT. (EXECUTIVE has SAME GRILLE)

DASH (BONNEVILLE)

(NO MORE VENTURA MODELS, BUT AVAIL. AS $106. OPTION IN CATALINA LINE.)

BONNEVILLE

$3770.

$3900.

125" WB (3802 BLT.) (44241 BLT.)

4-DR. H/T

BONNEVILLE 4-DR. SEDAN $4746. (DASH ABOVE) (WEST)

$4876. (WEST)

new 455 CID V8 (360 HP) (370 ") IS PONTIAC'S LARGEST ENGINE.

118" WB (65750 BLT.)

$4961. (WEST) $3985.

GRAND PRIX AND INTERIOR

PONTIAC 70

This is the way it's going to be.

PONTIAC

The First Catalina Brougham
H/T (8823 BLT.)
$4084. $4614.
(WEST)
CATALINA new 123" WB
350 or 400 CID V8 (250 or 265 HP)
GH 78 x 15 TIRES

Catalina
H/T (46257 BLT.) $3870.

The first
(1789 BLT.) $4706.
Grand Ville
CVT. $5236.
(WEST)

GRAND VILLE

SAFARI

4-DR. H/T
(30524 BLT.)

The First Grand Ville
$4566. $5096.
(WEST)

Bonneville RESEMBLES
GRAND VILLE, BUT BEARS
THESE MARKS
$4210.
UP

126" WB
455 CID V8 (280 or 325 HP)
IN BONNEVILLE, GRAND VILLE
TOTAL 1971 PROD. =
586,853

71
(INTRO.
9-29-70)
new
GRILLES

$4643. UP
Grand Safari
(9585 BLT.)

(SAFARI has GRILLE
LIKE CATALINA.)

REAR
71-115

Grand
Prix

118"
WB
400 CID
V8
(300 HP)

note
ONLY
2
HEADLIGHTS
ON
G-P

H/T (58325 BLT.)

G78 x 14
TIRES
GP H/T
5087.
(WEST)
$4557.

Pure
Pontiac!
PONTIAC 71

693

Pontiac

new ENERGY-ABSORBING SAFETY BUMPER

350 OR 400 CID V8 (160 OR 175 HP) IN CATALINA

400 OR 455 CID V8s (175 OR 185 HP) IN WAGONS

'72 Pontiac ...a cut above!

CONVERTIBLE $4596.

(2399 BLT.)

Catalina

123½" WB SEDAN $4229.

G78 × 15 TIRES

(83004 BLT.)

$3713.

$4640.

CVT. $5156. (2213 BLT.)

Grand Ville

OWN TAIL-LTS., BUT GRILLE LIKE BONNEVILLE

126" WB

new GRILLES

H78 × 15 TIRES, 455 CID V8 (185 OR 220 HP) IN BNVL., GR. VIL.

72 HP CUTS

(INTRO. 9-23-71)

Bonneville

SEDAN $4685. (9704 BLT.)

BONNE. 4-DR. H/T $4809. (15806 BLT.)

GP (BELOW) WITH 400 CID V8 (200 HP)

$4293. WESTERN PRICES SHOWN IN BLACK

Grand Prix.

Grand Prix

(91961 BLT.)

$4472. $4988. (WEST)

G78 × 14 TIRES (GP)

REAR

118" WB

FRONT

JULEP GREEN ONLY AVAIL. ON VENTURA, FIREBIRD EXC. T.A. →

JULEP GREEN

TOTAL 1972 PRODUCTION = 706,978

COLORS

PONTIAC 72

AVAILABLE 1973 COLORS

"AFRICAN CROSSFIRE MAHOGANY" TRIM

EXT. COLORS

| Starlight Black | Cameo White | Porcelain Blue | Admiralty Blue | Regatta Blue | Mesa Tan | Desert Sand | Golden Olive | Verdant Green | Slate Green | Brewster Green | Florentine Red | Ascot Silver | Burnished Umber |

HARMONIZING INT. COLORS →

White Black Blue Chamois Saddle Burgundy / White Black Blue Chamois Saddle Burgundy / White Black Blue Blue / White Black Blue Burgundy / White Black Blue Blue / White Black Chamois Saddle / White Black Chamois Saddle / White Black Chamois Saddle / White Black / White Black Saddle / White Black Saddle / White Black Burgundy / White Black Saddle Burgundy / White Black Saddle

PONTIAC 124" WB

4-DR. H/T (31,663 BLT.) $3938.

CATALINA FROM $4209.

GP

$4583. (153,899 BLT.) new OPERA WINDOW $4974.

REAR (BNVLLE.) SEDAN $4163. MORE COLORS

Valencia Gold / Burma Brown
White Black Saddle / White Black Saddle

$4292.

TOTAL 1973 PROD.=919,870

(new 116" WB)

GRAND PRIX

124" WB BONNEVILLE (GRAND VILLE GRILLE SIMILAR)

(RESTYLED)

73

350, 400 OR 455 CID V8s (150 TO 215 HP)

4-DR. H/T $4716.

LG. SIDE MIRRORS NOT STD. EQUIPMENT.

(17202 BLT.) 1973

new WIDE GRILLES (EXCEPT ON GP)

(46025 BLT.)

new "COLONNADE" H/T CPE. $4837.

$4692. UP

$4794. SEDAN CATALINA

(40654 BLT.)

CATALINA SAFARI (GRAND SAFARI ON NEXT PAGE)

400 OR 455 CID V8s (175-225 HP)

74 (RESTYLED)

$5498.

BONNEVILLE

4-DR. H/T $4639.

TOTAL 1974 PROD.= 580,045

new WRAPAROUND PARK./DIR. LIGHTS, ONLY ON GRAND VILLE.

GRAND VILLE

H/T

$5198. (6151 BLT.)

REAR

(CONT'D.)

$5495.

$4936. (99117 BLT.)

GRAND PRIX and DASH

WESTERN PRICES SHOWN IN BLACK

PONTIAC 73~74 (A)

Grand Prix instrument panel. Shown with available rally gauge cluster and Custom Sport wheel.

PONTIAC

BONNEVILLE BLOCK TWEED UPHOLSTERY
← (7639 BLT.)

3-SEAT WAGON WITH WOODGRAIN $5969. (5255 BLT.)
$5256.

(2894 2-SEAT WAGONS ALSO BLT.) PRICE = $5099.

74 B **(CONT'D.)**

Bonneville
Pontiac's original full-sized Wide Track
H/T $4572.

Grand Safari
Pontiac's full-sized station wagon

WAGON INTERIOR

1975 PONTIAC EXTERIOR FINISHES

A—STARLIGHT BLACK
Recommended interior colors:
Black, White, Sandstone, Saddle, Green, Blue, Burgundy

B—AUGUSTA GREEN
Recommended interior colors:
Black, White, Sandstone, Saddle

C—CAMEO WHITE
Recommended interior colors:
Black, White, Sandstone, Saddle, Green, Blue, Burgundy

D—ARCTIC BLUE
Recommended interior colors:
Black, White, Blue

E—STELLAR BLUE
Recommended interior colors:
Black, White, Blue

F—BIMINI BLUE
Recommended interior colors:
Black, White, Blue

G—CARMEL BEIGE
Recommended interior colors:
Black, White, Sandstone, Saddle

Catalina 123.4" WB
SEDAN $4612.

H—SANDSTONE
Recommended interior colors:
Black, White, Sandstone, Saddle

$5867. $5149. UP (WEST)

Catalina
Pontiac's lowest priced full-sized car.
$4700.

CATALINA SAFARI (3-SEAT)
H/T

V—STERLING SILVER
Recommended interior colors:
Black, White, Burgundy, Blue

J—GINGER BROWN
Recommended interior colors:
Black, White, Sandstone, Saddle

INTERIOR (40398 BLT.)

Z—PERSIMMON
Recommended interior colors:
Black, White, Saddle

75

(7320 BLT.)

N—ROMAN RED
Recommended interior colors:
Black, White

new SQUARE HEADLTS. ON SOME MODELS.
new GRILLES

L—LAKEMIST GREEN
Recommended interior colors:
Black, White, Green, Sandstone, Saddle

127" WB

$5433. UP **Grand Safari**

A—STARLIGHT BLACK
B—AUGUSTA GREEN
C—CAMEO WHITE
D—ARCTIC BLUE
E—STELLAR BLUE
F—BIMINI BLUE
G—CARMEL BEIGE
H—SANDSTONE
J—GINGER BROWN
K—OXFORD BROWN
L—LAKEMIST GREEN
M—ALPINE GREEN
N—ROMAN RED
P—HONDURAS MAROON
R—BUCCANEER RED
T—SUNSTORM YELLOW
U—FIRE CORAL BRONZE
V—STERLING SILVER
W—GRAYSTONE
X—TAMPICO ORANGE
Y—COPPER MIST
Z—PERSIMMON

U—FIRE CORAL BRONZE
Recommended interior colors:
Black, White, Sandstone, Saddle

Beautiful things are happening at your Pontiac dealer's!
400 CID V8 (170 OR 185 HP)
455 CID V8 (200 HP)

$5085. BNVL. COUPE OPERA WINDOW

RTS Radial Tuned Suspension

Bonneville
DASH

R—BUCCANEER RED
Recommended interior colors:
Black, White

Y—COPPER MIST
Recommended interior colors:
Black, White, Saddle

$5858.

TOTAL 1975 PROD. = 531,922

Grand Ville Brougham
Pontiac's most luxurious full-sized car.
126" WB

W—GRAYSTONE
Recommended interior colors:
Black, White, Sandstone, Saddle, Burgundy

K—OXFORD BROWN
Recommended interior colors:
Black, White, Sandstone, Saddle

(15686 BLT.)

M—ALPINE GREEN
Recommended interior colors:
Black, White, Green, Sandstone, Saddle

P—HONDURAS MAROON
Recommended interior colors:
Black, White, Burgundy

GRAND PRIX LJ TWO-TONE EXTERIOR FINISHES

P6—Dark Burgundy Lower, Honduras Maroon Hood & Deck Lid, Red Pinstriping and Burgundy Cordova Top.

B9—Dark Charcoal Lower, Sterling Silver Hood & Deck Lid, Red Pinstriping and Silver Cordova Top.

B2—Dark Charcoal Lower, Starlight Black Hood & Deck Lid, Red Pinstriping and Black Cordova Top.

GP DASH
(86582 BLT.)
116" WB

Grand Prix
Pontiac's classic personal car.

$5296. $6128. (WEST)

T—SUNSTORM YELLOW
Recommended interior colors:
Black, White, Sandstone, Saddle

X—TAMPICO ORANGE
Recommended interior colors:
Black, White, Sandstone, Saddle

PONTIAC 74 (B) ~ 75

696

PONTIAC

$5312.

$4767.

$5324. UP

Catalina Safari

Grand Safari

4-DR.
H/T

Bonneville

CATALINA
'A 4-DR. SEDAN ($5370.)
(WEST)
LOWEST PRICED FULL-SIZED PONTIAC.

76

new GRILLES

SJ

STD. GP COUPE $5377
SJ = $5802.
LJ = $6138.

Bonneville: 19 mpg Highway/13 mpg City (EPA)

CATALINA SIMILAR TO ABOVE CAR, BUT HAS 5 HVY. HORIZONTAL STRIPS ACROSS GRILLE.

400 and 450 CID V8s WITH HP AS IN 1975.

GP

STANDARD
Grand Prix. $4798*

WESTERN PRICE
$5377.)
(160 HP)

GP
350 CID

116"
WB

new "WATERFALL" GRILLE

(UNILLUSTRATED "LJ" has 2-TONE PAINT WITH SPECIAL STRIPING.)

DASH

$5120. UP
(228,430 BLT.)
GRAND PRIX

new GRILLE, WITH PCS. SPACED FURTHER APART.

new WHEELS

OTHER MODELS RESTYLED, DOWNSIZED (ON GP, LARGE
(SEE   CORNER
NEXT   LTS. REPL.
PG.)   BY *new* EXTRA
                              LT. BETWEEN
                              EACH PAIR OF
                              HEADLIGHTS,
                              AS SHOWN)

77
A

new 180 HP (SJ)

$5,109.*
(SALE)

PONTIAC ▼ THE MARK OF GREAT CARS

GRAND PRIX

REG. $5701. (LJ = $6064.)
(SJ = $6334.)   WESTERN PRICES

(CONT'D.
NEXT PAGE)

PONTIAC 76~77 (A)

697

Pontiac

This is the newest Bonneville since Wide-Track.

SEDAN new 116" WB

new DASH (GAUGES PLACED HIGH)

BONNEVILLE BROUGHAM (VINYL TOP)

WEST $6624.

$5992.

ALL-METAL TOP ↓ (47465 BLT.)

PONTIAC NAME ABOVE LTS.

new 231 CID V6 (105 HP)

77 **B** **(CONT'D.)**

new 301 CID V8 (135 HP)

TOTAL 1977 PROD. = 850,620

velour or

BONNEVILLE

BONNEVILLE

A beautiful new dash with easy-to-read gauges.

$5937. GRAND SAFARI WITH WOODGRAIN

INTERIOR

soft Morrokide

(CATALINA MODELS $5053. UP) (SEDAN)

3-SEAT GRAND SAFARI

(18304 BLT.)

PHANTOM VIEW, SHOWING HOW REAR DOOR OPENS SIDEWAYS OR SWINGS DOWN.

$6569. 1977

PONTIAC 77 (B)

698

Pontiac

CATALINA DASH $5484.

No austere dash for Catalina. With the new simulated walnut applique

Catalina SEDAN $5439.

(39707 BLT.)

Catalina

GRAND **Safari wagon** $7079.

CATALINA SAFARI FROM $6601. (12819 BLT.) $6011.

(9224 BLT.)

DASH

(13847 BLT.) $6319.

SEDAN (48647 BLT.)

$6023.

Bonneville

SALE: $5931.

(REG. $6608.) WEST

TOTAL 1978 PROD.= 900,380

SEDAN (36192 BLT.) $6784.

$7354.

Bonneville Brougham

301 CID V8 INCREASED TO 140 HP (V6 UNCHANGED)

1978 ▼ Pontiac's best year yet!

(GP RESTYLED) new 108" WB

FR/HR 78 x15 TIRES

new GRILLES 78

Grand Prix

(228,444 BLT.)

$5772.*

(REG. $6185.)

GP ORNAMENT

WESTERN PRICES SHOWN IN BLACK

GRAND PRIX DASH

GP

*25 mpg Highway, 18 City!

CATALINA

Catalina

← ORNAMENT

PONTIAC 78

699

PONTIAC

CATALINA and DASH

SEDAN
(28,121 BLT.)

new GRILLES

18 EPA ESTIMATE MPG **27** HWY ESTIMATE

79

$6076.
$6645.

V6 INCR. TO 115 HP (V8 UNCHANGED)

2-DR.
$6909. UP
$6593.

BONNEVILLE
AND. BNV. BROUGH.

SAFARI
2~SEAT
$7050.

3~SEAT
$7233.

SAFARI (16925 BLT.)

BNVL. and BNVL. BROUGH.
(179,416 BLT.)

WESTERN PRICES
SHOWN IN BLACK

GP "LJ"
(STRIPED)
WITH DE LUXE VINYL TOP

1979 TOTAL PROD. = 907,434

CLOSE-UP OF BONNEVILLE GRILLE, FRONT END

GRAND PRIX

LJ INTERIOR
$6555.

(210,050 GRAND PRIX H/Ts BLT.)

LJ
$6840.

195/75R14
205/70R14 (SJ)
TIRES

SJ =
$6814.

108" WB

$5454. UP (STD.)
FROM $6530.

231 CID V6
(115 HP)
EPA :

19 EPA EST MPG **25** HWY EST

THE 1979 PONTIACS ▼ OUR BEST GET BETTER

ALSO AVAIL : 301 CID
V8 (140/150 CID)

PONTIAC 79

700

PONTIAC

80

CATALINA
SEDAN (10408 BLT.)
$6761.
$7322. (WEST)

GAS MILEAGE =

(33/9 CATALINA COUPES BLT., AT $6703.)

231 CID V6 (115 HP)
OR *new 265* CID V8 (120 HP)

GRAND PRIX:			
20 EPA EST MPG	**27** HWY EST MPG	**362** MILES EST RANGE	**488** MILES HWY EST RANGE
GRAND LE MANS/GRAND LE MANS SAFARI:			
19 EPA EST MPG	**26** HWY EST MPG	**343** MILES EST RANGE	**470** MILES HWY EST RANGE

EPA HWY RANGE HWY. RANGE

BONNEVILLE INTERIOR

GIFTS

$7968.

↑ RESTYLED COUPE
(29/44 BLT. = BNVL. and BRM.)

BONNEVILLE BROUGHAM

BONNEVILLE and CATALINA NOW SHARE SAME GRILLE DESIGN.

Bonneville Brougham's available interior, with leather in the seating

↑ SEDAN
(47359 BLT. = BNVL. and BROUGHAM)

(LENGTH EXAGGERATED HERE)

$8160.

ACTUAL LENGTH

LEATHER SEATS AVAIL.

TOTAL 1980 PRODUCTION = 770,100

(2930 CATALINA SAFARIS BLT.)

(5309 BLT.)

SAFARI WAGON
(GRAND) (BONNEVILLE SERIES)

$7958.
$8570. (WEST) UP

(114,000 BLT.)

GRAND PRIX

LJ WITH OPT. T-BAR ROOF
$6621.~7597.

GP PRICES START AT $7096. (WEST)

More **P**ontiac **E**xcitement to the **G**allon — MPG

V6 OR *new 265* OR 301 CID V8 (120 OR 140 HP)

(WEST) { LJ = $7475.
{ SJ = $7993.

GP DASH

PONTIAC 80

PONTIAC COMPACTS **NEW**

new COMPACT CAR TEMPEST

TEMPEST

new 4-CYL. ENG. ADAPTED FROM THE RIGHT HALF OF A PONTIAC V8! *SLANTED*

FROM $**2329**. WEST COAST

2167.

TEMPEST new FOR 2438.

61 *new!*

61½ COUPE ROOF LINE

COUPES (STD. 6 PASS. or DLX. BUCKET SEATS) INTRO. IN MIDYEAR

112" wheelbase (THROUGH '63)

THE HOT TOPIC IS THE NEW TEMPEST BY PONTIAC

TROPHY 4 ENGINE

FOUR CYLINDERS

to **155 h.p.** (Or buy the 155 h.p. aluminum V-8 option.)

110 or 130 HP (STD.)

COUPE $**2113.** UP

4 (194.5 CID)

OR

V-8 (215 CID) 155 HP

Independent suspension at all wheels

CUSTOM (DLX.) '61½ COUPE has "TOWN CAR" REAR WINDOW.

FRONT ENGINE ⟷ REAR TRANSMISSION

PERFECT | BALANCE

PONTIAC'S TEMPEST
PICKED BY MOTOR TREND MAGAZINE AS
CAR OF THE YEAR

WITH
PONTIAC POWER STEERING (OPT.)

$**2113.**~**2622.** PRICE RANGE

STD. and *CUSTOM* MODELS
CALENDAR YEAR PRODUCTION = 115,945

SAFARI WAGON (REAR 3/4 VIEW)
$**2438.** TO **2622.**

PONTIAC COMPACTS 61

PONTIAC TEMPEST

STANDARD TEMPEST COUPE has BROAD BACKLIGHT, MINIMUM CHROME

COMPACTS $2186.

$2240.

new GRILLE

62

CUSTOM COUPE has "TOWN CAR" BACKLIGHT

$2297.

194½ CID 4 CYL. WITH 110, 115, 120, 140, OR 166 HP. 185-HP ALUMINUM V8 ALSO AVAIL. (215 CID)

new LE MANS $3200. (WEST COAST)

STD. WAGON

$2511. UP

The gas-saving "4" with Pontiac Punch!

LE MANS

MODELS:
COUPE (15,473 STD.)
SPT. ", CUSTOM (12,319 DLX.; 39,662 LE MANS)
4-DR. (16,057 STD.; 21,373 DLX.)

4 DR. WAGON (6504 STD.; 11,170 DLX.)
CONVERTIBLE (5076 DLX.; 15,559 LE MANS)
(CUSTOM = DLX.)

TOTAL 1962 PRODUCTION: 143,193

new TAIL LIGHTS 4 CYL. 195.4 CID (115-166 HP) TEMPEST (NAME RETURNS TO FRONT FENDER)

(10,135 BLT.) $2512. UP

AR 9186

$2241. UP

(28,221 BLT.)

CVT. WITH TOP DOWN $2142.

LE MANS

new 326 CID V8 ALSO AVAILABLE (260 HP)

$2418. (45,701 BLT.)

LE MANS has RECTANGULAR TAIL-LIGHTS, "LE MANS" ON FRONT FENDER.

new GRILLE

63

LE MANS CVT. (15,957 BLT.)

WITH TOP UP

TOTAL 1963 PRODUCTION: 143,6?6

LE MANS

Wide-Track Pontiac Tempest

PONTIAC COMPACTS 62~63

703

PONTIAC
COMPACTS
64
(RESTYLED)

$2313. SEDAN (19,427 BLT.)

$2259. SPT. COUPE (6365 BLT.)

Tempest

new 115" WB
new 215 CID
140-HP IN-LINE
O.H.V. 6

Tempest
CUSTOM
$2345.

SAFARI WAGON $2605. UP

CUST. SPT. CPE. (25,833 BLT.)

326 CID V8 ALSO AVAIL.
(250 OR 280 HP)

LE MANS SPT. CPE.
$2491.

(H/T $2556.)

(29,948 BLT.)
(31,317 BLT.)

$2399.

$2641.

CUSTOM CONVERTIBLE (7987 BLT.)

PONTIAC

1964

GTO ("GTO" APPEARS ON GRILLE) (new)

LE MANS

REAR DETAILS

CVT. (17,559 BLT.)
$2796.

$2259. ~ 3500. PRICE RANGE
TOTAL 1964 PRODUCTION: 250,328

GTO SPT. CPE. (7384 BLT.)	$3200.
H/T (18,422 BLT.)	3250.
CONVT. (6644 BLT.)	3500.

PONTIAC COMPACTS 64

PONTIAC

COMPACTS

$2605.

$2313.

(15,705 BLT.)

223
TEMPEST

SAFARI WAGON
(5622 BLT.)

Tempest

FROM
$2618.
(WEST COAST)

65

new GRILLES
new TAIL LIGHTS
2411.

H/T
(new)

CUSTOM H/T
(29,906 BLT.)
$2411.

(29906 BLT.)

140-HP 6 (215 CID)
OR
250-285 HP V8
(326 CID)

235
TEMPEST CUSTOM

H/T

SAFARI
4-DR. WAGON
(10,792 BLT.)
$2619.

LE MANS H/T
(60,548 BLT.)

SEDAN $2400. (25242 BLT.)

$2556.

LE MANS SPT. CPE.
(18,881 BLT.) $2491.

237
Le Mans

FRONT-END COMPARISON
OF LE MANS (left) and GTO (right)

CVT.
(13,897 BLT.)
$2797.

SEE
ALSO:
Pontiac

GTO CVT.
(11,311 BLT.) ➞

OFFICIAL PACE CAR·MOTOR TREND RIVERSIDE "500"
COURTESY OF
HURST

$3057.

GTO

TOTAL 1965 PRODUCTION:
326,019

GTO H/T (55,722 BLT.)
(GTO SPT. CPE. AVAIL.-8319 BLT.-$2751.)

$2816.

$2260. ~ 3057. PRICE RANGE

PLAIN TAIL LTS. ON ← LOW PRICED MODELS

TEMPEST OHC SPRINT

(SPRINT PKG.)

1966 PRODUCTION: 384,794

$2278. ~ 3082. PRICE RANGE

(230 CID OHC 6, 165 HP)
207 HP @ 5200 RPM, SPRINT
OR 326 CID V8 (250 HP)
115" WB

(160-MPH SPEEDOMETER and TACH. on SPRINT)

PONTIAC
COMPACTS

$2568.
LE MANS

$3006. (H/T)

CVT. FROM $3093. (WEST) $2665. (BASE PRICE)

(5557 BLT.)

66

(REAR) GTO

(TEMPEST, CUSTOM, LE MANS OR GTO MODELS)

1966

(78,109 BLT.)

GTO

GTO has RALLY LTS., "GTO" on GRILLE.

GTO has 389 CID V8 (335 HP)

The tiger scores again! Wide-Track Pontiac/'66

"GTO" MEANS "GRAN TURISMO OMOLOGATO"

CVT. $3425. (WEST)

(12,798 BLT.)

DELUXE STEER. WHEEL HAS HORN BUTTONS IN SPOKES.

$2341. ~ 3165. PRICE RANGE

1967 PROD. = 288,924

$3165.

/67

GTO CVT. (9517 BLT.)
$3547. (WEST)

HOOD SCOOP DETAIL

SAME HP AS 1966, EXCEPT new 215 HP IN SPRINT

$2935.

RALLY I

$3317. (WEST)

Pontiac GTO

67

(65,176 BLT.)

has F 70 x 14 TIRES

new GRILLES (TEMPEST FROM $2787.)

RALLY II

LE MANS

H/T $3094. (WEST)

7.75 x 14 TIRES

$2648. (75,965 BLT.)

PONTIAC COMPACTS 66~67

PONTIAC
COMPACTS
LE MANS

250 cɪᴅ OHC 6 (175 oʀ 215 HP)
350 cɪᴅ V8 (265 oʀ 320 HP)
oʀ 400 cɪᴅ V8
(265, 350 oʀ 360 HP)

TEMPEST

7.75/8.25 x 14" TIRES

H/T
(110,036
BLT.)
$2786.

new CONCEALED
WINDSHIELD
WIPERS

2 DR.
112" WB
116" = 4 DR.

TEMPEST
and
TEMPEST
CUSTOM
SHARE
LE MANS
STYLING.
$2509. UP

Wide-Track **1968** Pontiacs
RESTYLED **68**

GMAC
TIME PAYMENT
PLAN
General Motors Acceptance Corporation

$3101.

GTO has 400 cɪᴅ V8 (4 BBL)
(265 oʀ 350 HP)
3-SPEED HURST SHIFTER
AVAIL.

H/T
(77,704
BLT.)

←GTO

G-TO
has
new
CONCEALED
HEAD-
LIGHTS
CVT.
(9980 BLT.)
$3227.

We've just received our 4th Car of the Year award.

PONTIAC COMPACTS 68

PONTIAC COMPACTS

ALL RISE FOR **THE JUDGE**

"ENDURA" SCRATCH/DENT-RESISTANT FRONT END IS BODY-COLORED

SPOILER

The Judge: a special GTO by Pontiac

(64851 BLT.) **GTO** 3156

H/T $3544. (WEST)

69 new GRILLES

250 CID 6 (175 HP)
STD. 350 CID V8 (265 HP)

DASH (JUDGE)
RED-ORANGE IS STD. COLOR OF "JUDGE"
400 CID V8 (366-370 366 to 370 HP)

H/T (82,817 BLT.) **LE MANS** $2835.

H/T $3292. (WEST)

The year of the great Pontiac break away

$2510. ~ 3382. PRICE RANGE

GM MARK OF EXCELLENCE

WATER SPORTS

$3382.

ON-HOOD TACHOMETER and HURST SHIFTER ILLUSTRATED

GTO CONVERTIBLE (7436 BLT.)

G78 x 14" TIRES
400 CID V8 (350 HP) STD. IN GTO *

(* = 366 or 370 HP OPT.)

$3770. (WEST)

PONTIAC COMPACTS 69

PONTIAC
COMPACTS
LE MANS

TEMPEST FRONT DETAILS

70

$2735. UP

LE MANS SPORT has THIS DECORATION

$2891. SPORT CPE.

(1673 BLT.)

4-DR. H/T

$3083. (3657 BLT.)

H/T $2683.

(120883 BLT.)

(FINAL USE OF TEMPEST MODEL NAME)

TEMPEST SEDAN (9187 BLT.)

$2670.

INTERIOR

LE MANS SPORT

H/T $2953.

(58356 BLT.)

LE MANS FRONT DETAILS

PONTIAC

DM 70-36

250-cube, 155-hp six. You can also specify a 350-cube V-8, or one of two 400-cube V-8's (255 - 350 HP)

WAGON INTERIOR

REAR

$3328. (3823 BLT.)

LeMans Safari

(7165 BLT.)

$3092. 2-SEAT LeMans Wagon

GTO CVT.

$3492.

GTO
HEADLIGHTS NO LONGER CONCEALED

H/T

70-1000

$3267.
(36366 BLT.) GTO Hardtop Coupe

F78/ G78 x 14 TIRES

AVAIL. 455 CID V8 (335 HP; 310 NET HP) (350~370 HP AVAIL.)

THE JUDGE H/T

PONTIAC COMPACTS 70

PONTIAC
COMPACTS

new 2-WAY TAILGATE SWINGS ASIDE OR DOWN.

LeMans Wagon $3353. UP

250 CID 6 (145 HP) TO 455 CID V8 (335 HP; 310 NET HP)

(6311 2-SEAT)
(4363 3 SEAT)

71 T-37 H/T

THE JUDGE

$3840.

(357 BLT. and ONLY 17 JUDGE CONVERTIBLES) ($4070.)

(9497 BLT.)

LeMans

(29466)

COUPES 112" WB (116" OTHERS)

WAGON GRILLE

E78 x 14 TIRES

2807

GTO (CVT. ALSO AVAIL.) (661 BLT.) ($3676.)

new LOWEST-PRICED PONTIAC SERIES 111" WB

$3446.

DASH

(INTRO. SUMMER, 1971)

Ventura II

250 CID 6 (145 HP) OR 307 CID V8 (200 HP)

NEW $2488.

SEDAN (13803 BLT.) (21584, '72) ($2454., '72)

SPRINT COUPE
DISTINGUISHED BY HEAVY SIDE-STRIPE

COUPE (34681 BLT.) (51203, '72) $2458. ($2426., '72)

71½ -72 A

note DISTINCTIVE 4-PC. GRILLE, SINGLE HEADLTS.

$2654. (WEST)

PONTIAC   COMPACTS 71-72(A)

PONTIAC COMPACTS

Available: All Pontiac Models (except Trans AM)

J—BRASILIA GOLD

LeMans $3690.

$2814.

D—ADRIATIC BLUE

72

B "GTO" ON LOWER REAR FENDER

(19463 BLT.)
LeMANS 4-DOOR SEDAN

$2722.

(6855 BLT.)
LeMANS COUPE

$3598.

GTO

GTO HARDTOP COUPE

$2851. UP

(80383 HTs BLT.)

G—BRITTANY BEIGE

AVAIL.

L—SPRINGFIELD GREEN

R—CARDINAL RED

LE MANS
(WITH ENDURA FRONT END OPTION)

GTO has SAME FRONT AS ABOVE, EXCEPT FOR "GTO" INSTEAD OF "PONTIAC" ON GRILLE.

$2851. UP

H—SHADOW GOLD

LeMans
GT
H/T CPE.
(note SIDE TRIM)

$3378.

(5266 BLT.)
2-SEAT GRAND LE M. (GRAINED)

$4147.

M—WILDERNESS GREEN

$3228

$4104.

(FINAL LE M. CVT.) LeMANS SPORT CONVERTIBLE

LeMans Sport
(3438 BLT.)

(note THE DIFFERENCES AMONG GRILLES OF VARIOUS LE MANS TYPES ON THIS PAGE)

C—CAMEO WHITE

LeMans Station Wagons

N—REVERE SILVER

Luxury LeMans
(new)

$3319.

(8641 BLT.)
LUXURY LeMANS 4-DOOR HARDTOP

4-DR. H/T $4077.

STD. 350 CID V8 CUT TO 160 HP.

$3196.

400 OR 455 CID V8s ALSO AVAIL.

VINYL ROOF and CREST DETAIL ABOVE

2-DR. H/T $3954.

(37615 BLT.)

Available: Ventura xx, Firebird, Esprit, Formula, LeMans, GTO, Luxury LeMans, Grand Prix

E—QUEZAL GOLD
Recommended Interior Colors: Beige (Covert), Black, Ivory, Saddle, Tan

F—LUCERNE BLUE
Recommended Interior Colors: Black, Blue, Ivory, Pewter

S—ANACONDA GOLD
Recommended Interior Colors: Beige (Covert), Black, Ivory, Saddle, Tan

Y—MONARCH YELLOW
Recommended Interior Colors: Beige (Covert), Black, Ivory, Saddle, Tan

Z—SUNDANCE ORANGE
Recommended Interior Colors: Beige (Covert), Black, Ivory, Saddle, Tan

K—JULEP GREEN
Recommended Interior Colors: Beige (Covert), Black, Ivory, Saddle, Tan

Available: Ventura xx, Firebird, Esprit, Formula

9

(SMALLER COLOR SAMPLES ABOVE ARE AVAIL. ON MOST '72 PONTIACS.)

PONTIAC COMPACTS 72

PONTIAC

COMPACTS

250 CID 6 (100 HP)
new 350 CID V8
(150 HP)
$2603.
(26335 BLT.)
FROM
$2660.

'73 Ventura.

(VENTURA CUSTOM ALSO)

DASH

VENTURA NO LONGER KNOWN AS "VENTURA II" —
Ventura, Ventura Custom

new LOUVRED REAR QUARTER WINDOW DETAIL

(49/53 BLT.)

$2452. UP

new BUMPERS

new GRILLES

73 A

$3008. Introducing LeMans Sport Cpe.

(50999 BLT.)
$3867.

Le Mans.

(LUXURY LE MANS has 8 HEAVY VERT. GRILLE PCS.)

LUXURY LE MANS

(9377 BLT.)
(339/6 CPES. ALSO)

$3344. $4129. (CONT'D. NEXT PAGE)

Starlight Black | Mesa Tan | Burnished Umber

Cameo White | Porcelain Blue | Admiralty Blue | Regatta Blue | Desert Sand | Golden Olive | Verdant Green | Slate Green | Brewster Green | Florentine Red | Ascot Silver | Valencia Gold | Burma Brown | Buccaneer Red | Sunlight Yellow | Navajo Orange

LeMans Safari, LeMans Sport Coupe, Luxury LeMans, Grand Am, Catalina, Bonneville, Grand Ville, Grand Prix, Safari, and Grand Safari models.

Available all Ventura, Ventura Custom, Firebird, Esprit, and Formula models.

Available all LeMans.

1973 PONTIAC COLORS

PONTIAC COMPACTS 73 (A)

PONTIAC
COMPACTS

LE MANS 2-DR. COLONNADE H/T (68230 BLT.)
$2920.
G60 x 15 TIRLS

GTO PACKAGE
F70 x 14 TIRES

73 B

GRAND AM

CPE. 112" WB

(new)

$2920.

$4264.

$4969. (34443 BLT.)

$4353. 4-DR. (8691 BLT.)

$5058. (WEST)

Introducing the first Grand Am.

400 CID V8 (170 HP) GR 70 x 15 TIRES

Grand Am
(SIDE INSIGNIA)

WESTERN PRICES SHOWN IN BLACK

SOFT HUB

GRAND AM DASH

The Wide-Track people have a way with cars.

LE MANS DASH

Ventura
Pontiac's low-priced compact car.

Ventura Custom Sprint in Sunstorm Yellow.

250 CID 6 (100 HP)
350 CID V8 ← (150 HP OR 155 HP) →

LE MANS
2-DR. COLONNADE H/T

$3176.

Ventura Custom Hatchback Coupe in Carmel Beige.

74 A

VENTURA CUSTOM

new TAIL-LTS.

$3869.

new GRILLES

$3055.

VENTURA GTO
(CONT'D. NEXT PAGE)
PONTIAC COMPACTS 73-4

PONTIAC COMPACTS

WESTERN PRICES SHOWN *IN BLACK*

RTS Radial Tuned Suspension

$4114.

$4373.

(3004 BLT.)

LE MANS SAFARI (3-SEAT)
$4186.

Luxury LeMans

A hatchback wagon? Almost. This Luxury LeMans Safari liftgate allows easy loading in tight situations.

The Wide-Track people have a way with cars.

(25882 BLT.)

$3703.

74 (CONT'D.)
B

$4052. UP
LUXURY LE MANS SAFARI

FROM $4513.

(952 2-SEAT)
(1178 3-SEAT)

FROM $4806.
(13961 CPES.)
(3122 SEDANS)

Grand Am
new 175 HP
$4534.

Introducing the first subcompact Pontiac Astre.

140 CID 4
(78 HP)
(87 HP
IN "SJ"
MODELS)
97" WB

$2891.00*
(SALE)

(8339 BLT.)

37 MPG

Astre S Notchback Coupe

(REG. $3139.)

A78 × 13
TIRES
(40809 HATCHBACKS BLT.)

$2954. UP

ASTRE (new)

$3369.
(15332 WAGONS BLT. IN 3 MODELS)

SJ $3851.

(REG. $3139. UP)

ASTRE SJ
DASH (BELOW) has FULL
RALLY INSTRUMENTATION

75A
(new GRILLES)

$3686.

SJ SAFARI $3927.

BR 78 × 13

(CONT'D.
NEXT PAGE)

ST'D. SAFARI!

GT SAFARI!

The sporty Astre GT Safari gets a 2-bbl. carburetor, Rally wheels and gauges, a stiffer suspension, steel-belted radials, our Maximum Mileage System and some very sporty trim.

The luxurious Astre SJ Safari has our Radial Tuned Suspension with steel-belted radial tires. New finned Rally III wheels. Rally gauges. A 4-speed. And what has to be one of the plushest interiors ever put in an American subcompact.

PONTIAC COMPACTS 74 (B)-75 (A)

B—AUGUSTA GREEN | C—CAMEO WHITE
F—BIMINI BLUE | G—CARMEL BEIGE | H—SANDSTONE
M—ALPINE GREEN | P—HONDURAS MAROON | R—BUCCANEER RED
T—SUNSTORM YELLOW | U—FIRE CORAL BRONZE | X—TAMPICO ORANGE

PONTIAC

COMPACTS $3464. $4334

VENTURA CUSTOM 4-DR.

DASH (22068 SEDANS)

Pontiac strikes again.

$3432. UP

HATCHBACK $4302.

(10463 HATCHBACKS)

Ventura's standard instrument panel. The custom cushion steering wheel is standard on Ventura Custom, Sprint and SJ. It's available on Ventura.

VENTURA
250 CID 6 (105 HP)

$3829.

WESTERN PRICES SHOWN IN BLACK

Ventura SJ.

$4699. (CPE.)
4716. (HATCH.)
4824. (4-DR.)

75B (CONT'D.)

(34023 COUPES)

LeMans Safari (2393 BLT.)
(3-SEAT)
$5207.

$4749.

$4101.

Grand LeMans (19310 BLT.)

4688.

2-DR. COLONNADE (20636 BLT.)

LeMans $3590.

H/T CPE.

Pontiac 350 and 400 V-8s

350 CID V8 (155 HP)

$4605.

Grand LeMans Safari

$3612. (15065 BLT.) $4627.

$4882. $5401. (1501 BLT.) (3-SEAT)

$4976.

CPE. ROOF LINE

Grand Am.

DASH 71

1975

$5495.

Grand Am

(1893 BLT.) SEDAN

(NO MORE GRAND AMS UNTIL 1978)

400 CID V8 (170 HP)

Wheels and Wheel Covers

Options $4157.

Grand LeMans (4906 BLT.)

4-Door Colonnade Hardtop Sedan PONTIAC COMPACTS 75(B)

PONTIAC

COMPACTS

LE MANS

SED.   CPE.

DASH VENTURA

VENTURA GRILLE $3775.

DASH VENTURA

LE MANS DASH

$3590. UP

H/B CPE.

ASTRE $3064.

The Mark of Great Cars.

subcompact Astre

FR. $3377.

ASTRE $3306.

ASTRE

Sunbird

VENTURA
250 CID 6
260 CID V8
(BOTH 110 HP)
IN VENT. OR
LE M., GR. LE M.

140 CID 4 (70 HP)
(ASTRE OR SUNBIRD)

4101.

DASH
(GR. LE M.)

1976 PONTIAC GRAND LeMANS.

76

new GRILLES

$4928. UP

WB 97"
(231 CID
V6 AVAIL.)

(new)

(5357 BLT.)

ASTRE SAFARI WAGON   ASTRE HATCHBACK

$3784.

SUNBIRD SPORT HATCH

37 26   37 26

MPG/HIGHWAY   MPG/CITY   MPG/HIGHWAY   MPG/CITY

SUNBIRD

$4226

4101.

"IRON DUKE"
151 CID 87 HP 4-CYL.
ENG. (STD. 140 CID
has 84 HP)

77
A

new GRILLES

SPT. CPE.

THIS STYLE CPE. ALSO AVAIL. 1976

PHOENIX FROM $5060.
(2-DR.)

PHOENIX
(111.1" WB)

(NEW)
WITH
151 CID 4 (87 HP)
231 CID V6
(105 HP) OR
301 CID V8
(135 HP)

WESTERN PRICES
SHOWN
IN BLACK

PONTIAC ▼ THE MARK OF GREAT CARS

PONTIAC COMPACTS 76~77 (A)

PONTIAC
COMPACTS
77B
(CONT'D.)

GRAND LE MANS
and DASH

THE FINAL **Ventura**
$3650. UP

4-CYL., 231 CID V6 (105 HP), OR 301 CID V8 (135 HP)

$4635. UP (WEST)

$4742.

SEDAN (5584 BLT.)

$5520. (WEST)

$3541

SUNBIRD *new* 231 CID V6 $3590. UP

(18433 BLT.)

COUPE $4801.

Grand LeMans SEDAN **Resized**

(21252 BLT.)

85 HP 4 OR 105 HP V6 (SUNBIRD WAGON *has* ONLY 2 ROUND HEADLTS. and FEWER VERT. PCS. IN GRILLE.)

$4915.
$6186. (WEST)

new 108" W.B.

Phoenix 78

LE MANS DASH

REAR $4980. UP

Pontiac's best year yet!

27 mpg Hwy. 19 mpg City! These are EPA estimates for LeMans with its std. 3.8 litre (231 CID) 2-bbl. V-6 and available auto. trans.

LE MANS SAFARI WAGON

FROM $5866. (WEST)

$6091. UP (WEST) $5520. UP

(7767 COUPES, 2841 SEDANS)

(STD. LE MANS FROM $4427.)

GRAND AM RETURNS 301 CID V8 (140 HP)

108.1" WB

LE MANS GRILLE

PONTIAC COMPACTS 77(B)-78

PONTIAC
COMPACTS

SUNBIRD

A78 x 13
TIRES
(SINCE '76)

FROM $4276.

$4274.
(70647 BLT.)

Sunbird

DASH $4321.
(2902 BLT.)

SUNBIRD
"FORMULA"
PACKAGE
INCLUDES
EXTRAS SHOWN
(REAR SPOILER
ALSO)

SUNBIRD
SPORT SAFARI
$4633.
(INTRO. '78
@ $4181.)

WESTERN PRICES
SHOWN
IN BLACK

FORMULA

SOME MODELS
WITH
new GRILLES

79
A

SUNBIRD
GRILLE CLOSE-UP

SUNBIRD INT.

note AVAIL. VINYL-COVERED
LANDAU TOP on PHOENIX CPE.

(9233 BLT.) $4089.

$5274.

PHOENIX
INTERIOR
(CONT'D.
NEXT PAGE)

PHOENIX

$4689.

SEDAN
(2353
BLT.)

LJ $5874.

LJ GRILLE

27

PONTIAC COMPACTS 79 (A)

PONTIAC COMPACTS

OUR BEST GET BETTER

GRAND LE MANS SEDAN

$5430.

(28599 BLT.) $6410.

231 CID V6 (115 HP)
301 CID V8 (140 HP)

79
B
(CONT'D.)

$5031. UP

$6085.

LE MANS

COUPE (4021 BLT.) $5530.

$6338.

$5587. UP (GRAND SAFARIS ALSO)

(27517 BLT.)

SAFARI WAGON $6222. UP

REAR

GRAND AM
BUCKET SEATS (SEDANS ALSO, 1865 BLT. $5529.)

80
GRAND AM

GRAND AM DASH

new GRILLES
GRAND AM

151 CID 4 (86 HP)
231 CID V6 (115 HP)

8
0
A

COUPES ONLY (1647 GRAND AMS) $7504.

SUNBIRD
STD. CPE. $4915.

WITH STD. SIDE MIRROR and WHEEL COVERS

A78 x 13 TIRES (SINCE '76)

$4885. UP

You'll recognize this 'Bird by its distinctive tail feathers. Sunbird Sport Hatch, shown with available Formula Package.

SUNBIRD $5274. PLUS FORM. PKG.

SUNBIRD

(187,619 1980 SUNBIRDS, COUPES AND HATCHBACKS)

SPT. CPE. $5164.

(CONT'D. NEXT PAGE)

PONTIAC COMPACTS 79(B)~80(A)

PONTIAC
COMPACTS

PHOENIX

5-DR. HATCHBACK

ROUND-HUB STEERING WHEEL ALSO

PHOENIX

22 EPA ESTIMATE MPG **33** HWY ESTIMATE

$5465. UP

COUPE
(STD. 49485 BLT.)
(LJ 23674 BLT.)

REAR DETAIL (HBK.)

LJ WHEEL

151 CID 4 (90 HP)
173 CID V6 (115 HP)

80 B (CONT'D.)

PHOENIX

MORE **P**ONTIAC **MPG** TO THE **G**ALLON

(72875 BLT.)
(PLUS 32256 LJ HATCHBKS.)
5656. UP

$6682.

UPHOLST.

$5652.

DASH

LE MANS

COUPE

(9109 BLT.) $6799.

231 CID V6 (115 HP) OR
265 CID V8 (120 HP)

GRAND LE MANS

SEDAN (18561 BLT.)
$6120.

$8371. UP

GRAND LE MANS SAFARI
(14832 BLT.)

PONTIAC COMPACTS 80 (B)

GRAND LE MANS/GRAND LE MANS SAFARI:
19 EPA EST MPG **26** HWY EST MPG **343 MILES** EST RANGE **470 MILES** HWY EST RANGE

MORE **P**ONTIAC **MPG** **E**XCITEMENT TO THE **G**ALLON $7523.

PUP MOTOR CAR CO., SPENCER, WIS.

PUP

(1947-1949)

TOP SPEED 35~40 M.P.H.

50~60 AVG. MPG

1 OR 2 CYL., 7½ OR 10 HP

48-49

(WOODEN BODIES)

$500.

(PRICES APPROX.)

REAR ENGINE

$600.

AT NASH DEALERS

Rambler

6 CYL. (172.6 CID)

(1950 - 1969)

TOP DOWN

TOP UP

$1808., f.o.b.

(CVT. OR WAGON)

100" WB

all new

50

ENGINE: 172.6 CID 6 (82 HP)

(THROUGH '52)

"RAMBLER" NAME REVIVED BY NASH FOR THIS NEW COMPACT SERIES. CVT. INTRO. 3-50; WAGON 5-50

MODEL 5021
New Rambler Convertible Landau
(CUSTOM SERIES)

51-52

new "SUPER"

$1968. ('51) 2094. ('52)
MODEL 5127 (5227)

"COUNTRY CLUB" HARDTOP
INTRO. 6-51

SUBURBAN MODEL 5114 (5214)

('51) $1885.
('52) 2003.

57,555 RAMBLERS BLT. 1951; 53,055 RAMBLERS SOLD IN 1952

FIRST 2 DIGITS OF MODEL NUMBER INDICATE YEAR OF CAR

CONVERTIBLE CONTINUES $2119. ('52)

EST. PRODUCTION TOTAL : 1950 (21,674)

PUP / RAMBLER   50~52

RAMBLER $2150.

CUSTOM

5321 CVT.

5324 2-DR. WAGON $2119.

85 HP (90 with Hydra-Matic)

53

$2125.

5327 COUNTRY CLUB H/T

GREENBRIER

SUPER 2-DR. SUBURBAN IS LOWEST-PRICED : $**2003.**, f.o.b.

ENGINES : new 184 cid 6 (85 HP)
new 195.6 cid 6 (95 HP w. AUTO TRANS.)

TOTAL 1953 PRODUCTION : 41,825

$2003.~2150. PRICE RANGE

5406 CLUB SEDAN

new DE LUXE

NASH and HUDSON MERGE TO CREATE AMC (AMERICAN MOTORS CORP.) MAY 1, 1954

SUPER

$1800.

5417

$1550.

$1800.

5414 SUBURBAN WAGON

COUNTRY CLUB H/T

54

100" and 108" WB

Nash Motors, Division of
AMERICAN MOTORS CORP.
DETROIT, MICH.

$1980.

$1965.

5425 CUSTOM SEDAN

5421 CONVT.

CUSTOM

note LUGGAGE RACK AND DIP IN REAR ROOFLINE

TOTAL 1954 PROD. : 37,779

$2050.

REAR DETAILS (CROSS-COUNTRY)

new 4-DR. "CROSS-COUNTRY" WAGON (5428)
RAMBLER 53~54

RAMBLER a Whole **New Idea** in Automobiles

$1869.

5514

DELUXE 5515

ALL-WEATHER-EYE

SUPER SUBURBAN WAGON

NEW IDEA! *Touch this knob—and it will always be springtime in your Rambler. No cold in winter! No heat in summer! No dust or traffic roar! You breathe only fresh, filtered air. It's American Motors' All-Season Air Conditioning®— greatest health, comfort, safety feature of fifty years. Needs no trunk space. And you buy a Rambler so equipped for less than the price of an ordinary car!*
Patents applied for

PRICES START AT

$ **1585.**,
f.o.b.
(DLX. 2-DR.)

$1995.

5517-2
COUNTRY CLUB

CUSTOM H/T

$1995.

ON 9-22-55, FINAL AMC CAR ASSEMBLED AT EL SEGUNDO, CALIF. BRANCH FACTORY, *with* "DC-" SERIAL NUMBERS. KENOSHA, WIS. FACTORY CONTINUES *with* "D-" SERIAL NUMBERS AS USUAL.

new GRILLE *with* CRISS-CROSS PIECES

55

"FLEET" BUDGET MODEL 2 DR. SEDAN, 2-DR. WAGON *and* 4 DR. WAGON AVAIL.

195.6 CID 6 (90 OR 100 HP

$1585. ~ 2098.
PRICE RANGE

TOTAL 1955 PRODUCTION: 83,852

$2096.

INTERIOR (H/T)

CROSS-COUNTRY
5518

1955½, WITH "SPRING SPECIAL" TRIM

HUDSON RAMBLER

NASH RAMBLER
(DETERMINE BY NAME-PLATE ON GRILLE)

NOW AT *Nash* DEALERS AND HUDSON DEALERS EVERYWHERE

American Motors

RAMBLER 55

RAMBLER

You'll make the
Smart Switch for '56

Product of American Motors

AMERICAN MOTORS MEANS ⚡ MORE FOR AMERICANS

See Disneyland—great TV for all the family over ABC network.

YOU SAVE ON FIRST COST.
Model for model, Rambler is lowest-priced of all, with similar equipment, yet you get luxuries that rival the $5,000 cars—Power Brakes standard on custom models!

YOU SAVE ⅓ ON GASOLINE.
New Typhoon OHV engine, with 33% more power, delivers up to 200 more miles on a tankful than other low-price cars.

DE LUXE
5615

$1829.

SUPER
5618-1

$2230

America's lowest-priced 4-door station wagon, delivered at the factory, including federal taxes. State and local taxes (if any), white wall tires and optional equipment (if desired), extra.

new 120-HP SIX *with*
OVERHEAD VALVES

new BROADER GRILLE
ENCOMPASSES
HEADLIGHTS

56
(RESTYLED)
108" WB ON ALL

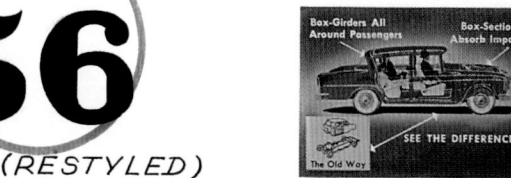

Make the Smart Switch to Double Safe Single Unit Car Construction. All-welded, twice as rigid with "double lifetime" durability—means higher resale value.

NOTE VARIATIONS
IN UPPER SIDE TRIM →

CUSTOM
SEDAN
5615-2

Make the Smart Switch to the car that out-corners, out-parks them all. Entirely new ride—first low-priced car with Deep Coil Springs on all four wheels.

$2059.

$1829.~2494.
PRICE RANGE

TOTAL 1956 PRODUCTION: 79,162
(OR 79,166)

"Make the Smart Switch to Rambler!"

$2224.

SPARE TIRE
AT
REAR
("CONTINENTAL
KIT")

new COLOR SPEAR SIDE~
MOULDINGS ON CUSTOM

2 VIEWS OF *new*
4-DOOR
H/T
5619-2

Make the Smart Switch to Airliner Reclining Seat luxury. You have a nap couch to keep children fidget-free on trips, relax grown-ups. Even a chaise longue!

new ROLL-DOWN REAR
DOOR WINDOW →
5618-2

New Rambler Cross Country Station Wagon! Enjoy more fun per mile and per dollar in America's lowest-priced four-door Custom Station Wagon.

CUSTOM

FLASH! RAMBLER TOPS MOBILGAS ECONOMY RUN FOR 2nd STRAIGHT YEAR! **24.35** m.p.g. with Hydra-Matic Drive!

$2329.

OVERDRIVE AVAIL.
RAMBLER 56

RAMBLER

(6) 5715-2
(V8) 5723-2

CUSTOM

new 190 H.P. V·8
And Economy 6

5718-1 (6)
5728-1 (V8)

$2213. (6)
2343. (V8)

(6) $2410. →
(V8) $2540.

5718-2 (6)
5728-2 (V8)
CROSS—COUNTRY
WAGON

SUPER

GEORGE ROMNEY
PRESIDENT, AMERICAN MOTORS
(UNTIL 2-62)

$2500. (6)
2630. (V8)

new REBEL V8

5739-2

255 HP
327 CID V8

↑ CUSTOM

AVAIL. AS REGULAR
OR HARDTOP
WAGON ↘

6.70 x 15

(1500 BLT.)
CUSTOM REBEL 4-DR. H/T $2786.

$1961. ~ 2786. PRICE RANGE

$2715.

5723-2 (V8)

ENGINES :
195.6 CID 6 (135 HP)
new 250 CID V8 (190 HP)
new 327 CID V8 (255 HP)

SIDE MOULDINGS
CHANGED

$2428.

57
20 MODELS

6.70 x 15

Rambler Custom

SMALL EXTRA PIECE
ADDED, IN TOP SECTION
OF GRILLE

5729-2 (V8)

114,084
RAMBLERS BLT.
CALENDAR YEAR, 1957

(91,469 MODEL YEAR)

RAMBLER

5802 OR 5806

new AMERICAN 6
(100" WB)
42,196 SOLD

5815

DE LUXE 6
$2047.

$1775., f.o.b. and up

5815-1

127 HP 6 SUPER

58

new GRILLES

new TAIL-FINS
(ON ALL BUT AMERICAN)

MORE THAN 100 IMPROVEMENTS!
22 MODELS

CUSTOM 6

215-HP REBEL V8

REAR DETAILS

INTRODUCED FOR 1958,
new AMERICAN and AMBASSADOR
MODELS have
OWN GRILLES, DIFFERENT
FROM THOSE OF
OTHER RAMBLERS.

$2532. →

REBEL V8
CUSTOM COUNTRY CLUB
4 DR. H/T

5829-2

DASH

5888-1 OR 2

new AMBASSADOR V8 117" WB
new = 4 HEADLIGHTS
270 HP
(THROUGH '59)

5889-2

$2822., f.o.b.

new "DEEP-DIP" RUSTPROOFING

ENGINES:
195.6 CID 6 (90 HP, AMERICAN; 127 HP, SIX; 138 HP- OPTIONAL)
250 CID V8 (215 HP)   (SAME ENGINES IN '59)
327 CID V8 (270 HP, AMBASSADOR)

$1775. ~ 3116. PRICE RANGE

TOTAL 1958 PRODUCTION: 186,227

RAMBLER 58

726

RAMBLER

5902
5906

New 100 inch wheelbase
Rambler American

$2060. UP STATION WAGON

AMERICAN

$1835

Suggested delivered price at Kenosha, Wisconsin, for 2-door sedan at left. State and local taxes, if any, automatic transmission and optional equipment, extra.

$2145.

SUPER

5915-1 $2268.

SIX

CUSTOM

$2383. 5915-2

5904-1
AMERICAN WAGON
(SUPER) IS new
90 HP

PUSH-BUTTON TRANS. AVAIL.

REBEL CROSS-COUNTRY
108" WB 5928-1 OR 2
SUPER-1 - $2692.
CUSTOM-2- 2807.

$1821. ~ 3116. PRICE RANGE

PRODUCTION:
363,372 (MODEL YEAR)
401,446 (AMC, CALENDAR YEAR

59

$2588.

REBEL

AMBASSADOR

$2587. UP
5985-1 OR 2

117" WB

270 HP V8

AMBASSADOR
CUSTOM
COUNTRY CLUB
4 DR. H/T

5929-2
COUNTRY
CLUB

INTERIOR

5989-2

DASH

RAMBLER 59

$2822.

727

RAMBLER

90 HP — AMERICAN — $2020. 6004

6005 DLX. 2-DR.

$1844.

DOORS NOW OPEN WIDER (75° INSTEAD OF 55°)

ROOF RACKS NOW ON ALL WAGONS

6002 $1781. and up

DLX.

$2098.

60

MODIFIED GRILLE (all except AMERICAN)

6015

6 DELUXE 108" WB 127 HP

6018 WAGON $2427.

6 SUPER SEDAN $2268. UP

6015-1 (6) 6025-1 (V8)

6015-2 (6) 6025-2 (V8) 2383. UP

CUSTOM COUNTRY CLUB 6019-2 (6) 6029-2 (V8)

$2458. UP

CUSTOM

new REAR FENDERS

V8 = 200 HP

6018 OR 6028 (-2 OR 4)

REAR COMPARTMENT DETAILS (WAGON)

3 WIDE SEATS, 5 BIG DOORS. The tailgate is a fifth door with outside key lock so children can't open from inside. Rear seat passengers step in—no scrambling over seats or tailgate.

new "COMPOUND WRAP-AROUND" WINDSHIELD on AMBASSADOR

WAGON (6 or 8-PASS.) 6088-1 TO 4

2881. and up

$2822. UP

AMB. CUSTOM COUNTRY CLUB 6089-2

AMBASSADOR V-8

BY RAMBLER

The New Standard of Basic Excellence in Luxury Cars

ENGINES:
AMERICAN 195.6 CID 6 (90 HP)
SIX 195.6 CID 6 (127 HP) (OPTIONAL 138 HP)
REBEL 250 CID V8 (200 HP) (" 215 HP)
AMBASSADOR 327 CID V8 (250 HP) (OPT. 270 HP)

434,704 RAMBLERS SOLD 1960. AMC 1960 CALENDAR YEAR, TOTAL = 485,745

RAMBLER 60

RAMBLER

6104

$1894. DLX.

6105

DLX.

6108 4-DR. WAGONS also

$2080.

6107-2
" -5

$2369.
and up

All New! A Convertible

"THE NEW WORLD STANDARD OF BASIC EXCELLENCE"

new Ceramic-Armored Muffler

$1831.~3111. PRICE RANGE

1961
MODEL YEAR TOTAL: 370,685

AMER. PRICES START AT
1831.
(6102)

AMERICAN 6
L-HEAD 90 (OR
125 HP OHV IN

AMERICAN WAGON REAR DETAILS

61 (RESTYLED)

SIX, REBEL REPLACED BY
CLASSIC 6 and V8

new CLASSIC 6 OR V8
127 OR 138 HP 6
6

$2098. UP

OR
200 OR 215 HP
V8

$2816. UP

CLASSIC DELUXE

CLOSE DETAIL OF CLASSIC FRONT END →

CLASSIC CUSTOM
6108-2 (6)
6128-4 (V8)
(CLASSIC 2-DR. WAGONS also)

...New! First acoustical ceiling of molded fiber glass

6188-1,2 OR 4

$2841. UP

CUSTOM 400 SEDAN JOINS AMBASSADOR LINE

AMBASSADOR V8
250 OR 270 HP
$2682. UP

Rambler
World Standard of Compact Car Excellence

6185-5

RAMBLER 61

RAMBLER

6205

6208 **$2130.**

1962 RAMBLER AMERICAN
DELUXE 4-DOOR SEDAN
(Also offered in Custom series)

$1895.

RAMBLER AMERICAN DELUXE 4 DOOR STATION WAGON
(Also offered in Custom series)

6206 **$1846.**
90 HP 6

1962 RAMBLER AMERICAN
DELUXE 2-DOOR CLUB SEDAN
(Also offered in Custom and "400" series)

6208 **$2130.**

RAMBLER AMERICAN "400" 4-DOOR STATION WAGON
(Also offered in Deluxe and Custom series)

$2344.

6207-5
AMERICAN "400" CVT.

$1832.~3023. PRICE RANGE

new GRILLES **62**

ENGINES:
195.6 CID 6 (90, 125, 127 OR 138 HP)
327 CID V8 (250 OR 270 HP)

$2150.
6216-2

1962 RAMBLER CLASSIC CUSTOM 2-DOOR CLUB SEDAN new
(Also offered in Deluxe and "400" series)

$2349.
6215-5

CLASSIC 400

new DOUBLE SAFETY BRAKES with
TANDEM MASTER CYLINDER

6218-5

1962 CLASSICS ARE 6 CYL. (127 OR 138 HP)

$2640.

RAMBLER CLASSIC 6 "400" CROSS COUNTRY STATION WAGON

$2760.
6288-2

1962 RAMBLER AMBASSADOR
CUSTOM 4 DOOR STATION WAGON

WB CUT TO 108"

250 OR 270 HP
AMB. V8s

AMBASSADOR 400
AND INTERIOR

$2605.

6285-5

AMC PROD., 1962 CALENDAR YEAR: 454,784

1962 RAMBLERS, MODEL YEAR: 423,104

RAMBLER 62

RAMBLER

TOP QUALITY AT
AMERICA'S LOWEST PRICE! $1846

Manufacturer's suggested retail price for the '63 Rambler American "220" Two-Door Sedan. Optional equipment, transportation, and state and local taxes, if any, extra. An award-winning Rambler value!

6302
220

AMERICAN 6
100" WB

6305
220
$1895.

(129,655 AMERICANS BLT.)

6304
$2081.

6306-5
440
$2040.

$2245.

$2281.
6309-7

440-H H/T
(with 138-HP OHV 6)

440 CVT.
$2344

6307-5

DASH

63

(CLASSICS and AMB.
TOTALLY RESTYLED)

6315-2
660

CLASSIC
6 OR V8*
new 112" WB

* OPTIONAL 198-HP
V8 (STARTING
3-1-63)

$2349.
770

6315-5
(321,916 CLASSICS BLT.)

770
6318-5
$2640.

New! Hidden storage compartment in wagon

SLOGAN:
The New Shape Of Quality

6388-2

880 CROSS
COUNTRY

990
WAGON
SIMILAR

New! Curved glass side windows ... far easier entry!

250 or 270 HP
AMBASSADOR V8
new 112" WB

$2606.

6386-5
2-DR.

(28,794 AMBASSADORS BLT.)

$2815.
990

AMBASSADOR has
LOWER BODY BAND

6385-5
SEDAN

WINNER OF
MOTOR TREND
AWARD
CAR OF THE YEAR $2660.

$1832. ~ 3018. PRICE RANGE

EXCEPT FOR '63½ CLASSIC V8,
(SAME ENGINES and HP AS IN 1962)
RAMBLERS, 1963 MODEL YR.: 428,346
AMC TOTAL PRODUCTION,
1963 CALENDAR YEAR: 480,365

RAMBLER 63

731

RAMBLER

new AMER. WAGON RESEMBLES A SEDAN *with* GRAFTED-ON REAR SECTION

6406

220

6408

6407-5

220

AMERICAN

6.00 x 14 TIRES (15" OPT.)

$2057.

330

6405-2

440-H
6409-7

(VI. TOP IN BLK., WHITE, GOLD OR TURQ.)

440

TO 138 HP

$2446.
6418

AMERICAN

TOTALLY RESTYLED (new 106" WB)

$2292.

$2651.

6418-5

770

660

2-DR.

550

CLASSIC (6 has 127 OR 138 HP)

112" WB

64

$2206.

6416-2

770

4-DR.
6415-5

$2360.

6489-5

990-H
(INTERIOR BELOW)

6488-5

FRESH NEW SPIRIT OF '64!

DASH (W/O AIR CONDITIONING)

$2985.

990

250 OR 270 HP

112" WB

AMBASSADOR

990

DASH (WITH AIR CONDITIONING)

RAMBLER 1964 PRODUCTION : 379, 412
    (MODEL YEAR)
AMC CALENDAR YEAR PRODUCTION : 393, 863
  CLASSIC = 321, 916   AMBASSADOR = 28, 794
 AMERICAN = 151, 969

ENGINES :
    195.6 CID 6 (90, 125, 127, 138)
    232 CID 6 (145 HP IN CLASSIC "TYPHOON" H/T)
    287 CID V8 (198 HP)
    327 CID V8 (250 OR 270 HP)

RAMBLER 64

RAMBLER

220 6506

$2396. — 6508-2   6509-7   American 440-H

$1979.

American 6

New! 3 different sizes of cars
New! 3 different wheelbases
New! 7 spectacular powerplants:
New Torque Command Sixes-
most advanced engines! Big V-8's

L-HEAD
195.6 CID
6 STILL
AVAIL. IN
AMERICAN
(90 HP @
3000 RPM)
(125 HP OHV ALSO)

65

330

2418.
6507-5

DASH (AMERICAN)
412,736 RAMBLERS SOLD 1965

AMERICAN
GRILLE NOW
VERTICALLY
SPLIT INTO
4 HORIZ.
SECTIONS

CVTS. NOW IN ALL 3 LINES $2727. →

6518-5
Rambler Classic 770 Station Wagon

CVT. (3882 BLT.)
195.6 OR 232 CID OHV 6s with
125 OR 155 HP

440

CVT.
6517-5
(4953 BLT.)

770

$2436.

SEE ALSO:
MARLIN

CLASSIC 770

199 OR 232 CID 6
(128, 145, 155 HP)
198 HP
with 287 CID
V8

6519-5
Rambler Classic 770 Hardtop

CLASSIC
770 SEDAN
DASH

GRILLE
CLOSE-
UPS

CLAS.

ALSO AVAIL. with
327 CID,
270-HP V8
ALSO USED IN
AMB.)

CLASSIC 112" WB CONT'D.,
BUT AMBASSADOR WB
INCREASED TO 116".

6515-5

6587-5

AMB.
(new HEADLIGHTS
VERTICALLY
STACKED)

6589-7

990

AMBASSADOR V8

$2837. →

SLOGAN:

THE
SENSIBLE SPECTACULARS

AMBASSADOR

1965

990-H
DASH

1965 RAMBLER MODEL YEAR PRODUCTION: 324,669

AMC CALENDAR YEAR PRODUCTION: 346,367

SEE "AMERICAN MOTORS" SECTION FOR '65 TO '69 MODELS.

$1979. ~ 2955. PRICE RANGE

RAMBLER 65

Rambler American 106" WB (THROUGH '69)

220
(STANDARD MODEL) DOES NOT HAVE CHROME STRIP ALONG SIDES.

440 WAGON
$2477.

AMC DEALERS ADVERTISED AS THE "FRIENDLY GIANT KILLERS"

66

440 CVT. $2486.
$2704. (WEST COAST)

GRILLE NOW SPLIT INTO ONLY 3 HORIZONTAL SECTIONS.

RACING STRIPES ON HOOD ARE NOT STD. EQUIPMENT.

$2588. (WEST COAST)
$2370.

new Rogue H/T
6 OR V8

199 CID 6 (128 HP) OR ROGUE 290 CID V8 (200 HP)
6.45/6.95 × 14 TIRES

TOTAL 1966 SALES = 265,712

440 4-DR.
$2259.

$2611. CVT.

ROGUE

THIS '67 ROGUE IS THE FINAL CONVERTIBLE IN AMERICAN SERIES.

$2073.

DASH

67

220 2-DR.

1967

HORIZONTAL GRILLE PCS. ARE NOW UNBROKEN, (AS THEY WERE IN 1964.)
TOTAL 1967 SALES = 237,785

199 CID 6 (128 HP); 232 CID 6 (145 HP) OR 290 CID V8 (225 HP)

DASH

4-DR. 2024.

220

$1946.
220
2-DR.
$2179.
(WEST COAST)

68

(INTRO. 9-26-67)
(259,346 SOLD)

new
SINGLE HEAVY
HORIZONTAL
CHROME STRIP ACROSS
GRILLE (OTHER HORIZ.
PCS. ARE BLACK)

68-220

440 AND ROGUE HAVE BRIGHT METAL BETWEEN TAIL LTS.

106" WB CONT'D.

(FINAL USE OF "RAMBLER AMERICAN" NAME)
REPLACED 9-25-69 BY AMC "HORNET" FOR 1970

69

(INTRO. 10-1-68)

"RAMBLER"
NAME
NO LONGER
APPEARS ON
GRILLE. SOME
VERTICAL PCS.
NOW ALSO
VISIBLE.

STD. 199 CID 6 (128 HP)
290 CID V8
(200
OR 225 HP)
232 CID 6
STD. IN
"ROGUE"
(145 HP)
BIG
new
390 CID V8
(315 HP)
IN
"SC/
RAMBLER
HURST"

Rambler $1,998
(SALE PRICE)
(RAMBLER 220, 440
and ROGUE RANGE IS
$2231. TO $2710.
RAMBLER 68~69

new
TRI-COLOR HOOD RAMBLEM

STUDEBAKER

$700.

CLUB SEDAN

Champion DeLuxe coupe

Folding seats give 5-passenger room in Champion Opera Coupe—A welcome convenience for families with small children or frequent extra guests. When not in use, the two extra seats fold up out of the way against the coupe rear wall. Tilting the front seat forward allows the extra passengers to get in and out easily.

PRICES BEGIN AT
$660
(COUPE)

40 **A** 110" WB (TO '46)

lowest~price car

1940 Studebaker Champion 2G

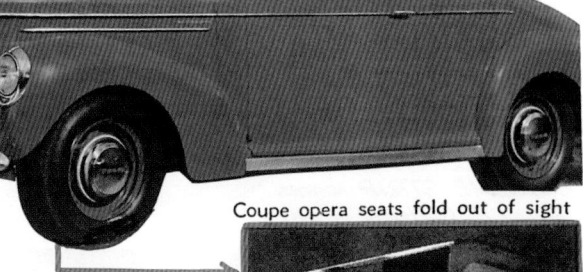

$740.
OPERA CPE.

Coupe opera seats fold out of sight

DELUXE 4~DR. SEDAN INTERIOR

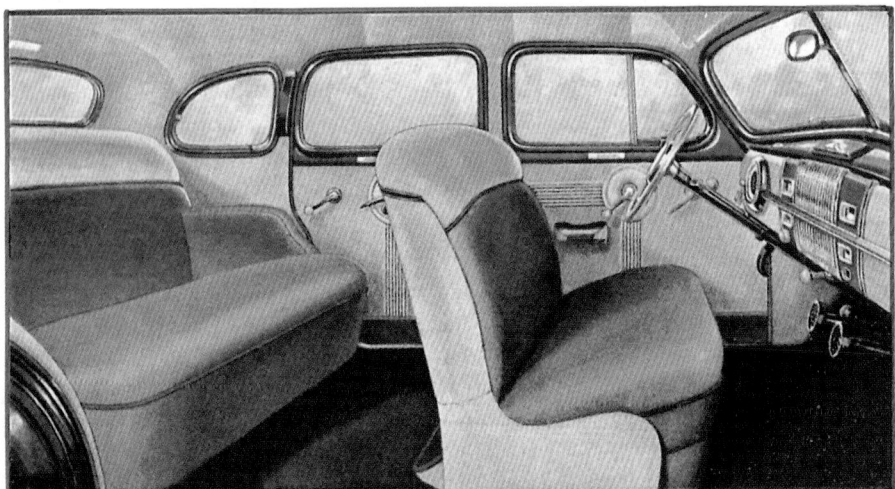

New Studebaker Delux-tone Models
NEXT YEAR'S STYLES NOW

164.3 CID 6, 78 HP (SINCE '39)

(CONT'D. NEXT PAGE)

40 STUDEBAKER (A)

Studebaker

Three Lines of Cars, Champion, Commander, President

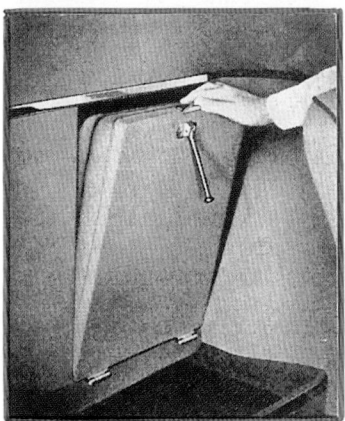

OPERA SEATS FOLDED AWAY

Front door trim on Commander and President

Champion instrument board

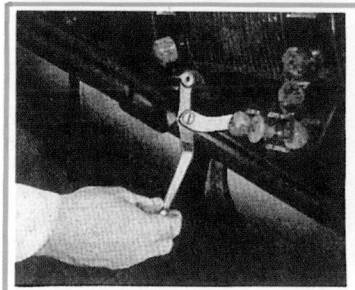 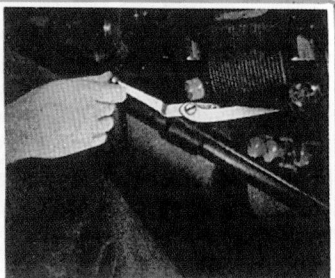

Hood is locked by lever on steering column

engine

			CID		HP
Champion	6	164.3	CID	78	HP
Commander	6	226.2		90	
President	8	250.4		110	

CHAMPION (66264 BLT.)

		110" WB
cpe 3P	$ 660	
cpe 5P	696	
club sdn	700	
Cruising Sedan 4d	740	
DeLuxe cpe 3P	705	
DeLuxe cpe 5P	740	
DeLuxe club sdn	745	
DeLuxe Cruising Sedan 4d	785	

COMMANDER (34477 BLT.)

		116½" WB
Custom cpe 3P	895	
club sdn	925	
Cruising Sedan 4d	965	

PRESIDENT (6444 BLT.)

		122" WB
cpe 3P	1,025	
club sdn	1,055	
Cruising Sedan 4d	1,095	

President 8 6C

$1055.

CLUB SEDAN

40.

B

LOA

COMMANDER

SLIDING REAR QUARTER WINDOWS IN COMMANDER and PRESIDENT SEDANS

CRUISING SEDAN $965.

Commander Cruising Sedan, $965, delivered at factory

Door handles are smartly aligned with belt moulding

40 STUDEBAKER (B)

1941 Studebaker
coupe $710. UP

3G

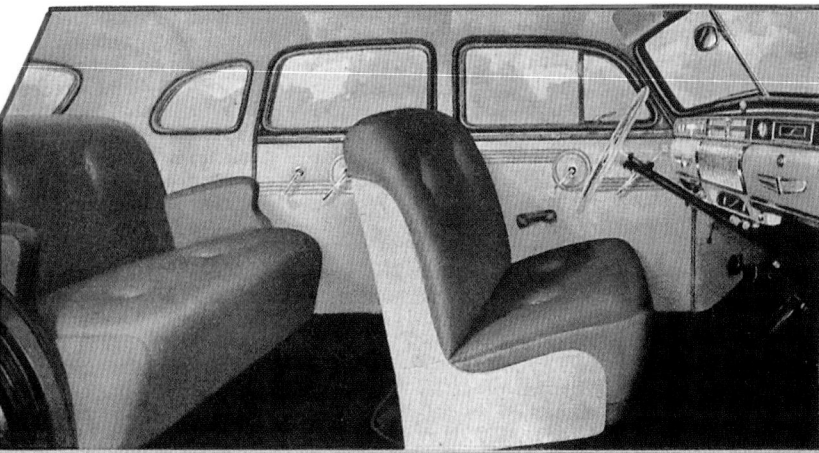

"Most beautiful interiors in any car!" That's what many discerning motorists say about this luxurious Studebaker Champion. Three contrasting-color fabrics, upholstered over foam-rubber cushions, are obtainable in Custom Deluxe Studebaker Champions at small added cost. Studebaker Delux-tone Champions feature five unusual two-tone exterior finishes and three attractive two-tone interiors.

Studebaker Champion
84910 BUILT

new 169.6 CID (THROUGH '54)

new 80 HP (THROUGH '49)

THIS BELTLINE CONTRASTING COLOR STRIPE OPTIONAL AT EXTRA COST.

CHAMPION CUSTOM CLUB SEDAN

Studebaker Champion 6, 3G

THE LOWEST PRICED
6-CYLINDER SEDAN IN AMERICA *

$730.

(*=UNTIL THE 1941½ FORD 6 APPEARED, WITH 2-DR. SEDAN AT $720.)

RESTYLED 41 A

Studebaker Commander 6, 11A

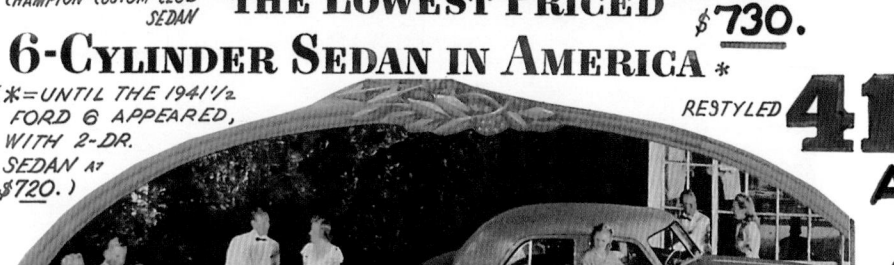

Studebaker President 8, 7G

sedans CHAMPION

$795.

(CONT'D. NEXT PAGE)
41 STUDEBAKER (A)

738

Studebaker

Commander 6, 11A . . . President Similar

COMMANDER 6

new 119" WB
(10 '52)
41996
BUILT

Studebaker Commander 6, 11A

smart new **STUDEBAKER LAND CRUISER**

AVAILABLE ON COMMANDER SIX OR PRESIDENT EIGHT CHASSIS

Studebaker President 8, 7G

PRESIDENT 8

6994 BUILT

41 B

CONT'D.

New

1941½ "SKYWAY" MODELS
START SPRING, 1941, IN
COMMANDER 6 and
PRESIDENT 8 SERIES

SMART 1941 STUDEBAKER

Illustrated: Skyway Series President Eight Sedan Coupe, $1210 delivered at factory

ABOVE = SKYWAY
PRESIDENT 8
SEDAN COUPE

$1210.

New

117
11P

new 124½" WB
(THRU '42)

$1260.
SKYWAY PRESIDENT 8
LAND CRUISER

41 STUDEBAKER (B)

PRICES BEGIN AT $810
for a Champion Business Coupe

NEW 1942 Studebaker Champion

(PRICES VARY, DURING SEASON)

FOR AMERICA'S DEFENSE
Studebaker is building an unlimited quantity of airplane engines, military trucks and other matériel

TAILLIGHT and DIRECTIONAL SIGNAL

ON CMNDR. 6, PRESIDENT 8

$840.

CHAMPION CUSTOM 2-DR. CLUB SEDAN

Range selector of the Turbo-matic drive, optional on Commander and President

42

new GRILLES

Fluid Coupling With Automatic Clutch Optional on Commander and President . . . New Style Features

$1045.

Commander Custom Cruising Sedan

4.1 GEAR RATIO (4.56 WITH OVERDRIVE)

SKYWAY SYMBOL

PRESIDENT 8 LAND CRUISER $1276.

SKYWAY SERIES   Commander

FINAL STUDE STRAIGHT-8s.

42 STUDEBAKER

TOTAL 1942 PROD.: 50678

Radio and Climatizer controls are compactly grouped

STUDEBAKER

169.6 cid 6 (80 HP)
"5~G"
SKYWAY CHAMPION is ONLY SERIES AVAIL.

EARLY **46** "5~G"

RARE!
(AVAIL. ONLY TO MAY, '46)

110" WB

"DOUBLE DATER" COUPE (1285 BLT.)

$916., f.o.b.
(INCREASED TO $1044.)

DASH

CLOSE UP OF GAUGES (UNRESTORED)

NEW BUMPERS, HIGHER BELT TRIM

ALSO AVAIL.
BUSINESS COUPE
(2465 BLT.)
$1002.
2 DR. CLUB SEDAN
(5000 BLT.)
$1046.

4~DR. CRUISING SEDAN (10525 BLT.)

PHOTOS OF 1946 SEDAN RECENTLY RESCUED FROM A WRECKING YARD (A RARE "SURVIVOR!")

AWAITING RESTORATION
(19275 TOTAL 1946 MODELS)

brand new

DESIGN

NEW WHEELBASES

CHAMPION "6~G" DELUXE SEDAN   new 112" WB $1478.

Starlight COUPE

$1877.

CHAMPION STRLT. CPE. has 1-PC. WINDSHIELD, UNLIKE OTHER CHAMPION MODELS
(SAME HP FIGS. SINCE '41)

14-A
←COMMANDER→   SEDAN

119" WB
226.2 cid 6
(94 HP)

ENGINE 6~CYL. L~HEAD

169.6 cid (80 HP) IN CHAMPION

PRODUCTION
CHAMPION (105,097 BLT.)
COMMANDER (56,399 BLT.)
161,496 TOTAL

$1761.

COMMANDER REGAL DE LUXE

TOTALLY and DRAMATICALLY RESTYLED!!

47 EARLY INTRO. MAY, 1946

DASH

(CAST~METAL)
note= GRILLE OF COMMANDER DIFFERS COMPLETELY FROM CHAMPION (STAMPED GRILLE.)

REGAL DE LUXE LAND CRUISER
(LONG WHEELBASE SEDAN IN COMMANDER SERIES)

DETAILS OF 2-DOOR SEDAN (CHAMP. REGAL DE LUXE) $1520.

$2043.

123" WHEELBASE

STUDEBAKER   46~47

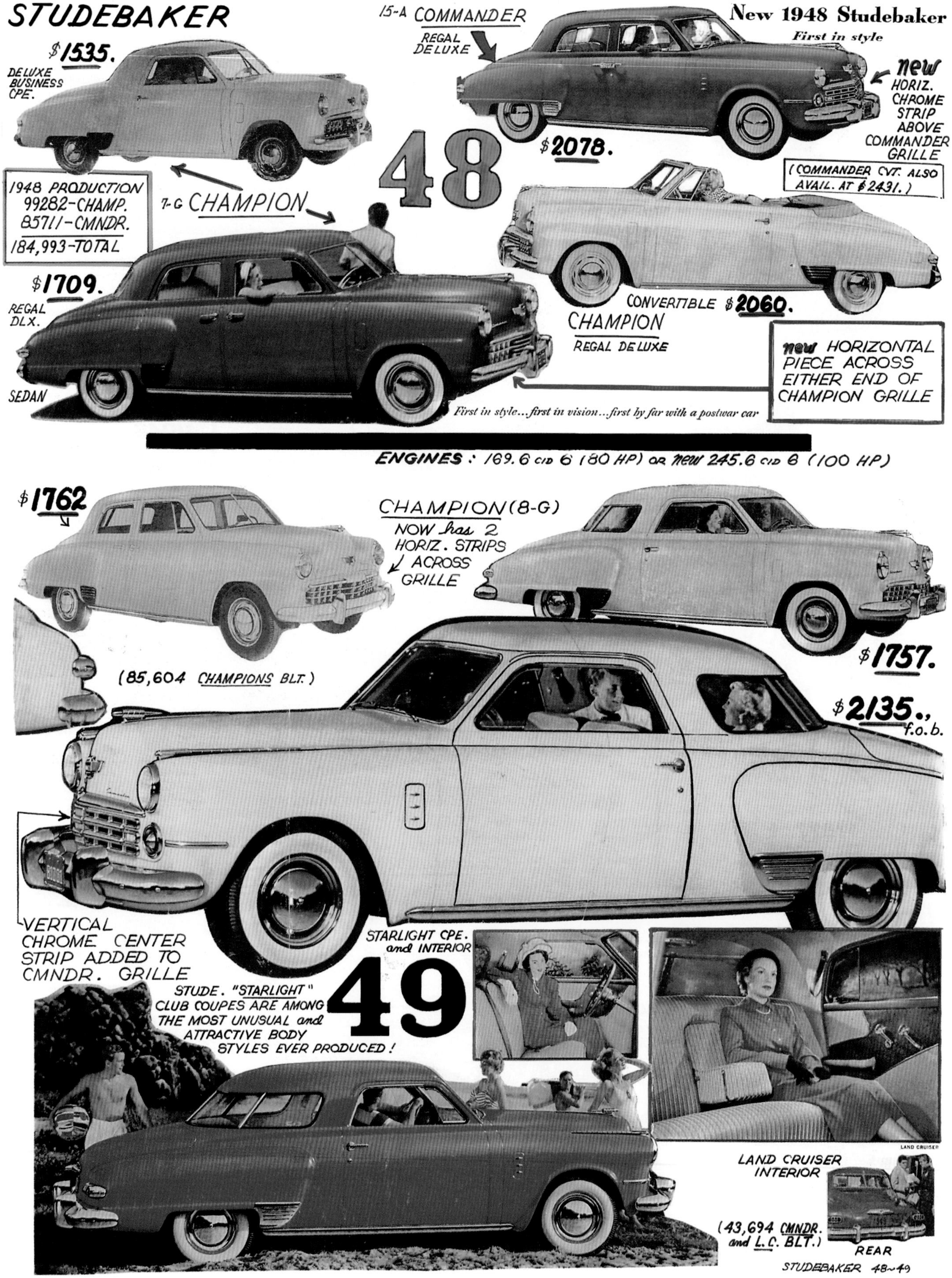

STUDEBAKER

$1535.
DELUXE BUSINESS CPE.

15-A COMMANDER
REGAL DELUXE

New 1948 Studebaker
First in style

$2078.

new HORIZ. CHROME STRIP ABOVE COMMANDER GRILLE

(COMMANDER CVT. ALSO AVAIL. AT $2431.)

48

1948 PRODUCTION
99282-CHAMP.
85711-CMNDR.
184,993-TOTAL

7-G CHAMPION

$1709.
REGAL DLX.

SEDAN

CONVERTIBLE **$2060.**
CHAMPION
REGAL DELUXE

new HORIZONTAL PIECE ACROSS EITHER END OF CHAMPION GRILLE

First in style...first in vision...first by far with a postwar car

ENGINES : 169.6 CID 6 (80 HP) or *new* 245.6 CID 6 (100 HP)

$1762

CHAMPION (8-G)
NOW *has* 2 HORIZ. STRIPS ACROSS GRILLE

(85,604 CHAMPIONS BLT.)

$1757.

$2135.,
f.o.b.

VERTICAL CHROME CENTER STRIP ADDED TO CMNDR. GRILLE

STARLIGHT CPE. and INTERIOR

STUDE. "STARLIGHT" CLUB COUPES ARE AMONG THE MOST UNUSUAL *and* ATTRACTIVE BODY STYLES EVER PRODUCED !

49

LAND CRUISER INTERIOR

(43,694 CMNDR. and L.C. BLT.)

REAR

STUDEBAKER 48~49

STUDEBAKER **new** "BULLET~NOSE" FRONT   the "next look" in cars

$1419. UP

BUSINESS COUPE

$1676

CHAMPION REGAL DE LUXE 6

CHROME ALONG ROCKER PANEL

Studebaker

new 6.40 x 15" IIRLS

(270,604 CHAMPIONS BLT.)

50 lowest price

CHAMPION CUSTOM 6-PASS. 2-DOOR SEDAN AS SHOWN

$1487.50

2-DR.

$1566.

CHAMPION DLX. (9-G)

new 113" WB

has RUBBER PAD ON REAR FENDER, BUT NO CHROME ALONG ROCKER PANEL.

NO RUBBER PAD ON FENDER, NO HOOD ORNAMENT.

$2013.

(17~A) COMMANDER   new 120" WB

$2024.

(72,562 COMMANDERS BLT., INCLUDING LAND CRUISER)

LAND CRUISER 124" WB

$2187.

America likes this "next look" in interiors —Fabulously fine nylon cord upholstery, introduced into motoring by Studebaker, is standard in the 1950 Land Cruiser and regal de luxe Commander. Land Cruiser is shown.

1950 PRICE RANGE $1419. ~ 2328.

(CHAMP. CUSTOM 3-PASS. CPE.)   (CMNDR. REGAL DLX. CVT.)

America likes Studebaker's new driving thrill—Every 1950 Studebaker handles with light-touch ease—rides so smoothly it almost completely abolishes travel fatigue. A new kind of coil spring front suspension.

STUDEBAKER 50

STUDEBAKER

new 115" WB (ON ALL BUT LAND CRUISER)

CHAMPION REGAL SEDAN

$1833.

Studebaker Champion

CHAMP. CUSTOM HAS NO HOOD ORNAMENT. CHAMP. DELUXE HAS ORNAMENT.

DLX. 3-WINDOW BUSINESS COUPE
$1643. →

L-HEAD 169.6 cid 6 (85 HP) OR 232.6 CID

51

new O.H.V. V8 ENGINE ALSO AVAIL. (120 HP)

6.40 x 15 TIRES

CHAMPION DE LUXE 6 (10-G) 85 HP

$1744.

(REGAL CHAMP. has LEATHER TRIM INSIDE DOORS.)

A brand new V-8 (233 CID) *Commander*

STATE CMNDR. CVT.

$2381. has

120 h.p. @4000 (THROUGH '54)

"BULLET NOSE" GRILLE SOMEWHAT MODIFIED FROM '50.

new GRILLE IS FLUSH WITH FRONT END

FINER PCS. IN GRILLE

$2143.

STATE CMNDR. SEDAN

COMMANDER LAND CRUISER

$2289.

new SHORTER 119" WB on L.C.

"STUDEBAKER...THE THRIFTY ONE FOR '51"

$1561. ~ 2381. PRICE RANGE   STUDEBAKER 51

CHAMPION = 144,286 BLT.; **CMNDR./L.C.** = 124,280 BLT.
6   V8

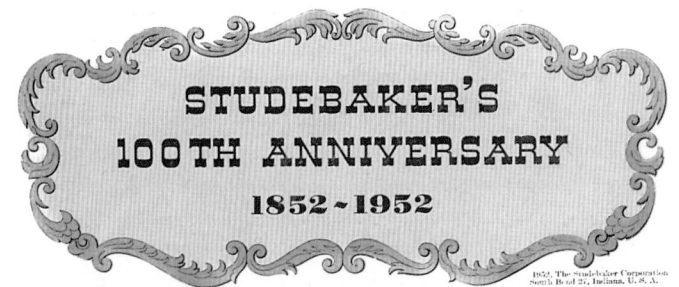

STUDEBAKER'S 100TH ANNIVERSARY

1852~1952

1952, The Studebaker Corporation
South Bend 27, Indiana, U. S. A.

REGAL COMMANDER

$2121.

REGAL CHAMPION OR STATE COMMANDER CVTS. AVAIL.

$2273. OR 2548.

PACE CAR
AT 1952 INDY 500 RACE

52

FRONT END RESTYLED

$2365.

LAND CRUISER

1952 PRODUCTION:
CHAMPION = 101,390
COMMANDER, L.C. = 84,849

BODY DESIGN BASICALLY AS BEFORE, BUT CONTROVERSIAL "BULLET NOSE" DISCONTINUED IN FAVOR OF A MORE CONVENTIONAL (BUT EXTREMELY BROAD) GRILLE

"STARLINER" H/T is new

AVAIL. IN CHAMP. OR CMNDR. SERIES

CHAMPION PRICES START AT $1735.

$2488.

STATE COMMANDER STARLINER

See Studebaker for '52

$2172.

(2-DR.)

EDITED PHOTOS (IN ADS) CAUSE PASSENGERS IN CARS TO APPEAR UNUSUALLY SMALL, IN COMPARISON TO THE CAR. (THIS MAKES THE CAR LOOK LARGER.)

$2208.

STATE COMMANDER

See and drive the Studebaker Starliner—It's America's smartest "hard-top"—available either as a Champion or a Commander V-8.

$1735.~2548. PRICE RANGE

52

Studebaker

REGAL CHAMPION
STARLINER
H/T

CHAMPION PRICES START AT
$1735.

85 HP @ 4000 RPM

170 CID 6 (THROUGH '54)

MEANS CHAMP. 6 H/T

53 $2116.

(TOTALLY RESTYLED)

1 new DESIGN WINS FASHION ACADEMY AWARD

new 116½" WB (120½" on CPE, H/T and LAND CRUISER)

$2488.

$1735.~2374. PRICE RANGE

MEANS CMNDR. V8

NO MORE CONVERTIBLES AVAILABLE (UNTIL '60 LARK)

1953 PROD.:

CHAMP. = 93,807
COM., L.C. = 76,092

CALENDAR YEAR PRODUCTION = 186,844

6.40 × 15 TIRES (6)
6.70 × 15 WAGON (6)
7.10 × 15 (V8)

| 1954 PRODUCTION: | CHAMPION | 51,431 |
| | COMMANDER, L.C. | 76,092 |

SAME ENGINES SINCE '51

STATION WAGON INTRODUCED!

$1758.~2556. PRICE RANGE

VERTICAL PIECES ADDED TO GRILLE FOR 1954.

STUDEBAKERS, SINCE LATE 1930s, ARE Styled by *Raymond Loewy*

CHAMPION

CHAMPION PRICES START AT $1758. (COUPE)

54 new GRILLE

COMMANDER

$2136. UP

new CONESTOGA WAGON (116½" WB) $2556.

LAND CRUISER

STUDEBAKER 53~54

$2438.

STUDEBAKER

$1741. ~ 3253. PRICE RANGE

6 CYL. has 101 HP @ 4000 RPM (new 186 CID THROUGH '58)

CHAMPION CUSTOM

A BIG NEW CHAMPION
America's No. 1 economy car!
Now more marvelous than ever!

$2125.
REGAL
H/T

CHAMPION PRICES
START AT $ 1741.
2 - DR.

new GRILLE (with HEAVY CHROME BORDERS)

55

CHAMPION DE LUXE

$1875.

$2127.
(CMNDR.)

INTERIOR

COUPES

COMMANDER

Now in the low price field!
A sensationally high-powered
NEW COMMANDER V-8

$2094.

(6-CYL. OR V8 WAGONS)

COMMANDER REGAL
CONESTOGA

SPEEDSTER

$3253.

$2445.

COMMANDER H/T
DETAILS

$2282.

STATE
PRESIDENT
$2456.

NEW!

AMERICA'S SMARTEST TWO-TONING!

PRESIDENT

The first dynamic headliners of the
great Studebaker-Packard alliance!
Sensationally powered '55 Studebakers!
Amazingly low introductory prices!

$2381.

ENGINES : new 185.6 CID 6 (101 HP) CHAMPION
new 224.3 CID V8 (140 HP) EARLY '55 COMMANDER
new 259.2 CID V8 (162 HP) LATER "   " (175 HP) PRESIDENT
(185 HP) EARLY '55 SPEEDSTER; "   " PRESIDENT

1955 PRODUCTION :
CHAMPION 6 = 50,368
COMMANDER V8 = 58,792
new PRESIDENT V8 = 24,666

STUDEBAKER 55

747

Studebaker

CHAMPION PRICES START AT $1841.

Craftsmanship with a Flair

PELHAM 6

CHAMPION 6 $1885.

wagons

$2232.

PARKVIEW V8 $2354.

CMNDR. V8 $1986.

$2101.

$3610.

FLIGHT HAWK 6

POWER HAWK V8

SKY HAWK V8

(3610. BLT.)

Hawks $4071.

FRONT DETAILS OF COMMANDER V8

NEW DUAL EXHAUSTS · Built into the bumper for more style, more class than you've ever seen in a low price car. Ready for 4-barrel carburetion to boost mileage and power.

The Golden Hawk

GOLDEN HAWK V8 (275 HP)

(4071. BLT.)

FRONTS RESTYLED **56**

$2235. SEDAN

PRESIDENT V8

CLASSIC SEDAN *has* ROCKER PANEL TRIM

"CLASSIC" SEDAN $2489.

259, 289 OR 352 CID V8s

PRESIDENT V8 195 HP * @ 4500 RPM

new 12-VOLT ELECTRICAL SYSTEM

NEW CYCLOPS-EYE SPEEDOMETER

* 210 HP *with* 4-BBL. CARB.

PRESIDENT PINEHURST V8

$2529.

ENGINES:
185.6 CID 6 (101 HP)
259.2 V8 (170 or 185 HP)
289 CID V8 (195, 210 or 225 HP)
352 CID V8 (275 HP)

CALENDAR YEAR PRODUCTION: 82,955

$1741.~4071. PRICE RANGE

STUDEBAKER 56

Studebaker

CHAMP. SCOTSMAN IS A new BUDGET-PRICED MODEL with MINIMUM of CHROME and PLAINEST INTERIOR

101 HP

W-1 SEDAN

2-DR.,
6-CYL.
WAGONS
SCOTSMAN (116½" WB)
PELHAM (118½" WB)

← PLAIN, PAINTED HUB CAPS,
6.40 × 15 TIRES

57-G
CHAMPION SCOTSMAN 6
(new)
PRICES START AT
$1776.
(2-DR.)

57A
(RESTYLED)

116½" WB ON MOST

57-G (6 CYL.)
57-H (8 CYL.)

CHAMPION DE LUXE 6
$2171.

STUDEBAKER
1957

$2505.

D-4
PARKVIEW 2-DR. WAGON

PROVINCIAL 4 DR. WAGON
P-4

$2561.

COMMANDER
F-2 (CUSTOM)
F-4 (DELUXE)

$2407.
PRESIDENT
W-6

$2246. (DLX.)

Studebaker-
Packard
CORPORATION

Where pride of Workmanship comes first!

BROADMOOR 4-DR. WAGON
P-6

$2666.

| 170 HP V8 RAISED TO 180 HP |
| 185 HP V8 RAISED TO 195 HP |

OTHER ENGINES AS IN 1956

STUDEBAKER 57(A)

SILVER HAWK (15,318 BLT.)
GOLDEN HAWK (4356 ")
TOTAL 1957 STUDEBAKER PRODUCTION:
74,738 (CALENDAR YEAR: 67,394)
(1957 HAWKS on NEXT PAGE)

STUDEBAKER

289 CID (275 HP @ 4800 RPM)
V8
GOLDEN
HAWK
H/T

K-7

$2263.

C-3
SILVER HAWK COUPE

186 CID 6
(101 HP)

$3185.

OR
210, 225 HP V8s
(289 CID)

57 B (CONT'D.)

Golden Hawk

(10,325 CHAMPIONS BLT.)

Studebaker Commanders and Champions

58

4 HEADLIGHTS
ON SOME
MODELS

101 TO
275 HP

(SAME HP AS '57)
THE FINAL GOLDEN HAWK (878 BLT.)
$3282.

180-HP CMNDR.

" Studebaker cars take on a
completely new luxury look for 1958!"

SCOTSMAN 6
PRICES START AT $1795.
(20,870
SCOTSMANS
BLT.)

NOTICE
STRIKING
DIFFERENCES
IN APPEARANCE
BETWEEN THE
LT.-OVER-DK.
AND
DK.-OVER-LT.
HARDTOPS

REAR DETAILS
(SEDAN)

$2639.
Studebaker President

1958

The Hawk-inspired PRESIDENT
STARLIGHT for 1958
H/T

10,442 PRESIDENTS BLT. (4 DR. SEDAN and H/T)

$2695.

Studebaker-Packard
CORPORATION
Where pride of Workmanship comes first!

CALENDAR YEAR PRODUCTION:
55,175

STUDEBAKER 57(B)~58

750

STUDEBAKER

59
6-(2417 BLT.)
V8-(5371 ")

170 CID 6 (90 HP @ 4000) OR 259 CID V8s (180 OR 195 HP @ 4500)

SEE ALSO: **LARK**

(STARTING 1959, LOWER-PRICED MODELS USE LARK NAME)

HAWK 6 PRICES START AT **$2360.**

$2495. (V8)

6 OR V8
SILVER HAWK (C-6)

1959

120½" WB

60
(3939 BLT.)

3 NEW STRIPS ON SIDE OF REAR FENDER

NEW 289 CID V8 RETURNS TO HAWK AS ONLY AVAIL. ENG. (210 OR 225 HP @ 4500 RPM)

$2650.

C-6 HAWK

6.70 × 15 TIRES

61
6.70 × 15" TIRES

(3340 BLT.)

NEW TRIM DESIGN ALONG REAR FENDERS

$2650.
$2677.

HAWK

(C-6)

62
NEW HAWK GT

(K-6)
$3095.

NEW ROOFLINE

120½" WB

(8388 BLT.)

(RESTYLED)

NEW CLASSIC-STYLE GRILLE WITH HEAVY CHROME BORDERS

$3424.
WEST COAST

(UP $27. IN '63)

63
NEW GRILLE DESIGN WITH DECORATIVE CRISS-CROSS STRIPS ADDED

$3095.

HAWK GT

(4634 BLT.)

NEW AVANTI
$4445.

WEST COAST
$4759.

AVANTI INTRO. DURING '62 109" WB 289 CID V8 (240 OR 290 HP)

(3834 BLT.)

STUDEBAKER (and LARK) **CALENDAR YEAR PRODUCTION:**
1959 = 153,823   1960 = 105,902   1961 = 78,664
1962 = 86,974   1963 = 67,918

HAWK GT (1963) HAS 289 CID V8 (210, 225, 240 OR 290 HP)

STUDEBAKER 59~63

STUDEBAKER

$4445.

6.00, 6.50 OR 6.70 × 15 TIRES

AVANTI V8

"LARK" DESIGNATION PHASED OUT DURING 1964.

113" WB

109" WB

(809 BLT.)

64

ENGINES:
169.6 CID 6 (112 HP)
259.2 CID V8 (180 OR 195 HP)
289 CID V8 (210, 225, 240, 290 HP)
new 304½CID V8 (280 OR 335 HP)

109" WB

COMMANDER

$2303.

CHALLENGER (109" WB)

(AVAIL. 1964 ONLY)
112 HP 6 OR 180 HP V8

113" WB ON CRUISER V8

$2048. UP
$2417. WEST COAST

120" WB

1964

FINAL GRAN TURISMO HAWK
(1767 BLT.)

$2966.

TOTAL 1965 PRODUCTION: 19,435
$2125. ~ 2890. PRICE RANGE

CHEVROLET ENGINES NOW USED
194 CID 6 (120 HP)
283 CID V8 (195 HP)
(SAME ENGINES IN 1966)

STUDE. PRODUCTION CONTINUES ONLY AT THE CANADIAN BRANCH FACTORY, FOR '65-66, (HAMILTON, ONT.)

DETAILS OF WAGONAIRE ILLUSTR. AT RIGHT

TOPSIDE LUGGAGE RACK (OPT.)

BRAKE RELEASE

Wagonaire

(V8) $2695.

TAILGATE STEP

65 A

6 CYL. CHEV. OHV ENG. (V8 ON NEXT PG.)

COMMANDER

"the Common-Sense Car"

(UNFOLDS AND LOWERS)

$2230.

$2581. (6 CYL.)
WEST COAST

(CONT'D.)
STUDEBAKER 64~65(A)

INTERIOR

752

Studebaker
THE COMMON-SENSE CAR

CRUISER INTERIOR FEATURES

Exclusive Beauty Vanity in glove compartment—(opt.).

Daytona *Sports* SEDAN

$2405. (6)
2500. (V8)

DAYTONA INTER.

CLOSER DETAIL OF DASH

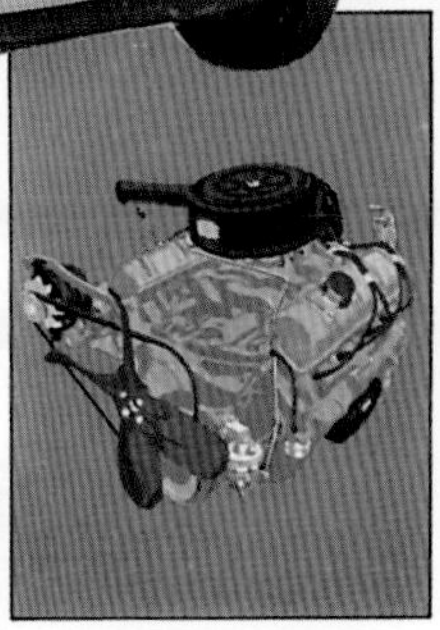

V8 NOW has 195 HP

← FINAL YEAR of 4 HEADLIGHTS

$2610. →

WEST COAST:
$2985. →

Cruiser

S = 6
V = V8

PRICES START AT $2060.

WEST COAST
$2465. (COMMANDER 6 2-DR.)

194 CID, 120-HP 6
or 283 CID, 195-HP V8

FINAL STUDEBAKERS HAVE THIS GRILLE.

Studebaker
AUTOMOTIVE SALES CORPORATION

LAST
Cars BY ST.-P.

66

$2555. UP

109" or 113" WB (SINCE 1962, ON LARK and LARK-BASED MODELS)

TOTAL 1966 PRODUCTION = 8947
$2060. ~ 2695. PRICE RANGE

STUDEBAKERS DISCONTINUED MARCH, 1966

STUDEBAKER 65(B) ~ 66

THUNDERBIRD

(INTRO. FALL, 1954, FOR 1955)

Ford

(MODEL 40)

55

"CLASSIC" T-BIRDS AVAIL. *with* REMOVABLE HARD TOP OR CVT. TOP (THROUGH '57)

ALL *with* V-8 O.H.V. ENGINES (292 CID)

193 HP (198 HP w. A.T.)
16,155 BLT.

102" WB (THROUGH '57)

6.70 × 15 TIRES (THROUGH '56)

$2944.

15,631 BLT.

$3151.

2 ENGINES NOW AVAILABLE :
292 CID V8 (202 HP) OR
new 312 CID V8 (215 HP, OVERDRIVE) (225 HP, A/T)

INTERIOR

40-B

REMOVABLE H/T has *new* PORTHOLES (EXCEPT EARLY MODELS)

56

40-A

new 7.50 × 14 TIRES

57

NAME MOVED TO FRONT FENDERS

new GRILLE; BUMPERS, TAIL-LIGHTS MODIFIED

$3408.

new WHEEL COVERS

new DASH

21,380 BLT.

292 CID V8 (212 HP) OR
312 CID V8 (245, 270, 285 OR 300 HP)

THUNDERBIRD 55~57

THUNDERBIRD

new H/T (35,758 BLT.) $3631.

NOW with 4 HEADLIGHTS

58 (TOTALLY RESTYLED)

REAR DETAILS

300 HP (THROUGH '65) new 352 CID V8

Exclusive "Panel Console"

DASH 63-A

76-A

new 113" WB $3929.

CVT. (2134 BLT.)

The car everyone would love to own!

$3696. $3979.

CVT. 76-A

H/T 63-A

(57,195 BLT.)

HORIZONTAL PCS. ON new GRILLE and BETWEEN TAIL-LIGHTS

new 8.00×14 TIRES

59

new 430 CID V8 (350 HP) OPTIONAL

new SIDE TRIM EACH YEAR

T-59

(VT. (10,261 BLT.)

6 TAIL-LIGHTS IN 1960

$4222.

CVT.

new GRILLE DETAILS

9 VERTICAL CHROME BANDS ON EA. REAR FENDER (1960 ONLY)

60

new GRILLE, 6 ROUND TAIL LIGHTS

REAR DETAILS

sliding sun roof (new)

$3755.

63A H/T (78,447 BLT.) (ALSO AVAIL.=63-B GOLD TOP H/T=2536 BLT.)

APPROX. $3900.

'60 THUNDERBIRD
THE WORLD'S MOST WANTED CAR

76A CONVERTIBLE (11,860 BLT.)

TOTAL 1960 PRODUCTION: 92,843

THUNDERBIRD 58~60

THUNDERBIRD

63A H/T (62,535 BLT.)
76A CVT. (10,516 BLT.)

ALL HAVE 390 cid V8
(300 HP)

Swing-Away Steering Wheel glides out of
your way for easier, more graceful entrances
and exits—yet locks safely in place before
you can drive.

(OPTIONAL)

'61 THUNDERBIRD
UNIQUE IN ALL THE WORLD
CVT. $ **4637.**

PACE CAR AT 1961
INDY 500 RACE

61
(TOTALLY
RESTYLED)

H/T $ **4170.**

unmistakably New, unmistakably Thunderbird

8.00 x 14"
TIRES

$ **4321.**

new BODY TYPES and MODEL NUMBERS in 1962

$ **4398.**

LANDAU
(new)

HARDTOP

CVT.
(7030 BLT.)

$ **5552.**

ORIG.
$5439.

$ **4511.**
(WEST COAST)

with
VINYL
TOP and
DECORATIVE LANDAU IRONS

Thunderbird

Sports Roadster
(new)
(1427 BLT.)

new GRILLE

62

(69 554 BLT.)
H/Ts = MODEL 83
CVTS. = MODEL 85
(8457 BLT.)

new SPTS. RDST.
has TWIN TONNEAU
CAPS (as illustrated)

unique in all the world

390 cid V8 (300 or 340 HP)

THUNDERBIRD 61~62

(SAME ENGINES AS IN 1962)

THUNDERBIRD

$4529. TO $5648.
WEST COAST PRICE RANGE

H/T 83   (42,806 BLT.)

$4445.

113" WB

63

(14,139 BLT.)

INTERIOR
(OFFERING
WOOD-GRAIN
EFFECTS)

LANDAU $4548.
87

CVT. 85

(5913 BLT.)

$4912.

$4445.~5563. PRICE RANGE

final
SPORT
ROADSTER
89
(455 BLT.)

113.2" WB
(THROUGH '66)

390 CID V8 (300 HP)
(THROUGH '65)

H/T $4486.
(60,552 BLT.)

64
(RESTYLED)

CVT.
(9198 BLT.)
$4953.
new
8.15 × 15
TIRES

new
WIDE TAIL-LIGHTS
with T-BIRD EMBLEM
$4589.

LANDAU H/T
(22,715 BLT.)

new DASH

A PRODUCT OF
Ford
MOTOR COMPANY

PRICED
FROM
$4486.

(IN '64 and
'65)
H/T
(42,652
BLT.)

LANDAU

LIGHT OR DARK TOP COVERING AVAIL.

INTERIOR with
new WOOD-
GRAIN
EFFECTS

CONVERTIBLE
(6846 BLT.)
$4953.

new 5
VERTICAL STRIPS
ON EACH TAIL-LIGHT

2
VERSIONS OF
LANDAU H/Ts:
LANDAU (STD.) $4589.
(20,974 BLT.)
LIMITED ED. SPEC. LANDAU
(4500 BLT.) $4639.

65

GRILLE SLIGHTLY CHANGED.
THUNDERBIRD EMBLEM AT FRONT and BACK END,
INSTEAD OF NAME.

THUNDERBIRD 63~65

FINAL THUNDERBIRD CONVERTIBLE PRICED AT $4879. (5049 BLT.)

$4483.

THUNDERBIRD

113" WB

(15,633 BLT.)

(WEST COAST) $5005.

66 new GRILLE; new TAIL-LIGHTS

TOWN HARDTOP

Highway Pilot CONTROL TOWN LANDAU H/T (35,105 BLT.)

H/T (13,389 BLT.) $4426.

$4584.

SEQUENTIAL TURN SIGNALS IN FULL-WIDTH TAIL-LIGHTS

PROD.: 69,176 (CALENDAR YR., 72,734)

390 CID V8 (315 HP)

(IN TOWN H/T) OVERHEAD CONSOLE with WARNING LIGHTS

Stereo-Tape System... Overhead Safety Control Panel →

TOWN LANDAU H/T TOP DETAILS

1967 PROD.: 77,956 (CALENDAR YR., 59,640)

H/T (15,567 BLT.)

(WEST COAST FR. $5144.)

4 DR. **NEW**

$4603.

(24,967 BLT.)

note HOW A SIDE SECTION OF TOP OPENS WITH REAR DOOR

67A (RESTYLED) (INTRO. 9-30-66)

DASH

(4 DR. DETAILS on NEXT PAGE)

THUNDERBIRD 66~67

THUNDERBIRD
$4825.

67 (B) (CONT'D.)
(LANDAU 2-DR. ALSO AVAIL.)

new CONCEALED HEADLIGHTS IN new GRILLE

new 115" WB (2-DR.)
117" WB (4-DR.)

(INTRO. 9-22-67)

LANDAU 4-DOOR is new
(WEST COAST) $5366.

INTERIOR

1968 PRODUCTION:
64,931

68

H/T 2-DR. FROM $5263.
(WEST)

new SIDE SAFETY LIGHTS

$4924.

new GRILLE

new 429 CID V8 (360 HP)

8.15/8.45×15 TIRES

4-DR. LANDAU $5471.
(WEST)

$4964.

OPTIONAL SUN ROOF

2-DR. $5359.
2-DR. LANDAU 5499.
4-DR. LANDAU 5578.
(WESTERN PRICES)

1969 PRODUCTION:
49,272

2-DR. (FORMAL ROOFLINE) LANDAU
(27,664 BLT.)

new 8.55×15 TIRES

69
new GRILLE

(INTRO. 9-27-68)

STD. 2-DR. ROOFLINE
(5913 BLT.)   4-DR.

(15,695 BLT.)

INTERIOR

THUNDERBIRD   67(B)-69

**FOR 1970:
A
NEW FLIGHT
OF BIRDS**

Soaring into the '70's far ahead of the rest . . . 1970 Thunderbird.

THUNDERBIRD

114.7 (115") WB
(117.2" on 4-DR.)

'70

CLOSE-UP OF THE UNUSUAL POINTED FRONT END ('70 ONLY)

H/T
$4961.
(5116 BLT.)

ALSO 36847 2-DR. LANDAUS $5104.

8401 4-DR. LANDAUS $5182.

Because there is no such thing as a flock of Thunderbirds. And the '71 Bird is the most individual yet. With standard features that make it unique, like power front disc brakes, Select Shift Cruise-O-Matic Transmission, AM radio, power steering, power ventilation, more. With Thunderbird options like steel-belted Michelin tires; power-operated Sunroof; Tilt Steering Wheel; Rear Window Electric Defrost; Automatic Fingertip Speed Control; computerized Sure-Track brake control system. Individuality is alive and well, and ready to fly.

stereosonic tape system; air conditioning with automatic temperature control, you name it.

'71 new GRILLE

$5295.

FINAL YEAR FOR 4-DR. $5516. (6553)

(20356 BLT.)

9146 BLT.

STD. H/T ROOFLINE

new LANDAU ROOFLINE (LANDAU IRONS ELIMINATED)

America's most distinctive personal-luxury car offers many luxuries. First among these is choice. Thunderbird lets you choose between two beautiful rooflines: the formal Landau, or the sleek hardtop. And you have the choice of two-door or four-door Thunderbirds

429 CID V8 (360 HP)

5438.

THUNDERBIRD 70-71

THUNDERBIRD

72

HP CUT TO 212

new 120.4" WB

215 R15 TIRES

FRONT END TOTALLY RESTYLED

(INTRO. 9-24-71)

2-DR. H/T is ONLY TYPE NOW AVAIL. = $5730.
WESTERN PRICE

INTERIOR

PAINTED DISC WHEEL COVERS ALSO

(57814 BLT.)
$5293.

ALL-HORIZONTAL GRILLE PCS.

RESTYLED 73-76

FEW CHANGES, 1973~1976

1973=(87269 BLT.)	$6437. ($6170, EARLY '73)
1974=(58443)	7330.
1975=(42685)	7701.
1976=(52905, PLUS 30 "COMMEMORATIVE" MODELS) $7790.

Deluxe Wheel Covers

Simulated Wire Wheel Covers

Deep-Dish Aluminum Wheels Standard with Copper Luxury Group

Wide White Sidewall Tires

1975 WHEEL CHOICES (new)

INSTRUMENT PANEL ('73)

new (1974) 460 CID V8

194 HP IN 1975

20TH ANNIV. "SILVER" OR "COPPER" '75 MODELS AVAIL.

('75)

('73)

new OPERA WINDOWS

new ORNAMENT ATOP HOOD

THUNDERBIRD 72~76

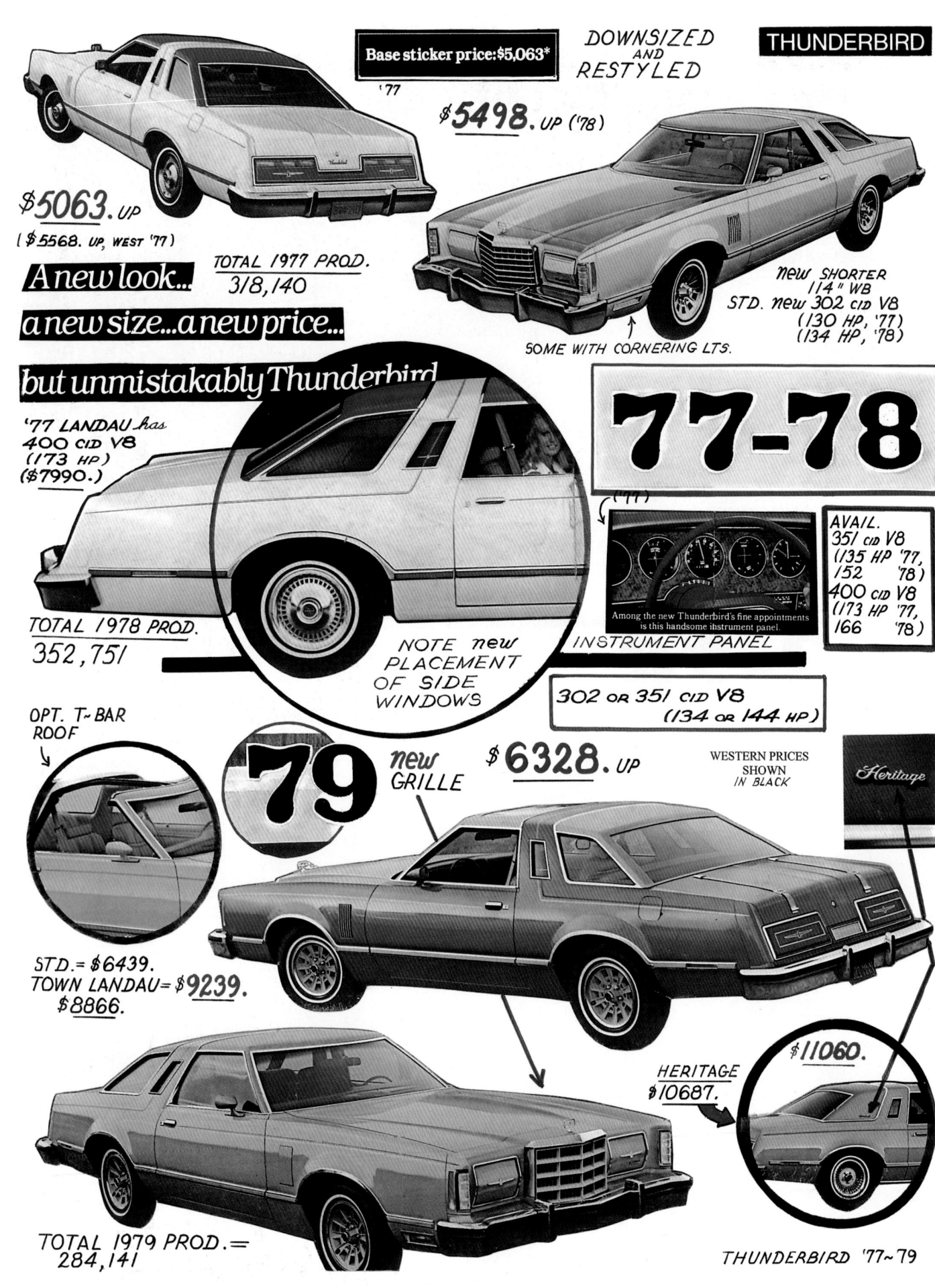

Base sticker price:$5,063*

'77

DOWNSIZED
AND
RESTYLED

$5498. UP ('78)

$5063. UP
($5568. UP, WEST '77)

A new look...

a new size...a new price...

TOTAL 1977 PROD.
318,140

new SHORTER
114" WB
STD. new 302 CID V8
(130 HP, '77)
(134 HP, '78)

SOME WITH CORNERING LTS.

but unmistakably Thunderbird

'77 LANDAU has
400 CID V8
(173 HP)
($7990.)

77-78

('77)

AVAIL.
351 CID V8
(135 HP '77,
152 '78)
400 CID V8
(173 HP '77,
166 '78)

Among the new Thunderbird's fine appointments
is this handsome instrument panel.

INSTRUMENT PANEL

TOTAL 1978 PROD.
352,751

NOTE new
PLACEMENT
OF SIDE
WINDOWS

302 OR 351 CID V8
(134 OR 144 HP)

OPT. T~BAR
ROOF

79 new
GRILLE

$6328. UP

WESTERN PRICES
SHOWN
IN BLACK

Heritage

STD.= $6439.
TOWN LANDAU= $9239.
$8866.

HERITAGE
$10687.

$11060.

TOTAL 1979 PROD.=
284,141

THUNDERBIRD '77~79

762

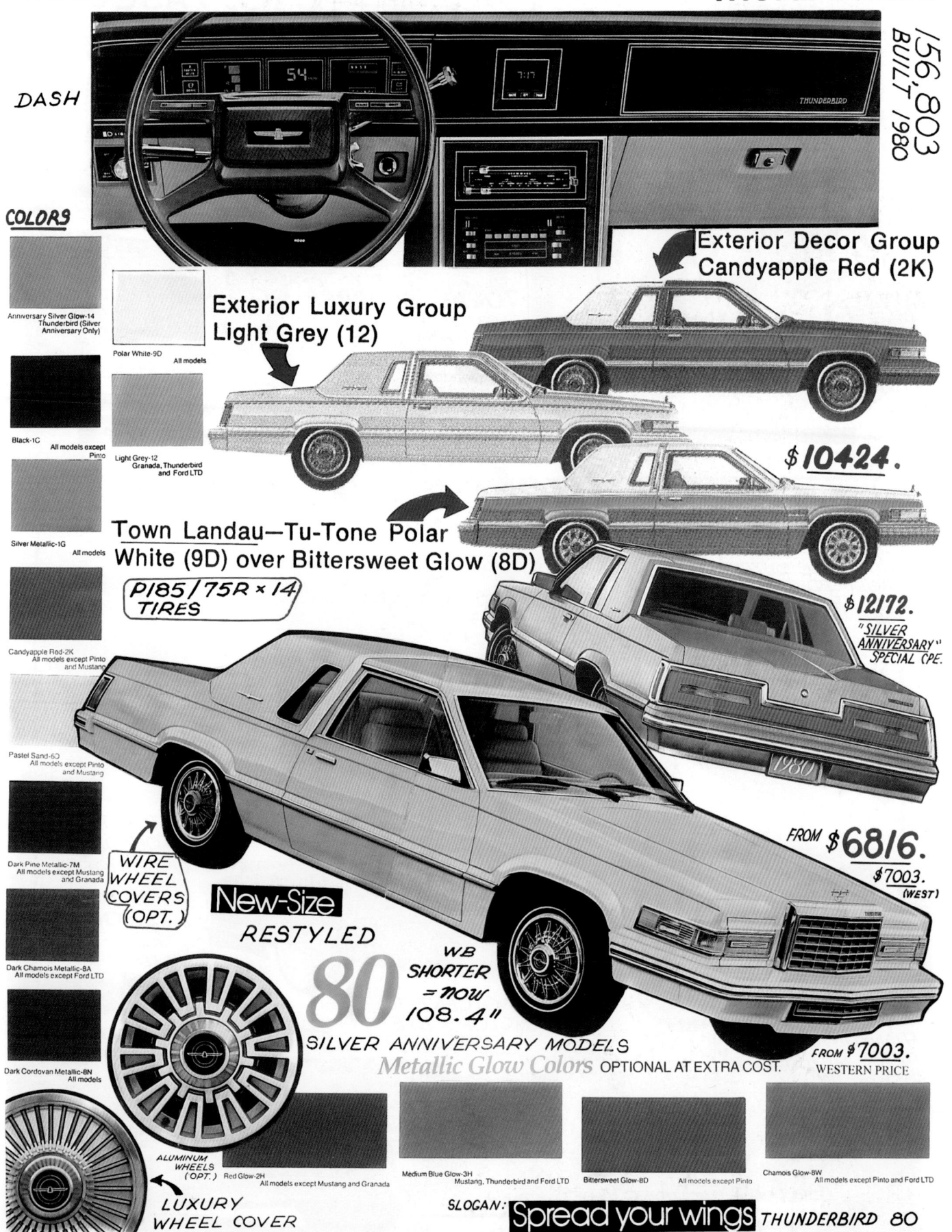

115 OR 131 HP = new 255 CID V8, OR 302 CID V8

THUNDERBIRD

156,803 BUILT 1980

DASH

COLORS

Anniversary Silver Glow-14
Thunderbird (Silver Anniversary Only)

Polar White-9D
All models

Black-1C
All models except Pinto

Light Grey-12
Granada, Thunderbird and Ford LTD

Silver Metallic-1G
All models

Candyapple Red-2K
All models except Pinto and Mustang

Pastel Sand-6D
All models except Pinto and Mustang

Dark Pine Metallic-7M
All models except Mustang and Granada

Dark Chamois Metallic-8A
All models except Ford LTD

Dark Cordovan Metallic-8N
All models

Exterior Luxury Group
Light Grey (12)

Exterior Decor Group
Candyapple Red (2K)

$10424.

Town Landau—Tu-Tone Polar
White (9D) over Bittersweet Glow (8D)

P185/75R × 14 TIRES

$12172.
"SILVER ANNIVERSARY" SPECIAL CPE.

FROM $6816.
$7003. (WEST)

WIRE WHEEL COVERS (OPT.)

New-Size RESTYLED

80 WB SHORTER = now 108.4"

SILVER ANNIVERSARY MODELS
Metallic Glow Colors OPTIONAL AT EXTRA COST.

FROM $7003.
WESTERN PRICE

ALUMINUM WHEELS (OPT.)

Red Glow-2H
All models except Mustang and Granada

Medium Blue Glow-3H
Mustang, Thunderbird and Ford LTD

Bittersweet Glow-8D
All models except Pinto

Chamois Glow-8W
All models except Pinto and Ford LTD

LUXURY WHEEL COVER

SLOGAN: **Spread your wings** THUNDERBIRD 80

763

(1948)

$7500. DERHAM BODY →

TASCO V8

AMER. SPTS. CAR CO.,
HARTFORD, CONN.

(1947-1948)

INTERNATIONAL MOTOR CAR CO.,
SAN DIEGO, CALIF.

MERCURY CHASSIS

TRUNK IS IN THE FRONT

('48)

TOWNE SHOPPER
63" WB   (116" LONG)
2 CYL. OWN REAR ENGINE
WT. 600 lbs.   (10.6 HP)
ALUMINUM BODY

$595.

('47)

4.00 x 8" TIRES   50 MPH   40~50 MPG

Tucker '48

THE TUCKER CORP., 7401 S. CICERO, CHICAGO, ILL. (1946-1949)

PRINCIPAL OUTPUT PRODUCED DURING 1947, BUT KNOWN AS 1948 MODELS, OR EVEN 1949!

REAR

PRESTON TUCKER (FOUNDER) (1903-1956)

SUGGESTED PRICE IN $2500. RANGE (MUCH LESS THAN MFRS. ACTUAL COST!)

6 - CYL. 335 cid HORIZ. OPPOSED FRANKLIN/TUCKER REAR ENGINE (166 HP)

TURNING (CENTER) "CYCLOPS EYE" HEADLIGHT

RARE! ONLY 53 BUILT, INCLUDING PILOT MODELS.

SYMBOL OF SAFETY

T ~ TUCKER

CRASH COWL

126" WB

Valiant (1960~1976)

NEW FROM CHRYSLER

$2053. (52,788 BLT.)

new INCLINED 6-CYL. 170 CID O.H.V. ENGINE 101 HP @ 4400 RPM or 148 HP @ 5200 RPM

106½" WB (THROUGH '62) PLYMOUTH'S new COMPACT CAR

V-100

V100 WAGON (13,946 BLT.) $2365. UP

V-200

V-200s have EXTRA SIDE CHROME TRIM.

$2053.~2566. PRICE RANGE

(21043 BLT.)

4-DR. (106,515 BLT.)

V-200

60 new!

QXI-L OR QXI-H

$2130.

1960

(25,695 BLT.) 4-DR.

V-100

225 CID PLYMOUTH 6 CYL. ENGINE ALSO AVAIL. (145 HP @ 4000 RPM)

$2423. V-200 WAGON (10,794 BLT.)

$2014.

new H/T

$2137.

V-200

1961

61

RVI-L OR RVI-H

DASH

V-200

H/T (18,586 BLT.)

note GRILLE CHANGE

FINAL YEAR FOR 148-HP VERSION OF SMALL ENGINE

4-DR. (59,056 BLT.)

V-200

$2110.

TOTAL 1961 PRODUCTION: 120,848

CALENDAR YEAR PRODUCTION: 122,275

(SAME ENGINES AS IN 1960)

$2014.~2423. PRICE RANGE

VALIANT 60~61

765

VALIANT
$2285. $**2590.** (WEST COAST)

V-100 WAGON

V-200 HAS SIDE TRIM

(55,789 BLT.) $**2087.**

V-200

(5932 BLT.)

$**2381.**

SV1

62

new GRILLES

(8055 BLT.)

SV1-L (V-100)
SV1-H (V-200)
SV1-P (SIGNET)

(25,586 BLT.)

new SIGNET (has FRONT BUCKET SEATS)

VALIANT

SIGNET has ▽ INSIGNIA on DARK GRILLE

$**2230.** $ **2538.** (WEST COAST)

CALENDAR YEAR PROD.: 153,248

$**1910.**

(new 18-GALLON FUEL TANK)
(32,761 BLT.)

Valiant V-100 2-door sedan/metallic green

ENGINE

new CONVTS.

106" WB

TRANSMISSION PUSHBUTTONS

63

TV1

(TOTALLY RESTYLED)

13M-82

SIGNET CVT.

Valiant V-200 4-door station wagon/dark metallic blue

MODELS: 1963

V-100			V-200			SIGNET	
2 DR. (32,761)	$1910.		2 DR. (10,605)	$2035.		H/T (30,857)	$2230.
4 DR. (54,617)	1973.		4 DR. (57,029)	2097.		CVT. (9154 BLT.)	
4 DR. WAGON (5932 BLT.)	2268.		CVT. (7122)	2340.			2454.
			4 DR. WAGON (11,147)	2392.			

VALIANT 62~63

CALENDAR YEAR PRODUCTION: 221,677

VALIANT

note THAT THIS LATER SERIES CONVERTIBLE has LESS REAR BRIGHTWORK and DIFFERENT DECK EMBLEM FROM "SIGNET" ILLUSTR. ON PRECEDING PAGE

63½

Valiant presents
AMERICA'S LOWEST-PRICED CONVERTIBLE...$2340*

Barracuda (new) (INTRO. 4-2-64)

$2375.
(23,443 BLT.)
6 CYL. OR V8

WEST COAST PRICE
$2670.
(6)

$2215.
WEST COAST

2-DR. $1921.

V-100
(35,403 BLT.)

Valiant V-100 2-Door Sedan

$2388.
↓ V-200

64

VVI-L (V-100)
VVI-H (V-200)
VVI-P (SIGNET 200)
VVI-P29 (BARRACUDA)

$2256.
$2549.
WEST COAST
↓
SIGNET

H/T

SIGNET CVT.
(7636 BLT.)

$2473.

new GRILLE with "PLYMOUTH" NAMEPLATE ABOVE

(37,736 BLT.)

Valiant/64 style
Best all-around compact

$1921. ~ 2473.
PRICE RANGE

ENGINES :
170 CID SLANT-6 (101 HP)
225 CID " " (145 HP)
new 273 CID V8 (180 HP)
@ 4200 RPM

VALIANT 63½ ~ 64

VALIANT

$2487.

BARRACUDA
(64,596 BLT.)

$2801. (V8)
(WEST COAST)

65
new GRILLE

ALL-VINYL SEATS IN "100."

6 and V8 ENGINE SPECS. AS BEFORE, EXCEPT THAT new OPTIONAL 10.5 COMPRESSION VERSION of V8 is ALSO AVAIL., with 235 HP @ 5200 RPM

$2004.   100
2-DR.
(40,434 BLT.)

$2476.

$2195.

200

$2127.
2 DR.

Plymouth Valiant 200 4-Door Station Wagon
(6133 BLT.)

6 CYL.:
AVI-L (100)
AVI-H (200)
AVI-P (SIGNET)
AVI-P29 (BARRACUDA)
(V8s have "AV2" PREFIXES)

(41,642 BLT.)   200

1965

(8919 BLT.)

The Roaring '65s*

$2340.

DASH

Valiant Signet
H/T

(10,999 BLT.)

new FLAT-PROFILE AIR CONDITIONER

CVT.
(2578 BLT.)

$2561.
$2004. TO $2561. PRICE RANGE

CALENDAR YEAR PRODUCTION:
VALIANT = 139,436
BARRACUDA = 54,855

$2234. TO $2932.
(WEST COAST PRICES)
* = SLOGAN APPLIES TO PLYMOUTH ALSO.

VALIANT 65

Valiant 66

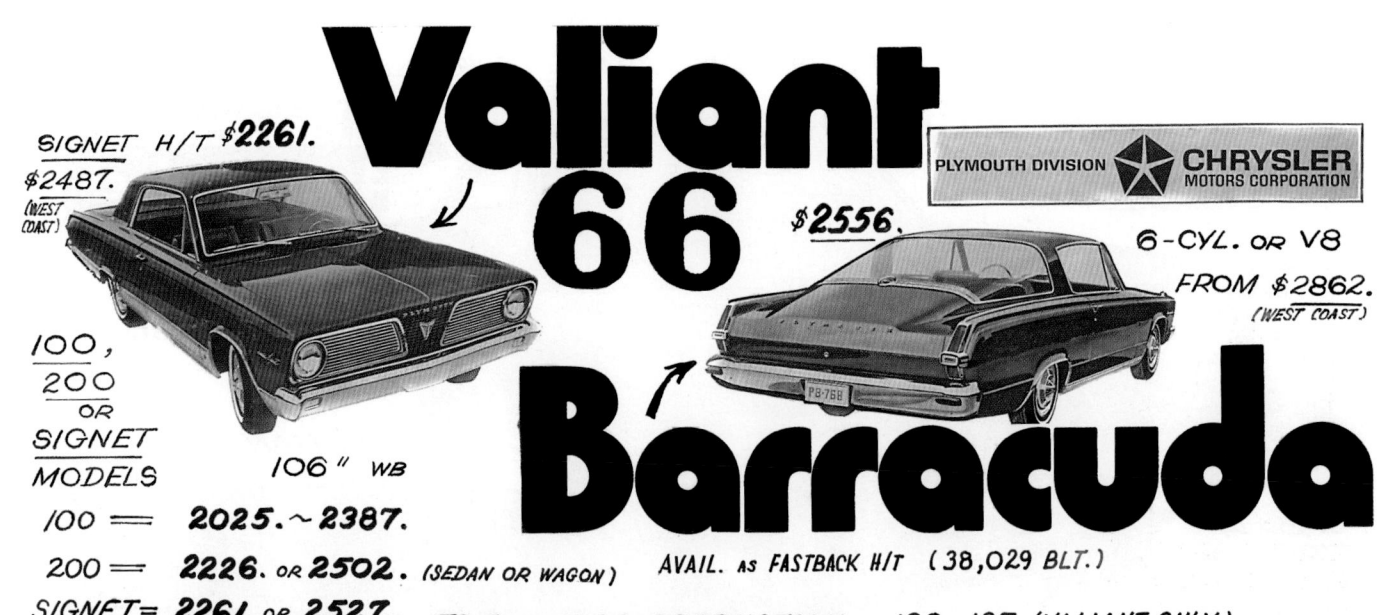

SIGNET H/T $2261.
$2487. (WEST COAST)

PLYMOUTH DIVISION — CHRYSLER MOTORS CORPORATION

$2556.

6-CYL. OR V8
FROM $2862. (WEST COAST)

Barracuda

100, 200 OR SIGNET MODELS
106" WB

100 = 2025. ~ 2387.
200 = 2226. OR 2502. (SEDAN OR WAGON)
SIGNET = 2261. (H/T) OR 2527. (CVT.)

AVAIL. AS FASTBACK H/T (38,029 BLT.)

TOTAL 1966 PRODUCTION: 138,137 (VALIANT ONLY)

(SINCE 1964)

DASH

TAIL-LT.

('67 BARRACUDA INTRO. 11-25-66)
new 108" WB
('67 VALIANT INTRO. 9-29-66)

67
new GRILLE

$2117.   100
2-DR. $2346. WEST COAST

(29,093 BLT.)

100 (WITH 200 DECOR OPTION)
(NOTE SIDE CHROME)

$2163. UP

$2308.

$2262.

100 REAR

4-DR. $2537.
SIGNET

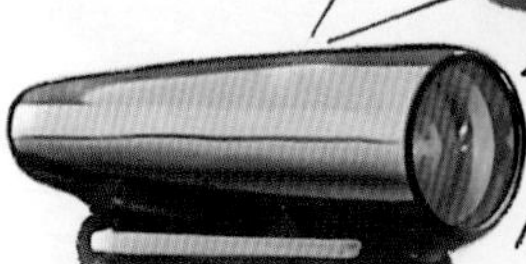

TURN SIGNAL INDICATOR IS VISIBLE TO DRIVER

'67

2-DR. $2491.

(200 ELIMINATED AS A MODEL SERIES)

TOTAL 1967 PRODUCTION: 108,969 VALIANTS; 62,534 BARRACUDAS (NOW IN 3 BODY TYPES)
FASTBACK - CVT. - H/T
VALIANT 66~67

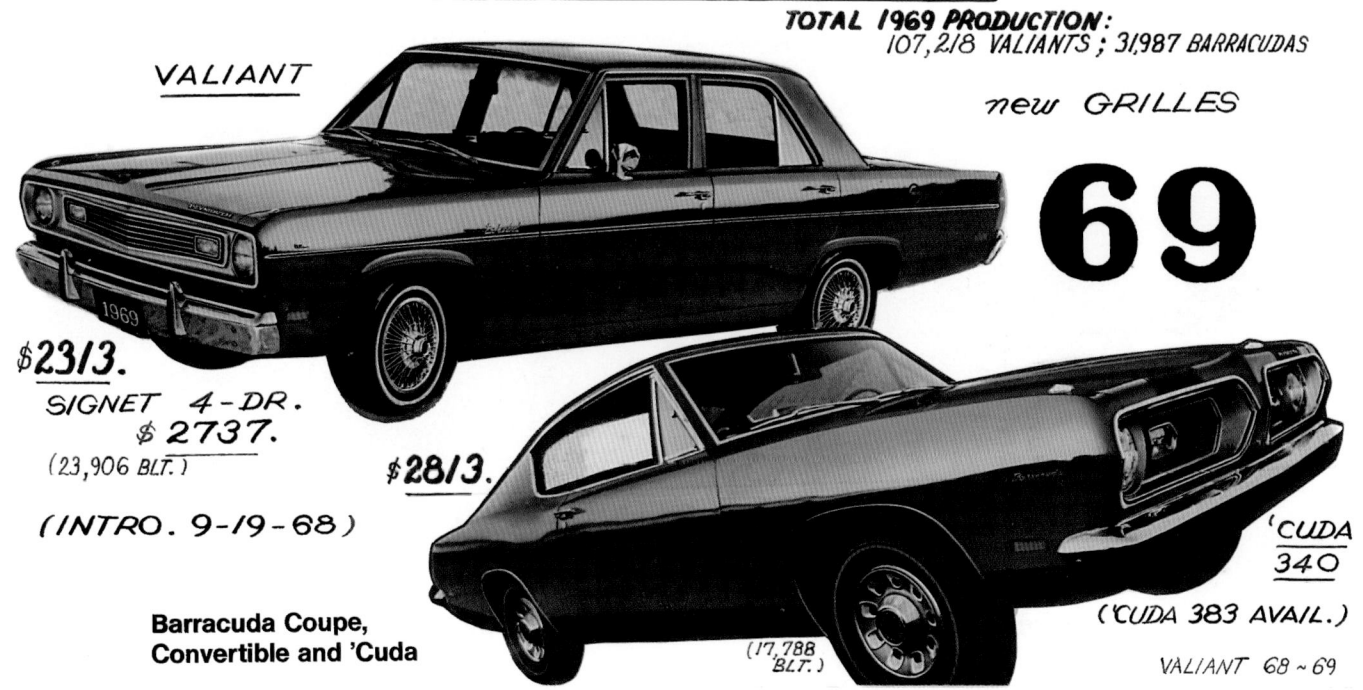

TOTAL 1968 PRODUCTION: 110,795 VALIANTS; 44,014 BARRACUDAS

Valiant

BARRACUDA $2605. H/T (19,997 BLT.)

FR. $2936. ('WEST COAST)

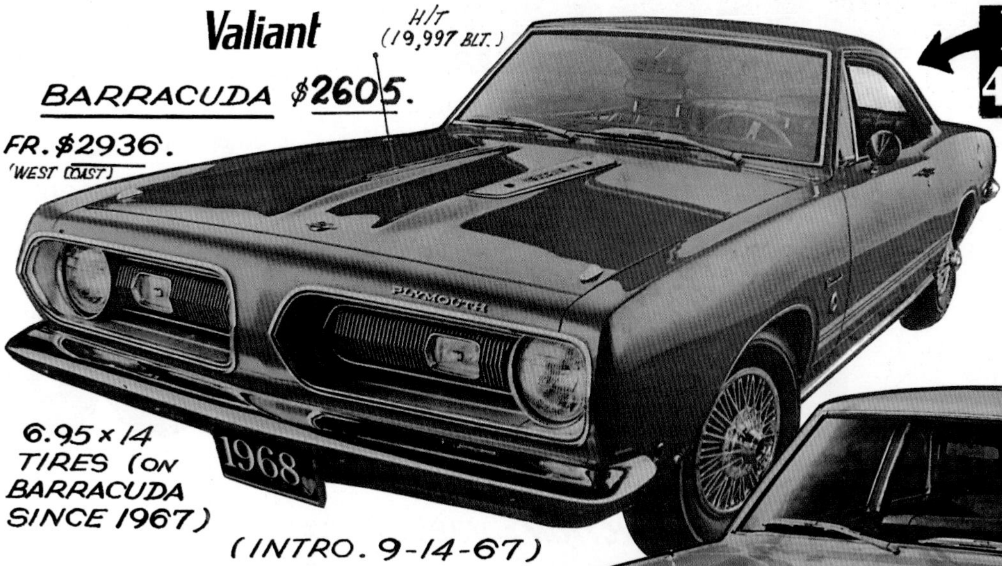

Barracuda. 4 new engines.

225 CID 6 (145 HP)

318, 340, 383 CID V8s (FROM 230 HP)

6.95 × 14 TIRES (ON BARRACUDA SINCE 1967)

(INTRO. 9-14-67)

68

VALIANT SIGNET 2-DR. $2633. (WEST COAST) (6265 BLT.)

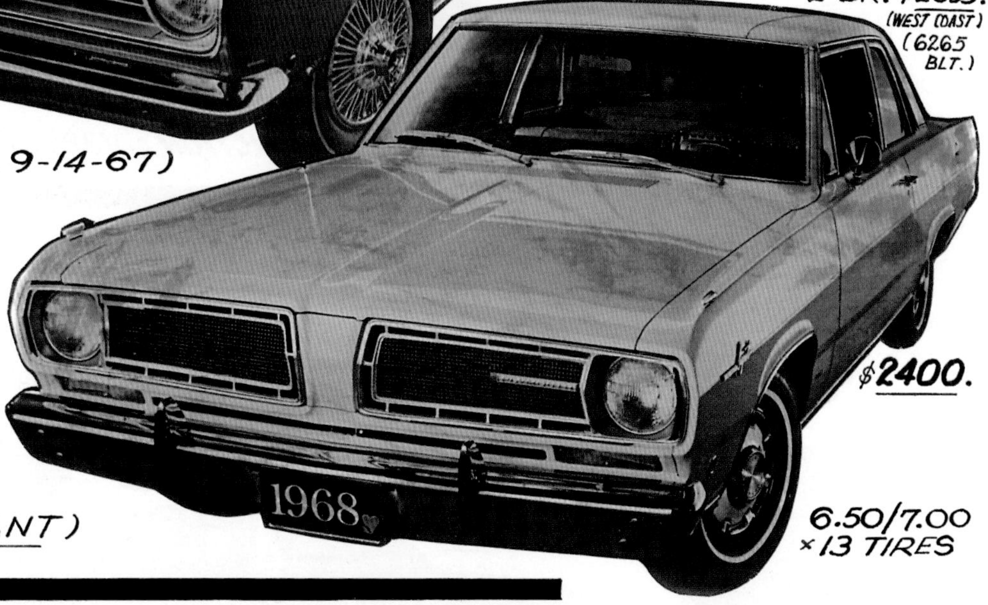

new GRILLES

(FINAL YR. FOR SPLIT GRILLE ON VALIANT)

$2400.

6.50/7.00 × 13 TIRES

ENGINES: 170 CID SLANT-6 (115 HP); 225 CID SLANT-6 (145 HP); 273 CID V8 (190 HP); 340 CID V8 (275 HP); 383 CID V8 (330 HP) (340 and 383 V8s OPTIONAL, BARRACUDAS ONLY)

V-100, SIGNET OR BARRACUDA

108" WB (SINCE '67)

TOTAL 1969 PRODUCTION: 107,218 VALIANTS; 31,987 BARRACUDAS

VALIANT

new GRILLES

69

$2313.

SIGNET 4-DR. $2737. (23,906 BLT.)

$2813.

(INTRO. 9-19-68)

'CUDA 340

('CUDA 383 AVAIL.)

(17,788 BLT.)

Barracuda Coupe, Convertible and 'Cuda

VALIANT 68 ~ 69

Valiant

VALIANT/
DUSTER
DASH

(50810 BLT.)
$2250.

The Gold Duster—Special Version of The Popular Duster

Valiant SEDAN

1970

1970

1970

2-DR. VALIANT NOW KNOWN AS

Duster
(24817 2-DR. H/Ts)
(192,375 FASTBACK COUPES)

Barracuda is so popular that sales are up 53%.

DUSTER CARTOON DECALS

DUSTER "340" WITH 340 CID V8 (275 HP)

70 (INTRO. 9-23-69)

6 OR V8

PLYMOUTH "HEART" NECKTIE USED IN ADVERTISING

new MODELS (RESTYLED)

new "HEMI 'CUDA" H/T

Barracuda

$3034.

CONVERTIBLE (1554 BLT.)

WITH "AIR GRABBER" (and 426 CID V8 = 425 HP)

$2934.

Barracuda is America's lowest priced sporty car.

2-DR. H/T (25651 BLT.)
$2764.

new GRAN COUPE (H/T) (8/83 BLT.)

VALIANT 70

(596 GRAN CVTS. ALSO)

108" WB ON ALL

Valiant

COLORS

Winchester Gray Metallic · Glacial Blue Metallic · True Blue Metallic · Evening Blue Metallic · In-Violet Metallic* · Rallye Red · Amber Sherwood Metallic · Sherwood Green Metallic · Sassy Grass Green*

Autumn Bronze Metallic · Bahama Yellow* · Tunisian Tan Metallic · Tor-Red* · Sno White · Formal Black · Curious Yellow* · Gold Leaf Metallic · Tawny Gold Metallic

1971 Valiant
Valiant 4-Door Sedan
1971
(42660 BLT.)

VALIANT DASH

DASH

DUSTER 340

DUSTER
(173,592 BLT.)

AVAIL. REAR SPOILER FOR DUSTER 340 DECK ←
1971

Option

71 (INTRO. 9-15-70) (VALIANT)

SCAMP
(new)
111"
WB
1971
↑
(48253 BLT.)

340
PLYMOUTH
DUSTER
GOOD/YEAR
POLYGLAS

DUSTER 340
WITH AVAILABLE BLACK DECORATED HOOD

GRILLE DIFFERS FROM STD. DUSTER.

'cuda
(6228 BLT.)

new 6-PORT GRILLE
(BARRACUDA'S 1971 MODEL INTRO. 10-6-70)

(1014 BLT.)

PLYMOUTH

(THE FINAL BARRACUDA CVT.)
(+374 'CUDA CVTS BLT.)

DUSTER
1971
DUSTER

DUSTER
VALIANT 71

772

Valiant

Coming through with the kind of car America wants.

WITH SIDE STRIPE and "DUSTER" DECAL AT FRONT END of STRIPE

212,331 STD. DUSTER COUPES BLT.

$2287. UP

(INTRO. 9-28-71)

72 A

Valiant $2363.

(52911 BLT.)

Valiant 4-Door Sedan

1972 Plymouth Duster

WITH SIDE TRIM STRIP and CHROME "DUSTER" LETTERING on COWL

SCAMP CLOTH-AND-VINYL SEAT (OPT.)

STD. SCAMP BLACK VINYL SEAT

Valiant Scamp

Twister Package. A lot of extras for your Duster including rear quarter panel designation and hood paint treatment.

REAR FENDER

HOOD

CLOCK/TACHOMETER AVAIL. AS OPTION IN 1971

(49470 BLT.)

$2528.

new WH. COVERS

VALIANT 72(A)

BUMPER GUARDS

NAME ADDED

Valiant

'CUDA
(7828 BLT.)
$3029.
($3761., WEST)

'Cuda 2-Door Hardtop

Rallye Instrument Cluster. What you see is what you get on Barracuda and Cuda.

STD. BARRACUDA VINYL SEATS (ALSO AVAIL. IN OTHER COLORS

Barracuda & 'Cuda

BARRACUDA (10622 BLT.) $2710. new GRILLE

72 B (CONT'D.)

Interiors

BARRACUDA SEATS

VALIANT BENCH SEAT

OPT. VALIANT, DUSTER and DUSTER 340 SEAT WITH ARM RESI

Duster and Duster 340 standard cloth-and-vinyl bench seat. Available in three colors.

Duster

DUSTER HAS SLIGHTLY ALTERED REAR (DUSTER NAME AT VERY CENTER, PLY. NAME OFF LID.)

DUSTER 340 (15681 BLT.) $2742.

Winchester Gray Metallic · Blue Sky · Basin Street Blue · True Blue Metallic · Rallye Red · Amber Sherwood Metallic · Sherwood Green Metallic · Mojave Tan Metallic

AVAIL. COLOR CHOICES

Chestnut Metallic · Tor-Red* · Spinnaker White · Lemon Twist* · Honeydew · Gold Leaf Metallic · Tawny Gold Metallic · Formal Black
*Optional at extra cost

SPECIAL TOP ON Gold Duster.

VALIANT 72 (B)

Valiant 'CUDA

$3120. ($3860., WEST)

NO MORE 6~CYL. BARRACUDAS OR 'CUDAS

Barracuda (11587 BLT.)

$2935. ($3675., WEST)

(10626 BLT.)

ENGINES*

198 c.i.d. 6 (100 HP)
225 c.i.d. 6 (110 HP)
318 c.i.d. V8 (150 HP)
340 c.i.d. V8 (240 HP)

*SAME ENGINES and HP as 1972

73

16½~ GALLON GAS TANK

new GRILLE NOW MATCHES BODY COLOR.
new SAFETY BUMPERS

F 70 x 14 TIRES

SCAMP'S GRAINED DASH OPTIONAL IN VALIANT / DUSTER MODELS.

vinyl roof Gold Duster.

new REAR STYLING

(249,243 BLT.)

DUSTER

(61826 BLT.)

VALIANT SEDAN

$2447. ($2687., WEST)

new GRILLES and SAFETY BUMPERS

$2376. (2616., WEST)

Duster 340 (15731 BLT.)
$2822.

Plymouth Duster 340
Extra care in engineering...it makes a difference.

($3093., WEST)

SCAMP (53792 BLT.)
$2617. ($2857., WEST) VALIANT 73

Valiant

$3288.

DUSTER 360
(REPLACES "340") 360 CID V8 (190 HP)

7 4

(RALLYE DASH with LARGE ROUND GAUGES STILL AVAIL.)

DUSTER/VALIANT/BARRACUDA EXTERIOR COLORS

Powder Blue	Dark Moonstone M
Lucerne Blue Metallic	Sienna Metallic
Rallye Red	Spinnaker White
Burnished Red Metallic	Formal Black
Frosty Green Metallic	Golden Fawn
Deep Sherwood Metallic	Yellow Blaze
Avocado Gold Metallic	Golden Haze Met.
Sahara Beige	Tahitian Gold Met.

NOTE: Due to occasional printing irregularities, the above may vary slightly from actual hues. See your Plymouth Dealer for accurate color chips.

Standard Scamp Instrument Panel—Optional on Duster and Valiant

Space Duster

1974

1974

DUSTER

TWISTER PACKAGE

For those buyers who want good handling and an extra sporty looking car but with a smaller displacement engine—Twister's the answer. With unique upper-body side tape stripes, deck lower panel tape applique, and bright drip moldings,

$2829.

E70 x 14

1974

DUSTER
(277,409 BLT., INCLUDING "360")

GOLD DUSTER

Valiant Brougham
CRUSHED VELOUR INTERIOR ➡

Valiant Brougham
(new)

1974

BARRACUDA
(6745 BLT.)
$3067.

REAR RESTYLED

VALIANT
(127,430 BLT., INCL. BROUGHAM)

SCAMP
(51,699 BLT.)
$3077.

(4989 BLT.)

'CUDA

$3252.

FINAL YR. FOR BARRACUDA and 'CUDA

VALIANT 74

776

Valiant / VOLARE

The style of a European sedan. At the price of an American compact. Valiant Brougham.

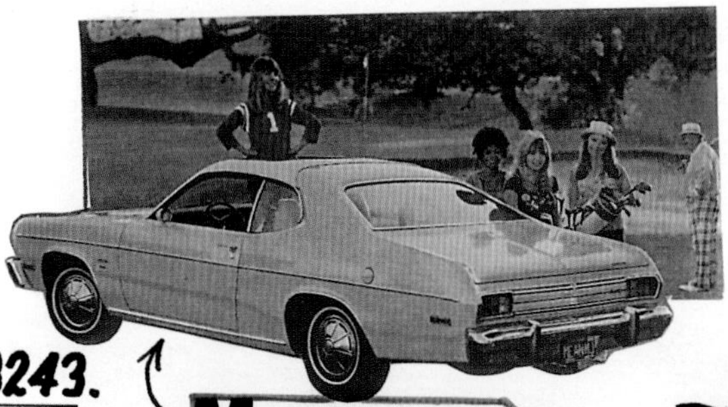

(17803 BLT., 1975) $**4139.**

$**3243.** UP (1975)

(SCAMP H/T STILL AVAIL.)

More car in a small car. That's par for Duster.

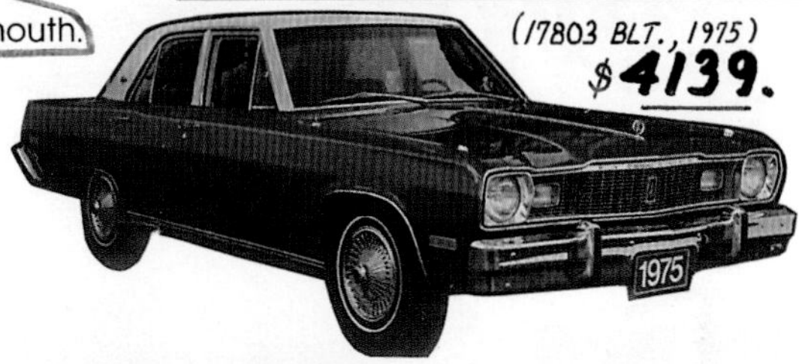

75-76

FINAL VALIANTS and DUSTERS. (REPLACED BY new VOLARE AFTER 1976.)

Plymouth

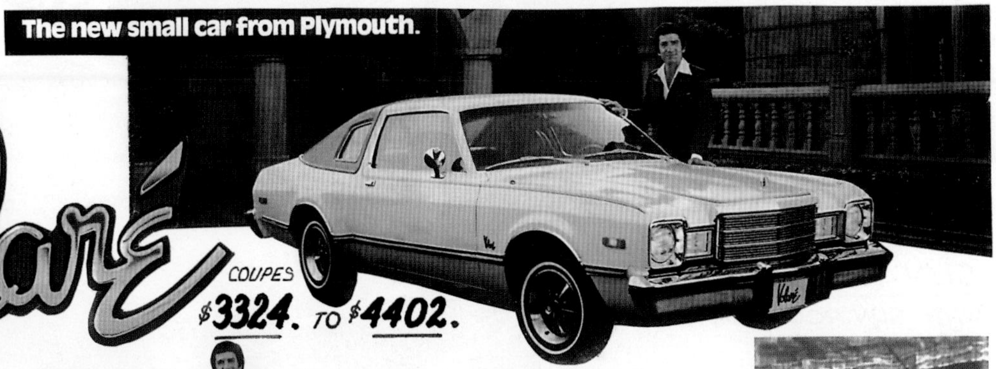

The new small car from Plymouth.

Volaré

COUPES $**3324.** TO $**4402.**

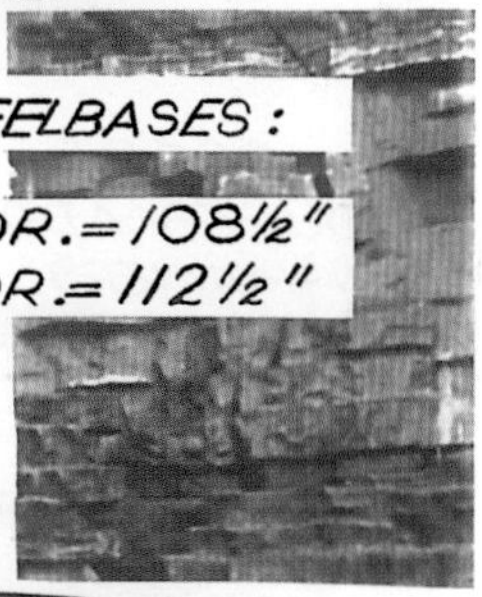

RESTYLED, and ½" LONGER WHEELBASES:

2-DR. = 108½"
4-DR. = 112½"

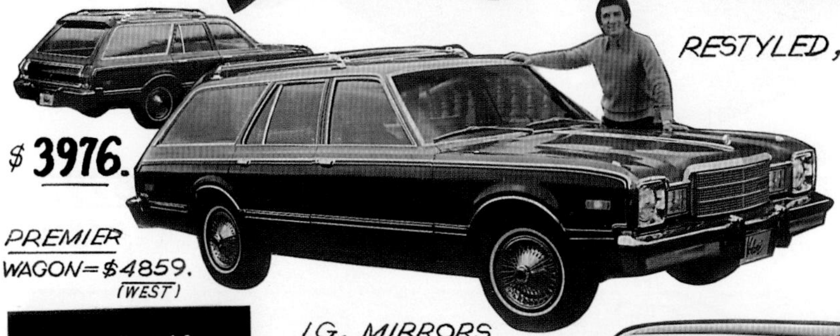

76 NEW

$**3976.**

PREMIER WAGON = $4859. (WEST)

The accent is on comfort... and space.

LG. MIRRORS OPTIONAL, USED WHEN HAULING TRAILERS

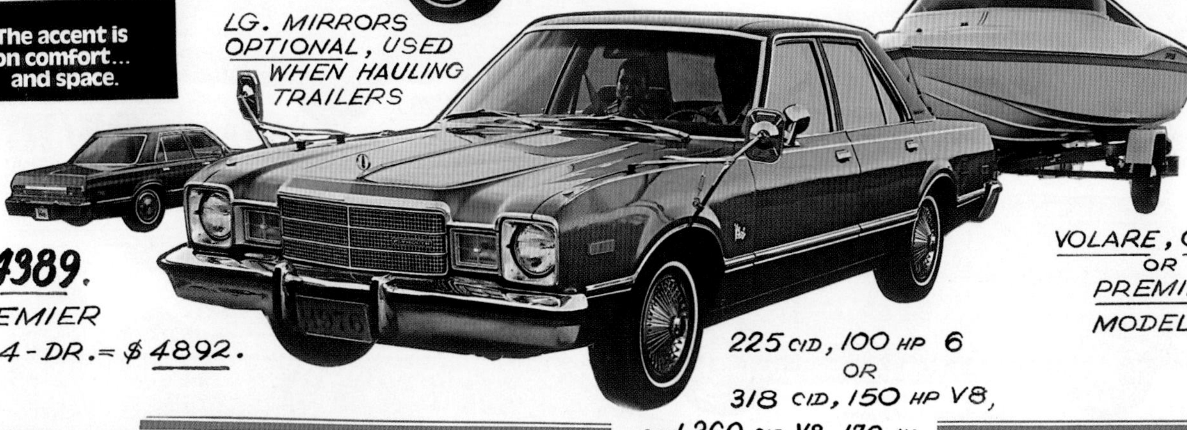

VOLARE, CUSTOM OR PREMIER MODELS

$**4389.**

PREMIER 4-DR. = $4892.

225 CID, 100 HP 6 OR 318 CID, 150 HP V8, and 360 CID V8, 170 HP

1976 PRODUCTION FIGURES

VALIANT SCAMP SPECIAL H/T (4018)
    "   DUSTER CPE. (34681)
    "   SEDAN (40079)
    "   SCAMP H/T (DLX.) (6908)
VOLARE SPT. CPE. (37024); SEDAN (23058)

VOLARE WAGON (46065)
   "   CUSTOM SPT. CPE. (31252)
   "   "   SEDAN (36407)

VOLARE PREM. CPE. (31475)
   "   PREMIER SED. (37131)
   "   "   WAGON (49507)

VALIANT '75~76 ; VOLARE '76

Volaré

ROAD RUNNER

PREMIER WAGON

OPERA WINDOWS

SPORT COUPE

Volaré Premier 4-Door Sedan

Volaré. The small car with the accent on comfort.

77

(382,418 VOLARES BLT. 1977)

$VOLARÉS 3

The new Volaré T-Bar Roof

NOTE THAT SOME 1977 VOLARES DON'T HAVE HOOD ORNAMENTS, IF NOT IN PREMIER SERIES

SUN RUNNER
(WITH SUN ROOF OR T-BAR

COUPES = $3570. TO $4305.

SEDANS = $3619. TO $4354.

WAGONS = $3941. TO $4271.

new SPORT COUPES ADDED ("FUN-RUNNERS")

FRONT RUNNER

78-79

new GRILLE WITH "WAFFLE" PATTERN

DUSTER CPL. RETURNS ('79)

COUPES FROM 4387. ('79)

4-DR. SEDAN

$3899. ('78)
$4504. ('79)

COUPES FROM $3771. ('78)

PRODUCTION
('78)
COUPES — 74818 ('78)
63620 ('79)
SEDANS — 100,718 ('78)
95383 ('79)
WAGONS — 81242 ('78)
50683 ('79)

225 c/d 6
318 c/d V8
(1979 LAST YR. 360 c/d V8 IS OFFERED IN VOLARE LINE.)

25/18* MPG HWY MPG CITY
$4362**

WAGONS FROM $4241. ('78)
$5110. ('79)

Volaré. America's first choice in wagons.

Don't Give Up.
Get a New Plymouth Volaré

19/14* MPG HWY MPG CITY
$4427**
Price includes optional automatic transmission.

** = SALE PRICE

PREMIER WAGON

1978

$5672., WEST

VOLARE 77~79

778

Volaré

VINYL SEATS STD. IN WAGONS (OPT. IN SEDANS)

ROAD-RUNNER →

COUPE

WITH PREMIER PKG.

(GRAINED) PREMIER WAGON ↖

Volaré Wagon Premier Package Includes all Custom features plus dark colonial walnut woodtone appliques on body sides and liftgate with bright sur-round moldings; Premier nameplates, hood ornament and deluxe wheel covers.

(19910 WAGONS BLT.)
$5022. UP

CUSTOM WAGON

Volaré Wagon Custom Package Includes all wagon features plus belt, upper door frame, wheel-opening and sill moldings. Plus "Custom" nameplates.

Standard in Volaré two- and four-door models is this cloth-and-vinyl bench seat, offered in blue, red or cashmere.

VOLARÉ TWO-DOOR. VALUE AT ITS BEST.

Sporty plaid cloth bucket seats are available in the Duster coupe. Offered in blue, red or cashmere.

INTERIOR TRIM

80 (FINAL VOLARE)

225 HP 6 (90 HP) OR 318 CID V8 (120 HP)

SEDANS FROM $5150. (55606 BLT.)

WITH ARM REST

DASH

new GRILLE

DUSTER CPE.

CPES. FROM $5033. (34256 BLT.)

(REPLACED BY 1981 RELIANT)

FRONT SIDE SAFETY LIGHTS NOW VERTICAL, and AT FENDER CORNER.

VOLARE 80

COLORS

Natural Suede Tan	Burnished Silver Metallic
Baron Red	Crimson Red Metallic
Graphic Red (coupe only)	Teal Tropic Green Metallic
Nightwatch Blue	Frost Blue Metallic
Mocha Brown Metallic	Spinnaker White
Light Cashmere	Teal Frost Metallic
Formal Black	(Upper) Frost Blue Metallic (Lower) Nightwatch Blue
(Upper) Light Cashmere (Lower) Natural Suede Tan	(Upper) Burnished Silver Metallic (Lower) Baron Red

WILLYS
FOR 1940

WILLYS ~
OVERLAND, INC.
TOLEDO, OH.

new 102" WB

$495

for Speedway Coupe*, illustrated below
DeLuxe Coupe $590*, Four-Door DeLuxe Sedan $620*
*All prices f.o.b. Toledo. Federal, State and
local taxes (if any), and transportation, extra.

4 CYLINDERS
134.2 CID
(SINCE 1933)
new
61 HP

40
RESTYLED

A

440
SERIES

WILLYS DOES IT BETTER !

1940 WILLYS
PRODUCTION =
26698

BODY and BRAKE CONSTRUCTION

Four-Door Speedway Sedan, illustrated above. $545*

Joseph W. Frazer, President of WILLYS~OVERLAND

WILLYS SPEEDWAY SEDAN — A
luxurious, four-door sedan
of astonishing beauty. Easy
to handle, thrilling to drive.
A family car for folks interested in thrift . . **$560***
(DeLuxe Model $635*)

note
EXTRA
HOOD CHROME
and
BUMPER
GUARDS ON
DE LUXE
←

(CONT'D.
NEXT
PAGE)

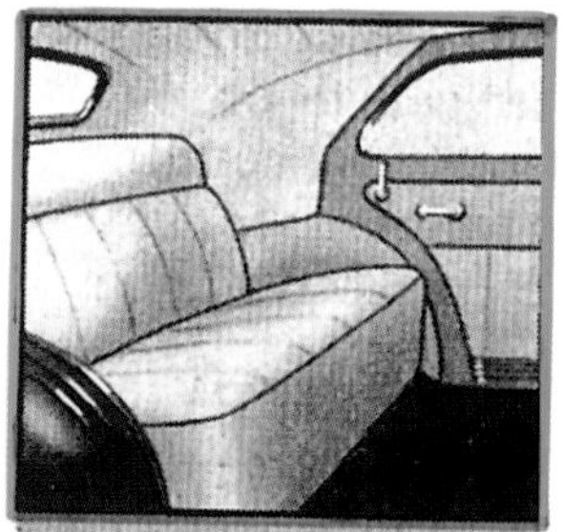

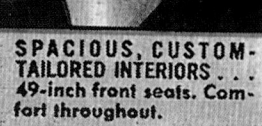

SPACIOUS, CUSTOM-
TAILORED INTERIORS . . .
49-inch front seats. Com-
fort throughout.

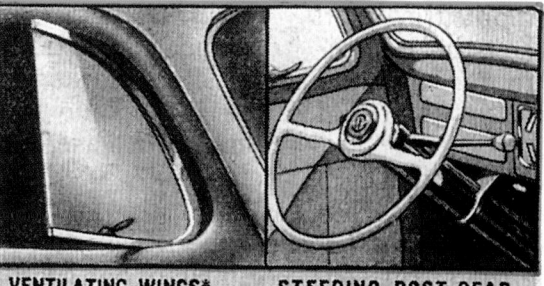

VENTILATING WINGS* . . .
Draft control . . . Safety
Glass in all windows.

STEERING-POST GEAR-
SHIFT* . . . Below natural-
grip Steering Wheel.
*Standard equipment on all DeLuxe models

40~41 WILLYS

WILLYS

AMERICA'S LOWEST PRICED FULL-SIZE CAR...
NOW HAS A THREE FULL YEAR OR

100,000 MILE GUARANTEE!

40 B

THE 4 SCARCEST MODELS SHOWN HERE

NEW

An amazing new policy... Joseph W. Frazer, President of Willys-Overland Motors, Inc., announces a new guarantee of 100,000 miles, or three full years — on 1940 Willys passenger and commercial cars — a remarkable tribute to a great new car!

WILLYS STATION WAGON— Beautiful, roomy, the 6-passenger Willys Station Wagon is today's smartest transportation. Sturdy enough to earn its keep—safety glass windows all-around **$795***

DELUXE WAGON ALSO AVAIL. IN 1941 and 1942.

RARE!·:· MID~SEASON MODEL: A New Californian (BELOW)

WILLYS HALF-TON CAB PICK-UP— Speedy, agile, economical to use, this great commercial car, like all 1940 Willys models, is guaranteed for three full years or 100,000 miles! Only **$535***

The new Willys Californian, now on display in the show rooms of the Transport Motor Co. here, Northern California Willys distributing organization, is the latest model to make its bow to San Francisco motorists. Built in the California plant of Willys-Overland Motors, Inc., it is styled to meet the discriminating tastes of Western automobile owners. Included among its features are a large amount of chromium trim on the hood and body and roll-pillow type cushions in two-tone mohair and broadcloth combination.

WILLYS PANEL DELIVERY— Ruggedly built, this beautiful truck is powerful and super-economical to run. Cab-Over-Engine design

VAN · · **$799***

* f.o.b., Toledo. Federal, State and local taxes (if any) and transportation extra.

3~PASS. COUPE

$634. and up

FOG LIGHTS NOT STD. EQUIPMENT

TOP-LINE PLAINSMAN SERIES IS new

41 A

new 104" WB (THRU 1951)

GRILLE NOT DIVIDED IN CENTER IN 1941.

1941 and 1942 KNOWN AS

WILLYS AMERICAR

1-OF-A-KIND 2-TONE PAINT on SPECIAL ORDER

(1941 SEDAN ON NEXT PAGE)

40~41 WILLYS
(B) (A)

WILLYS

new 63 HP (THRU '42) 1950)

← *ACTUAL PHOTO*

GLAMORIZED ARTIST'S CONCEPTION →

SEDAN = { SPEEDWAY — $674. / DE LUXE —— 720. / PLAINSMAN — 771. }

441 SERIES

41 B (CONT'D.)

AMERICAR

REAR

AMERICAR

THE PEOPLE'S CAR

TOTAL 1941~1942 PROD.: 28935

22~35 M.P.G.

COUPE RETAINS 2~PC. REAR WINDOW

442 SERIES

5.50 x 16" TIRES

THE NEW 1942

WILLYS

4-DR. SEDAN FROM $745.

MILITARY USE ONLY

The Jeep

(INTRO. 1941)

WITH SAME 4~CYL. "GO~DEVIL" ENG. AS WILLYS CAR

Ford, Willys Agree To Manufacture Jeeps

WASHINGTON (INS).—In a move to double the production of the army's "jeep" trucks, the war department Saturday announced that the Ford Motor company, and the Willys-Overland Motors, Inc., of Toledo, will join in turning out this type of vehicle.

The agreement between the two companies, the first of its kind to be negotiated by two American auto manufacturers since the World war, provides that the Ford company will make available the huge facilities of its River Rouge plant at Dearborn, Mich., for the production of a vehicle identical to the model now being manufactured by Willys. The latter company will furnish complete drawings, licenses, patents and other manufacturing information without cost.

LET'S GO! U.S.A. KEEP 'EM FLYING!

SAVE GAS FOR UNCLE SAM
DRIVE A FUEL-SAVING
WILLYS AMERICAR

42 — new HEAVIER VERTICAL PC. AT CENTER OF GRILLE

AVAIL. IN 3 SERIES:

SPEEDWAY FROM $737.

DE LUXE " 812.

PLAINSMAN FROM 863.

OVERDRIVE STD. ON PLAINSMAN, OPTIONAL ON OTHERS.

41~42 WILLYS

782

WILLYS 'Jeep'

WILLYS-OVERLAND, TOLEDO, OHIO

UNIVERSAL JEEP (4-W-D)

MILITARY STYLE ('46)

← $1146.

EARLY MODEL ('46)

Station Wagon

CLARK & COMPANY

All-Steel Station Wagon (new) ENGINE

MILITARY JEEPS INTRO. '41

46-47

(JEEP LT. TRUCKS ALSO AVAIL.)

CJ-2A SERIES

$1565.

('47)

"Jeep Station Wagon" ON HOOD

104" WB

the **Jeepster**

$1765.

(new) →

134.3 CID 4 L-HEAD (63 HP)

ALSO AVAIL. IN 1949: 134.3 CID 4 (F-HEAD, 72 HP) 148.5 CID 6 (72 HP)

REAR

48-49

JEEPSTER PRODUCED 1948 TO 1953. REVIVED 1967 BY KAISER JEEP.

104" WB

(10,326 BLT., 1948) (1949: 4 CYL. 2307; 6 CYL. 653) PRICE REDUCED IN 1949.

'Jeep' Station Sedan

6 CYL. only

has IMITATION WICKER PANELING →

DEEP UPHOLSTERED SEATS, interior roominess and road-leveling wheel suspension add to the smooth, luxurious riding comfort of the 'Jeep' Station Sedan.

$1865.

6.70 x 15

(PREVIOUS 4-CYL. STATION WAGON ALSO CONT'D. $1625.)

WILLYS 46~49

WILLYS 'Jeep'

JEEPSTER PRODUCTION:
4 CYL. (4066) 6 CYL. (1778)
(1950~1951)

2-W-D WAGON (4 CYL.)
$1783.

($2204. WITH 4-W-D)

('51)

('50) LATER SER.

JEEPSTER
$1603. UP ('50)   **$1597.** UP ('51)

6.50 x 15" TIRES

new GRILLE (EARLY '50 has '49-STYLE GRILLE.)

50-51

4 CYL. OR 6

OVERDRIVE OPTIONAL

FIRST NON-JEEP WILLYS CAR PRODUCED SINCE 1942 MODELS:

VARIOUS JEEPS, JEEP WAGONS and JEEPSTERS CONTINUE

MILITARY JEEP

The Revolutionary New Aero Willys

108" WB

AERO-WING
('52 ONLY)

ALL AEROS are 2 DR. SEDANS EXCEPT EAGLE (H/T)

AERO-ACE

52

AERO-LARK has 6-CYL. L-HEAD engine; WING, ACE, EAGLE have HURRICANE 6 F-HEAD.   JEEP WAGONS, JEEPSTERS also

DETAILS OF F-HEAD COMBUSTION CHAMBER

New Hurricane 6 Engine. F-head design with 7.6 compression, one of the world's most efficient power plants.

1952 PRODUCTION:	AERO-LARK (7474)	$1731.	(652-K SERIES, MODEL KA2~675)
31,363 TOTAL	AERO-WING (12,819)	1989.	652-L " " LA1~675
(NOT INCL. JEEPS, WAGONS OR JEEPSTERS)	AERO-ACE (8706)	2074.	652-M " " MA1~685
	AERO-EAGLE (2364)	2155.	" " " " MC1~685
161 CID 6 (75 HP, LARK; 90 HP, OTHER AEROS.)			CALENDAR YR. PRODUCTION: 35,954

WILLYS 50~52

Willys Aero

FIFTIETH YEAR
ANNIVERSARY OF
WILLYS-OVERLAND

$1732.

AERO LARK
4 OR 6 CYL.
(7692 BLT.)

NO HOOD ORNAMENT ON LARK $1646.

2-DR. (8205 BLT.)
AERO-LARK DELUXE ↗

4-DR. AEROS NOW AVAIL.
53
$1861.

AERO-ACE $2038.
4-DR. (7475 BLT.)

AERO-FALCON 4-DR. (3117 BLT.)
(REPLACES '52 AERO-WING) (AERO-FALCON 2-DR. RESEMBLES LARK DLX.)
(2 DR. ALSO) FALCON and LARK 6 HAVE 75 HP.

$1963. (4988 BLT.)
AERO-ACE 2-DR.

ACE H/T ALSO AVAIL. (ILLUSTR. AT LOWER RIGHT) (ACE and EAGLE HAVE 90 HP.)

AERO-EAGLE H/T

AERO EAGLE H/T (7018 BLT.) $2157.

JEEP 4 (4-W-D)   *Station Wagon*

JEEP 6 DELUXE (2-W-D) SERIES 685

SERIES 4 x 475

$2304. ($1862. W/O 4-W-D)
(4-W-D)   (SERIES 475)

$1949.
WILLYS, CALENDAR YEAR 35,146

LOW-PRICED AERO-LARK NOW AVAIL. WITH 134.2 CID 4 (72 HP), AS WELL AS WITH THE 161 CID 6 (75 HP) ALL OTHER AEROS W. 6 CYL. ENGINES

TOTAL 1953 PRODUCTION : 42,057

THE NEW
1954
Aero **WILLYS**

(LARK AVAIL. WITH
134 CID 4 OR 161 OR
226.2 CID 6)

KW
Kaiser-Willys Sales Div.
Willys Motors, Inc.

1954
KAISER/
WILLYS
MERGER

(11 BLT.)
↑
REAR SPARE TIRE

AERO EAGLE CUSTOM

27% MORE POWER (115 90 OR 72 HP)

LARK, ACE
OR EAGLE
MODELS

$2222.
↓

AERO FALCON
NO LONGER
AVAIL.

54

new HOODED HEADLTS.,
new SEGMENTED
TAIL LIGHTS
new HUBCAPS
$1737. UP

Eagle DeLuxe

EAGLE
DE LUXE
H/T
(84 BLT.)

4 OR 6 CYL.

PRODUCTION =
11,856
CALENDAR YEAR
9339

WIDER OPENING
TOP DOOR GIVES
**WIDEST OPENING OF
ANY STATION WAGON
IN ITS FIELD**

WAGON has
new GRILLE

4 x 175
$2304.

6 CYL.
2WD 4WD
$1973./2399.

SER. 685

MANY JEEPS WITH
FOUR-WHEEL-DRIVE
CAN BE RECOGNIZED
BY PLAIN WHEEL HUBS (BELOW)

1955 WILLYS PRODUCTION = 6565
CALENDAR YEAR = 4778
1955 AERO MODELS CUSTOM (3112 BLT.); ACE (659 BLT.); BERMUDA (2215 BLT.)
2 OR 4 DR.   4-DR.   H/T

ENGINES: 161 CID 6 (90 HP)
OR 226.2 CID 6 (115 HP) IN ACE;
OPT. IN CUSTOM OR BERMUDA

(2822 BLT.)
$1795.
4-DR.

CUSTOM
↓

4 OR 6 CYL.

NO HUBCAPS ON
THIS 4-W-D WAGON

4-W-D

all-new
GRILLE,
TAIL-
LIGHTS
and
TRIM

(2215
BLT.)
new↗
BERMUDA H/T
$1997.

55

"AERO"
FINAL WILLYS CAR
BUILT IN U.S.A.,
BUT JEEP PRODUCTION
CONTINUES. KAISER JEEPS
BLT. 1963 TO 1969. AMERICAN
MOTORS CORP. BEGAN BUILDING
JEEPS (SINCE START OF 1970
MODEL SEASON.) MFD. BY CHRYSLER
CORP. SINCE 1987.   WILLYS 54~55

MICHAEL, MARK and STEVIE   2

MICHAEL, MARK and STEVIE   3

MICHAEL, MARK and STEVIE   13

MICHAEL, MARK and STEVIE   15

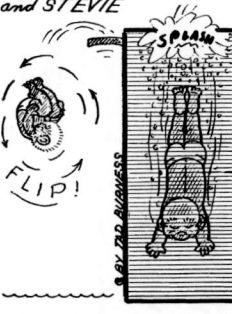

MICHAEL, MARK and STEVIE   19

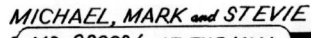
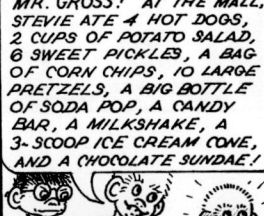

MICHAEL, MARK and STEVIE

MICHAEL, MARK and STEVIE

MICHAEL, MARK and STEVIE

MICHAEL, MARK and STEVIE

MICHAEL, MARK and STEVIE

MICHAEL, MARK and STEVIE   MARCH 4

DEPOSIT = DEPÓSITO (SPANISH)

MICHAEL, MARK and STEVIE   MARCH 27

DELIGHT = ALEGRIA (SPANISH)

MICHAEL, MARK and STEVIE   APRIL 12

AUDIENCE = AUDITORIO (SPANISH)   APRIL 13

MICHAEL, MARK and STEVIE

MAGNETIC (PERSONALITY) = CARISMÁTICO (SPANISH)

MICHAEL, MARK and STEVIE   JUNE 20

HEAD = CABEZA (SPANISH)

About the Author

One might call the work of Tad Burness the window on history, especially regarding his prolific work with automobiles and trucks in his syndicated newspaper series the Auto Album.

"I first got the idea for Auto Album in 1962, having been interested in cars ever since childhood." wrote Burness in his introduction to his book Ultimate Auto Album in 2001. "After four years, I was able to get Auto Album syndicated in the Spring of 1966."

In addition to his dedication to the subject, Burness also injects elements of pop culture into his work including mention of old songs, radio and television programs and period backgrounds creating a period feeling about the popular and rare vehicles he highlights.

Following the success of his syndicated newspaper feature, he published the book Cars of the Early Twenties in 1968. In 1973, the first of his popular Spotter's Guide series, featuring selected years of particular makes, was published featuring American cars from 1940 through 1965. Another book focused on American cars from 1920 through 1939.

Other Burness works over the years have highlighted imported cars, vans, trucks, pickups, buses, plus Ford and Chevrolet vehicles.

In 2001, three of his books appeared through Krause Publishing including Classic Railroad Advertising: Riding the Rails Again, Ultimate Auto Album: An Illustrated History of the Automobile and Ultimate Truck and Van Spotter's Guide: 1925-1990.

His interest in offering period-correct homes in his work with the Auto Album features produced led to the 2003 publication of The Vintage House Book: Classic American Homes 1880-1980, also by Krause Publishing, the forerunner of KP Books, part of the international F + W Publishing organization.

American Car Spotter's Guide will be his 28th book and his first all-color guide.

Tad lives in Pacific Grove, California, with his wife, Sandra, and their daughter, Tammy.

KP Books Standard Catalogs

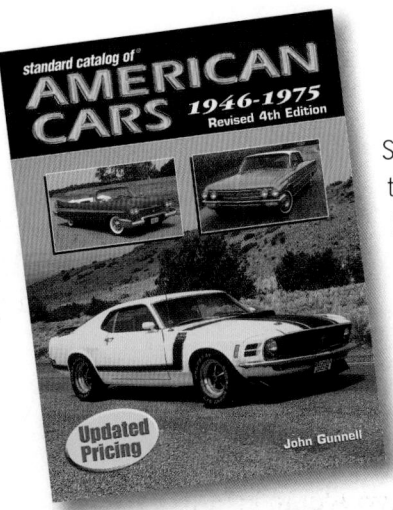

Standard Catalogs are THE place to look for history, photos, buyer's guide information, technical specifications and pricing in one easy-to-use book. You'll also get serial number information, VIN decoding, original equipment lists, factory prices, production totals, engine data and current collector pricing.

Standard Catalog of® V-8 Engines 1906-2002
Item# VEE1 • $24.95

Standard Catalog of® American Cars 1976-1999
Item# AD03 • $34.95

Standard Catalog of® American Cars 1946-1975
Item# AC04R • $34.95

Standard Catalogs by Marque

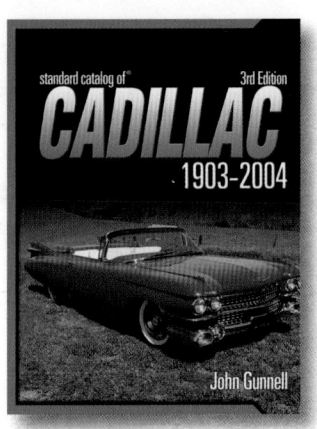

Standard Catalog of® Buick 1903-2004
Item# AK03 • $24.99

Standard Catalog of® Cadillac 1903-2004
Item# AL03 • $27.99

Standard Catalog of® Chevrolet 1912-2003
Item# AV03 • $24.99

Standard Catalog of® Chrysler 1914-2000
Item# AY02 • $22.95

Standard Catalog of® Ford 1903-2003
Item# AF03 • $24.95

Standard Catalog of® Pontiac 1926-2002
Item# APO02 • $21.95

Standard Catalogs for Imports

Standard Catalog of® Ferrari 1947-2003
Item# FERI1 • $24.99

Standard Catalog of® Imported Cars 1946-2002
Item# AI02 • $32.95

Standard Catalog of® Volkswagen, 1946-2004
Item# VOLK1 • $24.99

Standard Catalogs by Model

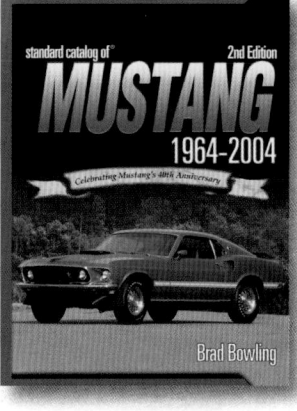

Standard Catalog of® Camaro 1967-2002
Item# CMRO1 • $24.95

Standard Catalog of® Chevelle 1964-1987
Item# CHVL1 • $24.99

Standard Catalog of® Corvette 1953-2005
Item# VET02 • $24.99

Standard Catalog of® Firebird 1967-2002
Item# BIRD1 • $24.95

Standard Catalog of® GTO 1961-2004
Item# GTL1 • $24.99

Standard Catalog of® Mustang 1964-2004
Item# MUS02 • $24.99

Standard Catalog of® Thunderbird 1955-2004
Item# TBRD1 • $24.99

Standard Catalogs for Trucks

Standard Catalog of® American Light-Duty Trucks
Item# PT03 • $34.95

Standard Catalog of® Jeep 1940-2003
Item# JPSC1 • $24.99

Standard Catalog of® Light-Duty Dodge Trucks 1917-2002
Item# LDDG1 • $24.95

Standard Catalog of® Light-Duty Ford Trucks 1905-2002
Item# LDFT1 • $24.95

kp books
an imprint of F+W Publications, Inc.
700 E. State St. • Iola, WI 54990-0001

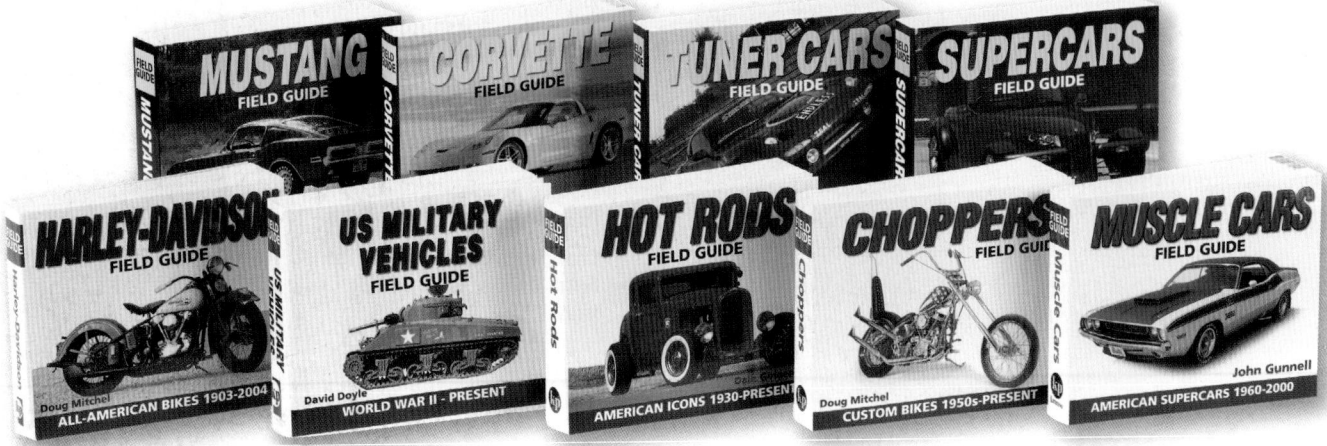